BASIC AND CONTEMPORARY ISSUES IN DEVELOPMENTAL PSYCHOLOGY

BASIC AND CONTEMPORARY ISSUES IN DEVELOPMENTAL PSYCHOLOGY

Paul Henry Mussen
University of California, Berkeley

John Janeway Conger
University of Colorado School of Medicine

Jerome Kagan
Harvard University

Harper & Row, Publishers
New York   Evanston   San Francisco   London

Sponsoring Editor: George A. Middendorf
Project Editor: Robert Ginsberg
Designer: Rita Naughton
Production Supervisor: Will C. Jomarrón

Previously published under the title **Readings in Child Development and Personality**

Basic and Contemporary Issues in Developmental Psychology

Library of Congress Cataloging in Publication Data

Mussen, Paul Henry, ed.
    Basic and contemporary issues in developmental psy-
chology.

    Published in 1965 and 1970 under title: Readings in
child development and personality.
    Includes index.
    1. Child study—Addresses, essays, lectures.
I. ·Conger, John Janeway, joint ed. II. Kagan, Jerome,
joint ed. III. Title. [DNLM: 1. Psychology. BF713
M989b]
BF721.M878   155.4   74-15243
ISBN 0-06-044706-0

Contents

⭐ MADE CLASS PRESENTATION

★ MADE CLASS PRESENTATION

Part I

Basic Issues

Chapter 1

The Concept of Stage

There is considerable controversy surrounding the issue of how best to describe the growth of various psychological systems. One can appreciate the problem by contrasting the growth of a butterfly with that of a leaf. Once a leaf has grown from its form as a seed, it never changes its basic shape or organization while it grows larger; growth seems to be continuous, with no transformations in shape. By contrast, the butterfly passes through several dramatically different forms—or stages—before it reaches its adult organization. The mature form of a maple leaf can be predicted easily from an early version, but it would be difficult to guess that the caterpillar and the butterfly are part of the life history of the same creature. We do not know which psychological systems grow like leaves, continuously without marked transformations, and which grow like butterflies, passing through different stages.

Most psychologists believe that cognitive systems have a stagelike growth and take the theory of Jean Piaget as their model. The central idea in a stage view of development is that the form of a child's thought changes **qualitatively** with age and that stages follow each other in a fixed sequence. More specifically, the definition of **stage** has two components: First, it refers to a set of psychological processes that emerge together during particular periods of development. Second, the sequence of emergence of each set is fixed, or "invariant." This means that the stages succeed each other in a constant order.

A weaker version of the stage idea states that cognitive development consists of the emergence of very specific competences—or processes—that are displayed initially in a limited number of situations. With growth, each of these competences becomes elaborated and is applied to an increasing number of problem situations until, years after its initial appearance, it is applied spontaneously in such a wide range of contexts that it is regarded as a generalized ability.

For example, Piaget has suggested that a child who is not yet in the stage of "concrete operations" (about 7 years of age) cannot mentally manipulate his knowledge of some past event. He bases this view, in part, on the fact that a 5-year-old cannot draw on paper the route he follows when he walks to kindergarten, even though he walks there every day. The weaker view implies that although the 5-year-old cannot mentally manipulate this knowledge, he can manipulate simpler experiences mentally. For example, there is evidence to suggest that a 5-year-old can manipulate—in his mind—his memory of a simple geometric form yet be unable to draw the route he follows to a familiar place.

The debate about the "abruptness" of stages in development is closely related to the basic issue of whether there is continuity or discontinuity in nature. Consider the breaking of a wave on the seashore. To a person standing on the beach, the breaking of a wave appears to be a discontinuous event, for suddenly there is white froth whereas moments before there was none. However, someone with a sensitive device to measure water pressure would have noted a gradual increase in pressure, starting many yards out from shore, which eventually culminated in the breaking of the wave. This person would see the breaking of the wave as part of a continuous phenomenon. Hence, at the surface or manifest level there seems to be discontinuity, while hidden below the surface nature seems to be continuous. Should we describe the development of hidden abilities in terms of manifest surface discontinuities or in terms of disguised, hidden continuities? This is a source of debate and discussion among developmental psychologists. The two articles presented in this chapter address this issue.

The paper by J. H. Flavell, who is a stage theorist, questions the idea that stages develop abruptly rather than gradually. He notes that the traditional view of stages implied qualitative rather than quantitative changes, sudden (abrupt) rather than gradual alterations. Flavell suggests that competences may develop more evenly than previously thought and that an ability may not achieve its final level of maturity until long after the "stage" is presumably over. He hypothesizes a longer "fermenting" time for the completion of a stage, which is a fresh way to view stages in intellectual development.

The paper by L. Kohlberg and C. Gilligan applies the stage notion to the reasoning of the adolescent, especially his moral reasoning. The authors believe there is a special stage of adolescent thinking, closely related to Piaget's stage of formal operational thinking, that is characterized by heightened subjectivity and a concern with one's own thought processes. The authors outline their view of the "stages" in moral development; they suggest that there is a universal, invariant sequence of "moral reasoning," by which they mean that **how the child thinks** about what is good and bad, in contrast to **what he thinks** is good or bad, advances in stages. Kohlberg and Gilligan believe there should be more emphasis on moral reasoning in public school curricula. They criticize the tendency in our society to oppose "intellect" and "emotion" and suggest that society should be concerned with the development of the whole child, rather than just his specialized achievements. Aiding the adolescent to find his own identity and moral ideology should be part of the schools' mission.

#1

Stage-Related Properties
of Cognitive Development

John H. Flavell

The aim of this paper is to refine and elaborate upon some earlier proposals (Flavell, 1970a; Flavell & Wohlwill, 1969) regarding the typical

NOTE: This article was written during a year's leave at the Center for Advanced Study in the Behavioral Sciences, Stanford, California. The author would like to express his deepest appreciation to the Center and its staff for providing just the sort of atmosphere that would tempt one to write a perhaps overspeculative "think piece" like this one. He is also most grateful to fellow Center Fellows Eleanor Maccoby, Donald Davidson, Amelie Rorty, John Rawls, Robert Glaser, Howard and Tracy Kendler, Albert Bandura, and above all, Walter Reitman for numerous thought-provoking interchanges concerning the nature of cognitive development and related topics. He is likewise much indebted to Eleanor J. Gibson, Jacqueline J. Goodnow, Adrien Pinard, Jan Smedslund, and Joachim F. Wohlwill for their highly thoughtful criticisms of an earlier draft of the paper.

SOURCE: Reprinted, in abridged form, from *Cognitive Psychology,* vol. 2, no. 4 (October 1971), 421–453, by permission of the author and the publisher. Copyright © 1971 by Academic Press, Inc.

course of human cognitive growth. The vehicle for presenting these views will be an analysis of the concept of cognitive-developmental stage and related matters, carried out primarily within the framework of Piaget's theory. As will be seen, this strategy of exposition does not stem from a deep and abiding faith in the empirical reality of "stages" (especially as they are frequently conceived), or in their ultimate theoretical utility, or in Piaget's views concerning them. Moreover, the present analysis will not even touch upon some of the important problems and issues concerning stages that more systematic treatments would routinely include (Flavell & Wohlwill, 1969; Kessen, 1962; Piaget, 1955; Pinard & Laurendeau, 1969), such as, for example, the question of the possible developmental mechanisms or processes by which the child advances within or between stages. Rather, the present expositional strategy arises from the fact that careful thought as to just what could and could not reasonably be said of stages seems to lead naturally to some general conclusions about how cognitive development usually proceeds, conclusions that need not apply only to Piagetian-type acquisitions and, in fact, conclusions that may even serve to blur and weaken their point of origin, the stage concept itself.

The procedure for elaborating these ideas will be to define a particular conception of "cognitive-developmental stage" and then try to estimate how closely it accords with ontogenetic reality. This conception is a deliberate caricature: a more extreme and sharply drawn picture of what "stage" implies than anyone would actually subscribe to, perhaps, it is nonetheless—like all caricatures—a highly recognizable, larger-than-life sort of image. It will be presented vis-à-vis a real example that has been elaborately defined and much studied, namely, Piaget's stage of concrete operations. In all that follows, the word "item" will be used as a suitably noncommittal and generic term for any sort of cognitive acquisition that a developmental psychologist might define and study. Thus, an "item" might be a structure, skill, concept, rule, strategy, operation, belief, attitude, or any other cognitive element, large or small, that he has isolated for consideration. Since the purpose of this paper is to make "true in general" sorts of assertions about the course of human cognition development (concerning how *most* of cognitive development proceeds, or how it *usually* progresses), the objects of these assertions also must be kept appropriately abstract and nonspecific.

Assume that a psychological X-ray of some child revealed the presence of all cognitive items that are supposed to define full membership in this particular stage, that is, all of the individual logical and infralogical operations constituting the various concrete-operational groupings and groups (e.g., Flavell, 1963, Chap. 5). The present characterization (or "caricaturization") of "stage"

would claim that at least four things are true of (1) these items. First, the items do not exist in the child's cognitive repertoire as psychologically isolated and unrelated abilities, but rather interact with one another in specified ways in the course of being utilized by the child; accordingly, it is legitimate to describe them as organized into one (2) or more cognitive *structures*. Second, the items and their structural organizations are qualitatively rather than just quantitatively different from those defining previous stages of the child's cognitive evolution; they are genuine developmental novelties, not merely more efficient or otherwise improved versions of what had already been (3) achieved. Third, each individual item functioned at asymptotic, adult-level proficiency as soon as it functioned at all, i.e., as soon as it could be said to have been "acquired" in any sense. Thus, for instance, as soon as the child could logically multiply any classes in any task setting, he was capable of performing this particular concrete operation on all the sets of classes and in all the task (4) settings that he would ever be capable of. Finally, all of his concrete-operational items made this abrupt, quantum-jump transition into the repertoire simultaneously. According to these last two assertions, therefore, the child was never "in" the stage of concrete operations in an ambiguous or qualified way, either in the sense of having only a rudimentary command of some given operation (third assertion) or in the sense of possessing only some of those operations at a given time (fourth assertion).

Overdrawn though it may be (with regard to the last two assertions, particularly), this conception does conjure up an image of "stage" something like the one I suspect that most people have: namely, of an abrupt and synchronized metamorphosis to a decidedly novel set of components and component interrelationships. Furthermore, something like this conception often seems to be implicit when people theorize and do research on the question of whether developmental changes are typically continuous or discontinuous, gradual or abrupt and step-like, quantitative or qualitative, synchronous or sequential (Flavell, 1970a; Flavell & Wohlwill, 1969). As a recent example, in the final chapter of her book on perceptual learning and development (1969), Eleanor Gibson argues that perceptual development does not proceed by stages, and the notion of "stage" she has in mind clearly resembles the one sketched above, even to the point of using the process of metamorphosis in insects as an analogy. An attempt will now be made to examine and evaluate each of the four components of this conception in the light of anything we know or can infer about how human cognitive development actually proceeds.

1. QUALITATIVE CHANGES

State-to-stage development entails qualitative rather than quantitative changes in thinking. It has recently been argued that cognitive development as a whole, including of course stage-to-stage transitions, exhibits changes of both a qualitative and a quantitative sort (Flavell & Wohlwill, 1969, pp. 76–78). Examples from Piaget's concrete-operational stage are not hard to find. For instance, the best current evidence indicates that the typical, say, nine-year-old is given to making transitive inferences (e.g., if shown only that A < B and B < C, he is likely to conclude that A < C must also be the case), whereas the typical four-year-old is not (e.g., Murray & Youniss, 1968). . . .

. . . . .

2. ABRUPTNESS

The development of individual stage-specific items is characteristically abrupt rather than gradual; that is, there is a zero-order transition period between the initial appearance of each item and its state of functional maturity. Figure 1 presents a visual model of this view of item development (Figure 1a), together with two alternative models (Figures 1b and 1c). The abscissas in Figure 1 show the defined age periods for three major stages of cognitive development, such as Piaget's

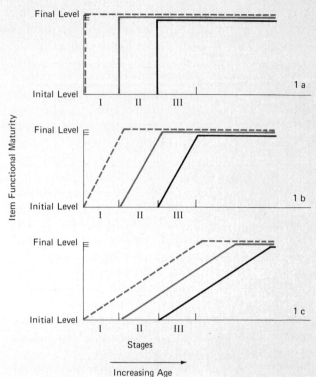

Figure 1 Three models of the developmental course of individual stage-specific cognitive items.

sensory-motor, concrete-operational, and formal-operational stages. Since the developmental course of individual stage-specific items is the only question under discussion here, each stage is counterfactually represented as entailing the development of but a single item. The ordinates then represent the "functional maturity" of each stage's item, i.e., the extent to which the subject can evoke and use it successfully in appropriate circumstances, relative to his final level of competence in this regard (this concept will be further explicated below). It is assumed that the item developed in an earlier stage continues in the repertory when the item proper to the next stage develops, as is the case for the major Piagetian stages.

There are two things to be noticed about the model of development shown in Figure 1a. First, it highlights the static, essentially a developmental connotation that the word "stage" tacitly has for most people: one is "in" a particular stage because, and for just so long as, one *continues* to behave in some particular fashion; developmental *changes* in behavior are largely relegated to the "period of transition" from one stage to the next. If these "periods of transition" are taken to be of essentially null duration (as in Figure 1a), the view that stages emerge abruptly rather than gradually, leads logically to the rather paradoxical conclusion that the individual spends virtually all of his childhood years "being" rather than "becoming." Second, the termination of any stage is defined not by the cessation of developmental change in the stage-specific item (this change having both commenced and ceased at the *beginning* of the stage), but simply by the abrupt emergence of the succeeding stage.

(2)

Figure 1b represents a very different conception of developmental stages. According to this view, a stage is a period during which the stage-specific item gradually increases in functional maturity, with this maturity finally being achieved in full at the close of the period. The end of a given stage is therefore defined both by the initial development of the next stage's item and by the just-completed development of its own item, the latter constituting a "natural," intrinsic-to-that-stage termination marker. Wholly unlike the case in Model 1a, a stage here is not a state but a process—it is *itself* the "period of transition." To be sure, the stage-specific item does finally achieve the steady properties of Model 1a, but by that time the child is classified as having entered the next subsequent stage. Notice also that statements like, "This child is in stage X," are far less useful for purposes of behavioral prediction than in the previous model, because whether or not the child will behave in a stage X fashion on a given occasion will jointly depend upon the specifics of the test situation and upon how far the child has progressed in his mastery of item X.

Figure 1c depicts a more extreme version of the gradual-development model. It asserts that a stage-specific item achieves its final level of functional maturity only after, and perhaps only well after, the child has begun the development of the next stage's item. Unlike both preceding models, this one asserts that items from two or more stages can undergo developmental change concurrently. Like Model 1a and unlike Model 1b, the conclusion of stage X is marked here only by the beginning of stage X + 1; that is, it is not additionally marked by the simultaneous completion of X's development, as in Model 1b.

Since the three models lie on a common continuum of abruptness-gradualness, one can of course readily imagine intermediary models, for instance, a compromise between 1a and 1b wherein item X achieves its asymptotic functional maturity during the first half of stage X, thus yielding an image of stages that is half process, half state. It should also be mentioned that the linearity of the growth curves in Figures 1b and 1c represents nothing more than a graphic convenience on the writer's part, and should not be taken seriously. And finally, there is, of course, no presumption that all children negotiate the various stages at the same ages, nor indeed, that all children must attain any given later stage at all.

Which of the three models comes closest to developmental reality? The existing research literature on the development of Piagetian and other cognitive items strongly indicates that Model 1a can immediately be ruled out of contention. It is, of course, possible to conceive of the child's initial, maiden effort to apply an item as an abruptly occurring developmental emergent, although a deeper understanding of the developmental background of that effort might well reduce one's impression of abruptness (e.g., Pinard & Laurendeau, 1969, p. 147). The subsequent transition from first effort to functional maturity is quite another matter, however:

> Everything we know about intellectual development continually forces us to distinguish between the potential generality of any cognitive tool and

the child's current ability to exploit that potential. Although it is still far from clear just how the developmental lag between early buddings and later blossomings ought to be conceptualized . . . it is simply a fact that the full evolution of any cognitive item almost invariably looks more like an extended process than a punctate episode (Flavell, 1970a, pp. 1038–1039).

Model 1a has much to commend it on formal grounds. It lends a meaning to "stage" that is conceptually clear, theoretically strong, operationally useful, and quite congruent with the ordinary-language meaning of that term. Unfortunately, that developing system we call the child just does not seem to conform to it.

Model 1b is a much more plausible contender, stressing as it does the view that a stage really defines the end points of an item's birth-to-maturity evolution: "For a single operation within the concrete-operational period, then, the best statement would seem to be that this period is the segment of childhood *during which,* or *by the end of which,* this particular kind of operation *acquires* much of the generality and stability that it has in adulthood" (Flavell, 1970a, p. 1039). Excepting the weasel words "much of," added only out of habitual caution, this quotation both describes and endorses Model 1b. Piaget himself also appears to endorse it in the course of describing his own particular criteria for stage progressions. The fourth of these criteria is stated as follows:

> A stage thus comprises both a level of *preparation,* on the one hand, and of *achievement,* on the other. For example, in the case of formal operations, the stage of preparation would be the entire period from 11 to 13–14 years and the achievement would be the state or level [*palier*] of equilibrium which is obtained at the end of that period (Piaget, 1955, p. 35, my translation; see also Pinard & Laurendeau, 1969, pp. 129–136).

Model 1b may in fact turn out to be the most accurate description of how some items develop. For most items, however, I currently think that something resembling Model 1c gives a more realistic picture. To explain why, it is necessary to examine the notion of "functional maturity" more closely.

In the present state of our knowledge, to assert that a child "possesses," or "has developed," a given cognitive item is to be either unclear or arbitrary: unclear if no specification is made of the particular task setting or settings in which the child successfully applied the item; arbitrary if such specification is provided. As Lipsitt (1967) has pointed out, much the same is true for the assertion that an S has "learned" something in a laboratory setting. The problem is that, while both the facts and our intuitions suggest that there are different, age-related "degrees" to which a child may possess an item, and conceivably even different "ways" of possessing it, there appears to be as yet no good theoretical language for describing and ordering these "degrees" and "ways." It is, however, possible to demarcate in a very rough way two general classes of abilities or processes which jointly determine the child's developmental status vis-à-vis an item, i.e., determine the extent to which that item has attained functional maturity within his cognitive repertoire (for an alternative set of distinctions here, see Smedslund, 1969, p. 239).

(1) One class refers to the evocability or operational availability of the item as a candidate solution procedure for the child, once that item has in at least a rudimentary way become part of his repertoire. Low evocability would mean that only a very small, "easy" subset of the entire range of tasks or problems soluble by that item will as yet stimulate the child to retrieve the item from long-term memory and attempt to use it as a solution procedure; high evocability would mean that the item is now readily retrieved for possible use with respect to most relevant problems, even when the item-to-problem fit is partly camouflaged by task or other variables. The second class refers to the child's ability, once having sensed this item-to-problem fit, to utilize the item effectively in solving the problem. The two classes can operate independently in determining the prob-

ability of problem solution. I may be fully aware that, say, it is my knowledge of algebra, rather than some other knowledge, that should be brought to bear on the solution of a particular (B) problem, and yet be unable to utilize that knowledge, fully or even partly, in my solution attempts. Conversely, it might not occur to me that it is this sort of knowledge rather than some other that the problem calls for, even though I might be quite capable of utilizing it successfully once made aware of this fact. The psychological interdependencies between the two are probably quite marked, however. For instance, problems constructed in such a way as to render nonobvious the applicability of an item may have a better than even chance of posing difficulties for the effective utilization of that item, given recognition of its applicability.

Something like this distinction between evocation and utilization processes proves useful in accounting for a variety of cognitive-developmental phenomena. Flavell and Wohlwill have incorporated a similar distinction into a crude model of how Piagetian logical operations might evolve (1969, pp. 98–99), taking their lead from the psycholinguist's differentiation between "competence" and "performance" (Chomsky, 1965). Flavell, Botkin, Fry, Wright, and Jarvis (1968, Chap. 7) have argued that children who have acquired some degree of role-taking ability can nonetheless fail to take another's perspective in a particular situation because they may simply not recognize the necessity of doing so in this situation (an evocation problem) as well as for the more obvious reason that this particular perspective may be too difficult for them to "compute" (a utilization problem). Similarly, it has proven necessary to distinguish "production deficiencies" from "mediation deficiencies" in explaining young children's failure to use mnemonic devices like verbal rehearsal in memory tasks (Flavell, 1970b). Thus, the child's problem might be that, in effect, the idea of rehearsing the recall items simply does not (A) occur to him (a production deficiency, or evoca-

tion failure), or it might be that, the idea having occurred to him either spontaneously or via instruction, he simply cannot rehearse with much mnemonic profit (a mediation deficiency, or utilization failure). For a cognitive item as uncomplicated as the verbal rehearsal of stimulus names, both common sense and the research evidence (Flavell, 1970b) suggest that most of the child's problem lies on the evocation (production) side. However, utilization difficulties would likely figure much more prominently in the case of more complex intellectual items, as, for instance, the role-taking skills and Piagetian operations mentioned above. It should be reiterated that "evocation" and "utilization" refer to whole complexes of skills or processes. This is obvious in the case of utilization, but is equally true for evocation. To be able to make psychological contact with just the right segment (item) of one's store of knowledge and skills when confronted with a problem may implicate virtually all of the processes (information retrieval processes, pattern recognition processes, etc.) that contemporary students of adult cognition find so complex and hard to model (Reitman, 1970). Indeed, the writer is far from sure that an "evocation" versus "utilization" parsing will finally provide the most useful theoretical segmentation here, although it serves well enough for present purposes.

"Functional maturity" can now be defined as the highest level of evocability and utilizability that an item ever achieves in an individual's lifetime. This definition, of course, makes the term a relative rather than absolute concept, since it makes reference to real thinkers rather than to some idealized cognitive automation. It naturally follows that, among those individuals who acquire any command of a particular item at all (and of course not all individuals need do so), "functional maturity" could mean anything from minimal competence to a level of mastery approximating that of the aforementioned automation; for a single individual, moreover, whatever level of maturity had finally been achieved could subsequently diminish through such regressive influences as item disuse and aging effects. In short, we have here the familiar problem of trying to relate (abstract, idealized) "Development" to (concrete, real) "Developments."

Let us stipulate for the sake of getting on with things, however, that the individual we will be talking about is going to grow up to be the perennial college sophomore, thus the normative "adult S" of psychological research. What is suggested here is that, for such individuals, *it is the usual case that a stage-specific item continues to develop towards whatever eventually constitute its functional maturity after one or more subsequent stages are in process.* This is the reason why one finds it much more comfortable to say, for instance, that pre-operational thinking normally *begins* its development around age two than to say that sensory-motor intelligence has *completed* its development at that time. Consider a random example of a sensory-motor acquisition: the ability to discover new means for achieving a concrete goal through active experimentation, e.g., to discover that a stick can be used to fetch an out-of-reach object (Flavell, 1963, pp. 117–118). It is surely true that this sort of ability continues to be refined and perfected long after the child has left the sensory-motor period; indeed, its development probably persists well into adulthood for many individuals. The reason one stops referring to the child as "sensory-motor" after age two, is that the most *homo sapiens* type "intelligent" things he can do are now of a different sort, not because sensory-motor skills have reached functional maturity. To put it more generally, what really determines the agreed-upon termination date for any cognitive-developmental stage is the beginning emergence of new skills, skills which impress us as the best, highest-level cognitive act the subject can now put on; the fact that we now turn our attention to the new act does not mean that the old one has stopped being perfected.

. . . .

3. CONCURRENCE

The various items which define a given stage develop concurrently, i.e., in synchrony with one another. As with the other putative components of the stage concept dealt with here, this one has been most extensively discussed and debated in connection with Piaget's concrete-operational stage (Flavell, 1970a; Flavell & Wohlwill, 1969; Pinard & Laurendeau, 1969; Wohlwill, 1963, 1966); we shall therefore examine it primarily within this context. It turns out that there are some very troublesome ambiguities and problems latent in this simple and straight-forward-looking assertion, and its validity cannot be assessed without some preliminary discussion of these.

One source of ambiguity has to do with the degree to which, or the sense in which, Piaget's theory is believed to predict the synchronous development of concrete operations (Flavell, 1970a; Pinard & Laurendeau, 1969). Certainly, Piaget's writings often convey an image of the entire ensemble of concrete-operational skills marching lockstep into the child's repertoire. At the same time, there is frequent mention of *décalages* or systematic age gaps in the cognitive conquest of this versus that concrete-operational concept, e.g., conservation of mass regularly attained before conservation of weight. Some have argued that the theory logically demands either relatively little in the way of within-stage developmental synchrony (Flavell & Wohlwill, 1969; Wohlwill, 1966), or essentially none at all (Flavell, 1970a). In contrast, Pinard and Laurendeau (1969, pp. 136–145) believe that it does require considerable developmental concurrence, but of a specific sort. Whether or not the theory really does require it (see below), the sort of concurrence they describe articulates Piaget's own vision of how concrete operations actually develop. According to Pinard and Laurendeau, all the operations from all of the concrete-operational groupings and groups which are potentially applicable to a particular concept ("length," or "class," or "weight," etc.) develop synchronously, but with "develop" restricted to mean *only* the process of becoming applicable *to that concept.* Thus, the child should simultaneously acquire the ability to apply diverse operations X_1, X_2, etc. to concept A, and the same should be true with respect to concept B. Since there might be an age lag or *décalage* in the cognitive management of A versus B, however, the theory allows for a certain limited form of item nonconcurrence. Thus, in the present example, there need not be developmental synchrony between X_1 (A) and X_2 (B), nor between X_2 (A) and X_1 (B), although there should be between X_1 (A) and X_2 (A), and between X_1 (B) and X_2 (B). Pinard and Laurendeau refer to this as an "intraconcept" as contrasted with "interconcept" (complete) form of developmental concurrence. In the quoted example that follows, various concrete operations or operational structures described by the theory precede the concepts or task behaviors (set in parentheses) they allegedly underlie or "mediate" in the domain of weight:

> It is thus that—to recall one of the two examples cited by Piaget in this connection—the construction of the concept of weight would simultaneously imply, at about the age of nine years: the mastery of groupings of simple addition and of vicariances (conservation of weight); of addition of asymmetrical (seriation of weight) and symmetrical (transitivity of equivalences) relations; of bi-univocal multiplication of relations or of classes (concept of density by the combination of weight and substance); of co-univocal multiplication (conservation of the weight of the particles of flour in the dilated corn); and finally, of the corresponding quantitative groupings, by a fusion of classes and relations (pp. 138–139).

Let us henceforth specify that the italicized sentence which leads this section (*The various items . . .*) be taken to mean the kind of concurrence that Pinard and Laurendeau describe, and assume that it fairly represents Piaget's position on the matter. There nonetheless remain some hidden unclarities in the sentence. These stem

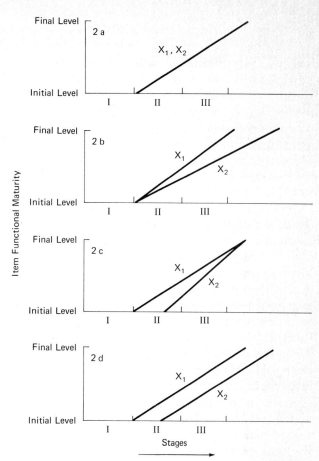

Figure 2 Four possible interpretations of developmental concurrence between two same-stage cognitive items.

from the fact that "developmental concurrence" can mean several rather different things if it is accepted that the course of an item's development is anything like its representation in Figure 1c. Figure 2 depicts the four principal ways in which the developmental courses of two same-stage items (in the present discussion, two concrete-operational skills) might conceivably be related. Figure 2a portrays the strongest possible kind of concurrence, specifying that the two items both begin and terminate their development simultaneously. As noted earlier, nothing is claimed about the shape of any of the hypothetical growth curves presented in this essay, and thus it matters not for our purposes whether the two curves in Figure 2a be regarded as congruent throughout their entire length, as shown here, versus being separated or bowed out in the middle, sinuous and interweaving, etc. What is important is that the two most salient aspects of these or any developmental processes—initiation and termination—are here conceived as strictly concurrent for items X_1 and X_2. The concurrence is less complete in the case of Figure 2b and c, with either emergence (2b) or functional maturity (2c) being taken as chronologically synchronous, but not both. Thus, in both cases there exist intervals in the subject's childhood when one item is in process of developmental change and the other not, and hence an absence of concurrence for these intervals.

It is clear that "developmental concurrence" can be an ambiguous expression once the acquisition of an item is regarded as an extended process (Figures 1b and 1c) rather than an instantaneous, quantum-like jump (Figure 1a). In particular, to say that "there is (exists) developmental concurrence" between two acquisition processes does not differentiate among Models 2a–2c. Nor does it distinguish these from 2d, nor, in fact, 2a–2d from the *different*-stage developments represented by the dotted, solid, and dashed lines in Figure 1c (the stage I item is after all, still developing during a time interval in which the stage III item is developing, and hence the two are for a time "developing concurrently").

What specific type or degree of concurrence do people have in mind, then, when they talk about items of the same stage developing "simultaneously" or "together"? The answer is, not surprisingly, that they generally do not have anything very specific in mind, because the distinctions represented in Figures 1 and 2 have not entered into their thinking on the matter. It is possible, with the following bit of conceptual legerdemain,

to interpret the Pinard–Laurendeau–Piaget position as favoring the very strong conception of concurrence represented by Figure 2a. If, as they argue, the whole set of concrete operations becomes initially (and simultaneously) applicable only to domain A, and later (simultaneously) applicable to domain B as well, and still later (simultaneously) applicable to domain C as well; and if this process of generalization is taken to represent, in my terms, successive moments in the developmental movement toward functional maturity of these operations (an increase in their evocability and utilizability across the range of relevant problems); then it seems to follow that all operations are conceived as being at comparable points in this developmental movement throughout its entire course—at first emergence, at all intermediate levels of functional maturity, and at the latter's achievement. However, the actual phraseology used by Pinard and Laurendeau, as well as that of their quoted excerpts from Piaget, is variable and probably indeterminate with respect to the kind or degree of concurrence meant: "all the forms of groupings *appear* at the same time"; "the . . . groupings appear to be *constituted* at about the same time"; ". . . would simultaneously imply . . . the *mastery of* . . ." (Pinard & Laurendeau, 1969, p. 138, my italics). It is barely possible that Model 2b, or even Model 2c, would be regarded by these authors as not wholly incongruent with the Genevan conception of stage development, although Model 2d would clearly be considered discordant with it.

. . . . .

4 STRUCTURES

Stage-specific items become organized and interrelated to form cognitive structures. The term "cognitive structure" currently suffers from a bad case of overuse and underdefinition. Its overuse is partly the result of its enormous utility as a slogan or professional password. People who invoke it approvingly can also be counted on to salute Piaget, Chomsky, and their ilk; people to whom it is anathema are rather likely to swear allegiance to Skinner's army or some similar counterforce. One gets the impression that neither faction very often employs it with any really clear and precise meaning in mind, and that it all too often functions as a substitute, rather than a tool, for developmental analysis. What *is* a "cognitive structure," anyway? Let us begin by looking at dictionary meanings. *Webster's Third New International Dictionary* (1965) and *A Comprehensive Dictionary of Psychological and Psychoanalytical Terms* (English and English, 1958) are both useful in this respect. According to my reading of these two sources, the really central and essential meaning of "cognitive structure" ought to be a set of cognitive items that are somehow interrelated to constitute an organized whole or totality; to apply the term "structure" correctly, it appears that there must be, at minimum, an ensemble of two or more *elements* together with one or more *relationships* interlinking these elements. There also appear to be at least two additional, secondary properties. One is that such organizations of cognitive items are relatively stable, enduring affairs, rather than merely temporary arrangements. The other, closely related, is that a structure is to be regarded as the common, underlying basis of a variety of superficially distinct, possibly even unrelated-looking behavioral acts; to use Werner's (1937) terminology, structures are akin to the "processes" which give rise to a variety of cognitive "achievements."

To return . . . to the topic statement: is it really the case that stage-specific cognitive items do tend eventually to interrelate to form cognitive structures? It is hard to doubt it. Whenever one looks for examples of cognitive items one discerns psychologically real and measurable connections among the entities found. Sensory-motor actions get coordinated into intricate systems of hierarchical and sequential (e.g., means-ends) relationships. Concepts interlink to form conceptual networks, and derive their meanings from these networks (Flavell, 1970a). The rules implicitly controlling linguistic and other cognitive outputs operate in specified combinations to constitute systems of rules. It is difficult even to conceive of a viable organism so designed that each of its actions, concepts, rules, etc., exists and operates in strict functional isolation and independence from all others—i.e., as an ensemble of "elements" with no "interlinking relationships" among them. If the denial of this conception be the minimum criterion for a disbelief in the existence of cognitive structures, one suspects that very few contemporary students of human behavior would qualify as nonbelievers. People do of course disagree about the sorts of structures that the child's cognitive behavior reflects during this or that developmental period; there may also be a more fundamental disagreement as to whether a theoretical concern with structures is a profitable scientific move at a given point in the history of the field. I submit, however, that virtually nobody who believes in the reality of cognitive items at all seriously believes that the natural state of such items is functional isolation versus functional interdependence.

. . . .

SUMMARY AND CONCLUSIONS

Stage-to-stage development is most conspicuously marked by genuinely qualitative changes in the child's repertoire of cognitive "items" (cognitive skills, rules, strategies, etc.). Such development also entails cognitive modifications of a more quantitative sort, however, and these may play an important role in the genesis of the more dramatic, stage-defining, qualitative changes.

The items that define a stage develop gradually rather than abruptly. Moreover, the typical item probably does not achieve its final level of "functional maturity" (defined in terms of the item's evocability and utilizability as a solution procedure) until *after* the conventional termination age of the stage in which it is supposed to begin its development. For example, a concrete-operational item like transitive inference probably continues to be perfected as an instrument of reasoning well after the generally accepted end point of the concrete-operational stage (age 10–11 years). In short, the development of cognitive items not only appears to be characteristically gradual rather than abrupt, it may prove to be even more gradual than most of us had supposed.

The fact that the acquisition period of a stage-specific item appears to constitute an extended temporal interval rather than a temporal point renders ambiguous the notion of developmental synchrony or concurrence. That is, to say that two stage-specific items "develop concurrently" could now mean that they begin their development at the same time, or conclude it (achieve functional maturity) synchronously, or both, or even neither (i.e., have developmental courses which show some chronological overlap, but only in the middle regions). Two conclusions were drawn with respect to interitem concurrence, after having somewhat arbitrarily restricted the term to mean only the synchronous emergence (i.e., the synchronous *initial* development) of two or more items. First, items from the same stage may often emerge in an invariant or near-invariant sequence rather than concurrently, although important methodological problems cloud the research evidence on this point. Second, a stage theory such as Piaget's does not in any event logically require anything but a very loose sort of item concurrence at most, and research attempts at establishing strict concurrences have been accordingly misguided in rationale.

It is in the nature of cognitive items to become functionally interrelated in various ways as they develop, and therefore "cognitive structure" must have real referents in human cognitive developments. An analysis of Piaget's claims about the development of cognitive structures suggests that, among other difficulties, some of these claims may not really be empirically testable at all; this would not necessarily prevent them from being otherwise useful to an empirical enterprise, e.g., in suggesting fruitful directions for new research.

Some might argue that the analysis presented in this essay seriously erodes the concept of cognitive-developmental stage. The claim that stage-specific items develop very gradually and asyncronously, they might say, amounts to no less than a tacit denial of the very concept of stage, and also perhaps, an implicit rejection of the fundamental tenets of Piaget's theory. I personally find it profitless to think in the terms ("denial," "rejection") of such arguments. Our task is, after all, not to contend with this concept and that theorist, but to seek a clearer picture of developmental reality, to try to understand how development actually proceeds. If the clearer picture should reveal "stage" to be a less simple and straightforward notion than we used to think it was, or if the picture should fail to square with something Piaget has said, so be it—it simply means that developmental psychology is showing the normal developmental course of any science.

References

Braine, M. D. S. The ontogeny of certain logical operations: Piaget's formulation examined by nonverbal methods. *Psychological Monographs*, 1959, 73, (5 Whole No. 475).

Bruner, J. S., Olver, R. R., & Greenfield, P. M., et al., *Studies in cognitive growth*. New York: Wiley, 1966.

Chomsky, N. *Aspects of the theory of syntax*. Cambridge, MA: M.I.T. Press, 1965.

Coon, R. C., & Odom, R. D. Transitivity and length judgments as a function of age and social influence. *Child Development*, 1968, 39, 1133–1144.

Donaldson, M. *A study of children's thinking*. London: Tavistock Publications, 1963.

English, H. B., & English, A. C. *A comprehensive dictionary of psychological and psychoanalytical terms*. New York: Longmans, Gren, 1958.

Flavell, J. H. *The development psychology of Jean Piaget*. Princeton, NJ: Van Nostrand, 1963.

Flavell, J. H. Concept development. In P. H. Mussen (Ed.), *Carmichael's manual of child psychology*. New York: Wiley, 1970. Pp. 983–1059. (a)

Flavell, J. H. Developmental studies of mediated memory. In H. W. Reese & L. P. Lipsitt (Eds.), *Advances *in child development and behavior.* Vol. 5. New York: Academic Press, 1970. Pp. 182–211 (b).

Flavell, J. H. An analysis of cognitive-development sequences. Division 7 Presidential address presented at the meeting of the American Psychological Association, Miami Beach, September 1970. (c)

Flavell, J. H. An analysis of cognitive-developmental sequences. Unpublished monograph, 1971.

Flavell, J. H., Botkin, P. T., Fry, C. L., Jr., Wright, J. W., & Jarvis, P. E. *The development of role-taking and communication skills in children.* New York: Wiley, 1968.

Flavell, J. H., & Wohlwill, J. F. Formal and functional aspects of cognitive development. In D. Ekind & J. H. Flavell (Eds.), *Studies in cognitive development: essays in honor of Jean Piaget.* New York: Oxford University Press, 1969. Pp. 69–120.

Gelman, R., & Weinberg, D. H. The relationship between liquid conservation and compensation. Unpublished paper, 1971.

Gibson, E. J. *Principles of perceptual learning and development.* New York: Appleton-Century-Crofts, 1969.

Hunter, I. M. L. The solving of three-term series problems. *British Journal of Psychology,* 1957, 48, 286–298.

Johnson, D. M. *The psychology of thought and judgment.* New York: Harper & Row, 1955.

Kessen, W. "Stage" and "structure" in the study of children. *Society for Research in Child Development Mongraphs,* 1962, 27, 65–82. (Serial N. 83)

Klahr, D., & Wallace, J. G. An information processing analysis of some Piagetian experimental tasks. *Cognitive Psychology,* 1970, 1, 358–387.

Lipsitt, L. P. "Stages" in developmental psychology. Comments from a round-table discussion at the meeting of the Eastern Psychological Association, Boston, April 1967.

Miller, S. A. Contradiction, surprise, and cognitive change: the effects of disconfirmation of belief on conservers and nonconservers. Unpublished doctoral dissertation, University of Minnesota, 1971.

Murray, J. P., & Youniss, J. Achievement of inferential transitivity and its relation to serial ordering. *Child Development,* 1968, 39, 1259–1268.

Pascual-Leone, J. A mathematical model for the transition rule in Piaget's developmental stages. Research Report, Grant NRC APA 234 (Canada), York University, 1968.

Piaget, J. Les stades du développement intellectuel de l'enfant et de l'adolescent. In P. Osterrieth et al., *Le problème des stades en psychologie de l'enfant.* Paris: Presses Universitaires de France, 1955. Pp. 33–42.

Piaget, J. *The psychology of intelligence.* Patterson, NJ: Littlefield, Adams, 1960.

Piaget, J. *Le structuralisme.* Paris: Presses Universitaires de France, 1968.

Piaget, J. Piaget's theory. In P. H. Mussen (Ed.), *Carmichael's manual of child psychology.* Vol. 1. New York: Wiley, 1970. Pp. 703–732.

Piaget, J., & Inhelder, B. Intellectual operations and their development. In P. Fraisse & J. Piaget (Ed.), *Experimental psychology: its scope and method.* Vol. VIII. *Intelligence.* New York: Basic Books, 1969. Chap. 24. (a)

Piaget, J., & Inhelder, B. *The psychology of the child.* New York: Basic Books, 1969. (b)

Pinard, A., & Laurendeau, M. "Stage" in Piaget's cognitive-developmental theory: exegesis of a concept. In D. Elkind & J. H. Flavell (Eds.), *Studies in cognitive development: essays in honor of Jean Piaget.* New York: Oxford University Press, 1969. Pp. 121–170.

Reitman, W. What does it take to remember? In D. A. Norman (Ed.), *Models of human memory.* New York: Academic Press, 1970. Pp. 469–509.

Smedslund, J. Concrete reasoning: a study of intellectual development. *Society for Research in Child Development Monographs,* 1964, 29, No. 2. (Serial No. 93)

Smedslund, J. Psychological diagnostics. *Psychological Bulletin,* 1969, 71, 237–248. Webster's third new international dictionary of the English language (unabridged). Springfield, MA: Merriam, 1965.

Werner, H. Process and achievement. *Harvard Educational Review,* 1937, 7, 353–368.

Wohlwill, J. F. Piaget's system as a source of empirical research. *Merrill-Palmer Quarterly,* 1963, 9, 253–262.

Wohlwill, J. F. Piaget's theory of the development of intelligence in the concrete-operations period. *American Journal of Mental Deficiency, Monograph Supplement,* 1966, 70, No. 4.

Wohlwill, J. F. *The study of behavioral development.* In preparation.

The Adolescent as a Philosopher

The Discovery of the Self in a Postconventional World

Lawrence Kohlberg

Carol Gilligan

The central themes of this essay are first, the definition of adolescence as a universal stage of development; second, the way in which the universal features of adolescence seem to be acquiring unique colorings in the present era in America; and third, the implications of these changes for education. . . .

THE MEANING OF THE STAGE CONCEPT— ILLUSTRATED FROM THE PRESCHOOL YEARS

To understand the universal meanings of adolescence as a stage and its implications for education, it will help to examine briefly an earlier stage and its implications for education, one more thoroughly understood than the stage of adolescence. Almost all cultures implicitly recognize two great stages or transformations in development. Adolescence, the second transformation, traditionally terminated compulsory schooling. The first transformation occurring from five to seven years of age initiated compulsory schooling.[1] This five-to-seven shift is termed the "onset of the latency period" by Freudian theory, the onset of concrete logical thought by Piaget. As embodied in educational thought, the Freudian interpretation of the five-to-seven shift implied letting the child grow, letting him work through his fantasies until he had repressed his sexual instincts and was ready to turn his energies into formal learning. This Freudian interpretation of the preschool stage suffered both from lack of confirmation by empirical research and from irrelevance to the intellectual development and everyday behavior with which the schools were

SOURCE: Reprinted, in abridged form, from *Twelve to Sixteen*, eds. J. Kagan and R. Coles (New York: Norton, 1972), pp. 144–179, by permission of the author and the publisher.

concerned. When the Great Society decided to do something for the disadvantaged child, the Freudian "let him work through his Oedipus complex" implications of the five-to-seven shift were dismissed as a luxury for the wealthy. Programs of preschool intellectual stimulation and academic schooling were initiated, with the expectation of long-range effects on intelligence and achievement. These programs failed to fulfill their initial hope of changing general intellectual maturity or long-range achievement.[2]

One reason they failed was because they confused specific teaching and learning with the development of new levels of thinking truly indicative of cognitive maturity. The evidence of limitations of these early education programs, together with growing positive research evidence of the existence of cognitive stages, convinced early educators of the reality of the stage transformation at the age five to seven. The stage transformation of the period five to seven is now conceived in quite a different way than in the vogue of Freudian education. In the Freudian view, the preschooler was in a stage of domination of thought by sexual and aggressive fantasies. The new stage which succeeded this was defined negatively as latency, rather than positively. Under the influence of Piaget, more recent thinking sees the preschool child's fantasy as only one aspect of the preschooler's pattern of prelogical thought. In the prelogical stage, subjective appearance is not fully distinguished from "reality"; the permanent identities of things are not differentiated from their momentary transformations. In the prelogical stage view, the preschool child's special fantasy is not the expression of an instinct later repressed but of a cognitive level of thought. The decline of fantasy in the years five to seven, longitudinally documented by R. Scheffler,[3] is not a repression; it is closely related to the positive development of concrete logical patterns of thought.

The child's changed orientation to reality in the five-to-seven period is part of the development of concrete logical operations then. During this period the child develops the operations of categorical classifications, of serial ordering, addition, subtraction, and inversion of classes and relations. This development occurs in the absence of schooling in African and Taiwanese villagers in much the same way that it occurs in the American suburban child.[4]

As a concrete example, Piaget and the writers have asked children if they had had a bad dream and if they were frightened when they woke up from their bad dream.[5] Susie, aged four, said she dreamt about a giant and answered, "Yes, I was scared, my tummy was shaking and I cried and told my mommy about the giant." Asked, "Was it a real giant or was it just pretend? Did the giant just seem to be there, or was it really there?" she answered, "It was really there but it left when I woke up. I saw its footprint on the floor."

According to Piaget, Susie's response is not to be dismissed as the product of a wild imagination, but represents the young child's general failure to differentiate subjective from objective components of his experience. Children go through a regular series of steps in their understanding of dreams as subjective phenomena. The first step, achieved before five by most American middle-class children, is the recognition that dreams are not real events. The next step, achieved soon thereafter, is the realization that dreams cannot be seen by others. The third step is the notion that dreams are internal (but still material) events.

By the ages six to eight children are clearly aware that dreams are thoughts caused by themselves. To say such cognitive changes define stages implies the following things:

1. That young children's responses represent not mere ignorance or error, but rather a spontaneous manner of thinking about the world that is qualitatively different from the way we adults think and yet has a structure of its own.
2. The notion of different developmental

structures of thought implies consistency of level of response from task to task. If a child's response represents a general structure rather than a specific learning, then the child should demonstrate the same relative structural levels in a variety of tasks.

3. The concept of stage implies an invariance of sequence in development, a regularity of stepwise progression regardless of cultural teaching or circumstance. Cultural teaching and experience can speed up or slow down development, but it cannot change its order or sequence.

The concept of stage, then, implies that both the youngest children's conceptions of the dream as real and the school age children's view of the dream as subjective are their own; they are products of the general state of the child's cognitive development, rather than the learning of adult teachings.

Cross-cultural studies indicate the universality of the basic sequence of development of thinking about the dream, even where adult beliefs about the meaning and significance of dreams is somewhat different from our own.[6] While the stage of concrete operations is culturally universal and in a sense natural, this does not mean it is either innate or that it is inevitable and will develop regardless of environmental stimulation. In the United States, the doctrine of stages was assumed for some time to mean that children's behavior unfolded through a series of age-specific patterns, and that these patterns and their order were wired into the organism. This indeed was the view of Gesell and Freud, and Americans misunderstood Piaget as maintaining the same thing. The implications of the Gesellian and Freudian theory for early education were clear; early teaching and stimulation would do no good since we must wait for the unfolding of the behavior, or at least the unfolding of the readiness to learn it.

In contrast, Piaget used the existence of stages to argue that basic cognitive structures are not wired in, but are general forms of equilibrium re-sulting from the interaction between organism and environment. If children have their own logic, adult logic or mental structure cannot be derived from innate neurological patterning because such patterning should hold also in childhood. (It is hardly plausible to view a succession of logics as an evolutionary and functional program of innate wiring.) At the same time, however, Piaget argued that stages indicate that mental structure is not merely a reflection of external physical realities or of cultural concepts of different complexities. The structure of the child's concepts in Piaget's view is not only less complex than the adult's, it is also different. The child's thought is not just a simplified version of the adult's.

Stages, or mental structures, then, are not wired into the organism though they depend upon inborn organizing tendencies. Stages are not direct reflections of the child's culture and external world, though they depend upon experience for their formation. Stages are rather the products of interactional experience between the child and the world, experience which leads to a restructuring of the child's own organization rather than to the direct imposition of the culture's pattern upon the child. While hereditary components of I.Q., of the child's rate of information processing, have some influence on the rate at which the child moves through invariant cognitive sequences, experiential factors heavily influence the rate of cognitive-structural development.[7] The kind of experience which stimulates cognitive stage development is, however, very different from the direct academic teaching of information and skills which is the focus of ordinary schooling. Programs of early education which take account of cognitive stages, then, look neither like the permissive "let them grow" nursery school pattern nor like the early teaching programs popular in the sixties. They are a new form now coming into being.[8]

2 COGNITIVE SIGNS IN ADOLESCENCE

The older children get, the more difficult it is to distinguish universal stage changes from sociocultural transitions in development. We said that the core phenomenon of adolescence as a stage (1) was the discovery of the subjective self and sub- (2) jective experience and a parallel questioning of adult cultural reality. The manifestations of this discovery, however, are heavily colored not only by historical and cultural variations, but also by previous patterns of life history of the child.

In our first section, we discussed one manifestation of the discovery of the self, the discovery of the body and its sexual drives. In part this is, of course, a biological universal, the physical growth spurt marking adolescent puberty and an accompanying qualitatively new sex drive. If there is anything which can be safely said about what is new in the minds of adolescents, it is that they, like their elders, have sex on their minds. These changes, of course, have been the focus of Freudian thinking about adolescence as a stage. If anything, however, Freudian thinking has underestimated the novel elements of sexual experience in adolescence. For the Freudian, early adolescent sexuality is the reawakening of early childhood sexuality previously latent, with a consequent resurrection of oedipal feeling. Although it is true that adolescent sexuality bears the stamp of earlier experience, it is not the resurrection of earlier sexual feelings. Adolescent sexual drive is a qualitatively new phenomenon.[9]

While sexual drives are awakened at puberty, there are vast individual and cultural variations in the extent to which they determine the adolescent's behavior and experience. Sexuality is a central concern for the self of some fourteen-year-olds; it is something deferred to the future of others. What is common for all, however, is an intensified emotionality whether experienced as sexual or not. This emotionality, too, is now experienced as a part of the self, rather than as a correlate of objective events in the world. C. Ellinwood studied the age development of the verbal experiencing and expression of emotion in projective tests and in free self-descriptions. She found that prior to adolescence (aged twelve or so), emotions were experienced as objective con-

comitants of activities and objects. The child experienced anger because events or persons were bad; he experienced affection because persons were good or giving; he felt excitement because activities were exciting or fun. At adolescence, however, emotions are experienced as the result of states of the self rather than as the direct correlate of external events.[10]

The difference may perhaps be clarified by reference to middle-class drug experiences. Occasionally, a psychological preadolescent may take drugs, as he may drink beer or sneak cigarettes. When he does this, he does this as an activity of an exciting forbidden and grown-up variety. For the adolescent drug-taker, drugs represent rather a vehicle to certain subjective moods, feelings, and sensations. In many cases, the drug experience is a vehicle for overcoming depression, felt as an inner subjective mood. In any case, drug-taking is not an activity with an objective quality; it is a mode of activating subjective inner feelings and states. The same is true of such activities as intensive listening to music, an activity characteristically first engaged in at early adolescence (ages eleven to fourteen). The rock, folk-rock, and blues music so popular with adolescents is explicitly a presentation of subjective mood and is listened to in that spirit.

Associated with the discovery of subjective feelings and moods is the discovery of ambivalence and conflicts of feeling. If feelings are objective correlates of external good and bad events, there can be little tolerance and acceptance of feeling hate and love for the same person, of enjoying sadness and feeling sad about pleasure. Ellinwood's study documents that adolescents are consciously expressing such ambivalence, which is of course the stock in trade of the blues and folk-rock music beamed to them.

We have spoken of the adolescent discovery of subjective moods and feelings as linked to puberty. More basically, it is linked to the universal cognitive stages of Piaget. We have said that the five-to-seven transition is defined by Piaget as the transition to *abstract, reflective* thought. More exactly, it is the transition from logical inference as a set of *concrete operations* to logical inference as a set of *formal operations* or "operations upon operations." "Operations upon operations" imply that the adolescent can classify classification, that he can combine combinations, that he can relate relationships. It implies that he can think about thought, and create thought systems or "hypothetico-deductive" theories. This involves the logical construction of all possibilities—that is, the awareness of the observed as only a subset of what may be logically possible. In related fashion, it implies the hypothetico-deductive attitude, the notion that a belief or proposition is not an immediate truth but a hypothesis whose truth value consists in the truth of the concrete propositions derivable from it.

An example of the shift from concrete to formal operations may be taken from the work of E. A. Peel.[11] Peel asked children what they thought about the following event: "Only brave pilots are allowed to fly over high mountains. A fighter pilot flying over the Alps collided with an aerial cable-way, and cut a main cable causing some cars to fall to the glacier below. Several people were killed." A child at the concrete-operational level answered: "I think that the pilot was not very good at flying. He would have been better off if he went on fighting." A formal-operational child responded: "He was either not informed of the mountain railway on his route or he was flying too low also his flying compass may have been affected by something before or after take-off this setting him off course causing collision with the cable."

The concrete-operational child assumes that if there was a collision the pilot was a bad pilot; the formal-operational child considers all the possibilities that might have caused the collision. The concrete-operational child adopts the hypothesis that seems most probable or likely to him. The formal-operational child constructs all possibilities and checks them out one by one.

As a second example, we may cite one of Piaget's tasks, systematically replicated by D. Kuhn, J. Langer, and L. Kohlberg.[12] The child is shown a pendulum whose length may vary as well as the number of weights attached. The child is asked to discover or explain what determines the speed of movement (or "period") of the pendulum. Only the formal-operational child will "isolate variables," that is, vary length holding weight constant, and so forth, and arrive at the correct solution (for example, that period is determined by length). Success at the task is unrelated to relevant verbal knowledge about science or physics, but is a function of logical level.

In fact the passage from concrete to formal operations is not an all or none phenomenon. There are one or two substages of formal operations prior to the full awareness of all possibilities just described. These substages are described in Table 1, which presents an overview of the Piaget cognitive stages. For simplifying purposes. we may say that for middle-class Americans, one stage of formal operations is reached at age ten to thirteen, while the consideration of all possibilities is reached around fifteen to sixteen. At the first formal-operational stage, children became capable of reversing relationships and ordering relationships one at a time or in chains, but not of abstract consideration of all possibilities. (They are capable of "forming the inverse of the reciprocal," in Piaget's terminology; but not of combining all relationships.) A social thinking example of failure to reverse relationships is shown in concrete-operational children's responses to the question: "What does the Golden Rule tell you to do if someone comes up on the street and hits you?" The typical answer is "hit him back, do unto others as they do unto you." The painful process of the transitional formal-operational child in response to the question is given by the fellowing response: "Well for the Golden Rule you have to like dream that your mind leaves your body and goes into the other person, then it comes back into you and you see it like he does and you act like the way you saw it from there."[13]

Table 1. Piaget's eras and stages of logical and cognitive development

ERA I (AGE 0–2) THE ERA OF SENSORIMOTOR INTELLIGENCE

Stage 1. Reflex action.

Stage 2. Coordination of reflexes and sensori-motor repetition (primary circular reaction).

Stage 3. Activities to make interesting events in the environment reappear (secondary circular reaction).

Stage 4. Means/ends behavior and search for absent objects.

Stage 5. Experimental search for new means (tertiary circular reaction).

Stage 6. Use of imagery in insightful invention of new means and in recall of absent objects and events.

ERA II (AGE 2–5) SYMBOLIC, INTUITIVE, OR PRELOGICAL THOUGHT

Inference is carried on through images and symbols which do not maintain logical relations or invariances with one another. "Magical thinking" in the sense of (a) confusion of apparent or imagined events with real events and objects and (b) confusion of perceptual appearances of qualitative and quantitative change with actual change.

ERA III (AGE 6–10) CONCRETE OPERATIONAL THOUGHT

Inferences carried on through system of classes, relations, and quantities maintaining logically invariant properties and which *refer to concrete objects*. These include such logical processes as (a) inclusion of lower-order classes in higher order classes; (b) transitive seriation (recognition that if $a > b$ and $b > c$, then $a > c$); (c) logical addition and multiplication of classes and quantities; (d) conservation of number, class membership, length and mass under apparent change.

Substage 1. Formation of stable categorical classes.

Substage 2. Formation of quantitative and numerical relations of invariance.

ERA IV (AGE 11 TO ADULTHOOD) FORMAL-OPERATIONAL THOUGHT

Inferences through logical operations upon propositions or "operations upon operations." Reasoning about reasoning. Construction of systems of all possible relations or implications. Hypothetico-deductive isolation of variables testing or hypotheses.

Substage 1. Formation of the inverse of the reciprocal. Capacity to form negative classes (for example, the class of all not-crows) and to see relations as simultaneously reciprocal (for example, to understand that liquid in a U-shaped tube holds an equal level because of counterbalanced pressures).

Substage 2. Capacity to order triads of propositions or relations (for example, to understand that if Bob is taller than Joe and Joe is shorter than Dick, then Joe is the shortest of the three).

Substage 3. True formal thought. Construction of all possible combinations of relations, systematic isolation of variables, and deductive hypothesis-testing.

We have described Piaget's stage of formal operations as a logical stage. What is of special importance for understanding adolescents, however, is not the logic of formal operations, but its epistemology, its conception of truth and reality. In the previous section we said that the child's attainment of concrete operations at age six to seven led to the differentiation of subjective and objective, appearance and reality. The differentiation at this level was one in which reality was equated with the physical and the external. We cited the child's concept of the dream, in which the unreality of the dream was equivalent to its definition as an inner mental event with no physical external correlate. The subjective and the mental are to the concrete-operational child equated with fantasies, with unrealistic replicas of external physical events. The development of formal operations leads, however, to a new view of the external and the physical. The external and the physical are only one set of many possibilities of a subjective experience. The external is no longer the real, "the objective," and the internal the "unreal." The internal may be real and the external unreal. At its extreme, adolescent thought entertains solipsism or at least the Cartesian cogito, the notion that the only thing real is the self. I asked a fifteen-year-old girl: "What is the most real thing to you?" Her unhesitating reply was "myself."

.　　.　　.　　.

. . . It seems that for all adolescents the discovery of the subjective is a condition for aesthetic feeling in the adult sense, for the experience of nature as a contemplative experience, and for religiosity of a mystical variety. It is probably the condition for adolescent romantic love as well. This whole constellation of experiences is called romantic because it is centered on a celebration of the self's experience as the self enters into union with the self's counterpart outside. The common view of romanticism as adolescent, then, is correct in defining the origins of romanticism in the birth of the subjective self in adolescence. . . .

MORAL STAGES IN ADOLESCENCE AND THEIR RELATION TO COGNITIVE STAGES

. . . To understand the adolescent's social thinking, however, we need to be aware not only of logical stages but also of stages of moral judgment. In our research, we have found six definite and universal stages of development in moral thought. In our longitudinal study of seventy-six American boys from preadolescence, youths were presented with hypothetical moral dilemmas, all deliberately philosophical, some of them found in medieval works of casuistry.

On the basis of their reasoning about these dilemmas at a given age, each boy's stage of moral thought could be determined for each of twelve basic moral concepts, values, or issues. The six stages of moral thought are divided into three major levels, the *preconventional,* the *conventional,* and the *postconventional* or autonomous.

While the preconventional child is often "well-behaved" and is responsive to cultural levels of good and bad, he interprets these labels in terms of their physical consequences (punishment, reward, exchange of favors) or in terms of the physical power of those who enunciate the rules and labels of good and bad. This level is usually occupied in the middle class by children aged four to ten.

The second or conventional level usually becomes dominant in preadolescence. Maintaining the expectation and rules of the individual's family, group, or nation is perceived as valuable in its own right. There is concern not only with conforming to the individual's social order, but also in maintaining, supporting, and justifying this order.

The postconventional level is first evident in adolescence and is characterized by a major thrust toward autonomous moral principles which have validity and application apart from authority of the groups or persons who hold them and apart from the individual's identification with those persons or groups.

Within each of these three levels there are two discernable stages. At the preconventional level we have: Stage 1: Orientation toward punishment and unquestioning deference to superior power. The physical consequences of action regardless of their human meaning or value determine its goodness or badness. Stage 2: Right action consists of that which instrumentally satisfies one's own needs and occasionally the needs of others. Human relations are viewed in terms like those of the market place. Elements of fairness, reciprocity, and equal sharing are present, but they are always interpreted in a physical, pragmatic way. Reciprocity is a matter of "you scratch my back and I'll scratch yours," not of loyalty, gratitude, or justice.

At the conventional level we have: Stage 3: Good-boy-good-girl orientation. Good behavior is that which pleases or helps others and is approved by them. There is much conformity to stereotypical images of what is majority or "natural" behavior. Behavior is often judged by intention—"he means well" becomes important for the first time and is overused. One seeks approval by being "nice." Stage 4: Orientation toward authority, fixed rules, and the maintenance of the social order. Right behavior consists of doing one's duty, showing respect for authority, and maintaining the given social order for its own sake. One earns respect by performing dutifully.

5A) At the postconventional level we have: Stage 5A: A social contract orientation, generally with legalistic and utilitarian overtones. Right action tends to be defined in terms of general rights and in terms of standards which have been critically examined and agreed upon by the whole society. There is a clear awareness of the relativism of personal values and opinions and a corresponding emphasis upon procedural rules for reaching consensus. Aside from what is constitutionally agreed upon, right or wrong is a matter of personal values and opinion. The result is an emphasis upon the legal point of view, but with an emphasis upon the possibility of changing law in terms of rational considerations of social utility, rather than freezing it in the terms of Stage 4, law and order. Outside the legal realm, free agreement and contract are the binding elements of obligation. This is the official morality of American government, and finds its ground in the thought of 5B) the writers of the Constitution. Stage 5B: Orientation to internal decisions of conscience but with- 6) out clear rational or universal principles. Stage 6: Orientation toward ethical principles appealing to logical comprehensiveness, universality, and consistency. These principles are abstract and ethical (the Golden Rule, the categorical imperative); they are not concrete moral rules like the Ten Commandments. Instead, they are universal principles of justice, of the reciprocity and equality of human rights, and of respect for the dignity of human beings as individual persons.

These stages are defined by twelve basic issues of moral judgment. On one such issue, Conscience, Motive Given for Rule Obedience or Moral Action, the six stages look like this:

1. Obey rules to avoid punishment.
2. Conform to obtain rewards, have favors returned, and so on.
3. Conform to avoid disapproval, dislike by others.
4. Conform to avoid censure by legitimate authorities and resultant guilt.

5A. Conform to maintain the respect of the impartial spectator judging in terms of community welfare.
5B. Conform to avoid self-condemnation.

In another of these moral issues, the value of human life, the six stages can be defined thus:

1. The value of a human life is confused with the value of physical objects and is based on the social status or physical attributes of its possessor.
2. The value of a human life is seen as instrumental to the satisfaction of the needs of its possessor or of other persons.
3. The value of a human life is based on the emphathy and affection of family members and others toward its possessor.
4. Life is conceived as sacred in terms of its place in a categorical moral or religious order of rights and duties.
5. Life is valued both in terms of its relation to community welfare and in terms of being a universal human right.
6. Belief in the sacredness of human life as representing a universal human value of respect for the individual.

We call our types "stages" because they seem to represent an invariant developmental sequence. True stages come one at a time and always in the same order.

All movement is forward in sequence and does not skip steps. Children may move through these stages at varying speeds, of course, and may be found half in and half out of a particular stage. An individual may stop at any given stage and at any age, but if he continues to move, he must move in accord with these steps. Moral reasoning of the conventional or Stage 3–4 kind never occurs before the preconventional Stage 1 and Stage 2 thought has taken place. No adult in Stage 4 has gone through Stage 6, but all Stage 6 adults have gone at least through 4.

While the evidence is not complete, our study

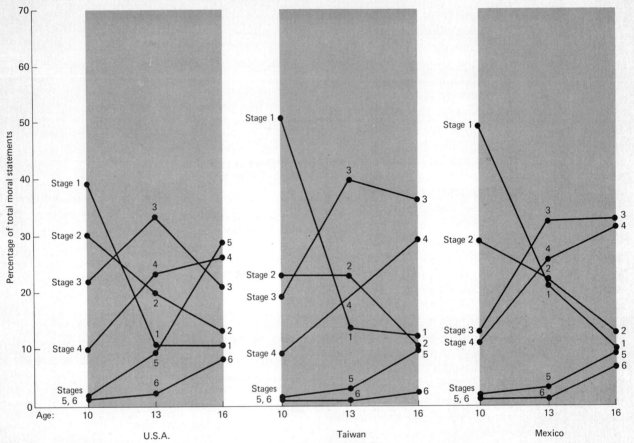

Figure 1   Middle-class urban boys in the U.S., Taiwan and Mexico. At age 10 the stages are used according to difficulty. At age 13, Stage 3 is most used by all three groups. At age 16 U.S. boys have reversed the order of age 10 stages (with the exception of 6). In Taiwan and Mexico, conventional (3–4) stages prevail at age 16, with Stage 5 also little used.

strongly suggests that moral change fits the stage pattern just described. Figures 1 and 2 indicate the cultural universality of the sequence of stages which we found. Figure 1 presents the age trends for middle-class urban boys in the United States, Taiwan, and Mexico. At age ten in each country, the order of use of each stage is the same as the order of its difficulty or maturity. In the United States, by age sixteen the order is the reverse, from the highest to the lowest, except that Stage 6 is still little used. The results in Mexico and

Taiwan are the same, except that development is a little slower. The most conspicuous feature is that at the age of sixteen, Stage 5 thinking is much more salient in the United States than in Mexico or Taiwan. Nevertheless, it is present in the other countries, so we know that this is not purely an American democratic construct.

Why should there be such a universal invariant sequence of development? In answering this question, we need first to analyze these developing social concepts in terms of their internal logi-

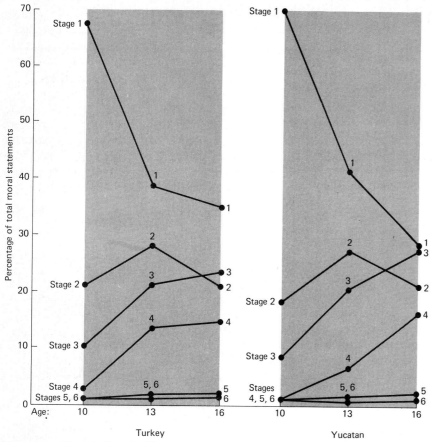

Figure 2   Two isolated villages, one in Turkey, the other in Yucatan, show similar patterns in moral thinking. There is no reversal of order, and preconventional (1–2) thought does not gain a clear ascendancy over conventional stages at age 16.

cal structure. At each stage, the same basic moral concept or aspect is defined, but at each higher stage this definition is more differentiated, more integrated, and more general or universal. When one's concept of human life moves from Stage 1 to Stage 2 the value of life becomes more differentiated from the value of property, more integrated (the value of life enters an organizational hierarchy where it is "higher" than property so that one steals property in order to save life) and more universalized (the life of any sentient being is valuable regardless of status or property). The same advance is true at each stage in the hier-

archy. Each step of development, then, is a better cognitive organization than the one before it, one which takes account of everything present in the previous stage, but making new distinctions and organizing them into a more comprehensive or more equilibrated structure.

What is the relation of moral stage development in adolescence to cognitive stage development? In Piaget's and our view, both types of thought and types of valuing (or of feeling) are schemata which develop a set of general structural characteristics representing successive forms of psychological equilibrium. The equilibrium of

Table 2. Relations between Piaget logical stages and Kohlberg moral stages (all relations are that attainment of the logical stages is necessary, but not sufficient, for attainment of the moral stage)

LOGICAL STAGE	MORAL STAGE
Symbolic, intuitive thought	Stage O: The good is what I want and like. *OWN PHYSICAL NEEDS*
PRE-MORAL Concrete operations, Substage 1	Stage 1: Punishment-obedience orientation. *AVOIDANCE OF PERSONAL PUNISHMENT*
Categorical classification	
PRE-ADOLESCENT Concrete operations, Substage 2	Stage 2: Instrumental hedonism and concrete reciprocity. *RECIPROCAL PHYSICAL NEEDS*
Reversible concrete thought	
Formal operations, Substage 1	Stage 3: Orientation to interpersonal relations of mutuality. *ESTEEM FROM OTHERS*
Relations involving the inverse of the reciprocal	
ARCHIE BUNKER LAW & ORDER Formal operations, Substage 2	Stage 4: Maintenance of social order, fixed rules, and authority. *LETTER OF LAW*
Formal operations, Substage 3	Stage 5A: Social contract, utilitarian law-making perspective. *SPIRIT (PURPOSE) OF LAW*
POST-COVENTIONAL, PRINCIPLED, CONSCIENCIOUS	Stage 5B: Higher law and conscience orientation. *OWN PHILO VITAE*
UNIVERSAL ETHICAL JUDGEMENT	Stage 6: Universal ethical principle orientation. *UNIVERSAL GOOD*

affective and interpersonal schemata, justice or fairness, involves many of the same basic structural features as the equilibrium of cognitive schemata logically. Justice (portrayed as balancing the scales) is a form of equilibrium between conflicting interpersonal claims, so that "in contrast to a given rule imposed upon the child from outside, the rule of justice is an imminent condition of social relationships or a law governing their equilibrium."[14]

What is being asserted, then, is not that moral judgment stages are cognitive—they are not the mere application of logic to moral problems—but that the existence of moral stages implies that normal development has a basic cognitive-structural component.

The Piagetian rationale just advanced suggests that cognitive maturity is a necessary, but not a sufficient condition for moral judgment maturity. While formal operations may be necessary for principled morality, one may be a theoretical physicist and yet not make moral judgments at the principled level.

. . . Kuhn, Langer, and Kohlberg found that 60 per cent of persons over sixteen had attained formal operational thinking (by their particular measures).[15] Only 10 per cent of subjects over sixteen showed clear principled (Stages 5 and 6) thinking, but all these 10 per cent were capable of formal-operational logical thought. More generally, there is a point-to-point correspondence between Piaget logical and moral judgment stages, as indicated in Table 2. The relation is that attainment of the logical stage is a necessary but not sufficient condition for attainment of the moral stage. As we shall note in the next section, the fact that many adolescents have formal logical capacities without yet having developed the corresponding degree of moral judgment maturity is a particularly important background factor in some of the current dilemmas of adolescents.

④ ADOLESCENT QUESTIONING AND THE PROBLEM OF RELATIVITY OF TRUTH AND VALUE

The cornerstone of a Piagetian interpretation of adolescence is the dramatic shift in cognition from concrete to formal operations by which old conceptions of the world are restructured in terms of a new philosophy. Piaget defined the preschool child as a philosopher, revolutionizing child psychology by demonstrating that the child at each stage of development actively organizes his experience and makes sense of the physical and social world with which he interacts in terms of the classical categories and questions of philosophers concerning space, time, causality, reality, and so on. It is, however, only in adolescence that the child becomes a philosopher in the formal or traditional sense. This emergence of philo-

AMONG ALL NATIONS THERE IS ONLY ONE RIGHT WAY AMONG MANY WAYS BOTH IN THEORY & IN FACT.

sophic questioning has been studied most carefully in the moral realm.

The transition from preconventional to conventional morality generally occurs during the late elementary school years. The shift in adolescence from concrete to formal operations, the ability now to see the given as only a subset of the possible and to spin out the alternatives, constitutes the necessary precondition for the transition from conventional to principled moral reasoning. It is in adolescence, then, that the child has the cognitive capability for moving from a conventional to a postconventional, reflective, or philosophic view of values and society.

The rejection of conventional moral reasoning begins with the perception of relativism, the awareness that any given society's definition of right and wrong, however legitimate, is only one among many, both in fact and theory. To clarify the issue of moral relativism as perceived by an adolescent, we will consider some adolescent responses to the following dilemma:

> In Europe, a woman was near death from a very bad disease, a special kind of cancer. There was one drug that the doctors thought might save her: It was a form of radium that a druggist in the same town had recently discovered. The drug was expensive to make, but the druggist was charging ten times what the drug cost him to make. He paid $200 for the radium and charged $2,000 for a small dose of the drug. The sick woman's husband, Heinz, went to everyone he knew to borrow the money, but he could only get together about $1,000 which was half of what it cost. He told the druggist that his wife was dying, and asked him to sell it cheaper or let him pay later. But the druggist said, "No, I discovered the drug and I'm going to make money from it." Heinz got desperate and broke into the man's store to steal the drug for his wife.

Should the husband have done that? Was it right or wrong? Bob, a junior in a liberal private high school, says:

> There's a million ways to look at it. Heinz had a moral decision to make. Was it worse to steal or let his wife die? In my mind I can either condemn

him or condone him. In this case I think it was fine. But possibly the druggist was working on a capitalist morality of supply and demand.

I went on to ask Bob, "Would it be wrong if he did not steal it?

> It depends on how he is oriented morally. If he thinks it's worse to steal than to let his wife die, then it would be wrong what he did. It's all relative, what I would do is steal the drug. I can't say that's right or wrong or that it's what everyone should do.

Bob started the interview by wondering if he could answer because he "questioned the whole terminology, the whole moral bag." He goes on:

> But then I'm also an incredible moralist, a real puritan in some sense and moods. My moral judgment and the way I perceive things morally changes very much when my mood changes. When I'm in a cynical mood, I take a cynical view of morals, but still whether I like it or not, I'm terribly moral in the way I look at things. But I'm not too comfortable with it.

Here are some other juniors from an upper-middle-class public high school:

> Dan: Immoral is strictly a relative term which can be applied to almost any thought on a particular subject . . . if you have a man and a woman in bed, that is immoral as opposed to if you were a Roman a few thousand years ago and you were used to orgies all the time, that would not be immoral. Things vary so when you call something immoral, it's relative to that society at that time and it varies frequently. [Are there any circumstances in which wrong in some abstract moral sense would be applicable?] Well, in that sense, the only thing I could find wrong would be when you were hurting somebody against their will.

> Elliot: I think one individual's set of moral values is as good as the next individual's . . . I think you have a right to believe in what you believe in, but I don't think you have a right to enforce it on other people.

> John: I don't think anybody should be swayed by the dictates of society. It's probably very much up to the individual all the time and there's no general principle except when the views of society seem to conflict with your views and your opportunities

at the moment and it seems that the views of society don't really have any basis as being right and in that case, most people, I think, would tend to say forget it and I'll do what I want.

The high school students just quoted are, from the point of view of moral stage theory, in a transitional zone. They understand and can use conventional moral thinking, but view it as arbitrary and relative. They do not yet have any clear understanding of, or commitment to, moral principles which are universal, which have a claim to some nonrelative validity. Insofar as they see any "principles" as nonrelative, it is the principle of "do your own thing, and let others do theirs." This "principle" has a close resemblance to the "principles" characteristic of younger children's Stage 2 instrumental egoistic thinking. The following examples of a ten-year-old naïve egoist and a college student transition relativistic response are more clearly of this instrumental egoistic form.

> Jimmy (American city, age 10): It depends on how much he loved his wife. He should if he does. [If he doesn't love her much?] If he wanted her to die, I don't think he should. [Would it be right to steal?] In a way it's right because he knew his wife would die if he didn't and it would be right to save her. [Does the druggist have the right to charge that much if no law?]Yes, it's his drug, look at all he's got invested in it. [Should the judge punish?] He should put him in jail for stealing and he should put the druggist in because he charged so much and the drug didn't work.

> Roger (Berkeley Free Speech Movement student, age 20): He was a victim of circumstances and can only be judged by other men whose varying value and interest frameworks produce subjective decisions which are neither permanent nor absolute. The same is true of the druggist. I'd do it. As far as duty, a husband's duty is up to the husband to decide, and anybody can judge him, and he can judge anybody's judgment. If he values her life over the consequences of theft, he should do it. [Did the druggist have a right?] One can talk about rights until doomsday and never say anything. Does the lion have a right to the zebra's life when he starves? When he wants sport? Or when he will take it at will? Does he consider rights? Is

man so different? [Should he be punished by the judge?] All this could be avoided if the people would organize a planned economy. I think the judge should let him go, but if he does, it will provide less incentive for the poorer people to organize.

Cognitive-developmental stages are stages of structure, not of content. The stages tell us *how* the child thinks concerning good and bad, truth, love, sex, and so forth. They do not tell us *what* he thinks about, whether he is preoccupied with morality or sex or achievement. They do not tell us what is on the adolescent's mind, but only how he thinks about what is on his mind. The dramatic changes in adolescence are not changes in structure, but changes in content. The adolescent need not know or care he is going from conventional to principled moral thinking, but he does know and care that sex is on his mind. In this sense cognitive structural stages may be contrasted with both psychosexual and Eriksonian stages.[16]

. . . .

IMPLICATIONS FOR EDUCATION

We said earlier that the five-to-seven shift has been traditionally represented in education by the beginning of formal schooling. The traditional educational embodiment of the adolescent shift has been a different one, that of a two-track educational system dividing adolescents into two groups, an elite capable of abstract thought and hence of profiting from a liberal education and the masses who are not. At first, this division was made between the wealthy and those who went to work. As public high schools developed, the tracking system instead became that of an academic school or lycee leading to the university and a vocational school. The clearest formulation of this two-track system as based on the dawn of abstract thought was found in the British 11+ system. Based on his score on an intelligence test given at the dawn of adolescence, a child was assigned to either a grammar (academic) or a modern (vocational-commercial) high school.

The aristocratic tracking system just described rested on the assumption that the capacity for abstract thought is all or none, that it appears at a fixed age, and that it is hereditarily limited to an elite group in the population. The evidence on formal operational thought does not support these assumptions. However, when democratic secondary education ignored the existence of the adolescent cognitive shift and individual differences in their attainment, real difficulties emerged. Most recently this ignoral occurred in the wave of high school curriculum reform of the late fifties and early sixties in America, the "new math," the "new science," and the "new social studies." These curricula reforms were guided by the notion that more intellectual content could be put into high school and that this content should not be factual content and rote skills, but the basic pattern of thinking of the academic disciplines of mathmematics, physics, or social science. The focus was to be upon understanding the basic logical assumptions and structure of the discipline and the use of these assumptions in reflective or critical thinking and problem-solving. Clearly the new curricula assumed formal-operational thought, rather than attempting to develop it. Partly as a result of this ignoral, some of the most enlightened proponents of the new curricula became discouraged as they saw only a subgroup of the high school population engaging with it. The solution we have proposed is that the new curricula be reformulated as tools for developing principled logical and moral thought rather than presupposing it. . . .[17]

The difficulties and failures of the new curricula and of the general movement to democratize higher learning or liberal education, then, is not due to hereditary differences in capacity used to justify the two-track system. They represent, instead, the failure of secondary education to take developmental psychology seriously. When stage development is taken seriously by educators as an aim, real developmental change can occur through education.

In saying this, we return to the thought of John Dewey which is at the heart of a democratic educational philosophy. According to Dewey, education was the stimulation of development through stages by providing opportunities for active thought and active organization of experience.

> The only solid ground of assurance that the educator is not setting up impossible artificial aims, that he is not using ineffective and perverting methods, is a clear and definite knowledge of the normal end and focus of mental action. Only knowledge of the order and connection of the stages in the development of the psychical functions can, negatively, guard against those evils, or postively, insure the full maturation and free, yet, orderly, exercises of the physical powers. Education is precisely the work of supplying the conditions which will enable the psychical functions, as they successively arise, to mature and pass into higher functions in the freest and fullest manner. This result can be secured only by a knowledge of the process of the development, that is only by a knowledge of "psychology."[18]

Besides a clear focus on development, an aspect of Dewey's educational thought which needs revival is that school experience must be and represent real life experience in stimulating development. American education in the twentieth century was shaped by the victory of Thorndike over Dewey. Achievement rather than development has been its aim. But now the achieving society, the achieving individual, and even the achievement tests are seriously questioned, by adults and adolescents alike. If development rather than achievement is to be the aim of education, such development must be meaningful or real to the adolescent himself. In this sense education must be sensed by the adolescent as aiding him in his search for identity, and it must deal with life. Neither a concern with self or with life are concerns opposed to intellectuality or intellectual development. The opposition of "intellect" and "life" is itself a reflection of the two-track system in which a long period of academic education provided a moratorium for leisurely self-crystallization of an adult role identity by the elite while the masses were to acquire an early adult vocational identity, either through going to work or through commitment to a vocation in a vocational high school.

. . . .

. . . If education is to promote self-development, ego development must be seen as one side of an education whose other side consists of the arts and sciences as philosophically conceived. We have pointed to the need for defining the aims of teaching the arts and sciences in developmental terms. In this sense one basic aim of teaching high school science and mathematics is to stimulate the stage of principled or formal-operational logical thought, of high school social studies, the stimulation of principled moral judgment. A basic aim of teaching literature is the development of a stage or level of aesthetic comprehension, expression, judgment. Behind all of these developmental goals lie moral and philosophic dimensions of the meaning of life, which the adolescent currently questions and the school needs to confront. The adolescent is a philosopher by nature, and if not by nature, by countercultural pressure. The high school must have, and represent, a philosophy if it is to be meaningful to the adolescent. If the high school is to offer some purposes and meanings which can stand up to relativistic questioning, it must learn philosophy.

References

1. S. H. White, "Some General Outlines of the Matrix of Developmental Changes Between Five to Seven Years," *Bulletin of the Orton Society,* 20 (1970), 41–57.
2. L. Kohlberg, "Early Education: A Cognitive-Developmental Approach," *Child Development,* 39 (December 1968), 1013–1062; A. R. Jensen, "How Much Can We Boost I.Q. and Scholastic Achievement?" *Harvard Educational Review,* 39 (1969), 1–123.
3. R. Scheffler, "The Development of Children's Orientations to Fantasy in the Years 5 to 7," unpublished Ph.D. dissertation, Harvard University, 1971.
4. L. Kohlberg, "Moral Education in the School," *School Review,* 74 (1966), 1–30; Kohlberg, "Early Education."
5. Kohlberg, "Moral Education in the School."
6. *Ibid.*
7. . Cognitive stage maturity is different from I.Q., a separate factor, though the two are correlated. (See L. Kohlberg and R. DeVries, "Relations between Piaget and Psychometric Assessments of Intelligence," in C. Lavatelli, ed., *The Natural Curriculum* [Urbana: University of Illinois Press, 1971].) General impoverishment of organized physical and social stimulation leads to retardation in stage development. Culturally disadvantaged children tend to be somewhat retarded compared to middle-class children with the same I.Q.'s in concrete-operational logic. Experimental intervention can to some extent accelerate cognitive development if it is based on providing experiencs of cognitive conflict which stimulate the child to reorganize or rethink his patterns of cognitive ordering.
8. Kohlberg, "Early Education."
9. Kohlberg, "Moral Education in the School."
10. C. Ellinwood, "Structural Development in the Expression of Emotion by Children," unpublished Ph.D. dissertation, University of Chicago, 1969.
11. E. A. Peel, *The Psychological Basis of Education,* 2d ed. (Edinburgh and London: Oliver and Boyd, 1967).
12. D. Kuhn, J. Langer, and L. Kohlberg, "The Development of Formal-Operational Thought: Its Relation to Moral Judgment," unpublished paper, 1971.
13. Another example of transitional stage response is success on the question: "Joe is shorter than Bob, Joe is taller than Alex, who is the tallest?" The transitional child can solve this by the required reversing of relations and serial ordering of them but will fail the pendulum task.
14. J. Piaget, *The Moral Judgment of the Child* (Glencoe, Ill.: Free Press, 1948; originally published in 1932).
15. Taken from Kuhn, Langer, and Kohlberg, "The Development of Formal-Operational Thought."
16. J. Loevinger, "The Meaning and Measurement of Ego Development," *American Psychology* (1966), 195–206.
17. L. Kohlberg and A. Lockwood, "Cognitive-Developmental Psychology and Political Education: Progress in the Sixties," speech for Social Science Consortium Convention, Boulder, Colorado, 1970;

L. Kohlberg and E. Turiel, "Moral Development and Moral Education," in G. Lesser, ed., *Psychology and Educational Practice* (Chicago: Scott, Foresman, 1971).

18. J. Dewey, *On Education: Selected Writing*, ed. R. D. Archambault (New York: The Modern Library, republished 1964).

Chapter 2

Resilience of Development

During the last 20 years the research of comparative psychologists, ethologists, and child psychologists has shown that the experiences of the infant and young child have powerful immediate effects on his behavior, temperament, and knowledge. The stronger view that early experiences also have long-lasting effects on later functioning emerged when research with animals demonstrated that apparently irreversible changes in behavior could be produced by specific early experiences. Imprinting in birds and the production of severely abnormal behavior in rhesus monkeys raised with inanimate wire mothers are two popular examples.

These provocative findings seemed to make Freud's emphasis on the extreme importance of the parent-infant interaction persuasive and strengthened the psychologist's belief that the events of infancy could seriously constrain future functioning. Reports of these findings seeped into popular magazine articles and implied that what happened to the infant and very young child could have an influence that extended long into the future. Everyone now acknowledges that the infant's development is influenced by his environment from the moment he is born. But there is more debate about the additional supposition that first dispositions are highly resistant to change, a supposition that at the moment does not have unequivocal support. We do not know how resilient—or how responsive to change—the child is because most children do not experience abrupt dramatic changes in their environment as they grow from infancy through adolescence.

One reason why most psychologists, parents, and educators are disposed to believe in the long-term effects of early experience is that each of us feels a compelling sense of continuity and connectedness when we reflect on our past and the experiences of our childhood. This sense of the past's continuous contribution to the present is part of our need to regard our lives as coherent and past decisions as part of a rationally causal chain.

More speculatively, belief in the extended power of early experience may be a derivative of one of the central maxims of Western Protestantism: Prepare for the future! Applying this maxim to human development, parents might believe that treating children optimally during the early years of life would assure the establishment of healthy attitudes and behaviors that would protect them from the traumas of adolescence and adulthood. Proper early treatment, like vaccination, would act as an inoculation against future strain. As we indicated earlier, it is difficult to disprove this view because the majority of children remain with their families in much the same environmental contexts from birth to late adolescence. As a result, psychological differences among 16-year-olds from different families could just as well be due to events that occurred during the years 6 to 12 or 12 to 16 as to experiences that occurred during the first three years of life.

Recently there have been several important experiments indicating that many of the dramatic effects of early experience may be reversible. This chapter concerns two of those studies. H. F. Harlow and his colleague, S. J. Suomi, placed male monkeys in isolation for the first six months of life. After removal from isolation, their behavior was disturbed: They showed immobility, fear, and withdrawal. To rehabilitate these monkeys, they were placed in cages with infant female monkeys three months younger than themselves. Surprisingly, after six months of interaction with the young females, the behavior of the formerly isolated monkeys was virtually indistinguishable from that of the younger monkeys. Their disturbed behaviors disappeared and they showed normal social behaviors. It appeared that they had been rehabilitated, suggesting that the extreme effects of a half year of isolation in infancy were reversible.

The second paper, by J. Kagan and R. E. Klein, is based on study of Guatemalan children from an isolated farming village. Because of cultural mores, infants receive a minimal amount of variety in external stimulation during the first year of life, and because of poor nutrition and illness they are of generally poor health. As a result of both these factors, infants are seriously retarded in psychological development between 1 and 1½ years of age. However, after their first year of life, when they are regularly allowed to leave the dark, isolated huts in which they live, they begin to experience the greater variety and challenge inherent in the natural environment. By the time they reach 10 and 11 years of age, they become gay, alert, competent children whose performance on selected cognitive abilities is comparable to that of middle-class American children.

These two studies suggest that there may be more resilience in human development than many psychologists had formerly surmised.

Social Rehabilitation of Isolate-Reared Monkeys

Stephen J. Suomi

Harry F. Harlow

Numerous researches have indicated that 6 or more months of total social isolation initiated at birth produces profound and apparently permanent social deficits in rhesus monkey subjects. Monkeys so reared fail to develop appropriate play, aggressive, sexual, and maternal behaviors but instead exhibit self-directed abnormalities such as self-clasping, huddling, and stereotypic rocking behaviors. Previous experi-

NOTE: This research was supported by United States Public Health Service Grants MH-11894 and RR-00167 from the National Institutes of Health to the University of Wisconsin Primate Laboratory and Regional Primate Research Center, respectively. The authors express their appreciation to S. David Kimball and Hal Treharne who collected most of the data, to Carole Mohr who helped to summarize the data, and to Helen Lauersdorf who supervised the final preparation of the manuscript.

mentation designed to rehabilitate isolate-reared subjects has not been successful. The present experiment successfully rehabilitated monkeys that spent the first 6 months of life in total social isolation. Following removal from isolation subjects were permitted to interact with socially normal monkeys 3 months chronologically younger than themselves. Within a few weeks isolate disturbance behaviors decreased substantially and were replaced by elementary socially directed activity. After 6 months of such exposure, the isolate subjects were virtually indistinguishable from their younger controls both in terms of absence of disturbance behaviors and sophistication of social behaviors. The process of the observed recovery and its implications for theoretical interpretations of the effects of isolation rearing are discussed.

The devastating effect of total social isolation upon monkey behavior is an exceptionally well-documented finding in primate behavioral re-

[A] search. Although 3 months of total social isolation from birth has yielded only transient and reversible behavioral effects (Boelkins, 1963; Griffin & [B] Harlow, 1966), isolation for the first 6 months of life or more has consistently resulted in profound and permanent psychopathology (Harlow, Dodsworth, & Harlow, 1965; Harlow & Harlow, 1962; Harlow, Harlow, Dodsworth, & Arling, 1966; Mason, 1963; Rowland, 1964; Sackett, 1968a; Senko, 1966). Upon emergence from total social isolation, monkeys fail to exhibit age-appropriate social and exploratory behavior. Instead, their behavioral repertoire is dominated by self-directed activities, including self-clasping, self-mouthing, huddling, and stereotypic rocking. Such abnormalities persist as the subjects mature. Appropriate sexual responses are virtually absent among adult isolate-reared monkeys, and those females artificially inseminated typically display inadequate maternal behavior toward their initial offspring. Aggressive behavior of isolate-reared monkeys is commonly self-directed or, when it occurs in social situations, inappropriately directed.

In contrast, isolation rearing apparently has little effect upon monkey learning capability. Although isolates are slower to adapt to most learning test situations (Harlow, Schiltz, & Harlow, 1969) and to extinguish certain nonreinforced behaviors previously operantly conditioned (Gluck, 1970), these deficits may be attributed to performance rather than intellectual variables. Once properly adapted to a Wisconsin General Test Apparatus, isolate-reared subjects solve complex learning problems as readily as do feral-born monkeys (Singh, 1969). *(WILD, UNTAMED)*

Two theoretical explanations for the socially destructive effects of isolation for monkeys have dominated the literature, although neither has had (1) its origin in primate research. The "critical period" approach (Scott, 1962), initially an embryological concept and more recently applied by ethologists to avian attachment behavior (e.g., Lorenz, 1965), postulates that subjects progress *(BIRDLIKE)*

through critical periods of social development. According to a strict interpretation of the theory, a subject denied appropriate social stimulation during a critical period will be rendered incapable of subsequent normal social development. A second theoretical position, stemming from research (2) using canine subjects (Fuller & Clark, 1966), maintains that the bizarre behavior patterns exhibited by monkeys removed from isolation is the result of "emergence trauma," that is, a shock precipitated by an abrupt shift from an unstimulating environment to one of relatively high complexity.

In view of the apparent discrepancy between intellectual and social effects of isolation rearing and of the alternative theoretical explanation posited, numerous attempts to rehabilitate isolate-reared monkeys have been initiated. Virtually all of these efforts have been summarily unsuccessful, a result consistent with critical period theory. For example, researches designed to shape appropriate social behavior in isolate-reared monkeys via aversive conditioning procedures produced only limited behavioral changes which failed to generalize beyond the experimental situation (Sackett, 1968b). Efforts to alleviate postulated emergence trauma via gradual introduction to environments of increasing complexity did not achieve significant rehabilitation of isolate social behaviors (Clark, 1968; Pratt, 1969). Repeated exposure to socially competent age-mates also had little apparent therapeutic success (Harlow, Dodsworth, & Harlow, 1965). In fact, such exposure may have actually exaggerated isolate disturbance behavior. By 6 months of age, well-socialized monkeys have developed complex patterns of social interaction, including vigorous play and socially directed aggression. They will typically attack any stranger monkey introduced to their social group, and only if the stranger reciprocates the attack will it be "accepted" and mutual play follow. The monkey that does not fight back continues to be the victim of aggression. In retrospect, it is not surprising that isolate-reared subjects were consistently attacked when exposed to well-socialized peers, nor is it surprising that these isolates failed to exhibit significant social recovery.

However, there exist data suggesting that isolate-reared subjects may be responsive to certain social agents and that exposure to such agents may have positive therapeutic value. Isolate-reared mothers who eventually submitted to their infants' efforts to maintain ventral contact usually exhibited adequate maternal behavior toward subsequent offspring (Harlow & Harlow, 1968). Also, monkeys exposed to heated surrogates upon emergence from isolation showed significant decreases in disturbance behavior after contacting the surrogates.[1] In neither case was social rehabilitation complete. The isolate mothers continued to exhibit incompetent sexual behavior, and the isolates exposed to surrogates failed to develop a sophisticated social repertoire.

It seems obvious that any experimental effort designed to rehabilitate isolates via social exposure requires effective social agents or "therapists." What types of monkeys could be appropriate therapists? In view of the above data, one might select animals who would predictably initiate social contact with an isolate without displaying social aggression, and who themselves would exhibit simple social responses which gradually would become more sophisticated. Such requirements are fulfilled by socially experienced monkeys only 3 or 4 months old, for at this age clinging responses still form an integral part of their social repertoire, play is in the primary stage of development, and aggressive behavior has not yet matured. In accord with these fundamental social considerations, the following rehabilitation study was initiated.

METHOD

Subjects

·ISOLATES Isolate subjects were four male rhesus monkeys (*Macaca mulatta*) born within a 2-week period.

[1] H. F. Harlow and S. J. Suomi, manuscript in preparation.

They were separated from their mothers at birth and maintained in the laboratory nursery (see Blomquist & Harlow, 1961) until their mean age was 10 days, when they were placed in individual isolation chambers (see Rowland, 1964) which effectively denied them physical and visual access to all social agents. The isolate subjects remained in the chambers until their mean age was 6 months.

·THERAPISTS Therapist subjects were four female rhesus monkeys, also born within a 2-week period, but 3 months subsequent to the isolates. They were separated from their mothers at birth and maintained in the laboratory nursery for the first 30 days. They were then placed in individual quadrants of a quad cage, described by Suomi and Harlow (1969), and each monkey was provided with a heated simplified surrogate (see Harlow & Suomi, 1970). In addition, the therapists were permitted 2 hours of mutual social interaction 5 days per week. During three sessions per week they interacted as pairs within the quad cage; during the remaining two 2-hour sessions per week they interacted as a group of four in a social playroom, described by Rosenblum (1961).

Procedure

·POSTISOLATION BASE-LINE PERIOD When the mean ages of the isolates and therapists were 6 and 3 months, respectively, the isolates were removed from their chambers. All subjects were then placed in individual quadrants of two quad cages, with two isolates and two therapists in each cage. The therapists retained their surrogates and continued to receive 2 hours of social interaction 5 days per week as described above, while the isolates were not permitted to interact socially with other monkeys or with surrogates. The postisolation base-line period lasted 2 weeks.

·POSTISOLATION THERAPY PERIOD Immediately after the base-line period, the following therapy procedure was initiated: (a) In therapy weeks 1–4, each isolate was allowed to interact with the therapist monkey adjacent to its quadrant for 2 hours per day, 3 days per week. (b) In therapy weeks 5–6, pair interaction (one isolate-one therapist) continued as described in a. In addition, the isolates were placed in the playroom with the therapists 1 hour per day, 2 days per week, in groups of four (two isolates, two therapists). (c) In therapy weeks 7–11, pair interaction (one isolate-one therapist) was reduced to two 2-hour sessions per week. The playroom sessions were expanded to three 1-hour sessions per week. (d) In therapy weeks 12–26, pair interaction was discontinued and replaced by two 2-hour sessions per week during which time all four members of each quad cage (two isolates, two therapists) were permitted free interaction within the quad cage. Playroom interaction continued as in *c*.

To summarize, following removal from isolation, the isolates were housed individually for a period of 2 weeks in order to assess postisolation behavioral levels. Twenty-six weeks of therapy followed. The first 4 weeks of therapy consisted of isolate-therapist interaction within the quad cage. Beginning at the fifth week, the isolates were also permitted social interaction with therapist and with each other in the playroom.

Data Collection

Beginning at 30 days of age, every subject was observed for two 5-minute periods, 5 days per week. Subject behaviors falling into each of 14 categories were measured for presence or absence during each of the twenty 15-second intervals which comprised the 5-minute session. The following behavioral categories were employed: self-groom (discrete, self-directed picking and/or spreading of the fur), self-mouth (oral contact, exclusive of biting, with any part of own body), self-bite (specific, vigorous, self-directed biting), self-clasp (clasping of any part of own body with hand(s) and/or foot (feet)), huddle (self-enclosed, fetallike position, incorporating any or all patterns of self-clasp, self-embrace, or lowered head), rock (repetitive, nonlocomotive forward and backward movement), spasm (single or repetitive convulsive jerk involving a major part of the body), stereotypy (identical body movements maintained in a rhythmic and repetitive fashion for at least three cycles), locomotion (ambulation of one or more full steps), environmental exploration (tactual and/or oral manipulation by subject or inanimate objects), vocalization (any sound emitted by subject), ventral cling (contact of own ventral body surface with another subject and/or surrogate), social contact (tactual and/or oral contact with another subject and/or surrogate, exclusive of ventral cling or play), and play (any socially directed play activity, including rough and tumble, approach-withdraw, and noncontact play). For each observation session, data consisted of 14 modified frequency scores, one for every behavioral category, each representing the total number of 15-second intervals during which behavior encompassed by the category was observed.

The observations were made between 9:00 A.M. and 5:00 P.M. by one of four testers, each of whom had been trained to a rigorous laboratory reliability criterion prior to the beginning of the experiment. Each subject's two daily observations were distributed as follows:

For isolate subjects (*a*) at 1–6 months there were two observations of each subject in the isolation chamber; (*b*) at 6–6½ months (postisolation base line) there were two observations of the subject in the individual quadrant of the quad cage; (*c*) at 6½–12½ months (therapy period) there was one observation of each subject in the individual quadrant of the quad cage and one observation of each subject in the social situation (either the quad cage or playroom) to which it had been assigned that day.

For therapist subjects at 1–9½ months there was one observation of each subject in the individual quadrant of the quad cage, the other of the subject in the social situation (either the quad cage or playroom) to which it had been assigned that day.

Data Analysis

Inspection of the data indicated that behaviors encompassed by four categories—self-groom, self-bite, spasm, and vocalization—were infrequently exhibited by any subjects, and therefore these categories were not analyzed statistically. Subject scores of the remaining 10 categories—self-mouth, self-clasp, huddle, rock, stereotype, locomotion, environmental exploration, and the social categories of ventral cling, social contact, and play—were analyzed in three stages.

First, behaviors of all subjects were traced from the end of the first to the sixth month of life in order to assess isolation effects during the period of confinement. For each of the above seven nonsocial categories, individual subject scores were summed over three 7-week periods, representing behaviors observed from 30 to 80 days, from 80 to 130 days, and from 130 to 180 days of age. Category means for each subject were calculated for each time period, representing the average number of 15-second intervals per observation session during the time block that behaviors encompassed by the category were observed. For each category the above means were subjected to a two-way repeated-measures analysis of variance, with group (isolate versus therapist) as the independent variable and time block as the repeated measure. The means were then compared by use of Duncan's new multiple-range test (Duncan, 1955), employing the Time Block × Subjects Within Groups mean square from the analysis of variance as the test denominator variance term. For the sake of parsimony, only the results of the Duncan tests are presented in this article.[2]

[2]The analysis of variance summary tables may be obtained from the authors upon request.

(2) Second, behavioral levels exhibited by the isolate subjects during the 2-week postisolation base line were directly compared to those observed during the final 50 days of isolation in order to determine possible "emergence trauma" effects. Two-tailed t tests were employed, one for each of the above nonsocial categories, to test for differences between category means calculated for the two time periods.

(3) Finally, behavioral changes transpiring during the therapy period were examined. Home-cage behaviors of each isolate and control subject were summed for every category over each of the three 60-day projects which comprised the therapy period. Category means were calculated for each subject as above, and the means were subjected to two-way repeated-measures analyses of variance, with groups as the independent variable and time block as the repeated measure, then compared by use of Duncan tests. Behaviors recorded during the quad cage interaction periods and during the playroom interaction sessions were separately analyzed in a similar fashion. Again, only the results of the Duncan tests are presented, although the complete analyses may be obtained from the authors upon request.

RESULTS

Three unequivocal findings emerged from the data analysis. First, isolate subjects developed significant behavioral abnormalities during the period of social isolation. Second, the isolate subjects exhibited virtually no trace of "emergence trauma" upon removal from isolation. Third and most important, the isolates showed significant recovery, in terms of both nonsocial and social behaviors in all testing situations during the course of the therapy period.

Isolation Period Behaviors

As shown by Table 1, which presents the group means obtained from isolation period observations and the results of the Duncan tests, during the first 2 months of life isolate and therapist monkeys failed to differ significantly on any measure except locomotion, with the isolates locomoting less than the controls ($p < .05$). During the third and fourth months, the only significant group difference was in self-mouthing, with the therapists exhibiting higher levels ($p < .05$). How-

Table 1. Duncan test analysis for isolation period

CATEGORY	I	T
Self-mouth		
Period 1	9.5	7.7
Period 2	7.4	10.7
Period 3	10.2	9.0
Self-clasp		
Period 1	.8	.1
Period 2	3.1	.5
Period 3	5.8	.7
Huddle		
Period 1	1.1	.6
Period 2	4.2	.7
Period 3	4.9	1.9
Rock		
Period 1	.1	.6
Period 2	.3	.6
Period 3	2.2	.4
Stereotypy		
Period 1	.2	.1
Period 2	1.2	.1
Period 3	2.6	.0
Locomotion		
Period 1	10.2	13.3
Period 2	11.4	13.4
Period 3	11.4	13.3
Environmental exploration		
Period 1	7.4	8.9
Period 2	8.6	10.9
Period 3	8.1	11.5

Note.—I = isolate subjects, T = therapist subjects; Period 1 = 30–80 days, Period 2 = 81–130 days, Period 3 = 131–180 days of age. Significant differences: Self-mouth—T – 2 > T – 1,I – 2, $p < .05$. Self-clasp—I – 3 > I –1, T – 1, T – 2, T – 3, $p < .01$; I – 3 > I – 2, $p < .05$. Huddle—I – 3 > I – 1, $p < .05$. Rock—I – 3 > I – 1, I – 2, T – 1, T – 2, T –3, $p < .05$. Stereotypy—I – 3 > I – 1, T – 1, T – 2, T – 3, $p < .01$; I – 3 > I – 2, $p < .05$; I – 2 > T – 3, $p < .05$. Locomotion— I – 1 < T – 1, T – 2, T – 3, $p < .05$. Environmental exploration—T – 3 > T – 1, I – 1, I – 2, I – 3, $p < .05$; T – 2 > I – 1, $p < .05$.

ever, during the final 2 months of the isolation period marked behavioral differences between isolates and therapists became evident. The isolates exhibited significantly higher levels of self-clasping ($p < .01$), rocking ($p < .05$), and stereotypy ($p < .01$) than the therapists, changes which reflected increases over previous levels by the isolates rather than decreases by the therapists. These behaviors have consistently been found in the past to differentiate isolate-reared monkeys from more adequately socialized controls. During this time period the isolates also exhibited lower levels of exploration than the therapists ($p < .05$). Thus, although the analysis disclosed few differences between isolate and therapist levels of behavior early in life, by 6 months of age the isolates were clearly exhibiting gross behavioral abnormalities in comparison with their therapist controls.

2. Postisolation Base-Line Behaviors

Comparison of the isolates' postisolation behavioral levels with their counterparts during the immediately preceding isolation period gave little indication of significant change following removal from isolation. No significant differences for any category were disclosed by the t tests. Thus, the data failed to substantiate the occurrence of measurable emergence trauma among the isolate subjects in this experiment. Rather, the isolates' abnormal behaviors, having developed during the period of isolation, remained at existing levels when the monkeys were removed from isolation.

3. Therapy Period Behaviors

The data from all three testing situations offered convincing evidence that significant gains were achieved by the isolate subjects during the therapy period. When first removed from their isolation chambers they exhibited high levels of disturbance behaviors and low levels of social behaviors, typical for monkeys socially isolated for the first 6 months of life. By the end of the therapy period, however, their behavioral levels were virtually indistinguishable from those of the socially competent therapist monkeys.

1) ·BEHAVIOR DURING QUAD CAGE THERAPY That the isolates exhibited significant recovery in the quad cage interaction situation during the therapy period was evident from the results of the appropriate Duncan tests. During the first 60 days of the therapy period, isolate subjects exhibited significantly higher levels of self-mouthing ($p < .05$), self-clasping ($p < .01$), huddling ($p < .05$), and rocking ($p < .05$) behaviors and lower levels of locomotion ($p < .05$), clinging ($p < .05$) than the therapist monkeys. These differences disappeared as the therapy period progressed, largely resulting from changes in isolate rather than therapist levels of behavior. From the sixty-first to the one hundred and twentieth day of therapy the two groups of monkeys differed significantly only with respect of locomotion, with the isolates exhibiting lower levels ($p < .05$). During the final 60 days of the therapy period there were no significant group differences on any of the category measures in the quad cage interaction situation.

2) ·BEHAVIOR DURING PLAYROOM THERAPY As in the quad cage interaction sessions, the isolate subjects exhibited significant behavioral recovery during the playroom therapy sessions. Initially in the playroom they showed significantly higher levels of self-mouth, self-clasp, huddle, and rock and significantly lower levels of locomotion, exploration, clinging, social contact, and play than the therapist monkeys (all $ps < .01$). During the fifty-first to the one hundredth day of the therapy period detectable group differences vanished except for categories of self-clasp, for which the isolates showed higher levels than the therapists ($p < .01$) and locomotion, clinging, and play, for which the therapists exhibited higher levels ($p < .05$, $p < .05$, and $p < .01$, respectively). During the final 50 days of playroom therapy the only category to yield significant group differences was self-clasp, with isolates showing higher levels ($p < .05$). The convergence of isolate-therapist behavioral levels over time resulted primarily from changes in isolate rather than therapist levels. Thus, although 9 behavior categories differentiated isolates from therapists during the first days of playroom therapy, the groups were behaviorally equivalent by the end of the therapy period save for the isolates' elevated levels of self-clasping, and for this behavior the isolates showed a significant decline

during the therapy period (0–50 days of therapy > 51–100 days of therapy > 101–150 days of therapy, $ps < .01$).

3) ·BEHAVIOR IN HOME QUADRANTS Except for the specific interaction sessions, all subjects were individually housed in quadrants of the quad cages during the 6 months of the therapy period. Analysis of home quadrant behavioral levels during this period indicated that the isolates' recovery in the presence of the therapist monkeys generalized to home-cage behaviors in the absence of physical contact with the therapists.

During the first 60 days of the therapy period isolates displayed significantly higher levels of self-mouth ($p < .05$), self-clasp ($p < .01$), huddle ($p < .01$), rock ($p < .01$), and stereotypy ($p < .01$) and significantly lower levels of locomotion ($p < .05$) and exploration ($p < .01$) than the therapist monkeys. During the middle 60 days of the therapy period, group differences were evident only for the behaviors of self-mouth ($p < .05$) and self-clasp ($p < .01$), with isolates exhibiting higher levels of both behaviors. During the final 60 days of the therapy period, no significant group differences for any category were disclosed by the analysis.

DISCUSSION

The primary finding of this experiment was that monkeys reared in total social isolation for the first 6 months of life exhibited significant recovery of virtually all behavioral deficits across all testing situations after appropriate therapeutic treatment. Reversal of the isolation syndrome to an equivalent degree over a range of situations had not been previously achieved or approached via any experimental procedures.

Some previous rehabilitative attempts used social agents but failed to reverse the isolation syndrome. We feel that the crucial factor for successful rehabilitation in the present study was intrinsic to the nature of the social agents employed. As well as the same species as the iso-lates, these agents were chosen specifically in terms of behaviors they could be predicted to exhibit consistently and spontaneously at appropriate stages of the therapy program. Behavioral predictions were based upon years of research examining the normal social development of the rhesus monkey.

A sequential, subjective account of the actual rehabilitative process early in the therapy period illustrates the appropriateness of the therapist choice. The isolate subjects did not exhibit spontaneous recovery during initial exposures to the younger, socially normal monkeys, a fact that is not surprising since no isolate monkey had shown spontaneous recovery in previous experimental situations. Rather, the therapist monkeys actively initiated the first social interactions, and only then did the isolates gradually exhibit improvement. Specifically, the therapist monkeys' initial responses to the isolates were to approach and cling, while the isolates were typically immobile and withdrawn. Only after clinging had been initiated did the isolates reciprocate, and only when the therapists had directed play responses toward the isolates did isolate play behavior emerge. Once these interaction patterns were established, the isolates themselves initiated play bouts with progressively increasing frequency.

Although the process of rehabilitation was essentially continuous, it is possible to delineate (1) two stages of isolate recovery. The first stage involved breaking down previously established patterns of abnormal, self-directed behaviors such as self-huddling and stereotypic rocking. This was achieved primarily through the clinging efforts of the therapist monkeys. An isolate receiving intimate social contact cannot effectively continue to rock and self-huddle. The breaking down of entrenched self-directed activity permitted the isolate subjects to engage in alternative behaviors, which took the form of elementary social contact, exploration, and locomotion.

(2) The second stage involved developing the simple behaviors described above into a more complex, socially appropriate behavioral repertoire.

Again, the therapists apparently provided the crucial stimulation as they themselves developed a complex social repertoire in the course of normal maturation. With respect to these behavior patterns, isolate recovery was substantial.

Previous rehabilitative attempts which initially exposed isolate subjects to complex social stimulation failed to break down self-directed activity exhibited by the isolates, and recovery did not follow. Also, exposure to a surrogate was demonstrated to reduce isolate disturbance behavior, but because a surrogate cannot provide complex social stimulation those isolate subjects never developed complex social behaviors in the presence of a surrogate. In contrast, the present study provided the isolate subjects with a set of social stimuli designed to reduce self-directed activity, followed by a set of stimuli gradually increasing in social sophistication. In this case, the same group of therapist monkeys provided both types of stimulation and provided them in the appropriate temporal sequence during the course of their own normal social maturation.

These results suggest that a reexamination of traditional theoretical interpretations of isolation-rearing effects is required. The data from the present study are inconsistent with a strict interpretation of the critical period position, which implies that once a so-called critical period has transpired without social stimulation, normal social behaviors can never develop. The present results yield empirical testimony that relatively normal social development can occur following 6 months of total social isolation from birth provided that the isolates are exposed to appropriately selected social stimulation. One can conclude [A] that either the first 6 months of life do not constitute a critical period for socialization of the rhesus [B] monkey or that strict critical periods do not exist for this species. We prefer the latter interpretation. While it is obvious from numerous researches that the first 6 months of life are indeed critical for socialization under usual circumstances, a more apt terminology for this chrono-

logical span might be "sensitive period" or "sensitive phase" (Hinde, 1966).

Also, the postisolation base-line data do not specifically support an emergence trauma interpretation of isolation-rearing effects. Rather, the monkeys socially isolated in this study had developed obvious behavioral anomalies prior to emergence, but the data analysis disclosed no significant increments in these abnormalities following emergence. We do not claim that emergence from isolation has no behavioral consequences. The actual analysis compared preeemergence behavioral levels with those encompassing a 2-week period following removal from isolation and may well have masked actual effects exhibited during the initial postisolation hours. However, acknowledgment of behavioral changes resulting from shifts in the environment is a far cry from attribution of persisting behavioral deficiencies to the process of environmental change.

It is appropriate at this point to express a certain degree of caution regarding the findings of this study, particularly in light of the absence of a group of control isolate-reared monkeys not exposed to therapists, although, in a sense, a decade of isolation research using monkeys provides an impressive body of control data. The above procedures resulted in a reversal of the isolation syndrome during the course of the experiment. However, since the isolate subjects have not yet reached physical maturity, assessment of their adult social capability is not possible at the present time. Further, the exact procedure described above may not be appropriate for monkeys subjected to longer periods of social isolation, nor will the procedure necessarily be effective if not instituted soon after the period of isolation.

Nevertheless, the fact that the isolates in this study did show marked social gains suggests that the *potential* for adequate social development is not necessarily destroyed by the isolation experience. Rather, the actual relationship between isolation rearing and social behavior may, in fact, be similar to the relationship between isolation rearing and learning capability. Previous researches have demonstrated that while isolation produces performance deficits in learning situations, intellectual capability remains relatively intact in monkey subjects. Apparently, adequate adaptation is required for adequate performance. With respect to social behavior, it may well be that previous studies have reported performance deficits only, that social capability remains viable despite the isolation experience, and that the requirement for rehabilitation is merely appropriate social stimulation. If this finding generalizes not only to other forms of early experience but also to other species, then the implications of the present experimentation for reversal of psychopathological behavior attributed to inadequate early experience become enormous.

References

Blomquist, A. J., & Harlow, H. F. The infant rhesus monkey program at the University of Wisconsin Primate Laboratory. *Proceedings of the Animal Care Panel,* 1961, 11, 57–64.

Boelkins, R. C. The development of social behavior in the infant rhesus monkey following a period of social isolation. Unpublished master's thesis, University of Wisconsin, 1963.

Clark, D. L. Immediate and delayed effects of early, intermediate, and late social isolation in the rhesus monkey. Unpublished doctoral dissertation, University of Wisconsin, 1968.

Duncan, D. B. Multiple range and multiple *F* tests. *Biometrics,* 1955, 11, 1–42.

Fuller, J. L., & Clark, L. D. Genetic and treatment factors modifying the postisolation syndrome in dogs. *Journal of Comparative and Physiological Psychology,* 1966, 61, 251–257.

Gluck, J. P. Successive acquisitons and extinctions of bar pressing: The effects of differential rearing in rhesus monkeys. Unpublished master's thesis, University of Wisconsin, 1970.

Griffin, G. A., & Harlow, H. F. Effects of three months of total social deprivation on social adjustment and learning in the rhesus monkey. *Child Development,* 1966, 37, 533–547.

Harlow, H. F., Dodsworth, R. O., & Harlow, M. K. Total social isolation in monkeys. *Proceedings of the National Academy of Sciences,* 1965, 54, 90–96.

Harlow, H. F., & Harlow, M. K. The effect of rearing conditions on behavior. *Bulletin of the Menninger Clinic,* 1962, 26, 213–224.

Harlow, H. F., & Harlow, M. K. Effects of various mother-infant relationships on rhesus monkey behaviors. In B. M. Foss (Ed.), *Determinants of infant behavior.* Vol. 4. London: Methuen, 1968.

Harlow, H. F., Harlow, M. K., Dodsworth, R. O., & Arling, G. L. Maternal behavior of rhesus monkeys deprived of mothering and peer associations in infancy. *Proceedings of the American Philosophical Society,* 1966, 110, 58–66.

Harlow, H. F., Schiltz, K. A., & Harlow, M. K. Effects of social isolation on the learning performance of rhesus monkeys. In C. R. Carpenter (Ed.), *Proceedings of the Second International Congress of Primatology.* Vol. I. New York: Karger, 1969.

Harlow, H. F., & Suomi, S. J. The nature of love—simplified. *American Psychologist,* 1970, 25, 161–168.

Hinde, R. A. *Animal behavior.* New York: McGraw-Hill, 1966.

Lorenz, K. *Evolution and modification of behavior.* Chicago: University of Chicago Press, 1965.

Mason, W. A. Social development of rhesus monkeys with restricted social experience. *Perceptual and Motor Skills,* 1963, 16, 263–270.

Pratt, C. L. The developmental consequences of variations in early social stimulation. Unpublished doctoral dissertation, University of Wisconsin, 1969.

Rosenblum, L. A. The development of social behavior in the rhesus monkey. Unpublished doctoral dissertation, University of Wisconsin, 1961.

Rowland, G. L. The effects of total isolation upon learning and social behavior of rhesus monkeys. Unpublished doctoral dissertation, University of Wisconsin, 1964.

Sackett, G. P. Abnormal behavior in laboratory reared rhesus monkeys. In M. W. Fox (Ed.), *Abnormal behavior in animals.* Philadelphia: Saunders, 1968. (a)

Sackett, G. P. The persistence of abnormal behavior in monkeys following isolation rearing. In R. Porter (Ed.), *The role of learning in psychotherapy.* London: Churchill. 1968. (b)

Scott, J. P. Critical periods in behavioral development. *Science,* 1962, 138, 949–958.

Senko, M. G. The effects of early, intermediate, and late experiences upon adult macaque sexual behavior. Unpublished master's thesis, University of Wisconsin, 1966.

Singh, S. D. Urban monkeys. *Scientific American.* 1969, 221, 108–115.

Suomi, S. J., & Harlow, H. F. Apparatus conceptualization for psychopathological research in monkeys. *Behavioral Research Methods and Instrumentation,* 1969, 1, 247–250.

Cross-Cultural Perspectives on Early Development

Jerome Kagan

Robert E. Klein

Most American psychologists believe in the hardiness of habit and the premise that experience etches an indelible mark on the mind not easily erased by time or trauma. The application of that

NOTE: This article was presented by J. Kagan as an invited address to the annual meeting of the American Association for the Advancement of Science, Washington, D.C., December 26, 1972. The research reported in this article was supported by the Association for the Aid of Crippled Children, Carnegie Corporation of New York, Grant HD-4299 and Contract PH 43-65-640 from the National Institute of Child Health and Human Development, and Grant GS-33048, Collaborative Research on Uniform Measures of Social Competence, from the National Science Foundation.

Requests for reprints should be sent to Jerome Kagan, Department of Psychology and Social Relations, Harvard University, William James Hall, 33 Kirkland Street, Cambridge, Massachusetts 02138.

assumption to the first era of development leads to the popular view that psychological growth during the early years is under the strong influence of the variety and patterning of external events and that the psychological structures shaped by those initial encounters have a continuity that stretches at least into early adolescence. The first part of that hypothesis, which owes much of its popularity to Freud, Harlow, and Skinner, has strong empirical support. The continuity part of the assumption, which is more equivocal, is summarized in the American adage, "Well begun is half done."

Many developmental psychologists, certain of the long-lasting effects of early experience, set out to find the form of those initial stabilities and the earliest time they might obtain a preview of the child's future. Although several decades of research have uncovered fragile lines that seem to travel both backward and forward in time, the breadth and magnitude of intraindividual continuities have not been overwhelming, and each seems to be easily lost or shattered (Kagan & Moss, 1962; Kessen, Haith, & Salapatek, 1970). A recent exhaustive review of research on human infancy led to the conclusion that "only short term stable individual variation has been demonstrated; . . . and demonstrations of continuity in process—genotype continuity—have been rare indeed [Kessen et al., 1970, p. 297]." Since that evaluation violates popular beliefs, the authors noted a few pages later:

> In spite of slight evidence of stability, our inability to make predictions of later personality from observations in the first three years of life is so much against good sense and common observation, to say nothing of the implication of all developmental theories, that the pursuit of predictively effective categories of early behavior will surely continue unabated [p. 309].

The modest empirical support for long-term continuity is occasionally rationalized by arguing that although behaviors similar in manifest form might not be stable over long time periods, the underlying structures might be much firmer (Kagan, 1971). Hence, if the operational manifestations of those hidden forms were discerned, continuity of cognitive, motivational, and affective structures would be affirmed. However, we recently observed some children living in an isolated Indian village on Lake Atitlan in the highlands of northwest Guatemala. We saw listless, silent, apathetic infants; passive, quiet, timid 3-year-olds; but active, gay, intellectually competent 11-year-olds. Since there is no reason to believe that living conditions in this village have changed during the last century, it is likely that the alert 11-year-olds were, a decade earlier, listless, vacant-staring infants. That observation has forced us to question the strong form of the continuity assumption in a serious way.

The data to be presented imply absence of a predictive relationship between level of cognitive development at 12–18 months of age and quality of intellectual functioning at 11 years. This conclusion is not seriously different from the repeated demonstrations of no relation between infant intelligence quotient (IQ) or developmental quotient (DQ) scores during the first year of life and Binet or Wechsler IQ scores obtained during later childhood (Kessen et al., 1970; Pease, Wolins, & Stockdale, 1973). The significance of the current data, however, derives from the fact that the infants seemed to be more seriously retarded than those observed in earlier studies, their environments markedly less varied, and the assessment of later cognitive functioning based on culture-fair tests of specific cognitive abilities rather than culturally biased IQ tests.

Moreover, these observations suggest that it is misleading to talk about continuity of any psychological characteristic—be it cognitive, motivational, or behavioral—without specifying simultaneously the context of development. Consider the long-term stability of passivity as an example. The vast majority of the infants in the Indian village were homogeneously passive and retained this characteristic until they were five or six years old. A preschool child rarely forced a submissive posture on another. However, by eight years of age, some of the children became dominant over others because the structure of the peer group required that role to be filled. Factors other than early infant passivity were critical in determining that differentiation, and physical size, strength, and competence at valued skills seemed to be more important than the infant's disposition. In modern American society, where there is much greater variation among young children in degree of passivity and dominance, a passive four-year-old will always encounter a large group of dominant peers who enforce a continuing role of submissiveness on him. As a result, there should be firmer stability of behavioral passivity during the early years in an American city than in the Indian village. But the stability of that behavior seems to be more dependent on the presence of dominant members in the immediate vicinity than on some inherent force within the child.

Continuity of a psychological disposition is not solely the product of an inherited or early acquired structure that transcends a variety of contexts. The small group of scientists who champion that view of stability—we have been among them—envision a small box of different-colored gems tucked deep in the brain, with names like intelligent, passive, irritable, or withdrawn engraved on them. These material entities guarantee that, despite behavioral disguises, an inherent set of psychological qualities, independent of the local neighborhood and knowable under the proper conditions, belongs to each individual. This belief in a distinct and unchanging mosaic of core traits—an identity—is fundamental to Western thought and is reflected in the psychological writings of Erik Erikson and the novels of popular Western writers. Only Herman Hesse, who borrowed the philosophy of the East, fails to make a brief for personal identity. *Siddhartha, Magister Ludi,* and *Narcissus and Goldmund* are not trying to discover "who they are" but are seeking serenity, and each appreciates the relevance of setting in that journey.

A secondary theme concerns the interaction of maturation and environment, an issue that has seized academic conversation because of the renewed debate surrounding the inheritance of intelligence. But there is a broader issue to probe. The majority of American psychologists remain fundamentally Lockean in attitude, believing that thought and action owe primary allegiance to experience and that reinforcements and observations of models set the major course of change. Despite Piaget's extraordinary popularity, the majority of American psychologists do not believe that maturation supplies the major impetus for psychological growth during the childhood years. We have forgotten that many years ago Myrtle McGraw (1935) allowed one twin to climb some stairs and prevented his co-twin from practicing that skill. This homely experiment occurred only

a few years after Carmichael (1926) anesthetized some *Amblystoma* embryos to prevent them from swimming. The twin not allowed to climb was behind his partner in learning this skill, but he eventually mastered it. Carmichael's embryos swam perfectly when the anesthetic was pumped out of the tank. In both instances, the organisms could not be prevented from displaying species-specific properties.

Our observations in these Indian villages have led us to reorder the hierarchy of complementary influence that biology and environmental forces exert on the development of intellectual functions that are natural to man. Separate maturational factors seem to set the time of emergence of those basic abilities. Experience can slow down or speed up that emergence by several months or several years, but nature will win in the end. The capacity for perceptual analysis, imitation, language, inference, deduction, symbolism, and memory will eventually appear in sturdy form in any natural environment, for each is an inherent competence in the human program. But these competences, which we assume to be universal, are to be distinguished from culturally specific talents that will not appear unless the child is exposed to or taught them directly. Reading, arithmetic, and understanding of specific words and concepts fall into this latter category.

This distinction between universal and culturally specific competences implies a parallel distinction between absolute and relative retardation. Consider physical growth as an illustration of this idea. There is sufficient cross-cultural information on age of onset of walking to warrant the statement that most children should be walking unaided before their second birthday. A three-year-old unable to walk is physically retarded in the absolute sense, for he has failed to attain a natural competence at the normative time. However, there is neither an empirical nor a logical basis for expecting that most children, no matter where they live, will develop the ability to hunt with a spear, ride a horse, or play football. Hence, it is not reasonable to speak of absolute retardation on these skills. In those cultures where these talents are taught, encouraged, or modeled, children will differ in the age at which they attain varied levels of mastery. But we can only classify a child as precocious or retarded relative to another in his community. The data to be reported suggest that absolute retardation in the attainment of specific cognitive competences during infancy has no predictive validity with respect to level of competence on a selected set of natural cognitive skills at age 11. *The data do not imply that a similar level of retardation among American infants has no future implication for relative retardation on culture-specific skills.*

THE GUATEMALAN SETTINGS

The infant observations to be reported here were made in two settings in Guatemala. One set of data came from four subsistence farming Ladino villages in eastern Guatemala. The villages are moderately isolated, Spanish speaking, and contain between 800 and 1,200 inhabitants. The families live in small thatched huts of cane or adobe with dirt floors and no sanitary facilities. Books, pencils, paper, and pictures are typically absent from the experience of children prior to school entrance, and, even in school, the average child has no more than a thin lined notebook and a stub of a pencil.

A second location was a more isolated Indian village of 850 people located on the shores of Lake Atitlan in the northwest mountainous region of the country. Unlike the Spanish-speaking villages, the Indians of San Marcos la Laguna have no easy access to a city and are psychologically more detached. The isolation is due not only to geographical location but also to the fact that few of the women and no more than half of the men speak reasonable Spanish. Few adults and no children can engage the culture of the larger nation, and the Indians of San Marcos regard themselves as an alien and exploited group.

The Infant in San Marcos

During the first 10–12 months, the San Marcos infant spends most of his life in the small, dark interior of his windowless hut. Since women do not work in the field, the mother usually stays close to the home and spends most of her day preparing food, typically tortillas, beans, and coffee, and perhaps doing some weaving. If she travels to a market to buy or sell, she typically leaves her infant with an older child or a relative. The infant is usually close to the mother, either on her lap or enclosed on her back in a colored cloth, sitting on a mat, or sleeping in a hammock. The mother rarely allows the infant to crawl on the dirt floor of the hut and feels that the outside sun, air, and dust are harmful.

The infant is rarely spoken to or played with, and the only available objects for play, besides his own clothing or his mother's body, are oranges, ears of corn, and pieces of wood or clay. These infants are distinguished from American infants of the same age by their extreme motoric passivity, fearfulness, minimal smiling, and, above all, extraordinary quietness. A few with pale cheeks and vacant stares had the quality of tiny ghosts and resembled the description of the institutionalized infants that Spitz called marasmic. Many would not orient to a taped source of speech, not smile or babble to vocal overtures, and hesitated over a minute before reaching for an attractive toy.

An American woman who lived in the village made five separate 30-minute observations in the homes of 12 infants 8–16 months of age. If a particular behavioral variable occurred during a five-second period, it was recorded once for that interval. The infants were spoken to or played with 6% of the time, with a maximum of 12%. The comparable averages for American middle-class homes are 25%, with a maximum of 40% (Lewis & Freedle, 1972). It should be noted that the infant's vocalizations, which occurred about 6% of the time, were typically grunts lasting less than a second, rather than the prolonged babbling typical of middle-class American children. The infants cried very little because the slightest irritability led the mother to nurse her child at once. Nursing was the single, universal therapeutic treatment for all infant distress, be it caused by fear, cold, hunger, or cramps. Home observations in the eastern villages are consonant with those gathered in San Marcos and reveal infrequent infant vocalization and little verbal interaction or play with adults or older siblings. The mothers in these settings seem to regard their infants the way an American parent views an expensive cashmere sweater: Keep it nearby and protect it but do not engage it reciprocally.

One reason why these mothers might behave this way is that it is abundantly clear to every parent that all children begin to walk by 18 months, to talk by age 3, and to perform some adult chores by age 10, despite the listless, silent quality of infancy. The mother's lack of active manipulation, stimulation, or interactive play with her infant is not indicative of indifference or rejection, but is a reasonable posture, given her knowledge of child development.

COMPARATIVE STUDY OF INFANT COGNITIVE DEVELOPMENT

Although it was not possible to create a formal laboratory setting for testing infants in San Marcos, it was possible to do so in the eastern Ladino villages, and we shall summarize data derived from identical procedures administered to rural Guatemalan and American infants. Although the infants in the Ladino villages were more alert than the Indian children of San Marcos, the similarities in living conditions and rearing practices are such that we shall assume that the San Marcos infants would have behaved like the Ladino children or, what is more likely, at a less mature level. In these experiments, the Guatemalan mother and child came to a special laboratory equipped with a chair and a stage that simulated

the setting in the Harvard laboratories where episodes were administered to cross-sectional groups of infants, 84 American and 80 Guatemalan, at $5\frac{1}{2}$, $7\frac{1}{2}$, $9\frac{1}{2}$, and $11\frac{1}{2}$ months of age, with 10–24 infants from each culture at each age level.

Before describing the procedures and results, it will be helpful to summarize the theoretical assumptions that govern interpretation of the infant's reactions to these episodes. There appear to be two important maturationally controlled processes which emerge between 2 and 12 months that influence the child's reactions to transformations of an habituated event (Kagan, 1971, 1972). During the first six weeks of life, the duration of the child's attention to a visual event is controlled by the amount of physical change or contrast in the event. During the third month, the infant shows prolonged attention to events that are moderate discrepancies from habituated standards. Maintenance of attention is controlled by the relation of the event to the child's schema for the class to which that event belongs. The typical reactions to discrepancy include increased fixation time, increased vocalization, and either cardiac deceleration or decreased variability of heart rate during the stimulus presentation. These conclusions are based on many independent studies and we shall not document them here (Cohen, Gelber, & Lazar, 1971; Kagan, 1971; Lewis, Goldberg, & Campbell, 1970).

However, at approximately eight–nine months, a second process emerges. The infant now begins to activate cognitive structures, called hypotheses, in the service of interpreting discrepant events. A hypothesis is viewed as a representation of a relation between two schemata. Stated in different language, the infant not only notes and processes a discrepancy, he also attempts to transform it to his prior schemata for that class of event and activates hypotheses to serve this advanced cognitive function. It is not a coincidence that postulation of this new competence coincides with the time when the infant displays object permanence and separation anxiety, phenomena that require the child to activate an idea of an absent object or person.

There are two sources of support for this notion. The first is based on age changes in attention to the same set of events. Regardless of whether the stimulus is a set of human masks, a simple black and white design, or a dynamic sequence in which a moving orange rod turns on a bank of three light bulbs upon contact, there is a U-shaped relation between age and duration of attention across the period 3–36 months, with the trough typically occurring between 7 and 12 months of age (Kagan, 1972).

The curvilinear relation between age and attention to human masks has been replicated among American, rural Guatemalan, and Kahlahari desert Bushman children (Kagan, 1971; Konnor, 1973; Sellers, Klein, Kagan, & Minton, 1972). If discrepancy were the only factor controlling fixation time, a child's attention should decrease with age, for the stimulus events become less discrepant as he grows older. The increase in attention toward the end of the first years is interpreted as a sign of a new cognitive competence, which we have called the *activation of hypotheses.*

A second source of support for this idea is that the probability of a cardiac acceleration to a particular discrepancy increases toward the end of the first year, whereas cardiac deceleration is the modal reaction during the earlier months (Kagan, 1972). Because studies of adults and young children indicate that cardiac acceleration accompanies mental work, while deceleration accompanies attention to an interesting event (Lacey, 1967; Van Hover, 1971), the appearance of acceleration toward the end of the first year implies that the infants are performing active mental work, or activating hypotheses.

Since increased attention to a particular discrepancy toward the end of the first year is one diagnostic sign of the emergence of this stage of cognitive development, cultural differences in attention to fixed discrepancies during the first year might provide information on the developmental maturity of the infants in each cultural group.

METHOD

Block Episode

Each child was shown a 2-inch wooden orange block for six or eight successive trials (six for the two older ages, and eight for the two younger ages) followed by three or five transformation trials in which a 1½-inch orange block was presented. These transformations were followed by three representations of the original 2-inch block.

Light Episode

The child was shown 8 or 10 repetitions of a sequence in which a hand moved an orange rod in a semicircle until it touched a bank of three light bulbs which were lighted upon contact between the rod and the bulbs. In the five transformation trials that followed, the hand appeared but the rod did not move and the lights lit after a four-second interval. Following the transformations, the original event was presented for three additional trials.

During each of the episodes, two observers coded (a) how long the infant attended to the event, (b) whether the infant vocalized or smiled, and (c) fretting or crying. Intercoder reliability for these variables was over .90.

RESULTS

The Guatemalan infants were significantly less attentive than the Americans on both episodes, and the cultural differences were greater at the two older than at the two younger ages. Figures 1 and 2 illustrate the mean total fixation time to four successive trial blocks for the two episodes. The four trial blocks were the first three standard trials, the last three standards, the first three transformations, and the three return trials.

The American infants of all ages had longer fixation times to the block during every trial block (F ranged from 30.8 to 67.3, $df = 1/154$, $p < .001$). The American infants also displayed longer fixations to the light during every trial block (F ranged from 9.8 to 18.4, $df = 1/141$, $p < .01$). However, it is important to note that at 11½ months, the Amer-

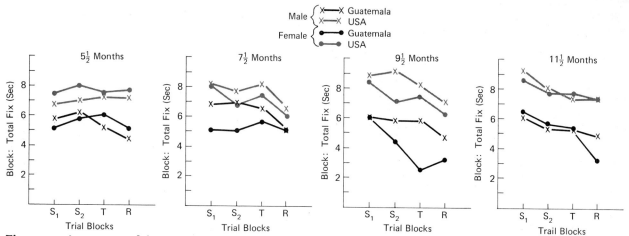

Figure 1 Average total fixation time to the block episode by age and culture.

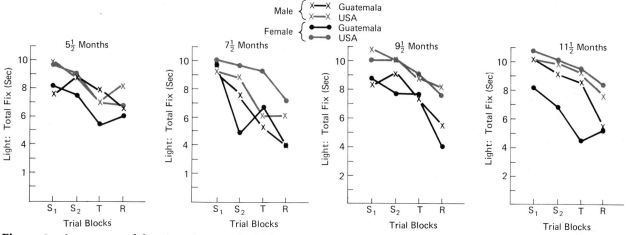

Figure 2 Average total fixation time to the light episode by age and culture.

ican children maintained more sustained attention to the return of the standard than the Guatemalans, who showed a drop in fixation time toward the end of the episode. These data suggest that more of the American than of the Guatemalan infants had entered the stage of activation of hypotheses. Since the Ladino infants appeared more mature than the San Marcos children, it is possible that the American one-year-olds were approximately three months advanced over the San Marcos children in this cognitive function.

ADDITIONAL ASSESSMENTS OF DEVELOPMENTAL STATUS

We collected, under less formal conditions in the home, additional information on the developmental status of the San Marcos infant. Not one of the 12 infants between 8 and 16 months reached for an attractive object they watched being hidden, although many would, with considerable hesitation, reach for a visible object placed close to their hands. Furthermore, none of these 12 infants revealed facial surprise following a sequence in which they watched an object being hidden under a cloth but saw no object when that cloth was removed. These observations suggest an absolute retardation of four months in the display of behavioral signs diagnostic of the attainment of object permanence.

A third source of data is based on observations of stranger anxiety. Each of 16 infants between 8 and 20 months was observed following the first exposure to a strange male (the senior author). The first age at which obvious apprehension and/or crying occurred was 13 months, suggesting a five-month lag between San Marcos and American infants. Finally, the information on nonmorphemic babbling and the onset of meaningful speech supports a diagnosis of absolute retardation. There was no marked increase in frequency of babbling or vocalization between 8 and 16 months among the 12 San Marcos infants observed at home, while comparable observations in American homes revealed a significant increase in babbling and the appearance of morphemic vocalizations for some children. Furthermore, many parents remarked that meaningful speech typically appears first at $2\frac{1}{2}$ years of age, about one year later than the average display of first words in American children.

These data, together with the extremely depressed, withdrawn appearance of the San Marcos infants, suggest retardations of three or more months for various psychological competences that typically emerge during the first two years of life. With the exception of one 16-month-old boy, whose alert appearance resembled that of an American infant, there was little variability among the remaining children. Since over 90% were homogeneously passive, nonalert, and quiet, it is unlikely that the recovery of intellectual functioning to be reported later was a result of the selective mortality of a small group of severely retarded infants.

RESILIENCE OF COGNITIVE DEVELOPMENT

The major theme of this article is the potential for recovery of cognitive functions despite early infant retardation. When the San Marcos child becomes mobile at around 15 months he leaves the dark hut, begins to play with other children, and provides himself with cognitive challenges that demand accommodations. Since all children experience this marked discontinuity in variety of experience and opportunity for exploration between the first and second birthday, it is instructive to compare the cognitive competence of older Guatemalan and American children to determine if differences in level of functioning are still present.

The tests administered were designed to assess cognitive processes that are believed to be part of the natural competence of growing children, rather than the culturally arbitrary segments of knowledge contained in a standard IQ test. We tried to create tests that were culturally fair, recognizing that this goal is, in the extreme, unattainable. Hence, the tests were not standardized instruments with psychometric profiles of test–retest reliabilities and criterion validity studies. This investigation should be viewed as a natural experiment in which the independent variable was degree of retardation in infancy and the dependent variables were performances on selected cognitive instruments during childhood. We assume, along with many psychologists, that perceptual analysis, recall and recognition memory, and inference are among the basic cognitive functions of children (even though they do not exhaust that set), and our tests were designed to evaluate those processes.

Tests of recall and recognition memory, perceptual analysis, and perceptual and conceptual inference were given to children in San Marcos, the Ladino villages, an Indian village close to Guatemala City and more modern than San Marcos, Cambridge, Massachusetts, and to two different groups of children living in Guatemala City. One of the Guatemala City settings, the "guarderia," was a day care center for very poor children. The second group, middle-class children attending nursery school, resembled a middle-class American sample in both family background and opportunity. Not all tests were administered to all children. The discussion is organized according to the cognitive function assessed, rather than the sample studied. The sample sizes ranged from 12 to 40 children at any one age.

Recall Memory for Familiar Objects

The ability to organize experience for commitment to long-term memory and to retrieve that information on demand is a basic cognitive skill. It is generally believed that the form of the organization contains diagnostic information regarding cognitive maturity for, among Western samples, both number of independent units of information and the conceptual clustering of that information increase with age.

A 12-object recall task was administered to two samples of Guatemalan children. One group lived in a Ladino village 17 kilometers from Guatemala City; the second group was composed of San Marcos children. The 80 subjects from the Ladino village were 5 and 7 years old, equally balanced for age and sex. The 55 subjects from San Marcos were between 5 and 12 years of age (26 boys and 29 girls).

The 12 miniature objects to be recalled were common to village life and belonged to three conceptual categories: animals (pig, dog, horse, cow), kitchen utensils (knife, spoon, fork, glass), and clothing (pants, dress, underpants, hat). Each child was first required to name the objects, and if the child was unable to he was given the name. The child was then told that after the objects had been randomly arranged on a board he would have 10 seconds to inspect them, after which they would be covered with a cloth, and he would be required to say all the objects he could remember.

Table 1 contains the average number of objects recalled and the number of pairs of conceptually similar words recalled—an index of clustering— for the first two trials. A pair was defined as the temporally contiguous recall of two or more items of the same category. A child received one point for reporting a pair of contiguous items, two points for three contiguous items, and three points

Table 1. Mean number of objects and pairs recalled

AGE	TRIAL 1		TRIAL 2	
	RECALL	PAIRS	RECALL	PAIRS
LADINO VILLAGE				
5	5.2	2.1	5.4	2.1
7	6.7	3.3	7.8	3.7
INDIAN VILLAGE				
5–6	7.1	3.4	7.8	3.8
7–8	8.6	3.4	8.3	3.6
9–10	10.3	4.9	10.3	4.3
11–12	9.6	3.4	10.1	3.6

for contiguous recall of four items. Hence, the maximum clustering score for a single trial was nine points. As Table 1 reveals, the children showed a level of clustering beyond chance expectation (which is between 1.5 and 2.0 pairs for recall scores of seven to eight words). Moreover, recall scores increased with age on both trials for children in both villages (F ranged from 11.2 to 27.7, $p < .05$), while clustering increased with age in the Ladino village ($F = 26.8$, $p < .001$ for Trial 1; $F = 3.48$, $p < .05$ for Trial 2).

No five- or six-year-old in either village and only 12 of the 40 seven-year-olds in the Ladino village were attending school. School for the others consisted of little more than semiorganized games. Moreover, none of the children in San Marcos had ever left the village, and the five- and six-year-olds typically spent most of the day within a 500-yard radius of their homes. Hence, school attendance and contact with books and a written language do not seem to be prerequisites for clustering in young children.

The recall and cluster scores obtained in Guatemala were remarkably comparable to those reported for middle-class American children. Appel, Cooper, McCarrell, Knight, Yussen, and Flavell (1971) presented 12 pictures to Minneapolis children in Grade 1 (approximately age 7) and 15 pictures to children in Grade 5 (approximately age 11) in a single-trial recall task similar to the one described here. The recall scores were 66%

for the 7-year-olds and 80% for the 11-year-olds. These values are almost identical to those obtained in both Guatemalan villages. The cluster indices were also comparable. The American 7-year-olds had a cluster ratio of .25; the San Marcos 5- and 6-year-olds had a ratio of .39.[1]

Recognition Memory

The cultural similarity in recall also holds for recognition memory. In a separate study, 5-, 8-, and 11-year-old children from Ladino villages in the East and from Cambridge, Massachusetts, were shown 60 pictures of objects—all of which were familiar to the Americans but some of which were unfamiliar to the Guatemalans. After 0-, 24-, or 48-hours delay, each child was shown 60 pairs of pictures, one of which was old and the other new, and was asked to decide which one he had seen. Although the 5- and 8-year-old Americans performed significantly better than the Guatemalans, there was no statistically significant cultural difference for the 11-year-olds, whose scores ranged from 85% to 98% after 0-, 24-, or 48-hours delay (Kagan et al., 1973). (See Table 2.) The remarkably high scores of the American 5-year-olds have also been reported by Scott (1973).

A similar result was found on a recognition memory task for 32 photos of faces, balanced for sex, child versus adult, and Indian versus Caucasian, administered to 35 American and 38 San Marcos children 8–11 years of age. Each child initially inspected 32 chromatic photographs of faces, one at a time, in a self-placed procedure. Each child's recognition memory was tested by showing him 32 pairs of photographs (each pair was of the same sex, age, and ethnicity), one of which was old and the other new. The child had to state which photograph he had seen during the inspection phase. Although the American 8- and 9-year-olds performed slightly better than the Guatemalans (82% versus 70%), there was no significant cultural difference among the 10- and 11-year-olds (91% versus 87%). Moreover, there was no cultural difference at any age for the highest performance attained by a single child.[2] The favored interpretation of the poorer performance of the younger children in both recognition memory studies is that some of them did not completely understand the task and others did not activate the proper problem-solving strategies during the registration and retrieval phases of the task.

It appears that recall and recognition memory are basic cognitive functions that seem to mature in a regular way in a natural environment. The cognitive retardation observed during the first year does not have any serious predictive validity for these two important aspects of cognitive functioning for children 10–11 years of age.

Perceptual Analysis

The Guatemalan children were also capable of solving difficult Embedded Figures Test items. The test consisted of 12 color drawings of familiar objects in which a triangle had been embedded as part of the object. The child had to locate the hidden triangle and place a black paper triangle so that it was congruent with the design of the drawing. The test was administered to rural Indian children from San Marcos, as well as to rural In-

Table 2. Mean percentage of correct responses

| | AMERICANS | | | GUATEMALANS | | |
| | AGE | | | | | |
DELAY	5	8	11	5	8	11
0 hours	92.8	96.7	98.3	58.4	74.6	85.2
24 hours	86.7	95.6	96.7	55.8	71.0	87.0
48 hours	87.5	90.3	93.9	61.4	75.8	86.2

Note. Percent signs are omitted.

[1]The cluster index is the ratio of the number of pairs recalled to the product of the number of categories in the list times one less than the number of words in each category.

[2]These photographs were also used in an identical procedure with 12 Kipsigis-speaking 10- and 11-year-olds from a rural village in eastern Kenya. Despite the absence of any black faces in the set, the percentage of items recognized correctly was 82 for this group of African children.

dians living close to Guatemala City (labeled Indian₁ in Figure 3), the Ladino villages, and two groups from Guatemala City. (See Figure 3.)

The Guatemala City middle-class children had the highest scores and, except for San Marcos, the rural children, the poorest. The surprisingly competent performance of the San Marcos children is due, we believe, to the more friendly conditions of testing. This suggestion is affirmed by an independent study in which a special attempt was made to maximize rapport and comprehension of instructions with a group of rural isolated children before administering a large battery of tests. Although all test performances were not facilitated by this rapport-raising procedure, performance on the Embedded Figures Test was improved considerably. It is important to note that no five- or six-year-old was completely incapable

of solving some of these problems. The village differences in mean score reflect the fact that the rural children had difficulty with three or four of the harder items. This was the first time that many rural children had ever seen a two-dimensional drawing, and most of the five-, six-, and seven-year-olds in San Marcos had had no opportunity to play with books, paper, pictures, or crayons. Nonetheless, these children solved seven or eight of the test items. Investigators who have suggested that prior experience with pictures is necessary for efficient analysis of two-dimensional information may have incorrectly misinterpreted failure to understand the requirements of the problem with a deficiency in cognitive competence. This competence seems to develop in the world of moving leaves, chickens, and water.[3] As with recall and recognition memory, the performance of the San Marcos child was comparable to that of his age peer in a modern urban setting.

Perceptual Inference

The competence of the San Marcos children on the Embedded Figures Test is affirmed by their performance on a test administered only in San Marcos and Cambridge and called Perceptual Inference. The children (60 American and 55 Guatemalan, 5–12 years of age) were shown a schematic drawing of an object and asked to guess what that object might be if the drawing were completed. The child was given a total of four clues for each of 13 items, where each clue added more information. The child had to guess an object from an incomplete illustration, to make an inference from minimal information (see Figures 4 and 5).

There was no significant cultural difference for the children 7–12 years of age, although the American 5- and 6-year-olds did perform significantly better than the Indian children. In San

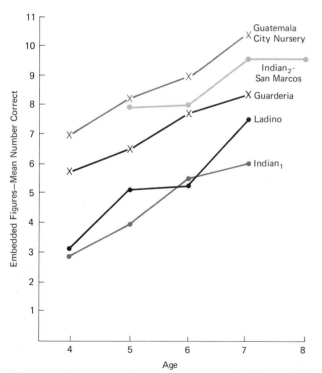

Figure 3 Mean number correct on the Embedded Figures Test.

[3]This conclusion holds for Embedded Figures Test performance, and not necessarily for the ability to detect three-dimensional perspective in two-dimensional drawings.

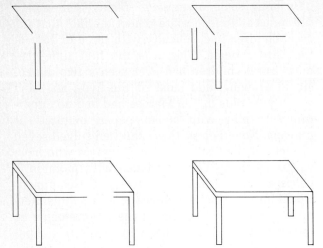

Figure 4 Sample item from the Perceptual Inference Test.

Marcos, performance improved from 62% correct on one of the first two clues for the 5- and 6-year-olds to 77% correct for the 9–12-year-olds. The comparable changes for the American children were from 77% to 84%. (See Figure 6.)

Familiarity with the test objects was critical for success. All of the San Marcos children had seen hats, fish, and corn, and these items were rarely missed. By contrast, many American children failed these items. No San Marcos child not attending school, and therefore unfamiliar with books, correctly guessed the book item, whereas

Figure 5—Sample item from the Perceptual Inference Test.

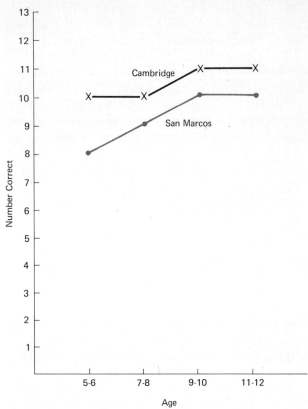

Figure 6 Number correct on the Perceptual Inference Test.

most of those in school guessed it correctly. As with memory and perceptual analysis, the retardation seen during infancy did not predict comparable retardation in the ability of the 11-year-old to make difficult perceptual inferences.

Conceptual Inference
The San Marcos child also performed well on questions requiring conceptual inference. In this test, the child was told verbally three characteristics of an object and was required to guess the object. Some of the examples included: What has wings, eats chickens, and lives in a tree? What moves trees, cannot be seen, and makes one cold? What is made of wood, is used to carry things, and allows one to make journeys? There was im-

proved performance with age; the 5- and 6-year-olds obtained an average of 9 out of 14 correct, and the 11- and 12-year-olds obtained 12 out of 14 correct. The San Marcos child was capable of making moderately difficult inferences from both visual and verbal information.

DISCUSSION

This corpus of data implies that absolute retardation in the time of emergence of universal cognitive competences during infancy is not predictive of comparable deficits for memory, perceptual analysis, and inference during preadolescence. Although the rural Guatemalan infants were retarded with respect to activation of hypotheses, alertness, and onset of stranger anxiety and object permanence, the preadolescents' performance on the tests of perceptual analysis, perceptual inference, and recall and recognition memory were comparable to American middle-class norms. Infant retardation seems to be partially reversible and cognitive development during the early years more resilient than had been supposed.

One potential objection to this conclusion is that the tests were too easy for the Guatemalan 11-year-olds and that is why cultural differences were absent. There are two comments that can be addressed to that issue. First, it is not intuitively reasonable to argue that the ability to remember 60 photographs of objects, classify an object from a few sketchy lines, or detect the triangle hidden in a two-dimensional drawing is "easy" for children who rarely see photographs, pencils, crayons, or books. Second, we deliberately assessed cognitive functions that we believe all children should master by the time they are preadolescents. The fact that many 11-year-olds approached the ceiling on some tests is support for the basic premise of this article, namely, that infant retardation does not prevent a child from eventually developing basic cognitive competences.

This result is surprising if one believes that each child is born with a certain level of general intellectual competence that is stable from infancy through adulthood. If, on the contrary, one assumes that each stage of development is characterized by a different profile of specific competences and there is no necessary relation between early emergence of the capacities of infancy and level of attainment of the quite different abilities characteristic of childhood, then these results are more reasonable. There is no reason to assume that the caterpillar who metamorphoses a bit earlier than his kin is a better adapted or more efficient butterfly.

Consideration of why the rural Guatemalan children lagged behind the urban children on some tests during the period five through nine years of age comprises a second implication of these data. It will be recalled that on the embedded figures and recognition memory tests the performance of rural children was several years behind both the American and Guatemala City middle-class children. The differences were minimal for the object recall and perceptual inference tests. The approximately three-year lag in performance is paralleled by comparable differences between lower- and middle-class children in urban Western cities. For example, Bosco (1972) found that middle-class first and third graders were able to tolerate smaller interstimulus intervals in a backward masking procedure than lower-class children, but this difference had vanished among sixth-grade children. Similarly, Bakker (1971) compared good and poor readers from urban centers in Holland on a task that required operating simultaneously on two items of information in a temporal integration task. The poor readers performed less well than the good readers at ages six to eight, but were comparable to the good readers during the preadolescent years.

We interpret these results as indicating that the urban lower-class children, like the younger, rural Guatemalans, were not able to mobilize proper problem-solving strategies necessary for task solution, but achieved that level of competence by 11 years of age. Some of these strategies include focused attention, rehearsal of task information and instructions, awareness of and understanding the problem to be solved, maintenance of problem set, and the ability to remember critical information elements in the problem and to operate on that information. It is believed that these functions may emerge a little later in some groups of children than in others, but that they are operative in all children by 11–12 years of age. In a recently completed study with Patricia Engle, we found that among rural Guatemalan children, 5 through 11 years of age, the rate of improvement in performance on three memory tasks (memory for numbers, memory for sentences, and auditory blending) was greatest between 9 and 11 years of age, whereas White (1970), using comparable data from American children, found that the greatest rate of improvement was between 5 and 7 years of age—a lag of about three years.

These data have implications for America's educational problems. There is a tendency to regard the poor test performances of economically impoverished, minority group 6-year-olds in the United States as indicative of a permanent and, perhaps, irreversible defect in intellectual ability —as a difference in quality of function rather than slower maturational rate. The Guatemalan data, together with those of Bosco and Bakker, suggest that children differ in the age at which basic cognitive competences emerge and that experiential factors influence the time of emergence. Economically disadvantaged American children and isolated rural Guatemalan children appear to be from one to three years behind middle-class children in demonstrating some of the problem-solving skills characteristic of Piaget's stage of concrete operations. But these competences eventually appear in sturdy form by age 10 or 11. The common practice of arbitrarily setting 7 years— the usual time of school entrance—as the age when children are to be classified as competent or incompetent confuses differences in maturational rate with permanent, qualitative differences in intellectual ability. This practice is as logical as classifying children as reproductively fertile or sterile depending on whether or not they have reached physiological puberty by their thirteenth birthday.

When educators note correctly that poor children tend to remain permanently behind middle-class children on intellectual and academic performance, they are referring to the relative retardation on the culturally specific skills of reading, mathematics, and language achievement described earlier. That relative retardation is the product of the rank ordering of scores on achievement and IQ tests. The fact that relative retardation on these abilities is stable from age five on does not mean that the relatively retarded children are not growing intellectually (when compared with themselves), often at the same rate as economically advantaged youngsters.

The suggestion that basic cognitive competences, in contrast to culturally specific ones, emerge at different times and that the child retains the capacity for actualization of his competence until a late age is not substantially different from the earlier conclusions of Dennis and Najarian (1957). Although the 49 infants 2–12 months of age living in poorly staffed Lebanese institutions were seriously retarded on the Cattell developmental scale (mean developmental quotient of 68 compared with a quotient of 102 for a comparison group), the $4\frac{1}{2}$–6-year-olds who had resided in the same institution all their lives performed at a level comparable to American norms on a memory test (Knox Cubes) as well as on Porteus mazes and the Goodenough Draw-a-Man Test.

Of more direct relevance is Dennis's (1973) recent follow-up study of 16 children who were adopted out of the same Lebanese institution between 12 and 24 months of age—the period during which the San Marcos infant leaves the unstimulating environment of the dark hut—with an average developmental quotient of 50 on the Cattell Infant Scale. Even though the assessment of later intellectual ability was based on the culturally biased Stanford-Binet IQ test, the average IQ, obtained when the children were between 4 and 12 years of age, was 101, and 13 of the 16 children had IQ scores of 90 or above.

Additional support for the inherent resiliency in human development comes from longitudinal information on two sisters who spent most of their infancy in a crib in a small bedroom with no toys.[4] The mother, who felt unable to care for her fourth child, restricted her to the room soon after birth and instructed her eight-year-old daughter to care for the child. One year later, another daughter was born, and she, too, was placed in a crib with the older sister. These two children only left the room to be fed and, according to the caretaking sister who is now a married woman in her twenties, the two infants spent about 23 hours of each day together in a barren crib. When the authorities were notified of this arrangement, the children were removed from the home and taken to a hospital when the younger was $2\frac{1}{2}$ and the older $3\frac{1}{2}$ years old. Medical records reveal that both children were malnourished, severely retarded in weight and height, and seriously retarded psychologically. After a month in the hospital, following considerable recovery, both sisters were placed in the care of a middle-class family who had several young children. The sisters have remained with that family for the last 12 years and regard the husband and wife as their parents. One of us (J. K.) tested the sisters five times when they were between 4 and 9 years of age, and recently interviewed and tested both of them over a two-day period when they were $14\frac{1}{2}$ and $15\frac{1}{2}$ years old.

The younger sister has performed consistently better than the older one over the last 10 years. The IQ scores of the younger girl have risen steadily from a Stanford-Binet IQ of 74 at age $4\frac{1}{2}$ (after two years in the foster home) to a Wechsler Full Scale IQ of 88 at age 14. The older girl's

[4]The authors thank Meinhard Robinow for information on these girls.

scores have also improved, but less dramatically, from a Stanford-Binet IQ of 59 at age 5 to a Wechsler IQ of 72 at age 15. The author also administered a lengthy battery of tests, some of which were discussed earlier. On the Perceptual Inference Test, the percentage correct was 85 for the younger sister and 61 for the older sister. On the Recognition Memory for Photographs, the percentages were 94 for both. On the Embedded Figures Test, the percentages were 92 and 100, and on the recall memory for objects, the percentages were 92 and 83 for the younger and older sister, respectively. Moreover, the interpersonal behavior of both girls was in no way different from that of the average rural Ohio adolescent—a group the author came to know well after seven years of work in the area. Although there is some ambiguity surrounding the competence of the older girl, the younger one performs at an average level on a wide range of tests of cognitive functioning, despite $2\frac{1}{2}$ years of serious isolation.

These data, together with the poor predictive relation between scores on infant developmental tests and later assessments of intellectual functioning, strengthen the conclusion that environmentally produced retardation during the first year or two of life appears to be reversible. The importance of the Guatemalan data derives from the fact that the San Marcos 11-year-olds performed so well, considering the homogeneity and isolation of their childhood environment. Additionally, there is a stronger feeling now than there was in 1957 that environmentally produced retardation during the first two years may be irreversible, even though the empirical basis for that belief is no firmer in 1972 than it was in 1957.

More dramatic support for the notion that psychological development is malleable comes from recent experimental studies with animals. Several years ago Harlow's group demonstrated that although monkeys reared in isolation for the first six months displayed abnormal and often bizarre social behaviors, they could, if the experimenter were patient, solve the complex learning problems normally administered to feral-born monkeys. The prolonged isolation did not destroy their cognitive competence (Harlow, Schiltz, & Harlow, 1969). More recently, Suomi and Harlow (1972) have shown that even the stereotyped and bizarre social behavior shown by six-month-old isolates can be altered by placing them with female monkeys three months younger than themselves over a 26-week therapeutic period. "By the end of the therapy period the behavioral levels were virtually indistinguishable from those of the socially competent therapist monkeys [Suomi & Harlow, 1972, p. 491]."

This resiliency has also been demonstrated for infant mice (Cairns & Nakelski, 1971) who experienced an initial 10 weeks of isolation from other animals. Compared with group-reared mice of the same strain, the isolated subjects were hyperreactive to other mice, displaying both extreme withdrawal and extreme aggressiveness. These investigators also attempted rehabilitation of the isolates by placing them with groups of mice for an additional 10 weeks, however, after which their behavior was indistinguishable from animals that had never been isolated.

> By the seventieth day after interchange, the effects of group therapy were complete, and animals that had been isolated for one hundred days following weaning were indistinguishable from animals that had never been isolated [Cairns & Nakelski, 1971, p. 363].

These dramatic alterations in molar behavior are in accord with replicated reports of recovery of visual function in monkeys and cats deprived of patterned light soon after birth (Baxter, 1966; Chow & Stewart, 1972; Wilson & Riesen, 1966). Kittens deprived of light for one year recovered basic visual functions after only 10 days in the experimenter's home (Baxter, 1966); kittens who had one or both eyes sutured for close to two years were able to learn pattern discriminations with the deprived eye only after moderate training (Chow & Stewart, 1972).

If the extreme behavioral and perceptual se-

quelae of isolation in monkeys, cats, and mice can be altered by such brief periods of rehabilitative experience, it is not difficult to believe that the San Marcos infant is capable of as dramatic a recovery over a period of nine years. These data do not indicate the impotence of early environments, but rather the potency of the environment in which the organism is functioning. There is no question that early experience seriously affects kittens, monkeys, and children. If the first environment does not permit the full actualization of psychological competences, the child will function below his ability as long as he remains in that context. But if he is transferred to an environment that presents greater variety and requires more accomodations, he seems more capable of exploiting that experience and repairing the damage wrought by the first environment than some theorists have implied.

These conclusions do not imply that intervention or rehabilitation efforts with poor American or minority group preschool children are of no value. Unlike San Marcos, where children are assigned adult repsonsibilities when they are strong and alert enough to assume them, rather than at a fixed age, American children live in a severely age graded system, in which children are continually rank ordered. Hence, if a poor four-year-old falls behind a middle-class four-year-old on a culturally significant skill, like knowledge of letters or numbers, he may never catch up with the child who was advanced and is likely to be placed in a special educational category. Hence, American parents must be concerned with the early psychological growth of their children. We live in a society in which the relative retardation of a four-year-old seriously influences his future opportunities because we have made relative retardation functionally synonymous with absolute retardation. This is not true in subsistence farming communities like San Marcos.

These data suggest that exploration of the new and the construction of objects or ideas from some prior schematic blueprint must be inherent properties of the mind. The idea that the child carries with him at all times the essential mental competence to understand the new in some terms and to make a personal contribution to each new encounter is only original in our time. Despite the current popularity of Kant and Piaget, the overwhelming prejudice of Western psychologists is that higher order cognitive competences and personality factors are molded completely by the environment. Locke's image of an unmarked tablet on which sensation played its patterned melody has a parallel in Darwin's failure to realize, until late in his life, that the organism made a contribution to his own evolution. Darwin was troubled by the fact that the same climate on different islands in the Galapagos produced different forms of the same species. Since he believed that climatic variation was the dynamic agent in evolution he was baffled. He did not appreciate that the gene was the organism's contribution to his own alteration. Western psychologists have been blocked by the same prejudice that prevented young Darwin from solving his riddle. From Locke to Skinner we have viewed the perfectibility of man as vulnerable to the vicissitiudes of the objects and people who block, praise, or push him, and resisted giving the child any compass on his own. The mind, like the nucleus of a cell, has a plan for growth and can transduce a new flower, an odd pain, or a stranger's unexpected smile into a form that is comprehensible. This process is accomplished through wedding cognitive structures to selective attention, activation of hypotheses, assimilation, and accommodation. The purpose of these processes is to convert an alerting unfamiliar event, incompletely understood, to a recognized variation on an existing familiar structure. This is accomplished through the detection of the dimensions of the event that bear a relation to existing schemata and the subsequent incorporation of the total event into the older structure.

We need not speak of joy in this psychological mastery, for neither walking nor breathing is performed in order to experience happiness. These properties of the motor or autonomic systems occur because each physiological system or organ naturally exercises its primary function. The child explores the unfamiliar and attempts to match his ideas and actions to some previously acquired representation because these are basic properties of the mind. The child has no choice.

The San Marcos child knows much less than the American about planes, computers, cars, and the many hundreds of other phenomena that are familiar to the Western youngster, and he is a little slower in developing some of the basic cognitive competences of our species. But neither appreciation of these events nor the earlier cognitive maturation is necessary for a successful journey to adulthood in San Marcos. The American child knows far less about how to make canoes, rope, tortillas, or how to burn an old milpa in preparation for June planting. Each knows what is necessary, each assimilates the cognitive conflicts that are presented to him, and each seems to have the potential to display more talent than his environment demands of him. There are few dumb children in the world if one classifies them from the perspective of the community of adaptation, but millions of dumb children if one classifies them from the perspective of another society.

References

Appel,, L. F., Cooper, R. G., McCarrell, N., Knight, J. S., Yussen, S. R., & Flavell, J. H. The developmental acquisition of the distinction between perceiving and memory. Unpublished manuscript, University of Minnesota–Minneapolis, 1971.

Bakker, D. J. *Temporal order in disturbed reading.* Rotterdam: Rotterdam University Press, 1972.

Baxter, B. L. Effect of visual deprivation during postnatal maturation on the electroencephalogram of the cat. *Experimental Neurology,* 1966, 14, 224–237.

Bosco, J. The visual information processing speed of lower middle class children. *Child Development,* 1972, 43, 1418–1422.

Cairns, R. B., & Nakelski, J. S. On fighting in mice: Ontogenetic and experiential determinants. *Journal of Comparative and Physiological Psychology*, 1971, 74, 354–364.

Carmichael, L. The development of behavior in vertebrates experimentally removed from the influence of external stimulation. *Psychological Review*, 1926, 33, 51–58.

Chow, K. L., & Stewart, D. L. Reversal of structural and functional effects of longterm visual deprivation in cats. *Experimental Neurology*, 1972, 34, 409–433.

Cohen, L. B., Gelber, E. R., & Lazar, M. A. Infant habituation and generalization to differing degrees of novelty. *Journal of Experimental Child Psychology*, 1971, 11, 379–389.

Cole, M., Gay, J., Glick, J. A., & Sharp, D. W. *The cultural context of learning and thinking.* New York: Basic Books, 1971.

Dennis, W. *Children of the Crèche.* New York: Appleton-Century-Crofts, 1973.

Dennis, W., & Najarian, P. Infant development under environmental handicap. *Psychological Monographs*, 1957, 71(7, Whole No. 436).

Harlow, H. F., Schiltz, K. A., & Harlow, M. K. The effects of social isolation on the learning performance of rhesus monkeys. In C. R. Carpenter (Ed.), *Proceedings of the Second International Congress of Primatology.* Vol. 1. New York: Karger, 1969.

Kagan, J. *Change and continuity in infancy.* New York: Wiley, 1971.

Kagan, J. Do infants think? *Scientific American*, 1972, 226(3), 74–82.

Kagan, J., Klein, R. E., Haith, M. M., & Morrison, F. J. Memory and meaning in two cultures. *Child Development*, 1973, 44, 221–223.

Kagan, J., & Moss, H. A., *Birth to maturity.* New York: Wiley, 1962.

Kessen, W., Haith, M. M., & Salapatek, B. H. Human infancy: A bibliography and guide. In P. H. Mussen (Ed.), *Carmichael's manual of child psychology.* (3rd ed.) Vol. 1. New York: Wiley, 1970.

Konnor, M. J. Development among the Bushmen of Botswana. Unpublished doctoral dissertation, Harvard University, 1973.

Lacey, J. I. Somatic response patterning in stress: Some revisions of activation theory. In M. H. Appley & R. Trumbull (Eds.), *Psychological stress: Issues in research.* New York: Appleton-Century-Crofts, 1967.

Lewis, M., & Freedle, R. *Mother-infant dyad: The cradle of meaning.* (Research bulletin RB72-22) Princeton, N.J.: Educational Testing Service, 1972.

Lewis, M., Goldberg, S., & Campbell, H. A developmental study of learning within the first three years of life: Response decrement to a redundant signal. *Monograph of the Society for Research in Child Development*, 1970, 34(No. 133).

McGraw, M. B. *Growth: A study of Johnny and Jimmy.* New York: Appleton-Century, 1935.

Pease, D., Wolins, L., & Stockdale, D. F. Relationship and prediction of infant tests. *Journal of Genetic Psychology*, 1973, 122, 31–35.

Scott, M. S. The absence of interference effects in preschool children's picture recognition. *Journal of Genetic Psychology*, 1973, 122, 121–126.

Sellers, M. J., Klein, R. E., Kagan, J., & Minton, C. Developmental determinants of attention: A cross-cultural replication. *Developmental Psychology*, 1972, 6, 185.

Suomi, S. J., & Harlow, H. F. Social rehabilitation of isolate reared monkeys. *Developmental Psychology*, 1972, 6, 487–496.

Van Hover, K. I. S. A developmental study of three components of attention. Unpublished doctoral dissertation, Harvard University, 1971.

White, S. H. Some general outlines of the matrix of developmental changes between 5 and 7 years. *Bulletin of the Orton Society*, 1970, 21, 41–57.

Wilson, P. D., & Riesen, A. H. Visual development in rhesus monkeys neonatally deprived of patterned light. *Journal of Comparative and Physiological Psychology*, 1966, 61, 87–95.

Chapter 3

Continuity and Discontinuity

The degree of continuity displayed by aspects of human personality is a highly controversial issue. However, the concept of continuity has three different meanings. The first, (1) **rank-order** continuity, holds that the child retains his relative rank for a particular attribute within a particular cohort over a particular period of time. The stability of IQ, grade-point average, and achievement-test scores from kindergarten through high school are examples of rank-order continuity. An 8-year-old Chicago child who scores in the thirtieth percentile for reading comprehension will probably remain between the twentieth and fourtieth percentile if he remains in Chicago or any other American city for the next 10 years. However, if that child moves to a rural school in western Kenya, his position will probably change from the thirtieth to the eightieth percentile and there will be a discontinuity in his relative ability, even though his absolute competence had not changed. Statements about continuity based on maintenance of a rank are always relative to the reference group with whom the child is being compared.

(2)   Continuity has a different meaning when it refers to the child's tendency to display the same hierarchical organization of behavioral dispositions over time. Imagine a 4-year-old boy who consistently withdraws in preference to attacking when he is threatened by a peer. We can ask whether this disposition to withdraw rather than attack will remain stable over a 5- or 10-year period. This is called **ipsative** continuity. Although his rank for the disposition to withdraw might change dramatically if he joins a group of children who withdraw even more frequently than he, as long as his individual tendency to with-

POSITION

BEHAVIOR

draw in preference to attacking remains stable, we would be justified in saying that his behavior displays ipsative continuity.

(3) The third and most profound meaning of continuity is most often called **psychological epigenesis.** It asks whether there is a necessary relation between a set of processes or performances at one time and a successive set at some time in the future. For example, *SET OF ATTITUDE* some psychologists believe that an infant who is closely attached to his mother at age 3 will be highly dependent on her at age 5. Most research on continuity in human development tends to be rank-order continuity, occasionally ipsative continuity and rarely epigenetic.

(1) The first reading in this chapter describes an early longitudinal study from the Fels Research Institute, in which J. Kagan and H. A. Moss showed that if a behavior was congruent with the sex-role stereotypes of the culture, it showed rank-order continuity. If it deviated from this sex-role stereotype, it showed no rank-order stability from childhood through young adulthood. Hence, aggressive behavior was moderately stable from age 10 to adulthood for males but not for females, while passive and dependent behavior was moderately stable from childhood to adulthood for females but not for males.

(2 & 3) An important longitudinal study of personality continuity was also being carried out during the same period at the Institute for Child Development at the University of California at Berkeley under the direction of J. W. Macfarlane. In the two papers included in this chapter, she summarizes her views regarding continuity in personality development. She suggests that earlier investigators tended to give insufficient emphasis to the resilience of the individual to recover from early trauma. In her own studies, she found that predictions of later development were often incorrect because too much weight had been given to pathological components present in the child and not enough weight had been given to those processes that were conducive to growth. There was a tendency to assume more stability than was warranted. Macfarlane argues that we must appreciate the value of stressful experiences which, in time, alter people and make them both more complex and more mature.

Birth to Maturity

Jerome Kagan

Howard A. Moss

Many childhood behaviors have short lives and are replaced or dropped long before maturity. Fear of the dark, for example, is associated with a specific period in the development of the child, and we are not surprised when it vanishes from the behavioral scene. However, people have long believed that many adult motives, attitudes, and behaviors originate during childhood and, once established, become permanent parts of an individual's behavioral repertoire. This belief is supported by various private recollections and personal reports, but more substantial evidence has been difficult to come by. The only way to discover which childhood behaviors are marked for future use and which will be lost along the way is through systematic longitudinal studies, in which the behavior of a given group of children over a long period of time is observed, recorded, and analyzed.

The investigation summarized here, which was carried out at the Fels Research Institute, in Yellow Springs, Ohio, is one such study. It is based in part on longitudinal data concerning the personality development of eighty-nine children, forty-five girls and forty-four boys, who from birth through early adolescence participated in a long-term research project at the institute, and in part on follow-up data regarding their personalities as young adults. The purpose of the investigation was to compare the two sets of data in an attempt to relate the functioning of the child to the psychological status of the adult or, in more technical terms, to study the selective stability of behavior from childhood through early adulthood.

SUBJECTS AND METHODS

The eighty-nine subjects in our investigation had joined the Fels project between 1929 and 1939. They came from sixty-three families, all white and most of them middle class. About three-fourths of the parents were high school graduates and almost half had attended college. The fathers included roughly equal numbers of laborers, farmers, small businessmen, white-collar workers, and professionals. In religious background, fifty-three families were Protestant, nine were Catholic, and one was Jewish.

Assessment: Birth Through Adolescence

The children were interviewed, observed, and tested repeatedly over the years from birth through the mid-teens. Table 1 summarizes the information obtained for a typical child in the sample. The narrative summaries of observations of the child at home, in school, and at the institute proved to be the richest and most accurate source of data on the child's personality development.

We divided this material into four age periods: birth to age three, three to six, six to ten, and ten to fourteen. These divisions roughly correspond to important developmental periods. The first three years include infancy and early social training. Years three to six, the preschool years, involve the child's first contacts with children his own age and his early attempts to become less dependent on his parents. The next four years call for adjustment to school, the establishment of interests and skills, and the develop-

Table 1. Summary of longitudinal information obtained on a typical child

TYPE OF INFORMATION	SETTING AND METHOD OF RECORDING	TYPICAL FREQUENCY
1. Observation of child and mother	(a) Half-day observation of child and mother in home. Observations summarized in narrative style	Twice yearly from birth to age 6. Annually from age 6 to 12.
	(b) Observation of child in Fels Experimental Nursery School and Day Camp; half-day sessions for 3 weeks. Observations summarized in narrative style and numerical ratings.	Twice yearly from age 2½ to 5. Annually from age 6 to 10.
	(c) Interview with child. Interview summarized in narrative style.	Annually from age 6 to 12.
	(d) Interview with mother with narrative summary.	Annually from child's birth to adolescence.
	(e) Observation of child in school with narrative summary.	Twice yearly from 1st to 8th grade.
2. Personality tests	(a) Selected stimuli from the Thematic Apperception Test.	Every third year from age 8½ to 17½.
	(b) Rorschach Test.	Every third year from age 8½ to 17½.
	(c) Minnesota Multiphasic Personality Inventory.	Once during adolescence— age 17.
	(d) Kuder Preference Record.	Once during adolescence— age 17.
3. Mental development tests	(a) Gesell Development Schedule.	6, 12, 18, and 24 months
	(b) Merrill-Palmer Infant Test.	18, 24, and 30 months.
	(c) Stanford-Binet Intelligence Test.	2½, 3, 3½, 4, 4½, 5, 6, 7, 8, 9, 10, 11, 12, and 14 years.
	(d) Wechsler-Bellevue IQ Test.	Age 13 and 17.
	(e) Primary Mental Abilities Test.	Age 17.
4. Mental testing of mother and father	Otis IQ Test.	One administration.

ment of friendships with other children of the child's own sex. During the preadolescent years, ten to four-teen, heterosexual interests develop, vocational choice begins to emerge, and modes of defensive reaction to anxiety-arousing situations are firmly established.

We had decided to organize the investigation around four major classes of behavior: behavior re-lated to motives, anxiety, defenses against anxiety, and social interaction. Within those general classes, we constructed forty-eight specific variables, on which each child was to be rated by means of a seven-point rating scale. These ratings were made by Howard Moss. He read each child's file and rated all children at birth to age three, three to six, six to ten, and ten to fourteen, in that order. These four sets of ratings became our primary source of historical data on the children.

The files on which the ratings were based did not include test information, and it should be stresed that Dr. Moss had no knowledge of any subject's perform-ance on any test. Nor was he acquainted with their psychological status as adults. Special precautions were taken to ensure that he would learn nothing about the subjects except what he read in the narra-tive reports.

Assessment: Early Adulthood

From July 1957 through October 1959, seventy-one of the eighty-nine subjects for whom longitudinal ratings had been made participated in an adult assessment program. It had two parts, an interview and a formal testing schedule. On the basis of the tape-recorded interviews, each adult was rated on variables similar to those used for childhood behavior. The testing program included a modified ink blot task, selected cards from the Thematic Apperception Test, a self-rating inventory, conceptual sorting tasks, a task involving the recognition of slides flashed briefly on a screen, the Wechsler-Bellevue IQ Test (Form I), and measures of reactivity of the autonomic nervous sys-tem. The interviews always took place before the series of tests, and they were conducted by Jerome Kagan. At the time of the interview, he had no knowl-edge of any longitudinal or test information on the subjects. This precaution insured that the childhood data would influence neither the interview itself nor later evaluations of the adults.

Thus the ratings based on longitudinal childhood data and the ratings based on adult interviews were completely independent of each other. Since the pri-mary purpose of the research was to relate child and adult personality dispositions, this independence was mandatory.

SELECTED RESULTS

When all the data had been collected, tabulated, and analyzed, we found that some of our hunches about the continuity of behavior from childhood to adulthood were verified; others were clearly refuted. Equally important were unexpected dis-coveries that suggested leads for future research and had implications for educational practices. We cannot summarize all the results here, but there are several conclusions that should be singled out for attention.

The Influence of Sex Typing

The most dramatic and consistent finding of the study was that many of the behaviors exhibited by the child during the period from six to ten years of age, and a few from the period three to six, were moderately good predictors of related behavior during early adulthood. Passive with-drawal from stress, dependence on family, ease of anger-arousal, involvement in intellectual mas-tery, social anxiety, sex-role identification, and sexual behavior in adulthood were each related to reasonably similar behavioral tendencies dur-ing the early school years. Figure 1 summarizes the stability of these seven classes of responses from childhood to adulthood. These results offer strong support to the popular notion that many characteristics of the adult personality begin to take form early in childhood.

However, it should be noted that the degree of continuity in all seven response classes was strongly influenced by traditional standards of masculinity and femininity. For example, passive girls were more likely to become passive adults than were passive boys, whereas angry boys were more likely than angry girls to become hostile adults. In our culture passive and dependent be-havior are subject to consistent cultural disap-proval for men but not for women. Direct aggres-sive retaliation, frequent sexual behavior, and a low threshold for anger, on the other hand, are frowned on in females; males are given greater license in these areas. It is not surprising, there-

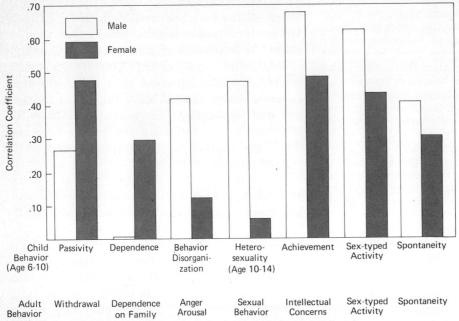

Figure 1   Continuity of behavior from childhood to adulthood.

fore, that childhood passivity and dependency were related to passive and dependent behavior during adulthood in women but not in men, and that childhood rages and frequent dating during preadolescence predicted adult aggressive and sexual predispositions, respectively, in men but not in women.

Some families did not consciously attempt to mold the children in strict accordance with traditional sex-role standards, but the children apparently responded to social pressure from outside the family. Aggressive and sexually active girls learned to inhibit direct expression of aggressive and sexual behavior; dependent boys gradually stopped making dependent overtures to others.

Intellectual mastery and the adoption of sex-typed interests are approved for both sexes, and both types of behavior showed considerable continuity in males and females from the early school years through adulthood. In some cases, even preschool behavior was related to a similar disposition in adulthood. For example, the preschool girl's involvement in achievement tasks successfully predicted her concern with intellectual mastery in adulthood.

Some forms that childhood behavior took during adulthood seemed to be determined in part by the sex-role appropriateness of the childhood behavior. Passivity in boys predicted noncompetitiveness, sexual anxiety, and social apprehension in adult men, but not direct dependent overtures to parents or love objects. A tendency toward rage reactions in young girls predicted intellectual competitiveness, masculine interests, and dependency conflict in adult women, but not direct expression of aggression. It appears that a childhood behavior is likely to lead to similar behavior in adulthood only when the early behavior fits traditional sex roles. When it conflicts with sex-role standards, the motive is more likely to be expressed later through substitute behaviors that are socially more acceptable than the original ones.

The relevance of sex-role identification in directing behavioral choices is supported by investigations indicating that the child begins to differentiate masculine and feminine characteristics and activities, as defined by his culture, at a very early age. Even three-year-olds are aware of the different interests and appearances of males and females. Comprehension of the world is much like a game of twenty questions in which the child tries to understand new experiences by categorizing them, broadly at first and then by successively narrow labels. One of the first questions a child asks about an object or activity seems to be whether it is masculine or feminine. Having determined the answer to that question, he adjusts his behavior accordingly. One of us recalls a conversation between his three and one-half year old daughter (D) and a female college student (S):

D: What are you studying?
S: Psychology, for your daddy.
D: Are you going to be a psychologist?
S: Yes.
D: Are you going to be a mother?
S: Yes, I think so.
D: (after a puzzled pause): Well, you can't be a psychologist and a mother too.

Social-class membership places constraints on the behavior the child sees as suitable for one of his sex. An interest in art and music, for example, is more acceptable to middle-class than to lower-class men, and vocational aspirations are, of course, strongly influenced by social class. Thus knowledge of the sex and social class of a child allows one to make a strikingly large number of predictions about his future interests, goals, vocational choice, and tendencies regarding dependent, aggressive, sexual, and mastery behavior. The face that a person shows the world depends to a large extent on what he thinks the world expects from one of his sex and social class.

The preceding discussion assumes that many people are motivated to behave in ways that fit an idealized model of the "masculine" man or the "feminine" woman. This assumption locates both the goals of motives and the incentive to move toward them in the cognitive system of the individual rather than in the outside world. Psychologists in the behavioral tradition, by contrast, define both the conditions that create motives (and drives) and the rewards that gratify them primarily in terms of external events. For example, they might say that rejection arouses a motive whose goal is the receipt of love. Although we do not deny the usefulness or validity of this orientation, it seems necessary to acknowledge a need, perhaps unique to human beings, to act and believe in ways that fit previously established, internal standards. Each person has a mental picture of the person he would like to be and the goals he would like to reach—an idealized model of himself. Any behavior or belief that increases the discrepancy between the person's perception of himself as he is and his picture of himself as he wants to be provokes anxiety and is likely to be shunned; any behavior that seems to bring the actual and the idealized selves into closer correspondence is pleasing and likely to be practiced.

It would appear that the desire to be an ideal male or an ideal female, as defined by the individual, is an essential part of every man's model of himself. An important determinant of the acceptability, and thus of the occurrence, of a given behavior is its position on a cognitive dimension ranging from "highly masculine" to "highly feminine."

REVIEWER'S EMPHASIS

The Early School Years: A Critical Period

Some adult behavior—especially withdrawal (in women), involvement in task mastery, social spontaneity, and the adoption of sex-typed interests—has clear antecedents in the individual's behavior from age six to ten, but the relation of adult behavior to behavior before age six is far less clear. This suggests that important changes in the child's behavioral organization take place between the ages of six and ten. The significant events of this period include: (1) identification with parents and attempts to adopt the parents' values and imitate their behavior; (2) the realization that mastering intellectual skills is both a cultural requirement and a source of satisfaction; and (3) the establishment of relationships with other children. The last experience forces the child to accommodate himself, at least to some degree, to the values and expectations of his peers. In some children, this strengthens tendencies toward dominance, social spontaneity, and positive self-evaluation; in others, such as those whose peers reject them, it can lead to social anxiety, social submission, and a sense of ineffectiveness. Some children in the latter group try to compensate by developing their competence in areas that do not require interaction with other children. Those who are unable to do that continue to anticipate failure when faced with challenges of various sorts.

The first four years of contact with the school and with other children seem to crystallize behavioral tendencies that some children maintain through young adulthood. Children who display intense strivings for mastery between ages six and ten are likely to maintain this behavioral posture; on the other side of the coin, withdrawal from anticipated failure, especially among girls, grows rapidly during the early school years once it has begun. These findings have implications for educational practices. For example, selecting bright, highly motivated fourth graders for special educational programs involves little risk that the children will suddenly stop trying. Similarly, children who tend to withdraw from tasks during the first few grades are likely to continue to do so, and remedial or therapeutic intervention should probably take place earlier than it usually does at present.

The Sleeper Effect

The bombardment of atomic nuclei or the reaction of hydrochloric acid with a base leads to effects that are immediate—sometimes even too fast to measure. In psychological development, however, the effects of specific early experiences are often not evident until long periods of time have passed.

For instance, the assumption that a good relationship between mother and infant is necessary for the development of satisfactory interpersonal relationships cannot be verified until the child is six or seven and beginning to have relationships with other children and adults.

One way to detect a time lag between cause and effect is to find a stronger relationship between one variable measured early and another measured late in development than between similar variables measured closer together in time. This set of circumstances—which we have called the "sleeper effect"—came up twice in our material. For boys, passivity and fear of bodily harm during the period from birth to age three and a tendency toward minimal body movement from three to six were each better predictors of love-object dependence in adulthood than were later assessments of these childhood variables. In the second case of the "sleeper effect," certain maternal practices during the first three years of life were more closely related to the child's preadolescent and adult behavior than were evaluations of similar parental practice in later childhood. These findings require different explanations.

Passivity and fear of harm in the young boy are probably less disguised during the preschool years than at later ages. As he grows up, the boy learns to inhibit the open expression of passivity and fear as immature, disapproved behavior. Thus an assessment of predispositions to passivity and anxiety about bodily harm based on behavior at age six is likely to be less sensitive than one based on behavior at age two or three. During the earlier period the child's defenses are weaker, and he is less able or less strongly motivated to prevent immature, anxiety-based reactions. However, a hidden predisposition to passivity may remain during the school years and gain expression, perhaps in behavior that is not obviously passive, during adolescence and adulthood.

The reasons for the "sleeper effect" of certain behaviors by mothers are more complicated. A highly critical maternal attitude toward daughters before the age of three predicted adult achievement behavior, but a critical maternal attitude toward daughters from three to six and from six to ten showed a negligible relation to achievement behavior in adult women. Similarly, maternal protection of a daughter during infancy predicted adult withdrawal from stress, but protectiveness from three to six and from six to ten showed no relation to adult withdrawal.

One explanation for these results rests on the fact that the nature of the interaction between mother and child becomes more reciprocal with time. That is, the degree to which the child's actions have the power to change the mother's behavior increases with the child's age: a six-year-old is more likely to produce a major change in his mother's behavior toward him than is a two-year-old.

Beginning at the child's birth, if not before, a mother typically establishes expectations as to what her child should be like and what standards his behavior should meet. The greater the discrepancy between her expectations and her evaluation of the child's behavior, the greater the likelihood that she will exert pressure of some sort on the child in an attempt to bring his behavior into line with her expectations. During infancy the child's "personality" is fairly ambiguous, and the discrepancy between the mother's standard and what she perceives in the child is necessarily small. The mother sees the child as she would like to see him; he is primarily an object to be acted upon. Her behavior toward the infant, therefore, is relatively uncontaminated by the child's own behavior. With a ten-year-old, things are likely to be different. To illustrate, a mother's concern with the intellectual achievement of her two-year-old (dissatisfaction with his verbal development, for example) is likely to be based primarily on her own needs and values, whereas a critical attitude toward the academic performance of a ten-year-old may be based on the fact that he is failing in school. Similarly, encouragement of independence in or overprotection toward a

ten-year-old may be newly developed reactions to a child's excessive dependence or fragile defenses. Excessive permissiveness or protectiveness toward a three-year-old, on the other hand, probably reflects fundamental maternal attitudes.

Mothers who were hypercritical during the first three years were usually dissatisfied with their daughters' intellectual development and lack of autonomy. These mothers often resented the child's dependency and rewarded mastery and independence. When the child began to achieve intellectually and to behave more independently at age nine or ten, the mother became less critical: the girl's adoption of the traits valued by the mother led to a decrease in the mother's criticism of the child. Thus the high correlation between maternal hostility or protection during infancy and adult behavior in women could be due to the fact that these practices during the first three years, by comparison to similar practices at age ten, are a more sensitive index of the mother's basic attitudes toward the child and therefore of her more lasting effect on the child's developing behavior.

The maternal behaviors that showed the "sleeper effect" most clearly were protection and hostility toward infant daughters. An extremely protective attitude was characteristic of mothers who wished to infantilize their children. A critical attitude was characteristic of mothers who wanted early autonomy and independence for their daughters. The daughters of these two types of mothers developed personalities that realized their mothers' expectations. The daughters of protective mothers were, as adults, passive, afraid of social interaction, noncompetitive, and involved in traditional feminine interests. Those of critical mothers gained independence from the family at an early age and retained this orientation through adolescence into adulthood.

Without a longitudinal research design, it is difficult to pair up causes and effects that are separated by time. Longitudinal research taxes even a scientist's capacity to tolerate delay of gratification, but we believe the results of our investigation demonstrate the value of continuous study of the developing child. We need more standard measures, more rigorous theory, and perhaps a series of five- to ten-year longitudinal studies aimed at specific developmental hypotheses. With these advantages we should become more adept at wresting from nature the secrets of human development.

From Infancy to Adulthood

Jean Walker Macfarlane

This paper gives an overview of the GS findings, describing stability and change in different areas of development and underscoring cases where early predictions were accurate and others where difficulties during childhood had maturity-inducing effects.

The Guidance Study has followed a group of infants through childhood and adolescence to age eighteen and has seen them at age thirty when they were facing adult tasks, including guidance of their own infants, children, and adolescents toward responsible adulthood.

In a short article we cannot give detail on the methods used; but it is clear that with our objectives we had to repeat systematically over the years a wide range of measurements covering biological, environmental, familial, and behavioral aspects of the growing organism. Direct measures such as developmental X rays, body-build measures, mental tests, and projective tests were used; also interviews furnished materials as seen by parents, teachers, brothers, sisters, the child himself, and the professional interviewers (clinical psychologists and physicians). Classmate appraisal was secured by sociometrics and cumulative achievement from yearly school records.

RELEVANT FINDINGS

Now let us look at some of the things we have learned that are relevant to you as persons and as teachers dealing wih children from kindergarten to or into junior high school. Let us look at the predictive usefulness of some of our tools in different developmental aspects. Physical measures,

SOURCE: Reprinted, in abridged form and with references deleted, from *Childhood Education,* vol. 39 (March 1963), 336–342. Reprinted by permission of Jean Walker Macfarlane and the Association for Childhood Education International, 3615 Wisconsin Avenue, N.W., Washington, D.C. Copyright © 1963 by the Association.

such as height, were much more predictive over a long age span than mental test measures, which in turn clearly excelled personality measures. Interage correlations, which indicate how stable in group position its members are, showed in respect to height for ages three and eighteen, correlations in the .70s; whereas mental test measures at these two ages were around .40. Even for three-year periods, few of our personality measures reached correlations of .40. Additionally, with increasing age, mental test correlations steadily climbed, as Bayley and Sontag also have found; that is, children were becoming more stabilized in mental test performance with age. For three-year periods three to six, four to seven, five to eight, . . . , nine to twelve, mental test interage correlations were .55, .59, .70, .76, .79, and .85, the last (nine to twelve) reaching the correlations for height of ages three to six. Not only is a centimeter a cleaner measuring device than a composite IQ or a personality variable, but it is also clear that growth in height precedes in time the other developmental aspects. In our sample of 248 cases, girls on the average reached half of their terminal height by twenty months, boys by twenty-six months; whereas by twenty and twenty-six months, respectively, a small proportion of eventual mental capacity had been disclosed and, save for constitutionally determined temperamental variables, very little of the durable patterns of adaptation we call personality characteristics is evident.

The variability of mental test scores is perhaps more meaningfully shown in terms of IQ changes for individuals. For the eight tests given between ages six and eighteen, 15 percent of our children showed a range of less than ten IQ points; 58 percent, fifteen IQ points or more; one of three, twenty IQ points or more; one of ten, a range of thirty IQ points or more; and one of 222, a fifty-or-more IQ-point spread. Clearly little reliance can be placed on one test, especially at the earlier years, in spite of the fact that three-fourths of the boys and girls for these eight tests showed an *average* change of less than ten IQ points.

When details of the history and the life situation at the time of the test were inspected, it was clear that any given IQ was a functional composite of native ability; the intellectual interests and stimulation in a child's home; the verbal values of his environment; *and* his attitude toward mental achievement and toward the examiner; his confidence or lack of it in his ability; his habits of heightened functioning or letdown under stress; his interpersonal ease or lack of it; the saliency of current emotional problems, both within and outside of the mental test situation; the nature of the test; and so forth.

There is, of course, for the group a definite and significant relationship between tested intelligence and the level of attained education; but one *of the striking findings is the number of men whose poor records on mental tests and school grades, some even into high school, completely belie the creative intelligence demands of their present positions.* An illustration of such will be seen among examples of poor prediction.

HOW A PERSON MATURES

We have been forced to the conclusion from our long study that the only way one grows up, matures, and learns to accept and to be comfortable with oneself and to approach one's potential is by having maturing experiences along the whole life span. Of course, the nature of the problems to be solved, the learning to be acquired, the coping devices to be mastered vary with a person's age, potential ability, physical makeup, temperament, and health. They vary with his stage of physical maturity, whether he is in a rapidly growing phase as, for example, in infancy, in preschool years, or in adolescent years. Likewise what he learns varies with what the persons in his environment, with their personalities and values—parents, teachers, brothers, sisters, classmates—permit, encourage, demand, reward him for, and/or punish him for. Of course, the impact of his trainers upon him varies with both the nature of his trainers and their training procedures as they mesh with his own nature. Pressure that is too heavy for the child's ability or methods too offensive to his temperament may result in great variations in his learned responses. One child is motivated to greater effort; another becomes anxious, brittle, and erratic; another defends himself with unmovable stubbornness; another rebels with defiant misbehavior; another ineptly and tonelessly "tries."

③ PREDICTIONS: INACCURATE AND ACCURATE

When we see the varieties of learning tasks with which they are confronted, the many incoherencies in the pressures put upon these differing organisms at different developmental periods, we still are not sure why so many of them turned out to be coherent adults. We were so aware of their uncertainties and dilemmas (and those of their parents and teachers) as they were growing up that seeing them as adults some twelve years later occasioned dramatic shock after shock. Close to 50 percent have turned out to be more stable and effective adults than any of us with our differing theoretical biases had predicted, some 20 percent were less substantial than we had predicted, and slightly less than a third turned out as predicted.

Our more accurate predictions were for those who early were overcontrolled, constricted compulsives whose defense patterns were so well entrenched that they became largely autonomous and presented an encapsulated system, or a hard shell, which appears to have protected them but, by denying them openness to many kinds of learning experiences, to have impoverished them. In a number of cases they were led to the choice of a mate who reinforced the previous encapsulating patterns. Another group of accurate predictions concerns the mentally retarded; a third group were youngsters who were subjected to variability of family treatment—for example, alternatingly so indulgent one moment and so harshly stripping them of confidence at another moment —that stable and integrated patterns have not been learned by age thirty. It is among the latter

group that the majority of our compulsive adult drinkers are recruited.

Let us next look at the very large group (nearly 50 percent) for whom, on the basis of persistent and what seemed to us overriding evidences of handicapping personality patterning or disorganization, we predicted crippled or inadequate adult personalities, who turned out better than any of us predicted, and especially the 10 percent who turned out far better than predicted and became mature, effective, and understanding adults or exceptionally creative ones. They are the first to admit that they are as surprised as we are and are willing that we give excerpts from their lives.

Without discussing the varieties of factors contributing to early patterns, we give a bare description of some of them early and late. Among this 10 percent are two who for years persistently spent all of their energies in defiance of regulations. Although having high IQs, both got marginal or failing grades throughout their schooling. After spending a considerable proportion of their school life "in the principal's office," each was finally expelled from public school—the girl at sixteen, the boy at fifteen. Both now are wise, steady, understanding parents who perceptively appreciate the complexities of life and have both humor and compassion for the human race. The woman, after getting some specialized training, contributes her time and considerable talents to the physically handicapped while her children are in school. The man is earning a good living for his family with his own business and functions as both mother and father to his motherless children. Each commented that "there must be easier ways" to grow up than having to go through such turmoil and waste of energies for so many years.

Another who defied our predictions at age thirty accurately described himself during the years previous to graduation from high school as a "listless oddball." His average IQ through year eighteen was around 100. He was held over three times in elementary school, finally graduated from high school at age twenty-one without college recommendations. He left the community, made

POOR STARTS BUT GREAT FINISHES

up high school deficiencies, and now is a highly talented architect, "living out a normal childhood through my children," is active in his community, and "life is exciting and satisfying." Obviously his tested IQs up through age eighteen were no measure of his true ability, although they corresponded with his grades.

(4) Another marginal grade-getter who was a social isolate and a self-centered, unhappy boy is now the manager of a large construction firm. He states that his primary satisfaction on the job is "feeding graded doses of increasing responsibility and difficulty in assigned jobs to the work staff and watching them grow in confidence as their competencies increase."

(5) Another—a large, awkward, early-maturing girl who labored under the weight of her size and shyness, feeling that she was a great disappointment to her mother—worked hard for her B average to win approval and was a pedestrian, uninteresting child and adolescent. She had periods of depression when she could see no point to living. Then, as a junior in college, she got excited over what she was learning (not just in grades to please her mother) and went on to get an advanced degree and to teach in college. Now she has taken time out to have and raise her children. Again we see an understanding, compassionate person, and one full of zest for living, married to an interesting, merry, and intelligent man she met in graduate school. "Life is now very good—but it took so very, very long to be comfortable and happy."

FACTORS LEADING TO ERRONEOUS PREDICTIONS

Why were our predictions wrong? As we look over the individual histories, several contributing factors seem to have led to erroneous predictive judgments.

1. It seems clear that we overweighted the troublesome and the pathogenic aspects and underweighted elements that were maturity-inducing. Since most personality theory has been derived from work with pathological groups, we were oversensitized to these aspects in respect to both overt and covert patterning and inadequately sensitized to the stabilizing and maturity-inducing aspects. Data on these last two aspects were available, but we failed to give them due weight, so preoccupied were we with current dilemmas.

2. We unquestionably overestimated the durability of those well-learned behaviors and attitudes that were characteristic and habitual response patterns over a substantial period of time. It appears that no matter how habitual these patterns were, if they were coping devices or instrumental acts that no longer were effective for desired ends in changed situations and with changing physiologies, by the vast majority they were dropped or modified. This relearning occurred not without some wear and tear nor without anxiety and erratic behavior during a trial-and-error relearning period. This is very clear both in adolescents and in their parents when previously learned patterns proved inadequate to emerging new needs and adequate new patterns had not as yet become stabilized.

3. Another thing we have learned is that no one becomes mature without living through the pains and confusions of maturing experiences. We have even observed experiences that we regarded as highly traumatic and therefore nonmaturing that our subjects as adults regard as forcing them to come to terms with what it was that they wanted and did not want out of their lives. These experiences enabled them in time to shift behavior in the direction of clarified goals and hence were in fact maturity-inducing experiences.

4. Still another thing that is clear is that many of our subjects did not achieve what Erikson (1956) calls "ego identity" until after marriage and parenthood forced them or presented an opportunity to them to fulfill a role that gave them a sense of worth, through responsibility to others, not open to them when they were on the receiving end in interpersonal relations as children and adolescents.

5. We had not sensed that long-continuous

patterns would be modified or converted into al-most the opposite characteristics. For example, it has been interesting to see how many of our over-dependents have converted their patterns into nurturant ones, yet not to an overnurturant ex-treme since they are aware that what they want to foster in their children is confidence, not over-dependence. One of our predictions was that our long overdependent boys with energetic dominant mothers would pick wives like their mothers and continue their patterns. For one or two we were right, but nearly all the dependent boys picked for wives girls who were lacking in confidence, thereby giving themselves a role as the proud male protector and giver of support. They thrived under this new non–self-centered change of status

with themselves. It does not seem a fortuitous happenstance that three of our four policemen were slow-maturing organisms with older, compe-tent siblings and at least one dominating parent, or that a number of our socially inept compen-satingly became supersalesmen where social skills were required.

6. Some subjects seem to be "late bloomers" or "slow jellers" who took a long time and a change of situation away from their community and family to work through early confusions or inhibitions and to achieve releases to be them-selves. Some subjects did not get consolidated until they had a job that encompassed what ear-lier had seemed conflicting needs or gave them "at last" a meaningful job they enjoyed.

GREG'S SUMMARY

1. MORE POSITIVE THAN NEGATIVE EMPHASIS
2.
3.
4.

#7 Perspectives on Personality Consistency and Change from the Guidance Study

Jean Walker Macfarlane

The participants of this symposium are all engaged in following the over-time flow of that multifaceted complex of coherencies, simply and naively accepted by the laity as "persons." As scientists, we are not satisfied with the laity's perceptions and descriptions nor with their simple explanatory concepts, valid as they may be. So we each take out a slice of this multifaceted complexity; we define "objectively" our own "relevant" personality variables and constructs; and we seek empirical or construct validity; a process which, I submit, is not unrelated to our own personalities and experiences.

Some of us, who are anal reductionists by temperament and training, firmly believe that, in

time, by the piling up of data from studies of small segments of this complexity and by using methods neat and clean, the major variances and coherencies can be ascertained and, like Humpty Dumpty in the nursery rhyme, can then be reassembled.

Others of us, who are oral incorporators by temperament, with a high tolerance for ambiguity and inclusion, and who are organismic ideographists by experience, just as firmly believe that the intensive study of individual "lives in process" over a long time span will disclose the *relevant* bioenvironmental-behavioral integrations and the major sources of continuity and change within and among individual personalities. Some of us are preoccupied with the development of internal "dynamic structure," others with the impinging pressures from the outside stimulus field, for example, with behavior settings, with social class,

SOURCE: Reprinted, in abridged form, from Jean Walker Macfarlane, "Perspectives on Personality Consistency and Change from the Guidance Study," *Vita humana,* 7 (Karger, Basel 1964), 115–126. Reprinted by permission.

and with interpersonal relations, especially with family members. Others of us are concerned with the developing processes of learning, perception, cognition, and motivation; still others of us with the emergence of psychodynamic patterns out of the enlarging circles of outer-inner and inner-outer transactions.

It is well at this neonatal stage of development of a science of personality that we should vary so in temperament, selective awareness, experience, and research preoccupations. Einstein warned that even in the field of physics there is no privileged position from which to make scientific observations, but that there is a responsibility to be aware of our positions in time and space. The late Alan Gregg, of the Rockefeller Foundation, had an opening gambit for grant applicants: "The only way I can judge a research project is by appraising the applicant's awareness of where he stands ... Let me tell you a story of the young engineer using surveying instruments for the first time. He suddenly shouted exuberantly, 'Eureka, I've found the rod!' but after a few moments quietly added, 'but where am I?' " Especially in the field of personality research it is important that investigators inspect more diligently the bases of their own selective awareness. To do so would clarify the events that have led to specific research programs from which come the data, data which in turn have led to reported findings and theoretical notions. To do so might even reduce current overgeneralization.

Our data collection procedure was to repeat systematically to age eighteen, on a normal sample of cases serially selected from the birth certificate registry, a wide range of measurements covering what we hoped were representative arrays of biological, environmental, familial, and overt-covert behavioral aspects of the growing organism.

Direct measures such as developmental X rays, body-build measures, mental tests, and projective tests were used; also interviews furnished materials as seen by parents, teachers, brothers,

sisters, the child himself, and the professional interviewers (clinical psychologists and physicians). Classmate appraisal was secured by sociometric techniques, and cumulative achievement was assessed from yearly school records.

At age thirty, a core group of measurements were repeated and the subjects and their spouses were interviewed to secure data for the appraisal of self-acceptance and morale; and competences and satisfactions on the job, as a husband or wife, and as a parent. The children of these subjects were also administered a schedule of measurements.

What one observes of change and continuity in personality depends upon the following:
1. Breadth and/or intensity of coverage.
2. Whether one's focus of attention is upon (a) the aspects in which all developing persons are like all others—the growing availability of functions with physical maturation, expanding attention span, increased learned skills and residuals, sharpened perceptual discriminations, expanding cognitive complexity, increasing ability to bind tension, and so on; (b) the ways in which individuals are like some other individuals—derived from analyses of subgroups or clusters of persons who are homogeneous with respect to certain behaviors or styles of coping, and by looking at the correlates of such behaviors in morphology, child-training practices, or social class; or (c) the unique patternings of coherence or change within individuals over time, through developmental periods, and across varying situations. Our study has attempted all three types of analyses.
3. The ages encompassed and the time span covered. Group findings show that interage correlations are a function of the time span and the age level for physical and mental measures, with correlations between physical measures far exceeding in magnitude correlations between mental measures in earlier years. For very few of the personality and behavioral variables we used did interage correlations even approach in magnitude those obtained for physical and mental measures.

Furthermore, they were often higher for an age span which straddled marked situational and biological changes (for example, adolescence) than for adjacent age levels. That is, the correlations for girls were higher on a number of behavior-personality variables between ages nine and fourteen years than between eleven and twelve years. Either our personality variables and measures were not as adequate as those for physical and mental growth, which is probable, and/or behavior-personality measures are more subject to variability in time of biological or situational stress and change, a point for which we have clear evidence.

4. Whether or not investigatory techniques, including interpersonal impacts, over a long time span, have added a significant new dimension to the child's and his family's life space. We have evidence from our two groups, the control group and intensively interviewed group, and from the adult testimony of many subjects that such new dimensions were added.

5. The nature of the organizing variables and concepts used, whether they are quantified descriptions referring to coping behaviors, specific to certain developmental stages or structural maturational levels or situations, or whether they are more encompassing inferential concepts. We tried to make our first order of analysis from quantified description. We hoped thereby to derive dimensions empirically so that we would not be left merely drawing inferences from inferences. The most consistent dimensions obtained by clusters of variables over a long time span (two to sixteen years) related to styles of behaviors: namely, reactive-expressive or retractive-inhibitive.

First, let us take an overall look at growing, developing organisms within their environmental contexts.

1. We found that important to personality were the *combinations* of biological statuses which varying organisms encompass in respect to morphology, rate of growth, sensory acuity, types of musculature, abilities, general sturdiness, state of health, natural tempo or motility level, thresholds of stimulatibilty, autonomic reactivity, levels of input tolerance, and temperament—combinations which gave rise both to very differing readinesses for stimulation acceptance or evasion, and to differing styles of overt-covert response patterning.

2. These varying organisms were not only stimulated to response, but these responses were also subjected to the regulatory procedures of parents, siblings, playmates, and teachers. Each of these persons had his own set of values, temperament, habits of showing affection, tempo, thresholds of stimulatibility, stabilized reaction patterns; and each of these persons had his own selective use of rewards, disapprovals, and punishments which changed with the child's age and which shifted with the trainer's moods, state of health, worries, and his preoccupations with aspects of living other than child regulating. Further, these stimulating and controlling persons gave rise to confusion in cues to the child, since they both gave affection and induced frustrations; they often acted very differently when alone with a child than when present with a spouse; and they often said one thing while facial expression showed they meant another. Some of these stimulating and controlling pressures were, and others were not, appropriate to the child's developmental readinesses or his input tolerances, or congenial to the needs of his temperament. In turn, the child's temperament, motility level, and behaviors were in or out of line with the trainer's expectancies, congenial or uncongenial to *their* needs and within or beyond *their* input tolerances.

Additionally, the individual was faced with myriad behavioral settings, differing subcultural pressures, and shifts in circumstances as well as shifts in the state of his biological organism. The complexity of the perceptual and learning tasks is enormous in ordering the priority of cues to respond to or to evade. The individual had the additional task of responding to this complexity in ways which, hopefully, would not bring on further distress. We submit that no experimentalist of sound mind in the fields of perception, learning, or cognition would attempt to order this contextual complexity of reality which the four-year-old struggles to order. We might well ask how *anyone* achieves even *relative* coherence. Yet it is clear that a majority do, albeit each in his own way and at his own speed.

Let us consider a few findings from individual lives that have forced us to look again at some of our theoretical notions. One inescapable lesson learned from 166 lives followed from babyhood to age thirty is the almost incredible capacity of the individual to process the welter of inner-outer stimulation; to program his overt-covert responses in ways that not only permit survival but permit growth in complexities of integrations and skills within his capacities and need systems; and still to have surplus energies with which to explore, to seek stimulation, and to enjoy a wide range of activities. Obviously, if catastrophic discontinuities occur, especially at vulnerable periods, or if biological functioning becomes seriously impaired, or if he is subjected to harsh and capricious pressures beyond his tolerance levels, or if most of his coping attempts are punished or derided, the individual may explode into erratic behavior. He may become immovably resistant, may develop psychosomatic disorders, or may become immobilized.

Our adult outcome data, however, show that for many persons early roadblocks were in time bypassed; or compensatory satisfactions were secured; or changed situations permitted resumption of or change in direction of growth. In fact, many of the most outstandingly mature adults in our entire group, many who are well integrated, highly competent, and/or creative, who are clear about their values, who are understanding and accepting of self and others, are recruited from those who were confronted with very difficult situations and whose characteristic responses during childhood and adolescence seemed to us to compound their problems. Among these were chronic rebels who were expelled from school, bright academic failures, one socially inept girl with blood pressure 4+ sigmas above the mean (now one sigma below), hostile dependents, unhappy withdrawn schizoids. They include one full-blown adolescent schizophrenic, who, without benefit of psychotherapy, now functions perceptively, creatively, and competently as a wife, mother, home builder, gardener, and community participant.

From their retrospective accounts at age thirty, these individuals were very convincing that behaviors we had regarded as disruptive to growth and stability had, in fact, provided them with essential maturity-inducing benefits. To quote one former rebel, "Granted that my defiance of authority precluded a college education. I desperately needed approval, even if it was from as maladjusted kids as I was. Yet I can see positive results, too. To maintain my rebel status called for a commitment that demanded my disciplined *all* of intelligence and stamina which, I believe, has contributed to my adult strength and to my self-confidence in tackling later tough problems. I hope my children find less wasteful ways to mature—but who knows?"

The following comment was made by a recovered schizophrenic: "The only stabilizing aspect of my life during that period was the undeviating and all-enveloping homicidal fantasies against my mother. I believe they prevented my complete disintegration until I could escape my home and achieve other methods of handling my strains."

Our theoretical expectations were also rudely jarred by the adult status of a number of our subjects who early had had easy and confidence-inducing lives. As children and adolescents, they were free of severe strains, showed high abilities and/or talents, excelled at academic work and were the adulated images of success. Included among these were boy athlete leaders and good-looking, socially skillful girls. One sees among them at age thirty a high proportion of brittle, discontented, and puzzled adults whose high potentialities have not been actualized, at least as of now.

As investigators, we were not always wrong! We did have several small groups whose adult status fulfilled theoretical expectations, some with severe organic impairment or deficts, physically and/or intellectually. There were a few cases where the loss of the warm, supporting parent during the preschool years, with no adequate substitute, was accompanied by somber withdrawal that has persisted into adulthood. There were some individuals from homes of unequivocal pathology where irrational pressures made integrations impossible and induced explosive behavioral escapes or repression and denial, with their toll of strain and restriction of coping flexibility. As an example, a vulnerable organism (a boy who had acute allergies), subjected to unpredictable sado-masochistic fluctuations in one or both parents, was left with such an unresolved love-hate tie that it was carried over into his new adult family and was often accompanied by acute depressive swings and/or compulsive drinking. In one case, the incoherent ambivalences have found supportive outlet in the John Birch Society.

Next, a few statements regarding needs for theory modification as I see them.

1. It seems clear that personality theories based upon pathological samples (essentially neurotic) need modification if they are to be useful for prediction for the larger number of developing persons. The currently expanding studies of normal persons and of the talented and creative, should help to trim our past overgeneralizations derived from our sample limitations. This is true even though all of us are aware that the initial and basic impetus to personality theory and research has come from the study of disrupted persons.

2. We had not appreciated the maturing utility of many painful, strain-producing, and confusing experiences which in time, if lived through, brought sharpened awareness, more complex integrations, better skills in problem solving, clarified goals, and increasing stability. Nor had we been aware that early success might delay or possibly forestall continuing growth, richness, and competence. It is not clear whether early success, reinforced by the projections of others trying to identify with success, led to unreal expectations and to a disproportionate draining of energies into maintaining an image, whether early success caused fixation on goals inappropriate to adult demands, or sidetracked development from other needed areas, or whether there was not enough stress to temper strength and induce development. We need to look at and to try to conceptualize the configurations of what kinds of stress, in what graded doses, with what compensating supports, at what developmental periods, and in what kinds of organisms, forestall maturity and strength or facilitate them. The recent expansion of interest in ego psychology appears as one important shift of emphasis in a useful direction.

3. Our experience confirms that the early years of family intimacy, of learning to control body functions, of discovering what overt behaviors are both permissible and useful in coping, comprise a highly important period, especially to basic self-confidence and affective trust, or their lack. Our data show that subsequent problem-solving periods (as all periods are) are also highly important.

Adolescence is reported by a substantial number of our subjects as their most confusing period and the time of lowest morale. It presented not only marked changes in biochemistry, with heightened reactivity and new sensory intensities, but was also a period of struggle to establish status with peers of the same and opposite sex. It was a period of driving urgency for independent selfhood (while being still dependent) and, simultaneously, a period of increased and anxiety-laden pressures from parents for high scholastic and/or social achievement. It was for many individuals a confusing period of establishing priorities among the competing pressures and needs. The priorities to which these adolescents gave time and energies, while accelerating certain competences, retarded or even precluded growth in other aspects. Here, too, we need better conceptualization of the dynamics of competing needs.

For many persons, <u>parenthood</u> turns out to be a very important period for consolidating identity and for expanding maturity. For others, it is a period marked by reactivation of unsolved problems from their early or adolescent past. For many girls, parenthood meant an expanding fulfillment, especially for those who were able to give their children a richer and a less straining environment than the one they had had. Among many of our rebels and our hostile dependent boys, parenthood offered an opportunity, not open to them when they were on the receiving end as children and adolescents, for responsibility to and nurturance of others, an opportunity which permitted dramatic modification of long-established behavioral habits and induced new feelings of self-worth which liberated potentials for other adult tasks. It seems clear that learning theory which ignores differing personality needs, and personality theory which ignores adult capacity for learning in new situations, could profit by modification.

May I add a final personal note. With my strange combinations of personality characteristics and early experiences, involvement in a long longitudinal, multidiscipline study of personality has offered an intellectually exciting, frustrating, humility-inducing, but highly satisfying life. If, on the other hand, the investigator's personality is one that needs neatness and early closure, he should think long and hard before entering the field of personality, longitudinally observed.

SUMMARY

(1) This paper presents a few of the concepts which have survived or have been modified in the course of studying personality continuity and change in a normal sample of persons over a long (2) time span—from infancy to age thirty. In the personality field, programming of research is peculiarly related to the temperament, experience, theoretical predictions, and sensitivities of the in- (3) vestigator. The great advantage of long-term longitudinal research is that it permits verification, refinement, or discard of previous theories and ideas.

(1) We have found from a review of life histories that <u>certain deficits of constitution and/or environment, and certain unsolvable interpersonal conflicts have long-term effects upon the individual, up to age thirty.</u> We have also found that (2) <u>much of personality theory based on pathological samples is not useful for prediction for the larger number of persons.</u> Many of our most mature and competent adults had severely troubled and confusing childhoods and adolescences. Many of our highly successful children and adolescents have failed to achieve their predicted potential. It is clear that we need more sophisticated theory that will help us weight the relevant components—the types of stress, the compensating supports, in various types of organisms, at the various developmental periods—if we are to predict which combinations of factors forestall and which combinations facilitate maturity and strength.

Chapter 4

The Role of Biology in Development

Many psychologists are now coming to the view that biological factors play an important role in monitoring development. A generation ago it was assumed that the child was a tabula rasa and that personality and cognitive development were under the primary influence of experience. We now realize that biology has an important influence in development. Biological factors predispose certain children to psychosis and determine sequences in intellectual development, both in school-age children and young infants.

(1)   In the first article in this chapter, J. Kagan suggests that the changes in the factors which control the distribution of the infant's attention are partly the result of a bio-

[A] logical program. Physical contrast is initially the prime basis for recruiting and main-

[B] taining attention in the newborn and very young infant. Somewhere around the second month of life, discrepancy from schemata (i.e., an event that is slightly different from the child's experiences) becomes an important determinant of sustained attention, and toward the end of the first year a new ability to activate hypotheses emerges as a salient force.

[C] This progression from contrast through discrepancy to activation of hypotheses seems to form an invariant sequence, with experience determining how early or late each of these competences will emerge.

(2)   In the second paper, S. H. White discusses important maturational changes that occur between 5 and 7 years of age. He believes there is a set of cognitive competences that mature during this time. The child is able to hold in memory complicated instructions for problems; he shows an increased ability to inhibit inappropriate behaviors;

and he seems aware of his problem-solving processes. He is less dependent on others, and he is able to inhibit impulsive behavior. There is good reason to believe that the emergence of these competences is controlled, in part, by maturation.

(3)   In the third article, A. A. Ehrhardt and S. W. Baker suggest that the tendency for boys to display more rough-and-tumble play and more aggressiveness than girls may be partly hormonal, for such behaviors can be increased in females who have had great amounts of androgens while being carried by their mothers. The authors suggest that some of the behavioral differences between or within sexes are influenced by biological variables. They do not result solely from different experiences.

#8 *Do Infants Think?*

Jerome Kagan

The sturdiest knowledge we have about the development of infants is the exquisitely invariant order in which they master complex motor coordinations. Most infants can accurately reach for an object by the age of six months, can sit erect by eight months, can crawl by 10 months, can stand by 12 months and can walk steadily by 15 months. Although there are slight differences in the ages at which these abilities are attained, the sequences of events is rarely altered. This fact has tempted some psychologists to propose that deviations from the normal attainment of motor coordinations may be indicative of more general dimensions of intelligence. Except for the 7 percent or so of the infants who are retarded in their passing of these milestones because of damage to the central nervous system, there is no strong relation between the age at which these super-reflexes emerge and the child's later language capacity, richness of memory and problem-solving abilities. In spite of the obvious developmental control of the universal motor patterns, most psychologists have not been interested in asking if early cognitive functioning is similarly yoked to the maturation of the central nervous system.

My colleagues and I at Harvard University have been working in the area of infant cognition for some 10 years. Initially we believed, as many other psychologists do, that mental phenomena are much more plastic than motor skills and are influenced primarily by experience. The data we have collected, however, have forced us to adopt the view that certain cognitive processes in infants are to a large extent controlled by maturation. When we say that aspects of cognitive de-

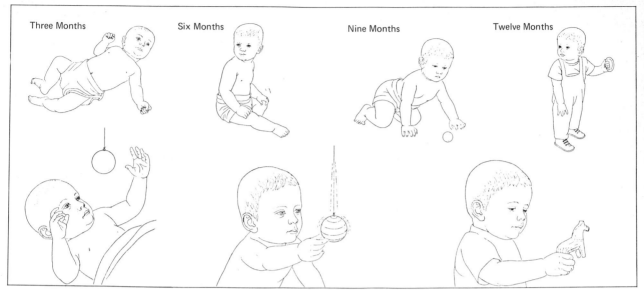

Figure 1 Development of motor abilities in infants (*top row*) is controlled by maturation of the nervous, muscular and other body systems. Most infants can roll over at about three months of age, sit erect between six and eight months, crawl by 10 months and stand by 12 months. The order of motor development is rarely altered. Certain cognitive developments (*bottom row*) appear to be linked to maturation of the central nervous system. As early as the second month infants begin forming "schemata," or mental representations, of events and objects. For the next six months they pay attention to events and objects that differ moderately from these schemata. They pay less attention to familiar or totally novel events. At about eight or nine months appear the first signs of active mental work, in which the infant tries to generate hypotheses to explain novel events.

velopment are controlled by maturation, we mean that biological factors limit the earliest appearance of certain functions, that the order of appearance, given the appropriate inducing environment, is controlled by the growth of the central nervous system. This does not mean that experience is irrelevant.

In our studies the primary measures of the infant's cognitive processes are selected kinds of behavior that accompany attention to an interesting event. By "attention" we do not mean the brief two-second orienting reaction of an infant to any sudden change in stimulus energy but rather the duration of sustained orientation that follows the initially orienting response. We believe that during the period of sustained orientation an infant

more than 30 days old is trying to build a representation of the event. The duration of sustained attention is a rough index of how easy or how difficult it is for him to understand a new experience.

The attention of newborn infants is attracted by objects that move or have sharp contours and light-dark contrast. These perceptual preferences seem to be inherent in the structure of the visual system. A two-day-old infant is more attentive to a moving or intermittently flashing light than to a steady light; he looks longer at a solid black figure on a white background than at a low-contrast gray figure. The rate of stimulus change is also important during this first era of growth. If a stimulus is introduced too rapidly, the infant may become fearful. Similarly, as Richard Kearsley of Harvard has found, if an unexpected sound, say 70 decibels of "white" noise, reaches maximum intensity within a few milliseconds, a newborn infant closes his eyes, starts and shows an increase in heart rate, all of which are signs of a de-[B]fensive response. If the same sound reaches its maximum intensity in two seconds, the infant then opens his eyes, looks around and is likely to show a decrease in heart rate, all of which are signs of interest.

The attention-recruiting power of contrast, which is maximal at birth or soon after, loses its force to a second property as early as the second month. As a result of the infant's encounters with the environment he acquires mental representations of events. We call these representations schemata. Toward the end of the second month the infant begins paying more attention to stimuli that differ moderately from those he usually encounters. The functional relation between duration of attention and the nature of the external event is summarized by the discrepancy principle: events that are moderately different from an infant's schema elicit longer spans of attention than either totally familiar events or totally novel events. Moreover, we suggest that the time of emergence of the infant's special reaction to discrepancy is controlled by maturational processes.

There is some controversy over the nature of the relation between the degree of discrepancy and the duration of attention. We believe it is curvilinear; others believe that increasing discrepancy is correlated with increasing attention. We do not have a way to measure degree of discrepancy, and we must be satisfied—only temporarily, we hope—with the qualitative statement that a discrepant stimulus is one that shares some aspects with its referent. A novel stimulus shares very few attributes with the standard or none at all. This definition always assumes the perspective of the viewer: an event that is novel to a six-month-old may be only mildly discrepant to a 26-month-old.

Data from several investigations directly support the curvilinear nature of the discrepancy principle or at least reveal that the infant reacts differently to a discrepant event compared with a novel event. In one experiment the infant was shown a two-inch orange cube on six separate occasions. Then the infant was shown either a smaller orange cube (a discrepant event) or a yellow rippled cylinder (a novel event). Infants between seven and 12 months, particularly females, became excited by the discrepant small cube and showed their excitement by vocalization; the appearance of the novel rippled cylinder did not induce any vocalization.

A more direct demonstration of the discrepancy principle in auditory perception has been achieved recently by Dennis K. Kinney of Harvard. He had groups of seven-and-a-half-month-old infants listen to repetitions of four-syllable phrases spoken in a distinctive rhythm. There were four groups of infants, and each group heard repetitions of a different phrase. After eight repetitions of the phrase all the infants then heard exactly the same four-syllable phrase. For one group the final phrase was identical with the one they had been hearing. For two groups the final phrase was either slightly or moderately discrepant from the repeated phrase. For the fourth group the final phrase was markedly different from the original and could be classified as novel.

Two measures of attention were used: orientation of the head and eyes toward the sound source and a decrease in heart rate. The infants who heard the slightly or moderately discrepant spoken phrase displayed a longer orientation to the sound source and a lower heart rate than the infants who heard either the identical phrase or the novel one (see Figure 2). Both measures are indicators of the degree to which the infants were attempting to understand the new event or, to put it differently, how much attention was invested in the changed phrase.

An equally convincing example in visual perception of the curvilinear relation between dis-

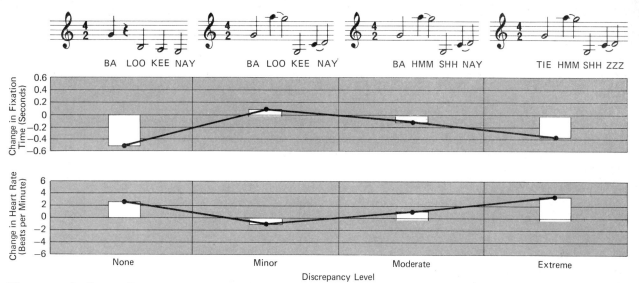

Figure 2 Auditory discrepancy test involved four groups of seven-and-a-half-month-old infants. Each group listened to a different spoken rhythmical phrase (*top*). After eight repetitions all then heard the first phrase. Attention paid to the last stimulus varied according to the discrepancy of the phrase (*abscissa*). The slightly discrepant phrase drew the most attention as evidenced by the increase in orientation to the sound source (*top graph*) and the decrease in heart rate (*bottom graph*), both indicators of attention.

crepancy and attention is provided by a study of four-month-old infants. Initially they were shown an arrangement of three colored geometrical objects in a "mobile." Each infant was exposed to 12 half-minute viewings of the mobile, and the amount of attention, as measured by fixation time, was recorded. Then some mothers were given a mobile to hang above the child's crib for 30 minutes a day for three weeks. Other mothers did not receive a mobile. All the mothers were asked to bring the infant back in three weeks for further testing. At home some infants saw a mobile with the same arrangement of shapes they had viewed initially in the laboratory. Other infants saw mobiles at home that differed from the original either slightly, moderately or greatly.

Each infant was then returned to the laboratory and was shown the same arrangement of objects he had seen three weeks earlier. The duration of sustained attention again was measured,

and changes in attention between the first and the second viewing were assessed. Infants who had not been shown a mobile at home exhibited virtually no change in their attention to the objects. Infants who had seen moderately discrepant mobiles at home paid more attention to the laboratory stimulus than infants who had seen novel mobiles or mobiles with only minor variations. In short, the moderately discrepant mobile attracted more attention than one with great discrepancy or slight discrepancy (see Figure 3).

The discrepancy principle may help to explain the regular occurrence of fear responses in very young animals. A novel event rarely engenders fear, whereas a discrepant event often does engender it. Eric A. Salzen of the University of Liverpool has shown that alteration in the immediate environment of chicks gave rise to fear only in animals raised in a normal environment. Chicks reared in isolation and deprived of seeing

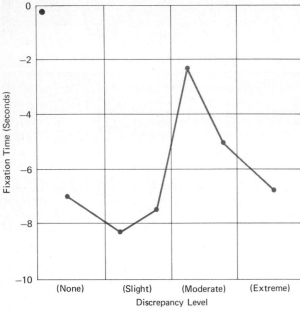

Figure 3 Visual discrepancy study with four-month-old infants involved measuring the amount of attention (eye fixation) given to an arrangement of geometrical objects. After baseline measurements were made in the laboratory the infants were returned home with special "mobiles" to be hung above their crib for 30 minutes a day. Some infants had an arrangement identical with what they had viewed in the laboratory. Others had slightly, moderately or extremely discrepant arrangements. A control group had no home mobile. After three weeks changes in attention to the initial arrangement were determined. There was no change in the attention span of infants who did not view a mobile at home (*black dot*). Of the infants who had viewed a mobile at home, those with the moderately discrepant mobiles showed the smallest drop in attention. Infants who had identical or similar mobiles showed the greatest drop in attention. Extreme discrepancy also drew less attention.

any moving objects did not respond fearfully to a moving object such as a cardboard cylinder. Chicks that had lived under normal conditions did respond fearfully to the moving cylinder. We believe chicks raised in isolation perceived the moving object as a novel event and were not alerted by it. Chicks from the normal environment had developed a schema for moving objects and had some basis for regarding the moving cardboard cylinder as being discrepant. Because they could not assimilate this discrepant event they reacted with fear. Research on "imprinting" in birds also suggests that a bird does not fear a decoy on hatching but does react with fear a few days after the animal has had the opportunity to become familiar with its environment. It is the relation between an external event and a schema for that event that seems to be the critical determinant in provoking fear, as well as attracting and maintaining attention.

One of the significant problems in this area of research is how to quantify degree of discrepancy. Currently this classification is done after the fact. There are some hints that for visual discrepancy, at least in infants, the shape and arrangement of elements are among the important dimensions to be quantified. Joseph Fagan of Case Western Reserve University has found that if six-month-old infants are repeatedly shown a pair of identical objects and minutes later one of the objects is altered either in shape or in arrangement, the infant looks longer at the changed member of the pair. For auditory perception rhythm seems to be as critical as the nature of the sounds in the recruiting of attention.

We believe the essential dimensions to be quantified for both visual and auditory events are the distribution of the stimulus elements in space and in time. This approach is intuitively attractive because of the history of the physical sciences. Chemistry had a major breakthrough in understanding when it was found that compounds could be classified by the spatial arrangement of atoms. Chemists assigned related names to compounds that had the same basic architecture but differed in minor ways. Physics used the arrangement of energy bands to classify complex sights and sounds. We are suggesting that psychology requires an analogous set of constructs that describes the spatial and temporal distribution of the events that comprise its basic forms.

Two empirical facts require the postulation of a third process that begins to control attention toward the end of the first year. Duration of attention to masklike representations of the human face decreases from two to nine months of age because the child's schema for a face becomes more mature and the masks become less discrepant. From nine to 36 months, however, duration of attention to the same facial masks increases. The U-shaped curve of this relation held true not only for American children but also for children living in extremely isolated rural areas of eastern Guatemala and for Bushman children living in isolated regions of the Kalahari Desert in Africa. If discrepancy from schema exerted the major control over attention, then the amount of attention should have continued to decrease after the first year as the infant's schema of the human face became better formed and the masks became increasingly less discrepant.

In order to explain the unexpected increase in attention toward the end of the first year, we postulated the emergence of a new cognitive structure or process. We call this presumed structure a hypothesis. The child, we suggest, tries to mentally transform the discrepant event into the form with which he is familiar, the familiar form being the schema. The cognitive structure involved in this mental transformation is the hypothesis. To be able to recognize that a sequence of high-pitched sounds is human speech rather than a birdsong requires schemata for the human voice and for birdsongs. On the other hand, the interpretation of why the speech is unusual requires the generation of hypotheses, which is an attempt to understand why the event is odd and how it might be related to the event that generated the original schema.

A quite different set of facts also supports the idea that "activation of hypotheses" emerges toward the end of the first year. Observations in varied cultural settings suggest that between eight and 15 months children are likely to show fear when they are separated from their primary caretaker.

The extensive studies with infant monkeys by Harry F. Harlow and Margaret Kuenne Harlow of the University of Wisconsin have tempted psychologists to assume that fear following separation reflects the intensity of the infant's attachment to his mother [see "Love in Infant Monkeys," by Harry F. Harlow; Scientific American, June, 1959]. With human infants the intensity of attachment of the infant to his mother often is measured by how long the infant cries when he is separated from her. Our experiments suggest that crying may not necessarily index intensity of attachment but can be the result, at least in part, of the infant's inability to interpret the discrepant event described by watching his mother leave him alone, or with a stranger, in an unfamiliar situation. The arousal of fear under these conditions seems to be caused by the same mechanism that elicits fear in much younger infants, namely an encounter with a discrepant event that cannot be assimilated, interpreted, rejected or destroyed.

Milton Kotelchuck of Harvard recorded on videotape the responses of children between the ages of six and 21 months to the departure of their parents in the presence of a female stranger. The observations were made in a living-room setting that included toys appropriate to the age of the child. During the first three minutes the child was with both his father and his mother, who sat near the wall while the child played. Then one parent left the room. After three minutes a female stranger entered and three minutes later the second parent departed, leaving the child alone with the stranger.

The episodes were repeated several times. In every case when the stranger entered the room, the infant looked more often at the stranger than at either of his parents, indicating that even the youngest child could discriminate the stranger

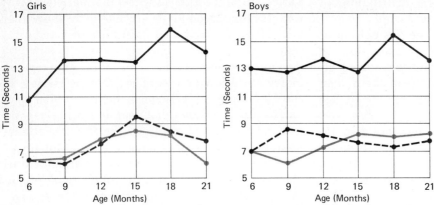

Figure 4 Arrival of a stranger drew more attention (*black curve*) from both male and female infants than arrival of either mother alone (*dashed curve*) or father alone (*gray curve*). Infants 18 months old paid the most attention following the stranger's arrival.

from the parents (see Figure 4 and Figure 5). The presence of the stranger when neither parent was present produced little crying or other signs of fear in infants either six or nine months old. Among infants either 12 or 15 months old the presence of the stranger alone caused the most crying and the most marked inhibition of play. At 18 and 21 months the infants cried less and showed less inhibition of play in the presence of the stranger.

The most marked inhibition of play, a sensitive sign of fear, occurred when the child was left alone with the stranger. We suggest that these behavioral signs of fear were the result of the child's inability to understand where his parents were or whether or not they would return. The hypotheses he generated to understand this discrepant event were insufficient, and faced with an unresolved discrepancy the child became frightened.

These data are relevant to the earlier assumption that the process of activating hypotheses does not emerge until the end of the first year, since we have to ask why Kotelchuck did not find much separation fear in the six-month-old infants. We know that four- and five-month-old infants

will cry and show signs of distress to discrepant events they cannot assimilate. We can partly resolve the paradox if we analyze the nature of the discrepancy. The fear displayed by the one-year-old infant following the departure of his parents may be due to the activation of hypotheses that cannot be resolved involving the immediate future: What will happen to me? Will my parents return? What will the stranger do? If the child has no answer to these troublesome hypotheses, he may become afraid, stop playing and begin to cry. The cause of his distress is uncertainty generated by unanswered questions about the future rather than direct encounter with an unusual, external event.

In cultures where a mother carries her young child for most of the day (as she does in parts of Uganda and Central America) a four-month-old infant will cry when he is removed from his mother. This crying is unlikely to be mediated by the same class of discrepancy that elicits crying in a one-year-old infant when he is left alone in a room. The fear at four months is a result of the discrepant kinesthetic and tactile stimuli that follow separation from the mother's body and not the activation of hypotheses as to her where-

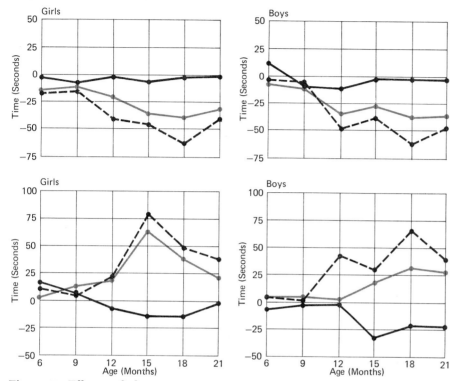

Figure 5 Effects of departure, as measured by change in infants' play (*upper graph*) and change in crying (*lower graph*) during the first minute after departure, are shown. In infants younger than nine months the departure of the mother (*dashed curve*) or the father (*gray*) or the stranger (*black*) resulted in a relatively small change in playing and crying. In older infants the departure of mother or father resulted in a large decrease in play and a large increase in crying; departure of the stranger resulted in less crying.

abouts or the probability of her returning. Therefore crying following separation from the parent may be mediated at different ages by qualitatively different sources of discrepancy.

The strongest support for the notion that a one-year-old is capable of generating hypotheses about his experiences comes from studies of heart-rate changes in response to discrepant events. John and Beatrice Lacey of the Fels Research Institute have found that when an adult looks at or listens to an interesting stimulus, his heart rate decreases; when he is actively thinking —either memorizing verbal material or perform-

ing arithmetical calculations—his heart rate increases. Recently Kathleen van Hover of the National Institute of Mental Health has extended the validity of this finding for children from six to 10 years old. The children showed an acceleration of heart rate in response to memory problems and a deceleration in heart rate to orienting and search situations for both visual and auditory tasks (see Figure 6).

The relation between active mental work and heart-rate acceleration observed in children and adults may hold for infants as well. Since generating hypotheses is a form of mental work, there

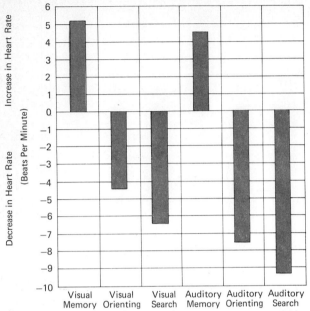

Figure 6 Heart rate and mental activity in children 6 to 10 years of age are related in this graph. Mental activities such as memorizing or calculating increase the heart rate. Paying attention to an event, either by looking or by listening, decreases the heart rate.

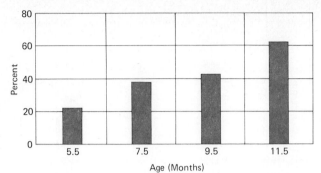

Figure 7 Heart-rate increase of infants who have just heard a discrepant sound is linked to age. Here the percentage of infants in each age group who exhibited cardiac acceleration is shown. A larger proportion of the older infants showed a rise in heart rate in response to the discrepant event. This could be a sign of greater mental activity in older infants.

should be a rise in the heart rate of infants as they become maturationally able to activate these structures. This prediction was affirmed in a study of infants ranging in age from 5½ months to 11½ months. The infants heard from eight to 12 repetitions of a meaningful phrase of speech followed by a discrepant speech phrase. The older the infant, the more likely his heart rate was to increase in response to the discrepant stimulus, suggesting active mental work in the form of activation of hypotheses (see Figure 7). In another study infants of the same age range heard repetitions of a nonsense phrase followed by a different nonsense phrase. Again the discrepant event produced the greatest rise in heart rate in the older infants. Moreover, there was an increasing tendency with age for infants to vocalize more after the discrepant speech phrase had ended than during its presentation (see Figure 8). This behavior suggests

that the older infants were working, in a cognitive sense, on the speech that had just terminated and their vocalization during this period was a reflection of the excitement that accompanied the work.

When the initial series of phrases is spoken by a male voice and the discrepant series is spoken by a female voice, older infants did not show an acceleration of heart rate. Similarly, infants do not show a rise in heart rate if the series is an ascending scale played on a cello and the discrepant series is a random arrangement of the same notes. This may mean that the infant does not perceive these events as discrepant transformations of the standard and thus does not attempt to generate hypotheses to assimilate the new stimulus.

Philip Zelazo of Harvard recorded eye fixation and changes in heart rate of 11½-month-old infants as they watched a toy car roll down an incline and knock over a plastic object. After a few trials some infants began to anticipate the car's motion and looked toward the object. In 73 percent of the anticipatory fixations Zelazo found an accompanying increase in heart rate. There was a decrease in heart rate in only 14 percent of the

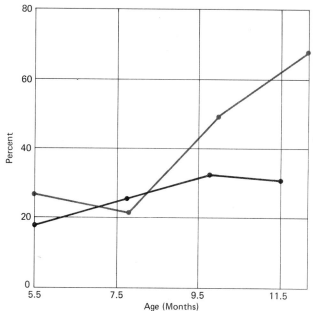

Figure 8 Increase in vocalization following a discrepant event also is linked to the age of the infant. The percentage of infants in each age group who vocalized during the stimulus (*black curve*) did not vary much. A large proportion of older infants vocalized after the stimulus had ended (*gray curve*). The poststimulus vocalization could be an indication that the older infants were engaged in some mental activity related to the discrepant event.

cases. If the increased heart rate means the same thing in infants as it does in older children, namely an increase in mental activity, it is reasonable to suggest that the child begins thinking about unusual events toward the end of his first year of life.

The suggestion that eight to nine months marks the maturational frontier when infants begin to generate hypotheses is supported by the fact that intra-individual continuity of behavior changes toward the end of the first year. We recently completed a long-term study of 180 firstborn infants whose reactions to a set of visual and auditory stimuli were assessed at four, eight, 13 and 27 months of age. We found virtually no relation between attentiveness or vocalization at four or eight months and attentiveness or speech in the same child at 27 months. We found moderate stability of these reactions, however, when we compared the kinds of behavior displayed at 13 and 27 months. These data suggest that the relation of attentional phenomena to mental structure changes toward the end of the first year.

Both theoretical and practical implications flow from these findings. It appears that before an infant is a year old he has become a thinking creature who activates cognitive structures to resolve discrepancies and solve problems. Over the past 20 years many students of child development have held a different view. For example, the eminent Swiss psychologist Jean Piaget has argued that during the first 18 months of life an infant knows the world only in terms of his sensory impressions and motor activities. Cognitive development, says Piaget, begins after the sensorimotor period ends. These results provide a mild challenge to his view. The infant may be more thoughtful than most psychologists have surmised.

A second implication takes the form of a suggestion to developmental physiologists and anatomists to search for important changes in the function and structure of the central nervous system between eight and 12 months of age. The infant becomes consistently reactive to discrepancy between two and three months, and the emergence of this competence is accompanied by a cluster of biological phenomena (including a mature form of the visual evoked potential and consistent occurrence of sleep spindles in the electroencephalogram). Nine months seems to be a frontier that announces the child's ability to generate simple hypotheses, but the existing literature does not mention a comparable set of biological changes in the central nervous system. We suggest that this new competence is dependent on correlated changes in the brain. A new cluster of biological phenomena should appear at that time. It would seem appropriate for neurophysiologists and developmental anatomists to look for changes in the structure and function of the central nervous system of infants between eight months and one year old.

(3)   The final suggestion is more practical. Up to six months of age the differences among infants in motor and cognitive development are fairly independent of the child's social class, his ethnic origin and even some aspects of his rearing conditions. By one year of age, however, differences in rearing experience seriously affect cognitive functioning. This means that pediatricians and psychologists might assess the reactions of one-year-old infants to discrepant stimuli to obtain information about their developmental status, particularly the status of infants who may have been exposed to psychic risks or who suffer from metabolic or structural defects.

ATTENTION

HEARTBEAT RATE

Concentration in reading
        is lost
    if the material is either
            { too old   & ∴ too boring, or
            { too novel & ∴ too incomprehensible,

                both being ∴ too irrevelant.

Some General Outlines of the Matrix of Developmental Changes Between Five and Seven Years

Sheldon H. White

This paper discusses an exploration of the large literature of developmental change over the age range from five to seven years. The analysis was set in motion by some findings of change in children's learning in this age range (White, 1966a) and its ultimate aim is to try to understand the mechanisms of children's learning in a broad context . . . that is, in the context of the cognitive and developmental mechanisms which regulate what the child can absorb from his experience. I have been led by the analysis into some newer research lines, an attempt to survey the co-incidence of a number of behavior changes in the

Research supported by Grant OE5-10-239 from the Office of Education.

SOURCE: Reprinted from *Bulletin of the Orton Society*, 20 (1970), 41–57, by permission of the author and the publisher.

same child (Super and White, 1970), and some studies of children's ability to order series of pictures into a representation of a temporal sequence (White and Evans, 1970), but I will speak here primarily about the literature analysis.

One good justification for a literature review in this area age range is the situation created by the sheer diversity and quantity of reported research findings. That diversity makes it impossible for any research program to explore all the signs of change at this time, and it has led to some segregation among channels of facts and hypotheses dealing with the age range. In the present paper, continuing several previous efforts (White, 1965, 1966b, 1968), I hope to explore further the literature of change.

To a psychologist, what is most interesting about this age range is its association with the emergence in some strength of adult-like posers of reasoning, symbolization, or operational thought. Historically, psychologists have sustained a largely-frustrated preoccupation with the analysis of man's higher faculties. We have had diverse theories about them. We have had a psychometry of intelligence. We have had a polyglot research literature on reasoning, abstraction, concept formation, and symbolism. And yet it all does not seem to have jelled into a satisfying and cohesive picture. Now we find, again and again in the literature, the conclusion that a higher level of thought is emergent in the seven year old, that conclusion arising out of a hundred-odd particularities of behavior change.

The theoretical possibilities offered by this have already been significantly capitalized upon by developmental theorists. We owe many of our more cogent and satisfying analyses of Mind to developmental theorists who have analyzed events within and without this age range—to [A] Freud, with his descriptions of the strata of child-[B] hood thought and emotion; to Vygotsky, with his account of the juxtaposition of language and [C] thought; to Werner; and, in greatest detail and [D] most incisively, to Piaget's many-faceted account of the moves from preoperational to operational thought. None of these theorists see the abstract faculty as a novelty of the 5–7 age range, without antecedent or subsequent elaboration, but all emphasize the significance of prominent qualitative changes in the observables at this time.

Why does one find so many sharp changes in the child's behavior in the five to seven age range? There are probably several reasons.

1. For reasons of convenience and interest, developmental psychologists have devoted a great deal of research effort to this time of development—more, by far, than to any other era of the life span. We have, here, a richer body of material in which to look for sharp changes.

2. There is every reason to believe that the child's training environment changes significantly at this time. Societies with institutionalized education typically place children in school between the ages of five and seven, and it may also be true that underdeveloped societies may change their indoctrination of the child at this time (White 1968a).

3. There appears to be a factor under development in this age range which is in part a genuine change in the child and in part an artifact which enhances and distorts many signs of change. At five or six, the child seems to develop abilities which enable him to cooperate significantly more adequately with the fixed-procedure kind of psychological experiment. This may mislead us, because we tend to interpret observed changes in the child according to the way we interpret the experiment we have put to him. We may conclude that there is a change in learning or perception or motivation when it might be more accurate to say that there is a change in the child's competence as an experimental subject, whether the experiment is about learning or perception or motivation.

4. Fourth, and finally, there must be maturational developments at this time as one basis of the observed changes. There is a positivistic tradition, particularly prominent in American developmental psychology, which acts to hold off appeals to maturational factors as an explanation of age changes as long as possible (White, 1968b). To redress the balance, it seems worthwhile to go over certain information which definitely suggests the basis in maturation—specifically, the kind of ontogenetic corticalization process envisaged by Hughlings Jackson, in which lower-order cognitive mechanisms become inhibited and supplanted by substitute higher-order mechanisms in the course of development (White, 1968b).

To begin with, the age range from five to seven appears to be the terminus of a sensitive period for the development of human intelligence. There is a treatise by Bloom (1964) which has developed this thesis from psychometric information—specifically, from the fact that correlations between early and late IQ measures level off to a high and

(OPPOSED) { ONTOGENY = BIOLOGICAL DEVELOPMENT OF THE INDIVIDUAL ; LIFE CYCLE OF A SINGLE ORGANISM

PHYLOGENY = ORIGIN & EVOLUTION OF A DIVISION, GROUP, OR RACE OF ANIMALS OR PLANTS stable asymptote at age seven. Corroborative information suggests that the physiological supports of intelligence acquire a new kind of invulnerability in this age range. This evidence, partially reviewed elsewhere (White, 1968a), draws upon clinical surveys of several kinds of pathology in childhood—the effects of hospitalization, diabetes, phenylketonuria, febrile convulsions, and childhood autism. Each line of evidence says in some way that the child shows intellectual or neurological vulnerability until the 5–7 period, after which there is a hardening of the child's status. Considering the kinds of evidence at hand, it is unlikely that these hardenings are established by other than maturational developments.

(2) One confronts, second, information which indicates that the developmental progressions of the child in this age range are often reversed in old age. There are several behavioral characteristics for which, specifically, a "five to seven" shift in childhood is matched by a "seven to five" shift in old age. Preschoolers and the aged show a common tendency to lapse into "position habits" (stereotyped response to the same position again and again) during a discrimination problem (Levinson and Reese, 1967); they give a characteristic reaction on the face-hand test (i.e., not "noticing" the more distal of two simultaneously-applied touches) different from that of older children and younger adults (Cohn, 1951; Fink and Bender, 1953; Pollack and Fink, 1962); they are relatively less sensitive to the verbal transformation effect, illusory changes in the same words heard over and over again (Warren, 1961, 1968; Warren and Warren, 1966); they are not as susceptible to classical conditioning (Razran, 1933; Braun and Geiselhart, 1959). Other characteristics, which show trends but seemingly not sharp changes during early ontogenesis show inverse trends in old age: a general slowing of reaction in all situations (Lynn, 1962); a slowing of habituation (Kazmiin and Fedorov, 1951); a decline in EEG alpha frequency (Axelrod, 1962); and a general decline in the ability to deal with embedded figures (Axel-

rod, 1962). Beyond the material which links the events of the preschool period with those of old age, there is other research that does not quite enter the preschool period—that begins the study of the child at age six—and that has demonstrated development during youth and a corresponding dissolution in old age. In the latter case, I am thinking particularly of the several excellent cross sectional studies of the life span reported by the comparative-developmental group at Clark University (Comalli, Wapner, and Werner, 1959, 1962; Wapner, Werner, and Comalli, 1960; Comali, 1965). All these data suggest a resurgence of preschool cognitive characteristics in the aged. Pelz, Pike, and Ames (1962) have shown some differential diagnosis of intactness among the aged using preschool and early school instruments.

This second body of data, the regression data, suggest a maturational improvement at the base of the changes in childhood. If one were to argue that the childhood progressions arise only through learning or training, one would seemingly have to invent an old age fraught with very specialized kinds of extinction or forgetting.

[2] There is a second implication of these regression data. If components of the cognitive system which organizes the child's response to the world re-emerge in old age, then one must assume that to some significant degree that cognitive system has persisted, superseded, in the eras of later childhood and adulthood.

Both arguments, so far, present indicative arguments in support of maturational causation. Can we go further? Can we give some shape or form to these imaginary maturational events? Recently, Esther Milner (1967) has provided us with a bold book in which—working in the spirit of Hughlings Jackson and C. Judson Herrick and Myrtle McGraw to whom she dedicates the effort —she attempts to survey what is known about the maturation of the human brain and then aligns the ontogenesis of personality with this information.

CORTICAL = PERTAINING TO THE BRAIN CORTEX

Data summarized in Milner indicate a substantial completion of cortical maturation by age six—particularly the parietal, occipital, and temporal lobes. (It is at six, as she puts it, that the "human principle" comes to be dominant over the "mammalian principle.") The frontal areas grow rapidly until age six but are left to do somewhat more after that age range. One might expect, then, that important behavioral transitions might be aligned with virtually complete organization of the temporal, occipital, and parietal cortex. Our knowledge of the functions of these areas in the human has been given to us largely by neurological examination of the brain-damaged adult. With all the shortcomings of clinical neurological material—the fact that damage is never neuroanatomically neat, the fact that functions are not neatly localized in the brain—there is nevertheless a mass of clinical material which by now has sketched out connections between cortical areas and the constructive processes of thought and action. Verbal descriptions of thought disorders due to cortical misfunction regularly parallel verbal descriptions of the preschool child's thought. To some extent, the preschool child might be considered an "organic" patient, small, with good prognosis.

We do not yet have many investigations which have studied changes in the normative incidence of various neurological signs during human development, nor related such signs to cognitive functions. There are suggestions that such information might be useful. Koppitz (1960) has reported that children under five regularly show signs of organicity on the Bender-Gestalt test, showing a pattern of disorder which in the neurological literature would be called "constructional apraxia" and linked with parietal symptomatology. Vygotsky's (1962) block-sorting test for children's concept formation has, as we know, been used subsequently as a test for organicity of function. The children's imperfect treatment of the block-sorting follows a syndrome which in the neurological literature has been called "amorpho-

synthesis," again linked with the parietal lobes. There are resemblances between disorders of left-right sense and finger localization found in aphasia and that found among young children (Benton, 1959). And, finally, one must make brief allusion to a vast literature which suggests that the dyslexic syndrome is associated, on the one hand, with developmental immaturity and on the other, with some of the specific neurological signs found in disorders of the parieto-occipital areas. (Money, 1962; Critchley, 1964; Thompson, 1966). If we can ever achieve a coherent understanding of the symptomatology of dyslexia, we will surely advance in our understanding of the maturational substrate of thought development.

To summarize, one feels compelled to argue on the basis of the pattern of the literature that there must be—as one among several factors—a maturational substrate underlying the behavior changes between five and seven. One might construe the maturational component in terms of functions assigned to parietal and occipital cortex in humans. But any attempt to explain the diverse phenomena of change in this age range in any terms must depend upon the crystallization of the phenomena, some attempt to find simpler structure ruling the diverse experimental data. A few years ago, when first surveying a more limited portion of the literature, an attempt at summary was made, yielding a list of genotypic changes (White, 1965).

My purpose, in the remainder of this paper, is to present and discuss a revised set of summarizations, based in some part on residual dissatisfactions with the first effort and re-analysis of the set originally offered, but stemming in larger part from a more extended inquiry into the relevant literature.

Let me first outline what will be taken up in more detail. The following trends are suggested in the literature:

First, a sharply enhanced ability to form a system of behavior in accord with a proposition

APRAXIA = COMPLETE OR PARTIAL LOSS OF MEMORY OF HOW TO PERFORM CERTAIN COMPLEX MUSCULAR MOVEMENTS, RESULTING FROM BRAIN DAMAGE.

offered to the child and, then, an ability to maintain the proposition over an extended period of time.

Second, an increase in inhibitory mechanisms manifesting itself in diverse ways.

Third, an increase in the access of certain kinds of memory or awareness to verbal or voluntary processes.

Fourth, the ability to superpose dimensionalization on the concrete situation, so that the child does not so much deal with events as with events-in-context.

Fifth, a relative decline in what might be regarded as affective dependence upon other humans and, together with that, the ascension of what might be called competitive dependence.

Sixth, an increase in speed of reaction and speed of recognition.

Development and Maintenance of a Proposition

As a way of introducing the first of these factors, let me first discuss the problem of cooperation with experiments alluded to earlier. A good many of us use fixed-procedure experiments with children, in which instructions are given to the child which project a target for a following sequence of encounters with events. He is to try to choose the picture which rings the bell, he is to find the embedded figure; he is to associate to the word he hears the first word he thinks of; he is to state whether two figures are similar or dissimilar. One such experiment with which I am familiar is the discrimination-learning experiment. This is a simple procedure imported from animal work for use with preschool children. The child is shown a pair of stimuli again and again, choosing one or the other each time and being rewarded or nonrewarded, until he always chooses the rewarded one. While I have long used certain precautions in this kind of experiment, only recently have I thought about the implications of those precautions.

To get optimum cooperation of a child with this procedure, it is usually wise to establish certain conditions:

1. One must have "rapport" with a preschool child. One must bypass a noticeable component of "stranger anxiety" for many children and, for a good many more, one must signal warmth with conversation in friendly tones.

2. One arranges as simplified a visual environment as possible. The apparatus is large and dominates the child's field of view. As much as possible distraction and other interesting visual material are gotten out of the way.

3. One never gives lengthy verbal instructions. The shorter the instructions, the better. The instructions must be mixed with actual motor rehearsal of the moves the child will make during the course of the procedure.

4. When one begins the learning procedure, one takes care to "notice" in some marked way the first few times the child behaves correctly. One says "Good!" or praises the child. One does this because one is not completely sure the child knows what he is supposed to do, and this praise is intended to supplement the instructions. Apart from this, the experimenter tries to "hide" from the child's vision or, if visible, he tries to keep his face expressionless, so that the child will be led to attend to what satisfies the test and not to what will satisfy the experimenter.

5. Periodically throughout the learning task, in my work at about ten-trial intervals, one gives the child a sentence or a phase which recalls his goal to him.

6. After a long period of non-success, near the end of a task or at its conclusion, one praises the child as a way of making him feel successful, and to indicate that one's friendly feelings for the child continue.

My impression is that most experimenters who work with preschool children use techniques somewhat like those just described. Generally, there seems much less need for the precautions for the child of primary school age.

Consider what these precautions represent. [1] First, they take pains to engage the child in a motivation springing from friendship; we will [2] have more to say about this later. Second, they do not leave it to the child to construct a motor routine from a verbal prescription. Instead, rather quickly, a motor routine is "shaped" by instruction and modelling, and then guided for several [3] trials into the task. Third, the goals toward which the motor routine is directed–the specifications of what end-state the motor routine is to seek to bring about—are continually refreshed for the child. By doing this, and by our attempt to keep the environment free of distractions, we recognize the extreme fragility of the child's hold on the target of his efforts.

Even with such precautions, a significant proportion of preschool children will "fail" the discrimination learning task. The youngest of them will lapse into long strings of position habits, or other stereotypes. The older preschoolers may or may not show stereotypies, but if they have not stumbled into solution within the first ten or twenty trials, it is more likely than not that they will go out to 80 or more trials without solution. They will show what has been called a "failure set." This presumes discouragement, but discouragement is only occasionally evident and most often is not. One might presume instead that the child has simply lost sight of his target, his end-state, and remains content to exercise his motor routine, accepting those rewards which chance may bring.

During this age range, there is varied evidence of this sort. The child improves in ability to hold the plan which is to guide his behavior, without lapsing back into an unguided motor routine. In the younger child, the sheer passage of time is apt to dissipate the plan, or else the plan is attacked by the inner and outer distractions which time brings.

1) In an experiment by Annett (1959) in which children were asked to sort 16 pictures according to category, there was evidence of a sharp increase of "within category" sorting between 6 and 7, accompanied by a marked decrease in the percentage of subjects who could not sustain sorting at all.

2) In an experiment by Koppitz (1960) asking children to reproduce Bender-Gestalt figures, and in studies by Olson (1968) examining children's ability to draw a diagonal, children at five and under showed substantial inability to complete construction following the model.

3) In a number of experiments (Walk and Saltz, 1965; White, 1966a; Gollin, 1961; Turnure, 1965) it has been shown that moderate distraction interferes with the ability of the five year old child to form a solution to the discrimination problem while not interfering with that of a seven year old.

4) In an experiment by Birch (1966), preschool children in three age groups were asked simply to hold down a lever and were timed until they released the lever; the older the children, the longer the timed duration of the instruction. In an older experiment by Miles (1933), children were asked to watch for a jack-in-the-box, and the duration of their gaze was timed. Again, the older the children, the longer the instructional set held.

These latter studies are reminiscent of older attention span studies and, as everyone knows, statements about the brevity of children's attention span are very misleading. Even the one or two year old will show surprisingly sustained attention span in free play. The meaning of the attention span experiments is, I think, related to the point being made here. It is with respect to a proposition or plan placed upon the child by others, and one not periodically prompted by visual or verbal reminders, that attention span is brief.

•ACCUMULATION OF A PROPOSITION There appear to be two other changes related to the weakness in sustaining a proposition during encounters. First, there may be something like an inverse deficit, a weakness in cumulating a proposition through a series of encounters. A series of experiments by Zinchenko and his associates (Tarakanov and Zinchenko, 1960; Chzhi-Jsin, Zinchenko, and Ruzskaya, 1960) have shown that there is a significant improvement in the child's ability to recognize a visual form by tactual exploration at age 5. Blank and Bridger (1966) have reported similar findings. From such reports, one might reach a more general conclusion that there is a kind of bidirectional improvement in this age range: first, the ability to sustain a proposition to guide successive behavior segments and, second, the ability to integrate successive behavior segments to form a proposition.

•REDUCTION OF STEREOTYPY We have said, earlier, that in the discrimination experiment the plan seems to dissipate from the child's behavior, leaving behind a rather empty set of "motor routine" behaviors. It is interesting that the motor routine is sustained. The child has caught the rhythm of the experiment and so, trial after trial, he senses when he is to deliver an act and, on schedule, he continues to give it. There is evidence of stereotypies in the execution of this motor routine. Rieber (1966) has suggested that the position perseveration is a dominant stereotype of the child up to age four, and after four, agreeing with a number of other authors (Weir, 1964; Miller, Tu, and Moffat, 1969; Manley and Miller, 1968), there is a dominance of response alternation. One might suggest that these stereotypies might be something more than vacuum behavior, patterns manifest when the child has nothing else to do. They may have some active tendency to intrude in the very young child, perhaps if some accumulation of fatigue degrades his ability to inhibit them. White (1966a), Blank and Bridger (1966), and Brian and Goodenough (1941), in different sorts of experiments, have commented on the influence of response stereotyping in blocking more adaptive problem-solving in the preschool child.

The Development of the Inhibition of Impulsive Behavior

In an earlier presentation on the cognitive changes between five and seven years, the thesis was developed at some length that the 5–7 changes are associated with a pervasive inhibitory factor involving, in the most structural sense, the inhibition of a juvenile logic so that an adult logic can assume direction of the child's behavior (White, 1965). It continues to be true that there is little direct evidence for the broad assertion. Broad assertions are rarely directly provable. But there are a number of minor signs showing changes in motor restraint and in what we call "inhibition of impulse."

Studies of sustained intellectual activity in human adults have suggested that the endurance of cognitive problem-solving time is accompanied by gradually rising gradients of arousal. Malmo (1965) and his associates at Montreal have reported on an extended research program using a diversity of tasks in which, repeatedly, rising gradients of muscle tension were found as adults carried through their tasks to completion, the tension dissipating after completion. Kahneman (e.g. Kahneman, Beatty and Pollack, 1967) has reported similar gradients of pupillary dilation. In the one attempt to extend such research to children, Elliot (1965) was not able to find comparable gradients in six year olds. There is some reason to believe that such gradients are associated with a physiological device to protect the task (Malmo, 1965) and there is, further, some reason to believe that such gradients may be dependent upon an inhibition of motor activity.

There have been several clinical surveys which have reported that the peak incidence of tics in children occurs at seven years of age (Mackay et al., 1955–1956). In animal studies it has been shown that the incidence of tics is greatly augmented by restraint of motor behavior.

3) A large cross-sectional survey of children's behavior problems by Macfarlane, Honzik, and Allen (1954) has noted that parents reported a marked dimunition of stealing and lying in children after age six. One might attribute this to the development of a superego at about this time, or, perhaps what amounts to the same thing, one might associate it with findings which relate children's attentiveness and motor stability in an experimental situation with their obedience and control as rated by the teacher in the classroom (Grim, Kohlberg, and White, 1968).

It was suggested earlier, that stereotypies disappear as an interfering factor in children's problem solving because the ability to inhibit them is improved in the course of development. Our second major factor underlying the diversity of behavior changes in the 5–7 age range is, it is suggested, an inhibition factor—an inhibition of impulse.

Accessibility of Certain Memories to a Verbal Level

Birch and his associates have provided us with several studies in support of the contention that an important improvement in cross-modal integration of sensory information is manifest in the child in the early school years (Birch and Lefford, 1962). These are interesting findings, consistent with information that it is the late-myelinating cortical association areas which mature at about this time. Among the ramifications of such heightened intersensory transfer may be some odd findings of changes in thought and memory at this time, each of which may be construed as an interpenetration of one kind of information upon another.

1) First, one might note here the conclusions of Kendler and Kendler (1962) that this age sees an integration of words with actions, similar to the conclusion of Vygotsky (1960) that egocentric speech becomes an internalized instrument of consciousness and reflection at this time.

2) Simmel (1966), studying the incidence of phantom limb phenomena at this time, has concluded that children at four never report sensing a phantom limb, children at eight always do.

3) Clinical findings among blind children suggest that children blinded before six never are able to report visual memories, while children blinded after six are able to do so (Singer, 1966).

Such findings suggest that information from other sense modalities only gradually become accessible to language report, but some further analysis is required. Children well before six can assign a name to a sight, a touch, or a felt muscle movement, and this is cross-modal integration. Indeed, cross-modal integration and the interpenetration of thought and language must be present from the very beginning of speech or what would there be for a child to speak about? What may be special about the 5–7 age range is that for the first time sustained sequences of experiences in other modalities can be transposed into language with the resulting language-melodies having a new kind of accessibility and permanence.[1]

[1]Such an ability to transpose may have some relevance to the capability of the child for reading . . . not reading as letter-by-letter decoding but the broader process by which a string of words is construed as an organization of ideas to form comprehension. In an ingenious experiment, Farnham-Diggory (1967) taught children pictographs and logographs for 8 words and then asked them to "read" simple sentences composed of the logographs. There were 80 children of differing ages, 30 of them brain-damaged. They were asked to synthesize the meanings of diagram-sequences representing "Clap hands," "Jump over block," "Walk around teacher," etc. The children had to act out the synthesis of the two- or three-logograph sentences. (Enactions of one logograph

MYELIN = WHITE, FATTY SUBSTANCE
    FORMING A SHEATH
    ABOUT CERTAIN NERVE FIBERS

Before this age range, perhaps, sequences in other modalities are not readily transposed into language and, when they are, they are not readily remembered. Perhaps it is this kind of missing mechanism which is at the basis of what Freud called infantile amnesia.

There are, in addition, findings in this age range which suggest that children may not continuously monitor their own speech. It has been noted that children before six are not disrupted in speech by delayed auditory feedback (White, 1965).

At first blush, all these findings on the integration of experience would seem contrary to the convincing arguments of a number of developmental theorists to the effect that the natural development of mentation is an undifferentiated amalgam and only later is separated into components.

However, it is likely that the contrast between integration and differentiation so posed is only an accidental contrast in labelling. Probably, the cross-modal integration of information is differentiative in effect. It may be the juxtaposition of information from diverse modalities which forms contrast and context for the data of each separate sense and, thus, leads to the experience of differentiation. The intuition of localized and well-specified contrast, in turn, may form a substrate for the subsequent intuition of a dimension running between opposites.

The notion of an "opposite" is subtle, basic to dimensionalization of experience, and probably requires a substantial differentiation of the notion of "difference." Two things that are "different" can only be "opposite" if: (a) they are alike in a well-specified way; (b) they are different in a way related to the given specification. The child probably does not first work out the specification. He probably first understands that things are to be considered as opposites . . . there are many signs that children lump together opposites in their thinking, as indeed there are signs that adults find opposites close together in theirs . . . and the intuition of dimension may simply be a gradual understanding of what they are opposite about.

④ **The Dimensionalization of Experience**

Between the ages of five and seven, one finds the crystallization of an organization of experience in terms of various conventional and logical dimensionalizations. There are many signs of this. The child is shown to be able to discriminate compass direction; he can reproduce order; he develops adult perceptual constancies; he understands his sex role; he is sensitive to his racial identification, and so forth. There are complicated issues surrounding the child's acquisition of the dimensionalization of his experience, and it does not seem wise to try to speak about these issues in passing except to note the importance of this development. Piaget's treatment of this trend culminating in the psycho-logic of operations is extensive and, one dares to say, completely definitive (cf., particularly, Piaget, 1957).

⑤ **Decline in Affective Dependence**

We pick up, as our next trend, a non-cognitive factor. Our discussion of the discrimination procedure, it will be recalled, laid particular emphasis on elements of warmth and rapport in the association with the preschool child. In the Piagetian theory, as in the treatments of children's thought by Zaporozhets and his associates, one meets steadily the proposition that the origins of thought are to be found in symbolized action. There are also studies suggesting that motivation and reward systems manifest a move from a direct to a symbolized level.

Zigler and Kanzer (1962) have noted a shift in

---

after another were scored negative.) The children had to make the action implied by the conjunction of the logographs. The data indicated that, ". . . it is not until the age range of 6–8 to 7–3 that normal children begin to demonstrate reliable proficiency in the ability to synthesize sentences from word symbols. . . . In the brain-damaged sample, proficiency comparable to that of the normals was not evident even by the age of 13."

this age range from a sensitivity to praise to a desire for competence. Their report seems typical of a number of others, all of which suggest that the rewards of the preschool child must be fairly immediate and sensual while the grade-school child comes to adopt an internal standard of performance. Thus, Crandall and Rabson (1969) have reported that boys at 6–8 years come to prefer to repeat tasks on which they have failed rather than those on which they have succeeded.

There have also been reports that one finds "genuine" competitiveness and the origins of the need for achievement in the first school years. Two-factor theories of dependency have become more popular recently (cf., Walters and Parke, 1965) and perhaps it might not be too fanciful to think of the changes in the child's attitude toward achievement as related to these. In the earlier years, desiring sensual rewards, the child's dependency upon others may be primarily assuaged by warmth and reassurance. In the later years, in our society, the form of his dependence may change to be reflected in a need for the esteem of others.

In his classic analysis of human entrepreneurial activity, McClelland (1961) traces the origin of n Achievement (need achievement) to early parental emphasis on self-reliance and mastery. The age placement of such parental emphasis seems important:

> . . . what is desirable in somewhat idealized terms, is a stress on meeting certain achievement standards somewhere between the ages of six and eight (at least according to the mothers' reports), neither too early for the boy's abilities nor too late for him to internalize those standards as his own. (McClelland, 1951, p. 345).

Need achievement may reflect a competitive, mastery-oriented construal of the child's dependency upon others. He comes to depend upon their esteem or respect. This construal seems characteristic of middle-class America but, as McClelland shows, it is by no means characteristic of all societies at all times. What may be broadly characteristic of all cultures is the symbolization of human interdependency for the child at this time. A social contract between the child and others is, in effect, written. It may rest on a metaphor of competition; it may rest, as Bronfenbrenner has suggested for the Russians, on a metaphor of self-abnegation and cooperation. In either case, a higher-order dependency need (a new intuition of equilibriar social "comfort") is thereby established.

6 Increase in Speed of Reaction and Speed of Recognition

The last of our six trends of change at this time is an increase in speed of reaction and speed of recognition. The quickening of reaction time with age has been found again and again; the evidence exists in the traditional textbooks in abundance and need not be detailed here. Not only simple motor reaction time, but time or reaction in all sorts of complex procedures quickens with age. (The trend is countermanded only under special circumstances. There is a counterposed slowing of reaction associated with the older child's tendency to be more reflective rather than impulsive in his reaction.)

Paralleling the quickening of time to movement there have been several studies showing a quickening of time to recognition. All these kinds of quickening in the child may very well be associated with an increase in the more rapid electroencephalographic waveforms with age (Milner, 1967). This seems particularly likely because Surwillo, in an elegant series of studies (Surwillo, 1961, 1963a, 1963b), has shown a high degree of association between EEG frequency and rate of reaction.

There is nothing marked about the age trends in speed of the child's reaction during the period we are discussing here, the 5–7 age range, but nevertheless it has occurred to me that an increase in speed of the child's inner and outer reaction to experience may have a great deal to do with the changes we have been discussing. There is an argument by McLaughlin (1962) that each of the successive Piagetian stages might be accounted for on the assumption that there are increments in the number of "bits" the child can simultaneously take into account. The general argument, which seems reasonable, is that the child can think about more complex issues, or more facets of a simple issue, as he grows older. Most of the trends we have been discussing have some imaginable relevance to such an argument.

It might here be suggested, as a hypothesis, that the amount of complexity one can handle is related to one's speed of inner reaction—one's speed in locating recognition, meaning, and association to an event. We have become accustomed recently to speaking of a "short-term memory" function, thinking of it as a holding of rehearsing function in the brain. All kinds of values are given for the duration of short-term memory; let us choose one of them arbitrarily—10 seconds—for this argument. The argument would simply be that the child with a long recognition time might be able to place one association to an event in his short-term memory simultaneously. What if the rectification and reconciliation of experience—the intersection of thought and language, the cross-modal integrations, the comparison of plan and activity, and so forth—all depend upon the ability of items of information to meet in the critical ten-second span? With the gradual increase in the child's speed of reaction with age, there might come about discontinuous changes in reasoning ability, as various threshold values are reached allowing more "bits" of information into the ten-second sector—now conceived of as a span of processing.[2]

Similarly, the decline of cognitive function in senescence—accompanied by a well-established slowing of reaction time and slowing of EEG frequencies—might come about because of an inverse process. Gradually, as reaction time becomes slower, fewer and fewer units might be taken into the processing time-sector, leading effectively to a deoperationalization of thought.

In the foregoing remarks, I have tried to present a summary of the diverse literature of behavior change in the 5–7 age range, not including mention of all of the literature and its ramifications, but concentrating on certain central tendencies, or factors, which seem suggested by the body of literature.

A few comments and we will be done:

It should be remarked, again, that these summarizations are based on an analysis of reported changes in this 5–7 age range. The hope is that one may capitalize upon the conspicuousness of cognitive change at this time, the many qualitative changes, to better construct the mechanisms of the adult logic. But the rudiments of juvenile and adult logic probably exist in infancy and both systems coexist in progressively elaborating form throughout the life span. Both systems learn, according to different laws. It is probably not true that abstract thought begins in the 5–7 age range nor that juvenile logic ceases. One sees only, in some situations, a shift in the usual dominance in the individual. This dominance may shift in either direction, in response to certain stimuli (in flashes of maturity in the young), or under stress (in regressions to immature behavior in the older individual).

---

[2]The suggestion is that words, associations, or ideas must come close together in time in order for cognitive blending or structuring to occur. This idea has cropped up recently from several diverse areas of inquiry in the psychological literature. One source that gives the reader some intuitive feeling for the notion comes from the consideration of sentence comprehension (and may well be a factor in the Farnham-Diggory findings discussed in an earlier footnote). "The computation of sentence structure evidently must take place within a certain limited period. If a sentence is uttered too slowly—say one word every five seconds—its structure collapses. The collapse of sentences has not to my knowledge been studied. But there is no doubt that it happens: sentences, to be understood, must be experienced within a certain span of time. Beyond this span, there is a string of words; within it, a sentence. Forgetting may in part be responsible for this effect, but it does not seem to be the entire story" (McNeill, 1968, pp. 182–183).

In this overview, it has not been possible to mention various features of the evidence which have led me to wonder recently if the shifts in this age range occur at the same time—or, possibly, in the same way—for males and females. The suspicion seems worth communicating. The vast majority of the data are undifferentiated according to sex and, where there is separate reporting for the sexes, there are very often not sex differences. However, sex differences do turn up from time to time and their nature has been such as to make me believe that the transition under discussion may here have been more accurately delineated for males than for females. This is an area in which the studies of developmental dyslexia may have a significant contribution to make.

References

Annett, M. The classification of instances of four common class concepts by children and adults. *British Journal of Educational Psychology*, 1959, 29, 223–236.

Axelrod, S. Cognitive tasks in several modalities. In R. H. Williams, C. Tibbitts, and W. Donahue (Eds.). *Processes of aging.* New York: Atherton, 1963.

Benton, A. L. *Right-left discrimination and finger localization.* New York: Hoeber, 1959.

Birch, D. Verbal control of nonverbal behavior. *Journal of Experimental Child Psychology*, 1966, 4, 266–275.

Birch, H. G., and Lefford, A. Intersensory development in children. *Monographs of the Society for Research in Child Development*, 1963, Serial No. 89.

Blank, M., and Bridger, W. H. Conceptual and crossmodal transfer in deaf and hearing children. *Child Development*, 1966, 37, 29–38.

Bloom, B. S. *Stability and change in human characteristics.* New York: Wiley, 1964.

Braun, H. W., and Geiselhart, R. Age differences in the acquisition and extinction of the conditioned eyelid response. *Journal of Experimental Psychology*, 1959, 57, 386–388.

Brian, C. R., and Goodenough, F. L. The relative potency of color and form perception at various ages. *Journal of Experimental Psychology*, 1929, 12, 197–213.

Chzhi-Jsin, Van, Zinchenko, V. P., and Ruzskaya, G. G. (Comparative analysis of touch and vision. Communication VIII. Some techniques of sensory training.) *Dokl. Acad. Nauk SSSR,* 1961, 5(4), 73–76.—from abstract prepared by H. Pick.

Cohn, R. On certain aspects of sensory organization of the human brain: A study of rostral dominance in children. *Neurology,* 1951, 1, 119–122.

Comalli, P. E. Cognitive functioning in a group of 80–90 year old men. *Journal of Gerontology*, 1965, 20, 14–17.

Comalli, P. E., Wapner, S., and Werner, H. Perception of verticality in middle and old age. *Journal of Psychology,* 1959, 47, 259–266.

Comalli, P. E., Wapner, S., and Werner, H. Interference of Stroop Color-Word Test in childhood, adulthood, and aging. *Journal of Genetic Psychology,* 1962, 100, 47–53.

Crandall, V. J., and Rabson, A. Children's repetition choices in an intellectual achievement situation following success and failure. *Journal of Genetic Psychology,* 1960, 97, 161–168.

Critchley, M. *Developmental dyslexia.* London: Heinemann, 1964.

Elliot, R. Physiological activity and performance: A comparison of kindergarten children with young adults. *Psychological Monographs,* 1964, Whole Number, 78.

Farnham-Diggory, S. Symbol and synthesis in experimental "reading," *Child Development,* 1967, 38, 221–231.

Fink, M., and Bender, M. B. Perception of simultaneous tactile stimuli in normal children. *Neurology,* 1953, 3, 27–33.

Gollin, E. S. Tactual form discrimination: A developmental comparison under conditions of spatial interference. *Journal of Psychology,* 1961, 51, 131–170.

Grim, P. F., Kohlberg, L., and White, S. H. Some relationships between conscience and attentional processes. *Journal of Personality and Social Psychology,* 1961, 51, 131–140.

Kahneman, D., Beatty, J., and Pollack, I. Perceptual deficit during a mental task. *Science,* 1967, 157, 218–219.

Kazmiin, G. I., and Fedorov, V. K. (1951) 14th Conference on Problems of Higher Nervous Activity. Moscow and Leningrad. Cited in Lynn, R. *Attention, arousal and the orientation reaction.* New York: Pergamon, 1966, p. 31.

Koppitz, E. M. The Bender Gestalt Test for children: A normative study. *Journal of Clinical Psychology,* 1960, 16, 432–435.

Levinson, B., and Reese, H. W. Patterns of discrimination learning set in preschool children, fifth-graders, college freshmen, and the aged. *Monographs of the Society for Research in Child Development*, 1967, 32, Serial No. 115.

Lynn, R. Aging and expressive movements: An interpretation of aging in terms of Eysenck's construct of Psychoticism. *Journal of Genetic Psychology*, 1962, 100, 77–84.

Mackay, R. W., Wortis, S. B., Baily, P., and Sugar, D. *Yearbook of neurology, psychiatry, and neurosurgery*. Chicago: Yearbook Publishers, 1955–1956. (Citation of study by Zansener)

Macfarlane, J., Allen, L., and Honzik, M. *A developmental study of behavior problems of normal children between 21 months and 14 years*. Berkeley: University of California Publications in Child Development, 1954.

Malmo, R. B. Physiological gradients and behavior, *Psychological Bulletin*, 1965, 64, 225–234.

Manley, S., and Miller, F. D. Factors affecting children's alternation and choice behavior. *Psychonomic Science*, 1968, 13, 65–66.

McClelland, D. C. *The achieving society*. New York: Free Press, 1967 (original, 1951).

McLaughlin, G. H. Psycho-logic: A possible alternative to Piaget's formulation. *British Journal of Educational Psychology*, 1963, 33, 61–67.

McNeill, D. Production and perception: The view from language. *Ontario Journal of Educational Research*, 1968, 10, 181–185.

Miles, K. A. Sustained visual fixation of preschool children to a delayed stimulus. *Child Development*, 1933, 4, 1–5.

Miller, F. D., Tu, J. D-W, Moffat, G. H., and Manley, S. Children's response alternation as a function of stimulus duration, age, and trials. *Psychonomic Science*, 1969, 15, 199–200.

Milner, E. *Human neural and behavioral development*. Springfield, Ill.: Charles C. Thomas, 1967.

Money, J. Reading disability: *Progress and research needs in dyslexia*. Baltimore: Johns Hopkins, 1962.

Olson, D. From perceiving to performing the diagonal. *Ontario Journal of Educational Research*, 1968, 10, 171–179.

Pelz, K., Pike, F., and Ames, L. B. A proposed battery of childhood tests for discriminating between different levels of intactness of function in elderly subjects. *Journal of Genetic Psychology*, 1962, 100, 23–40.

Piaget, J. *Logic and psychology*. New York: Basic Books, 1957.

Pollack, M., and Fink, M. Disordered perception of simultaneous stimulation of face and hand: A review

and theory. *Recent Advances in Biological Psychiatry*, 1962, 4, 362–369.

Razran, G. H. S. Conditioned responses in children: A behavioral and quantitative critical review of experimental studies. *Archives of Psychology*, 1933, No. 148.

Rieber, M. Response alternation in children under different schedules of reinforcement. *Psychonomic Science*, 1966, 4, 149–150.

Simmel, M. L. Developmental aspects of the body scheme. *Child Development*, 1966, 37, 82–95.

Singer, J. L. *Daydreaming*. New York: Random House, 1966.

Super, C., and White, S. H. Studies of the simultaneity of behavior change in the 5–7 age range. Manuscript in preparation, 1970.

Surwillo, W. W. Frequency of the "alpha" rhythm, reaction time and age. *Nature*, 1961, 191, 823–824.

Surwillo, W. W. The relation of simple response time to brain-wave frequency and the effects of age. *Electroencephalography and Clinical Neurophysiology*, 1963, 15, 105–114. (a)

Surwillo, W. W. The relation of response-time variability to age and the influence of brain wave frequency. *Electroencephalography and Clinical Neurophysiology*, 1963, 15, 1029–1032. (b)

Tarakanov, V. V., and Zinchenko, V. P. (Comparative analysis of touch and vision. Communication VI. Voluntary and involuntary memory of form at preschool age.) *Dokl. Akad. Nauk SSSR.*, 1960, 4(5), 49–52.—from abstract prepared by H. Pick.

Thompson, L. J. *Reading disability: Developmental dyslexia*. Springfield, Ill.: Charles C. Thomas, 1966.

Turnure, J. Children's reactions to distractions: A developmental approach. Unpublished Ph.D. Dissertation, Yale University, 1965.

Vygotsky, L. F. *Thought and language*. Cambridge, Mass.: M.I.T., 1962.

Walk, R. D., and Saltz, E. J. Discrimination learning with varying numbers of positive and negative stimuli by children of different ages. *Psychonomic Science*, 1965, 2, 95–96.

Walters, R. H., and Parke, R. D. The role of the distance receptors in the development of social responsiveness. In L. P. Lipsitt & C. C. Spiker (Eds.). *Advances in child behavior and development*, Vol. 2. New York: Academic Press, 1965.

Wapner, S., Werner, H., and Comalli, P. E. Perception of part-whole relationships in middle and old age. *Journal of Gerontology*, 1960, 15, 412–416.

Warren, R. M. Illusory changes in repeated words: Differences between young adults and the aged. *American Journal of Psychology*, 1961, 74, 506–516.

Warren, R. M. Verbal transformation effect and auditory perceptual mechanisms. *Psychological Bulletin,* 1968, 70, 261–270.

Warren, R. M., and Warren, R. P. A comparison of speech perception in childhood, maturity, and old age by means of the verbal transformation effect. *Journal of Verbal Learning and Verbal Behavior,* 1966, 5, 142–146.

Weir, M. W. Developmental changes in problem-solving strategies. *Psychological Review,* 1964, 71, 473–490.

White, S. H. Evidence for a hierarchical arrangement of learning processes. In L. P. Lipsitt & C. C. Spiker (Eds.). *Advances in child behavior and development,* Vol. 2. New York: Academic Press, 1965.

White, S. H. Age differences in reaction to stimulus variation. In O. J. Harvey (Ed.). *Flexibility, adaptability, and creativity.* New York: Springer, 1966. (a)

White, S. H. The hierarchical organization of intellectual structures. Paper presented at symposium, "The role of experience in intellectual development," American Association for the Advancement of Science convention, Washington, December, 1966. (b)

White, S. H. Changes in learning processes in the late preschool years. Paper presented at symposium, "Early learning," American Educational Research Association convention, Chicago, 1968. (a)

White, S. H. The learning-maturation controversy: Hall to Hull. *Merrill-Palmer Quarterly,* 1968, 14, 187–196. (b)

White, S. H., and Evans, J. A developmental study of children's assembly of picture sequences. Manuscript in preparation, 1970.

Zigler, E., and Kanzer, P. The effectiveness of two classes of verbal reinforcers in the performance of middle- and lower-class children. *Journal of Personality,* 1962, 30, 157–163.

Zinchenko, V. P., and Ruzskaya, A. G. (Comparative analysis of touch and vision. Communication VII. The observable level of perception of form in children of preschool age.) *Dokl. Akad Nauk, SSSR.,* 1960, 4(6), 85–88.—from abstract prepared by H. Pick.

Hormonal Aberrations and Their Implications for the Understanding of Normal Sex Differentiation

Anke A. Ehrhardt

Susan W. Baker

INTRODUCTION

This paper will deal with the origins of sex differences. My colleagues and I will direct our presentations specifically to behavioral sex differences rather than to more global concepts such as gender identity.

Before I begin to comment about the possible role of sex hormones in behavioral sex differentiation, I would like to make a few introductory remarks to give you some background information on how our studies fit into this whole discussion, why we should be concerned about biological variables at all in view of the overwhelming evidence of social-environmental factors, and why only rather recently hormonal effects became of interest for behavioral scientists.

Traditionally, research on sexual differentiation in the behavior of children has tackled the problem of etiology from various angles of environmental influences, as for instance, the effects of differential parental treatment of boys and girls, the influence of imitation patterns of boys and girls of their same-sexed parent and same-sexed peers, or the role of cognitive discrimination level in modeling behavior. The list of the different types of studies concerned with etiologic factors

The study was supported by a grant from the United Health Foundation of Western New York (#CL-10-CH-71), the Human Growth Foundation and the Variety Club of Buffalo, Tent No. 7. Children's Hospital of Buffalo, 219 Bryant Street, Buffalo, New York 14222. The patients in this sample were diagnosed and managed by Drs. Thomas Aceto, Jr., and Margaret MacGillivray of the Pediatric Endocrine Clinic at Children's Hospital. Their clinical cooperation is greatly appreciated. The data graphs were designed by the Department of Medical Illustrations, SUNY, Buffalo.

SOURCE: From a paper presented by Dr. A. Ehrhardt at the Society for Research in Child Development, Philadelphia, March 31, 1973. Printed with permission of the authors.

in the process of psychosexual differentiation could easily be prolonged and, I am sure, some of the other presentations will address themselves to various postnatal social variables.

There have been relatively few studies on the possible role of biological variables, such as hormonal effects. The reason is easily understood considering on the one hand the complexity of interaction between biological and social-environmental factors in all behavioral sex differences, and on the other hand, the relatively recent advances in biochemical and neurohormonal methodology.

There are two developmental time periods during which dramatic hormonal changes occur; one is before birth and the next is in adolescence. Since we are here mainly concerned with childhood behavioral sex differences, my presentation will be limited to the particular area of fetal hormones and their possible effects on the differentiation of the nervous system and, thus, on postnatal behavior. Let me mention in passing that the time from shortly after birth to early adolescence appears to be one of dormancy during which the sex hormone output does not differ significantly between normal girls and boys (see review by Boon, Keenan, Slaunwhite, & Aceto, 1972).

Before birth, the testes in the male start producing male hormones as soon as they have differentiated which takes place in the first trimester of pregnancy. The time span of human external genitalia differentiation, which is largely dependent on androgens, is fairly well established, while the critical phase for sexual differentiation of the central nervous system (CNS) is still being discussed. Recent experiments by Doerner and colleagues on the brain of the human fetus show that human hypothalamic differentiation goes through similar changes as described in the rat. Doerner suggests that the critical time for human hypothalamus differentiation lasts from week 14–16 to week 25 before birth (Doerner & Staudt, 1972).

ANIMAL RESEARCH

Let me come back to my topic, namely, fetal hormones and behavioral sex differentiation. The main push in research in this area comes from animal experimental evidence. Some of the conclusions based on numerous studies over the last 20 years can be summarized in a simplified way as follows: Most of the neurohormonal studies have been carried out on rats, mice, and rabbits; it has been clearly demonstrated that at a critical time before birth or around birth the presence of androgens, male hormones, has a long-term effect on the CNS, mediating sex-related behavior, such as mating and aggressive behavior; absence of androgens during the critical time of differentiation has a long-term effect on female behavior, such as female mating patterns, degree of aggression, and certain aspects of maternal behavior. (I will here not go into the more complicated story of hormonal manipulation with female hormones, estrogen, since it is not pertinent for our clinical studies.)

Rats and rabbits are a long way from people; monkeys are clearly closer related, so I will talk a little bit more about the one long-term study on rhesus monkeys (Goy, 1970) specifically designed to test out the effects of excess androgen before birth on female behavior. Pregnant rhesus monkeys were treated with testosterone. Their female offspring were physically masculinized and were born with a penis and empty scrotum. Internally, they were normally female. Their childhood play has been under long-term observation and has been compared with normal male monkeys and normal female monkeys. One has to know that there are clear-cut behavioral sex differences in monkeys that are not too dissimilar from those found in human beings. The fetally androgenized female monkeys were more similar to normal male monkeys than to normal female monkeys in rough-and-tumble play, fear grimacing, and dominance behavior. They were not exactly like males, but took rather an intermediate position between male and female behavior, suggesting that some aspects of childhood masculine play behavior is affected by the presence of fetal androgens.

② CLINICAL GROUPS

With this background information in mind, you will easily understand the basis for our studies on clinical extreme groups, in particular those on females with a known history of fetal androgenization, analogous to the Oregon rhesus monkeys, and on males with a known history of an excess of fetal androgen exposure.

Fetal androgenization chiefly occurs in two syndromes of human females, namely, in progestin-induced hermaphroditism and in the adrenogenital syndrome. In both groups, the genetic female fetus is exposed to an excess of androgens. The result is masculinization of the external genitalia, but unaffected normal female internal organs. The masculinization of the external genitalia can vary from an enlarged clitoris to a normal-appearing penis and empty scrotum.

The progestin-induced condition occurred predominantly in the fifties as an untoward side effect of treatment with progestinic drugs in mothers who had a history of habitual miscarriages. Postnatally, the affected child needs only surgical correction of the genitalia and no hormonal treatment.

The adrenogenital syndrome is transmitted as a recessive autosomal genetic trait. The source of androgenization is the individual's own hyperactive adrenal gland that begins producing too much of the adrenal's masculinizing hormone in utero and continues doing so after birth if not corrected with cortisone. The condition requires lifetime hormonal control with cortisone and early surgical feminization of the external genitalia.

The adrenogenital syndrome also occurs in genetic males who will be exposed to an excess of androgen before and after birth. The postnatal error of the adrenal cortex can be regulated with cortisone. If cortisone treatment is handled optimally, both girls and boys with the adrenogenital syndrome will grow up like normal children with usually a normal female or male puberty in adolescence.

CLINICAL STUDIES: METHODOLOGY

The studies of prenatal hormonal influences on behavior in human females were started at Johns Hopkins with John Money several years ago. At that time 10 girls with progestin-induced masculinization and 15 girls with the early-treated adrenogenital syndrome, between the ages 4 and 16, were evaluated and compared with matched normal control girls (Ehrhardt, 1973; Ehrhardt, Epstein, & Money, 1968; Ehrhardt & Money, 1967; Money & Eharhardt, 1972). Today, I will not go into details of the results in these earlier studies, but rather talk about a series of new studies carried out at the Children's Hospital of Buffalo in collaboration with Susan W. Baker.

The methods and, in particular, the problems with getting good measurements of sex-related behavior are still the same as in our earlier study. We were interested in long-term childhood behavior which we could assess in interviews with the mothers and children themselves. The interviews were conducted with the help of a semistructured interview schedule, recorded, and then transcribed. The items included in the schedule were general developmental and play behavior items intermixed with typical sex-related behavior such as toy preference, aggression, rehearsal of adult roles, clothes preferences, etc. The parents and children were told that the interviews served as a general devlopmental checkup. The transcribed interviews were rated according to coding scales with a range from two- to five-point ratings. The agreement between the mothers' and childrens' interviews has been found to be generally very high so that the answers can be pooled. Two people tabulated the data from the files. The comparison of patient and control groups were statistically tested with the Fisher Exact Test for four-fold tables after the rating scales for each item were dichotomized (for methodological details, see Ehrhardt, 1971).

③ FAMILY STUDY: FETALLY ANDROGENIZED GIRLS VERSUS UNAFFECTED FEMALE SIBLINGS

The sample for our family study in Buffalo consists of 27 patients, i.e., 17 females and 10 males, which is clearly a representative sample of the clinical population seen in the Pediatric Endocrine Clinic, considering that only 31 patients with this condition have been seen altogether since the clinic's inception 10 years ago. The age range is 4.3–19.9 years for the girls and 4.8–26.3 for the males, with most of the children in middle childhood and early adolescence. The unaffected sibling sample consists of 11 females and 16 males with comparable age ranges. Eighteen mothers and 14 fathers were seen in our office. The families came from social classes II–V, according to the Hollingshead Index, with a greater number from lower than middle and higher classes. The behavior data are only part of the whole family study, which had an additional goal, namely, the evaluation of intelligence and specific ability patterns (Baker & Ehrhard, 1974).

All children were under corrective treatment with replacement of cortisone.

The onset of cortisone treatment for the females occurred in 14 cases within the first year of life and happened usually shortly after birth. The other three patients were started on cortisone in the second, third, and fourth year of life, respectively. Surgical correction of the external genitalia varied with the following breakdown: 6 patients within the first year of life, 7 patients between ages 1 and 3 years, and 4 patients later than early childhood.

The data on the females are based on a comparison of the 17 patients versus all 11 unaffected female siblings and are derived from interviews with all patients and all mothers. Out of the vast amount of data, the following comparisons seem to be of special interest here.

One of the most consistent sex differences found in normal boys and girls has to do with rough-and-tumble play and aggression (Figure 1). Fetally androgenized girls show more frequently a higher level of intense physical energy expenditure than unaffected female siblings. The behavior was long-term and specific in the sense of a high degree of rough outdoor play. There was no significant difference between the two groups in frequency of starting fights, either verbal or physical. Since aggressiveness has been one of the

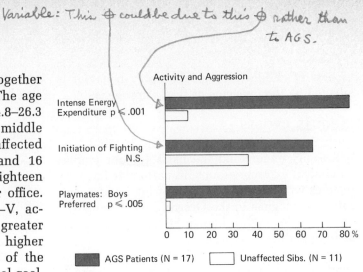

Figure 1

Handwritten margin note (top): Variable: This ↑ could be due to this ↑ rather than to AGS.

Figure labels: Activity and Aggression

Intense Energy Expenditure p ≤ .001

Initiation of Fighting N.S.

Playmates: Boys Preferred p ≤ .005

0 10 20 30 40 50 60 70 80 %

■ AGS Patients (N = 17)   □ Unaffected Sibs. (N = 11)

consistent sex differences in normal samples and since our items were relatively crude, we have obtained in the meantime, more detailed data (as yet unanalyzed) on fighting behavior on the basis of a special aggression scale. Thus, the result may be due to our assessment or it may mean that fetally androgenized girls conform with the less permissive standard for females concerning aggression. Fetally androgenized girls also more frequently prefer boys over girls if they have a choice in playmates, again on a long-term basis during all childhood.

The second cluster of pertinent results has to do with toy preference, interest in female vs. male adult roles and response to small infants (Figure 2). Studies on normal samples show that girls and boys differ in their toy preferences from an early age on. More girls prefer dolls, dollhouses, stoves, etc., and more boys prefer trucks, cars, guns. Fetally androgenized girls show a conspicuously low interest in dolls and tend to choose boys' toys. They show generally very little interest in future roles as bride and mother and tend to be more concerned with job careers, while unaffected females display both rehearsal of wedding and marriage plus career interests.

There is a lack of studies on the response of girls and boys toward small infants. One assumes that girls more frequently like to handle and take care of small babies, such as with younger sib-

Handwritten margin note (bottom): due to { innateness or conditioning?

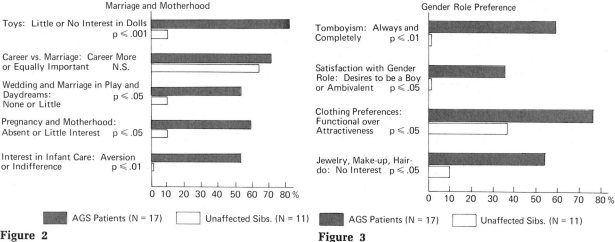

Figure 2

Figure 3

lings or during baby-sitting. Fetally androgenized girls significantly more often show aversion or indifference when presented with small infants, while all unaffected siblings were rated to have a moderate or strong interest in small babies.

The next cluster of items has to do with gender role preference and with more arbitrary sex differences, such as interest in appearance (Figure 3). If a girl tends to rough-and-tumble play, prefer boys and boys' toys, then she is traditionally identified as a tomboy. Fifty-nine percent among the patients were identified by themselves and others as a tomboy during all of their childhood, significantly different from the sample of unaffected siblings, in which nobody showed this complete and long-term pattern of tomboyism, although 27 percent were rated as having some tomboyish traits apparent at some time during their childhood.

Fetally androgenized girls had generally no conflict in their gender identity, although 35 percent thought that it may have been easier to be a boy if they had had a choice in the beginning. This ambivalence did not cause any particular problem, however.

The last two items relate to interest in clothes and appearance. Fetally androgenized girls preferred functional over attractive clothing and gen-

erally were not particular at all about the way they looked.

The results presented are almost in complete agreement with the earlier studies at Johns Hopkins in which patients were compared with normal matched girls from nonpatient families. Thus, even in sibling comparisons, when social class, intelligence of the parents, number of brothers, and other family characteristics are matched to a high degree for both patients and sibling controls, clear-cut behavior differences were found.

Let me now focus on what appears to be the central differences between girls with a history of fetal androgenization and normal girls. Exposure to high levels of androgen before birth may be related to a temperamental behavior set of a high energy expenditure level in rough-and-tumble play. This kind of behavior is more frequently seen in girls with a known history of exposure to an excess of androgens as well as in normal boys who also have high androgen exposure before birth. However, it obviously takes a social environment which allows or stimulates this kind of behavior, because, otherwise, all boys and all androgenized girls should show this kind of behavior. It seems that fetal androgens may make an individual prone to certain temperamental traits, but it probably will depend on other variables such as environmental factors, whether a certain observable behavior, such as rough-and-tumble play, occurs or does not. Preferring boys over girls as playmates is probably a secondary behavior related to the basic temperamental trait of high energy expenditure. If you like to play more rough games, you will find more boys to do it with.

2) The second central theme which may be related to fetal androgens is the response to the very young. As I said before, we know very little about sex differences in direct caretaking behavior, especially in childhood. Certainly men have also the capacity of responding to small infants and frequently do so, but it seems that women are prone to respond more readily and to a more intense degree to small infants than men and probably also girls more than boys in childhood. The same difference has been found in free observation studies in monkeys (Jay, 1963; Devore, 1963), and in experimental studies on rodents (see review by Lehrman, 1961). Girls who were exposed to androgens showed little interest in doll play, future children of their own, and caretaking of small infants. The difference is clearly in degree and not one of total absence vs. presence.

FAMILY STUDY: BOYS WITH THE ADRENOGENITAL SYNDROME VERSUS UNAFFECTED MALE SIBLINGS

We have a standard against which we can—at least to a certain degree—evaluate our assumptions of masculine behavior in the study on the females. Although no direct comparisons between the females and males have been made, the same appropriately modified interview schedules were used for the unaffected males vs. adrenogenital boys who were exposed to more than normal androgens before birth. The behavioral data are based on 9 patients and 11 unaffected brothers. One patient of the original sample of 10 was excluded because both he and his mother were functioning at a mentally retarded level.

Cortisone treatment was initiated in six pa-tients within the first month of life. The other three patients were started on cortisone in their fifth, seventh, and eighth year of life, respectively. These latter three patients had signs of a precocious male puberty at the onset of treatment. Five of the original 16 unaffected brothers who came in for IQ testing were not any more available for the behavior study. The two samples, of patients and unaffected male siblings, are comparable in age.

Let me start with the cluster on toy preferences and interest in future roles as husband and father. There are no significant differences between boys with an excess of androgens vs. boys with the presumably normal male amount of androgens. The frequency of no interest in dolls was 82 and 89 percent respectively, in groups of male siblings and male patients. Thus, in both groups of males, very few boys are interested in dolls and other girls' toys. In both groups, some boys have thoughts and fantasies of becoming a father, although much less than the percentage of unaffected females who are concerned with becoming a mother. Eighteen percent of male siblings manifested an interest in fatherhood and 56 percent of male patients. The difference was not significant. The same is true for boys who like to handle their little brothers or sisters and other small infants, although to a lesser degree than the unaffected females who scored 100 percent in the moderate and strong category. More adrenogenital males rehearsed wedding and marriage in play and daydreams than male siblings (56 vs. 18 percent respectively), but the difference was not significant. Both groups expressed less interest than the female sibling control group.

2) The next cluster deals with satisfaction with the male sex role (clearly prefers being a boy), which is 100 percent in both groups. There is a total absence of effeminacy in both groups and most of them are rated or rate themselves as extremely masculine. All boys prefer boys' clothes and approximately half in each sample have no interest in their appearance while the other half

have a moderate or strong interest in clothes and looking attractive. Interest in appearance per se is, thus, not specifically feminine and the finding that fetally androgenized girls are so extremely low on this item is somewhat surprising. There was no difference between adrenogenital boys or male siblings on mothers' rating of masculinity. Over two-thirds of both groups were rated as extremely masculine.

The last cluster of items shows the only significant difference between the adrenogenital boys and unaffected brothers. Boys with a history of an excess of androgen show more frequently an intense energy expenditure level in sports and rough outdoor activities (78 percent vs. 18 percent male siblings, $p \leq .05$), while there are more unaffected boys who show a moderate or periodic interest in sports and rough activities. The result is in agreement with the finding in the fetally androgenized girls, who show more frequently intense outdoor activity measured at the standard for normal girls. Furthermore, there are 56 percent in the affected boys and 36 percent in the normal brothers who are described as initiators in fighting, verbally or physically. The percentages are not too different from the female samples, which may be due to the crude measurements as mentioned before. And last, almost all boys prefer males over girls to play with if they have a choice (89 percent of patients vs. 100 percent of male siblings).

The results on the male samples suggest that an additional amount of androgen before and in some cases also after birth above the normal male level does not appear to affect the behavior much, except perhaps for an even higher degree of rough outdoor and sport activities. Apparently, a certain amount of androgen is enough as a basis for masculine behavior. Excess androgen above a certain critical level may have no additional effect on behavior.

The study on the males also shows that we are right in some of our assumptions on what comprises masculine behavior. Boys usually did not play with dolls, and they had a lesser interest in play rehearsal of future roles as husbands and fathers than girls in becoming one day a bride and a mother. They also showed less frequently a positive response to small infants. They uniformly liked boys' clothes and preferred to be a boy, although a strong interest in appearance is not specific for the female sex. Boys preferred almost always males as playmates. Compared to normal females, they showed more rough outdoor energy expenditure, but did not seem to be more frequently initiators of fights, at least on the basis of their own and their mothers' statements.

CONCLUSION: NORMAL SEX DIFFERENCES

The behavior of extreme groups is not only studied for reason of clinical management and treatment. It also may magnify or point to hypotheses for questions of normal behavior. It seems to us that one can draw several hypotheses from our findings on girls and boys with a known history of exposure to high levels of fetal androgens:

1. We know that normal girls and boys differ in the amount of androgens they are exposed to before birth. Behavioral sex differences have been found in normal samples, in rough-and-tumble play, which we find difficult to attribute *solely* to differential parental treatment of the sexes. The finding that girls and boys with an excess of androgen before birth show a tendency to more intense energy expenditure of that kind compared to normal girls and normal boys, respectively, strengthens the hypothesis that fetal and/or postnatal hormones may be one factor in triggering that kind of a temperament difference between boys and girls.

2. Caretaking behavior as seen in play with dolls has been found as a consistent behavioral sex difference. Undoubtedly, imitation of other females is an important factor for girls to show a higher degree of it. We know

TRADITIONAL IDEAS ON MALE-FEMALE BEHAVIOR VERIFIED FOR THE MOST PART

very little directly about sex differences in childhood in response to small infants. Animal studies suggest that although the potential for parental behavior is present in both sexes, females tend to respond to small offspring sooner and with a more complete behavior pattern. Hormonal manipulation during the critical time of differentiation of the CNS has resulted in some animals in "masculinizing" or "feminizing" the type of response to small offspring.

Fetally androgenized girls are clearly different from normal girls in their lack of interest in doll and house play, in interest in marriage, and in their response to small infants. Although, undoubtedly, social factors influence this kind of behavior to a large degree, our studies suggest that fetal hormones may play a part in the intensity of response in maternal behavior or some aspects of it.

Alternatively, one has to consider that the environment may have contributed to the behavior differences between patients and unaffected siblings. Families go through a traumatic time around birth when they have a baby girl with a genital abnormality. We interviewed the parents in great detail about possible lurking fears. Although one cannot exclude the parents' attitude as a possible contributing factor, it seems unlikely that a temperamental set of behavior can be modified as uniformly as found in our and previous studies (Ehrhardt & Baker, 1974). The attitudes within the parent sample varied greatly: Some did not appear to have any concerns whatsoever and were proud of their daughter's energetic, tomboyish behavior; others expressed some worries, usually, however, not related to rough-and-tumble play, but rather to future sexual attractions. In this context, it is important to mention that the behavior pattern found in fetally androgenized girls was clear-cut and significantly different from other girls, but still within the range of acceptable normal behavior. The pa-

tients are too young to make a definitive statement concerning homosexuality. Since most of the teenage girls were already romantically interested in boys, however, it seems unlikely that we will find a significantly higher frequency of lesbianism in girls with a history of fetal hormonal androgenization.

Let me close with one other point. Our studies on clinical groups may not only have certain implications for behavior sex differences *between* the sexes, but also suggest that hormones may play a part in behavior differences *within* the sexes. Alice Rossi (1973) speculated first on the basis of some of our data that possibly slight variations of fetal androgens may be related to variations of physical toughness, lack of maternalism and career orientation, within the samples of normal women. This hypothesis is hard to examine and, thus, hard to prove or disprove at the present time. It raises interesting speculations, however, which may be investigated when finer biochemical measurements become possible.

References

Baker, S. W., and Ehrhardt, A. A. 1974. Prenatal androgen, intelligence and cognitive sex differences. In: R. C. Friedmann (ed.). *Sex Differences in Behavior.* New York: Wiley & Sons, in press.

Boon, D. A., Keenan, R. E., Slaunwhite, W. R., Jr., and Aceto, T., Jr. 1972. Conjugated and unconjugated plasma androgens in normal children. *Pediatric Research,* 6:111–118.

DeVore, I. 1963. Mother-infant relations in free-ranging baboons. In: H. L. Rheingold (ed.). *Maternal Behavior in Mammals.* New York: Wiley & Sons.

Doerner, G., and Staudt, J. 1972. Vergleichende morphologische Untersuchungen der Hypothalamus-differenzierung bei Ratte und Mensch. *Endokrinologie,* 59:152–155.

Ehrhardt, A. A. 1971. Der Einfluss von foetalen Hormonen auf Intelligenz und geschlechtsspezifisches Verhalten. In E. Duhm (ed.). *Praxis der Klinischen Psychologie,* Band II. Göttingen: Verlag fuer Psychologie. Dr. C. J. Hogrefe.

Ehrhardt, A. A. 1973. Maternalism in fetal hormonal and related syndromes. In: J. Zubin and J. Money (eds.). *Contemporary Sexual Behavior: Critical Issues in the 1970's.* Baltimore: The Johns Hopkins Press.

Ehrhardt, A. A., and Baker, S. W. 1974. Fetal androgen, human CNS differentiation and behavior sex differences. In: R. C. Friedmann (ed.). *Sex Differences in Behavior.* New York: Wiley & Sons, in press.

Ehrhardt, A. A., Epstein, R., and Money, J. 1968. Fetal androgens and female gender identity in the early-treated adrenogenital syndrome. *Johns Hopkins Medical Journal,* 122:160–167.

Ehrhardt, A. A., and Money, J. 1967. Progestin-induced hermaphroditism: IQ and psychosexual identity in a study of ten girls. *Journal of Sex Research,* 3:83–100.

Goy, R. W. 1970. Experimental control of psychosexuality. *Philosophical transactions of the Royal Society of London,* 259:149–162.

Jay, P. 1963. Mother-infant relations in langurs. In: H. L. Rheingold (ed.). *Maternal Behavior in Mammals.* New York: Wiley & Sons.

Lehrman, D. S. 1961. Hormonal regulation of parental behavior in birds and infrahuman mammals. In: W. C. Young (ed.). *Sex and Internal Secretions.* Baltimore: Williams & Wilkins.

Money, J., and Ehrhardt, A. A. 1972. *Man and Woman, Boy and Girl.* Baltimore: The Johns Hopkins Press.

Rossi, A. 1973. Maternalism, sexuality, and the new feminism. In: J. Zubin and J. Money (eds.). *Contemporary Sexual Behavior: Critical Issues in the 1970's.* Baltimore: The Johns Hopkins Press.

Chapter 5

Memory

As recently as 20 years ago, it was believed that there was only one basic memory process and that all information which was attended to was "registered." If children differed in their ability to recall the past, it was due to interference in recall, not to differences in basic "memory." We now know that view is incorrect. There are at least three, and perhaps more, memory processes, beginning with primary sensory memory (which lasts less than a second) through short-term memory (which has a life of 20 to 30 seconds) to long-term memory (which is potentially permanent). We also know that memory is influenced by many factors, three of which are (1) the strategies the child uses to organize the information when he first attends to it, (2) his tendency to rehearse the information that he organizes, and (3) his strategies of retrieval. There are remarkable differences in recall memory between young children and adults. Adults can recall a string of eight or nine numbers, while 3- and 4-year-olds can recall only two or three. We do not know if this is a function of organization, rehearsal, retrieval or all three.

In the first paper in this chapter, E. Neimark and her colleagues N. S. Slotnick and T. Ulrich show that one of the reasons why young children are inferior in recall to older children and adults is that they do not organize the information presented to them. In their study, children in grades 1, 3, 4, 5, and 6 and college students were given 24 pictures belonging to four different categories and told to memorize them. The investigators watched the subjects to see if they organized the pictures during the time they were studying them. The older children were more likely to rearrange the pictures spontaneously into the four categories. As might be expected, this tendency to organize the pictures into concepts was paralleled by an increase in the number of objects the subjects could recall spontaneously.

2)   In the second article, S. Rossi and M. C. Wittrock show that there are also age differences in the process of remembering past experiences. Young children—2 years old— tend to recall words that rhyme; 3-year-olds tend to recall words that are syntactically related (dogs-bark, men-work); and 4-year-olds tend to recall words by their conceptual category (fruits, parts of the body). It is possible that one reason for the age differences in recall is the older child's more efficient strategy of organizing information, both as he processes it and when he retrieves it.

3)   The child's ability to recall past information is typically poorer than his ability to recognize past experience. Children who can recall only 3 or 4 of 12 pictures they have seen can usually recognize all 12. In the study by A. L. Brown and M. S. Scott, recognition memory for large numbers of pictures was tested in children 3 to 5 years of age. Their ability to recognize pictures they had seen a few minutes earlier was remarkably high—over 98 percent correct. When there were delays of 1, 2, 7, or 28 days between the inspection of the pictures and when they were tested, there was only a slight drop in recognition memory performance, from 98 percent at 1 day to 78 percent at 28 days.

Development of
Memorization Strategies

Edith Neimark

Nan S. Slotnick

Thomas Ulrich

On developmental tasks, the instructions and materials may be identical for all subjects but what the subject does with them changes qualitatively with age. In support of this assumption, children in Grades 1, 3, 4, 5, 6, and college were given 24 pictures to memorize for free recall during a 3-minute study interval. Ratings of the subject's organizing of material during the study interval were a nonlinear function of age. Recall measures (number of correct recalls, clustering, and duration of recall) were also systematically related to age. Data were interpreted as evidence that memorization is not an isolated skill but, rather, one of many manifestations of an individual's characteristic age-related approach to problems.

NOTE: This research was conducted under support from Grant No. HD01725-05. The authors are grateful to Harold Wickholm and his staff at Grandview Elementary School, Piscataway, New Jersey, for their continuing cooperation in providing space and subjects. Deborah F. Weisman assisted in analysis of the data. Requests for reprints should be sent to E. D. Neimark, Douglass College, New Brunswick, New Jersey 08903.

SOURCE: From *Developmental Psychology*, vol. 5, no. 3 (1971), 427–432. Copyright © 1972 by the American Psychological Association. Reprinted by permission.

We are in the throes of a revolution in theoretical approaches to the study of memory. The recent literature is full of articles reflecting an increasing awareness that memorizing is not a rote process of reading into storage more or less iconic traces of the material to be learned but, rather, that it is an active process of transforming and restructuring, in many respects akin to problem solving. If this assumption is correct, then one would expect to find the transforming and restructuring techniques employed by a subject to be largely a function of the repertoire of techniques available to him, that is, his stage of cognitive development. A number of recent developmental studies of learning show this to be the case (e.g., Inhelder, 1969; Moely, Olson, Halwes, & Flavell, 1969; Wapner & Rand, 1968). Previous research has generally compared groups of elementary school children. The present experiment includes an adult group in order to provide a more complete picture of developmental changes in memorization for free recall in a task employed by Moely et al. (1969).

METHOD

Materials

The materials to be learned consisted of 24 pictures from the Peabody Picture Vocabulary Test which could be categorized into four classes of six pictures each: bear, camel, cow, dog, goat, horse; bicycle, boat, bus, car, train, truck; chair, crib, lamp, sink, stove, table; jacket, mitten, purse, shoe, sock, tie. Three decks of the 24 cards were prepared by Xeroxing each picture, cutting it to a 3-square-inch size and laminating it in plastic film. All decks were arranged in the same standardized random order. In addition, there was a practice deck of five Peabody pictures similarly prepared: pear, bat, broom, apple, crayons.

Subjects

There were six groups of 20 volunteers each. It was not possible to get an even division of boys and girls in each group so sex could not be included as an experimental variable. Since Moely et al. (1969) found no significant sex differences, and since the present authors' data do not suggest any, this is probably not a serious loss.

The elementary school subjects were white middle class students at a public elementary school selected from among a pool of volunteers for IQs in the normal range of 95–115. The children in Grades 1, 3, and 6 did only the memory task; those in Grades 4 and 5 were part of a longitudinal study of problem-solving skills who did the memory task in conjunction with a problem-solving task.[1] The college group was selected from among introductory psychology students at Rutgers University and Douglass College who served as part of a course requirement. Mean CA in months was

[1]These children attend the same school and fall within the same IQ range. They differ from the first, third, and sixth graders only in having participated in research on development of problem-solving skills since fall of 1968.

79.95, 105.90, 118.65, 128.00, 143.18, and 237.05 for Grades 1, 3, 4, 5, 6, and college, respectively. Number of girls in the group was 13, 7, 10, 11, 11, 12 for Grades 1 through college, respectively. Each child was tested individually during the spring of 1970.

Procedure

The five pictures of the practice series were spread in a row and the child was asked to name each of them. He was then told: "Now we are going to play a memory game. You study these pictures and try to remember them. After one minute, I'll cover them up and you tell me what they were." After recall of the five practice pictures (even the first graders recalled all five correctly), the subject was told: "Now we'll play the memory game again with a lot of pictures." The experimenter then went quickly through the deck having the subject identify each picture and correcting where necessary. Thereupon the experimenter continued:

> Now I'm going to put all of the pictures on the table. When I have finished you will have three minutes to study them. You may move them around in a different order, pick them up, make notes, or do anything you like to help you learn them. After three minutes, I'll take them, and any notes you have made, away and you will try to name as many of them as you can. You don't have to learn them in any special order.

The pictures were placed on the table in five rows of five cards each (four in the last row). During the 3-minute inspection period the experimenter made notes on the subject's behavior and comments. At the end of 3 minutes the cards were collected and the experimenter recorded (a) the subject's recall in order and (b) the total recall time from onset of the recall period to the subject's saying he was through. The procedure was repeated with the second deck along with a reminder of the instructions and the encouragement to learn all 24. A third trial was given when the subject had not attained perfect recall on the second trial. At the completion of each trial, the subject was asked to describe how he had gone about learning the pictures and his answer was recorded.

RESULTS

Means and standard deviations of number of items correctly recalled on each trial are summarized in Table 1 (once the subject attained 24 he was given a score of 24 for subsequent trials).

Table 1. Means and standard deviations of response measures on successive trials

MEASURE	GRADE											
	1		3		4		5		6		COLLEGE	
	M	SD	M	SD	M	SD	M	SD	M	SD	M	SD
No. recalled												
Trial 1	8.7	2.27	12.2	3.35	15.0	3.75	16.3	3.99	16.6	3.45	22.2	2.88
Trial 2	11.1	2.36	16.8	3.88	18.8	3.28	20.0	3.38	20.4	3.45	23.6	.99
Trial 3	12.7	3.76	18.5	3.59	20.3	2.90	22.3	2.49	21.8	2.71	23.9	.22
Clustering												
Trial 1	.45	.27	.43	.23	.52	.33	.61	.27	.68	.25	.91	.18
Trial 2	.40	.27	.46	.17	.50	.22	.62	.24	.70	.29	.95	.13
Trial 3	.34	.19	.46	.18	.56	.22	.65	.26	.76	.22		
Organization rating												
Trial 1	.0	.0	.10	.45	.80	.83	.90	1.02	1.10	.97	2.05	.82
Trial 2	.05	.22	.35	.59	.65	.88	.95	1.00	1.15	.93	2.45	.51
Trial 3	.15	.49	.30	.57	.60	.94	.85	1.09	1.05	1.00		
Recall time (in sec.)												
Trial 1	101	29	138	41	136	40	110	35	114	33	94	40
Trial 2	153	47	185	53	214	53	166	45	144	47	66	43

Analysis of variance comparison of these data yields highly significant ($p < .01$) F ratios for between groups, F 46.3, $df = 5/114$; between trials, $F = 187.7$, $df = 2/228$; and for the Trial × Group interaction, $F = 4.65$, $df = 10/228$. A Newman-Kuels test of between-group differences shows that each group is significantly different from the adjacent group except for Grade 5 versus Grade 6. The data values are very similar to those reported by Moely et al. (1969) despite the fact that they varied list length with age. Apparently, within limits, amount learned is relatively unaffected by number of items on the list for supracapacity list lengths.

That recall performance improves with age is hardly surprising; the pattern of performance, however, suggests that more than quantitative differences are involved. The number of subjects for whom recall on Trial n + 1 equalled or exceeded recall on Trial n was 12, 16, 17, and 19 for Grades 1, 3, 4, and 5, respectively.[2] No first grader attained criterion at the end of three trials (maxi-

[2] For sixth graders and college students all 20 were as good or better on Trial n + 1 as compared to Trial n.

mum recall was 19) whereas 2, 3, 10, 9, and 19 subjects in Grades 3 to college did so. Although 11 college students attained criterion on Trial 1, none of the school children did so. The correlation between CA and number correctly recalled on Trials 1–3, respectively, is .75, .68, and .62.

The Bousfield clustering measure employed by Moely et al. (1969) was computed for recall data of each subject on each trial and is summarized in Table 1 (only 2 college subjects had a third trial). Once again, the obtained values are very similar to those reported by Moely et al. Since the minimum possible score is zero (and the maximum possible 1.0), even the youngest subjects evidence some clustering although the amount increases with age. Analysis of variance comparison of first trial data shows that age-group differences are significant beyond the .01 level of confidence: $F = 9.74$, $df = 5/114$ (the F for trials and Trials × Age was not statistically significant in comparison for school children who had three trials). A Newman-Kuels comparison indicates significantly more clustering in the recall of Grades 5 and over than in Grades 1 and 3; furthermore, college students show significantly more clustering than grade-school children. The correlation of CA and clustering on Trials 1–2, respectively, is .51 and .62.

In order to provide a quantitative measure of subject's deliberate organizing during the 3-minute study period, his rearrangement of cards during this interval (supplemented by his report of study strategy where it was articulated) was rated on a 4-point rating scale analogous to the strategy rating scale employed on problem-solving tasks for subjects in the longitudinal study mentioned earlier. Criteria for the ratings are as follows: 0 for no systematic rearrangement, 1 for organization of *part* of the material (e.g., putting together all animals or all animals and all clothing but not differentiating among the other pictures, or forming four nonexhaustive classes), 2 for an organization—almost always four classes of six pictures each—which encompassed all 24 pictures, and 3 for an elaborated exhaustive organization which imposed order within classes as well as between classes (e.g., alphabetizing or forming of pairs). Ratings were assigned at the time of testing. These data are summarized in Tables 1 and 2.

A repeated-measures analysis of variance of ratings over trials did not yield a significant main effect or interaction effect for trials; differences among age groups are significant beyond the .01 level, $F = 27.10$, $df = 5/114$. A Newman-Kuels analysis of group means indicates that (a) children in Grades 1 and 3 do less deliberate organizing than older children; (b) children in Grades 5 and 6 are significantly better than children in Grade 4 or lower; and (c) college students show significantly more deliberate organizing than elementary school children. The correlation of CA and organization rating on Trials 1–2, respectively, is .66 and .73.

Although there is a high positive correlation, $r = .71$, between clustering score and organization rating on Trial 1, clustering per se is insufficient evidence of deliberate organizing. Children in Grades 1 and 3 do show some clustering on their first recall trial but, as can be seen from

Table 2. Frequency distribution of organization ratings

GRADE	RATING LEVEL			
	0	1	2	3
1				
Trial 1	20			
Trial 2	19	1		
Trial 3	18	1	1	
3				
Trial 1	19		1	
Trial 2	15	4	1	
Trial 3	15	4	1	
4				
Trial 1	9	6	5	
Trial 2	12	3	5	
Trial 3	14		6	
5				
Trial 1	11		9	
Trial 2	10	1	9	
Trial 3	12		7	1
6				
Trial 1	8	2	10	
Trial 2	7	3	10	
Trial 3	9	1	10	
COLLEGE				
Trial 1	2		13	5
Trial 2			11	9
Trial 3			11	9

Table 2, only one third grader appeared to be deliberately organizing material. At the other extreme, after the first trial all college subjects imposed at least an ordering into classes with nine subjects employing a within-category ordering as well. Among the intermediate age groups only one fifth-grade girl attained an elaborated (third level) ordering although by Grade 6 50% of the group employ a between-category (second level) organization. Clustering during recall antedates deliberate organization for learning. Organization appears to be a better determinant of recall; it correlates .74 with number recalled whereas clustering correlates .58 with number recalled.

Although time spent in recall only measures time from start to completion or giving up, it sheds some additional light on recall behavior. Data for the first two trials are summarized in Table 1. Analysis of variance comparison of Trial 1 recall times shows a significant difference among age groups, $F = 4.56$, $df = 5/114$; a Newman-Kuels comparison shows this difference to result from the significantly faster recall of college students as compared with Grades 3 and 4. If recall were simply a process of emptying the contents of an immediate memory store, then duration should be a function of number of items recalled and increase with age as a result. This is not the case. There is a negative correlation between duration of recall and both amount recalled ($r = .33$) and age ($r = -.56$). Many children, especially among the third and fourth graders, sit there obviously searching for additional items before giving up. Their spontaneous comments suggest that they are aware not only of the number of missing items but also of their nature: "There are more animals." These long periods of sitting and struggling appear to be attributable to insufficient organization schemes for coding into memory and to relatively little practice in the use of whatever coding schemes are in their repertoire. College students, on the other hand, are highly skilled at committing long lists of nonsense to memory; their efficient schemes enable prompt and accurate recall whose speed increases over trials. As might be expected from the assumption that efficiently organized mnemonic encoding promotes rapid recall, recall duration is negatively correlated with both organization rating $r = -.45$, and index of clustering, $r = -.43$.

DISCUSSION

The procedure employed in this experiment was very similar to that of Moely et al. (1969) with three exceptions: (a) they presented 16 pictures to the first graders, 20 to the third graders, and 24 to the fifth graders whereas the present authors presented 24 pictures to all groups; (b) Moely et al. allowed 2 minutes for each study session whereas 3 were allowed in the present study and (c) the experimenter was present during study periods. Despite these procedural differences not only did the authors replicate their findings that number of items correctly recalled and amount of clustering in recall are an increasing function of age, but, also, the absolute values obtained for all measures are very similar to the values reported by them. Furthermore, although the authors did not take careful tallies of their six categories, qualitative aspects of the subject's behavior during study trials appeared to be very similar: deliberate rehearsal (either by reciting aloud or by pointing to pictures) is present even among first graders; and most children do some rearrangement of the pictures, although systematic sorting into category classes is very infrequent before Grade 4. Another interesting strategy employed by 2, 1, 1, 4 and 5 children in Grades 1–6, respectively, is to segregate out the items omitted on the previous recall trial for more concentrated rehearsal. The inclusion of an adult group and of an additional measure of deliberate organization of material provides evidence that development of mnemonic strategies continues beyond the grade-school level. College students have a well-structured system for organizing material which is applied immediately and efficiently. Thus, there are at least two marked shifts in the subject's approach to a simple memorizing task: one occurring roughly around Grade 3 and the second between Grade 6 and college.

A general algorithm for list memorization requires two structural features: (a) an exhaustive organization for efficient encoding of each list item and (b) a mechanism for keeping track on readout, that is, knowing what has been recalled and what is yet to come. The young child seems unaware of either requirement. After scanning each of the items in turn he thinks he "has them"; a number of the younger children announced that they were ready before the end of the first 3-minute study interval.[3] On recall they appeared surprised at the paucity of their output and scanned the test room for associative cues to trigger the remaining items. It is almost as though they confused recognition with recall. Older children, who are better practiced in noting properties and forming classes, appear to be more aware of the structure inherent in the list as evidenced by their clustering in recall, but they do not yet use the structure as a deliberate encoding scheme. Rather, the categories are called into play during recall in an attempt to supply missing items through logical guessing: "TV set?" "Kangaroo?" etc. Nor do they recall what they have already said, as indicated by frequent requests for verification: "Did I say 'jacket'?" They, too, look about the room for objects to serve as reminders. College students, on the other hand, not only deliberately organize into categories at the outset, but also encode within them at a more abstract level, that is, items are no longer treated as pictures of objects but are spontaneously transformed into words, and organizing schemes capitalize upon their properties qua words. Partial or exhaustive alphabetizing is common at this age but nonexistent among sixth graders. Of course, only six items per category is within the immediate memory span; had a longer list been used it is possible that intracategory organization would have been even more frequent among college students.

The development of memorization for free recall seems to parallel the pattern of cognitive development from preoperational thought to concrete operations and from concrete operations to formal operations (Piaget & Inhelder, 1969) with respect to component activities and ages of transition. This close correspondence suggests to us that development of memory skills is at least part of the more comprehensive process of cognitive development; or possibly that development of procedures for systematic deliberate storage and retrieval of information may be one of the basic processes underlying cognitive development. A direct assessment over a wide age range of the relation between spontaneous imposition of organization upon information (Neimark, 1970; Neimark & Slotnick, 1970) and mnemonic organization is now in progress.

References

Flavell, J. H., Friedrichs, A. G., & Hoyt, J. D. Developmental changes in memorization processes. *Cognitive Psychology,* 1970, 1, 324–340.

Inhelder, B. Memory and intelligence in the child. In D. Elkind & J. B. Flavell (Eds.), *Studies in cognitive development.* New York: Oxford University Press, 1969.

Moely, B. M., Olson, F. S., Halwes, T. G., & Flavell, J. B. Production deficiency in young children's clustered recall. *Developmental Psychology,* 1969, 1, 26–34.

Neimark, E. D. Model for a thinking machine: An information-processing framework for the study of cognitive development. *Merrill-Palmer Quarterly,* 1970, 16, 345–368.

Neimark, E. D., & Slotnick, N. S. Spontaneous imposition of organization: A developmental study. Paper presented at the meeting of the Eastern Psychological Association, Atlantic City, April 1970.

Piaget, J., & Inhelder, B. *The psychology of the child.* New York: Basic Books, 1969.

Wapner, S., & Rand, G. Ontogenetic differences in the nature of organization underlying serial learning. *Human Development,* 1968, 11, 249–259.

---

[3]Direct objective evidence on the subject's ability to evaluate his own readiness for recall is provided by Flavell, Friedrichs, and Hoyt (1970). They found accuracy of assessment to improve with age over Grades N, K, 2, and 4. The first graders in the present study were similar in this respect to Flavell et al.'s kindergarten children.

#12 Developmental Shifts in Verbal Recall Between Mental Ages Two and Five

Sheila Rossi

M. C. Wittrock

MA = MENTAL AGE

A developmental progression in children's bases for organizing words in free recall was investigated. The hypothesized developmental progression began with rhyming responses peaking at MA 2, followed by syntactical, clustering, and serial ordering responses reaching their peaks at MA 3, MA 4, and MA 5, respectively. 2 stimulus lists of 12 words were presented individually to 144 children. It was found as hypothesized that in free recall: (1) rhyming reached its peak proportion at MA 2; (2) syntactical responses reached their highest proportion at MA 3; (3) clustering reached its peak proportion at MA 4; (4) serial order-ing reached its peak at MA 5; (5) clustering showed a positive linear trend with intelligence; (6) intrusions showed a negative linear trend with intelligence; and (7) the most frequent responses at a given age were rhyming at MA 2, clustering at MA 3 and 4, and serial ordering at MA 5.

NOTE: This research was supported by a grant from the Ford Foundation. For reprints write to M. C. Wittrock, Department of Educational Psychology, University of Illinois, Urbana, Illinois 61801.

SOURCE: From *Child Development*, vol. 42, no. 1 (March 1971), 333–338. Copyright © 1971 by the Society for Research in Child Development, Inc. Reprinted by permission of the authors and the publisher.

Children between mental ages 2 and 5 show different organizations in their free recall of word lists. Organization by rhyming reaches its peak proportion of responses at MA 2 and declines thereafter (Entwisle 1966; Rossi 1966). Syntactical bases (e.g., men-work) of organization in free recall reach their highest proportion of responses at MA 3 and decline thereafter (Entwisle 1966; Rossi 1966). Clustering reaches its highest proportion at MA 4 (Rossi & Rossi 1965; Rossi & Wittrock 1967). Serial ordering of responses increases from MA 2 through MA 5 (Rossi & Rossi 1965).

The purpose of the research reported below was to examine in one study the developmental progression in bases of organizing free recall found in the studies mentioned above, all dealing with children of MA 2 through MA 5. From these earlier studies it was hypothesized that from MA 2 through MA 5 the above progression in bases of organizing free recall would occur.

The above sequence probably represents a development from concrete to abstract intellectual [A] functioning. Rhyming represents a concrete [B] response to the sound of words. Syntactical responses represent chaining based on the order in which words frequently follow each other in language usage. [C] Clustering represents a hierarchical grouping of words into a learned category or concept. [D] Serial ordering, although a less abstract response than clustering, may represent an increased intellectual ability to memorize short lists without using more sophisticated bases for grouping words, such as clustering.

METHOD

Subjects

The 144 subjects were divided into four levels of mental age (2, 3, 4, and 5), three levels of intelligence (low, average, and high), and sex. The children all attended public or private nursery schools in Los Angeles. They were each tested individually by the same examiner. They had no serious hearing or other physical anomalies to prevent them from following directions.

The respective means and standard deviations of the mental age groups were as follows: for MA 2, 27.0 and 2.5; for MA 3, 35.0 and 2.2; for MA 4, 48.5 and 3.6; and for MA 5, 61.7 and 5.0.

The means and standard deviations of the IQs of the low, average, and high intelligence groups were as follows. 84.4 and 3.9, 99.5 and 4.7, and 112.6 and 2.5, respectively.

Stimulus Material

The Peabody Picture Vocabulary test (Dunn 1965) was used to determine the verbal IQ levels of low (75–89), average (90–109), and bright (110–124) children; and their verbal developmental levels (MA 2, 3, 4, and 5). Two stimulus lists composed of different orders of the same 12 words were constructed. The words were selected to be familiar to the subjects and were all words of high frequency in the Thorndike-Lorge (1944) count of words in juvenile books. Each list consisted of two pairs of words which could be scored only as rhyming, syntactical, or clustering responses. These pairs of words are: (rhyming) sun-fun, hat-fat; (syntactical) dogs-bark, men-work; (clustering) peach-apple, leg-hand.

To avoid suggesting a way of organizing the words to the subject, the two words comprising a pair were never presented consecutively. There were no homonyms in the lists. The stimuli were presented aurally. The two stimulus lists are: (list 1) sun, hand, men, fun, leg, work, hat, apple, dogs, fat, peach, bark; and (list 2) dogs, peach, fat, bark, apple, hat, men, leg, fun, work, hand, sun.

Procedure

Each subject was tested individually in a quiet room of his school by the same examiner. The Peabody Picture Vocabulary test was administrated first to all subjects.

Then the recall lists were presented. The following instructions were given to each subject: "Now we are going to play another game. First, I am going to say some words, and you say them after me. Then, when we finish saying all the words, you tell me all you can remember. Then we'll do it one more time. All right?"

The examiner then read the list at a rate of one word every 3 or 4 seconds, recorded each response within a 2-minute recall period, and then repeated the procedure. From child to child, the order of presentation of the two lists was alternated.

The Peabody Picture Vocabulary test (Dunn 1965) was scored according to the manual. The responses to the stimulus lists were scored in pairs in the order they were recalled, as rhyming (sun-fun, hat-fat, or the reverse order), syntactical (men-work or dogs-bark), clustering (apple-peach, hand-leg, or in the reverse order), serial ordering (recalling two words serially from the stimulus list, i.e., sun-hand), or intrusions (words which were not on the stimulus lists).

RESULTS AND DISCUSSION

To control for number of words recalled, which increased with increases in MA and intelligence, the following ratio measures were used to obtain scores for each child. These were modeled after Bousfield's (1953) ratio of repetition for clustering, for example, $Pr/n - 1$, or pairs of words recalled contiguously which form a rhyming unit (*Pr*), over the number of words recalled minus one. Each subject's score was totaled over the two lists. Similar ratios for syntactical, clustering, and serial order responses were computed. Intrusions were scored individually rather than as a ratio because of their low frequency of occurrence. Because the above ratios were used for each measure, results will be discussed in terms of proportion of total responses for each level of MA.

By analyses of variance, multiple comparisons tests, and planned comparisons for linear and other trends, it was found, as predicted, that in proportion to other responses rhyming was higher at MA 2 than at any other MA ($df = 1/132$, $F = 19.59$, $p < .01$). Syntactical responses were higher at MA 3 than at any other MA ($df = 1/132$, $F = 26.36$, $p < .001$). Clustering was higher in proportion to other responses at MA 4 than at any other MA ($df = 1/132$, $F = 13.55$, $p < .01$). And serial ordering was higher in proportion to other responses at MA 5 than at any other MA ($df = 1/140$, $F = 47.10$, $p < .001$). Intrusions, however, showed no significant relation to MA (see Figure 1).

Clustering showed a positive linear trend with

intelligence ($df = 1/132$, $F = 7.68$, $p < .01$), while intrusions showed a negative linear trend with intelligence ($df = 1/132$, $F = 37.17$, $p < .01$). Rhyming showed an inverted V-function with intelligence ($df = 1/132$, $F = 8.32$, $p < .01$).

The developmental progression in bases for organizing free recall found in the earlier studies cited above was found again in this study. At MA 2, rhyming reached its peak proportion and was also the most frequent type of response to occur. At MA 3, syntactical responses reached their peak proportion, although clustering was the most frequent response. At MA 4, clustering responses reached their peak proportion and were also the most frequent type of response. At MA 5, serial ordering reached its peak and was also the most frequent type of response to occur (see Figure 2).

The progression of rhyming, syntax, clustering, and serial ordering, reaching their peak proportions in that order, probably represents different psychological processes acting simultaneously. In many ways, the progression is consistent with Piaget's theory of development and can be described as a development from concrete to abstract functioning and from perceptual to conceptual responding. In rhyming, the child responds to perceptual, intrastimulus properties, rather than to interstimulus properties. In syntactical recall, which at its peak proportion at MA 3 is still not so frequent a response as clustering at

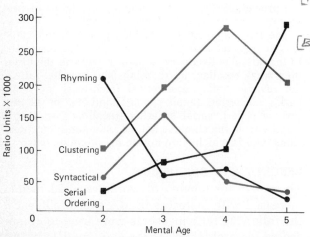

Figure 1 Proportion of rhyming, syntactical, clustering, and serial ordering responses to total responses by mental age.

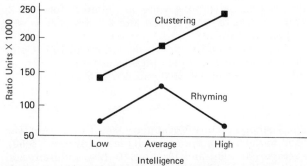

Figure 2 Proportion of rhyming and clustering responses to total responses, by level of intelligence.

MA 3, he is showing the first evidence of inter-stimulus organization. In this case the organization seems to be based upon previous learning of probabilities that one word frequently follows another word.

[c] Clustering represents the first example of inter-stimulus organization evidencing a hierarchical or conceptual grouping of words according to their common properties or common membership in one class. Abstraction and generalization are introduced with this type of organization.

[D] Serial ordering seems to be a more elementary type of interstimulus organization than clustering. Why it should occur more frequently than other responses at MA 5 in this study and in the earlier studies mentioned above is not known. It may mean only that at age 5 ability to memorize 12 words is sufficiently developed that grouping them into clusters requires more effort than memorizing them in serial order. We may not be sampling clustering which would occur with longer lists requiring an efficient organization to recall all their members.

A longitudinal study would help to establish the viability of the developmental progression indicated in this study and in the earlier studies mentioned above. It would also be useful to devise longer lists of words to find if there is a ceiling effect operating in these studies.

References

Bousfield, W. A. The occurrence of clustering in the recall of randomly arranged associates. *Journal of General Psychology,* 1953, 49, 229–240.

Dunn, L. M. *Expanded manual of the Peabody Picture Vocabulary test.* Minneapolis: American Guidance Service, 1965.

Entwisle, D. R. *World associations of young children.* Baltimore: Johns Hopkins University Press, 1966.

Rossi, E. L., & Rossi, S. I. Concept utilization, serial order, and recall in nursery school children. *Child Development,* 1965, 36, 771–779.

Rossi, S. I. Development of mediation in children between ages three and five as shown by free association rsponses. Unpublished paper, University of California, Los Angeles, 1966.

Rossi, S. I., & Wittrock, M. C. Clustering versus serial ordering in recall by four-year-old children. *Child Development,* 1967, 38, 1139–1142.

Thorndike, E. L., & Lorge, I. *The teacher's work book of 30,000 words.* New York: Bureau of Publications, Teachers College, Columbia University, 1944.

#13 # Recognition Memory For Pictures in Preschool Children

Ann L. Brown

Marcia S. Scott

EG { GOOD: SEEN + SEEN + RECOGNIZED
BETTER: SEEN + RECOGNIZED + RECOGNIZED

S = SUBJECT ?
E = EXPERIMENTER ?

THINGS CAN BE RECOGNIZED BETTER
WHIF THEY HAVE BEEN SEEN BEFORE;
THINGS CAN BE RECOGNIZED BETTER
WHIF THEY HAVE BEEN RECOGNIZED BEFORE.

Two continuous recognition experiments are reported in which the ability of children (CA 3–5) to recognize old pictures approximated that of adults. Thirty-three Ss were tested for immediate retention in Experiment 1. The probability of recognizing items recurring within the series was .98, with no decline in accuracy even with 50 items intervening between presentations. For 32 of these Ss long-term retention was also examined. Accuracy declined as a function of increasing retention interval (1, 2, 7, or 28 days). The probability of recognizing a twice-seen item declined from .98 at 1 day to .78 after 28 days but was only .84 and .56, respectively for items seen only once. The probability of incorrectly identifying a new stimulus as old was consistently low. Nine new Ss were tested in Experiment 2 where it was shown that the superiority of twice-seen items was related to both seeing the item twice and making an overt recognition response to that item on its recurrence.

Laboratory investigations of recognition memory for pictures have consistently reported impressive levels of performance for adult Ss (Nickerson, 1965; Shepard, 1967). Attempts to define a limit to recognition capacity have been restricted by the feasible length of experimental sessions rather than any inferred limitation of the S's ability (Standing, Conezio, & Haber, 1970). Studies with adult Ss also indicate excellent retention over long periods of time (Nickerson, 1968; Shep-

NOTE: This research was supported in part by U.S. Public Health Service Grant HD 02898 and U.S. Public Health Service Grant MH 07346 to the Children's Research Center, University of Illinois. The authors would like to express their appreciation to the staff and children of the Busy Bee Day Care Center, the Happi Time Day Care Center, and La Petite Academie, all of Champaign, Illinois.

SOURCE: From *Journal of Experimental Child Psychology*, vol. 11, no. 2 (1971), 401–412. Reprinted by permission.

ard, 1967). The efficiency of this recognition process suggests that familiar pictures must have ready access to long-term memory where they are permanently stored in content addressable locations (Shiffrin & Atkinson, 1969). A sophisticated voluntary control process is also implied by the efficiency with which recognition is confined to those pictures recurring within the experimental setting. Familiar pictures occurring for the first time within a session are seldom incorrectly identified as recurring items (Nickerson, 1965).

The developmental origins of both storage and retrieval processes in visual recognition memory have received comparatively little attention. Studies of recognition memory in children have been limited to tests of immediate retention with no more than 32 items intervening between presentations (Carterette & Jones, 1967; Corsini, Jacobus, & Leonard, 1969). Carterette & Jones did show improved performance in visual recognition of words between first and third grade children. However, the use of words as stimulus items confounded recognition efficiency with reading ability, an ability which would be expected to improve within the age range selected for study. No evidence of a developmental effect can be drawn from the Corsini et al. study which reported near perfect recognition accuracy for pictures in preschool children. The Corsini study was limited to tests of immediate retention, with a maximum of 20 intervening stimulus items. Neither of these studies examined long-term retention over considerable periods of time.

The degree to which both recognition capacity and the efficiency of its controlling processes are acquired by experience has yet to be determined. The studies of recognition memory in preschool children reported here attempted to extend both the number of stimulus items and the length of retention interval intervening between successive presentations of a test picture. Evidence of limited capacity was sought in Experiment 1 which attempted to define a limit to performance as a function of increased within and between ses-

sions retention intervals. The focus of Experiment 2 was a preliminary attempt to define one controlling process involved in recognition memory.

EXPERIMENT 1

METHOD

Subjects

Thirty-three preschool children, 16 boys and 17 girls, served as Ss in the immediate retention test. They ranged in age from 44 to 62 months with a mean of 52.7. One S refused to cooperate in the long-term retention test. Thus the data from thirty-two Ss, 16 boys and 16 girls, were included in the analyses of long-term retention.

Stimulus Materials

Colored pictures were cut out from children's books and pasted in the center of 14 × 6 in. black posterboard cards. The cards were then covered with transparent contact paper. The pictures were classified into four categories: people, animals, outdoor scenes and objects, household scenes and objects. Within each category an attempt was made to choose perceptually distinct pictures and no item occurred more than once (e.g., only one lion occurred in the animal category). An equal number of pictures from each category was used. There were 100 cards in the immediate retention experimental pack, consisting of 44 duplicates and 12 single pictures. For the long-term retention test, a stack of 72 pictures was used, consisting of 36 old and 36 new pictures. The old pictures were selected from the immediate retention experimental pack. The new pictures were taken from the same books and fell into the same stimulus categories as the old pictures. Each stimulus category occurred equally often as old and new items. A further pack of 10 cards was used in pretraining.

PROCEDURE

Immediate Retention Test

A continuous recognition task was used. The experimental series of 100 cards consisted of 44 test items which appeared twice and 12 filler items which appeared once. For purposes of clarification, an item will be referred to as new on its first occurrence and old on its second occurrence. The number of items intervening between the first and second presentation of an item will be referred to as the lag. The pictures were ordered so that 10 items recurred after each of 4 lags: 0, 5, 10, and 25, and 4 items recurred after the maximum lag of 50 items. Within each lag each stimulus category occurred approximately an equal number of times (e.g., either two or three times for lags 0, 5, 10, and 25), with each category occurring equally often across the entire series. Within each successive block of 25 cards, the proportion of old and new cards was kept approximately stable at 44% old to 56% new. Runs of more than three old or new items were avoided where possible. Within each successive block of 20 cards an equal number of lag 0 and 5 items occurred. Tests of the remaining lags were distributed as evenly as possible throughout the series, with the necessary restriction that a greater proportion of the long lag tests occurred in the latter part of the series. A set of 10 additional cards, with lags of 0, 2, and 5, was used in pretraining.

Each S was tested individually while seated at a small table next to the E. Both the pretraining and the experimental stacks of cards were placed face down in front of the S. Initial testing had revealed that if children of this age were required to respond like adults, with "old" to old pictures and "new" to new pictures, they were unable to understand the instructions. Therefore, each child was told to look at the pictures one at a time, and say "Yes" when he saw a picture that he had seen before and "No" when he saw a picture that he had not seen before. The E turned the cards one at a time and waited for the S's reaction. Approximately 5 sec were required to view and respond to each picture. During pretraining the E repeatedly stressed that the S must only say "Yes" to pictures that occurred before in the stack and this was further emphasized by returning to the first occurrence of an item each time a repeat occurred and showing the S that an identical picture had indeed occurred before. Following pretraining, the experimental series of 100 cards was presented but the E no longer indicated that the S's response was correct by returning to the first occurrence of a picture. Knowledge of results was not given, but periodically the E indicated that the S was "Doing fine." On completion of the series, the S chose a small reward item from a collection of 10¢ toys.

Long-Term Retention Test

The 32 Ss were randomly assigned to one of four interexperimental retention intervals of 1, 2, 7, or 28 days. There were eight Ss, four boys and four girls at each retention interval. The Ss were presented with the long-term retention stack of 72 pictures. The 32 old pictures consisted of the 12 filler items (seen once) and 24 tested items (seen twice) from the immediate retention test. All of the seen twice items had been correctly recognized as old on their recurrence in the immediate test. With this restriction, the seen twice items were selected so that five items came from each of the original 0, 5, 10, and 25 lags. The remaining four pictures had been lag 50 items. The stack was ordered so that runs of old and new items were determined by a Gellermann (1933) series. The pictures were presented one at a time in a continuous recognition task identical to that of the immediate test. The Ss were told, "This is a different stack of pictures. Some of the pictures you saw last time you played the game and some of them you have not seen before in the game." Again the Ss were required to say "Yes" to stimuli they had seen before (old stimuli) and "No" to pictures not previously seen (new stimuli). Each S received a 10¢ toy at the end of the testing session.

RESULTS

Immediate Retention Test

The general level of performance was high, with a mean of 98% correct responses. Performance as a function of lag remained at a consistently high level of accuracy, with 100, 95, 98, 95, and 100% correct responses, respectively, for the five lags of 0, 5, 10, 25, and 50.

Errors could be of two types; either an omission error, where the S failed to recognize the recurrence of a picture, or a false alarm error, where the S incorrectly identified a new stimulus as old. The total error mean of 1.43 consisted of a mean of 1.28 and .15, respectively, for omission and false alarm errors. Thus the probability of giving a response "old" (yes) to an old stimulus, $p(Ro \mid So)$ was .98 while the probability of giving a response "old" to a new stimulus, $p(Ro \mid Sn)$ was less than .01. Eighty-five percent of the Ss made no false alarm errors. The $p(Ro \mid Sn)$ did not increase as the sequence progressed.

Long-Term Retention Test

Three response measures were considered which corresponded to the probability of giving a response "old" (yes) to each of the three types of stimuli: stimuli seen twice, $p(Ro \mid So_2)$, stimuli seen once, $p(Ro \mid So_1)$ and new stimuli, $p(Ro \mid Sn)$. These probabilities are shown in Figure 1 where it can be seen that the $p(Ro \mid So_2)$ is very high for intervals up to 7 days (above .94) and even after 28 days is still .78. How-

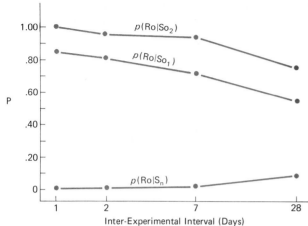

Figure 1 The probability of a response "old" to each of the stimulus types as a function of interexperimental interval. The values expressed on the abscissa are the log. days.

ever, the $p(Ro \mid So_1)$ is .84 after only 1 day and drops to .56 at 28 days.

A 2 × 4 mixed analysis of variance was conducted on the arcsine transformation of the proportion of old items correctly identified as old. The between subjects variable was the Interexperimental Retention Interval of 1, 2, 7, or 28 days. The within subjects variable was the Type of Item (seen once or twice). Longer retention intervals yielded lower proportions of correct recognition responses ($F(3,28) = 24.95$, $p < .001$). A consistently greater proportion of twice-seen items were correctly identified as old items ($F(1,28) = 60.92$, $p < .001$). This difference between the $p(Ro \mid So_2)$ and the $p(Ro \mid So_1)$ remained relatively constant over time resulting in a nonsignificant interaction of Retention Interval × Type of Item. The probabilities shown in Figure 1 were obtained by reconverting the mean arcsine proportion correct into probabilities.

In Figure 1 the probability of incorrectly labeling a new stimulus as old, $p(Ro \mid Sn)$, is also plotted. This false alarm score increased with time, and though negligible at intervals up to 7 days (below .02), it rose to .08 at 28 days. However, even after 28 days the $p(Ro \mid Sn)$ was still far less than either the $p(Ro \mid So_2)$ or the $p(Ro \mid So_1)$.

DISCUSSION

The immediate retention performance supports and extends the Corsini et al. (1969) finding of excellent recognition memory for pictures in pre-

school children. The present study extended the lag to 25 and 50 items with no decline in accuracy. Long-term retention paralleled that reported for adults (Nickerson, 1968). Recognition of twice-seen items was consistently superior to recognition of items seen only once in the immediate test. Alternative explanations of the superiority of twice-seen items are considered in Experiment 2.

The ability of preschool Ss to recognize large numbers of pictures recurring after considerable periods of time and many familiar items had intervened, suggests that phenomenal recognition capacity is not restricted to adults. However, the recognition scores reported here were based on an original stimulus pool of only 100 items, considerably less than the stimulus pools of 600 items used in the adult studies of Nickerson (1965) and Shepard (1967). The comparatively small stimulus pool was determined by the amount of time necessary to view the items. An experimental session of about 10 min duration was regarded as optimal for such young children. The ease of responding in all stages of the study indicated that the children were not being taxed beyond their capacity. It is probable that the stimulus pool could be increased for young children by introducing more than one experimental session, each of short duration. Such a method was used by Standing et al. (1970) to increase the stimulus pool for adults to more than 2500 pictures.

The false alarm score remained consistently low in both the immediate and long-term retention tests, and could only be considered a possible source of contamination at the 28-day retention interval. It is not possible to determine whether this consistently low false alarm score is typical of young children, or occurs only with the type and number of stimuli used in this experiment. However, not only does the false alarm score suggest that the hit rate recorded is a reasonably pure recognition measure, but it also reflects the ability of these preschool children to recognize as old only those stimuli that were re-

NUMBER OF CARDS USED BY KIDS WAS LESS THAN THE NUMBER USED BY ADULTS, BUT THE NUMBER USED BY ADULTS COULD BE INCREASED.

curring within the experimental sessions. This ability to limit recognition to test items is somewhat surprising in view of the particular stimuli selected for use in this study. Highly familiar pictures were taken from readily accessible children's books. Some *S*s spontaneously reported that they had "Seen that picture before at home," or "In my Snow White book." The combination of near perfect recognition accuracy and the almost total absence of false recognition of new items, not only implies an extensive capacity for storing visual information, but also the operation of a sophisticated voluntary control process (Atkinson & Shiffrin, 1968). This control process must confine the memory search to within an experimentally defined limited search set (Shiffrin, 1970) and exclude interference from more general search sets of similar familiar items. The efficiency of such voluntary control processes would appear to be an interesting subject for future research.

EXPERIMENT 2

Long-term recognition of items that were originally seen twice is consistently superior to recognition of items seen only once, both for preschool children (Experiment 1) and adults (Nickerson, 1968). Two possible explanations of this finding were examined in Experiment 2. The first explanation is that each presentation of an item strengthens the original trace, or lays down an alternative trace in the memory store (Bjork, 1970); either process resulting in a more accessible trace which facilitates retrieval. Therefore, the difference between the $p(Ro \mid So_2)$ and the $p(Ro \mid So_1)$ could be due to the fact that simply seeing an item twice renders that item more resistant to decay. The second explanation of the superiority of twice-seen items is that these pictures had already been subjected to the process of retrieval in the immediate retention test. Subsequently, the test items were easier to recognize not only because they had occurred twice, but because they had also been classified as old when they recurred

in the immediate test. In contrast, the filler items occurred only once and were, therefore, never classified as old items.

In Experiment 2, an attempt was made to determine the separate effects of seeing an item twice, and labeling it as old on its second occurrence. A further group of preschool children were shown the stimuli of Experiment 1, but were not required to respond to a repeating item. Thus, they saw each test item twice, but were not required to label it as old when it recurred in the series.

METHOD

Subjects

Eight preschool children, four boys and four girls, served as *S*s. Their age range of 44 to 63 months (mean = 54 months) was comparable to that of the *S*s in Experiment 1. One additional *S* spontaneously responded "old" to recurring items and his data were treated separately. Two further *S*s were dropped from the study; one failed to complete the initial viewing of the 100 items, and one was unavailable at the designated retention interval.

Stimulus Materials

The stimuli were identical to those used in Experiment 1.

PROCEDURE

An initial viewing session was substituted for the immediate retention test of Experiment 1. The *S*s were shown the identical pretraining and experimental stacks of pictures. During pretraining the *S*s were told that some pictures would occur once and some twice, but they were instructed only to "Look at all the pictures carefully" as they would be required to remember them later. After a 7-day retention interval, the second session was conducted. Here the *S*s were shown the retention stack of 72 cards and were instructed to say which pictures they had seen before, following the procedure of the long-term retention test of Experiment 1. To ensure that the *S*s understood the procedure of responding "Yes" or "No," *E* repeated "Yes, that's the one you saw before," when the first old picture occurred. No difficulty in understanding the instructions was apparent. After each session the *S*s received 10¢ toys as rewards.

RESULTS

Analyses were performed on the retention performance which followed 7-days after the initial viewing period. When the results of Experiment 2 were considered separately, items seen twice were again significantly easier to recognize than items seen once. The $p(Ro \mid So_2)$ was .78 compared with the $p(Ro \mid So_1)$ of .69 ($t(7) = 2.79$, $p < .02$). The correlated t test was conducted on the arcsine transformed scores. The $p(Ro \mid Sn)$ was .03. Both the $p(Ro \mid So)$ and the $p(Ro \mid Sn)$ remained stable across trials.

To determine the relative effect of seeing an item twice and labeling it as old on its second presentation, the results of Experiment 2 were compared to those of the comparable 7-day retention group of Experiment 1. A 2 × 2 mixed analysis of variance was conducted on the arcsine transformation of the proportion of pictures correctly recognized as old. The within subjects variable was Type of Item (seen once or twice) and the between subjects variable was Experimental Condition (Experiments 1 or 2). The $p(Ro \mid So_2)$ was significantly higher than the $p(Ro \mid So_1)$, ($F(1,14) = 71.04$, $p < .001$). The Ss of Experiment 1 performed better than the Ss of Experiment 2 ($F(1,14) = 5.18$, $p < .05$). The interaction of Type of Item X Experimental Condition was also reliable ($F(1,14) = 9.60$, $p < .01$). This interaction is illustrated in Figure 2, where it can be seen that the Ss of Experiment 2 performed significantly less well on the items seen twice ($t(14) = 3.55$, $p < .01$), but their slight drop in performance on items seen once is not reliable ($t(14) = .47$, $p > .10$). Both t tests for independent means were conducted on the arcsine transformed scores. The probabilities shown in Figure 2 were obtained by reconverting the mean arcsine proportion correct into probabilities.

The data for the one S who spontaneously labeled repeating stimuli "old" were considered separately. For this S, the $p(Ro \mid So_2)$ was .98 and the $p(Ro \mid So_1)$ was .73. Inspection of Figure 2 reveals that these scores are more comparable to those reported in Experiment 1, where labeling was demanded by the experimental condition, than to the scores of Experiment 2, where such labeling was not required.

DISCUSSION

The fact that twice-seen items are easier to recognize than once-seen items is the combined result of seeing the item twice and responding "old" to that item on its recurrence. Merely seeing the item twice aids retention. This was confirmed by the findings of Experiment 2, where a significantly greater proportion of twice-seen items were recognized as old. Comparing performance on twice-seen items in Experiments 1 and 2, it becomes apparent that the fact that items are seen twice is not solely responsible for the greater $p(Ro \mid So)$ reported. The $p(Ro \mid So_2)$ at the 7-day retention interval of Experiments 2 was only .78, which more closely approximated the 28-day retention score of .79, than the 7-day retention score of .94 found in Experiment 1. This significantly better retention of twice-seen items under the conditions of Experiment 1 suggests that recognition is greatly facilitated if items are not only seen twice, but are classified as old when they reappear.

The superior retention of twice-seen items in Experiment 1 is open to several interpretations. It could be that the similarity of the two testing conditions facilitated performance for the Ss of Experiment 1. These Ss arrived at the long-term retention test with experience in responding "Yes" and "No" to old and new items gained in the original continuous recognition task. However, the Ss of Experiment 2, lacking this experience in their initial viewing task, were required to learn the correct method of responding during the retention test. This explanation receives little

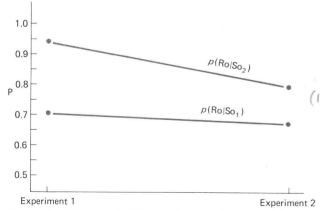

Figure 2 The probability of a response "old" to stimuli seen once and stimuli seen twice in Experiments 1 and 2.

support from either the ease of responding to instructions displayed by the Ss or the stability of performance measures over trials in the retention task. The $p(Ro \mid So)$ did not increase, nor did the $p(Ro \mid Sn)$ decrease over the session, both of which would be predicted if the Ss were gradually learning the "rules of the game" during the course of the retention task.

(2) A second interpretation of the superior retention of twice seen items in Experiment 1 would be to suggest that the procedure of forcing Ss to classify each item in the continuous recognition task, also forced them to attend more closely to each item as it occurred. The Ss of Experiment 2 were not required to classify each item and, therefore, paid less attention to items in the initial viewing period. This second explanation is refuted by the finding of no significant difference between the subsequent recognition of once-seen items in the retention tests of Experiments 1 and 2. A hypothesis which suggests that a decrease in attention in the initial viewing period is responsible for the poorer performance on twice-seen items, would also predict a decrement in performance on once-seen items. These filler items should also suffer from any lowering of attention in the initial task and should therefore show a comparable deficit in the retention task.

(3) If it is unlikely that either procedural differences or a general decrement in attention hypothesis can explain the superior retention of twice-seen items under the conditions of Experiment 1, then a third interpretation would be to suggest that the overt act of labeling a recurring item as "old" aids storage or retrieval of that item. A test item once labeled as old could be replaced in the memory store together with this information that the item is old. When a second recognition is required, the item has already been "tagged" old and stored as such. It has already been suggested that items in long-term memory are stored together with certain contextual, feature, or time tags (Anisfeld & Knapp, 1968; Kintsch, 1970; Shiffrin, 1970; and Yntema & Trask, 1963). There-

fore, one explanation of the superior recognition of a twice-seen item overtly labeled as old is that such an item was placed in the memory store, together with the tag "old," and that this tag aided retrieval.

The excellent recognition performance in both Experiments 1 and 2 indicates that further attempts to define a limited recognition capacity in preschool children would be as restricted as adult studies by experimental limitations on the S's viewing capacity rather than recognition ability. A promising alternate area of future research would be a systematic attempt to delineate the processes controlling storage and recognition of pictures in young children.

References

Anisfeld, M., & Knapp, M. Association, synonymity, and directionality in false recognition. *Journal of Experimental Psychology,* 1968, 77, 171–179.

Atkinson, R. C., & Shiffrin, R. M. Human memory: A proposed system and its control processes. In K. W. Spence & J. T. Spence (Eds.), *The psychology of learning and motivation: Advances in research and theory,* Vol. 2. New York: Academic Press, 1968.

Bjork, R. A. Repetition and rehearsal mechanisms in models of short-term memory. In D. A. Norman (Ed.), *Models of human memory.* New York: Academic Press, 1970.

Carterette, E. C., & Jones, M. H. Visual and auditory information processing in children and adults. *Science,* 1967, 156, 986–988.

Corsini, D. A., Jacobus, K. A., & Leonard, D. S. Recognition memory of preschool children for pictures and words. *Psychonomic Science,* 1969, 16, 192–193.

Gellermann, L. W. Chance orders of alternating stimuli in visual discrimination experiments. *Journal of Genetic Psychology,* 1933, 42, 207–208.

Kintsch, W. Models for free recall and recognition. In D. A. Norman (Ed.), *Models of human memory.* New York: Academic Press, 1970.

Nickerson, R. S. Short-term memory for complex meaningful visual configurations: A demonstration of capacity. *Canadian Journal of Psychology,* 1965, 19, 155–160.

Nickerson, R. S. A note on long-term recognition

memory for pictorial material. *Psychonomic Science,* 1968, 11, 58.

Shepard, R. N. Recognition memory for words, sentences, and pictures. *Journal of Verbal Learning and Verbal Behavior,* 1967, 6, 156–163.

Shiffrin, R. M. Memory search. In D. A. Norman (Ed.), *Models of human memory.* New York: Academic Press, 1970.

Shiffrin, R. M., & Atkinson, R. C. Storage and retrieval processes in long-term memory. *Psychological Review,* 1969, 76, 179–193.

Standing, L., Conezio, J., & Haber, R. N. Perception and memory for pictures: Single-trial learning of 2500 visual stimuli. *Psychonomic Science,* 1970, 19, 73–74.

Yntema, D. B., & Trask, F. P. Recall as a search process. *Journal of Verbal Learning and Verbal Behavior,* 1963, 2, 65–74.

Chapter 6

Language

One of the most significant developments in psychology during the past decade has been the increased interest in and investigation of the child's acqusition of language—his ability to understand, speak, and read the language of his community. The work of Noam Chomsky, Roger Brown, and other psycholinguists has emphasized the maturational basis for language acquisition. There seems to be a universal period, somewhere between 12 and 36 months, when all children begin to speak. Many assume that we will understand more about cognitive processes in general when we understand the rules by which children learn to use and comprehend language.

Although most psycholinguistic research has focused on grammatical development, there is growing interest in the semantic aspects of language, that is, the meaning of words and sentences. Since the acquisition of grammatical rules appears to be lawful, it is reasonable to assume that there is also lawfulness in the acquisition of semantic rules.

(1)   In the first selection in this chapter, K. Nelson reports her discovery of some of these rules. She studied 18 middle-class children from the time they spoke their first words, around their first birthday, to their first production of sentences, close to their second birthday. Nelson recorded the children's speech in their home settings and, additionally, tested all the children. She found that, initially, most of the words children use are names of objects (shoe, ball), types of animals (dog, cat), and specific people (mommy, daddy). By contrast they are less likely to use pronouns or action words and

rarely use adjectives that describe the attributes of objects. Nelson suggests that children tend to learn first the names of things that they play with and act upon (e.g., toys, keys) as well as objects that move (e.g., dogs, cats, cars). With few exceptions children tend initially to learn the names of small, manipulable or movable objects. In all cases these objects have the salient property of change. The author comes to the important conclusion that if the child does not know a word, he is not likely to imitate that word. More generally, the child must have first acquired some language before he will imitate the language of others. Hence minimal language skill comes before imitation, rather than imitation preceding spoken language. Nelson suggests that the child must first acquire some nonlinguistic, abstract categories or concepts for objects and people before he learns the words that apply to those categories. The child will be maximally receptive to learning the name of an object or animal if he first has acquired a schema for it. For example, we know that an infant possesses a good representation of the parts of a face by 6 months of age, four to six months before he will either say or understand the words **eyes, nose,** or **mouth.**

(2)   One controversy in the study of language concerns the meaning of the fact that ghetto black children tend to speak differently from middle-class white children. Some psychologists have interpreted that difference to imply a deficiency in cognitive processes in the black child. W. Labov argues against that view, suggesting that poor black children possess the same capacity for conceptual learning and use the same logic as middle-class children. He presents examples from the speech of black children to support his view that black language follows a set of rules which are slightly different from those of middle-class white English. Labov denies that poor black children are verbally deprived or have language deficiencies.

(3)   The fact that there are five or six times as many children from poor as from middle-class families who do not learn to read is an unsolved puzzle having serious social consequences. The article by D. Shankweiler and I. Liberman offers some clues as to the source of difficulty that first- and second-grade children encounter in learning to
[1] read. The authors suggest that the central problem is the inability to read individual words and that the problem of recognizing letters or comprehending long sentences is
[2] secondary. The beginning reader has trouble synthesizing successive syllables. He also
[3] has more difficulty with the middle and final sounds of words than with initial sounds

(final consonants are more frequently misread than initial consonants). Moreover, more [4] errors are made on vowels than on consonants. There is little correlation between the accuracy of perception of meaning through reading and the accuracy of perception of speech. Children who are good in one modality are not necessarily good in the other.

Structure and Strategy in Learning to Talk

Katherine Nelson

Most children at 1 year of age have begun to say one or two words. Most children by the age of 2 have begun to talk in short sentences. The present *Monograph* attempts to describe the process by which the child takes the first step and proceeds to the second. It also describes some problems met along the way and variations among children (and their parents) in solving these problems through the employment of varying strategies of selection and processing.

. . . . .

Subjects

A sample of 18 subjects was recruited from a pool of 160 mothers who had participated in a previous experiment in the Laboratory of Infancy Studies at Yale. These mothers represented a self-selection from among those whose babies were born in the Yale–New Haven Hospital together with volunteers recruited through newspaper advertisements.

The size of the sample was determined by the desire to have a group large enough for drawing meaningful generalizations yet small enough for a single observer to maintain personal knowledge of each mother-child pair. At the time the study began infants ranged from 10 to 15 months. For comparison purposes, the sample was divided into three equal age groups with the aim of recruiting seven children for each group, divided as equally as possible between the sexes. Mothers were invited by phone to participate in a study covering several months and involving frequent in-the-home visits. The first visit was spent in acquainting the mother with the purposes of the

SOURCE: Excerpted from *Monographs of the Society for Research in Child Development*, vol. 38, Ser. #149 (1973), 1–135, with footnotes and cross-references deleted. Copyright © by the Society for Research in Child Development, Inc. Reprinted with permission.

Table 1. Distribution of sample by age and sex

	AGE AT ONSET OF STUDY		
	GROUP I (14–15 MO)	GROUP II (12–13 MO)	GROUP III (10–11 MO)
Females	5	3	3
Males	2	2	3
Total	7	5	6

study in more detail, in explaining the collection of vocabulary data, and in obtaining preliminary information about the child and home. In this manner 19 subjects of appropriate ages were recruited; however, equal distribution by sex proved impossible to obtain. One subject subsequently withdrew from the study. This left a final sample of 18 who were divided, as shown in Table 1, by sex and age at the onset of the study.

All of the children lived in middle-class homes. Their parents ranged in educational level from high school only to professional degrees with a median of 16 years of schooling for the fathers and 15 for the mothers. The employment status of the fathers was white collar, business, and professional.

Time Span

The study was designed to cover the developmental sequence from learning of first words to production of early sentences. Thus a year-long sequence from approximately 1 year of age to 2 years was decided upon. However, as can be seen from the distribution in Table 1, some subjects were studied for slightly less than a year and some for slightly longer. The main part of the study ended for all subjects at 25 months. A follow-up visit at 30 months gathered supplementary language data.

Overall, each child was visited at home once a month (with a few missing observations because of illness, vacations, etc.) for a period ranging from ½ hour to 1 hour, during which vocabulary records were collected from the mother and discussed with her, and the child was observed in a structured setting or was given a test or partici-

pated in an experiment. All sessions were recorded on tape using a battery-powered stereophonic Sony Cassette recorder which allowed maximum mobility with a reasonably high quality of recording. Sessions were transcribed in ordinary English orthography, and no attempt was made to render the child's speech phonetically or to make any phonetic analysis. When there was any question regarding the interpretation of the child's utterances, they were interpreted by the author who was also the observer and experimenter at all sessions and could therefore supplement the taped record with the context of the observation. During the early phase of the study a second observer was also present. At 24 or 25 months the child was visited in his home for 2 hours, and a tape recording was made of mother-child interaction (and child-child interaction if siblings were present) in an unstructured free activity situation of 1½–2 hours of speech. These tapes formed the basis for the analysis of grammatical competence and mean length of utterance at age 2. The child was also given a concept development test at this age and was brought to the laboratory for the administration of the Bayley tests of infant development. At 30 months a follow-up visit was made to 16 of the 18 children still in the area, when another language sample was obtained and a Peabody Picture Vocabulary Test (PPVT) was given.

. . . . .

Analyses of Form

1. Words were classified according to their *content* or *reference* into classes related to the basic grammatical-form classes. These classes were subdivided into semantic categories. Insofar as possible, the child's use of the word determined its classification, although it was not always feasible to differentiate consistently among his uses. Because it is important to recognize that one cannot apply grammatical descriptions to single-word utterances, different terms are assigned here for this purpose. At this level detailed analyses have

not been made of the use of a particular word by a particular child across situations and over time. Thus if a mother reported that a child said "door" when he wanted to go outside, this was classified as an action word; if he said "door" when he touched the door but not in demand it was classified as a nominal. The mothers in this study on the whole reported that early words were used quite consistently to express a particular *function*, that is, reference, demand, etc. It has been often asserted that young children use a single word for a variety of different functional statements. This view was not strongly supported; the evidence on the contrary suggests that these children were quite consistent, not to say repetitive, in the use of the words they knew. This question deserves more direct and intensive study.

2. Words were classified according to their order of acquisition, so that for each child one could determine the composition of his vocabulary along an acquisition curve, and across children one could make comparisons as to kinds of words acquired at a particular point in the learning sequence defined by vocabulary growth (rather than chronological age). This approach was taken in order to determine if there were content and form regularities associated with development. It was also possible in this way to determine individual differences in learning rate.

An arbitrary cutoff for this vocabulary analysis was established at 50 words for the following reasons: (1) Mother's reports were in almost all cases reliable up to this vocabulary level but few mothers kept accurate records much beyond this point (rate of acquisition accelerates and monthly reporting intervals become too long to sustain). (2) The noted acceleration of words sometimes coincided with the construction of phrases and a comparison within a defined period of primarily single-unit usage was desired. (3) Although all of the children in the study had produced 50 different words by the age of 2 years, the slower ones had vocabularies of approximately that size at the termination of the study.

The analyses that follow therefore concern regularities and variability within the 50-word vocabularies. The 50-word level was achieved by different children at ages ranging from 15 to 24 months. The mean age was 19.75; the time period covered (from first word to fiftieth) ranged from 4 to 13 months.

Grammatical Categories

I. Nominals
   Definition.—Words used to refer to the "thing world." May be used in labeling or demanding, in ostensive reference or relations involving agent or object.
   A. *Specific Nominals*
      Definition.—Words used to refer to only one exemplar of a category whether a proper name (i.e., a class with only one member) or not.
      1. People (*Mommy*)
      2. Animals (*Dizzy*—name of pet)
      3. Objects (*car*)
   B. *General Nominals*
      Definition.—Words used to refer to all members of a category whether child or adult defined.
      1. Objects (*ball, car*)
      2. Substances (*milk, snow:* includes all mass nouns)
      3. Animals and people (*doggie, girl*)
      4. Letters and numbers (*E, 2*)
      5. Abstractions (*God, birthday*)
      6. Pronouns (*he, that*)

II. Action Words
   Definition.—Words that describe, demand, or accompany action or that express attention or demand for attention. They may be used for notice, locative, or action relations.
   1. Descriptive (*go, bye-bye*)
   2. Demand (*up, out*)
   3. Notice (*look, hi*)
   In practice it proved impossible to determine reliably descriptive versus demand use from our records. Therefore, the quantitative analysis pools these two subcategories.

III. Modifiers
   Definition.—Words that refer to properties or qualities of things or events. They express recurrence, disappearance, attribution, location, and possession.

1. Attributes (*big, red, pretty*)
2. States (*hot, dirty, all gone*)
3. Locatives (*there, outside*)
4. Possessives (*mine*)

IV. Personal Social
Definition.—Words that express affective states and social relationships; these range from highly idiosyncratic to highly conventional (e.g., *thank you*). They do not express basic operations or relations.
1. Assertions (*no, yes, want, know*)
2. Social expressive (*please, ouch*)

V. Function Words
Definition.—Words that fulfill a solely grammatical function, words relating to other words.
1. Question words (*what, where*)
2. Miscellaneous functions (*is, to, for*)

Results of Word Analysis

When the total 50-word vocabularies for all children were classified according to this scheme the breakdown was as shown in Table 2. A few preliminary comments about the data are in order. First, the proportions of nominals, action words, and modifiers are similar to the counts made by others using similar schemes over the course of the past century. Specific names do *not* predominate here, although there were individual cases at all vocabulary levels of specific references (e.g., to the family car or to the child's blanket). The proportion of general object and substance names indicates that considerable "label learning" is going on. Action words are not as numerous as might be expected according to a theory of the salience of action in the life of the young child, but neither are they so absent that they can be considered a "secondary acquisition" (McNeill 1970a). Not all of these action words are verbs in adult language (e.g., *up*), but they clearly express an action reference. The modifier category is of great interest since it demonstrates on the language-learning level the salience of states or functions (*all gone, dirty, hot*) versus invariant attributes (*red, round, pretty*) to the young child at this point in his development (see Nelson 1972b, 1973). Words referring to states comprised 6% of

Table 2. Mean percentage of 50-word vocabularies by category ($N = 18$)

CATEGORY	%
I. Nominals:	
Specific:	
People	12
Animals	1
Objects	1
Total specific nominals	14
General:	
Objects	31
Substances	7
Animals and people	10
Letters and numbers	1
Abstractions	1
Pronouns	3
Total general nominals	51
II. Action words:	
Demand-descriptive	11
Notice	2
Total action	13
III. Modifiers:	
Attributes	1
States	6
Locatives	2
Possessives	1
Total modifiers	9
IV. Personal-social:	
Assertions	4
Social-expressive	4
Total personal-social	8
V. Function words:	
Question	2
Miscellaneous	2
Total function	4

Note. Percentages do not add up to 100 due to rounding.

the vocabularies and attributes less than 1%. It should also be noted that the personal-social words comprise a not insignificant proportion (8%) of the vocabularies of these young children.

. . . . .

. . . Table 3 gives a tabulation of all the words learned in six categories by all children during the 50-word period.

Table 3. Words acquired in the first 50-word vocabularies by semantic categories

CATEGORY AND WORD[a]	FREQUENCY[b]
Food and drink:	
Juice	12
Milk	10
Cookie	10
Water	8
Toast	7
Apple	5
Cake	5
Banana	3
Drink	3
Bread	2
Butter	2
Cheese	2
Egg	2
Pea(s)	2
(Lolli) pop	2
Candy	1
Clackers	1
Coffee	1
Cracker	1
Food	1
Gum	1
Meat	1
Melon	1
Noodles	1
Nut	1
Peach	1
Pickle	1
Pizza	1
Soda	1
Spaghetti	1
Total	90
Animals:	
Dog (variants)	16
Cat (variants)	14
Duck	8
Horse	5
Bear	4
Bird	4
Cow (variants)	4
Bee	1
Bug	1
Donkey	1
Frog	1
Goose	1
Monkey	1
Moose	1
Pig	1
Puppy	1
Tiger	1
Turkey	1
Turtle	1
Total	67
Clothes:	
Shoes	11
Hat	5
Socks	4
Boots	2
Belt	2
Coat	2
Tights	1
Slippers	1
Shirt	1
Dress	1
Bib	1
Total	31
Toys and play equipment:	
Ball	13
Blocks	7
Doll	4
Teddy bear	2
Bike	2
Walker	1
Swing	1
Total	30
Vehicles:	
Car	13
Boat	6
Truck	6
Bus	2
Plane	1
Choo choo	1
Total	29
Furniture and household items:	
Clock	7
Light	6
Blanket	4
Chair	3
Door	3
Bed	1
Crib	1
Pillow	1
Telephone	1
Washing machine	1
Drawer	1
Total	29

Table 3. (Continued)

CATEGORY AND WORD[a]	FREQUENCY[b]
Personal items:	
Key	6
Book	5
Watch	3
Tissue	1
Chalk	1
Pen	1
Paper	1
Scissors	1
Pocketbook	1
Money	1
Total	21
Eating and drinking utensils:	
Bottle	8
Cup	4
Spoon	2
Glass	1
Knife	1
Fork	1
Dish	1
Tray	1
Total	19
Outdoor objects:	
Snow	4
Flower	2
House	2
Moon	2
Rock	2
Flag	1
Tree	1
Map	1
Total	15
Places:	
Pool	3
Beach	1
School	1
Porch	1
Total	6

[a]Adult form of word used. Many words had several variant forms, in particular the animal words.
[b]Number of children in the sample who used the word in the 50-word acquisition sequence.

To borrow a technique from Leopold, it is instructive to look at the omissions from this list as well as what it includes. Under clothes there was no word for diaper, although all the children wore them. (Is diaper a baby taboo word?) Similarly lacking are pants, overalls, jackets, sweaters, mittens, pajamas, etc. The number of clothing items represented was but a fraction of those that the average child comes into contact with daily. The predominant words learned in this category (three-fifths) were those that the child can act on easily: his shoes, socks, and other footwear. It is these that he loves to take off and less frequently to put on.

Two-thirds of the furniture and household items were of less than "furniture size." There were no tables, sofas, bureaus, chests, televisions, stoves, refrigerators, windows, or, for that matter, pictures, vases, or ashtrays in this baby world. Only three of the children spoke of chair or any other seating item, and only two said bed or crib. Yet they sat in chairs, slept in beds, ate at tables.

Books were well represented (five instances), and there was a scattering of related items—chalk, paper, pen. Keys appeared (six instances) but not combs, brushes, toothbrushes, soap, towels. This was certainly not because of the relatively greater importance of keys in their lives.

The few outside and place items that appear were equally selective. Beach, pool, and snow can all be played in. But note that there was no rain, ice, or sun. There was only one lone tree, no grass, sidewalks, mailbox, or street; yet they all took at least occasional walks. There was no store, park, or playground, but they all had outings to these places. There were no rooms. Vehicles were notable for the absence of trains, but note also only one plane!

Frequency of personal experience, exposure to words, strength of need or desire cannot apparently explain the selection of these words. They are personal, selective, and for the most part action related. It is apparent that children learn the names of the things they can act on, whether they are toys, shoes, scissors, money, keys, blankets, or bottles as well as things that act themselves such as dogs and cars. They do not learn the names of things in the house or outside that are simply "there" whether these are tables, plates, towels, grass, or stores. With very few exceptions all the words listed are terms applying to manipulable or movable objects.

The common attribute of all of the most frequent early referents is that they have salient properties of change–that is, they do things (roll, run, bark, meow, go r-r-r and drive away). In this connection, sound is as relevant as movement; both exhibit temporal change. The omissions are in general of things that—however obvious and important—just sit there: sofas, tables, chests, windows, plates, overalls, trees, grass. The words that are learned are not only the ones the child acts upon in some way (shoes, bottle, ball) but also ones that do something themselves that the child only observes—trucks, clocks, buses, and all the animals. (Although some animal names referred to pictures rather than live or toy animals, the mother almost always gave the animal sound: e.g., "What does the tiger say? r-r-r." The sound rather than the picture thus may have defined the concept.) This general conclusion is of course in accord with cognitive theories (e.g., Piaget's) emphasizing the importance of the child's action to his definition of the world, but it implicates equally the importance of actions external to the child. Thus, the words the child learns reflect the child's mode of structuring the world. Their properties are those of high salience to the child exhibited either through his own interactions or through their apparent changes.

. . . . .

Imitation and Repetition

The place of imitation in language learning has a long and controversial history which will not be reviewed here. Although Ervin (1964) concluded that imitation is not progressive in grammatical constructions, she specifically denied that this implied no role in language learning for imitation. Indeed, she states, "In comprehension covert imitation may be important. Possibly imitation aids

in the acquisition of vocabulary or of phonetic mastery" (p. 172). Following this line, imitation will here be viewed as a potentially useful tool for solving certain tasks, in particular, one that is useful at certain points in vocabulary acquisition but not at others.

An outstanding characteristic of child talk is its sheer repetitiveness, which might be termed self-imitation, suggesting that imitation and repetition are somehow functionally related. The functional consequences of repetition, however, have been little analyzed. Is repetition also a strategy that is potentially useful at particular points in development, or is it an intraindividual stylistic variable?

Imitation Analysis

Imitation is a less intractable strategy from the point of view of the investigator than is comprehension. Like his free production, a child's imitations can be observed, although not always without ambiguity. What is to be counted as an imitation? Phonetic matching? Intonational form? Some kind of word contour or pattern? Fully *correct* imitation on the part of very young children is relatively rare (an observation that forms the basis for most contemporary imitation analyses), yet spontaneous partial imitation occurs frequently, especially at certain points in language learning.

An early attempt to have mothers elicit imitation from their children at about 12 months showed that few children were interested in the game at that age, even when the stimulus words were those they used themselves. There was thus very little "circular imitation" at the word level observed. A count of spontaneous imitation in the protocols of the children at that time showed a low level also (median of 2.75% of their utterances), although there were ambiguities of word form making the identification of imitation doubtful in some cases. Spontaneous imitation at this point was not related to acquisition of words. Yet it is a common observation that children will imitate the parent language. On what occasion? When is imitation a good strategy?

An imitation task was designed to probe this question. Two picture books were assembled showing 16 colorful pictures of familiar and less familiar objects. Each object was matched with a word of the following type: (1) correct name (e.g., *car* paired with a picture of car); (2) incorrect name (e.g., *banana* paired with a picture of car); (3) attribute (e.g., *red)*; (4) function (e.g., *swims)*. Each word was embedded in a statement of the following form: "See, it's [a] ————. Can you say ————?"

The mother was asked to read these sentences to the child and wait for a response. If the child did not repeat the correct word, the mother was to repeat the sentence twice (because of fussing and inattention this was not always possible).

With one exception, each child in the study participated in this experiment once or twice, always at 20–21 months and, for seven of the children, also at 18–19 months. The vocabulary range for the children studied was quite wide, ranging from nine to over 300 (estimated) words.

The child was scored for his imitation of the critical word. As usual, all sessions were taped, but the judgment was made at the time of the response as to its imitative quality. Responses fell into the following general categories:

1. No response. Child is attentive and participates by turning pages, etc., but does not name pictures or imitate mother.
2. Repetitive verbal response—nonimitative. Child repeats same sound in response to each picture.
3. Labeling. Instead of repeating word used by mother, child labels the object or part of the picture.
4. Imitation. Child repeats word used by mother, producing similar phonetic or general form.

Only the last category was considered imitative. Labeling responses were analyzed separately.

Total number of imitations were counted, yielding scores ranging from 0 to 16. Correlations with age and vocabulary level revealed a significant relation with vocabulary level at time of testing ($r =$ .58, $p < .005$), and a lower correlation with age ($r = .39$, $p < .05$). That is, the larger the child's vocabulary, the greater the imitation. This is apparent in the comparison of mean scores for those below the median vocabulary level of 55 words (2.9) compared to those above the median (10.3) (see Table 4). This difference is larger than that for the sample divided by median age.

Surprisingly, the number of imitations was no different for pictures that did *not* match the object word than for those that did (mean scores of 1.7 and 1.8, respectively). The correlation of object correct words with vocabulary level was .59, and for object incorrect it was .52, both significant at $p < .01$. The only difference between the types of words was that fewer imitations were given for attributes. These included color words and properties such as having feathers or fins, or being round or sharp.

The fact that correct object names were not more frequently imitated than other words is evidence against the hypothesis that imitation is an increasing function of association between object and its label. Also, object names were not more frequently imitated than were function words which were mostly verbs. Thus, neither the formal characteristics of the words nor of their pictured referents appeared to determine imitation in this situation.

An analysis of the response to words or pictures in each child's current active vocabulary is shown in Table 5. When the child used the stimulus word but had not learned the name for the pictured object, and when these were different (e.g., *car* paired with crib), he responded with an imitation 77% of the time. This compares to an imitative response 71% of the time for similar cases where the picture and the name were congruent and the word was known (e.g., *car* paired with car). Thus the child seemed willing to imi-

Table 4. Mean correct imitations by vocabulary level, age, and functional group

	PICTURE-WORD RELATIONSHIP					
	OBJECT CORRECT (N = 4)	OBJECT INCORRECT (N = 4)	FUNCTION (N = 4)	ATTRIBUTE (N = 4)	TOTAL (N = 16)	SD
Vocabulary level (median = 55 words):						
Below (N = 12)	0.8	0.7	1.0	0.4	2.9	3.9
Above (N = 12)	2.7	2.7	2.5	1.9	10.3	4.0
Age (median = 20 mo):						
Below (N = 12)	1.6	1.3	1.5	.9	5.4	5.1
Over (N = 12)	1.9	2.1	2.0	1.8	7.8	5.5
Functional group:						
Referential[a] (N = 10)	1.5	1.5	1.9	1.6	6.5	5.0
Expressive[a] (N = 7)	2.3	2.5	1.8	1.4	8.1	4.5
Total group (N = 24)[b]	1.8	1.7	1.7	1.2	6.6	5.4

[a]Scores for the 20-month test.
[b]Seven of the children were tested twice, and one was not tested.

Table 5. Imitative responses to stimulus names in child's active vocabulary

STIMULUS CATEGORY	N CASES	% RESPONSES	
		IMITATION	LABEL
No relevant words in vocabulary	156	45	...
Stimulus word in vocabulary:			
Picture matches word	48	71	...
Picture does not match word	22	77	...
Stimulus picture label in vocabulary:			
Picture does not match word	57	40	35

tate his mother's use of a known word even when it was highly discrepant from the known concept domain.

On the other hand, when the object label that matched the picture was in the active vocabulary and the stimulus word was not (e.g., *red* paired with *car*), the child was less likely to imitate (40% imitative responses) and was almost equally likely to label the picture with his object name (35% of the cases). In contrast, when neither word was in the child's vocabulary, imitative responses were given 45% of the time. Thus *imitation occurred with high frequency whenever the child knew the word to be imitated regardless of whether it was used appropriately;* and he imitated equally often words he did not know whether or not he had an appropriate label available. Imitation in this task then was controlled by familiarity of the word, not by its reference.

Of those seven children tested twice, one who was at the ceiling on the first test (16 points) decreased 1 point on the second; one child who scored 0 on the first test continued to score 0. The others (N = 5) all increased one or more points (mean = 4.25) over the 2-month period.

Thus the imitative task was correlated with

the child's general language development: the more advanced in terms of vocabulary, the more likely he was to imitate. Scores on this test also correlated significantly with all measures of language development (see Table 6) except age at 10 words. Further, the child was more likely to imitate words that he knew than words he did not know, *whether or not they matched the referent pictures.* Here we find evidence of imitation of familiar forms analogous to that found for grammatical constructions (Ervin 1964). However, it should be borne in mind that unfamiliar forms were also imitated by children at a critical level of vocabulary development, although less frequently. What evidence is there that such imitation is serving a functional role in development?

Spontaneous imitations in the final session at 24 months revealed a mean rate of 5.4% of the utterances. This compares to the 2.7% found at 14 months. However, this measure of spontaneous imitation differs strikingly from that of the imitation test. The correlation between test at 21 months and spontaneous use at 24 months is of a zero order, and spontaneous imitation at 2 years is *negatively* related to language progress. This raises the problem of whether spontaneously occuring imitation is different from evoked imitation, or whether imitation at 2 years is associated with retarded development while imitation at 21

months indicates advanced development. A definitive answer to this question cannot be given, but the tentative hypothesis proposed is that both are true.

Briefly, imitation of words can be viewed as an appropriate accommodative strategy for the problem of acquiring and expanding vocabulary entries. This is appropriate for the level of the more advanced children at 21 months but no longer at 24 months when the task for these children has shifted from word meaning to sentence building. It is also likely that the language "game" played in the imitation task is one that calls on such characteristics of the child as attention, cooperation, and sociability, whereas spontaneous imitation may represent an attempt (perhaps inadequate) at problem solving.

It appears that there is no general "propensity" to imitate verbal stimuli on the part of the prelinguistic child. Some minimal adequacy in vocabulary acquisition *precedes* the general imitative response to new words. The more words the child has above a minimum level, the more likely he is to imitate either old or new ones. A likely explanation of this result is that the child (or at least some children) discovers the imitative strategy once he is launched on the word-learning game. It is an accommodative strategy, in Piaget's terms. It is not, however, an advancing strategy.

Table 6. Correlation of strategy variables with indices of language progress

STRATEGY VARIABLES	MEAN	SD	CORRELATIONS					
			AGE 10W[a]	AGE 50W[a]	AGE 10P[a]	RATE	MLU-2	VOCAB.-2
Ref. Voc.	0.51	0.13	.16	.28	−.20	.39*	.06	.43*
Comp. I	0.25	0.14	.14	.79**	.50*	.76**	.59*	.65**
Comp. II	0.53	0.21	.50*	.22	.05	.34	.40	.65*
Prod. 20 mo.	69.2	34.1	.28	.42*	.38*	.45*	.62**	.61**
Imit. test 21 mo.	7.18	4.86	.14	.55**	.45*	.41*	.57**	.70**
Imit. 2 yr	0.05	0.04	.25	−.02	−.01	−.38	−.28	−.22
Rep. 2 yr	0.11	0.08	−.33	−.44*	−.58**	−.39*	−.57**	−.50*
Questions 2 yr	0.09	0.06	.37	.52*	.53*	.35	.36	.54*

[a]These correlations have been reversed in direction to reflect greater progress for positive numbers.
*$p < .05$.
**$p < .01$.

A child who imitates words is already well along in acquiring words; there is no evidence of a gradual shift or a period of imitative practice prior to rapid word acquisition.

. . . .

The child comes to language learning with a range of organizing hypotheses about the world in the form of schemata, categories, or concepts. Because this point is less generally accepted and has not been elaborated in the work presented here thus far, it is necessary to justify it in some detail at this point. The child is an active organizer of perceptual data. He builds primitive concepts (categories, schemata) that group common experiences on the basis of their defining characteristics (features) for him. A given concept may be based on one or many defining features. These characteristics of the world will be bound together by a structure or configuration (a schema). These structures must of course be based on sensory-motor experience, but they may represent fairly abstract—functional, not immediately apparent—knowledge. For example, cups are things to drink from whatever their size, shape, or color, and whether or not they are filled with liquid. This definition can be verified by observation of a 12-month-old child "pretending" to drink from an empty cup, thus demonstrating his knowledge of its membership in the class of cups. It is not enough simply to assert that his reaction to cups is determined by the perceptual feature [handle] or [cavity], although this certainly deserves exploration. Rather, one needs to know why the form of cup is attached to the action definition "drink from" and why *cup* is granted the status of a thing that can be named as well as acted upon, while other equally distinguishable sets of features ([smooth, bouncy, high, flat] bed) are not named. The proposal here is that *cup* represents a concept for the child, a structured set of features.

Concepts represent defined wholes, the most obvious examples of which are common objects.

However, even for young children concepts do not apply exclusively to objects as indicated by the vocabularies analyzed here. The position taken here is that those objects and events that do operate as concepts may be named; and that those objects that exhibit within-object variance are most likely to be conceptualized. Thus varying properties will be defining features of the concept *and therefore* defining features of the word meaning.

However, most important, this feature or these features must exist in a *form* that can be recognized as a whole configuration; a single feature or uniformed set of features can be neither conceptualized nor named. The young child does not learn *four-legged* or *striped* or *moves* but *doggie, zebra, car*. Note, however, the frequency with which the child does learn sounds, for example, *r-r-r, bow-wow, tick-tock*. These *stand* for the concept which they define, however; they are not themselves the concept.

This is not to imply that a single feature (e.g., [bark]) may not be recognized as a sign of the object, but this is different from applying a concept name to a feature of the concept. For example, one child learned *tick-tock* as his first object word (at 12 months). When the clock struck the hour he would say "tick-tock" and crawl to the room where the clock was, thus demonstrating that the sound stood for the object. When he heard the sound, he uttered the word and looked for the object, which itself (not the sound) was the embodiment of the concept.

The child then must have an existing schema or concept in order to learn a word that applies to it. If the words that the parents use do not apply to the domain of the schemata that the child has constructed, those words will not be learned. A simple example will illustrate this problem. A child may define all flat raised surfaces as things to bang on with an implement. The parents, however, may call some of these tables, one a box, another a workbench. The parents may also say, "Don't bang on the table—

here, bang on your workbench." The child will not at first be able to understand this message, and he will be hindered from learning either key word because of his divergent division of the word. Or, to take another case, the child may have constructed a category of "good" snack food which overlaps several of his mother's categories, as shown in Figure 1. Thus, the child will have difficulty learning the appropriate words in this case because his mother's words do not coincide with his own concept. Or this case may be one in which he overgeneralizes or extends his words to inappropriate instances, using cookie for all "good" food to the amusement of his hearers. (This hypothesis incidentally predicts that fussier or more difficult eaters will learn food words more slowly.) Similar examples will be found in the individual cases of children studied here.

Several writers recently have suggested that the young child begins to learn language through its meaning by applying what he already knows about the world to the language used by his parents. However, the present proposal differs in some important ways from other interpretations of this general position. Three in particular may be considered.

1. Naming specific people, objects, and events. It seems at first glance reasonable to suppose that the child begins with specific names for familiar

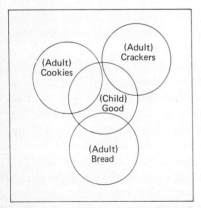

Figure 1 Relation of a hypothetical child concept of good snack food to relevant adult labels.

people and objects and then learns to generalize the names to broad categories as required by the nature of language. This in fact has been asserted as an explanation of the often rather late generalization of "daddy" to all men. And it appears to be a necessary assumption of S-R formulations (e.g., Skinner 1957; Staats 1971). However, the data here do not support such a progression: general terms are used from the first.

It should be noted, however, that some terms are used that are *more* specific than the adult terms rather than less so.

2. Applying words to semantic or perceptual features. In this view the child begins with terms applying to very general categories defined in terms of one or more features that are gradually differentiated through the addition of further semantic features. Clark (1973) has presented a persuasive account of this sort based on the young child's perceptual knowledge. She has attempted to account for overgeneralizations found in early language diary accounts—and their changes—through the gradual addition of semantic features to very general (one-feature) early categories. It should be noted, however, that this formulation adds very little to the concept formation view discussed below. It assumes that the child must learn what the relevant sets of features are in his language. And the only mode of organization suggested is that of feature additions provided through the language. The child possesses only a set of percepts from which to build. Moreover, unless one makes specific assumptions about which features are more primitive and therefore are to be acquired first, there is no reason to assume that a definition in terms of a single feature will be any more general than a definition in terms of many features. Dogs, for example, rather than being defined as [four-legged] (which of course also includes tables, chairs, and many other entities) may be defined as [barks], in which case the category will be quite specific and, until the child meets a seal, also correct. As noted above, it is frequently true that a child has a nar-

rower rather than a broader category for the adult term—*car* for toy cars but not real ones, for example, as shown in Figure 2—but this is difficult if not impossible to account for in terms of few general to more specific perceptual features.

3. The concept-formation view. In a classical concept-formation model one must conceive of the child's attending to (and producing) words before he attends to their meanings. That is, he is seen as learning the form of a word and then searching for its reference (see Brown 1958b). This is, however, a most unlikely sequence in that the word alone can have little salience or attraction compared to the nonlinguistic events to which it refers. . . . It is also a sequence that puts an enormous strain on memory and cognitive processing ability in that the child must hold in memory not only all of the instances of Word but all of the relevant attributes of these instances, until he has extracted the invariance common to all. Although there are common strategies for solving this problem (see, e.g., Bruner, Goodnow, & Austin 1956), their use implies a sophistication in and capacity for the use of problem-solving skills that have never been attributed to the infant. On the other hand, the present position avoids these problems by proposing that the child moves from concept to name, from those aspects of the world to which he already attends (and has organized into structural wholes) to the less salient linguistic invariance.

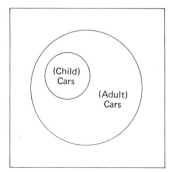

Figure 2 Relation of a hypothetical child concept of car to adult label.

In brief then, the concept-matching model proposed here asserts that the young child has a set of organized concepts referring to aspects of the world (objects, events, relationships), which are loosely organized into various concept domains (according to contexts, situations, interests), and are defined by the characteristics arising from the child's own experience. Such concepts may overlap to a greater or lesser degree with those referred to by the adult language, and the definitions attached to the words the child learns will initially reflect his own preexisting concepts. Thus these concepts will determine whether it is learned at all.

. . . . .

The major proposition implicit in the interaction notion is that there is no one way to learn language. Language learning poses a problem for the child, and, as with other complex problems, there is no single path to a solution. Although this point seems obvious, many investigations in emphasizing the general or universal have overlooked the lessons to be learned from the particular. The language problem is of course universal in human societies, and the components of its solution are universal. All children will learn a language as it is spoken by others in the speech community, whether by adults or children, and they will relate it to their own knowledge of the world. They will utilize a limited number of acquisition strategies. However, variations in preverbal cognitive organization, in language, in family patterns, and in physical environment will interact to produce a variety of difficult acquisition patterns in terms of both direction and rate characteristics. These different patterns may be useful in identifying more general characteristics of process. Having traced some of the variations in learning patterns that have emerged here, it therefore now becomes possible to identify some generalities of the process.

Summarized below are a set of hypotheses, drawn from the preceding analysis, regarding the major steps that the child takes in proceeding from zero language to communication competence. The major emphasis here is on aspects of the child's changing concept status, in accordance with the argument that the child's language-learning problem is always to match his concepts with the symbols used by the environment.

1. The child acquires his first n (productive) words by matching environmental labels to his own concepts (n is some unknown number between 10 and perhaps 100). The child's concepts can be defined by rules expressing the relations between critical attributes derived from his experiences and actions with objects, people, and events. In the present model the child begins with a relation derived from a schema; thus the relation is child-centered. It may not include all of the relevant invariant features of the concept. It will express only those features that are relevant to the child's actions or experiences with the objects or event. To return to an example given above, the child may eventually form a notion of "table" and be able to name it correctly by the rule: all flat raised surfaces suitable for banging *in conjunction with NO-NO.* Such rules are based on perceptual characteristics particularly salient to the primitive organization of the world, including shape, movement, noise, and other immediately experienced sensory qualities. Change (variance within objects) is a basic and important defining characteristic for the young child. Color, size, and utility to others are rarely the basis for the child's first concept definitions.

2. After the child has acquired n words that match his own concepts he may reverse the process and build a concept to match a word that others use to him. At this time he may also differentiate old concepts to match the usage of the environment. From this point on the dual process advances, but his use of the language will continue to be idiosyncratic to a greater or lesser degree. This internal versus external definition is in fact a significant dimension of cognitive style throughout life.

3. In addition to the conceptual base, the child will make a hypothesis about language function based on a primitive notion of how it is used around him. This hypothesis may be primarily referential or primarily expressive or it may (and eventually must) combine aspects of both. The theory emerges after the child has had some minimal experience with the language, and it helps to define which aspects of the previously organized world will be assigned names. The theory of function interacts with the primitive conceptual system to produce the individual characteristics of the child's early language.

4. For each produced word, the parents provide or fail to provide feedback indicating acceptance or rejection. The more closely the child's cognitive organization matches that of the parent model and the more tolerant of deviations the parents are, the more positive feedback the child will receive. Positive feedback is conducive to rapid acquisition of new words. A child may quickly acquire words for all of his nameable concepts under these conditions and will need, then, to advance cognitively in order to differentiate new concepts or relate old ones before making further language progress.

5. After this point, further progress in concept naming will depend upon the development of additional acquisition strategies appropriate to the stage of the problem solution and upon the use of helpful feedback and selection strategies by the parents. Both expressive and referential language functions must be developed.

The child's choice of problem-solving strategies appears to influence the initial progress to a relatively small extent. The use of some strategies—for example, comprehension and repetition—appears to be an epiphenomenon occurring together with other primary characteristics such as rapid or slow vocabulary growth. Other strategies—for example, imitation—appear to be used in general by children at particular points in the acquisition process; their use is functionally characteristic rather than individually determined. Still other strategies, such as high rate of production and question asking, are stylistic and appear with particular patterns of growth, such as match-referential-acceptance. Although they may be advancing strategies, they appear to be more determined by the language-learning pattern than to be themselves determining. They do not, for example, seem to differentiate among children within a particular pattern.

As a first approximation, then, it can be asserted that the child has a set of strategies available at the outset, which can be used in solving the concept-matching puzzle. Which will be used depends upon point in development, cognitive organization, language-function hypothesis, strategies used by the mother, and cognitive style of the child. It is not the choice of strategy that is critical but rather the factors that determine that choice. These strategies are viewed as processing mechanisms—mediators between environment and internal structure—and this mediating function is determined from two directions.

The place of comprehension in the production problem is an intriguing question that has received little attention here. We may speculate that the child initially learns to respond to commands, games, etc., without relating these words to his own conceptual system. After this he may learn to associate particular referents with his parent's words and thus form a dual system: "yours" (words associated with correct referents that I understand) and "mine" (words referring to my own concepts that I produce). The former set will not be widely generalized—the remarkable generalizations made by young children are based on their own concept domains and concept rules. Eventually these two systems will be brought into correspondence through the concept-matching and differentiating process. Some characteristics of the alien system linger on into adulthood—empty words associated with certain contexts but for which we do not have the correct concept rule, just as characteristics of our own idiosyncratic meaning systems persist.

The present model is concerned with and explains why the child begins with single language units: these express unitary and as yet unrelated concepts. As his ability to communicate aspects of his conceptual system advances he will need words and language structures to express relationships among concepts. This suggests that the language "milestone" of putting words together is symptomatic of a cognitive advance that enables the child to relate two concepts abstractly and simultaneously. (Earlier utterances may relate words to real objects and events [see Greenfield et al., 1973].) Thus, acquisition of syntax depends upon the ability to manipulate symbols for two concepts that are permanently or temporarily related. The relationship, like the concept, is prior to its expression. The expression of relationships will be matched to the language model in much the same way that concept domains are, although the earliest expressions will be constrained by child-defined rules. These rules have been the focus of much recent work on child language and, important as they are, will not be considered here. It will be asserted, however, that the earliest sentences (as opposed to learned phrases) express the child's own conjunction of concepts; complete grammatical forms for these conjunctions will be achieved through the concept-matching paradigm. A simple example will serve here. The child says at some point, "Daddy car," in order to express the intersection of *Daddy's* things and *car* and constrained by his original combining rules to a particular order for the construction. Having expressed this relation it becomes interesting and important to the child to match such a relationship in his mother's speech, and he will find "That's Daddy's hat" or "That's Johnny's car," thus identifying a more advanced model for his expression. Although one expects to find certain basic relationships expressed early by most children, one may account for great differences in the order of acquisition of particular forms by the variety of relationships that a child may wish to express. These considerations certainly predict that expansions should play a significant role in the child's acquisition of grammar, and the lack of firm relationships found thus far remains puzzling. However, it may be that a child who can express a relationship may find any similar expression in his mother's speech equally useful as a model. Alternatively, it may be that expansions are parent strategies that are useful to the child only at particular points in the language-learning sequence, just as is the child's strategy of imitation. Or, all parents may use expansions to a degree that is optimally useful for the child, thus eliminating any explanatory variance.

The implications of this model for the relation of cognition to language development are implicit in all that has been said thus far. First, the basic prerequisite of language learning is conceptualization (a point emphasized by Lenneberg [1967]). Thus, those children who are more advanced in this process will be more advanced in language. Children who are intellectually deficient will be slow in all phases of learning to talk. Moreover, the present model shows why some children who are not inherently slow learners or poor conceptualizers may be slow in learning the language because of deviant early conceptual systems. The slight but consistent sex difference observed between boys and girls in the early years of language learning may be related to the fact that boys more frequently have conceptual organizations that differ from the standard reflected in their mother's language. For example, they may more often emphasize activity or affectivity rather than things and social relationships.

Such conceptual differenecs may also explain the language differences often observed between social classes (see Bernstein 1964, 1970). Two other factors, however, seem to be equally or perhaps more important in this connection. First is the type of language—that is, the language function—emphasized by the child. This factor, whether it emanates from the child or from the language environment, sets the range of topics that the child will initially talk about. Given the highly thing-oriented nature of Western thought and schooling, the child who talks about things (names them, describes them, relates them) to his parents will seem to be (correctly or not) cogni-

tively more advanced than the child who talks about his own needs and feelings and about social events. Second is the relative emphasis that the child learns to put on his own conceptualizations versus those of others. After his initial word learning, semantic development is a process of refining and adding categories to fit the culture. There remains, however, a great deal of variation in the degree to which the child relies upon his own conceptualizations and the degree to which he accepts those of others. Here the dimension of mother's control and direction of the language-acquisition process becomes extremely important. The greater her control, the more restricted the range of concepts that he will learn. Thus the process of parental education may persuade him that his own categories are not to be trusted and that he must rely upon parents and, later, teachers and scholars to define the world. Critics such as Holt (1967) assert that this is one of the main effects of our educational system. To the extent that the child is not so persuaded he will remain a creator of categories with the potential to make an original contribution to our understanding of the world. This dimension of parental control shows significant variation among mothers and is correlated with their educational achievement as well as with the child's language process, and with functional language type. Thus the dimension of accepting others' control of one's thought processes has its beginnings in the earliest language interchange—in the first interactions between mother and child—and has implications for cognitive functioning reaching far into the educational process and to the frontiers of science itself.

References

Anglin, J. M. *The growth of word meaning.* Cambridge, Mass.: M.I.T. Press, 1970.

Bayley, N. Development of mental abilities. In P. H. Mussen (Ed.), *Carmichael's manual of child psychology.* (3rd ed.) Vol. 1. New York: Wiley, 1970.

Bernstein, B. Elaborated and restricted codes: their social origins and some consequences. *American Anthropologist,* 1964, 66(Pt. 2), 55–69.

Bernstein, B. A sociolinguistic approach to socialization: with some reference to educability. In F. Williams (Ed.), *Language and poverty.* Chicago: Markham, 1970.

Bever, T. G. The cognitive basis for linguistic structures. In J. R. Hayes (Ed.), *Cognition and the development of language.* New York: Wiley, 1970.

Bloom, L. M. *Language development: form and function in emerging grammars.* Cambridge, Mass.: M.I.T. Press, 1970.

Bloom, L. M. One word at a time: the use of single word utterances before syntax. In T. E. Moore (Ed.), *Cognitive development and the acquisition of language.* New York: Academic Press, in press.

Brown, R. How shall a thing be called? *Psychological Review,* 1958, 65, 14–21. (a)

Brown, R. *Words and things.* New York: Free Press, 1958. (b)

Brown, R. The development of wh questions in child speech. *Journal of Verbal Learning and Verbal Behavior,* 1968, 7, 279–90.

Brown, R. *Psycholinguistics.* New York: Free Press, 1970.

Brown, R., & Bellugi, U. Three processes in the child's acquisition of syntax, *Harvard Educational Review,* 1964, 34(2), 133–151.

Brown, R.; Cazden, C.; & Bellugi, U. The child's grammar from I to III. In J. P. Hill (Ed.), *The Minnesota Symposium on Child Psychology.* Vol. 2. Minneapolis: University of Minnesota Press, 1969.

Brown, R., & Fraser, C. The acquisition of syntax. In U. Bellugi & R. Brown (Eds.), The acquisition of language. *Monographs of the Society for Research in Child Development,* 1964, 29 (1, Serial No. 92), 43–78.

Bruner, J. S. On cognitive growth I. In J. S. Bruner, R. R. Oliver, & P. M. Greenfield, *Studies in cognitive growth.* New York: Wiley, 1966.

Bruner, J. S.; Goodnow, J. J.; & Austin, G. A. *A study of thinking.* New York: Wiley, 1956.

Bruner, J. S.; Oliver, R. R.; & Greenfield, P. M. *Studies in cognitive growth.* New York: Wiley, 1966.

Cazden, C. B. The acquisition of noun and verb in inflections. *Child Development,* 1968, 39, 433–448.

Cazden, C. B. The neglected situation in child language research and education. In F. Williams (Ed.), *Language and poverty.* Chicago: Markham, 1970.

Chomsky, N. *Aspects of the theory of syntax.* Cambridge, Mass.: M.I.T. Press, 1965.

Clark, E. V. What's in a word? On the child's acquisition of semantics in his first language. In T. E. Moore (Ed.), *Cognitive development and the acquisition of language.* New York: Academic Press, 1973.

Collins, A. H., & Quillian, M. R. Retrieval time from semantic memory. *Journal of Verbal Learning and Verbal Behavior,* 1969, 8, 240–247.

Darley, F. L., & Winitz, H. Age of first word: review of research. *Journal of Speech and Hearing Disabilities,* 1961, 26, 272–290.

Dewey, J. The psychology of infant language. *Psychological Review,* 1894, 1, 63–66.

Ervin, S. M. Imitation and structural change in children's language. In E. H. Lenneberg (Ed.), *New directions in the study of language.* Cambridge, Mass.: M.I.T. Press, 1964.

Ervin-Tripp, S. An overview of grammatical development. In D. Slobin (Ed.), *The ontogenesis of grammar.* New York: Academic Press, 1971.

Francis, H. Structure in the speech of a $2\frac{1}{2}$ year old. *British Journal of Educational Psychology,* 1969, 39, 291–302.

Friedlander, B. Z.; Jacobs, A. C.; Davis, B. B.; & Wetstone, H. S. Time sampling analysis of infants' natural language environments in the home. *Child Development,* 1972, 43, 730–40.

Gardner, R. A., & Gardner, B. T. Teaching sign language to a chimpanzee. *Science,* 1969, 165, 664–672.

Gibson, E. J. *Principles of perceptual learning and development.* New York: Appleton-Century-Crofts, 1969.

Gleason, J. B. Code switching in children's language. Paper presented at the NSF Conference on Developmental Psycholinguistics, Buffalo, New York, August 1971.

Greenfield, P. M. Who is "DADA": some aspects of the semantic and phonological development of a child's first words. *Language and Speech,* 1973.

Greenfield, P. M.; Smith, J. H.; & Laufer, B. Communication and the beginnings of language: the development of semantic structure in one-word speech and beyond. New York: Academic Press, in press.

Guillaume, P. *Imitation in children.* Trans. from French by E. P. Halperin. Chicago: University of Chicago Press, 1971. (Originally published 1926.)

Haith, M.; Kessen, W.; & Collins, D. Response of the human infant to level of complexity of intermittent visual movement. *Journal of Experimental Child Psychology,* 1969, 7, 52–69.

Halliday, M. A. K. Learning to mean. In E. & E. Lenneberg (Eds.), *Foundations of language development: a multidisciplinary approach.* In press.

Hess, R. D., & Shipman, V. Early experience and socialization of cognitive modes in children. *Child Development*, 1965, 36, 869–886.

Holt, J. *How children learn*. New York: Pitman, 1967.

Kagan, J. *Change and continuity in infancy*. New York: Wiley, 1971.

Katz, J. J., & Fodor, J. A. The structure of a semantic theory. *Language*, 1963, 39, 170–210.

Kessen, W. "Stage" and "structure" in the study of children. In W. Kessen & C. Kuhlman (Eds.), Thought in the young child. *Monographs of the Society for Research in Child Development*, 1962, 27(2, Serial No. 83), 65–82.

Kessen, W. The construction and selection of environments. In D. C. Glass (Ed.), *Environmental influences: biology and behavior series*. New York: Rockfeller University Press, 1969.

Kessen, W. The near future of research with young children. Paper prepared for the Office of Economic Opportunity, 1970.

Kessen, W. Early cognitive development: hot or cold? In T. Mischel (Ed.), *Cognitive development and epistemology*. New York: Academic Press, 1971.

Lenneberg, E. H. *Biological foundations of language*. New York: Wiley, 1967.

Leopold, W. K. *Speech development of a bilingual child*. Vol. 1. Evanston, Ill.: Northwestern University Press, 1939.

Leopold, W. K. *Speech development of a bilingual child*. Vol. 3. Evanston, Ill.: Northwestern University Press, 1949.

Lewis, M. M. *Infant speech*. London: Routledge & Kegan Paul, 1951.

Limber, J. The genesis of complex sentences. Paper presented at the NSF Conference on Developmental Psycholinguistics, Buffalo, New York, August 1971.

Lyons, J. *Introduction to theoretical linguistics*. Cambridge: Cambridge University Press, 1969.

McCarthy, D. Language development in children. In L. Carmichael (Ed.), *Manual of child psychology*. (2d ed.) New York: Wiley, 1954.

Macnamara, J. Parsimony and the lexicon. *Language*, 1971, 47, 359–374.

Macnamara, J. Cognitive basis of language learning in infants. *Psychological Review*, 1972, 79, 1–13.

McNeill, D. Developmental psycholinguistics. In F. Smith & G. A. Miller (Eds.), *The genesis of language*. Cambridge, Mass.: M.I.T. Press, 1966.

McNeill, D. Language before symbols: very early children's grammar. *Interchange*, 1970, 1(3), 127–133. (a)

McNeill, D. *The acquisition of language*. New York: Harper & Row, 1970. (b)

Menyuk, P. *The acquisiton and development of language*. Englewood Cliffs, N.J.: Prentice Hall, 1971.

Neisser, U. *Cognitive psychology*. New York: Appleton-Century Crofts, 1967.

Nelson, K. The relation of form recognition to concept development. *Child Development*, 1972, 43, 67–74. (a)

Nelson, K. The semantic structure of the earliest lexicons. Paper presented at the Eastern Psychological Association, Boston, April 1972. (b)

Nelson, K. Some evidence for the cognitive primacy of categorization and its functional basis. *Merrill-Palmer Quarterly*, 1973, 19, 21–39.

Olson, D. R. *Cognitive development: the child's acquisition of diagonality*. New York: Academic Press, 1970. (a)

Olson, D. R. Language and thought: aspects of a cognitive theory of semantics. *Psychological Review*, 1970, 77, 257–273. (b)

Palmer, F. H., & Rees, A. H. Concept training in two-year-olds; procedures and results. Paper presented at the biennial meeting of the Society for Research in Child Development, Santa Monica, California, March 1969.

Piaget, J. *Play, dreams and imitation*. Trans. from French by C. Gattegno & F. M. Hodgson, New York: Norton, 1962.

Posner, M. I., & Warren, R. E. Traces, concepts and conscious constructions. In A. W. Melton and E. Martin (Eds.), *Coding processes in human memory*. Washington, D.C.: Winston, 1972.

Schlesinger, I. M. Production of utterances and language acquisition. In D. Slobin (Ed.), *The ontogenesis of grammar*. New York: Academic Press, 1971.

Shipley, E.; Smith, C. S.; & Gleitman, L. A study in the acquisition of syntax: free responses to verbal commands. *Language*, 1969, 45, 322–342.

Skinner, B. F. *Verbal behavior*. New York: Appleton-Century-Crofts, 1957.

Slobin, D. I. (Ed.) *A field manual for cross-cultural study of the acquisition of communicative competence*. Berkeley: University of California Press, 1967.

Snow, C. E. Mothers' speech to children learning language. *Child Development*, 1972, 43, 549–565.

Staats, A. W. Linguistic-mentalistic theory versus an explanatory S-R learning theory of language development. In D. Slobin (Ed.), *The ontogenesis of grammar*. New York: Academic Press, 1971.

Starr, S. The discrimination of syntactical errors in children under $2\frac{1}{2}$ years of age. Unpublished doctoral dissertation, Boston University, 1972.

Stern, C., & Stern, W. The language of children. In

A. L. Blumenthal, *Language and psychology*. New York: Wiley, 1970.

Stern, W. *Psychology of early childhood*. New York: Holt, 1930.

Suton-Smith, B., & Rosenberg, B. G. *The sibling*. New York: Holt, Rinehart & Winston, 1970.

Toman, W. The duplication theorem of social relationships as tested in the general population. *Psychological Review*, 1971, 78(5), 380–390.

Tracy, F. *The psychology of childhood*. Boston: Heath, 1893.

Velten, H. V. The growth of phonemic and lexical patterns in infant language. *Language*, 1943, 19, 281–292.

#15 # The Logic of
Nonstandard English

William Labov

In the past decade, a great deal of federally sponsored research has been devoted to the educational problems of children in ghetto schools. In order to account for the poor performance of children in these schools, educational psychologists have attempted to discover what kind of disadvantage or defect they are suffering from. The viewpoint that has been widely accepted and used as the basis for large scale intervention programs is that the children show a cultural deficit as a result of an impoverished environment in their early years. Considerable attention has been given to language. In this area the deficit theory appears as the concept of verbal deprivation. Black children from the ghetto area are said to receive little

verbal stimulation, to hear very little well-formed language, and as a result are impoverished in their means of verbal expression. They cannot speak complete sentences, do not know the names of common objects, cannot form concepts or convey logical thoughts.

Unfortunately, these notions are based upon the work of educational psychologists who know very little about language and even less about black children. The concept of verbal deprivation has no basis in social reality. In fact, black children in the urban ghettos receive a great deal of verbal stimulation, hear more well-formed sentences than middle-class children, and participate fully in a highly verbal culture. They have the same basic vocabulary, possess the same capacity for conceptual learning, and use the same logic as anyone else who learns to speak and understand English.

· · · ·

SOURCE: Reprinted in abridged form, with permission of the author, from Chapter 5 of *Language in the Inner City*. Philadelphia: University of Pennsylvania Press, 1972. This paper was originally presented in 1969 at the 20th Annual Georgetown Round Table meeting on Linguistics and Language Studies, Washington, D.C.

VERBALITY AND VERBOSITY

The general setting in which the deficit theory arises consists of a number of facts which are known to all of us. One is that black children in the central urban ghettos do badly in all school subjects, including arithmetic and reading.

. . . . .

The most extreme view which proceeds from this orientation—and one that is now being widely accepted—is that lower-class black children have no language at all. The notion is first drawn from Basil Bernstein's writings that "much of lower-class language consists of a kind of incidental 'emotional' accompaniment to action here and now" (Jensen 1968, p. 118). Bernstein's views are filtered through a strong bias against all forms of working-class behavior, so that middle-class language is seen as superior in every respect—as "more abstract, and necessarily somewhat more flexible, detailed and subtle" (p. 119).

. . . . .

Here, for example, is a complete interview with a black child, one of hundreds carried out in a New York City school. The boy enters a room where there is a large, friendly, white interviewer, who puts on the table in front of him a toy and says: "Tell me everything you can about this." (The interviewer's further remarks are in parentheses).

[12 seconds of silence]
(What would you say it looks like?)
[8 seconds of silence]
A space ship.
(Hmmmm.)
[13 seconds of silence]
Like a je-et.
[12 seconds of silence]
Like a plane.
[20 seconds of silence]
(What color is it?)
Orange. (2 seconds) An' whi-ite. (2 seconds) An' green.
[6 seconds of silence]

(An' what could you use it for?)
[8 seconds of silence]
A je-et.
[6 seconds of silence]
(If you had two of them, what would you do with them?)
[6 seconds of silence]
Give one to some-body.
(Hmmm. Who do you think would like to have it?)
[10 seconds of silence]
Cla-rence.
(Mm. Where do you think we could get one of these?)
At the store.
(Oh ka-ay!)

We have here . . . defensive, monosyllabic behavior. . . .What is the situation that produces it? The child is in an asymmetrical situation where anything he says can literally be held against him. He has learned a number of devices to avoid saying anything in this situation, and he works very hard to achieve this end.

. . . . .

If one takes this interview as a measure of the verbal capacity of the child, it must be as his capacity to defend himself in a hostile and threatening situation. But unfortunately, thousands of such interviews are used as evidence of the child's total verbal capacity, or more simply his verbality. It is argued that this lack of verbality explains his poor performance in school. Operation Head Start and other intervention programs have largely been based upon the deficit theory— the notions that such interviews give us a measure of the child's verbal capacity and that the verbal stimulation which he has been missing can be supplied in a preschool environment.

. . . . .

The view of the black speech community which we obtain from our work in the ghetto areas is precisely the opposite from that reported by Deutsch or by Bereiter and Engelmann. We see a child bathed in verbal stimulation from morning to night. We see many speech events which depend upon the competitive exhibition of verbal skills—sounding, singing, toasts, rifting, louding–a whole range of activities in which the individual gains status through his use of language (see Labov, et al., 1968, section 4.2). We see the younger child trying to acquire these skills from older children, hanging around on the outskirts of older peer groups, and imitating this behavior to the best of his ability. We see no connection between verbal skill in the speech events characteristic of the street culture and success in the schoolroom.

.   .   .   .

Our work in the speech community makes it painfully obvious that in many ways working-class speakers are more effective narrators, reasoners, and debaters than many middle-class speakers who temporize, qualify, and lose their argument in a mass of irrelevant detail. Many academic writers try to rid themselves of that part of middle-class style that is empty pretension, and keep that part that is needed for precision. But the average middle-class speaker that we encounter makes no such effort; he is enmeshed in verbiage, the victim of sociolinguistic factors beyond his control.

I would like to contrast two speakers dealing with roughly the same topic—matters of belief. The first is Larry H., a fifteen-year-old core member of the Jets, being interviewed by John Lewis. Larry is one of the loudest and roughest members of the Jets, one who gives the least recognition to the conventional rules of politeness. For most readers of this paper, first contact with Larry would produce some fairly negative reactions on both sides. It is probable that you would not like him any more than his teachers do. Larry causes trouble in and out of school. He was put back from the eleventh grade to the ninth, and has been threatened with further action by the school authorities.

JL: What happens to you after you die? Do you know?

Larry: Yeah, I know. (What?) After they put you in the ground, your body turns into—ah—bones, an' shit.

JL: What happens to your spirit?

Larry: Your spirit—soon as you die, your spirit leaves you. (And where does the spirit go?) Well, it all depends . . . (On what?) You know, like some people say if you're good an' shit, your spirit goin' t'heaven . . . 'n' if you bad, your spirit goin' to hell. Well, bullshit! Your spirit goin' to hell anyway, good or bad.

JL: Why?

Larry: Why? I'll tell you why. 'Cause, you see, doesn' nobody really know that it's a God, y'know, 'cause I mean I have seen black gods, pink gods, white gods, all color gods, and don't nobody know it's really a God. An' when they be sayin' if you good, you goin' t'heaven, tha's bullshit, 'cause you ain't goin' to no heaven, 'cause it ain't no heaven for you to go to.

Larry is a paradigmatic speaker of the Black English Vernacular (BEV) as opposed to standard English. His grammar shows a high concentration of such characteristic BEV forms as negative inversion ("don't nobody know . . ."), negative concord ("you ain't goin' to no heaven . . ."), invariant *be* ("when they be sayin' . . ."), dummy *it* for standard *there* ("it ain't no heaven . . ."), optional copula deletion ("if you're good . . . if you bad . . .") and full forms of auxiliaries ("I have seen . . ."). The only standard English influence in this passage is the one case of "doesn't" instead of the invariant "don't" of BEV. Larry also provides a paradigmatic example of the rhetorical style of BEV: he can sum up a complex argument in a few words, and the full force of his opinions come through without qualification or reservation. He is eminently quotable, and his interviews give us many concise statements of the BEV point of view. One can almost say that Larry speaks the BEV culture (see Labov, et al. 1968, vol. 2, pp. 38, 71–73, 291–92).

It is the logical form of this passage which is

of particular interest here. Larry presents a complex set of interdependent propositions which can be explicated by setting out the standard English equivalents in linear order. The basic argument is to deny the twin propositions:

(A) If you are good, *(B)* then your spirit will go to heaven.

(∿A) If you are bad, *(C)* then your spirit will go to hell.

Larry denies *(B)* and asserts that if *(A)* or *(∿A)*, then *(C)*. His argument may be outlined as follows:

1. Everyone has a different idea of what God is like.
2. Therefore nobody really knows that God exists.
3. If there is a heaven, it was made by God.
4. If God doesn't exist, he couldn't have made heaven.
5. Therefore heaven does not exist.
6. You can't go somewhere that doesn't exist.

(∿B) Therefore you can't go to heaven.
(C) Therefore you are going to hell.

The argument is presented in the order: *(C)*, because (2) because (1), therefore (2), therefore *(∿B)* because (5) and (6). Part of the argument implicit: the connection (2) therefore *(∿B)* leaves unstated the connecting links (3) and (4), and in this interval Larry strengthens the propositions from the form (2) "Nobody knows if there is . . ." to (5) "There is no . . . ." Otherwise, the case is presented explicitly as well as economically. The complex argument is summed up in Larry's last sentence, which shows formally the dependence of *(∿B)* on (5) and (6):

An' when they be sayin' if you good, you goin' t'heaven (the proposition, if *A*, then *B*),

Tha's bullshit (is absurd),

'cause you ain't goin' to no heaven (because *B)*

'cause it ain't no heaven for you to go to (because (5) and (6)).

This hypothetical argument is not carried on at a high level of seriousness. It is a game played with ideas as counters, in which opponents use a wide variety of verbal devices to win. There is no personal commitment to any of these propositions, and no reluctance to strengthen one's argument by bending the rules of logic as in the (2)-(5) sequence. But if the opponent invokes the rules of logic, they hold. In John Lewis's interviews, he often makes this move, and the force of his argument is always acknowledged and countered within the rules of logic. In this case, he pointed out the fallacy that the argument (2)-(3)-(4)-(5)-(6) leads to *(∿C)* as well as *(∿B)*, so it cannot be used to support Larry's assertion *(C)*:

> JL: Well, if there's no heaven, how could there be a hell?
> Larry: I mean—ye-eah. Well, let me tell you, it ain't no hell, 'cause this is hell right here, y'know! (This is hell?) Yeah, this is hell right here!

Larry's answer is quick, ingenious, and decisive. The application of the (3)-(4)-(5) argument to hell is denied, since hell is here, and therefore conclusion *(C)* stands. These are not ready-made or preconceived opinions, but new propositions devised to win the logical argument in the game being played. The reader will note the speed and precision of Larry's mental operations. He does not wander, or insert meaningless verbiage. The only repetition is (2), placed before and after (1) in his original statement. It is often said that the nonstandard vernacular is not suited for dealing with abstract or hypothetical questions, but in fact speakers from the black community take great delight in exercising their wit and logic on the most improbable and problematical matters. Despite the fact that Larry H. does not believe in God, and has just denied all knowledge of him, John Lewis advances the following hypothetical question:

> JL: . . . but, just say that there is a God, what color is he? White or black?
> Larry: Well, if it is a God . . . I wouldn' know what color, I couldn' say—couldn' nobody say what color he is or really *would* be.

JL: But now, jus' suppose there was a God—
Larry: Unless'n they say . . .
JL: No, I was jus' sayin' jus' suppose there is a God, would he be white or black?
Larry: . . . He'd be white, man.
JL: Why?
Larry: Why? I'll tell you why. 'Cause the average whitey out here got everything, you dig? And the nigger ain't got shit, y'know? Y'unnerstan'? So—um—for—in order for *that* to happen, you know it ain't no black God that's doin' that bullshit.

No one can hear Larry's answer to this question without being convinced that they are in the presence of a skilled speaker with great "verbal presence of mind," who can use the English language expertly for many purposes. Larry's answer to John Lewis is again a complex argument. The formulation is not standard English, but it is clear and effective even for those not familiar with the vernacular. The nearest standard English equivalent might be: "So you know that God isn't black, because if he was, he wouldn't have arranged things like that."

The reader will have noted that this analysis is being carried out in standard English, and the inevitable challenge is: why not write in BEV, then, or in your own nonstandard dialect? The fundamental reason is, of course, one of firmly fixed social conventions. All communities agree that standard English is the proper medium for formal writing and public communication. Furthermore, it seems likely that standard English has an advantage over BEV in explicit analysis of surface forms, which is what we are doing here. We will return to this opposition between explicitness and logical statement in subsequent sections on grammaticality and logic. First, however, it will be helpful to examine standard English in its primary natural setting, as the medium for informal spoken communication of middle-class speakers.

Let us now turn to the second speaker, an upper-middle-class, college-educated black man (Charles M.) being interviewed by Clarence Robins in our survey of adults in Central Harlem.

CR: Do you know of anything that someone can do, to have someone who has passed on visit him in a dream?
Charles: Well, I even heard my parents say that there is such a thing as something in dreams some things like that, and sometimes dreams do come true. I have personally never had a dream come true. I've never dreamt that somebody was dying and they actually died (Mhm) or that I was going to have ten dollars the next day and somehow I got ten dollars in my pocket (Mhm). I don't particularly believe in that, I don't think it's true. I do feel, though, that there is such a thing as—ah—witchcraft. I do feel that in certain cultures there is such a thing as witchcraft, or some sort of *science* of witchcraft; I don't think that it's just a matter of believing hard enough that there is such a thing as witchcraft. I do believe that there is such a thing that a person can put himself in a state of *mind* (Mhm), or that—er—something could be given them to intoxicate them in a certain—to a certain frame of mind—that—that could actually be considered witchcraft.

Charles M. is obviously a good speaker who strikes the listener as well-educated, intelligent, and sincere. He is a likeable and attractive person, the kind of person that middle-class listeners rate very high on a scale of job suitability and equally high as a potential friend. His language is more moderate and tempered than Larry's; he makes every effort to qualify his opinions, and seems anxious to avoid any misstatements or overstatements. From these qualities emerge the primary characteristic of this passage—its verbosity. Words multiply, some modifying and qualifying, other repeating or padding the main argument. The first half of this extract is a response to the initial question on dreams, basically:

1. Some people say that dreams sometimes come true.
2. I have never had a dream come true.
3. Therefore I don't believe (1).

Some characteristic filler phrases appear here: *such a thing as, some things like that,* and *par-*

ticularly. Two examples of dreams given after (2) are afterthoughts that might have been given after (1). Proposition (3) is stated twice for no obvious reason. Nevertheless, this much of Charles M.'s response is well-directed to the point of the question. He then volunteers a statement of his beliefs about witchcraft which shows the difficulty of middle-class speakers who (a) want to express a belief in something but (b) want to show themselves as judicious, rational, and free from superstitions. The basic proposition can be stated simply in five words:

"But I believe in witchcraft."

However, the idea is enlarged to exactly 100 words, and it is difficult to see what else is being said. In the following quotations, padding which can be removed without change in meaning is shown in parentheses.

(1) "I (do) feel, though, that there is (such a thing as) witchcraft." *Feel* seems to be a euphemism for "believe."

(2) "(I do feel that) in certain cultures (there is such a thing as witchcraft)." This repetition seems designed only to introduce the word *culture,* which lets us know that the speaker knows about anthropology. Does *certain cultures* mean "not in ours" or "not in all"?

(3) "(or some sort of *science* of witchcraft.)" This addition seems to have no clear meaning at all. What is a "science" of witchcraft as opposed to just plain witchcraft? The main function is to introduce the word *science,* though it seems to have no connection to what follows.

(4) "I don't think that it's just (a matter of) believing hard enough that (there is such a thing as) witchcraft." The speaker argues that witchcraft is not merely a belief; there is more to it.

(5) "I (do) believe that (there is such a thing that) a person can put himself in a state of mind . . . that (could actually be considered) witchcraft." Is witchcraft as a state of mind different from the state of belief, denied in (4)?

(6) "or that something could be given them to intoxicate them (to a certain frame of mind) . . . ." The third learned word, *intoxicate,* is introduced

by this addition. The vacuity of this passage becomes more evident if we remove repetitions, fashionable words and stylistic decorations:

But I believe in witchcraft.
I don't think witchcraft is just a belief.

A person can put himself or be put in a state of mind that is witchcraft. Without the extra verbiage and the "OK" words like *science, culture,* and *intoxicate,* Charles M. appears as something less than a first-rate thinker. The initial impression of him as a good speaker is simply our long-conditioned reaction to middle-class verbosity. We know that people who use these stylistic devices are educated people, and we are inclined to credit them with saying something intelligent. Our reactions are accurate in one sense. Charles M. is more educated than Larry. But is he more rational, more logical, more intelligent? Is he any better at thinking out a problem to its solution? Does he deal more easily with abstractions? There is no reason to think so. Charles M. succeeds in letting us know that he is educated, but in the end we do not know what he is trying to say, and neither does he.

In the previous section I have attempted to explain the origin of the myth that lower-class black children are nonverbal. The examples just given may help to account for the corresponding myth that middle-class language is in itself better suited for dealing with abstract, logically complex, or hypothetical questions. These examples are intended to have certain negative force. They are not controlled experiments. On the contrary, this and the preceding section are designed to convince the reader that the controlled experiments that have been offered in evidence are misleading. The only thing that is controlled is the superficial form of the stimulus. All children are asked "What do you think of capital punishment?" or "Tell me everything you can about this." But the speaker's interpretation of these requests, and the action he believes is appropriate in response is completely uncontrolled. One can view these test stimuli as requests for information, commands for action, threats of punishment, or meaningless sequences of words. They are probably intended as something altogether different—as requests for display, but in any case the experimenter is normally unaware of the problem of interpretation. The methods of educational psychologists such as used by Deutsch, Jensen, and Bereiter follow the pattern for animal experiments where motivation is controlled by simple methods as withholding food until a certain weight reduction is reached. With human subjects, it is absurd to believe that identical stimuli are obtained by asking everyone the same question.

Since the crucial intervening variables of interpretation and motivation are uncontrolled, most of the literature on verbal deprivation tells us nothing about the capacities of children. They are only the trappings of science, approaches which substitute the formal procedures of the scientific method for the activity itself. With our present limited grasp of these problems, the best we can do to understand the verbal capacities of children is to study them within the cultural context in which they were developed.

It is not only the black vernacular which should be studied in this way, but also the language of middle-class children. The explicitness and precision which we hope to gain from copying middle-class forms are often the product of the test situation, and limited to it. For example, it was stated in the first part of this paper that working-class children hear more well-formed sentences than middle-class children. This statement may seem extraordinary in the light of the current belief of many linguists that most people do not speak in well-formed sentences, and that their actual speech production, or performance, is ungrammatical. But those who have worked with any body of natural speech know that this is not the case. Our own studies (Labov 1966) of the grammaticality of everyday speech show that the great majority of utterances in all contexts are complete sentences, and most of the rest can be reduced to grammatical form by a small set of editing rules. The proportions of grammatical sentences vary with class backgrounds and styles. The highest percentage of well-formed sentences are found in casual speech, and working-class speakers use more well-formed sentences than middle-class speakers. The widespread myth that most speech is ungrammatical is no doubt based upon tapes made at learned conferences, where we obtain the maximum number of irreducibly ungrammatical sequences.

It is true that technical and scientific books are written in a style which is markedly middle-class. But unfortunately, we often fail to achieve the explicitness and precision which we look for in such writing, and the speech of many middle-class people departs maximally from this target. All too often, standard English is represented by a style that is simultaneously overparticular and vague. The accumulating flow of words buries rather than strikes the target. It is this verbosity which is most easily taught and most easily learned, so that words take the place of thoughts, and nothing can be found behind them.

When Bernstein (e.g., 1966) describes his elaborated code in general terms, it emerges as a subtle and sophisticated mode of planning utterances, where the speaker is achieving structural variety, taking the other person's knowledge into account, and so on. But when it comes to describing the actual difference between middle-class and working-class speakers (Bernstein 1966), we are presented with a proliferation of "I think," of the passive, of modals and auxiliaries, of the first-person pronoun, of uncommon words, and so on. But these are the bench marks of hemming and hawing, backing and filling, that are used by Charles M., the devices which so often obscure whatever positive contribution education can make to our use of language. When we have discovered how much of middle-class style is a matter of fashion and how much actually helps us express ideas clearly, we will have done ourselves a great service. We will then be in a position to say what standard grammatical rules must be taught to nonstandard speakers in the early grades.

. . . .

LOGIC

For many generations, American schoolteachers have devoted themselves to correcting a small number of nonstandard English rules to their standard equivalents, under the impression that they were teaching logic. This view has been reinforced and given theoretical justification by the claim that BEV lacks the means for the expression of logical thought.

Let us consider for a moment the possibility that black children do not operate with the same logic that middle-class adults display. This would inevitably mean that sentences of a certain grammatical form would have different truth values for the two types of speakers. One of the most obvious places to look for such a difference is in the handling of the negative, and here we encounter one of the nonstandard items which has been stigmatized as illogical by schoolteachers—the double negative, or as we term it, *negative concord*. A child who says "He don't know nothing" is often said to be making an illogical statement without knowing it. According to the teacher, the child wants to say "He knows nothing" but puts in an extra negative without realizing it, and so conveys the opposite meaning, "He does not know nothing," which reduces to "He knows something." I need not emphasize that this is an absurd interpretation. If a nonstandard speaker wishes to say that "He does not know *nothing*," he does so by simply placing contrastive stress on both negatives as I have done here ("He *don't* know *nothing*") indicating that they are derived from two underlying negatives in the deep structure. But note that the middle-class speaker does exactly the same thing when he wants to signal the existence of two underlying negatives: "He *doesn't* know *nothing*." In the standard form with one underlying negative ("He

doesn't know anything"), the indefinite *anything* contains the same superficial reference to a preceding negative in the surface structure as the nonstandard *nothing* does. In the corresponding positive sentences, the indefinite *something* is used. The dialect difference, like most of the differences between the standard and nonstandard forms, is one of surface form, and has nothing to do with the underlying logic of the sentence.

We can summarize the ways in which the two dialects differ:

	Standard English, SE	Black English Vernacular, BEV
Positive:	He knows something.	He know something.
Negative:	He doesn't know anything.	He don't know nothing.
Double Negative:	He *doesn't* know *nothing*.	He *don't* know *nothing*.

This array makes it plain that the only difference between the two dialects is in superficial form. When a single negative is found in the deep structure, standard English converts *something* to the indefinite *anything;* BEV converts it to *nothing*. When speakers want to signal the presence of two negatives, they do it the same way. No one would have any difficulty constructing the same table of truth values for both dialects. English is a rare language in its insistence that the negative particle be incorporated in the first indefinite only. The Anglo-Saxon authors of the Peterborough Chronicle were surely not illogical when they wrote *For ne waeren nan martyrs swa pined alse he waeron,* literally, "For never weren't no martyrs so tortured as there were." The "logical" forms of current standard English are simply the accepted conventions of our present-day formal style. Russian, Spanish, French, and Hungarian show the same negative concord as nonstandard English, and they are surely not illogical in this. What is termed "logical" in standard English is of course the conventions which are habitual. The distribution of negative concord in English dialects can be summarized in this way (Labov, et al. 1968, section 3.6; Labov 1968):

1. In all dialects of English, the negative is attracted to a lone indefinite before the verb: "Nobody knows anything," not "Anybody doesn't know anything."
2. In some nonstandard white dialects, the negative also combines optionally with all other indefinites: "Nobody knows nothing," "He never took none of them."
3. In other white nonstandard dialects, the negative may also appear in preverbal position in the same clause: "Nobody doesn't know nothing."
4. In Black English Vernacular, negative concord is obligatory to all indefinites within the clause, and it may even be added to preverbal position in following clauses: "Nobody didn't know he didn't" (meaning, "Nobody knew he did").

Thus all dialects of English share a categorical rule which attracts the negative to an indefinite subject, and they merely differ in the extent to which the negative particle is also distributed to other indefinites in preverbal position. It would have been impossible for us to arrive at this analysis if we did not know that black speakers are using the same underlying logic as everyone else.

Negative concord is more firmly established in Black English Vernacular than in other nonstandard dialects. The white nonstandard speaker shows variation in this rule, saying one time, "Nobody ever goes there" and the next, "Nobody never goes there." Core speakers of the BEV vernacular consistently use the latter form. In repetition tests which we conducted with adolescent blacks (Labov, et al. 1968, section 3.9), standard forms were repeated with negative concord. Here, for example, are three trials by two thirteen-year-old members (Boot and David) of the Thunderbirds:

Model by interviewer: "Nobody ever sat at any of those desks, anyhow."
Boot:
　(1) Nobody never sa—No [whitey] never sat at any o' tho' dess, anyhow.
　(2) Nobody never sat any any o' tho' dess, anyhow.
　(3) Nobody as ever sat at no desses, anyhow.
David:
　(1) Nobody ever sat in-in-in-in- none o'—say it again?
　(2) Nobody never sat in none o' tho' desses anyhow.
　(3) Nobody—aww! Nobody never ex—Dawg!

It can certainly be said that Boot and David fail the test; they have not repeated the sentence correctly—that is, word for word. But have they failed because they could not grasp the meaning of the sentence? The situation is in fact just the opposite; they failed because they perceived only the meaning and not the superficial form. Boot and David are typical of many speakers who do not perceive the surface details of the utterance so much as the underlying semantic structure, which they unhesitatingly translate into the vernacular form.

Model:
　I asked Alvin if he knows how to play basketball.
Boot:
　I ax Alvin do he know how to play basketball.
Money:
　I ax Alvin if—do he know how to play basketball.
Model:
　I asked Alvin whether he knows how to play basketball.
Larry F:
　(1) I axt Alvin does he know how to play basketball.
　(2) I axt Alvin does he know how to play basketball.

Here the difference between the words used in the model sentence and in the repetition is striking. Again, there is a failure to pass the test. But it is also true that these boys understand the standard sentence, and translate it with extraordinary speed into the BEV form, which is here the regular Southern colloquial form.

To pass the repetition test, Boot and the others have to learn to listen to surface detail. They do not need a new logic; they need practice in paying attention to the explicit form of an utterance rather than its meaning. Careful attention to surface features is a temporary skill needed for language learning—and neglected thereafter by competent speakers.

.   .   .   .

Linguists are in an excellent position to demonstrate the fallacies of the verbal deprivation theory. All linguists agree that nonstandard dialects are highly structured systems. They do not see these dialects as accumulations of errors caused by the failure of their speakers to master standard English. When linguists hear black children saying "He crazy" or "Her my friend," they do not hear a primitive language. Nor do they believe that the speech of working-class people is merely a form of emotional expression, incapable of expressing logical thought.

.   .   .   .

When linguists say that BEV is a system, we mean that it differs from other dialects in regular and rule-governed ways, so that it has equivalent ways of expressing the same logical content. When we say that it is a separate subsystem, we mean that there are compensating sets of rules which combine in different ways to preserve the distinctions found in other dialects. Thus as noted above BEV does not use the *if* or *whether* complementizer in embedded questions, but the meaning is preserved by the formal device of reversing the order of subject and auxiliary.

.   .   .   .

Linguists now agree that teachers must know as much as possible about the Black English Vernacular as a communicative system.

.   .   .   .

The exact nature and relative importance of the structural differences between BEV and standard English are not in question here. It is agreed that the teacher must approach the teaching of the standard through a knowledge of the child's own system. The methods used in teaching English as a foreign language are recommended, not to declare that BEV is a foreign language, but to underline the importance of studying the native dialect as a coherent system for communication. This is in fact the method that should be applied in any English class.

.   .   .   .

That educational psychology should be strongly influenced by a theory so false to the facts of language is unfortunate; but that children should be the victims of this ignorance is intolerable. It may seem that the fallacies of the verbal deprivation theory are so obvious that they are hardly worth exposing. I have tried to show that such exposure is an important job for us to undertake. If linguists can contribute some of their available knowledge and energy toward this end, we will have done a great deal to justify the support that society has given to basic research in our field.

.   .   .   .

References

Alatis, J., ed. *Georgetown Monographs in Language and Linguistics, No. 22.* Washington, D.C.: Georgetown University Press, 1970.

Bereiter, C., and Engelmann, S. *Teaching Disadvantaged Children in the Preschool.* Englewood Cliffs, N.J.: Prentice-Hall, 1966.

Bereiter, C.; Englemann, S.; Osborn, Jean; and Reidford, P. A. An academically oriented preschool for culturally deprived children. In F. Hechinger, ed., *Pre-school Education Today.* New York: Doubleday, 1966.

Bernstein, B. Elaborated and restricted codes: Their social origins and some consequences. In A. G. Smith, ed., *Communication and Culture.* New York: Holt, Rinehart & Winston, 1966.

Blum, A. The sociology of mental illness. In J. Douglas, ed., *Deviance and Respectability.* New York: Basic Books, (in press).

Caldwell, Bettye M. What is the optimal learning environment for the young child? *American J. Orthopsychiatry* 1967, 37: 8–21.

Chomsky, N. *Aspects of the Theory of Syntax.* Cambridge, Mass.: M.I.T. Press, 1965.

Coleman, J. S., et al. *Equality of Educational Opportunity.* Washington, D.C.: U.S. Office of Education, 1966.

Deutsch, M., and associates. *The Disadvantaged Child.* New York: Basic Books, 1967.

Deutsch, M.; Katz, I.; and Jensen, A. R., eds., *Social Class, Race, and Psychological Development.* New York: Holt, Rinehart & Winston, 1968.

Gans, H. *The Urban Villagers.* New York: Free Press, 1962.

Heber, R. Research on education and habilitation of the mentally retarded. Paper read at Conference on Sociocultural Aspects of Mental Retardation, June 1968, Peabody College, Nashville, Tenn.

Jensen, A. R. Social class and verbal learning. In M. Deutsch, et al., eds., *Social Class, Race, and Psychological Development.* New York: Holt, Rinehart & Winston, 1968.

———. How much can we boost IQ and scholastic achievement? *Harvard Educational Review* 1969, 39: 1–123.

Labov, W. On the grammaticaly of everyday speech. Paper presented at the annual meeting of the Linguistic Society of America, December 1966, New York.

———. Some sources of reading problems for Negro speakers of nonstandard English. In A. Frazier, ed., *New Directions in Elementary English.* Champaign, Ill.: National Council of Teachers of English, 1967. Also reprinted in J. C. Baratz and R. W. Shuy, eds., *Teaching Black Children to Read.* Washington, D.C.: Center for Applied Linguistics, 1969.

———. Negative attraction and negative concord in four English dialects. Paper presented at the annual meeting of the Linguistic Society of America, December 1968, New York.

———. Contraction, deletion, and inherent variability of the English copula. *Language* 1969, 45: 715–62.

Labov, W.; Cohen, P.; Robins, C. A preliminary study of the structure of English used by Negro and Puerto Rican speakers in New York City. Final report, U.S. Office of Education Cooperative Research Project No. 3091, 1965.

Labov, W.; Cohen, P.; Robins, C.; and Lewis, J. A study of the nonstandard English of Negro and Puerto Rican speakers in New York City. Final report, U. S. Office of Education Cooperative Research Project No. 3288 Vols. 1, 2. Mimeographed. Columbia University, 1968.

Labov, W., and Robins, C. A note on the relation of reading failure to peer-group status in urban ghettos. *The Teachers College Record* 1969, 70: 396–405.

Langer, T. S., and Michaels, S. T. *Life Stress and Mental Health.* New York: Free Press, 1963.

Rosenthal, R., and Jacobson, Lenore. Self-fulfilling prophecies in the classroom: teachers' expectations as unintended determinants of pupils' intellectual competence. In M. Deutsch, et al., eds., *Social Class, Race, and Psychological Development.* New York: Holt, Rinehart & Winston, 1968.

United States Commission of Civil Rights. *Racial Isolation in the Public Schools,* Vol. 1. Washington, D.C.: U.S. Government Printing Office, 1967.

Whiteman, M., and Deutsch, M. Social disadvantage as related to intellective and language development. In M. Deutsch, et al., eds., *Social Class, Race, and Psychological Development.* New York: Holt, Rinehart & Winston, 1968.

Wilmott, P. *Adolescent Boys of East London.* London: Routledge & Kegan Paul, 1966.

LANGUAGE = WHAT IS THOUGHT
SPEECH = " " SAID

LANGUAGE &/OR SPEECH
   CAN BE A TOOL OF NON-COMMUNICATION* AS WELL AS OF COMMUNICATION

*AS IN AMERICAN POLITICS
ALSO AS IN WATERGATE TACTICS

Misreading: A Search for Causes

Donald Shankweiler

Isabelle Y. Liberman

Because speech is universal and reading is not, we may suppose that the latter is more difficult and less natural. Indeed, we know that a large part of the early education of the school child must be devoted to instruction in reading and that the instruction often fails, even in the most favorable circumstances. Judging from the long history of debate concerning the proper methods of teaching children to read [Mathews 1966], the problem has always been with us. Nor do we appear to have come closer to a solution: we are still a long way from understanding how children learn to read and what has gone wrong when they fail.

.   .   .   .   .

SOURCE: Reprinted, in abridged form, from *Language by Ear and Eye: The Relationships Between Speech and Reading*, edited by J. F. Kavanagh & I. G. Mattingly, by permission of the author and the M.I.T. Press, Cambridge, Massachusetts.

THE WORD AS THE LOCUS OF DIFFICULTY IN BEGINNING READING

One often encounters the claim that there are many children who can read individual words well yet do not seem able to comprehend connected text [Anderson and Dearborn 1952; Goodman 1968]. The existence of such children is taken to support the view that methods of instruction that stress spelling-to-sound correspondences and other aspects of decoding are insufficient and may even produce mechanical readers who are expert at decoding but fail to comprehend sentences. It may well be that such children do exist; if so, they merit careful study. Our experience suggests that the problem is rare, and that poor reading of text with little comprehension among beginning readers is usually a consequence of reading words poorly (i.e., with many errors and/or at a slow rate).

.   .   .   .   .

175

The purpose of our first experiment was to investigate whether the main source of difficulty in beginning reading is at the level of connected text or at the word level. We wished to know how well one can predict a child's degree of fluency in oral reading of paragraph material from his performance (accuracy and reaction time) on selected words presented in lists.

For a variety of children in the early grades, there is a moderate-to-high relationship between errors in reading words on word lists (see Tables 1 & 2) and performance on the Gray paragraphs. We would expect to find a degree of correlation between reading words and reading paragraphs (because the former are contained in the latter), but not correlations as high as the ones we did find if it were the case that many children can read words fluently but cannot deal effectively with organized strings of words. These correlations suggest that the child may encounter his major difficulty at the level of the word—his reading of connected text tends to be only as good or as poor as his reading of individual words. Put another way, the problems of the beginning reader appear to have more to do with the synthesis of syllables than with scanning of larger chunks of connected text.

. . . . .

The Error Pattern in Misreading

We examined the error rate in reading in relation to segment position in the word (initial, medial, and final) and in relation to the type of segment (consonant or vowel).

List 2 (Table 2) was designed primarily for that purpose. It consisted of 204 real-word CVC (or CCVC and CVCC) monosyllables chosen to give equal representation to most of the consonants, consonant clusters, and vowels of English. Each of the 25 initial consonants and consonant clusters occurred eight times in the list, and each final consonant or consonant cluster likewise occurred eight times. Each of eight vowels occurred approximately 25 times. This characteristic of equal

Table 1. Reading list 1: Containing reversible words, reversible letters, and primer sight words

1. of	21. two	41. bat
2. boy	22. war	42. tug
3. now	23. bed	43. form
4. tap	24. felt	44. left
5. dog	25. big	45. bay
6. lap	26. not	46. how
7. tub	27. yam	47. dip
8. day	28. peg	48. no
9. for	29. was	49. pit
10. bad	30. tab	50. cap
11. out	31. won	51. god
12. pat	32. pot	52. top
13. ten	33. net	53. pal
14. gut	34. pin	54. may
15. cab	35. from	55. bet
16. pit	36. ton	56. raw
17. saw	37. but	57. pay
18. get	38. who	58. tar
19. rat	39. nip	59. dab
20. dig	40. on	60. tip

opportunities for error within each constant and vowel category enables us to assess the child's knowledge of some of the spelling patterns of English.

The manner of presentation was the same as for List 1 (Table 1). The responses were recorded and transcribed twice by a phonetically trained person. The few discrepancies between first and second transcription were easily resolved. Although it was designed for a different purpose, List 1 also gives information about the effect of the segment position within the syllable upon error rate and the relative difficulty of different kinds of segments. We therefore analyzed results from both lists in the same way; and as we shall see, the results are highly comparable. . . .

We have chosen to use phonetic transcription[1] rather than standard orthography in noting down the responses, because we believe that phonetic tabulation and analysis of oral reading errors has

---

[1] In making the transcription, the transcriber was operating with reference to the normal allophonic ranges of the phonemic categories in English.

powerful advantages that outweigh the traditional problems associated with it. If the major sources of error in reading the words are at some linguistic level, as we have argued, phonetic transcription of the responses should greatly simplify the task of detecting the sources of error and making them explicit. Transcription has the additional value of enabling us to make a direct comparison between errors in reading and in oral repetition.

Table 2. Reading list 2: Presenting equal opportunities for error on each initial consonant,* medial vowel, and final consonant*

help	teethe	than	jots	thus
pledge	stoops	dab	shoots	smelt
weave	bilk	choose	with	nudge
lips	hulk	thong	noose	welt
wreath	jog	puts	chin	chops
felt	shook	hood	rob	vim
zest	plume	fun	plot	vet
crisp	thatch	sting	book	zip
touch	zig	knelt	milk	plop
palp	teeth	please	vest	smug
stash	moot	this	give	foot
niece	foot's	that	then	chest
soothe	jeeps	dub	plug	should
ding	leave	vast	knob	clots
that's	van	clash	cook	rasp
mesh	cheese	soot	love	shops
deep	vets	sheath	posh	pulp
badge	loops	stop	lisp	wedge
belk	pooch	cob	nest	hatch
gulp	mash	zen	sulk	says
stilt	scalp	push	zips	watch
zag	thud	cleave	would	kelp
reach	booth	mops	tube	sheathe
stock	wreathe	hasp	chap	bush
thief	gasp	them	put	juice
coop	smoothe	good	rook	thieve
theme	feast	fuzz	loom	chaff
cult	jest	smith	judge	stuff
stood	chief	tots	breathe	seethe
these	god	such	whelp	gin
vat	clang	veldt	smash	zoom
hoof	dune	culp	zing	cliff
clog	wasp	wisp	could	plod
move	heath	guest	mob	rough
puss	tooth	bulk	clasp	nook
doom	lodge	silk	smudge	dodge
talc	jam	moose	kilt	thug
shoes	roof	smut	thing	cling
smooch	gap	soup	fog	news
hook	shove	fez	death	look
took	plebe	bing	goose	

*Consonant clusters are counted as one phoneme.

Table 3. Errors in reading in relation to position and type of segment. Percentages of opportunities for error

GROUP*	READING ABILITY	n	AGE RANGE	INITIAL CONSONANT	FINAL CONSONANT	ALL CONSONANTS	VOWEL
C_1	Good††	11	9–10	6	12	9	10
C_2	Poor††	11	9–10	8	14	11	16
B	Poor†	18	8–10	8	14	11	27
Clinic	Poor††	10	10–12	17	24	20	31

*The groups indicated by C_1 and C_2 comprise the upper and lower thirds of Group C in Table 1. Group B is the same as so designated in Table 1. The clinic group is not represented in Table 1.
†List 1 (Table 2)
††List 2 (Table 3)

Table 3 shows errors on the two word lists percentaged against opportunities as measured in four groups of schoolchildren. Group C_1 includes good readers, being the upper third in reading ability of all the third graders in a particular school system; Group C_2 comprises the lower third of the same third-grade population mentioned above; Group B includes the lower third of the entire beginning third grade in another school system; the clinic group contains 10 children, aged between 10 and 12, who had been referred to a reading clinic at the University of Connecticut. In all four groups, the responses given were usually words of English.

Table 3 shows two findings we think are important. First, there is a progression of difficulty with position of the segment in the word; final consonants are more frequently misread than initial ones. Second, more errors are made on vowels than on consonants. The consistency of these findings is impressive because it transcends the particular choice of words and perhaps the level of reading ability.

We will have more to say in a later section about these findings when we consider the differences between reading and speech errors. At this point, we should say that the substantially greater error rate for final consonants than for initial ones is certainly contrary to what would be expected by an analysis of the reading process in terms of sequential probabilities. If the child at the early stages of learning to read were able to utilize the constraints that are built into the language, he would make fewer errors at the end than at the beginning, not more. In fact, what we often see is that the child breaks down after he has gotten the first letter correct and can go no further.

. . . . .

. . . The perception of speech by reading has problems which are separate and distinct from the problems of perceiving speech by ear. We cannot predict the error rate for a given phoneme in reading from its error rate in listening. . . . As for the vowels, they are seldom misheard but often misread (suggesting, incidentally, that the high error rate on vowels in reading cannot be an artifact of transcription difficulties).

Accounting for the Differences in the Error Pattern in Reading and Speech

. . . There are major differences between error patterns in reading and speech. However, they should not be taken to mean that reading and speech are not connected. What they do tell us is that reading presents special problems that reflect the difficulties of the beginning reader in making the link between segments of speech and alphabetic shapes.

·WHY THE INITIAL SEGMENT IS MORE OFTEN CORRECT IN READING We have seen that there is much evidence to indicate that in reading the initial segment of a word is more often correct than succeeding ones, whereas in oral repetition the error rate for initial and final consonants is essentially identical.

One of us [I. Y. Liberman 1971] has suggested a possible explanation for this difference in distribution of errors within the syllable. She pointed out that in reading an alphabetic language like English, the child must be able to segment the words he knows into the phonemic elements that the alphabetic shapes represent. In order to do this, he needs to be consciously aware of the segmentation of the language into units of phonemic size. Seeing the word *cat,* being able to discriminate the individual optical shapes, being able to read the names of the three letters, and even knowing the individual sounds for the three letters, cannot help him in really reading the word (as opposed to memorizing its appearance as a sight word), unless he realizes that the word in his own lexicon has three segments. Before he can map the visual message to the word in his vocabulary, he has to be consciously aware that the word *cat* that he knows—an apparently unitary syllable—has three separate segments. His competence in speech production and speech perception is of no direct use to him here, because this competence enables him to achieve the segmentation without ever being consciously aware of it.[2]

. . . . .

SUMMARY AND CONCLUSIONS

In an attempt to understand the problems encountered by the beginning reader and children who fail to learn, we have investigated the child's misreadings and how they relate to speech. The first question we asked was whether the major barrier to achieving fluency in reading is at the level of connected text or in dealing with individual words. Having concluded from our own findings and the research of others that the word and its components are of primary importance, we then looked more closely at the error patterns in reading words.

[2]The idea of "linguistic awareness," as it has been called here, has been a recurrent theme in this conference. . . .

Since reading is the perception of language by eye, it seemed important to ask whether the principal difficulties within the word are to be found at a visual stage of the process or at a subsequent linguistic stage. We considered the special case of reversals of letter sequence and orientation in which the properties of visual confusability are, on the face of it, primary. We found that although optical reversibility contributes to the error rate, for the children we have studied it is of secondary importance to linguistic factors. Our investigation of the reversal tendency then led us to consider whether individual differences in reading ability might reflect differences in the degree and kind of functional asymmetries of the cerebral hemispheres. Although the evidence is at this time not clearly supportive of a relation between cerebral ambilaterality and reading disability, it was suggested that new techniques offer an opportunity to explore this relationship more fully in the future.

When we turned to the linguistic aspects of the error pattern in words, we found, as others have, that medial and final segments in the word are more often misread than initial ones and vowels more often than consonants. We then considered why the error pattern in mishearing differed from misreading in both these respects. In regard to segment position, we concluded that children in the early stages of learning to read tend to get the initial segment correct and fail on subsequent ones because they do not have the conscious awareness of phonemic segmentation needed specifically in reading but not in speaking and listening.

As for vowels in speech, we suggested, first of all, that they may tend to be heard correctly because they are carried by the strongest portion of the acoustic signal. In reading, the situation is different: alphabetic representations of the vowels possess no such special distinctiveness. Moreover, their embedded placement within the syllable and their orthographic complexity combine to create difficulties in reading. Evidence for the importance of orthographic complexity was seen in our data by the fact that the differences among vowels in error rate in reading were predictable from the number of orthographic representations of each vowel. However, we also considered the possibility that phonetic confusions may account for a significant portion of vowel errors, and we suggested how this hypothesis might be tested.

We believe that the comparative study of reading and speech is of great importance for understanding how the problems of perceiving language by eye differ from the problems of perceiving it by ear, and for discovering why learning to read, unlike speaking and listening, is a difficult accomplishment.

References

Anderson, I. H., and W. F. Dearborn, 1952. *The Psychology of Teaching Reading*. New York: Ronald Press.

Benton, A. I., 1962. Dyslexia in relation to form perception and directional sense. In *Reading Disability*, J. Money (ed.), Baltimore: Johns Hopkins Press.

Biemiller, A., 1970. The development of the use of graphic and contextual information as children learn to read. *Reading Res. Quart.*, 6:75–96.

Bryden, M. P., 1965. Tachistoscopic recogniton, handedness, and cerebral dominance. *Neuropsychologia* 3:1–8.

———, 1970. Laterality effects in dichotic listening: Relations with handedness and reading ability in children. *Neuropsychologia*, 8:443–450.

Chomsky, N., and M. Halle, 1968. *The Sound Pattern of English*. New York: Harper and Row.

Christenson, A., 1969. Oral reading errors of intermediate grade children at their independent, instructional, and frustration reading levels. In *Reading and Realism*, J. A. Figurel (ed.), Proceedings of the International Reading Association, 13:674–677.

Conrad, R., 1964. Acoustic confusions in immediate memory. *Brit. J. Psych.* 55:75–83.

Conrad, R. Speech and reading. In this volume.

Crowder, R. Visual and auditory memory. In this volume.

Daniels, J. C., and H. Diack, 1956. *Progress in Reading*. Nottingham: University of Nottingham Institute of Education.

Doehering, D. G., 1968. *Patterns of Impairment in Specific Reading Disability*. Bloomington: Indiana University Press.

Fries, C. C., 1962. *Linguistics and Reading*. New York: Holt, Rinehart and Winston.

Fujisaki, H., and T. Kawashima, 1969. On the modes and mechanisms of speech perception. *Annual Report of the Divison of Electrical Engineering*. Engineering Research Institute, University of Tokyo, No. 1.

Gibson, E. J., 1965. Learning to read. *Science,* 148: 1066–1072.

Gibson, E. J., J. J. Gibson, A. D. Pick, and R. Osser, 1962. A developmental study of the discrimination of letter-like forms. *J. Comp. Physiol. Psych.* 55:897–906.

Goodman, K. S., 1965. A linguistic study of cues and miscues in reading. *Elementary English*, 42:639–643.

———, 1968. The psycholinguistic nature of the reading process. In *The Psycholinguistic Nature of the Reading Process*, K. S. Goodman (ed.), Detroit: Wayne State University Press.

Gough, P. B. One second of reading. In this volume.

Hochberg, J., 1970. Attention in perception and reading. In *Early Experience and Visual Information Processing in Perceptual and Reading Disorders*, F. A. Young and D. B. Lindsley (eds.), Washington: National Academy of Sciences.

Huey, E. B. 1908. *The Psychology and Pedagogy of Reading*. New York: Macmillan. Reprinted. Cambridge: MIT Press, 1968.

Jastak, J., 1946. *Wide Range Achievement Test (Examinter's Manual)*. Wilmington: C. L. Story.

Katz, L., and D. A. Wicklund, 1971. Word scanning rate for good and poor readers. *J. Ed. Psych.* 62:138–140.

Kimura, D. 1967. Functional asymmetry of the brain in dichotic listening. *Cortex*, 3:163–178.

Kimura, D., 1961. Cerebral dominance and the perception of verbal stimuli. *Canad. J. Psych.* 15:166–171.

Kolers, P. A., 1970. Three stages of reading. In *Basic Studies on Reading*, H. Levin (ed.), New York: Harper & Row.

Kolers, P. A., and D. N. Perkins, 1969. Orientation of letters and their speed of recognition. *Perception and Psychophysics* 5:275–280.

Liberman, A. M., 1968. Discussion in *Communicating by Language: The Reading Process*. J. F. Kavanagh (ed.), Bethesda, Md.: National Institute of Child Health and Human Development, pp. 125–128.

———, 1970. The grammars of speech and language. *Cog. Psych.* 1:301–323.

Liberman, A. M., F. S. Cooper, D. Shankweiler, and M.

Studdert-Kennedy, 1967. Perception of the speech code. *Psych. Rev.* 74:431–461.

Liberman, I. Y., 1971. Basic research in speech and lateralization of language: Some implications for reading disability. *Bull. Orton Soc.* 21:71–87.

Liberman, I. Y., D. Shankweiler, C. Orlando, K. S. Harris, and F. B. Berti, 1971. Letter confusions and reversals of sequence in the beginning reader: Implications for Orton's theory of developmental dyslexia. *Cortex* 7:127–142.

Mathews, M., 1966. *Teaching to Read Historically Considered.* Chicago: University of Chicago Press.

Mattingly, I. G. Reading, the linguistic process, and linguistic awareness. In this volume.

Mattingly, I. G., and A. M. Liberman, 1970. The speech code and the physiology of language. In *Information Processing in the Nervous System,* K. N. Leibovic (ed.), New York: Springer.

Orlando, C. P., 1971. Relationships between language laterality and handedness in eight and ten year old boys. Unpublished doctoral dissertation, University of Connecticut.

Orton, S. T., 1925. "Word-blindedness" in school children. *Arch. Neurol. Psychiat.* 14:581–615.

———, 1937. *Reading, Writing and Speech Problems in Children.* New York: W. W. Norton.

Savin, H. B. What the child knows about speech when he starts to read. In this volume.

Schale, F. C., 1964. Changes in oral reading errors at elementary and secondary levels. Unpublished doctoral dissertation, University of Chicago. Summarized in *Acad. Theo. Quart.* 1966, 1:225–229.

Shankweiler, D., 1964. Developmental dyslexia: A critique and review of recent evidence *Cortex,* 1:53–62.

Shankweiler, D., and M. Studdert-Kennedy, 1967. Identification of consonants and vowels presented to left and right ears. *Quart. J. Exp. Psych.* 19:59–63.

Spache, G. D., 1963. *Diagnostic Reading Scales (Examiner's Manual).* Monterey: California Test Bureau.

Sparrow, S. S., 1968. Reading disability: A neuropsychological investigation. Unpublished doctoral dissertation, University of Florida.

Sternberg, S., 1967. Two operations in character recognition: Some evidence from reaction time measures. *Perception and Psychophysics,* 2:45–53.

Studdert-Kennedy, M., in press. The perception of speech. In *Current Trends in Linguistics,* Vol. XII, T. A. Sebeok (ed.), The Hague: Mouton. Also has appeared in *Haskins Laboratories Status Reports on Speech Research,* 23 (1970), pp. 15–48.

Health and Human development, p. 206.

Venezky, R. L., 1968. Discussion in *Communicating by Language: The Reading Process,* J. I. Kavanagh (ed.), Bethesda, Md.: National Institute of Child Health and Human Development, p. 206.

Vernon, M. D., 1960. *Backwardness in Reading.* Cambridge: Cambridge University Press.

Weber, R., 1968. The study of oral reading errors: A survey of the literature. *Reading Res. Quart.* 4:96–119.

———, 1970. A linguistic analysis of first-grade reading errors. *Reading Res. Quart.* 5:427–451.

Weir, R. H., and R. L. Venezky, 1968. Spelling-to-sound patterns. In *The Psycholinguistic Nature of the Reading Process,* K. S. Goodman (ed.), Detroit: Wayne State University Press.

Woodworth, R. S., 1938. *Experimental Psychology.* New York: Holt, Chapter 28.

Zangwill, O. L., 1960. *Cerebral Dominance and Its Relation to Psychological Function.* Edinburgh: Oliver & Boyd.

Zurif, E. B., and G. Carson, 1970. Dyslexia in relation to cerebral dominance and temporal analysis. *Neuropsychologia* 8:351–361.

Chapter 7

Intelligence

Although intelligence has been a key concept in psychology throughout most of the history of the discipline, there is no generally accepted definition of it. Different theorists and authors of mental tests use the term **intelligence** in very different ways.

Probably no one has had more influence on, or contributed more, theoretically and substantively, to our understanding of the development of intelligence than Jean Piaget of the University of Geneva, the author of the first article in this chapter. Piaget regards intelligence as the ability to adapt to the environment and new situations; to think, reason, and act in adaptive ways. In his own research, Piaget has observed children's behavior closely, centering his attention on discovering the developmental progress in such critical cognitive processes as reasoning, abstraction, concept formation, thinking, comprehension, and problem-solving. His emphasis is on developmental and age changes in these abilities, **not** on the assessment of individual differences in ability.

Piaget's theory traces the development of cognition from its roots in the infant's earliest primitive reflexes to the adult's complex, formal, logical thinking. The four major stages of cognitive development—**sensorimotor, preoperational, concrete operations, formal operations**—occur in an invariant sequence. Each of these stages is defined and described briefly in Piaget's article, and some explanations of such fundamental Piagetian concepts as schemata, conservation, and equilibration are also provided. According to Piaget the highest form of intelligence is logical thinking or reasoning, abilities that are manifested in the stage of formal operations, the highest level of intellectual development.

The traditional American approach to intelligence is a quantitative one, concerned primarily with the measurement of **individual differences.** Most authors of intelligence tests view intelligence as a broad, generalized, unitary factor—"mental ability," "ability to adapt," "ability to solve problems," or "ability to think rationally"—measured in terms of IQ (intelligence quotient).

(2) An excellent example of the quantitative approach to intelligence is found in the article by J. P. Guilford of the University of Southern California. Guilford maintains that each person possesses a unique composite of a great many different intellectual abilities. His statistical analysis indicates that each intellectual ability involves three components: (1) There is a **cognitive process** or **operation,** such as recognition, memory, generation of hypotheses, grouping of ideas into concepts, and evaluation; (2) such operations are applied to specific **contents,** for example, figures, symbols (letters and numbers), words (or sentences) and behaviors; and (3) the operations acting on the contents result in **products,** including units (words or ideas), classes or concepts, and relationships among units or classes. Intelligence, in Guilford's view, is like a cube consisting of 120 cells, each cell representing a unique intellectual ability.

(3) The mental test approach, focused on individual differences, has been the source of a great many controversies and critical social questions. One of the major controversies centers around the question of hereditary versus environmental (or nature versus nurture) contributions to intelligence test scores. An intense, heated argument developed recently when Arthur Jensen, a University of California professor of educational psychology, published his view that blacks may be genetically inferior intellectually to whites. He based his conclusion on the finding that blacks, on the average, score lower than whites in IQ. Most psychologists disagree with Jensen's interpretation of these data and argue that heredity and environment interact in the determination of IQ. The limits of the individual's ability, his **potential** may be strongly influenced by genetic factors, but the environment in which he lives determines whether—or to what degree—his potential becomes actualized.

In an excellent critique of the writings of Jensen, Eysenck, Herrnstein, and others, S. Scarr-Salapatek of the University of Minnesota discusses this difficult issue in a thorough, penetrating, and lucid way. She argues convincingly that there is no reason to believe that race differences in IQ scores are direct products of genetic differences between blacks and whites.

#17 *The Stages of the Intellectual Development of the Child*

Jean Piaget

A consideration of the stages of the development of intelligence should be preceded by asking the question, What is intelligence? Unfortunately, we find ourselves confronted by a great number of definitions. For Claparède, intelligence is an adaptation to new situations. When a situation is new, when there are no reflexes, when there are no habits to rely on, then the subject is obliged to search for something new. That is to say, Claparède defines intelligence as groping, as feeling one's way, trial-and-error behavior. We find this trial-and-error behavior in all levels of intelligence, even at the superior level, in the form of hypothesis testing. As far as I am concerned, this definition is too vague, because trial and error occurs in the formation of habits, and also in the earliest established reflexes: when a newborn baby learns to suck.

Karl Bühler defines intelligence as an act of immediate comprehension; that is to say, an insight. Bühler's definition is also very precise, but it seems to me too narrow. I know that when a mathematician solves a problem, he ends by having an insight, but up to that moment he feels, or gropes for, his way; and to say that the trial-and-error behavior is not intelligent and that intelligence starts only when he finds the solution to the problem, seems a very narrow definition. I would, therefore, propose to define intelligence not by a static criterion, as in previous definitions, but by the direction that intelligence follows in its evolution, and then I would define intelligence as a form of equilibration, or forms of equilibration, toward which all cognitive functions lead.

But I must first define equilibration. Equilibra-

SOURCE: Reprinted with permission from the *Bulletin of the Menninger Clinic*, vol. 26, no. 3 (1962), 120–145. Copyright © 1962 by The Menninger Foundation.

tion in my vocabulary is not an exact and automatic balance, as it would be in Gestalt theory; I define equilibration principally as a compensation for an external disturbance.

When there is an external disturbance, the subject succeeds in compensating for this by an activity. The maximum equilibration is thus the maximum of the activity, and not a state of rest. It is a mobile equilibration, and not an immobile one. So equilibration is defined as compensation; compensation is the annulling of a transformation by an inverse transformation. The compensation which intervenes in equilibration implies the fundamental idea of reversibility, and this reversibility is precisely what characterizes the operations of the intelligence. An operation is an internalized action, but it is also a reversible action. But an operation is never isolated; it is always subordinated to other operations; it is part of a more inclusive structure. Consequently, we define intelligence in terms of operations, coordination of operations.

Take, for example, an operation like addition: Addition is a material action, the action of reuniting. On the other hand, it is a reversible action, because addition may be compensated by subtraction. Yet addition leads to a structure of a whole. In the case of numbers, it will be the structure that the mathematicians call a "group." In the case of addition of classes which intervene in the logical structure it will be a more simple structure that we will call a grouping, and so on.

Consequently, the study of the stages of intelligence is first a study of the formation of operational structures. I shall define every stage by a structure of a whole, with the possibility of its integration into succeeding stages, just as it was prepared by preceding stages. Thus, I shall distinguish four great stages, or four final great periods, in the development of intelligence: first, the sensori-motor period before the appearance of language; second, the period from about two to seven years of age, the pre-operational period which precedes real operations; third, the period from seven to 12 years of age, a period of concrete operations (which refers to concrete objects); and finally after 12 years of age, the period of formal operations, or propositional operations.

SENSORI-MOTOR STAGE

Before language develops, there is behavior that we can call intelligent. For example, when a baby of 12 months or more wants an object which is too far from him, but which rests on a carpet or blanket, and he pulls it to get to the object, this behavior is an act of intelligence. The child uses an intermediary, a means to get to his goal. Also, getting to an object by means of pulling a string when the object is tied to the string, or when the child uses a stick to get the object, are acts of intelligence. They demonstrate in the sensori-motor period a certain number of stages, which go from simple reflexes, from the formation of the first habits, up to the coordination of means and goals.

Remarkable in this sensori-motor stage of intelligence is that there are already structures. Sensori-motor intelligence rests mainly on actions, on movements and perceptions without language, but these actions are coordinated in a relatively stable way. They are coordinated under what we may call schemata of action. These schemata can be generalized in actions and are applicable to new situations. For example, pulling a carpet to bring an object within reach constitutes a schema which can be generalized to other situations when another object rests on a support. In other words, a schema supposes an incorporation of new situations into the previous schemata, a sort of continuous assimilation of new objects or new situations to the actions already schematized. For example, I presented to one of my children an object completely new to him—a box of cigarettes, which is not a usual toy for a baby. The child took the object, looked at it, put it in his mouth, shook it, then took it with one hand and hit it with the other hand, then rubbed it on the edge of the crib, then shook it again, and gave the impression of trying to see if there were noise. This behavior is a way of exploring the object, of trying to understand it by assimilating it to schemata already known. The child behaves in this situation as he will later in Binet's famous vocabulary test, when he defines by usage, saying, for instance, that a spoon is for eating, and so on.

But in the presence of a new object, even without knowing how to talk, the child knows how to assimilate, to incorporate this new object into each of his already developed schemata which function as practical concepts. Here is a structuring of intelligence. Most important in this structuring is the base, the point of departure of all subsequent operational constructions. At the sensori-motor level, the child constructs the schema of the permanent object.

The knowledge of the permanent object starts at this point. The child is not convinced at the beginning that when an object disappears from view, he can find it again. One can verify by tests that object permanence is not yet developed at this stage. But there is there the beginning of a subsequent fundamental idea which starts being constructed at the sensori-motor level. This is also true of the construction of the ideas of space, of time, of causality. What is being done at the sensori-motor level concerning all the foregoing ideas will constitute the substructure of the subsequent, fully achieved ideas of permanent objects, of space, of time, of causality.

In the formation of these substructures at the sensori-motor level, it is very interesting to note the beginning of a *reversibility,* not in thought, since there is not yet representation in thought, but in action itself. For example, the formation of the conception of space at the sensori-motor stage leads to an amazing decentration if one compares the conception of space at the first weeks of the development with that at one and one-half to two years of age. In the beginning there is not one space which contains all the objects, including the child's body itself; there is a multitude of spaces which are not coordinated: there are the buccal space, the tactilokinesthetic space, the visual and auditory spaces; each is separate and each is centered essentially on the body of the subject and on actions. After a few months, however, after a kind of Copernican evolution, there is a total reversal, a decentration such that space becomes homogeneous, a one-and-only space that envelops the others. Then space becomes a container that envelops all objects, including the body itself; and after that, space is mainly coordinated in a structure, a coordination of positions and displacements, and these constitute what the geometricians call a "group"; that is to say, precisely a reversible system. One may move from A to B, and may come back from B to A; there is the possibility of returning, of reversibility. There is also the possibility of making detours and combinations which give a clue to what the subsequent operations will be when thought will supersede the action itself.

PRE-OPERATIONAL STAGE

From one and one-half to two years of age, a fundamental transformation in the evolution of intelligence takes place in the appearance of symbolic functions. Every action of intelligence consists in manipulating significations (or meanings) and whenever (or wherever) there is significations, there are on the one hand the "significants" and on the other the "significates." This is true in the sensori-motor level, but the only significants that intervene there are perceptual signs or signals (as in conditioning) which are undifferentiated in regard to the significate; for example, a perceptual cue, like distance, which will be a cue for the size of the distant object, or the apparent size of an object, which will be the cue for the distance of the object. There, perhaps, both indices are different aspects of the same reality, but they are not yet differentiated significants. At the age of one and one-half to two years a new class of significants arises, and these significants are differentiated in regard to their significates. These differentiations can be called symbolic functions.

The appearance of symbols in a children's game is an example of the appearance of new significants. At the sensori-motor level the games are nothing but exercises; now they become symbolic play, a play of fiction; these games consist in representing something by means of something else. Another example is the beginning of delayed imitation, an imitation that takes place not in the presence of the original subject but in its absence, and which consequently constitutes a kind of symbolization or mental image.

At the same time that symbols appear, the child acquires language; that is to say, there is the acquisition of another phase of differentiated significance, verbal signals, or collective signals. This symbolic function then brings great flexibility into the field of intelligence. Intelligence up to this point refers to the immediate space which surrounds the child and to the present perceptual situation; thanks to language, and to the symbolic functions, it becomes possible to invoke objects which are not present perceptually, to reconstruct the past, or to make projects, plans for the future, to think of objects not present but very distant in space—in short, to span spatio-temporal distances much greater than before.

But his new stage, the stage of representation of thought which is superimposed on the sensori-motor stage, is not a simple extension of what was referred to at the previous level. Before being able to prolong, one must in fact reconstruct, because behavior in words is a different thing from representing something in thought. When a child knows how to move around in his house or garden by following the different successive cues around him, it does not mean that he is capable of representing or reproducing the total configuration of his house or his garden. To be able to represent, to reproduce something, one must be capable of reconstructing this group of displacements, but at a new level, that of the representation of the thought.

I recently made an amusing test with Nel Szeminska. We took children of four to five years of age who went to school by themselves and came back home by themselves, and asked them if they could trace the way to school and back for us, not in design, which would be too difficult, but like a construction game, with concrete objects. We found that they were not capable of representation; there was a kind of motor-memory, but it was not yet a representation of a whole—the group of displacements had not yet been reconstructed on the plan of the representation of thought. In other words, the operations were not yet formed. There are representations which are internalized actions; but actions still centered on the body itself, on the activity itself. These representations do not allow the objective combinations, the decentrated combinations that the operations would. The actions are centered on the body. I used to call this egocentrism; but it is better thought of as lack of reversibility of action.

At this level, the most certain sign of the absence of operations which appear at the next stage is the absence of the knowledge of conservation. In fact, an operation refers to the transformation of reality. The transformation is not of the whole, however; something constant is always untransformed. If you pour a liquid from one glass to another there is transformation; the liquid changes form, but its liquid property stays constant. So at the preoperational level, it is significant from the point of view of the operations of intelligence that the child has not yet a knowledge of conservation. For example, in the case of liquid, when the child pours it from one bottle to the other, he thinks that the quantity of the liquid has changed. When the level of the liquid changes, the child thinks the quantity has changed—there is more or less in the second glass than in the first. And if you ask the child where the larger quantity came from, he does not answer this question. What is important for the child is that perceptually it is not the same thing any more. We find this absence of conservation in all object properties, in the length, surface, quantity, and weight of things.

This absence of conservation indicates essentially that at this stage the child reasons from the configuration. Confronted with a transformation, he does not reason from the transformation itself; he starts from the initial configuration, then sees the final configuration, compares the two but forgets the transformation, because he does not know how to reason about it. At this stage the child is still reasoning on the basis of what he sees because there is no conservation. He is able to master this problem only when the operations are formed and these operations, which we have already sensed at the sensori-motor level, are not formed until around seven to eight years of age. At that age the elementary problems of conservation are solved, because the child reasons on the basis of the transformation per se, and this requires a manipulation of the operation. The ability to pass from one stage to the other and be able to come back to the point of departure, to manipulate the reversible operations, which appears around seven to eight years of age, is limited when compared with the operations of the superior level only in the sense that they are concrete. That is to say, the child can manipulate the operations only when he manipulates the object concretely.

STAGE OF CONCRETE OPERATIONS

The first operations of the manipulation of objects, the concrete operations, deal with logical classes and with logical relations, or the number. But these operations do not deal yet with propositions, or hypotheses, which do not appear until the last stage.

Let me exemplify these concrete operations: the simplest operation is concerned with classifying objects according to their similarity and their difference. This is accomplished by including the subclasses within larger and more general classes, a process that implies inclusion. This classification, which seems very simple at first, is not acquired until around seven to eight years of age. Before that, at the pre-operational level, we do not find logical inclusion. For example, if you show a child at the pre-operational level a bouquet of flowers of which one half is daisies and the other half other flowers and you ask him if in this bouquet there are more flowers or more daisies, you are confronted with this answer, which seems extraordinary until it is analyzed: The child cannot tell you whether there are more flowers than daisies; either he reasons on the basis of the whole or of the part. He cannot understand that the part is complementary to the rest, and he says there are more daisies than flowers, or as many daisies as flowers, without understanding this inclusion of the subclass, the daisies, in the class of flowers. It is only around seven to eight years of age that a child is capable of solving a problem of inclusion.

Another system of operation that appears around seven to eight years of age is the operation of serializing; that is, to arrange objects according to their size, or their progressive weight. It is also a structure of the whole, like the classification which rests on concrete operations, since it consists of manipulating concrete objects. At this level there is also the construction of numbers, which is, too, a synthesis of classification and seriation. In numbers, as in classes, we have inclusion, and also a serial order, as in serializing. These elementary operations constitute structures of wholes. There is no class without classification; there is no symmetric relation without serialization; there is not a number independent of the series of numbers. But the structures of these wholes are simple structures, groupings in the case of classes and relations, which are already groups in the case of numbers, but very elementary structures compared to subsequent structures.

STAGE OF FORMAL OPERATIONS

The last stage of development of intelligence is the stage of formal operations or propositional operations. At about eleven to twelve years of age we see great progress; the child becomes capable of reasoning not only on the basis of objects, but also on the basis of hypotheses, or of propositions.

An example which neatly shows the difference between reasoning on the basis of propositions and reasoning on the basis of concrete objects comes from Burt's tests. Burt asked children of different ages to compare the colors of the hair of three girls: Edith is fairer than Susan, Edith is darker than Lilly; who is the darkest of the three? In this question there is seriation, not of concrete objects, but of verbal statements which supposes a more complicated mental manipulation. This problem is rarely solved before the age of 12.

Here a new class of operations appears which is superimposed on the operations of logical class and number, and these operations are the propositional operations. Here, compared to the previous stage, are fundamental changes. It is not simply that these operations refer to language, and then to operations with concrete objects, but that these operations have much richer structures.

The first novelty is a combinative structure; like mathematical structures, it is a structure of a system which is superimposed on the structure of simple classifications or seriations which are not themselves systems, because they do not involve a combinative system. A combinative system permits the grouping in flexible combinations of each element of the system with any other element of that system. The logic of propositions supposes such a combinative system. If children of different ages are shown a number of colored disks and asked to combine each color with each other two by two, or three by three, we find these combinative operations are not accessible to the child at the stage of concrete operations. The child is capable of some combination, but not of all the possible combinations. After the age of 12, the child can find a method to make all the possible combinations. At the same time he acquires both the logic of mathematics and the logic of propositions, which also supposes a method of combining.

A second novelty in the operations of propositions is the appearance of a structure which constitutes a group of four transformations. Hitherto there were two reversibilities: reversibility by inversion, which consists of annulling, or canceling; and reversibility which we call reciprocity, leading not to cancellation, but to another combination. Reciprocity is what we find in the field of a relation. If A equals B, by reciprocity B equals A. If A is smaller than B, by reciprocity B is larger than A. At the level of propositional operations a new system envelops these two forms of reversibility. Here the structure combines inversion and reversibility in one single but larger and more complicated structure. It allows the acquisition of a series of fundamental operational schemata for the development of intelligence, which schemata are not possible before the constitution of this structure.

It is around the age of 12 that the child, for example, starts to understand in mathematics the knowledge of proportions, and becomes capable of reasoning by using two systems of reference at the same time. For example, if you advance the position of a board and a car moving in opposite directions, in order to understand the movement of the board in relation to the movement of the car and to other movement, you need a system of four transformations. The same is true in regard to proportions, to problems in mathematics or physics, or to other logical problems.

The four principal stages of the development of intelligence of the child progress from one stage to the other by the construction of new operational structures, and these structures constitute the fundamental instrument of the intelligence of the adult.

#18 Three Faces of Intellect

J. P. Guilford

My subject is in the area of human intelligence, in connection with which the names of Terman and Stanford have become known the world over. The Stanford Revision of the Binet intelligence scale has been the standard against which all other instruments for the measurement of intelligence have been compared. The term IQ or intelligence quotient has become a household word in this country. This is illustrated by two brief stories.

[1] A few years ago, one of my neighbors came home from a PTA meeting, remarking: "That Mrs. So-And-So, thinks she knows so much. She kept talking about the 'intelligence *quota*' of the children; 'intelligence *quota*'; imagine. Why, everybody knows that IQ stands for 'intelligence *quiz*.'"

SOURCE: From *American Psychologist,* vol. 14, no. 8 (August 1959), 469–479. Copyright © 1959 by the American Psychological Association. Reprinted by permission.

[2] The other story comes from a little comic strip in a Los Angeles morning newspaper, called "Junior Grade." In the first picture a little boy meets a little girl, both apparently about the first-grade level. The little girl remarks, "I have a high IQ." The little boy, puzzled, said, "You have a what?" The little girl repeated, "I have a high IQ," then went on her way. The little boy, looking thoughtful, said, "And she looks like such a nice little girl, too."

It is my purpose to speak about the analysis of this thing called human intelligence into its components. I do not believe that either Binet or Terman, if they were still with us, would object to the idea of a searching and detailed study of intelligence, aimed toward a better understanding of its nature. Preceding the development of his intelligence scale, Binet had done much research on different kinds of thinking activities and

190

apparently recognized that intelligence has a number of aspects. It is to the lasting credit of both Binet and Terman that they introduced such a great variety of tasks into their intelligence scales.

Two related events of very recent history make it imperative that we learn all we can regarding the nature of intelligence. I am referring to the advent of the artificial satellites and planets and to the crisis in education that has arisen in part as a consequence. The preservation of our way of life and our future security depend upon our most important national resources: our intellectual abilities and, more particularly, our creative abilities. It is time, then, that we learn all we can about those resources.

Our knowledge of the components of human intelligence has come about mostly within the last 25 years. The major sources of this information in this country have been L. L. Thurstone and his associates, the wartime research of psychologists in the United States Air Forces, and more recently the Aptitudes Project at the University of Southern California, now in its tenth year of research on cognitive and thinking abilities. The results from the Aptitudes Project that have gained perhaps the most attention have pertained to creative-thinking abilities. These are mostly novel findings. But to me, the most significant outcome has been the development of a unified theory of human intellect, which organizes the known, unique or primary intellectual abilities into a single system called the "structure of intellect." It is to this system that I shall devote the major part of my remarks, with very brief mentions of some of the implications for the psychology of thinking and problem solving, for vocational testing, and for education.

The discovery of the components of intelligence has been by means of the experimental application of the method of factor analysis. It is not necessary for you to know anything about the theory or method of factor analysis in order to follow the discussion of the components. I should like to say, however, that factor analysis has no connection with or resemblance to psychoanalysis. A positive statement would be more helpful, so I will say that each intellectual component or factor is a unique ability that is needed to do well in a certain class of tasks or tests. As a general principle we find that certain individuals do well in the tests of a certain class, but they may do poorly in the tests of another class. We conclude that a factor has certain properties from the features that the tests of a class have in common. I shall give you very soon a number of examples of tests, each representing a factor.

THE STRUCTURE OF INTELLECT

Although each factor is sufficiently distinct to be detected by factor analysis, in very recent years it has become apparent that the factors themselves can be classified because they resemble one another in certain ways. One basis of classification is according to the basic kind of process or operation performed. This kind of classification gives us five major groups of intellectual abilities: factors of cognition, memory, convergent thinking, divergent thinking, and evaluation.

Cognition means discovery or rediscovery or recognition. Memory means retention of what is cognized. Two kinds of productive-thinking operations generate new information from known information and remembered information. In divergent-thinking operations we think in different directions, sometimes searching, sometimes seeking variety. In convergent thinking the information leads to one right answer or to a recognized best or conventional answer. In evaluation we reach decisions as to goodness, correctness, suitability, or adequacy of what we know, what we remember, and what we produce in productive thinking.

A second way of classifying the intellectual factors is according to the kind of material or content involved. The factors known thus far involve three kinds of material or content: the content may be figural, symbolic, or semantic. Figural content is concrete material such as is perceived through the senses. It does not represent anything

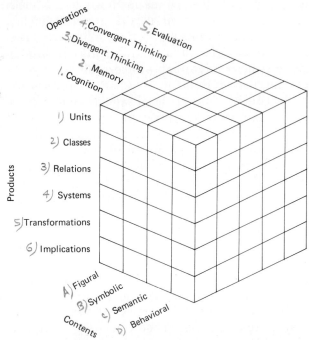

120 CUBES = 120 FACTORS = 120 ABILITIES

except itself. Visual material has properties such as size, form, color, location, or texture. Things we hear or feel provide other examples of figural material. Symbolic content is composed of letters, digits, and other conventional signs, usually organized in general systems, such as the alphabet or the number system. Semantic content is in the form of verbal meanings or ideas, for which no examples are necessary. BEHAVIORAL CONTENT*.

When a certain operation is applied to a certain kind of content, as many as six general kinds of products may be involved. There is enough evidence available to suggest that, regardless of the combinations of operations and content, the same six kinds of products may be found associated. The six kinds of products are: units, classes, relations, systems, transformations, and implications. So far as we have determined from factor analysis, these are the only fundamental kinds of products that we can know. As such, they may serve as basic classes into which one might fit all kinds of information psychologically.

The three kinds of classifications of the factors of intellect can be represented by means of a single solid model, shown in Figure 1. In this model, which we call the "structure of intellect," each dimension represents one of the modes of variation of the factors.[1] Along one dimension are found the various kinds of operations, along a second one are the various kinds of products, and along the third are various kinds of content. Along the dimension of content a fourth category has been added, its kind of content being designated as "behavioral." This category has been added on a purely theoretical basis to represent the general area sometimes called "social intelligence." More will be said about this section of the model later.

In order to provide a better basis for understanding the model and a better basis for accepting it as a picture of human intellect, I shall do

Figure 1 A cubical model representing the structure of intellect.

some exploring of it with you systematically, giving some examples of tests. Each cell in the model calls for a certain kind of ability that can be described in terms of operation, content, and product, for each cell is at the intersection of a unique combination of kinds of operation, content, and product. A test for that ability would have the same three properties. In our exploration of the model, we shall take one vertical layer at a time, beginning with the front face. The first layer provides us with a matrix of 18 cells (if we ignore the behavioral column for which there are as yet no known factors) each of which should contain a cognitive ability.

The Cognitive Abilities

We know at present the unique abilities that fit logically into 15 of the 18 cells for cognitive abilities. Each row presents a triad of similar abilities,

[1] For an earlier presentation of the concept, see Guilford (1956).

having a single kind of product in common. The factors of the first row are concerned with the knowing of units. A good test of the ability to cognize figural units is the Street Gestalt Completion Test. In this test, the recognition of familiar pictured objects in silhouette form is made difficult for testing purposes by blocking out parts of those objects. There is another factor that is known to involve the perception of auditory figures—in the form of melodies, rhythms, and speech sounds—and still another factor involving kinesthetic forms. The presence of three factors in one cell (they are conceivably distinct abilities, although this has not been tested) suggests that more generally, in the figural column, at least, we should expect to find more than one ability. A fourth dimension pertaining to variations in sense modality may thus apply in connection with figural content. The model could be extended in this manner if the facts call for such an extension.

The ability to cognize symbolic units is measured by tests like the following:

Put vowels in the following blanks to make real words:

P —— W —— R
M —— RV —— L
C —— RT —— N

Rearrange the letters to make real words:

R A C I H
T V O E S
K L C C O

The first of these two tests is called Disemvoweled Words, and the second Scrambled Words.

The ability to cognize semantic units is the well-known factor of verbal comprehension, which is best measured by means of a vocabulary test, with items such as:

GRAVITY means ——————
CIRCUS means ——————
VIRTUE means ——————

From the comparison of these two factors it is obvious that recognizing familiar words as letter structures and knowing what words mean depend upon quite different abilities.

For testing the abilities to know classes of units, we may present the following kinds of items, one with symbolic content and one with semantic content:

Which letter group does not belong?
XECM PVAA QXIN VTRO

Which object does not belong?
clam tree oven rose

A figural test is constructed in a completely parallel form, presenting in each item four figures, three of which have a property in common and the fourth lacking that property.

The three abilities to see relationships are also readily measured by a common kind of test, differing only in terms of content. The well-known analogies test is applicable, two items in symbolic and semantic form being:

JIRE : KIRE :: FORA : KORE KORA LIRE GORA GIRE
poetry : prose :: dance : music walk sing talk jump

Such tests usually involve more than the ability to cognize relations, but we are not concerned with this problem at this point.

The three factors for cognizing systems do not at present appear in tests so closely resembling one another as in the case of the examples just given. There is nevertheless an underlying common core of logical similarity. Ordinary space tests, such as Thurstone's Flags, Figures, and Cards or Part V (Spatial Orientation) of the Guilford-Zimmerman Aptitude Survey (GZAS), serve in the figural column. The system involved is an order or arrangement of objects in space. A system that uses symbolic elements is illustrated by the Letter Triangle Test, a sample item of which is:

d
b e
a c f ?

What letter belongs at the place of the question mark?

The ability to understand a semantic system

has been known for some time as the factor called general reasoning. One of its most faithful indicators is a test composed of arithmetic-reasoning items. That the phase of understanding only is important for measuring this ability is shown by the fact that such a test works even if the examinee is not asked to give a complete solution; he need only show that he structures the problem properly. For example, an item from the test Necessary Arithmetical Operations simply asks what operations are needed to solve the problem:

A city lot 48 feet wide and 149 feet deep costs $79,432. What is the cost per square foot?	A. add and multiply B. multiply and divide C. subtract and divide D. add and subtract E. divide and add

Placing the factor of general reasoning in this cell of the structure of intellect gives us some new conceptions of its nature. It should be a broad ability to grasp all kinds of systems that are conceived in terms of verbal concepts, not restricted to the understanding of problems of an arithmetical type.

Transformations are changes of various kinds, including modifications in arrangement, organization, or meaning. In the figural column for the transformations row, we find the factor known as visualization. Common measuring instruments for this factor are the surface-development tests, and an example of a different kind is Part VI (Spatial Visualization) of the GZAS. A test of the ability to make transformations of meaning, for the factor in the semantic column, is called Similarities. The examinee is asked to state several ways in which two objects, such as an apple and an orange, are alike. Only by shifting the meanings of both is the examinee able to give many responses to such an item.

In the set of abilities having to do with the cognition of implications, we find that the individual goes beyond the information given, but not to the extent of what might be called drawing conclusions. We may say that he extrapolates.

From the given information he expects or foresees certain consequences, for example. The two factors found in this row of the cognition matrix were first called "foresight" factors. Foresight in connection with figural material can be tested by means of paper-and-pencil mazes. Foresight in connection with ideas, those pertaining to events, for example, is indicated by a test such as Pertinent Questions:

> In planning to open a new hamburger stand in a certain community, what four questions should be considered in deciding upon its location?

The more questions the examinee asks in response to a list of such problems, the more he evidently forsees contingencies.

The Memory Abilities

The area of memory abilities has been explored less than some of the other areas of operation, and only seven of the potential cells of the memory matrix have known factors in them. These cells are restricted to three rows: for units, relations, and systems. The first cell in the memory matrix is now occupied by two factors, parallel to two in the corresponding cognition matrix: visual memory and auditory memory. Memory for series of letters or numbers, as in memory span tests, conforms to the conception of memory for symbolic units. Memory for the ideas in a paragraph conforms to the conception of memory for semantic units.

The formation of associations between units, such as visual forms, syllables, and meaningful words, as in the method of paired associates, would seem to represent three abilities to remember relationships involving three kinds of content. We know of two such abilities, for the symbolic and semantic columns. The memory for known systems is represented by two abilities very recently discovered (Christal, 1958). Remembering the arrangement of objects in space is the nature of an ability in the figural column, and remembering a sequence of events is the nature of a corresponding ability in the semantic column. The differentiation between these two abilities implies that a person may be able to say where he saw an object on a page, but he might not be able to say on which of several pages he saw it after leafing through several pages that included the right one. Considering the blank rows in the memory matrix, we should expect to find abilities also to remember classes, transformations, and implications, as well as units, relations, and systems.

3. The Divergent-Thinking Abilities

The unique feature of divergent production is that a *variety* of responses is produced. The product is not completely determined by the given information. This is not to say that divergent thinking does not come into play in the total process of reaching a unique conclusion, for it comes into play wherever there is trial-and-error thinking.

The well-known ability of word fluency is tested by asking the examinee to list words satisfying a specified letter requirement, such as words beginning with the letter "s" or words ending in "-tion." This ability is now regarded as a facility in divergent production of symbolic units. The parallel semantic ability has been known as ideational fluency. A typical test item calls for listing objects that are round and edible. Winston Churchill must have possessed this ability to a high degree. Clement Attlee is reported to have said about him recently that, no matter what problem came up, Churchill always seemed to have about ten ideas. The trouble was, Attlee continued, he did not know which was the good one. The last comment implies some weakness in one or more of the evaluative abilities.

The divergent production of class ideas is believed to be the unique feature of a factor called "spontaneous flexibility." A typical test instructs the examinee to list all the uses he can think of for a common brick, and he is given eight minutes. If his responses are: build a house, build a barn, build a garage, build a school, build a church, build a chimney, build a walk, and build a barbecue, he would earn a fairly high score for ideational fluency but a very low for spontaneous flexibility, because all these uses fall into the same class. If another person said: make a door stop, make a paper weight, throw it at a dog, make a bookcase, drown a cat, drive a nail, make a red powder, and use for baseball bases, he would also receive a high score for flexibility. He has gone frequently from one class to another.

A current study of unknown but predicted divergent-production abilities includes testing whether there are also figural and symbolic abilities to produce multiple classes. An experimental figural test presents a number of figures that can be classified in groups of three in various ways, each figure being usable in more than one class. An experimental symbolic test presents a few numbers that are also to be classified in multiple ways.

A unique ability involving relations is called "associational fluency." It calls for the production of a variety of things related in a specified way to a given thing. For example, the examinee is asked to list words meaning about the same as "good" or to list words meaning about the opposite of "hard." In these instances the response produced is to complete a relationship, and semantic content is involved. Some of our present experimental tests call for the production of varieties of relations, as such, and involve figural and symbolic content also. For example, given four small digits, in how many ways can they be related in order to produce a sum of eight?

One factor pertaining to the production of systems is known as expressional fluency. The rapid formation of phrases or sentences is the essence of certain tests of this factor. For example, given the initial letters:

$$W\text{——} \quad c\text{——} \quad e\text{——} \quad n\text{——}$$

with different sentences to be produced, the examinee might write "We can eat nuts" or "Whence came Eve Newton?" In interpreting the

4 B)
4 A)
factor, we regard the sentence as a symbolic system. By analogy, a figural system would be some
4 c)
kind of organization of lines and other elements,
and a semantic system would be in the form of a
verbally stated problem or perhaps something as
complex as a theory.

In the row of the divergent-production matrix
devoted to transformations, we find some very
5 A)
interesting factors. The one called "adaptive flexibility" is now recognized as belonging in the
figural column. A faithful test of it has been
Match Problems. This is based upon the common
game that uses squares, the sides of which are
formed by match sticks. The examinee is told to
take away a given number of matches to leave a
stated number of squares with nothing left over.
Nothing is said about the sizes of the squares to
be left. If the examinee imposes upon himself
the restriction that the squares that he leaves
must be of the same size, he will fail in his attempts to do items like that in Figure 2. Other
odd kinds of solutions are introduced in other
items, such as overlapping squares and squares
within squares, and so on. In another variation of
Match Problems the examinee is told to produce
two or more solutions for each problem.

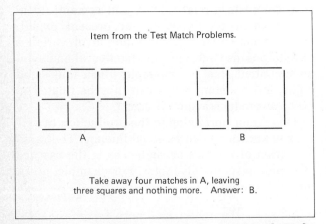

Item from the Test Match Problems.

A   B

Take away four matches in A, leaving
three squares and nothing more.   Answer: B.

Figure 2   A sample item from the test Match Problems. The problem in this item is to take away four
matches and leave three squares. The solution is
given.

5 c)
A factor that has been called "originality" is
now recognized as adaptive flexibility with semantic material, where there must be a shifting
of meanings. The examinee must produce the
shifts or changes in meaning and so come up with
novel, unusual, clever, or farfetched ideas. The
Plot Titles Test presents a short story, the examinee being told to list as many appropriate titles
as he can to head the story. One story is about a
missionary who has been captured by cannibals
in Africa. He is in the pot and about to be boiled
when a princess of the tribe obtains a promise for
his release if he will become her mate. He refuses
and is boiled to death.

In scoring the test, we separate the responses
into two categories, clever and nonclever. Examples of nonclever responses are: African Death,
Defeat of a Princess, Eaten by Savages, The Princess, The African Missionary, In Darkest Africa,
and Boiled by Savages. These titles are appropriate but commonplace. The number of such responses serves as a score for ideational fluency.
Examples of clever responses are: Pot's Plot, Pot-
luck Dinner, Stewed Parson, Goil or Boil, A Mate
Worse Than Death, He Left a Dish for a Pot,
Chaste in Haste, and A Hot Price for Freedom.
The number of clever responses given by an examinee is his score for originality, or the divergent production of semantic transformations.

Another test of originality presents a very
novel task so that any acceptable response is unusual for the individual. In the Symbol Production Test the examinee is to produce a simple
symbol to stand for a noun or a verb in each
short sentence, in other words to invent something like pictographic symbols. Still another test
of originality asks for writing the "punch lines"
for cartoons, a task that almost automatically
challenges the examinee to be clever. Thus, quite
a variety of tests offer approaches to the measurement of originality, including one or two
others that I have not mentioned.

Abilities to produce a variety of implications
are assessed by tests calling for elaboration of

given information. A figural test of this type provides the examinee with a line or two, to which he is to add other lines to produce an object. The more lines he adds, the greater his score. A semantic test gives the examinee the outlines of a plan to which he is to respond by stating all the details he can think of to make the plan work. A new test we are trying out in the symbolic area presents two simple equations such as $B - C = D$ and $z = A + D$. The examinee is to make as many other equations as he can from this information.

4. The Convergent-Production Abilities

Of the 18 convergent-production abilities expected in the three content columns, 12 are now recognized. In the first row, pertaining to units, we have an ability to name figural properties (forms or colors) and an ability to name abstractions (classes, relations, and so on). It may be that the ability in common to the speed of naming forms and the speed of naming colors is not appropriately placed in the convergent-thinking matrix. One might expect that the thing to be produced in a test of the convergent production of figural units would be in the form of figures rather than words. A better test of such an ability might somehow specify the need for one particular object, the examinee to furnish the object.

A test for the convergent production of classes (Word Grouping) presents a list of 12 words that are to be classified in four, and only four, meaningful groups, no word to appear in more than one group. A parallel test (Figure Concepts Test) presents 20 pictured real objects that are to be grouped in meaningful classes of two or more each.

Convergent production having to do with relationships is represented by three known factors, all involving the "eduction of correlates," as Spearman called it. The given information includes one unit and a stated relation, the examinee to supply the other unit. Analogies tests that call for completion rather than a choice between alternative answers emphasize this kind of ability. With symbolic content such an item might read:

pots   stop   bard   drab   rats   ?

A semantic item that measures eduction of correlates is:

The absence of sound is ———.

Incidentally, the latter item is from a vocabulary-completion test, and its relation to the factor of ability to produce correlates indicates how, by change of form, a vocabulary test may indicate an ability other than that for which vocabulary tests are usually intended, namely, the factor of verbal comprehension.

Only one factor for convergent production of systems is known, and it is in the semantic column. It is measured by a class of tests that may be called ordering tests. The examinee may be presented with a number of events that ordinarily have a best or most logical order, the events being presented in scrambled order. The presentation may be pictorial, as in the Picture Arrangement Test, or verbal. The pictures may be taken from a cartoon strip. The verbally presented events may be in the form of the various steps needed to plant a new lawn. There are undoubtedly other kinds of systems than temporal order that could be utilized for testing abilities in this row of the convergent-production matrix.

In the way of producing transformations of a unique variety, we have three recognized factors, known as redefinition abilities. In each case, redefinition involves the changing of functions or uses of parts of one unit and giving them new functions or uses in some new unit. For testing the ability of figural redefinition, a task based upon the Gottschaldt figures is suitable. Figure 3 shows the kind of item for such a test. In recognizing the simpler figure within the structure of a more complex figure, certain lines must take on new roles.

In terms of symbolic material, the following sample items will illustrate how groups of letters

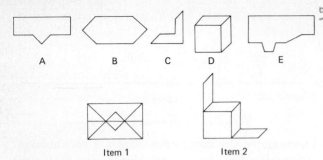

Figure 3 Sample items from a test Hidden Figures, based upon the Gottschaldt figures. Which of the simpler figures is concealed within each of the two more complex figures?

in given words must be readapted to use in other words. In the test Camouflaged Words, each sentence contains the name of a sport or game:

> I did not know that he was ailing.
> To beat the Hun, tin goes a long way.

5 c) For the factor of semantic redefinition, the Gestalt Transformation Test may be used. A sample item reads:

> From which object could you most likely make a needle?
>   A. a cabbage
>   B. a splice
>   C. a steak
>   D. a paper box
>   E. a fish

The convergent production of implications means the drawing of fully determined conclusions from given information. The well-known 6B) factor of numerical facility belongs in the symbolic column. For the parallel ability in the figural 6A) column, we have a test known as Form Reasoning, in which rigorously defined operations with figures are used. For the parallel ability in the 6C) semantic column, the factor sometimes called "deduction" probably qualifies. Items of the following type are sometimes used.

> Charles is younger than Robert
> Charles is older than Frank
> Who is older: Robert or Frank?

5 Evaluative Abilities

The evaluative area has had the least investigation of all the operational categories. In fact, only one systematic analytical study has been devoted to this area. Only eight evaluative abilities are recognized as fitting into the evaluation matrix. But at least five rows have one or more factors each, and also three of the usual columns or content categories. In each case, evaluation involves reaching decisions as to the accuracy, goodness, suitability, or workability of information. In each row, for the particular kind of product of that row, some kind of criterion or standard of judgment is involved.

In the first row, for the evaluation of units, the important decision to be made pertains to the identity of a unit. Is this unit identical with that 1A) one? In the figural column we find the factor long known as "perceptual speed." Tests of this factor invariably call for decisions of identity, for example, Part IV (Perceptual Speed) of the GZAS or Thurstone's Identical Forms. I think it has been generally wrongly thought that the ability involved is that of cognition of visual forms. But we have seen that another factor is a more suitable candidate for this definition and for being in the very first cell of the cognitive matrix. It is parallel to this evaluative ability but does not require the judgment of identity as one of its properties.

In the symbolic column is an ability to judge 1B) identity of symbolic units, in the form of series of letters or numbers or of names of individuals.

> Are members of the following pairs identical or not:
>   825170493 _____ 825176493
>   dkeltvmpa _____ dkeltvmpa
>   C. S. Meyerson _____ C. E. Meyerson

Such items are common in tests of clerical aptitude.

1C) There should be a parallel ability to decide whether two ideas are identical or different. Is the idea expressed in this sentence the same as the idea expressed in that one? Do these two proverbs express essentially the same idea? Such tests exist and will be used to test the hypothesis that such an ability can be demonstrated.

No evaluative abilities pertaining to classes have as yet been recognized. The abilities having to do with evaluation where relations are concerned must meet the criterion of logical consistency. Syllogistic-type tests involving letter symbols indicate a different ability than the same type of test involving verbal statements. In the figural column we might expect that tests incorporating geometric reasoning or proof would indicate a parallel ability to sense the soundness of conclusions regarding figural relationships.

The evaluation of systems seems to be concerned with the internal consistency of those systems, so far as we can tell from the knowledge of one such factor. The factor has been called "experiential evaluation," and its representative test presents items like that in Figure 4 asking "What is wrong with this picture?" The things wrong are often internal inconsistencies.

A semantic ability for evaluating transformations is thought to be that known for some time as "judgment." In typical judgment tests, the examinee is asked to tell which of five solutions to a practical problem is most adequate or wise. The solutions frequently involve improvisations, in other words, adaptations of familiar objects to unusual uses. In this way the items present redefinitions to be evaluated.

A factor known first as "sensitivity to problems" has become recognized as an evaluative ability having to do with implications. One test of the factor, the Apparatus Test, asks for two needed improvements with respect to each of several common devices, such as the telephone or the toaster. The Social Institutions Test, a measure of the same factor, asks what things are wrong with each of several institutions, such as tipping or national elections. We may say that defects or deficiencies are implications of an evaluative kind. Another interpretation would be that seeing defects and deficiencies are evaluations of implications to the effect that the various aspects of something are all right.[2]

SOME IMPLICATIONS OF THE STRUCTURE OF INTELLECT

For Psychological Theory

Although factor analysis as generally employed is best designed to investigate ways in which individuals differ from one another, in other words, to discover traits, the results also tell us much about how individuals are alike. Consequently, information regarding the factors and their interrelationships gives us understanding of functioning individuals. The five kinds of intellectual abilities in terms of operations may be said to represent five ways of functioning. The kinds of intellectual abilities distinguished according to varieties of test content and the kinds of abilities distinguished according to varieties of products suggest a classification of basic forms of information or knowledge. The kind of organism suggested by

Figure 4 A sample item from the test Unusual Details. What two things are wrong with this picture?

[2] For further details concerning the intellectual factors, illustrative tests, and the place of the factors in the structure of intellect, see Guilford (1959).

this way of looking at intellect is that of an agency for dealing with information of various kinds in various ways. The concepts provided by the distinctions among the intellectual abilities and by their classifications may be very useful in our future investigations of learning, memory, problem solving, invention, and decision making, by whatever method we choose to approach those problems.

2. For Vocational Testing

With about 50 intellectual factors already known, we may say that there are at least 50 ways of being intelligent. It has been facetiously suggested that there seem to be a great many more ways of being stupid, unfortunately. The structure of intellect is a theoretical model that predicts as many as 120 distinct abilities, if every cell of the model contains a factor. Already we know that two cells contain two or more factors each, and there probably are actually other cells of this type. Since the model was first conceived, 12 factors predicted by it have found places in it. There is consequently hope of filling many of the other vacancies, and we may eventually end up with more than 120 abilities.

The major implication for the assessment of intelligence is that to know an individual's intellectual resources thoroughly we shall need a surprisingly large number of scores. It is expected that many of the factors are intercorrelated, so there is some possibility that by appropriate sampling we shall be able to cover the important abilities with a more limited number of tests. At any rate, a multiple-score approach to the assessment of intelligence is definitely indicated in connection with future vocational operations.

Considering the kinds of abilities classified as to content, we may speak roughly of four kinds of intelligence. The abilities involving the use of figural information may be regarded as "concrete" intelligence. The people who depend most upon these abilities deal with concrete things and their

properties. Among these people are mechanics, operators of machines, engineers (in some aspects of their work), artists, and musicians.

In the abilities pertaining to symbolic and semantic content, we have two kinds of "abstract" intelligence. Symbolic abilities should be important in learning to recognize words, to spell, and to operate with numbers. Language and mathematics should depend very much upon them, except that in mathematics some aspects, such as geometry, have strong figural involvement. Semantic intelligence is important for understanding things in terms of verbal concepts and hence is important in all courses where the learning of facts and ideas is essential.

In the hypothesized behavioral column of the structure of intellect, which may be roughly described as "social" intelligence, we have some of the most interesting possibilities. Understanding the behavior of others and of ourselves is largely nonverbal in character. The theory suggests as many as 30 abilities in this area, some having to do with understanding, some with productive thinking about behavior, and some with the evaluation of behavior. The theory also suggests that information regarding behavior is also in the form of the six kinds of products that apply elsewhere in the structure of intellect, including units, relations, systems, and so on. The abilities in the area of social intelligence, whatever they prove to be, will possess considerable importance in connection with all those individuals who deal most with other people: teachers, law officials, social workers, therapists, politicians, statesmen, and leaders of other kinds.

3. For Education

The implications for education are numerous, and I have time just to mention a very few. The most fundamental implication is that we might well undergo transformations with respect to our conception of the learner and of the process of learning. Under the prevailing conception, the learner is a kind of stimulus-response device, much on the order of a vending machine. You put in a coin, and something comes out. The machine learns what reaction to put out when a certain coin is put in. If, instead, we think of the learner as an agent for dealing with information, where information is defined very broadly, we have something more analogous to an electronic computer. We feed a computer information; it stores that information; it uses that information for generating new information, either by way of divergent or convergent thinking; and it evaluates its own results. Advantages that a human learner has over a computer include the step of seeking and discovering new information from sources outside itself and the step of programming itself. Perhaps even these steps will be added to computers, if this has not already been done in some cases.

At any rate, this conception of the learner leads us to the idea that learning is discovery of information, not merely the formation of associations, particularly associations in the form of stimulus-response connections. I am aware of the fact that my proposal is rank heresy. But if we are to make significant progress in our understanding of human learning and particularly our understanding of the so-called higher mental processes of thinking, problem solving, and creative thinking, some drastic modifications are due in our theory.

The idea that education is a matter of training the mind or of training the intellect has been rather unpopular, wherever the prevailing psychological doctrines have been followed. In theory, at least, the emphasis has been upon the learning of rather specific habits or skills. If we take our cue from factor theory, however, we recognize that most learning probably has both specific and general aspects or components. The general aspects may be along the lines of the factors of intellect. This is not to say that the individual's status in each factor is entirely determined by learning. We do not know to what extent each factor is determined by heredity and to what extent by learning. The best position for educators to take is that possibly every intellectual factor can be developed in individuals at least to some extent by learning.

If education has the general objective of developing the intellects of students, it can be suggested that each intellectual factor provides a particular goal at which to aim. Defined by a certain combination of content, operation, and product, each goal ability then calls for certain kinds of practice in order to achieve improvement in it. This implies choice of curriculum and the choice or invention of teaching methods that will most likely accomplish the desired results.

Considering the very great variety of abilities revealed by the factorial exploration of intellect, we are in a better position to ask whether any general intellectual skills are now being neglected in education and whether appropriate balances are being observed. It is often observed these days that we have fallen down in the way of producing resourceful, creative graduates. How true this is, in comparison with other times, I do not know. Perhaps the deficit is noticed because the demands for inventiveness are so much greater at this time. At any rate, realization that the more conspicuously creative abilities appear to be concentrated in the divergent-thinking category, and also to some extent in the transformation category, we now ask whether we have been giving these skills appropriate exercise. It is probable that we need a better balance of training in the divergent-thinking area as compared with training in convergent thinking and in critical thinking or evaluation.

The structure of intellect as I have presented EPILOGUE
it to you may or may not stand the test of time. Even if the general form persists, there are likely to be some modifications. Possibly some different kind of model will be invented. Be that as it may, the fact of a multiplicity of intellectual abilities seems well established.

There are many individuals who long for the good old days of simplicity, when we got along with one unanalyzed intelligence. Simplicity certainly has its appeal. But human nature is exceedingly complex, and we may as well face that fact. The rapidly moving events of the world in which we live have forced upon us the need for knowing human intelligence thoroughly. Humanity's peaceful pursuit of happiness depends upon our control of nature and of our own behavior; and this, in turn, depends upon understanding ourselves, including our intellectual resources.

References

Christal, R. E. Factor analytic study of visual memory. *Psychol. Monogr.*, 1958, 72, No. 13 (Whole No. 466).

Guilford, J. P. The structure of intellect. *Psychol. Bull.*, 1956, 53, 267–293.

Guilford, J. P. *Personality.* New York: McGraw-Hill, 1959.

Unknowns in the IQ Equation

A Review of Three Monographs

Sandra Scarr-Salapatek

Environment, Heredity, and Intelligence. Compiled from the *Harvard Educational Review*. Reprint Series No. 2. Harvard Educational Review, Cambridge, Mass., 969. iv, 248 pp., illus. Paper, $4.95.

The IQ Argument. Race, Intelligence and Education. H. J. Eysenck. Library Press, New York, 1971. iv, 156 pp., illus. $5.95.

IQ. Richard Herrnstein, in the *Atlantic,* Vol. 228, No. 3, Sept. 1971, pp. 44–64.

IQ scores have been repeatedly estimated to have a large heritable component in United States and Northern European white populations (1). Indi-

source: Reprinted from *Science,* vol. 174 (December 17, 1971), 1223–1228, by permission of the author and the publisher. Copyright © 1971 by the American Association for the Advancement of Science.

vidual differences in IQ, many authors have concluded, arise far more from genetic than from environmental differences among people in these populations, at the present time, and under present environmental conditions. It has also been known for many years that white lower-class and black groups have lower IQ's, on the average, than white middle-class groups. Most behavioral scientists comfortably "explained" these group differences by appealing to obvious environmental differences between the groups in standards of living, educational opportunities, and the like. But recently an explosive controversy has developed over the heritability of between-group differences in IQ, the question at issue being: If individual differences within the white population as a whole can be attributed largely to heredity, is it not plausible that the average differences between social-class groups and between racial groups also reflect significant genetic differences? Can the former data be used to explain the latter?

To propose genetically based racial and social-class differences is anathema to most behavioral scientists, who fear any scientific confirmation of the pernicious racial and ethnic prejudices that abound in our society. But now that the issue has been openly raised, and has been projected into the public context of social and educational policies, a hard scientific look must be taken at what is known and at what inferences can be drawn from that knowledge.

The public controversy began when A. R. Jensen, in a long paper in the *Harvard Educational Review,* persuasively juxtaposed data on the heritability of IQ and the observed differences between groups. Jensen suggested that current large-scale educational attempts to raise the IQ's of lower-class children, white and black, were failing because of the high heritability of IQ. In a series of papers and rebuttals to criticism, in the same journal and elsewhere (2), Jensen put forth the hypothesis that social-class and racial differences in mean IQ were due largely to differences in the gene distributions of these populations. At least, he said, the genetic-differences hypothesis was no less likely, and probably more likely, than a simple environmental hypothesis to explain the mean difference of 15 IQ points between blacks and whites (3) and the even larger average IQ differences between professionals and manual laborers within the white population.

Jensen's articles have been directed primarily at an academic audience. Herrnstein's article in the *Atlantic* and Eysenck's book (first published in England) have brought the argument to the attention of the wider lay audience. Both Herrnstein and Eysenck agree with Jensen's genetic-differences hypothesis as it pertains to individual differences and to social-class groups, but Eysenck centers his attention on the genetic explanation of racial-group differences, which Herrnstein only touches on. Needless to say, many other scientists will take issue with them.

EYSENCK'S RACIAL THESIS

Eysenck has written a popular account of the race, social-class, and IQ controversy in a generally inflammatory book. The provocative title and the disturbing cover picture of a forlorn black boy are clearly designed to tempt the lay reader into a pseudo-battle between Truth and Ignorance. In this case Truth is genetic-environmental interactionism (4) and Ignorance is naive environmentalism. For the careful reader, the battle fades out inconclusively as Eysenck admits that scientific evidence to date does not permit a clear choice of the genetic-differences interpretation of black inferiority on intelligence tests. A quick reading of the book, however, is sure to leave the reader believing that scientific evidence today strongly supports the conclusion that U.S. blacks are genetically inferior to whites in IQ.

The basic theses of the book are as follows:

1. IQ is a highly heritable characteristic in the U.S. white population and probably equally heritable in the U.S. black population.
2. On the average, blacks score considerably lower than whites on IQ tests.
3. U.S. blacks are probably a non-random, lower-IQ, sample of native African populations.
4. The average IQ difference between blacks and whites probably represents important genetic differences between the races.
5. Drastic environmental changes will have to be made to improve the poor phenotypes that U.S. blacks now achieve.

The evidence and nonevidence that Eysenck cites to support his genetic hypothesis of racial differences make a curious assortment. Audrey Shuey's review (5) of hundreds of studies showing mean phenotypic differences between black and white IQ's leads Eysenck to conclude:

All the evidence to date suggests the strong and indeed overwhelming importance of genetic factors in producing the great variety of intellectual differences which we observe in our culture, and much of the difference observed between certain racial groups. This evidence cannot be argued away by niggling and very minor criticisms of details which do not really throw doubts on the major points made in this book [p. 126].

To "explain" the genetic origins of these mean IQ differences he offers these suppositions:

> White slavers wanted dull beasts of burden, ready to work themselves to death in the plantations, and under those conditions intelligence would have been counter-selective. Thus there is every reason to expect that the particular sub-sample of the Negro race which is constituted of American Negroes is not an unselected sample of Negroes, but has been selected throughout history according to criteria which would put the highly intelligent at a disadvantage. The inevitable outcome of such selection would of course be a gene pool lacking some of the genes making for higher intelligence [p. 42].

Other ethnic minorities in the U.S. are also, in his view, genetically inferior, again because of the selective migration of lower IQ genotypes:

> It is known [sic] that many other groups came to the U.S.A. due to pressures which made them very poor samples of the original populations. Italians, Spaniards, and Portuguese, as well as Greeks, are examples where the less able, less intelligent were forced through circumstances to emigrate, and where their American progeny showed significantly lower IQ's than would have been shown by a random sample of the original population [p. 43]. ✳

Although Eysenck is careful to say that these are not established facts (because no IQ tests were given to the immigrants or nonimmigrants in question?), the tone of his writing leaves no doubt about his judgment. There is something in this book to insult almost everyone except WASP's and Jews.

Despite his conviction that U.S. blacks are genetically inferior in IQ to whites, Eysenck is optimistic about the potential effects of radical environmental changes on the present array of Negro IQ phenotypes. He points to the very large IQ gains produced by intensive one-to-one tutor-ing of black urban children with low-IQ mothers, contrasting large environmental changes and large IQ gains in intensive programs of this sort with insignificant environmental improvements and small IQ changes obtained by Headstart and related programs. He correctly observes that, whatever the heritability of IQ (or, it should be added, of any characteristic), large phenotypic changes may be produced by creating appropriate, radically different environments never before encountered by those genotypes. On this basis, Eysenck calls for further research to determine the requisites of such environments.

Since Eysenck comes to this relatively benign position regarding potential improvement in IQ's, why, one may ask, is he at such pains to "prove" the genetic inferiority of blacks? Surprisingly, he expects that new environments, such as that provided by intensive educational tutoring, will not affect the black-white IQ differential, because black children and white will probably profit equally from such treatment. Since many middle-class white children already having learning environments similar to that provided by tutors for the urban black children, we must suppose that Eysenck expects great IQ gains from relatively small changes in white, middle-class environments.

This book is an uncritical popularization of Jensen's ideas without the nuances and qualifiers that make much of Jensen's writing credible or at least responsible. Both authors rely on Shuey's review (5), but Eysencks's way of doing it is to devote some 25 pages to quotes and paraphrases of her chapter summaries. For readers to whom the original Jensen article is accessible, Eysenck's book is a poor substitute; although he defends Jensen and Shuey, he does neither a service.

It is a maddeningly inconsistent book filled with contradictory caution and incaution; with hypotheses stated both as hypotheses and as conclusions; with both accurate and inaccurate statements on matters of fact. For example, Eysenck thinks evoked potentials offer a better measure of

✳ I do not agree that those who refused to conform to a suppressive system are less able or less intelligent.

"innate" intelligence than IQ tests. But on what basis? Recently F. B. Davis (6) has failed to find any relationship whatsoever between evoked potentials and either IQ scores or scholastic achievement, to which intelligence is supposed to be related. Another example is Eysenck's curious use of data to support a peculiar line of reasoning about the evolutionary inferiority of blacks: First, he reports that African and U.S. Negro babies have been shown to have precocious sensorimotor development by white norms (the difference, by several accounts, appears only in gross motor skills and even there is slight). Second, he notes that by three years of age U.S. white exceed U.S. black children in mean IQ scores. Finally he cites a (very slight) negative correlation, found in an early study, between sensorimotor intelligence in the first year of life and later IQ. From exaggerated statements of these various data, he concludes:

> These findings are important because of a very general view in biology according to which the more prolonged the infancy the greater in general are the cognitive or intellectual abilities of the species. This law appears to work even within a given species [p. 79].

Eysenck would apparently have us believe that Africans and their relatives in the U.S. are less highly evolved than Caucasians, whose longer infancy is related to later higher intelligence. I am aware of no evidence whatsoever to support a within-species relationship between longer infancy and higher adult capacities.

HERRNSTEIN'S SOCIAL THESIS

Thanks to Jensen's provocative article, many academic psychologists who thought IQ tests belonged in the closet with the Rorschach inkblots have now explored the psychometric literature and found it to be a trove of scientific treasure. One of these is Richard Herrnstein, who from a Skinnerian background has become an admirer of intelligence tests—a considerable leap from shaping the behavior of pigeons and rats. In contrast to Eysenck's book, Herrnstein's popular account in the *Atlantic* of IQ testing and its values is generally responsible, if overly enthusiastic in parts.

Herrnstein unabashedly espouses IQ testing as "psychology's most telling accomplishment to date," despite the current controversy over the fairness of testing poor and minority-group children with IQ items devised by middle-class whites. His historical review of IQ test development, including tests of general intelligence and multiple abilities, is interesting and accurate. His account of the validity and usefulness of the tests centers on the fairly accurate prediction that can be made from IQ scores to academic and occupational achievement and income level. He clarifies the pattern of relationship between IQ and these criterion variables: High IQ is a necessary but not sufficient condition for high achievement, while low IQ virtually assures failure at high academic and occupational levels. About the usefulness of the tests, he concludes:

> An IQ test can be given in an hour or two to a child, and from this infinitesimally small sample of his output, deeply important predictions follow— about schoolwork, occupation, income, satisfaction with life, and even life expectancy. The predictions are not perfect, for other factors always enter in, but no other single factor matters as much in as many spheres of life [p. 53].

One must assume that Herrnstein's enthusiasm for intelligence tests rests on population statistics, not on predictions for a particular child, because many children studied longitudinally have been shown to change IQ scores by 20 points or more from childhood to adulthood. It is likely that extremes of giftedness and retardation can be sorted out relatively early by IQ tests, but what about the 95 percent of the population in between? Their IQ scores may vary from dull to bright normal for many years. Important variations in IQ can occur up to late adolescence (8).

On a population basis Herrnstein is correct; the best early predictors of later achievement are ability measures taken from age five on. Predictions are based on correlations, however, which are not sensitive to absolute changes in value, only to rank orders. This is an important point to be discussed later.

After reviewing the evidence for average IQ differences by social class and race, Herrnstein poses the nature-nurture problem of "which is primary" in determining phenotypic difference in IQ. For racial groups, he explains, the origins of mean IQ differences are indeterminate at the present time because we have no information from heritability studies in the black population or from other, unspecified, lines of research which could favor primarily genetic or primarily environmental hypotheses. He is thoroughly convinced, however, that individual differences and social-class differences in IQ are highly heritable at the present time, and are destined, by environmental improvements, to become even more so:

> If we make the relevant environment much more uniform (by making it as good as we can for everyone), then an even larger proportion of the variation in IQ will be attributable to the genes. The average person would be smarter, but intelligence would run in families even more obviously and with less regression toward the mean than we see today [p. 58].

For Herrnstein, society is, and will be even more strongly, a meritocracy based largely on inherited differences in IQ. He presents a "syllogism" [p. 58] to make his message clear.

1. If differences in mental abilities are inherited, and
2. If success requires those abilities, and
3. If earnings and prestige depend on success,
4. Then social standing (which reflects earnings and prestige) will be based to some extent on inherited differences among people.

Five "corollaries" for the future predict that the heritability of IQ will rise; that social mobility will become more strongly related to inherited IQ differences; that most bright people will be gathered in the top of the social structure, with the IQ dregs at the bottom; that many at the bottom will not have the intelligence needed for new jobs; and that the meritocracy will be built not just on inherited intelligence but on all inherited traits affecting success, which will presumably become correlated characters. Thus from the successful realization of our most precious egalitarian, political and social goals there will arise a much more rigidly stratified society, a "virtual caste system" based on inborn ability.

To ameliorate this effect, society may have to move toward the socialist dictum, "From each according to his abilities, to each according to his needs," but Herrnstein sees complete equality of earnings and prestige as impossible because high-grade intelligence is scarce and must be recruited into those critical jobs that require it, by the promise of high earnings and high prestige. Although garbage collecting is critical to the health of the society, almost anyone can do it; to waste high-IQ persons on such jobs is to misallocate scarce resources at society's peril.

Herrnstein points to an ironic contrast between the effects of caste and class systems. Castes, which established artifical hereditary limits on social mobility, guarantee the inequality of opportunity that preserves IQ heterogeneity at all levels of the system. Many bright people are arbitrarily kept down and many unintelligent people are artifically maintained at the top. When arbitrary bounds on mobility are removed, as in our class system, most of the bright rise to the top and most of the dull fall to the bottom of the social system, and IQ differences between top and bottom become increasingly hereditary. The greater the environmental equality, the greater the hereditary differences between levels in the social structure. The thesis of egalitarianism surely leads to its antithesis in a way that Karl Marx never anticipated.

Herrnstein proposes that our best strategy, in the face of increasingly biological stratification, is publicly to recognize genetic human differences but to reallocate wealth to a considerable extent. The IQ have-nots need not be poor. Herrnstein does not delve into the psychological consequences of being publicly marked as genetically inferior.

Does the evidence support Herrnstein's view of hereditary social classes, now or in some future Utopia? Given his assumptions about the high heritability of IQ, the importance of IQ to social mobility, and the increasing environmental equality of rearing and opportunity, hereditary social classes are to some extent inevitable. But one can question the limits of genetic homogeneity in social-class groups and the evidence for his syllogism at present.

Is IQ as highly heritable throughout the social structure as Herrnstein assumes? Probably not. In a recent study of IQ heritability in various racial and social-class groups (9), I found much lower proportions of genetic variance that would account for aptitude differences among lower-class than among middle-class children, in both black and white groups. Social disadvantage in prenatal and postnatal development can substantially lower phenotypic IQ and reduce the genotype-phenotype correlation. Thus, average phenotypic IQ differences between the social classes may be considerably larger than the genotypic differences.

Are social classes largely based on hereditary IQ differences now? Probably not as much as Herrnstein believes. Since opportunities for social mobility act at the phenotypic level, there still may be considerable genetic diversity for IQ at the bottom of the social structure. In earlier days arbitrary social barriers maintained genetic variability throughout the social structure. At present, individuals with high phenotypic IQ's are often upwardly mobile; but inherited wealth acts to maintain genetic diversity at the top, and nongenetic biological and social barriers to phenotypic development act to maintain a considerable genetic diversity of intelligence in the lower classes.

As P. E. Vernon has pointed out (10), we are inclined to forget that the majority of gifted children in recent generations have come from working class, not middle-class, families. A larger percentage of middle-class children are gifted, but the working classes produce gifted children in larger numbers. How many more disadvantaged children would have been bright if they had had middle-class gestation and rearing conditions?

I am inclined to think that intergenerational class mobility will always be with us, for three reasons. First, since normal IQ is a polygenic characteristic, various recombinations of parental genotypes will always produce more variable genotypes in the offspring than in the parents of all social-class groups, especially the extremes. Even if both parents, instead of primarily the male, achieved social-class status based on their IQ's, recombinations of their genes would always produce a range of offspring, who would be upwardly or downwardly mobile relative to their families of origin.

Second, since, as Hernstein acknowledges, factors other than IQ—motivational, personality, and undetermined—also contribute to success or the lack of it, high IQ's will always be found among lower-class adults, in combination with schizophrenia, alcoholism, drug addiction, psychopathy, and other limiting factors. When recombined in offspring, high IQ can readily segregate with facilitating motivational and personality characteristics, thereby leading to upward mobility for many offspring. Similarly, middle-class parents will always produce some offspring with debilitating personal characteristics which lead to downward mobility.

Third, for all children to develop phenotypes that represent their best genotypic outcome (in current environments) would require enormous changes in the present social system. To improve and equalize all rearing environments would involve such massive intervention as to make Herrnstein's view of the future more problematic than he seems to believe.

RACE AS CASTE

Races are castes between which there is very litte mobility. Unlike the social-class system, where mobility based on IQ is sanctioned, the racial caste system, like the hereditary aristocracy of medieval Europe and the caste system of India, preserves within each group its full range of genetic diversity of intelligence. The Indian caste system was, according to Dobzhansky (11), a colossal genetic failure—or success, according to egalitarian values. After the abolition of castes at independence, Brahmins and untouchables were found to be equally educable despite—or because of—their many generations of segregated reproduction.

While we may tentatively conclude that there are some genetic IQ differences between social-class groups, we can make only wild speculations about racial groups. Average phenotypic IQ differences between races are not evidence for genetic differences (any more than they are evidence for environmental differences). Even if the heritabilities of IQ are extremely high in all races, there is still no warrant for equating within-group and between-group heritabilities (12). There are examples in agricultural experiments of within-group differences that are highly heritable but between-group differences that are entirely environmental. Draw two random samples of seeds from the same genetically heterogeneous population. Plant one sample in uniformly good conditions, the other in uniformly poor conditions. The average height difference between the populations of plants will be entirely environmental, although the individual differences in height within each sample will be entirely genetic. With known environments, genetic and environmental variances between groups can be studied. But racial groups are not random samples from the same population, nor are members reared in uni-

form conditions within each race. Racial groups are of unknown genetic equivalence for polygenic characteristics like IQ, and the differences in environments within and between the races may have as yet unquantified effects.

There is little to be gained from approaching the nature-nurture problem of race differences in IQ directly (13). Direct comparisons of estimated within-group heritabilities and the calculation of between-group heritabilities require assumptions that few investigators are willing to make, such as that all environmental differences are quantifiable, that differences in the environments of blacks and whites can be assumed to affect IQ in the same way in the two groups, and that differences in environments between groups can be "statistically controlled." A direct assault on race differences in IQ is vulnerable to many criticisms.

Indirect approaches may be less vulnerable. These include predictions of parent-child regression effects and admixture studies. Regression effects can be predicted to differ for blacks and whites if the two races indeed have genetically different population means. If the population mean for blacks is 15 IQ points lower than that of whites, then the offspring of high-IQ black parents should show greater regression (toward a lower population mean) than the offspring of whites of equally high IQ. Similarly, the offspring of low-IQ black parents should show less regression than those of white parents of equally low IQ. This hypothesis assumes that assortative mating for IQ is equal in the two races, which could be empirically determined but has not been studied as yet. Interpretable results from a parent-child regression study would also depend upon careful attention to intergenerational environmental changes, which could be greater in one race than the other.

Studies based on correlations between degree of white admixture and IQ scores *within* the black group would avoid many of the pitfalls of between-group comparisons. If serological genotypes can be used to identify persons with more and less white admixture, and if estimates of admixture based on blood groups are relatively independent of visible characteristics like skin color, then any positive correlation between degree of admixture and IQ would suggest genetic racial differences in IQ. Since blood groups have not been used directly as the basis of racial discrimination, positive findings would be relatively immune from environmentalist criticisms. The trick is to estimate individual admixture reliably. Several loci which have fairly different distributions of alleles in contemporary African and white populations have been proposed (14). No one has yet attempted a study of this sort.

h² AND PHENOTYPE

Suppose that the heritabilities of IQ differences within all racial and social-class groups were .80, as Jensen estimates, and suppose that the children in all groups were reared under an equal range of conditions. Now, suppose that racial and social-class differences in mean IQ still remained. We would probably infer some degree of genetic difference between the groups. So what? The question now turns from a strictly scientific one to one of science and social policy.

As Eysenck, Jensen, and others (14) have noted, eugenic and euthenic strategies are both possible interventions to reduce the number of low-IQ individuals in all populations. Eugenic (A) policies could be advanced to encourage or require reproductive abstinence by people who fall below a certain level of intelligence. The Reeds (15) have determined that one-fifth of the mental retardation among whites of the next generation could be prevented if no mentally retarded persons of this generation reproduced. There is no question that a eugenic program applied at the phenotypic level of parents' IQ would substantially reduce the number of low-IQ children in the future white population. I am aware of no studies in the black population to support a similar program, but some proportion of future retardation could surely be eliminated. It would be extremely

important, however, to sort out genetic and environmental sources of low IQ both in racial and in social-class groups before advancing a eugenic program. The request or demand that some persons refrain from any reproduction should be a last resort, based on sure knowledge that their retardation is caused primarily by genetic factors and is not easily remedied by environmental intervention. Studies of the IQ levels of adopted children with mentally retarded natural parents would be most instructive, since some of the retardation observed among children of retarded parents may stem from the rearing environments provided by the parents.

In a pioneering study of adopted children and their adoptive and natural parents, Skodak (16) reported greater *correlations* of children's IQ's with their natural than with their adoptive parents' IQ's. This statement has been often misunderstood to mean that the children's *levels* of intelligence more closely resembled their natural parents' which is completely false. Although the rank order of the children's IQ resembled that of their mother's IQ's, the children's IQ's were higher, being distributed, like those of the adoptive parents, around a mean above 100, whereas their natural mothers' IQ's averaged only 85. The children, in fact, averaged 21 IQ points higher than their natural mothers. If the (unstudied) natural fathers' IQ's averaged around the population mean of 100, the mean of the children's would be expected to be 94, or 12 points lower than the mean obtained. The unexpected boost in IQ was presumably due to the better social environments provided by the adoptive families. Does this mean that phenotypic IQ can be substantially changed?

Even under existing conditions of child rearing, phenotypes of children reared by low IQ parents could be markedly changed by giving them the same rearing environment as the top IQ group provide for their children. According to DeFries (17), if children whose parents average 20 IQ points below the population mean were reared in environments such as usually are pro-

EUGENICS = MOVEMENT DEVOTED TO SPECIES IMPROVEMENT VIA CONTROL OF HEREDITY ;

EUTHENICS = " " " " " " " " " " ENVIRONMENT.

vided only by parents in the top .01 percent of the population, these same children would average 5 points *above* the population mean instead of 15 points below, as they do when reared by their own families.

(B) Euthenic policies depend upon the demonstration that different rearing conditions can change phenotypic IQ sufficiently to enable most people in a social class or racial group to function in future society. I think there is great promise in this line of research and practice, although its efficacy will depend ultimately on the cost and feasibility of implementing radical intervention programs. Regardless of the present heritability of IQ in any population, phenotypes can be changed by the introduction of new and different environments. (One merit of Eysenck's book is the attention he gives to this point.) Furthermore, it is impossible to predict phenotypic outcomes under very different conditions. For example, in the Milwaukee Project (18), in which the subjects are ghetto children whose mothers' IQ's are less than 70, intervention began soon after the children were born. Over a four-year period Heber has intensively tutored the children for several hours every day and has produced an enormous IQ difference between the experimental group (mean IQ 127) and a control group (mean IQ 90). If the tutored children continue to advance in environments which are radically different from their homes with retarded mothers, we shall have some measure of the present phenotypic range of reaction (19) of children whose average IQ's might have been in the 80 to 90 range. These data support Crow's comment on h^2 in his contribution to the *Harvard Educational Review* discussion (p. 158):

> It does not directly tell us how much improvement in IQ to expect from a given change in the environment. In particular, it offers no guidance as to the consequences of a new kind of environmental influence. For example, conventional heritability measures for height show a value of nearly 1. Yet, because of unidentified environmental influ-

ences, the mean height in the United States and in Japan has risen by a spectacular amount. Another kind of illustration is provided by the discovery of a cure for a hereditary disease. In such cases, any information on prior heritability may become irrelevant. Furthermore, heritability predictions are less dependable at the tails of the distribution.

To illustrate the phenotypic changes that can be produced by radically different environments for children with clear genetic anomalies, Rynders (20) has provided daily intensive tutoring for Down's syndrome infants. At the age of two, these children have average IQ's of 85 while control-group children, who are enrolled in a variety of other programs, average 68. Untreated children have even lower average IQ scores.

The efficacy of intervention programs for children whose expected IQ's are too low to permit full participation in society depends on their long-term effects on intelligence. Early childhood programs may be necessary but insufficient to produce functioning adults. There are critical research questions yet to be answered about euthenic programs, including what kinds, how much, how long, how soon, and toward what goals?

Does h^2 Matter?

There is growing disillusionment with the concept of heritability, as it is understood and misunderstood. Some who understand it very well would like to eliminate h^2 from human studies for at least two reasons. First, the usefulness of h^2 estimates in animal and plant genetics pertains to decisions about the efficacy of selective breeding to produce more desirable phenotypes. Selective breeding does not apply to the human case, at least so far. Second, if important phenotypic changes can be produced by radically different environments, then, it is asked, who cares about the heritability of IQ? Morton (21) has expressed these sentiments well:

> Considerable popular interest attaches to such questions as "is one class or ethnic group innately superior to another on a particular test?" The rea-

sons are entirely emotional, since such a difference, if established, would serve as no better guide to provision of educational or other facilities than an unpretentious assessment of phenotypic differences.

I disagree. The simple assessment of phenotypic performance does not suggest any particular intervention strategy. Heritability estimates can have merit as indicators of the effects to be expected from various types of intervention programs. If, for example, IQ tests, which predict well to achievements in the larger society, show low heritabilities in a population, then it is probable that simply providing better environments [than] now exist will improve average performance in that population. If h^2 is high but environments sampled in that population are largely unfavorable, then (again) simple environmental improvement will probably change the mean phenotypic level. If h^2 is high and the environments sampled are largely favorable, then novel environmental manipulations are probably required to change phenotypes, and eugenic programs may be advocated.

The most common misunderstanding of the concept "heritability" relates to the myth of fixed intelligence: if h^2 is high, this reasoning goes, then intelligence is genetically fixed and unchangeable at the phenotypic level. This misconception ignores the fact that h^2 is a population statistic, bound to a given set of environmental conditions at a given point in time. Neither intelligence nor h^2 estimates are fixed.

It is absurd to deny that the frequencies of genes for behavior may vary between populations. For individual differences within populations, and for social-class differences, a genetic hypothesis is almost a necessity to explain some of the variance in IQ, especially among adults in contemporary white populations living in average or better environments. But what Jensen, Shuey, and Eysenck (and others) propose is that genetic racial differences are necessary to account for the current phenotypic differences in mean IQ between populations. That may be so, but it would be extremely difficult, given current methodological limitations, to gather evidence that would dislodge an environmental hypothesis to account for the same data. And to assert, despite the absence of evidence, and in the present social climate, that a particular race is genetically disfavored in intelligence is to scream "FIRE! . . . I think" in a crowded theater. Given that so little is known, further scientific study seems far more justifiable than public speculations.

Notes

1. For a review of studies, see L. Erlenmeyer-Kimling and L. F. Jarvik, *Science* 142, 1477 (1963). Heritability is the ratio of genetic variance to total phenotypic variance. Heritability is used in its broad sense of total genetic variance/total phenotypic variance.
2. The *Harvard Educational Review* compilation includes Jensen's paper, "How much can we boost IQ and scholastic achievement?," comments on it by J. S. Kagan, J. McV. Hunt, J. F. Crow, C. Bereiter, D. Elkind, L. J. Cronback and W. F. Brazziel, and a rejoinder by Jensen. See also A. R. Jensen, in J. Hellmuth, *Disadvantaged Child*. vol. 3 (Special Child Publ., Seattle, Wash., 1970).
3. P. L. Nichols, thesis, University of Minnesota (1970). Nichols reports that in two large samples of black and white children, seven-year WISC IQ scores showed the same means and distributions for the two racial groups, once social-class variables were equated. These results are unlike those of several other studies, which found that matching socio-economic status did not create equal means in the two racial groups [A. Shuey (5); A. B. Wilson, *Racial Isolation in the Public Schools*, vol. 2 (Government Printing Office, Washington, D.C., 1967)]. In Nichols' samples, prenatal and postnatal medical care was equally available to blacks and whites which may have contributed to the relatively high IQ scores of the blacks in these samples.
4. By interaction, Eysenck means simply $P = G + E$, or "heredity and environment acting together to produce the observed phenotype" (p. 111). He does not mean what most geneticists and behavior geneticists mean by interaction; that is, the *differential*

phenotypic effects produced by various combinations of genotypes and environments, as in the interaction term of analysis-of-variance statistics. Few thinking people are not interactionists in Eysenck's sense of the term, because that's the only way to get the organism and the environment into the same equation to account for variance in any phenotypic trait. How much of the phenotypic variance is accounted for by each of the terms in the equation is the real issue.

5. A. Shuey, *The Testing of Negro Intelligence* (Social Science Press, New York, 1966), pp. 499–519.

6. F. B. Davis, *The Measurement of Mental Capacity through Evoked-Potential Recordings* (Educational Records Bureau, Greenwich, Conn., 1972). "As it turned out, no evidence was found that the latency periods obtained . . . displayed serviceable utility for predicting school performance or level of mental ability among pupils in preschool through grade 8" (p. v).

7. *New York Times,* 8 Oct. 1971, p. 41.

8. J. Kagan and H. A. Moss, *Birth to Maturity* (Wiley, New York, 1962).

9. S. Scarr-Salapatek, *Science,* in press.

10. P. E. Vernon, *Intelligence and Cultural Environment* (Methuen, London, 1969).

11. T. Dobzhansky, *Mankind Evolving* (Yale Univ. Press, New Haven, 1962), pp. 234–238.

12. J. Thoday, *J. Biosocial Science* 1, suppl. 3, 4 (1969).

13. L. L. Cavalli-Sforza and W. F. Bodmer, *The Genetics of Human Populations* (Freeman, San Francisco, 1971), pp. 753–804. They propose that the study of racial differences is useless and not scientifically supportable at the present time.

14. T. E. Reed, *Science* 165, 762 (1969); *Am. J. Hum. Genet.* 21, 1 (1969; C. MacLean and P. L. Workman, paper at a meeting of the American Society of Human Genetics (1970, Indianapolis).

15. E. W. Reed and S. C. Reed, *Mental Retardation: A Family Study* (Saunders, Philadelphia, 1965); *Social Biol.* 18, supple., 42 (1971).

16. M. Skodak and H. WM. Skeels, *J. Genet. Psychol.* 75, 85 (1949).

17. J. C. DeFries, paper for the C.O.B.R.E. Research Workshop on Genetic Endowment and Environment in the Determination of Behavior (3–8 Oct. 1971, Rye, N.Y.).

18. R. Heber, *Rehabilitation of Families at Risk for Mental Retardation* (Regional Rehabilitation Center, Univ. of Wisconsin, 1969). S. P. Strickland, *Am Ed.* 7, 3 (1971).

19. I. I. Gottesman, in *Social Class, Race, and Psychological Development,* M. Deutsch, I. Katz, and A. R. Jensen, Eds. (Holt, Rinehart, and Winston, New York, 1968), pp. 11–51.

20. J. Rynders, personal communication, November 1971.

21. N. E. Morton, paper for the C.O.B.R.E. Research Workshop on Genetic Endowment and Environment in the Determination of Behavior (3–8 Oct. 1971, Rye, N.Y.).

22. I thank Philip Salapatek, Richard Weinberg, I. I. Gottesman, and Leonard I. Heston for their critical reading of this paper. They are not in any way responsible for its content, however.

Chapter 8

Motivation

What motivates the child's behavior? What needs and desires, what goals, provoke his actions and responses? These have been and continue to be critical questions for theorists and researchers in the fields of learning, personality development, and social psychology. Although some behaviors are motivated by basic drives such as hunger and thirst (labeled **primary** drives in traditional learning theory), most of man's actions appear to be aroused by motives that are not so obviously tied to biological states. There has been a continuing debate about what motives are most important and what goals people strive for most strongly. Earlier it was believed that the primary motive of man was to reduce tension and stimulation. In the light of a great deal of recent research evidence and theory, however, R. W. White and others have come to the view that human beings seek excitement and stimulation from the environment: Babies explore and manipulate both familiar and unfamiliar objects; novelty and variety appear to be enjoyable for their own sake.

(1)   In an important and stimulating paper, the first in this chapter, White marshaled many relevant findings from a variety of investigations that demonstrate that even very young babies exhibit a desire to be competent, to master or deal effectively with their own environment. He labels this desire **effectance motivation**, and he considers it an essential attribute of personality, evident early in life and closely related to such other basic and pervasive motives as curiosity, mastery, and achievement—that is, to the child's desire to master problems and increase his skills and capabilities.

The term **aggression** is used in two quite different ways in psychological literature:

(1) to describe the behavior that causes injury or anxiety to others (e.g., hitting, pushing, destroying property, quarreling) and (2) to designate the **intention** or motivation to hurt someone. The behavior is aggressive; the intention or desire is often labeled hostility.

Hostile motivation and aggressive behavior are not necessarily linked directly. Any particular aggressive act may have different motives or functions; it may be motivated by hostility, or it may be motivated by other factors. One child may hit another, not because the first is hostile toward him, but because he wants a toy that the other is holding; the aggressive act has an instrumental, not a hostile, goal (i.e., to obtain a nonaggressive goal, a toy). Nor does aggressive or hostile motivation necessarily lead to aggressive behavior. A child may feel very hostile toward his younger sister when she frustrates him, but he has learned that direct physical aggression toward her is punished, so he inhibits this kind of response.

In recent years the amount of overt violence and aggressive behavior in our society has burgeoned. What provokes such aggression? Does exposure to aggressive models on television or other mass media increase aggression in children? Under what conditions is the level of aggressive behavior likely to increase and what factors lead to its inhibition? What methods are most effective in modifying and reducing aggressive behaviors?

(2) The extensive research literature bearing on these socially relevant questions is reviewed and evaluated in the article written by N. Feshbach and S. Feshbach. The authors discuss the complex issues of parental and home influences on children's aggression, noting that "although parental punishment is intended to inhibit aggression, research has provided surprisingly little evidence of inhibitory effects" (p. 236). In fact, some studies indicate that sons and daughters of highly punitive parents are more aggressive than children of low punitive parents. The parent who uses physical aggression in punishing his child serves as an aggressive model.

There is a close relation between the **determinants** of aggression and the **means of controlling** it. Thus, the effects of punishment, violence in the mass media, and imitation of others can be considered antecedents of aggression but they are also potential **regulators** of aggressive behavior. Aggressive behavior can be modified by means of the cognitive processes of reviewing, restructuring, or reinterpreting a frustrating or distressing experience.

20

Motivation Reconsidered:
The Concept of Competence

Robert W. White

When parallel trends can be observed in realms as far apart as animal behavior and psychoanalytic ego psychology, there is reason to suppose that we are witnessing a significant evolution of ideas. In these two realms, as in psychology as a whole, there is evidence of deepening discontent with theories of motivation based upon drives. Despite great differences in the language and concepts used to express this discontent, the theme is everywhere the same: Something important is left out when we make drives the operating forces in animal and human behavior.

The chief theories against which the discontent is directed are those of Hull and of Freud. In their respective realms, drive-reduction theory and psychoanalytic instinct theory, which are

SOURCE: Reprinted, in abridged form, from *Psychological Review*, vol. 66 (1959), 297–333. Copyright © by the American Psychological Association. Reprinted by permission.

basically very much alike, have acquired a considerable air of orthodoxy. Both views have an appealing simplicity, and both have been argued long enough so that their main outlines are generally known. In decided contrast is the position of those who are not satisfied with drives and instincts. They are numerous, and they have developed many pointed criticisms, but what they have to say has not thus far lent itself to a clear and inclusive conceptualization. Apparently there is an enduring difficulty in making these contributions fall into shape.

In this paper I shall attempt a conceptualization which gathers up some of the important things left out by drive theory. To give the concept a name I have chosen the word *competence*, which is intended in a broad biological sense rather than in its narrow everyday meaning. As used here, competence will refer to an organism's capacity to interact effectively with its environment. In organisms capable of but little learning, this capacity might be considered an innate attribute, but in the mammals and especially man, with their highly plastic nervous systems, fitness to interact with the environment is slowly attained through prolonged feats of learning. In view of the directedness and persistence of the behavior that leads to these feats of learning, I consider it necessary to treat competence as having a motivational aspect, and my central argument will be that the motivation needed to attain competence cannot be wholly derived from sources of energy currently conceptualized as drives or instincts. We need a different kind of motivational idea to account fully for the fact that man and the higher mammals develop a competence in dealing with the environment which they certainly do not have at birth and certainly do not arrive at simply through maturation. Such an idea, I believe, is essential for any biologically sound view of human nature.

.   .   .   .

COMPETENCE AND THE PLAY
OF CONTENTED CHILDREN

A survey of the relevant literature shows considerable agreement about the kinds of behavior that are left out or handled poorly by theories of motivation based wholly on organic drives.[1] Repeatedly we find reference to the familiar series of learned skills which starts with sucking, grasping, and visual exploration and continues with crawling and walking, acts of focal attention and perception, memory, language and thinking, anticipation, the exploring of novel places and objects, effecting stimulus changes in the environment, manipulating and exploiting the surroundings, and achieving higher levels of motor and mental coordination. These aspects of behavior have long

[1]White's unabridged article contains a complete summary.—Ed.

been the province of child psychology, which has attempted to measure the slow course of their development and has shown how heavily their growth depends upon learning. Collectively they are sometimes referred to as adaptive mechanisms or as ego processes, but on the whole we are not accustomed to cast a single name over the diverse feats whereby we learn to deal with the environment.

I now propose that we gather the various kinds of behavior just mentioned, all of which have to do with effective interaction with the environment, under the general heading of competence. According to Webster, competence means fitness or ability, and the suggested synonyms include capability, capacity, efficiency, proficiency, and skill. It is therefore a suitable word to describe such things as grasping and exploring, crawling and walking, attention and perception, language and thinking, manipulating and changing the surroundings, all of which promote an effective—a competent—interaction with the environment. It is true, of course, that maturation plays a part in all these developments, but this part is heavily overshadowed by learning in all the more complex accomplishments like speech or skilled manipulation. I shall argue that it is necessary to make competence a motivational concept; there is a *competence motivation* as well as competence in its more familiar sense of achieved capacity. The behavior that leads to the building up of effective grasping, handling, and letting go of objects, to take one example, is not random behavior produced by a general overflow of energy. It is directed, selective, and persistent, and it is continued not because it serves primary drives, which indeed it cannot serve until it is almost perfected, but because it satisfies an intrinsic need to deal with the environment.

No doubt it will at first seem arbitrary to propose a single motivational conception in connection with so many and such diverse kinds of behavior. What do we gain by attributing motivational unity to such a large array of activities? We could, of course, say that each developmental sequence, such as learning to grasp or to walk, has its own built-in bit of motivation—its "ailment," as Piaget (1952) has expressed it. We could go further and say that each item of behavior has its intrinsic motive—but this makes the concept of motivation redundant. On the other hand, we might follow the lead of the animal psychologists and postulate a limited number of broader motives under such names as curiosity, manipulation, and mastery. I believe that the idea of a competence motivation is more adequate than any of these alternatives and that it points to very vital common properties which have been lost from view amidst the strongly analytical tendencies that go with detailed research.

In order to make this claim more plausible, I shall now introduce some specimens of playful exploration in early childhood. I hope that these images will serve to fix and dramatize the concept of competence in the same way that other images —the hungry animal solving problems, the child putting his finger in the candle flame, the infant at the breast, the child on the toilet, and the youhful Oedipus caught in a hopeless love triangle—have become memorable focal points for other concepts. For this purpose I turn to Piaget's (1952) studies of the growth of intelligence from its earliest manifestations in his own three children. The examples come from the first year of life, before language and verbal concepts begin to be important. They therefore represent a practical kind of intelligence which may be quite similar to what is developed by the higher animals.

As early as the fourth month, the play of the gifted Piaget children began to be "centered on a result produced in the external environment," and their behavior could be described as "rediscovering the movement which by chance exercised an advantageous action upon things" (1952, p. 151). Laurent, lying in his bassinet, learns to shake a suspended rattle by pulling a string that hangs from it. He discovers this result fortu-

itously before vision and prehension are fully coordinated. Let us now observe him a little later when he has reached the age of three months and ten days.

I place the string, which is attached to the rattle, in his right hand, merely unrolling it a little so that he may grasp it better. For a moment nothing happens. But at the first shake due to chance movement of his hand, the reaction is immediate: Laurent starts when looking at the rattle and then violently strikes his right hand alone, as if he felt the resistance and the effect. The operation lasts fully a quarter of an hour, during which Laurent emits peals of laughter [Piaget, 1952, p. 162].

Three days later the following behavior is observed.

Laurent, by chance, strikes the chain while sucking his fingers. He grasps it and slowly displaces it while looking at the rattles. He then begins to swing it very gently, which produces a slight movement of the hanging rattles and an as yet faint sound inside them. Laurent then definitely increases by degrees his own movements. He shakes the chain more and more vigorously and laughs uproariously at the result obtained [Piaget, 1952, p. 185].

Very soon it can be observed that procedures are used "to make interesting spectacles last." For instance, Laurent is shown a rubber monkey which he has not seen before. After a moment of surprise, and perhaps even fright, he calms down and makes movements of pulling the string, a procedure which has no effect in this case, but which previously has caused interesting things to happen. It is to be noticed that "interesting spectacles" consist of such things as new toys, a tin box upon which a drumming noise can be made, an unfolded newspaper, or sounds made by the observer such as snapping the fingers. Commonplace as they are to the adult mind, these spectacles enter the infant's experience as novel and apparently challenging events.

Moving ahead to the second half of the first year, we can observe behavior in which the child explores the properties of objects and tries out his repertory of actions upon them. This soon leads to active experimentation in which the child attempts to provoke new results. Again we look in upon Laurent, who has now reached the age of nine months. On different occasions he is shown a variety of new objects—for instance a notebook, a beaded purse, and a wooden parrot. His carefully observing father detects four stages of response: *(a)* visual exploration, passing the object from hand to hand, folding the purse, etc.; *(b)* tactile exploration, passing the hand all over the object, scratching, etc.; *(c)* slow moving of the object in space; *(d)* use of the repertory of action; shaking the object, striking it, swinging it, rubbing it against the side of the bassinet, sucking it, etc., "each in turn with a sort of prudence as though studying the effect produced" (1952, p. 255).

Here the child can be described as applying familiar tactics to new situations, but in a short while he will advance to clear patterns of active experimentation. At 10 months and 10 days Laurent, who is unfamiliar with bread as a nutritive substance, is given a piece for examination. He manipulates it, drops it many times, breaks off fragments and lets them fall. He has often done this kind of thing before, but previously his attention has seemed to be centered on the act of letting go. Now "he watches with great interest the body in motion; in particular, he looks at it for a long time when it has fallen, and picks it up when he can." On the following day he resumes his research.

> He grasps in succession a celluloid swan, a box, and several other small objects, in each case stretching out his arm and letting them fall. Sometimes he stretches out his arm vertically, sometimes he holds it obliquely in front of or behind his eyes. When the object falls in a new position (for example on his pillow) he lets it fall two or three times more on the same place, as though to study the spatial relation; then he modifies the situation. At a certain moment the swan falls near his mouth; now he does not suck it (even though this object habitually serves this purpose), but

drops it three times more while merely making the gesture of opening his mouth [Piaget, 1952, p. 269].

These specimens will furnish us with sufficient images of the infant's use of his spare time. Laurent, of course, was provided by his studious father with a decidedly enriched environment, but no observant parent will question the fact that babies often act this way during those periods of their waking life when hunger, erotic needs, distresses, and anxiety seem to be exerting no particular pressure. If we consider this behavior under the historic headings of psychology we shall see that few processes are missing. The child gives evidence of sensing, perceiving, attending, learning, recognizing, probably recalling, and perhaps thinking in a rudimentary way. Strong emotion is lacking, but the infant's smiles, gurgles, and occasional peals of laughter strongly suggest the presence of pleasant affect. Actions appear in an organized form, particularly in the specimens of active exploration and experimentation. Apparently the child is using with a certain coherence nearly the whole repertory of psychological processes except those that accompany stress. It would be arbitrary indeed to say that one was more important than another.

These specimens have a meaningful unity when seen as transactions between the child and his environment, the child having some influence upon the environment and the environment some influence upon the child. Laurent appears to be concerned about what he can do with the chain and rattles, what he can accomplish by his own effort to reproduce and to vary the entertaining sounds. If his father observed correctly, we must add that Laurent seems to have varied his actions systematically, as if testing the effect of different degrees of effort upon the bit of environment represented by the chain and rattles. Kittens make a similar study of parameters when delicately using their paws to push pencils and other objects ever nearer to the edge of one's desk. In all such examples it is clear that the child or animal is by no means at the mercy of transient stimulus fields. He selects for continuous treatment those aspects of his environment which he finds it possible to affect in some way. His behavior is selective, directed, persistent—in short, motivated.

Motivated toward what goal? In these terms, too, the behavior exhibits a little of everything. Laurent can be seen as appeasing a stimulus hunger, providing his sensorium with an agreeable level of stimulation by eliciting from the environment a series of interesting sounds, feels, and sights. On the other hand we might emphasize a need for activity and see him as trying to reach a pleasurable level of neuromuscular exercise. We can also see another possible goal in the behavior: the child is achieving knowledge, attaining a more differentiated cognitive map of his environment and thus satisfying an exploratory tendency or motive or curiosity. But it is equally possible to discern a theme of mastery, power, or control, perhaps even a bit of primitive self-assertion, in the child's concentration upon those aspects of the environment which respond in some way to his own activity. It looks as if we had found too many goals, and perhaps our first impulse is to search for some key to tell us which one is really important. But this, I think, is a mistake that would be fatal to understanding.

We cannot assign priority to any of these goals without pausing arbitrarily in the cycle of transaction between child and environment and saying, "This is the real point." I propose instead that the real point is the transactions as a whole. If the behavior gives satisfaction, this satisfaction is not associated with a particular moment in the cycle. It does not lie solely in sensory stimulation, in a bettering of the cognitive map, in coordinated action, in motor exercise, in a feeling of effort and of effects produced, or in the appreciation of change brought about in the sensory field. These are all simply aspects of a process which at this stage has to be conceived as a whole. The child appears to be occupied with the agreeable task of developing an effective familiarity with his environment. This involves discovering the effects he can have on the environment and the effects the environment will have on him. To the extent that these results are preserved by learning, they build up an increased competence in dealing with the environment. The child's play can thus be viewed as serious business, though to him it is merely something that is interesting and fun to do.

Bearing in mind these examples, as well as the dealings with environment pointed out by other workers, we must now attempt to describe more fully the possible nature of the motivational aspect of competence. It needs its own name, and in view of the foregoing analysis I propose that this name be *effectance*.

②EFFECTANCE

The new freedom produced by two decades of research on animal drives is of great help in this undertaking. We are no longer obliged to look for a source of energy external to the nervous system, for a consummatory climax, or for a fixed connection between reinforcement and tension-reduction. Effectance motivation cannot, of course, be conceived as having a source in tissues external to the nervous system. It is in no sense a deficit motive. We must assume it to be neurogenic, its "energies" being simply those of the living cells that make up the nervous system. External stimuli play an important part, but in terms of "energy" this part is secondary, as one can see most clearly when environmental stimulation is actively sought. Putting it picturesquely, we might say that the effectance urge represents what the neuromuscular system wants to do when it is otherwise unoccupied or is gently stimulated by the environment. Obviously there are no consummatory acts; satisfaction would appear to lie in the arousal and maintaining of activity rather than in its slow decline toward bored passivity. The motive need not be conceived as intense and powerful in the sense that hunger, pain, or fear can be powerful when aroused to high pitch. There are plenty of instances in which children refuse to leave their absorbed play in order to eat or to visit the toilet. Strongly aroused drives, pain, and anxiety, however, can be conceived as overriding the effectance urge and capturing the energies of the neuromuscular system. But effectance motivation is persistent in the sense that it regularly occupies the spare waking time between episodes of homeostatic crisis.

In speculating upon this subject we must bear in mind the continuous nature of behavior. This is easier said than done; habitually we break things down in order to understand them, and such units as the reflex arc, the stimulus-response sequence, and the single transaction with the environment seem like inevitable steps toward clarity. Yet when we apply such an analysis to playful exploration we lose the most essential aspect of the behavior. It is constantly circling from stimulus to perception to action to effect to stimulus to perception, and so on around; or, more properly, these processes are all in continuous action and continuous change. Dealing with the environment means carrying on a continuing transaction which gradually changes one's relation to the environment. Because there is no consummatory climax, satisfaction has to be seen as lying in a considerable series of transactions, in a trend of behavior rather than a goal that is achieved. It is difficult to make the word "satisfaction" have this connotation, and we shall do well to replace it by [the] "feeling of efficacy" when attempting to indicate the subjective and affective side of effectance.

It is useful to recall the findings about novelty: the singular effectiveness of novelty in engaging interest and for a time supporting persistent behavior. We also need to consider the selective continuance of transactions in which the animal or child has a more or less pronounced effect upon the environment—in which something happens as a consequence of his activity. Interest is not aroused and sustained when the stimulus field is so familiar that it gives rise at most to reflex acts or automatized habits. It is not sustained when actions produce no effects or changes in the stimulus field. Our conception must therefore be that effectance motivation is aroused by stimulus conditions which offer, as Hebb (1949) puts it, difference-in-sameness. This leads to variability and novelty of response, and interest is best sustained when the resulting action affects the stimulus so as to produce further difference-in-sameness. Interest wanes when action begins to have less effect; effectance motivation subsides when a situation has been explored to the point that it no longer presents new possibilities.

We have to conceive further that the arousal of playful and exploratory interest means the appearance of organization involving both the cognitive and active aspects of behavior. Change in the stimulus field is not an end in itself, so to speak; it happens when one is passively moved about, and it may happen as a consequence of random movements without becoming focalized and instigating exploration. Similarly, action which has effects is not an end in itself, for if one unintentionally kicks away a branch while walking, or knocks something off a table, these effects by no means necessarily become involved in playful investigation. Schachtel's (1954) emphasis on focal attention becomes helpful at this point. The playful and exploratory behavior shown by Laurent is not random or casual. It involves focal *attention* to some object—the fixing of some aspect of the stimulus field so that it stays relatively constant—and it also involves the focalizing of *action* upon this object. As Diamond (1939) has expressed it, response under these conditions is "relevant to the stimulus," and it is change in the *focalized* stimulus that so strongly affects the level of interest. Dealing with the environment means directing focal attention to some part of it and organizing actions to have some effect on this part.

In our present state of relative ignorance about the workings of the nervous system it is impossible to form a satisfactory idea of the neural basis of effectance motivation, but it should at least be clear that the concept does not refer to any and every kind of neural action.

It refers to a particular kind of activity, as inferred from particular kinds of behavior. We can say that it does not include reflexes and other kinds of automatic response. It does not include well-learned, automatized patterns, even those that are complex and highly organized. It does not include behavior in the service of effectively aroused drives. It does not even include activity that is highly random and discontinuous, though such behavior may be its most direct forerunner. The urge toward competence is inferred specifically from behavior that shows a lasting focalization and that has the characteristics of exploration and experimentation, a kind of variation within the focus. When this particular sort of activity is aroused in the nervous system, effectance motivation is being aroused, for it is characteristic of this particular sort of activity that it is selective, directed, and persistent, and that instrumental acts will be learned for the sole reward of engaging in it.

Some objection may be felt to my introducing the word *competence* in connection with behavior that is so often playful. Certainly the playing child is doing things for fun, not because of a desire to improve his competence in dealing with the stern hard world. In order to forestall misunderstanding, it should be pointed out that the usage here is parallel to what we do when we connect sex with its biological goal of reproduction. The sex drive aims for pleasure and gratification, and reproduction is a consequence that is presumably unforeseen by animals and by man at primitive levels of understanding. Effectance motivation similarly aims for the feeling of efficacy, not for the vitally important learnings that come as its consequence. If we consider the part played by competence motivation in adult human life we can observe the same parallel. Sex may now be completely and purposefully divorced from reproduction but nevertheless pursued for the pleasure it can yield. Similarly, effectance motivation may lead to continuing exploratory interests or active adventures when in fact there

is no longer any gain in actual competence or any need for it in terms of survival. In both cases the motive is capable of yielding surplus satisfaction well beyond what is necessary to get the biological work done.

In infants and young children it seems to me sensible to conceive of effectance motivation as undifferentiated. Later in life it becomes profitable to distinguish various motives such as cognizance, construction, mastery, and achievement. It is my view that all such motives have a root in effectance motivation. They are differentiated from it through life experiences which emphasize one or another aspect of the cycle of transaction with environment. Of course, the motives of later childhood and of adult life are no longer simple and can almost never be referred to a single root. They can acquire loadings of anxiety, defense, and compensation, they can become fused with unconscious fantasies of a sexual, aggressive, or omnipotent character, and they can gain force because of their service in producing realistic results in the way of income and career. It is not my intention to cast effectance in the star part in adult motivation. The acquisition of motives is a complicated affair in which simple and sovereign theories grow daily more obsolete. Yet it may be that the satisfaction of effectance contributes significantly to those feelings of interest which often sustain us so well in day-to-day actions, particularly when the things we are doing have continuing elements of novelty.

③ THE BIOLOGICAL SIGNIFICANCE OF COMPETENCE

The conviction was expressed at the beginning of this paper that some such concept as competence, interpreted motivationally, was essential for any biologically sound view of human nature. This necessity emerges when we consider the nature of living systems, particularly when we take a longitudinal view. What an organism does at a given moment does not always give the right clue as to what it does over a period of time. Discussing this problem, Angyal (1941) has proposed that we should look for the general pattern followed by the total organismic process over the course of time. Obviously this makes it necessary to take account of growth. Angyal defines life as "a process of self-expansion"; the living system "expands at the expense of its surroundings," assimilating parts of the environment and transforming them into functioning parts of itself. Organisms differ from other things in nature in that they are "self-governing entities" which are to some extent "autonomous." Internal processes govern them as well as external "heteronomous" forces. In the course of life there is a relative increase in the preponderance of internal over external forces. The living system expands, assimilates more of the environment, transforms its surroundings so as to bring them under greater control. "We may say," Angyal writes,

> that the general dynamic trend of the organism is toward an increase of autonomy. . . . The human being has a characteristic tendency toward self-determination, that is, a tendency to resist external influences and to subordinate the heteronomous forces of the physical and social environment to its own sphere of influence.

The trend toward increased autonomy is characteristic so long as growth of any kind is going on, though in the end the living system is bound to succumb to the pressure of heteronomous forces.

Of all living creatures, it is man who takes the longest strides toward autonomy. This is not because of any unusual tendency toward bodily expansion at the expense of the environment. It is rather that man, with his mobile hands and abundantly developed brain, attains an extremely high level of competence in his transactions with his surroundings. The building of houses, roads and bridges, the making of tools and instruments, the domestication of plants and animals, all qualify as planful changes made in the environment so that it comes more or less under control and serves our purposes rather than intruding

upon them. We meet the fluctuations of outdoor temperature, for example, not only with our bodily homeostatic mechanisms, which alone would be painfully unequal to the task, but also with clothing, buildings, controlled fires, and such complicated devices as self-regulating central heating and air conditioning. Man as a species has developed a tremendous power of bringing the environment into his service, and each individual member of the species must attain what is really quite an impressive level of competence if he is to take part in the life around him.

We are so accustomed to these human accomplishments that it is hard to realize how long an apprenticeship they require. At the outset the human infant is a slow learner in comparison with other animal forms. Hebb (1949) speaks of "the astonishing inefficiency of man's first learning, as far as immediate results are concerned," an inefficiency which he attributes to the large size of the association areas in the brain and the long time needed to bring them under sensory control. The human lack of precocity in learning shows itself even in comparison with one of the next of kin: as Hebb points out, "the human baby takes six months, the chimpanzee four months, before making a clear distinction between friend and enemy." Later in life the slow start will pay dividends. Once the fundamental perceptual elements, simple associations, and conceptual sequences have been established, later learning can proceed with ever increasing swiftness and complexity. In Hebb's words, "learning at maturity concerns patterns and events whose parts at least are familiar and which already have a number of other associations."

This general principle of cumulative learning, starting from slowly acquired rudiments and proceeding thence with increasing efficiency, can be illustrated by such processes as manipulation and locomotion, which may culminate in the acrobat devising new stunts or the dancer working out a new ballet. It is especially vivid in the case of language, where the early mastery of words and pronunciation seems such a far cry from spontaneous adult speech. A strong argument has been made by Hebb (1949) that the learning of visual forms proceeds over a similar course from slowly learned elements to rapidly combined patterns. Circles and squares, for example, cannot be discriminated at a glance without a slow apprenticeship involving eye movements, successive fixations, and recognition of angles. Hebb proposes that the recognition of visual patterns without eye movement

> is possible only as the result of an intensive and prolonged visual training that goes on from the moment of birth, during every moment that the eyes are open, with an increase in skill evident over a period of 12 to 16 years at least.

On the motor side there is likewise a lot to be cumulatively learned. The playing, investigating child slowly finds out the relationships between what he does and what he experiences. He finds out, for instance, how hard he must push what in order to produce what effect. Here the S-R formula is particularly misleading. It would come nearer the truth to say that the child is busy learning R-S connections—the effects that are likely to follow upon his own behavior. But even in this reversed form the notion of bonds or connections would still misrepresent the situation, for it is only a rare specimen of behavior that can properly be conceived as determined by fixed neural channels and a fixed motor response. As Hebb has pointed out, discussing the phenomenon of "motor equivalence" named by Lashley (1942), a rat which has been trained to press a lever will press it with the left forepaw, the right forepaw, by climbing upon it, or by biting it; a monkey will open the lid of a food box with either hand, with a foot, or even with a stick; and we might add that a good baseball player can catch a fly ball while running in almost any direction and while in almost any posture, including leaping in the air and plunging forward to the ground. All of these feats are possible because of

a history of learnings in which the main lesson has been the effects of actions upon the stimulus fields that represent the environment. What has been learned is not a fixed connection but a flexible relationship between stimulus fields and the effects that can be produced in them by various kinds of action.

One additional example, drawn this time from Piaget (1952), is particularly worth mentioning because of its importance in theories of development. Piaget points out that a great deal of mental development depends upon the idea that the world is made up of objects having substance and permanence. Without such an "object concept" it would be impossible to build up the ideas of space and causality and to arrive at the fundamental distinction between self and external world. Observation shows that the object concept, "far from being innate or ready-made in experience, is constructed little by little." Up to 7 and 8 months the Piaget children searched for vanished objects only in the sense of trying to continue the actions, such as sucking or grasping, in which the objects had played a part. When an object was really out of sight or touch, even if only because it was covered by a cloth, the infants undertook no further exploration. Only gradually, after some study of the displacement of objects by moving, swinging, and dropping them, does the child begin to make an active search for a vanished object, and only still more gradually does he learn, at 12 months or more, to make allowance for the object's sequential displacements and thus to seek it where it has gone rather than where it was last in sight. Thus it is only through cumulative learning that the child arrives at the idea of permanent substantial objects.

The infant's play is indeed serious business. If he did not while away his time pulling strings, shaking rattles, examining wooden parrots, dropping pieces of bread and celluloid swans, when would he learn to discriminate visual patterns, to catch and throw, and to build up his concept of the object? When would he acquire the many other foundation stones necessary for cumulative learning? The more closely we analyze the behavior of the human infant, the more clearly do we realize that infancy is not simply a time when the nervous system matures and the muscles grow stronger. It is a time of active and continuous learning, during which the basis is laid for all those processes, cognitive and motor, whereby the child becomes able to establish effective transactions with his environment and move toward a greater degree of autonomy. Helpless as he may seem until he begins to toddle, he has by that time already made substantial gains in the achievement of competence.

Under primitive conditions survival must depend quite heavily upon achieved competence. We should expect to find things so arranged as to favor and maximize this achievement. Particularly in the case of man, where so little is provided innately and so much has to be learned through experience, we should expect to find highly advantageous arrangements for securing a steady cumulative learning about the properties of the environment and the extent of possible transactions. Under these circumstances we might expect to find a very powerful drive operating to insure progress toward competence, just as the vital goals of nutrition and reproduction are secured by powerful drives, and it might therefore seem paradoxical that the interests of competence should be so much entrusted to times of play and leisurely exploration. There is good reason to suppose, however, that a strong drive would be precisely the wrong arrangement to secure a flexible, knowledgeable power of transaction with the environment. Strong drives cause us to learn certain lessons well, but they do not create maximum familiarity with our surroundings.

This point was demonstrated half a century ago in some experiments by Yerkes and Dodson (1908). They showed that maximum motivation did not lead to the most rapid solving of problems, especially if the problems were complex. For each problem there was an optimum level of motivation, neither the highest nor the lowest, and the optimum was lower for more complex tasks. The same problem has been discussed more recently by Tolman (1948) in his paper on cognitive maps. A cognitive map can be narrow or broad, depending upon the range of cues picked up in the course of learning. Tolman suggests that one of the conditions which tend to narrow the range of cues is a high level of motivation. In everyday terms, a man hurrying to an important business conference is likely to perceive only the cues that help him to get there faster, whereas a man taking a stroll after lunch is likely to pick up a substantial amount of casual information about his environment. The latent learning experiments with animals, and experiments such as those of Johnson (1953) in which drive level has been systematically varied in a situation permitting incidental learning, give strong support to this general idea. In a recent contribution, Bruner, Matter, and Papanek (1955) make a strong case for the concept of breadth of learning and provide additional evidence that it is favored by moderate and hampered by strong motivation. The latter "has the effect of speeding up learning at the cost of narrowing it." Attention is concentrated upon the task at hand and little that is extraneous to this task is learned for future use.

These facts enable us to see the biological appropriateness of an arrangement which uses periods of less intense motivation for the development of competence. This is not to say that the narrower but efficient learnings that go with the reduction of strong drives make no contribution to general effectiveness. They are certainly an important element in capacity to deal with the environment, but a much greater effectiveness results from having this capacity fed also from learnings that take place in quieter times. It is then that the infant can attend to matters of lesser urgency, exploring the properties of things he does not fear and does not need to eat, learning to gauge the force of his string-pulling when the only penalty for failure is silence on the part of the attached rattles, and generally accumulating for himself a broad knowledge and a broad skill in dealing with his surroundings.

The concept of competence can be most easily discussed by choosing, as we have done, examples of interaction with the inanimate environment. It applies equally well, however, to transactions with animals and with other human beings, where the child has the same problem of finding out what effects he can have upon the environment and what effects it can have upon him. The earliest interactions with members of the family may involve needs so strong that they obscure the part played by effectance motivation, but perhaps the example of the well fed baby diligently exploring the several features of his mother's face will serve as a reminder that here, too, there are less urgent moments when learning for its own sake can be given free rein.

In this closing section I have brought together several ideas which bear on the evolutionary significance of competence and of its motivation. I have sought in this way to deepen the biological roots of the concept and thus help it to attain the stature in the theory of behavior which has not been reached by similar concepts in the past. To me it seems that the most important proving ground for this concept is the effect it may have on our understanding of the development of personality. Does it assist our grasp of early object relations, the reality principle, and the first steps in the development of the ego? Can it be of service in distinguishing the kinds of defense available at different ages and in providing clues to the replacement of primitive defenses by successful adaptive maneuvers? Can it help fill the yawning gap known as the latency period, a time when the mastery of school subjects and other accomplishments claim so large a share of time and energy? Does it bear upon the self and the vicissitudes of self-esteem, and can it enlighten the origins of psychological disorder? Can it make adult motives and interests more intelligible and enable us to rescue the concept of sublimation from the difficulties which even its best friends have recognized? I believe it can be shown that existing explanations of development are not satisfactory and that the addition of the concept of competence cuts certain knots in personality theory. But this is not the subject of the present communication, where the concept is offered much more on the strength of its logical and biological probability.

④ SUMMARY

The main theme of this paper is introduced by showing that there is widespread discontent with theories of motivation built upon primary drives. Signs of this discontent are found in realms as far apart as animal psychology and psychoanalytic ego psychology. In the former, the commonly recognized primary drives have proved to be inadequate in explaining exploratory behavior, manipulation, and general activity. In the latter, the theory of basic instincts has shown serious shortcomings when it is stretched to account for the development of the effective ego. Workers with animals have attempted to meet their problem by invoking secondary reinforcement and anxiety reduction, or by adding exploration and manipulation to the roster of primary drives. In parallel fashion, psychoanalytic workers have relied upon the concept of neutralization of instinctual energies, have seen anxiety reduction as the central motive in ego development, or have hypothesized new instincts such as mastery. It is argued here that these several explanations are not satisfactory and that a better conceptualization is possible, indeed that it has already been all but made.

In trying to form this conceptualization, it is first pointed out that many of the earlier tenets of primary drive theory have been discredited by recent experimental work. There is no longer any compelling reason to identify either pleasure or reinforcement with drive reduction, or to think of motivation as requiring a source of energy external to the nervous system. This opens the way for considering in their own right those aspects of animal and human behavior in which stimulation and contact with the environment seem to be sought and welcomed, in which raised tension and even mild excitement seem to be cherished, and in which novelty and variety seem to be enjoyed for their own sake. Several reports are cited which bear upon interest in the environment and the rewarding effects of environmental feedback. The latest contribution is that of Woodworth (1958), who makes dealing with the environment the most fundamental element in motivation.

The survey indicates a certain unanimity as to the kinds of behavior that cannot be successfully conceptualized in terms of primary drives. This behavior includes visual exploration, grasping, crawling and walking, attention and perception, language and thinking, exploring novel objects and places, manipulating the surroundings, and producing effective changes in the environment. The thesis is then proposed that all of these behaviors have a common biological significance: they all form part of the process whereby the animal or child learns to interact effectively with his environment. The word *competence* is chosen as suitable to indicate this common property. Further, it is maintained that competence cannot be fully acquired simply through behavior instigated by drives. It receives substantial contributions from activities which, though playful and exploratory in character, at the same time show direction, selectivity, and persistence in interacting with the environment. Such activities in the ultimate service of competence must therefore be conceived to be motivated in their own right. It is proposed to designate this motivation by the term effectance, and to characterize the experience produced as a *feeling of efficacy*.

In spite of its sober biological purpose, effectance motivation shows itself most unambiguously in the playful and investigatory behavior of young animals and children. Specimens of such

behavior, drawn from Piaget (1952), are analyzed in order to demonstrate their constantly transactional nature. Typically they involve continuous chains of events which include stimulation, cognition, action, effect on the environment, new stimulation, etc. They are carried on with considerable persistence and with selective emphasis on parts of the environment which provide changing and interesting feedback in connection with effort expended. Their significance is destroyed if we try to break into the circle arbitrarily and declare that one part of it, such as cognition alone or active effort alone, is the real point, the goal, or the special seat of satisfaction. Effectance motivation must be conceived to involve satisfaction—a feeling of efficacy—in transactions in which behavior has an exploratory, varying, experimental character and produces changes in the stimulus field. Having this character, the behavior leads the organism to find out how the environment can be changed and what consequences flow from these changes.

In higher animals and especially in man, where so little is innately provided and so much has to be learned about dealing with the environment, effectance motivation independent of primary drives can be seen as an arrangement having high adaptive value. Considering the slow rate of learning in infancy and the vast amount that has to be learned before there can be an effective level of interaction with surroundings, young animals and children would simply not learn enough unless they worked pretty steadily at the task between episodes of homeostatic crisis. The association of interest with this "work," making it play and fun, is thus somewhat comparable to the association of sexual pleasure with the biological goal of reproduction. Effectance motivation need not be conceived as strong in the sense that sex, hunger, and fear are strong when violently aroused. It is moderate but persistent, and in this, too, we can discern a feature that is favorable for adaptation. Strong motivation reinforces learning in a narrow sphere, whereas moderate motivation is more conducive to an exploratory and experimental attitude which leads to competent interactions in general, without reference to an immediate pressing need. Man's huge cortical association areas might have been a suicidal piece of specialization if they had come without a steady, persistent inclination toward interacting with the environment.

References

Allport, G. W. *Personality: a psychological interpretation.* New York: Holt, 1937.

Allport, G. W. Effect: a secondary principle of learning. *Psychol. Rev.,* 1946, 53, 335–347.

Angyal, A. *Foundations for a science of personality.* New York: Commonwealth Fund, 1941.

Ansbacher, H. L., & Ansbacher, Rowena R. (Eds.) *The individual psychology of Alfred Adler.* New York: Basic Books, 1956.

Beach, F. A. Analysis of factors involved in the arousal, maintenance and manifestation of sexual excitement in male animals. *Psychosom. Med.,* 1942, 4, 173–198.

Beach, F. A. Instinctive behavior: reproductive activities. In S. S. Stevens (Ed.), *Handbook of experimental psychology.* New York: Wiley, 1951. Pp. 387–434.

Berlyne, D. E. Novelty and curiosity as determinants of exploratory behavior. *Brit. J. Psychol.,* 1950, 41, 68–80.

Berlyne, D. E. The arousal and satiation of perceptual curiosity in the rat. *J. comp. physiol. Psychol.,* 1955, 48, 238–246.

Berlyne, D. E. Attention to change, conditioned inhibition (S–R and stimulus satiation. *Brit. J. Psychol.,* 1957, 48, 138–140.

Berlyne, D. E. The present status of research on exploratory and related behavior. *J. indiv. Psychol.,* 1958, 14, 121–126.

Bibring, E. The development and problems of the theories of the instincts. *Int. J. Psychoanal.,* 1941, 22, 102–131.

Bruner, J. S., Matter, J., & Papanek, M. L. Breadth of learning as a function of drive level and mechanization. *Psychol. Rev.* 1955, 62, 1–10.

Bühler, C. The reality principle. *Amer. J. Psychother.,* 1954, 8, 626–647.

Bühler, K. *Die geistige Entwicklung des Kindes.* (4th ed.) Jena: Gustav Fischer, 1924.

Butler, R. A. Discrimination learning by rhesus monkeys to visual-exploration motivation. *J. comp. physiol. Psychol.,* 1953, 46, 95–98.

Butler, R. A. Exploratory and related behavior: a new trend in animal research. *J. indiv. Psychol.,* 1958, 14, 111–120.

Butler, R. A., & Harlow, H. F. Discrimination learning and learning sets to visual exploration incentives. *J. gen. Psychol.,* 1957, 57, 257–264.

Cofer, C. N. Motivation. *Ann. Rev. Psychol.,* 1959, 10, 173–202.

Colby, K. M. *Energy and structure in psychoanalysis.* New York: Ronald, 1955.

Dashiell, J. F. A quantitative demonstration of animal drive. *J. comp. Psychol.,* 1925, 5, 205–208.

Diamond, S. A neglected aspect of motivation. *Sociometry,* 1939, 2, 77–85.

Dollard, J., & Miller, N. E. *Personality and psychotherapy.* New York: McGraw-Hill, 1950.

Erikson, E. H. *Childhood and society.* New York: Norton, 1950.

Erikson, E. H. Growth and crises of the healthy personality. In C. Kluckhohn, & H. A. Murray (Eds.), *Personality in nature, society, and culture.* (2nd ed.) New York: Knopf, 1953. Pp. 185–225.

Fenichel, O. *The psychoanlytic theory of neurosis.* New York: Norton, 1945.

French, T. M. *The integration of behavior.* Vol. 1. *Basic postulates.* Chicago: Univer. Chicago Press, 1952.

Freud, Anna. The mutual influences in the development of ego and id: introduction to the discussion. In Ruth S. Eissler et al. (Eds.), *The psychoanalytic study of the child.* Vol. 7. New York: International Universities Press, 1952. Pp. 42–50.

Freud, S. *Wit and its relation to the unconscious.* New York: Moffat, Yard, 1961.

Freud, S. Formulations regarding the two principles in mental functioning. In *Collected papers.* Vol. 4. London: Hogarth and Institute of Psycho-analysis, 1925. Pp. 13–21. (a)

Freud, S. On narcissism: an introduction. In *Collected papers.* Vol. 4. London: Hogarth and Institute of Psycho-analysis, 1925. Pp. 30–59. (b)

Freud, S. Instincts and their vicissitudes. In *Collected papers.* Vol. 4. London: Hogarth and Institute of Psycho-analysis, 1925. Pp. 60–83. (c)

Freud, S. *The ego and the id.* (Trans. by J. Riviere.) London: Hogarth, 1927.

Freud, S. *Beyond the pleasure principle.* London: Hogarth, 1948.

Freud, S. *An outline of psychoanalysis.* (Trans. by J. Strachey.) New York: Norton, 1949.

Goldstein, K. *The organism.* New York: American Book, 1939.

Goldstein, K. *Human nature in the light of psychopathology.* Cambridge, Mass.: Harvard Univer. Press, 1940.

Gross, K. *The play of man.* (Trans. by E. L. Baldwin.) New York: Appleton, 1901.

Harlow, H. F. Mice, monkeys, men, and motives. *Psychol. Rev.,* 1953, 60, 23–32.

Harlow, H. F., Harlow, Margaret K., & Meyer, D. R. Learning motivated by a manipulation drive. *J. exp. Psychol.,* 1950, 40, 228–234.

Hartmann, H. Comments on the psychoanalytic theory of the ego. In Ruth S. Eissler et al. (Eds.), *The psychoanalytic study of the child.* Vol. 5. New York: International Universities Press, 1950. Pp. 74–95.

Hartmann, H. Notes on the theory of sublimation. In Ruth S. Eissler et al. (Eds.), *The psychoanalytic study of the child.* Vol. 10. New York: International Universities Press, 1955. Pp. 9–29.

Hartmann, H. Notes on the reality principle. In Ruth S. Eissler et al. (Eds.), *The psychoanalytic study of the child.* Vol. 11. New York: International Universities Press, 1956. Pp. 31–53.

Hartmann, H. *Ego psychology and the problem of adaptation.* (Trans. by D. Rapaport.) New York: International Universities Press, 1958.

Hartmann, H., Kris, E., & Loewenstein, R. Notes on the theory of aggression. In Ruth S. Eissler et al. (Eds.), *The psychoanalytic study of the child.* Vol. 3/4. New York: International Universities Press, 1949. Pp. 9–36.

Hebb, D. O. *The organization of behavior.* New York: Wiley, 1949.

Hebb, D. O. Drives and the c.n.s. (conceptual nervous system). *Psychol. Rev.,* 1955, 62, 243–254.

Hebb, D. O. The motivating effects of exteroceptive stimulation. *Amer. Psychologist,* 1958, 13, 109–113.

Hebb, D. O., & Thompson, W. R. The social significance of animal studies. In G. Lindzey (Ed.), *Handbook of social psychology.* Vol. 1. Reading, Mass.: Addison-Wesley, 1954. Pp. 532–561.

Hendrick, I. Instinct and the ego during infancy. *Psychoanalyt. Quart.,* 1942, 11, 33–58.

Hendrick, I. Work and the pleasure principle. *Psychoanalyt. Quart.,* 1943, 12, 311–329. (a)

Hendrick, I. The discussion of the instinct to master. *Psychoanalyt. Quart.* 1943, 12, 561–565. (b)

Hill, W. F. Activity as an autonomous drive. *J. comp. physiol. Psychol.,* 1956, 49, 15–19.

Johnson, E. E. The role of motivational strength in latent learning. *J. comp. physiol. Psychol.,* 1953, 45, 526–530.

Kagan, J. Differential reward value of incomplete and complete sexual behavior. *J. comp. physiol. Psychol.,* 1955, 48, 59–64.

Kagan, J., & Berkun, M. The reward value of running activity. *J. comp. physiol. Psychol.,* 1954, 47, 108.

Kardiner, A., & Spiegel, H. War stress and neurotic illness. New York: Hoeber, 1947.

Lashley, K. S. Experimental analysis of instinctive behavior. *Psychol. Rev.,* 1938, 45, 445–471.

Lashley, K. S. The problem of cerebral organization in vision. In H. Klüver, *Visual mechanisms.* New York: Jaques Cattell, 1942. Pp. 301–322.

Leuba, C. Toward some integration of learning theories: the concept of optimal stimulation. *Psychol. Rep.* 1955, 1, 27–33.

Lilly, J. C. Mental effects of reduction of ordinary levels of physical stimuli on intact, healthy persons. *Psychiat. res. Rep.,* 1956, No. 5.

Maslow, A. H. *Motivation and personality.* New York: Harper, 1954.

Maslow, A. H. Deficiency motivation and growth motivation. In M. R. Jones (Ed.), *Nebraska symposium on motivation 1955.* Lincoln, Neb.: Univer. Nebraska Press, 1955. Pp. 1–30.

McClelland, D. C., Atkinson, J. W., Clark, R. A., & Lowell, E. L. *The achievement motive.* New York: Appleton-Century-Crofts, 1953.

McDougall, W. *Introduction to social psychology.* (16th ed.) Boston: John Luce, 1923.

McReynolds, P. A restricted conceptualization of human anxiety and motivation. *Psychol. Rep.,* 1956, 2, 293–312. (Monogr. Suppl. 6.)

Miller, N. E. Learnable drives and rewards. In S. S. Stevens (Ed.), *Handbook of experimental psychology.* New York: Wiley, 1951. Pp. 435–472.

Miller, N. E. Central stimulation and other new approaches to motivation and reward. *Amer. Psychologist,* 1958, 13, 100–108.

Mittelmann, B. Motility in infants, children, and adults. In Ruth S. Eissler et al. (Eds.), *The psychoanalytic study of the child.* Vol. 9. New York: International Universities Press, 1954. Pp. 142–177.

Montgomery, K. C. The role of the exploratory drive in learning. *J. comp. physiol. Psychol.,* 1954, 47, 60–64.

Montgomery, K. C., & Monkman, J. A. The relation between fear and exploratory behavior. *J. comp. physiol. Psychol.,* 1955, 48, 132–136.

Morgan, C. T. *Physiological psychology.* New York: McGraw-Hill, 1943.

Morgan, C. T. Physiological mechanisms of motivation. In M. R. Jones (Ed.), *Nebraska symposium on motivation 1957.* Lincoln, Neb.: Univer. Nebraska Press, 1957. Pp. 1–35.

Mowrer, O. H. *Learning theory and personality dynamics.* New York: Ronald, 1950.

Munroe, R. *Schools of psychoanalytical thought.* New York: Dryden, 1955.

Murphy, G. *Personality: a biosocial approach to origins and structure.* New York: Harper, 1947.

Murray, H. A. *Explorations in personality.* New York and London: Oxford Univer. Press, 1938.

Murray, H. A., & Kluckhohn, C. Outline of a conception of personality. In C. Kluckhohn & H. A. Murray (Eds.), *Personality in nature, society, and culture.* (2nd ed.) New York: Knopf, 1953.

Myers, A. K., & Miller, N. E. Failure to find a learned drive based on hunger; evidence for learning motivated by "exploration." *J. comp. physiol. Psychol.,* 1954, 47, 428–436.

Nissen, H. W. A study of exploratory behavior in the white rat by means of the obstruction method. *J. genet. Psychol.,* 1930, 37, 361–376.

Olds, J., & Milner, P. Positive reinforcement produced by electrical stimulation of septal area and other regions of rat brain. *J. comp. physiol. Psychol.,* 1954, 47, 419–427.

Piaget, J. *The origins of intelligence in children.* (Trans. by M. Cook.) New York: International Universities Press, 1952.

Rapaport, D. *Organization and pathology of thought.* New York: Columbia Univer. Press, 1951.

Rapaport, D. On the psychoanalytic theory of thinking. In R. P. Knight & C. R. Friedman (Eds.), *Psychoanalytic psychiatry and psychology.* New York: International Universities Press, 1954. Pp. 259–273.

Rapaport, D. The theory of ego autonomy: a generalization. *Bull. Menninger Clin.,* 1958, 22, 13–35.

Rosvold, H. E. Physiological psychology. *Ann. Rev. Psychol.,* 1959, 10, 415–454.

Schachtel, E. G. The development of focal attention and the emergence of reality. *Psychiatry,* 1954, 17, 309–324.

Sheffield, F. D., & Roby, T. B. Reward value of a nonnutritive sweet taste. *J. comp. physiol. Psychol.,* 1950, 43, 471–481.

Sheffield, F. D., Roby, T. B., & Campbell, B. A. Drive reduction vs. consummatory behavior as determinants of reinforcement. *J. comp. physiol. Psychol.,* 1954, 47, 349–354.

Sheffield, F. D., Wulff, J. J., & Backer, R. Reward value of copulation without sex drive reduction. *J. comp. physiol. Psychol.,* 1951, 44, 3–8.

Skinner, B. F. *Science and human behavior.* New York: Macmillan, 1953.

Steller, E. The physiology of motivation. *Psychol. Rev.,* 1954, 61, 5–22.

Tolman, E. C. Cognitive maps in rats and men. *Psychol. Rev.,* 1948, 55, 189–208.

Welker, W. L. Some determinants of play and exploration in chimpanzees. *J. comp. physiol. Psychol.,* 1956, 49, 84–89.

Whiting, J. W. M., & Mowrer, O. H. Habit progression and regression—a laboratory study of some factors relevant to human socialization. *J. comp. Psychol.,* 1943, 36, 229–253.

Wolfe, J. B., & Kaplon, M. D. Effect of amount of reward and consummative activity on learning in chickens. *J. comp. Psychol.,* 1941, 31, 353–361.

Woodworth, R. S. *Dynamics of behavior.* New York: Holt, 1958.

Yerkes, R. M., & Dodson, J. D. The relation of strength of stimulus to rapidity of habit-formation. *J. comp. Neurol. Psychol.,* 1908, 18, 459–482.

Young, P. T. Food-seeking drive, affective process, and learning. *Psychol. Rev.,* 1949, 56, 98–121.

Young, P. T. The role of hedonic processes in motivation. In M. R. Jones (Ed.), *Nebraska symposium on motivation 1955.* Lincoln, Neb.: Univer. Nebraska Press, 1955. Pp. 193–238.

Zimbardo, P. G., & Miller, N. E. Facilitation of exploration by hunger in rats. *J. comp. physiol. Psychol.,* 1958, 51, 43–46.

Children's Aggression

21

Norma Feshbach

Seymour Feshbach

Every society is confronted with the task of training children so that they can participate in the transactions of social living without mutual aggression or self-destruction. For the younger child, this task is generally assigned by the society to his parents and teachers. They must help him learn to inhibit and control his impulsiveness and anger, to discriminate between situations in which aggression is appropriate and those in which it is not, and to discriminate between aggressive behaviors which are permissible and those which are frowned upon by the culture. This fundamental aspect of the socialization of the child has taken on increased significance as problems of violence and social disruption have become a major concern in contemporary society.

SOURCE: From *The Young Child: Reviews of Research,* ed. W. W. Hartup, vol. 2 (1972), 284–302. Washington, D.C.: National Association for the Education of Young Children. Reprinted with permission.

There has been considerable research on problems of aggression, reflecting the widespread interest in this area. And, while significant advances in our understanding of aggressive phenomena have been made, there is still substantial debate and uncertainty concerning the causes of aggression and the most effective means of controlling aggressive behavior (Feshbach, 1970).

The diversity of behaviors which are classified as "aggression" is one reason why progress in this area has been relatively slow. Hitting another child, striking an inflated doll figure, bursting a balloon, making a critical comment, are only a small sample of behaviors which have been labeled as aggressive. Unless one can demonstrate that these behaviors share common properties and functions, research using these varied instances of aggression is likely to yield conflicting findings.

In reviewing studies of aggression, it should

also be recognized that the same behaviors can have rather different functions. For example, when a child hits one of his peers on the playground, it is often difficult to ascertain whether his purpose was to obtain some material advantage or to hurt the other child. A child may strike a playmate because he wants a toy which the other child refuses to relinquish or because the aggressor dislikes or envies the child whom he has struck. In the first instance, the aggressive response is instrumental to the attainment of a nonaggressive goal—namely, obtaining the toy. Presumably, other kinds of instrumental responses, such as pleading, crying, or exchanging toys—if successful in achieving the child's goal— would have been equally satisfactory to the aggressor. In the second instance, the response is motivated by an aggressive goal—specifically, inflicting injury or pain. Behaviors whose major purpose is to hurt or damage a person, animal, or object has most often been considered by learning theorists (Dollard, Doob, Miller, Mowrer & Sears, 1939) and by psychoanalytic theorists (Freud, 1930; Freud, 1950) as expressions of aggressive drive or motivation.

Aggressive behaviors such as pushing, hitting, and shouting are also instrumental in purpose. As the child develops, he acquires a complex repertoire of instrumental verbal and motor behaviors which can be utilized to circumvent barriers and overcome obstacles in a nonaggressive manner. However, during the early years, physical aggression is a readily available response which the young child can use to achieve desired goals and during this period it is often difficult to distinguish between aggression and the reasonable assertion of self-interest. Indeed, popular usage of the term "aggressive" may carry either connotation, so that it can describe the assertive, active youngster as well as the more hostile child. Important tasks still remaining for social scientists include an analysis of the relation between assertiveness and aggression, and a study of the con-

ditions under which we can foster the former without reinforcing the latter.

The definition and description of aggression is an essential step toward understanding its development in children. It provides a framework from which one can proceed to examine the critical issues of causes or determinants, and the most effective methods for modifying and reducing aggressive behavior. There is an extensive research literature which relates to these issues. The principal findings will only be briefly summarized here, more extensive discussion being reserved for those research issues in which the authors have been most directly involved.

DETERMINANTS OF AGGRESSION
Theories of Aggression

Aggressive behavior is common to most animal species and appears to be related to biological processes (Lorenz, 1966; Moyer, 1967). Aggression is also a social act and a method of problem solving and, consequently, very much subject to the influence of experience and learning. Theories of aggression differ in the degree to which they emphasize biological as compared to psychological (learning and experience) determinants and also differ in the particular biological and psychological factors believed to be most critical in the development of aggression. Early psychoanalytic theorists such as Freud (1930) attributed aggressive behavior to biological instincts and suggested that the principal function of the child's experience is to shape the direction and form in which his innate aggressive impulses are expressed. It was assumed that the child is born with an aggressive drive but that the individuals toward whom he directs his aggression and the manner in which he expresses it are learned. Ethologists such as Lorenz (1966), who have mainly studied animals, favor a modified instinct view in which aggressive reactions are seen as innate responses to particular stimulus patterns. A rather different modification of the instinct position is found in the form of the "frustration-aggression hypothesis" which states that aggression is a highly probable response to a frustrating event. In this view, aggressiveness of a child is regarded as a function of the degree of frustration to which he has been subjected.

Conceptions of aggression as an instinct, or as a consequence of frustration, or as a reaction to a disturbing event such as threat or pain can be contrasted with theoretical positions which consider the learning experiences of the child to be the primary determinants of his aggressive behavior. Two principal mechanisms have been suggested as means by which the child acquires aggressive responses. Selective reinforcement, resulting in rewards for being aggressive, is one such mechanism (Brown & Elliot, 1965; Walters & Brown, 1963; Patterson, Littman & Bricker, 1967; Lovaas, 1961). Such rewards can be fairly obvious, as when parents or peers defer to an aggressive child. They can also be rather subtle, as in "negative attention-seeking." Here the parent may inadvertently reward the child, even while scolding him, if the object of the child's aggressive behavior is to obtain the parent's attention. The second learning process involved in the acquisition of aggressive behavior is imitation or modeling (Bandura & Huston, 1961; Bandura, Ross & Ross, 1961, 1963a, 1963b). The child, merely through observation of aggressive adult and peer models, may acquire aggressive response tendencies without being specifically reinforced for an aggressive act. However, while the child may learn an aggressive response through imitation, his performance of that response may be dependent on its subsequent reinforcement or punishment (Bandura, 1962).

2. Frustration-Aggression

Perhaps the most important and widely known explanation of aggressive behavior is the frustration-aggression hypothesis proposed by Dollard

and his associates (1939) three decades ago. Research bearing upon the hypothesis that frustration is causally linked to aggression has yielded conflicting and ambiguous results (Feshbach, 1970). Many authorities are prepared to discard the hypothesis (Bandura & Walters, 1963; Buss, 1961) while others maintain that it still has considerable merit (Berkowitz, 1962).

One of the reasons for the diversity of results on this issue is the inclusion of varying types and degrees of frustration. Studies of the relatively mild frustrations that are entailed in weaning and toilet training have yielded inconsistent findings. In general, there appears to be little relation between a child's aggressiveness and the severity with which he was weaned (Sears, Whiting, Nowles & Sears, 1953; Sears, Maccoby & Levin, 1957; Sewell, 1952) and the results obtained for toilet training and aggression are mixed (Sears et al., 1953; Sewell, 1952; Wittenborn, 1954). On the other hand, profound frustration, such as in parental rejection, is generally associated with a high degree of aggression (Feshbach, 1970).

Laboratory studies, in comparison to field studies of child-rearing practices, provide a better opportunity for controlling variations in frustrations. For ethical reasons, however, laboratory work has employed rather weak kinds of frustration such as performing a repetitive or difficult task (Jegard & Walters, 1960; Mussen & Rutherford, 1961; Yarrow, 1948). Consequently, it is difficult to determine whether the failure to find an increase in aggression following frustration is due to the mildness of the frustrations used in these studies or the inadequacy of the frustration-aggression hypothesis.

The type of frustration used appears to be a very important factor although it should be noted that different types of frustration may also involve different degrees of frustration. Several studies indicate that physical pain is a much stronger instigator of aggression than is criticism or blocking of a subject's response (Buss, 1963;

Graham, Charwat, Honig & Welty, 1951). The extent to which a frustration is intentional or accidental is also an important factor (Cohen, 1955; Pastore, 1952). One is more likely to get angry when tripped if it is perceived as deliberate rather than accidental.

Another dimension of frustration which has not been well investigated in children is the role of ego threat and humiliation. Clinical observations indicate that children may become deeply hurt or angered when embarrassed or threatened by loss of face or status. Several theorists (Maslow, 1941; Rosenzweig, 1944) have suggested that these types of frustrations are more powerful sources of aggression than the simple blocking of a child's desires. Further research is needed on classification and evaluation of the many possible modes of frustration.

A more detailed study of the types of children who respond to frustration with aggression is also needed. The few studies that bear on this issue (Block & Martin, 1955; Otis & McCandless, 1955) indicate that there are systematic relations between the type of response made to frustration and personality variables such as self-control and dominance. It would appear from these studies that the frustration-aggression hypothesis best applies to particular types of children as well as to particular types of frustrating experiences, and that one cannot assume that frustration necessarily increases aggressive tendencies in all children at all times.

3. Reinforcement

An aggressive response can be viewed as a habit which is learned in the same way that other habits are acquired. Studies of child-rearing practices strongly suggest that the learning process has an important role in the development of aggressive behavior (Becker, 1964) and laboratory experiments leave little doubt that aggression can be learned. The work of Bandura and his associates on the imitation of aggressive models has been previously reviewed in *The Young Child*

(Bandura, 1967). These pioneering studies and the research they have stimulated have provided significant insights into the processes by which a child may acquire aggressive response patterns from parental, teacher, peer, and other models (Bandura, Ross & Ross, 1961, 1963a, 1963b; Feshbach, 1967; Portuges & Feshbach, 1969). An important point made by these modeling studies is that aggressive behavior can be acquired without the prior performance and direct reinforcement of the behavior.

Even so, selective reinforcement of aggressive behaviors is a significant determinant of aggression, perhaps the most important single process influencing the acquisition and performance of an aggressive response. The dependence of an aggressive act upon the occurrence of a reinforcement is clearly demonstrated in a series of studies by Walters and his associates (Cowan & Walters, 1963; Hops & Walters, 1963; Walters & Brown, 1963). The reinforcement used was a marble given to the child for striking an inflated, automated Bobo doll. The results indicate that the acquisition of an aggressive response is subject to the same influences as other instrumental behaviors. Lovaas (1961), in a study of generalization effects, rewarded one group of nursery school children with a trinket whenever they made verbally aggressive responses to a doll figure, e.g., "doll should be spanked," "bad doll." Another group was reinforced for nonaggressive verbal remarks. Following the reinforcement training, the children were given an opportunity to play with a nonaggressive ball toy or with an apparatus which was so arranged that by depressing a lever the child would make one doll strike another on the head with a stick. The children in the group that had been reinforced for verbal aggression used the aggressive toy relatively more often than the children reinforced for nonaggressive verbal responses.

The insights gained in these laboratory studies have been fruitfully applied to the modification and study of aggression in more naturalistic settings. For example, Brown and Elliot (1965) successfully manipulated the aggressive behavior of three- to four-year-old preschool boys through the use of these operant reinforcement procedures. Nursery school teachers were instructed to ignore aggressive acts wherever possible and to direct their attention to nonaggressive, cooperative behaviors. This procedure was followed for two two-week treatment periods separated by a three-week interval. Changes in the behavior of the groups reflected a significant and substantial decline in both physical and verbal aggression during the second week of each treatment period.

The role of the nursery school experience in the acquisition of aggressive behaviors has also been studied by Patterson, Littman and Bricker (1967). Aggressive interactions occurring among three- to four-year-old children in two middle-class nursery schools were recorded for approximately 60 sessions over a 26-week period. For each aggressive act, a detailed notation was made of the specific action, the victim's reaction, and the teacher's behavior. The hypothesis was proposed that the "victim's" reaction would have a critical effect on the aggressor's subsequent behavior. If the victim complied with the aggressor's wish or otherwise reinforced the aggressive act, it was predicted that the aggressor would be more likely to aggress against that same child on a subsequent occasion. However, if the victim counter-attacked or the teacher intervened, it was predicted that the aggressive response would be temporarily suppressed and redirected to another child. It was also predicted that the frequency of aggressive interactions and victimizations would relate to the child's activity level and degree of social interaction.

The results strikingly confirmed these propositions. It was observed that the large majority of aggressive responses resulted in a positive reinforcement or gain for the aggressor. Those nonaggressive children who were socially active showed a marked increase in aggressive behavior after entering nursery school while the nonagres-sive children who engaged in little social interaction maintained a low level of aggression. These results point to the importance of the reinforcement process as a determinant of aggressive behavior and to the subtle and varied manner in which the nursery school setting can influence the development of aggression.

Parental and Home Influences

During the early years of a child's life, parents control the child's experiences of frustration and gratification, determine whether he is reinforced for aggressive or nonaggressive behavior, and serve as models for the child to imitate. For these reasons, there has been considerable interest in exploring the relations between various aspects of a child's home environment and the development of aggressive behavior. Unfortunately, this research area presents several problems. First one cannot manipulate and control child-rearing practices but must study their effects in the context of a large number of correlated influences. Particular parental behaviors, such as maternal rejection or severe punishment, do not operate in isolation but occur in conjunction with other aspects of the home environment. In addition, the child's behavior may well affect his parent's reactions to him so that it is sometimes difficult to determine whether a particular parental method of handling a child is a cause or is a result of the child's actions. Second, a variety of methods, all subject to varying degrees of distortion and other sources of error, have been used to assess parental attitudes and behaviors.

In spite of these methodological reservations, the research literature suggests several conclusions. Children who are unwanted by their parents, and who are given little affection and attention, are likely to develop hostile behavior patterns (Banister & Ravden, 1944; Goldfarb, 1945; Lowrey, Zilboorg, Bender, Brickner, Reeve, Lippman, Slavson & Slawson, 1943; Glueck & Glueck, 1950). A striking instance of this relation is reported by McCord, McCord and Howard (1961), who studied longitudinally a sample of nondelinquent, lower-class boys, beginning at nine years of age. They divided these boys into three groups: aggressive, normally assertive, and nonaggressive. A thorough analysis of the home experiences of these children yielded a very strong relation between exposure to a rejecting parent and aggressive behavior. Ninety-five percent of the aggressive boys were raised in homes where one or both parents was considered rejecting, whereas the majority of children classified as assertive and nonaggressive had parents who were warm and affectionate.

One controversial issue has been the relation between parental permissiveness and children's aggressive behavior. When evaluating the effects of parental discipline, the parent's basic attitude toward the child as well as the type of discipline employed must be taken into account. For example, permissiveness in a household with a rejecting parent appears to be associated with delinquency and other forms of aggressive, antisocial behavior (Bandura & Walters, 1959; Glueck & Glueck, 1950; McCord, McCord & Howard, 1961). Evidence from several of these studies strongly suggests that the critical factor is not the parental permissiveness but the lack of parental demands for conformity to social conventions. The parents of an aggressive boy may impose restrictions and punish deviant behavior while still failing to foster socially desirable behavior. Under these circumstances the child may know what he should not do, but have a poor conception of the kind of behaviors that his parents and society will approve.

Although parental punishment is intended to inhibit aggression, research has provided surprisingly little evidence of inhibitory effects. Theoretically, the use of strong punishment, especially physical punishment, can facilitate as well as discourage aggressive behavior. Since punishment is a source of frustration and pain, it may stimulate anger and aggressive tendencies. The parent who uses physical aggression in punishing his child is also serving as an aggressive model. The child, through imitation, may be acquiring aggressive response patterns although ostensibly being taught that aggression is bad. It is perhaps not surprising then that several investigators have found that severity of parental punishment for aggression is associated with the child's aggression in doll play (Hollenberg & Sperry, 1951; Sears et al., 1953) and in other forms of fantasy (Allinsmith, 1954; Whiting & Child, 1953; Wright, 1954).

The positive association between aggression and the severity with which aggressive behavior has been punished is not restricted to fantasy expressions of aggression. Greater use of physical punishment by parents of delinquent boys as compared to nondelinquent boys has been reported by the Gluecks (1950) and by Bandura and Walters (1959), and by mothers of aggressive as compared to nonaggressive boys by the McCords 1961) and Eron, Walder, Toigo and Lefkowitz (1963). In the latter study, the investigators asked a large sample of third graders to complete a form in which each child indicated members of his class who displayed various types of aggressive behavior. On the basis of these "peer-nominations," they were able to derive a reliable and useful measure of aggressiveness for every child in their sample. They also systematically interviewed the parents and obtained a measure of the severity of punishment used in disciplining aggression. Their results indicated that both boys and girls of highly punitive fathers or mothers had higher aggression scores than children of low punitive parents. While it is difficult to establish precisely what is "cause" and what is "effect" in this finding, the data nevertheless offer very little support for the old adage "spare the rod and spoil the child."

Sex Differences

There are two principal questions to be asked in regard to sex differences in aggression: What are the differences between males and females in degree and type of aggression? What are the factors responsible for these differences? The second question is addressed to the difficult problem of ascertaining the relative contribution of biological and social factors to these sex differences. Reviews of the research literature bearing on this complex issue (Maccoby, 1966; Mischel, 1970) indicate that social determinants are very powerful but that biological factors also appear to exert an influence in ways that are not yet well understood.

The description of sex differences in aggression would seem to be a fairly straightforward issue, certainly much simpler than the determination of the causes of sex differences in aggressive behavior. Despite the fact that males are widely recognized as the more aggressive of the two sexes, this generalization does not hold for all forms of aggressive behavior. There is considerable evidence that boys are more *physically* aggressive than girls. When other forms of aggression are measured, however, the findings are much less consistent. Several studies show greater verbal aggression in girls than in boys (Bach, 1945; Durrett, 1959; Muste & Sharp, 1947). A boy is more likely than a girl to hit but is not more likely to scold or insult another child.

Sears and his co-workers have made a further distinction between forms of aggressive behavior which are approved by society and forms of aggressive behavior which are disapproved or anti-social (Sears, 1961; Sears, Rau & Alpert, 1965). An example of behavior in which aggression can be expressed in a socially approved manner is the severity of a sentence advocated for a particular crime. Expressing aggression in a socially approved manner is a relatively indirect form of aggressive behavior but such activity may be considered aggressive since it results in painful consequences to another person. Although indirect, it may lead to satisfaction of aggressive impulses or feelings.

In the Sears studies, the differences obtained between boys and girls depended upon whether the measure was an index of anti-social or pro-

social aggression. Although the boys displayed stronger anti-social aggressive tendencies than the girls, the girls displayed stronger pro-social aggression. Additional evidence suggesting that girls make greater use of indirect forms of aggression than boys has been reported by Feshbach (1969). In the initial phase of this experiment, two-person groups consisting of six- to seven-year-old children were formed. Efforts were made to develop group cohesiveness between the two children by providing them with a club name, special badges, and an opportunity for free play with attractive toys. One week later, the same pair returned to the experimental room and a newcomer joined the group. For half the groups the newcomer was of the same sex as the original pairs while for the other half, the newcomer was of the opposite sex. The critical measure was the children's reaction to the newcomer: Girls were initially more unkind and unfriendly to the newcomer than boys, especially when the newcomer was of the opposite sex. Very little direct aggression, including physical aggression, was exhibited by either girls or boys and no significant sex difference was found on this dimension.

Additional evidence suggesting that girls tend to be more indirectly aggressive than boys is found in a study by Feshbach and Sones (1970). In this experiment, male and female adolescents who were close friends were formed into two-person groups to which a newcomer of the same sex was introduced. A problem-solving situation was employed to observe aggressive interactions and, in addition, the group members rated each other's personality. More negative reactions to the newcomer were evidenced by the girls than by the boys. The girls rated the newcomer less favorably than the boys and, on the behavioral interaction measures, displayed less friendly reactions to the newcomers.

Another study by Feshbach (1969) suggests one of the mechanisms by which the child's school experiences help to establish sex differences in aggression. Student teachers were presented with story situations depicting boys and girls displaying various personality characteristics. The teachers rated the children in the stories on a number of intellectual and preference dimensions. In general, the student teachers expressed the least preference for the independent, assertive child and for the flexible, nonconforming child. These behaviors were especially disapproved when displayed by girls, suggesting that direct, assertive reactions are less tolerated in girls than in boys. It is not surprising then that girls develop more indirect means for self-expression than boys do.

THE REGULATION OF AGGRESSION

There is a close relation between the determinants of aggression and the means for controlling aggression, and in a number of instances the distinction is an arbitrary one. For example, the effects of punishment, violence in the mass media, and the consequences of imitation can be examined both as potential causes of aggression or as potential regulators of aggression. The effects of exposure to the mass media are presented in this section, with attention directed to factors involved in the control and reduction of aggressive behavior. It is fully recognized, however, that the observation of violence in the media may stimulate children's aggressive behavior.

Inhibition of Aggression

The most obvious method of inhibiting a behavior is to punish it. Laboratory results indicate that punishment has a temporary suppressing effect upon aggressive responses (Hollenberg & Sperry, 1951) but, as mentioned earlier, the relation between punishment and aggression is complex. As we have said, the data suggest that the long-term effect of punishment, particularly physical punishment, may be the enhancement of aggression rather than its inhibition.

At the same time, the effects of punishment are by no means uniform. They may vary with the timing and type of punishment and with the consistency with which punishment is applied. There is some evidence that love-oriented, psychological punishment, as contrasted with physical punishment, may lead to the greater inhibition of direct aggression (Allinsmith, 1954; Sears, 1961) but much more research is required in order to specify the effects upon aggression of the many possible modes of punishment that parents and others employ.

Punishment is not the only method, of course, for training children to inhibit aggressive behavior. The internalization of moral standards, as reflected in the development of conscience, is also a mechanism for the control of aggression. The development of conscience has been shown to be related to such factors as parental warmth and parental use of reasoning as a technique of discipline; reasoning has also been shown to be related to the inhibition of aggression (Bandura & Walters, 1951; Baumrind, 1967; Sears, 1961). The child with a strong conscience is one who will refrain from carrying out a socially prohibited act, including an aggressive act, even when he knows he will not be discovered and that he need not fear punishment by external authority figures.

Associated with conscience development, but theoretically distinct from it, is the acquisition of self-control. Needless to say, children vary in their ability to inhibit aggressive behavior and other "acting out" tendencies. Several studies of preschool children have shown that children who were high in self-control, as evidenced by the ability to persist in a monotonous task and to delay gratification, were less aggressive than children who displayed weak capacities for self-control (Block & Martin, 1955; Livson & Mussen, 1957).

One should also expect greater control of aggression in children who are empathic and who have positive social feelings toward others. Contrary to expectation, Murphy (1937) found a positive correlation between teachers' ratings of sympathetic behaviors and aggression in nursery school children. However, aggression and sympathy can both be considered as manifestations of socially oriented behavior and could both be related to degree of social maturity during the preschool years. For the elementary school child, on the other hand, aggression is more likely an indication of social immaturity; consequently one would anticipate different findings for this age group. Results consistent with this expectation were reported by Feshbach and Feshbach (1968) in an investigation of the relation between empathy and aggression in preschool and first grade children. First, the children described their feelings after observing a sequence of slides depicting a similar age child experiencing various emotions (see Feshbach & Roe, 1968). Several series of slide sequences were presented depicting the affects of fear, anger, happiness, and sadness. The degree to which the child's self-reports of his emotional reactions matched the emotion conveyed by the stimuli constituted the measure of empathy. The measure of aggression was based on teacher ratings of the child's behavior in school. A positive relation, similar to that reported by Murphy (1937), was found between empathy and aggression for the younger age group. As predicted, the relation was reversed for the older children, with the more empathic children obtaining the lower ratings of aggression. Confirmation of the inverse relation between empathy and aggression was obtained for first and second grade children in a recent study (Huckaby, 1971). These data suggest that studying the development of empathy may be one fruitful approach to the problem of controlling aggressive behavior.

Catharsis

The concept of catharsis, which has its origin in Greek philosophical writing, usually refers to the tension-releasing properties of emotional expression. It has also been applied to the potential aggression reducing properties of aggressive play, aggressive fantasies, exposure to aggression on television and on films, and related experiences.

The critical question in regard to these experiences is whether they result in a decrease or an increase in subsequent aggression. On the basis of a "catharsis hypothesis," one would predict a decrease.

Contrary to the catharsis hypothesis, several studies have indicated that aggressive play tends to facilitate or increase children's aggression rather than serve as an outlet for aggressive tendencies (Feshbach, 1956; Kenny, 1953). Research on the effects of observing aggressive film content has been more extensive and, with certain exceptions, also has not supported the catharsis hypothesis. The predominant finding has been an increase in aggression following exposure to aggressive interactions on films (Bandura, Ross & Ross, 1963b; Hartmann, 1969; Lovaas, 1961; Mussen & Rutherford, 1961; Walters & Thomas, 1963). In all of the studies demonstrating increased aggression, however, rather brief film sequences were employed. Two studies employing lengthier motion pictures provided little evidence of either aggression enhancement or aggression reduction (Albert, 1957; Emery, 1959). In addition, the degree to which aggressive affect is aroused at the time a film is presented may be a critical variable in determining whether catharsis occurs. In almost all of the studies cited the subjects were essentially relaxed prior to presentation of the aggressive film.

Although these experiments provide insight into the various psychological influences of filmed content upon children, it is very difficult to generalize from these laboratory studies to the natural viewing situation; so many more variables operate under natural conditions. In an effort to reduce this gap, a study was carried out in which television exposure was experimentally varied over a six-week period (Feshbach & Singer, 1970). The subjects were boys ranging in age from 10 to 17 who were either attending a private school or who lived in a boys' home. Seven different institutions, three private schools and four boys' homes, participated in the project. Boys were randomly assigned within each institution to a television schedule containing predominantly aggressive programs or to a control treatment of predominantly nonaggressive programs. All subjects were required to watch a minimum of six hours of television a week and were permitted to view as much television as they wanted, provided they observed programs from the designated list. Measures of aggressive personality attributes, aggressive values, and aggressive fantasy were administered before and after the experimental period. In addition, daily behavior ratings were submitted for each boy by his immediate supervisors.

The differences in television exposure had little effect upon the children attending the private schools. However, the children in the boys' homes who had observed the aggressive programs displayed significantly *less* verbal and physical aggression toward peers and toward authority than the group who had observed predominantly nonaggressive television content. These effects were especially pronounced for boys who were initially impulsive and aggressive. The effects of the film exposure on aggressive values were less impressive but tended to be consistent with the differences found in the reports about aggressive behavior. Finally, the fantasy measure was the only index on which the aggressive TV group *increased* relative to the change in the nonaggressive TV group. This effect is readily attributable to generalization of the observed television story content to the fantasy story content.

These data offer little support for the view that exposure to aggressive content in television leads to an increase in aggressive behavior. Rather, the experimental findings are compatible with a catharsis hypothesis and suggest that the observation of aggression on television may help control and modulate the expression of aggressive impulses in some of those children who have strong aggressive tendencies. These findings must be interpreted with considerable caution and clearly cannot be generalized to girls or to younger children. They do, however, point to the need for extending laboratory research to more naturalistic settings.

Other Aggression Regulation Mechanisms

Aggression, as an instrumental response, can be unlearned as well as learned, and it is possible to train children to respond nonaggressively to situations which would ordinarily elicit an aggressive reaction (Davitz, 1952; Updegraff & Keister, 1957; Walters & Brown, 1963). An experiment by Davitz (1952) is particularly instructive in this regard. A series of seven training sessions were held for groups of seven- to nine-year-old children. Half the groups were praised for aggressive behavior while the other half were reinforced for cooperative responses. Following this initial training period, the children were exposed to a frustrating experience consisting of the loss of a candy and/or the interruption of a film as it approached its climax. A subsequent free play session revealed striking differences in behavior as a result of the experimental training program. Those children who had been trained to respond aggressively displayed more aggression in free play than the group trained in cooperative activities who, in contrast, responded more constructively.

This study and the modeling experiments cited previously (Bandura, Ross & Ross, 1961, 1963a; Walters & Brown, 1965) point to the potential use of selective reinforcement and exposure to nonaggressive models as procedures for modifying aggressive behavior. These methods aim at changing the child's response to a provoking stimulus situation. Another alternative is to modify the meaning of the stimulus for the child so that it is no longer perceived as provocative. This procedure has been effectively demonstrated in an experiment by Mallick and McCandless (1966) in which third graders, following frustration or nonfrustration, were randomly assigned to one of three treatments: "interpretation of frustration," aggressive play, or a control condition. The interpretation condition consisted of offering various rationalizations for the behavior of the person who frustrated the child; e.g., "He was upset at the time." Each child was then given the opportunity to interfere with or help the individual who frustrated him. While there was little difference between the aggressive play and control groups who had been frustrated, the "interpretation" group displayed significantly less aggression than either of the other two groups.

These results indicate that aggressive behavior can be modified by means of a cognitive process of reviewing and restructuring a frustrating, distressing experience. It is not clear how effective this method would be with preschool children whose capacities for reasoning and social understanding are much more limited than those of the older child. Nevertheless, this procedure is promising. It supplements the other methods available for controlling and reducing aggression in children. Such methods as cognitive re-orientation, behavior shaping, and the facilitation of empathy do not rely on punishment, fear, or guilt for producing behavior change and offer positive alternatives for the modification of children's aggression.

References

Albert, R. The role of mass media and the effect of aggressive film content upon children's aggressive response and identification choices. *Genet. Psychol. Monogr.*, 1957, 55, 221–285.

Allinsmith, B. B. Parental discipline and children's aggression in two social classes. *Dissertation Abstracts*, 1954, 14, 708.

Bach, G. R. Young children's play fantasies. *Psychol. Monogr.*, 1945, 59 (2).

Bandura, A. Punishment revisited. *J. consult. Psychol.*, 1962, 26, 298–301.

———. The role of modeling processes in personality development. In W. W. Hartup & N. L. Smothergill (Eds.), *The Young Child: Reviews of Research.* Washington: National Association for the Education of Young Children, 1967. Pp. 42–58.

Bandura, A. & Huston, A. Identification as a process

of incidental learning. *J. abnorm. soc. Psychol.*, 1961, 63, 311–318.

Bandura, A., Ross, D. & Ross, S. Transmission of aggression through imitation of aggressive models. *J. abnorm. soc. Psychol.*, 1961, 63, 575–582.

———. Imitation of film-mediated aggressive models. *J. abnorm. soc. Psychol.*, 1963, 66, 3–11 (a).

———. Vicarious reinforcement and imitative learning. *J. abnorm. soc. Psychol.*, 1963, 67, 601–607 (b).

Bandura, A. & Walters, R. H. *Adolescent Aggression.* New York: Ronald Press, 1959.

———. Aggression. In H. W. Stevenson (Ed.), *Sixty-Second Yearbook of the National Society for the Study of Education: Child Psychology.* Chicago: Univ. of Chicago Press, 1963. Pp. 364–415.

Banister, H. & Ravden, M. The problem child and his environment. *British J. Psychol.*, 1944, 34, 60–65.

Baumrind, D. Child care practices anteceding three patterns of preschool behavior. *J. genet. Psychol.*, 1967, 75, 43–88.

Becker, W. C. Consequences of different kinds of parental discipline. In M. L. Hoffman & L. W. Hoffman (Eds.), *Review of Child Development Research*, Vol. 1. New York: Russell Sage, 1964. Pp. 169–205.

Berkowitz, L. *Aggression: A Social Psychological Analysis.* New York: McGraw-Hill, 1962.

Block, J. & Martin, B. Predicting the behavior of children under frustration. *J. abnorm. soc. Psychol.*, 1955, 51, 281–285.

Brown, P. & Elliot, R. Control of aggression in a nursery school class. *J. exp. child Psychol.*, 1965, 2, 103–107.

Buss, A. H. *The Psychology of Aggression.* New York: Wiley, 1961.

———. Physical aggression in relation to different frustrations. *J. abnorm. soc. Psychol.*, 1963, 67, 1–7.

Cohen, A. R. Social norms, arbitrariness of frustration, and status of the agent of frustration in the frustration-aggression hypothesis. *J. abnorm. soc. Psychol.*, 1955, 51, 222–226.

Cowan, P. & Walters, R. Studies of reinforcement of aggression: I. Effects of scheduling. *Child Develpm.*, 1963, 34, 543–551.

Davitz, J. The effects of previous training on postfrustration behavior. *J. abnorm. soc. Psychol.*, 1952, 47, 309–315.

Dollard, J., Doob, L. W., Miller, N. E., Mowrer, O. H. & Sears, R. R. *Frustration and Aggression.* New Haven, Conn.: Yale Univ. Press, 1939.

Durrett, M. E. The relationship of early infant regulation and later behavior in play interviews. *Child Develpm.*, 1959, 30, 211–216.

Emery, F. E. Psychological effects of the western film:

A study in television viewing: II. The experimental study. *Human Relat.*, 1959, 12, 215–232.

Eron, L. D., Walder, L. O., Toigo, L. & Lefkowitz, M. M. Social class, parental punishment for aggression, and child aggression, *Child Develpm.*, 1963, 34, 849–867.

Feshbach, N. Variations in teachers' reinforcement styles and imitative behavior of children differing in personality characteristics and social background. C.S.E. Technical Report No. 2, 1967, Univ. of California, Los Angeles, 1967.

———. Sex differences in children's modes of aggressive responses toward outsiders. *Merrill-Palmer Qtrly.*, 1969, 15, 249–258.

———. Student teacher preferences for elementary school pupils varying in personality characteristics. *J. educ. Psychol.*, 1969, 60, 126–132.

Feshbach, N. & Roe, K. Empathy in six and seven year olds. *Child Develpm.*, 1968, 39, 133–145.

Feshbach, N. & Feshbach, S. The relationship between empathy and aggression in two age groups. *Develpm. Psychol.*, 1969, 1, 102–107.

Feshbach, N. & Sones, A. Sex differences in reactions of adolescents to outsiders. *Develpm. Psychol.*, 1971, 4, 3, 381–386.

Feshbach, S. The catharsis hypothesis and some consequences of interaction with aggressive and neutral play objects. *J. Pers.*, 1956, 24, 449–462.

———. The stimulating versus cathartic effects of a vicarious aggressive activity. *J. abnorm. soc. Psychol.*, 1961, 63, 381–385.

———. Aggression. In P. H. Mussen (Ed.), *Carmichael's Manual of Child Psychology*, 3rd Ed., Vol. 2. New York: Wiley, 1970. Pp. 159–259.

Feshbach, S. & Singer, R. *Television and Aggression.* San Francisco: Jossey-Bass, 1970.

Freud, A. Notes on aggression. *Yearbook of Psychoanalysis,* 1950, 6, 145–154.

Freud, S. *Civilization and its Discontents.* London: Hogarth, 1930 (2nd ed., 1957).

Glueck, S. & Glueck, E. *Unraveling Juvenile Delinquency.* Cambridge, Mass.: Harvard Univ. Press, 1950.

Goldfarb, W. Psychological privation in infancy and subsequent adjustment. *Am. J. Orthopsychiat.,* 1945, 15, 247–255.

Graham, F., Charwat, W., Honig, A. & Welty, P. Aggression as a function of the attack and the attacker. *J. abnorm. soc. Psychol.*, 1951, 56, 512–520.

Hartmann, D. P. Influence of symbolically modeled instrumental aggression and pain cues on aggressive behavior. *J. pers. soc. Psychol.,* 1969, 11, 280–288.

Hollenberg, E. H. & Sperry, M. S. Some antecedents of aggression and effects of frustration in doll play. *Personality,* 1951, 1, 32–43.

Hops, H. & Walters, R. H. Studies of reinforcement of aggression: II. Effects of emotionally-arousing antecedent conditions. *Child Develpm.*, 1963, 34, 553–562.

Huckaby, L. M. D. A developmental study of the relationship of negative moral-social behavior to empathy, to positive social behavior, and to cognitive moral judgment. Unpubl. doctoral dissertation, Univ. of California, Los Angeles, 1971.

Jegard, S. & Walters, R. H. A study of some determinants of aggression in young children. *Child Develpm.*, 1960, 31, 739–747.

Kenny, D. T. *An Experimental Test of the Catharsis Theory of Aggression.* Ann Arbor, Mich.: University Microfilms, 1953.

Livson, N. & Mussen, P. H. The relation of ego control to overt aggression and dependency. *J. abnorm. soc. Psychol.,* 1957, 55, 66–71.

Lorenz, K. *On Aggression.* New York: Harcourt, Brace & World, 1966.

Lovaas, O. Effect of exposure to symbolic aggression on aggressive behavior. *Child Develpm.*, 1961, 32, 37–55. (a)

———. Interaction between verbal and nonverbal behavior. *Child Develpm.*, 1961, 32, 329–336. (b)

Lowrey, L. G., Zilboorg, G., Bender, L., Brickner, R. M., Reeve, G. H., Lippman, H. S., Slavson, S. R. & Slawson, J. The treatment of aggression. Round Table. *Am. J. Orthopsychiat.*, 1943, 13, 384–441.

Mallick, S. K. & McCandless, B. R. A study of catharsis of aggression. *J. pers. soc. Psychol.,* 1966, 4, 591–596.

Maslow, A. H. Deprivation, threat and frustration. *Psychol. Rev.,* 1941, 48, 364–366.

McCord, W., McCord, J. & Howard, A. Familial correlates of aggression in non-delinquent male children. *J. abnorm. soc. Psychol.,* 1961, 62, 79–93.

Mischel, W. Sex-typing and socialization. In P. H. Mussen (Ed.), *Carmichael's Manual of Child Psychology,* Vol. 2. New York: John Wiley & Sons, 1970. Pp. 3–72.

Moyer, K. E. Kinds of aggression and their physiological basis. Report No. 67–12. Dept. of Psychology, Carnegie-Mellon Univ., Pittsburgh, Penn., 1967.

Murphy, L. B. *Social Behavior and Child Personality.* New York: Columbia Univ. Press, 1937.

Mussen, P. H. & Rutherford, E. Effects of aggressive cartoons in children's aggressive play. *J. abnorm. soc. Psychol.,* 1961, 62, 461–464.

Muste, M. & Sharpe, D. Some influential factors in the determination of aggressive behavior in pre-school children. *Child Develpm.*, 1947, 18, 11–28.

Otis, N. & McCandless, B. R. Responses to repeated frustrations of young children differentiated according to need area. *J. abnorm. soc. Psychol.*, 1955, 50, 349–353.

Pastore, N. The role of arbitrariness in the frustration-aggression hypothesis. *J. abnorm. soc. Psychol.*, 1952, 47, 728–731.

Patterson, G. R., Littman, R. A. & Bricker, W. Assertive behavior in children: A step toward a theory of aggression. *Monogr. Soc. Res. Child Develpm.*, 1967, 32 (5 & 6).

Portuges, S. & Feshbach, N. The influence of sex and socio-ethnic factors upon imitation of teachers by elementary school children. *Child Develpm.*, in press.

Rosenzweig, S. An outline of frustration theory. In J. McV. Hunt (Ed.), *Personality and the Behavior Disorders.* New York: Ronald Press, 1944. Pp. 379–388.

Sears, R. R. Relation of early socialization experiences to aggression in middle childhood. *J. abnorm. soc. Psychol.*, 1961, 63, 466–492.

Sears, R. R., Maccoby, E. E. & Levin, H. *Patterns of Child Rearing.* Evanston, Ill.: Row, Peterson, 1957.

Sears, R. R., Rau, L. & Albert, R. *Identification and Child Rearing.* Stanford: Stanford Univ. Press, 1965.

Sears, R. R. Whiting, J. W. M., Nowlis, V. & Sears, P. S. Some child rearing antecedents of aggression and dependency in young children. *Genet. Psychol. Monogr.*, 1953, 47, 135–236.

Sewell, W. H. Infant training and the personality of the child. *Am. J. of Sociol.*, 1952, 58, 150–159.

Updegraff, R. & Keister, M. E. A study of children's reactions to failure and an experimental attempt to modify them. *Child Develpm.*, 1937, 8, 241–248.

Walters, R. H. & Brown, M. Studies of reinforcement of aggression: III. Transfer of responses to an interpersonal situation. *Child Develpm.*, 1963, 34, 563–571.

Walters, R. H. & Thomas, E. Enhancement of punitiveness of visual and audio-visual displays. *Canadian J. Psychol.*, 1963, 17, 244–255.

Whiting, J. W. M. & Child, I. L. *Child Traning and Personality.* New Haven, Conn.: Yale Univ. Press, 1953.

Wittenborn, J. R. *The Development of Adoptive Children.* New York: Russell Sage, 1954.

Wright, G. O. Projection and displacement: A cross-cultural study of folk-tale aggression. *J. abnorm. soc. Psychol.*, 1954, 49, 523–28.

Yarrow, L. The effect of antecedent frustration on projective play. *Psychol. Monogr.*, 1948, 62 (293).

Chapter 9

Imitation, Identification, and Socialization

The term **socialization** refers to the process by which the individual acquires those be-havior patterns, beliefs, standards, and motivations that are valued and appropriate in his own familial, cultural, social, ethnic, and religious group. Early social learning is of cen-tral importance in this process; the child's first learning experiences stem from his inter-actions with members of his family. From infancy on, parents and others directly reward or reinforce appropriate and acceptable responses and punish actions they disapprove of or consider inappropriate. These parental reactions may have immediate and enduring effects on the development of personal characteristics, motives, and social behavior. Ad-ditionally, parental modeling and the child's imitation of the behavior of others enhance the process of socialization.

In studying parental patterns of reward, punishment, and modeling, investigators have generally focused on different kinds of home atmosphere—for example, authoritar-ian, permissive, or democratic—and their consequences for children. Thus, in the first paper in this chapter the investigator, D. Baumrind, describes three patterns of parental child-rearing practices—authoritative, authoritarian, and permissive. She shows how these patterns are related to various aspects of children's behavior and personality, particularly characteristics indicative of **instrumental competence,** that is, behavior that is independent and socially responsible. The results of her study clearly indicate that the development of responsibility and independent behavior in nursery school boys and girls is facilitated by parental modeling of socially responsible and self-assertive behavior and by firm policies in which the parents use reinforcement principles consistently, rewarding socially responsible behavior and punishing deviant responses. These policies are most effective if parental demands and sanctions are accompanied by explanations and reasons that reflect a set of principles that the parents practice as well as preach.

Not all aspects of the child's socialization and personality development are the outcomes of reward learning or imitation. Many complex behavior patterns, personality characteristics, motivations, ideals, and attitudes are acquired by means of **identification** with parents or other models. A child is said to be identified with a model when he believes that he is similar to that model. This belief may be increased through the child's adoption of the model's attributes. Since the child's models are generally carriers and exemplars of culturally approved behavior patterns, identification contributes very significantly to the process of socialization.

(2) In the second article in this chapter, E. M. Hetherington of the University of Virginia discusses parental variables that may affect the strength of identification. She also reports an interesting study of the effects of parental characteristics and child-rearing practices on parent-child similarities and children's sex-typing. These variables are generally considered to be, to a great extent, products of identification. The results of the study indicate that femininity in girls is associated with parental warmth, restrictiveness, psychological forms of discipline, father's masculinity, paternal dominance in the marriage, maternal approval of the feminine role, and reinforcement of feminine behaviors. Sex-typing in boys seems to be more highly influenced by paternal dominance and masculinity and maternal hostility. Dominance and warmth are important factors in both boys' and girls' identifications, but dominance is relatively more important for boys and warmth for girls.

Of course, children are not socialized exclusively by their parents; there are many other agents of socialization. When the child enters nursery school, he encounters many new people who will help socialize him. Nursery school teachers are, to some extent, like parents in reinforcing and thus strengthening some of the child's already established patterns of reaction. And, through their teaching and modeling they may also influence the child to modify some of his behavior, personality characteristics, and attitudes. As the child becomes more active socially and more highly oriented toward his peers, they inevitably become informal, unselfconscious agents of socialization, sometimes presenting new, attractive models for imitation and identification.

(3)   In the third paper in this chapter, A. Bandura and his colleagues at Stanford University demonstrate how peers may play a significant positive role in helping to modify children's undesirable behavior. Children's fears of dogs were dramatically reduced by exposing them to peer models approaching and playing with a dog in calm, friendly ways. The positive, fear-reduction effects were stable and lasting. Children who were initially fearful were soon willing to approach a familiar dog, and these approach responses generalized to another, unfamiliar dog.

22

Socialization and Instrumental Competence in Young Children

Diana Baumrind

For the past 10 years I have been studying parent-child relations, focusing upon the effects of parental authority on the behavior of preschool children. In three separate but related studies, data on children were obtained from three months of observation in the nursery school and in a special testing situation; data on parents were obtained during two home observations, followed by an interview with each parent.

In the first study, three groups of nursery school children were identified in order that the

NOTE: The research by the author reported in this paper was supported in part by research grant HD 02228 from the National Institute of Child Health and Development, U.S. Public Health Service.

SOURCE: Reprinted, in abridged form, from *The Young Child: Reviews of Research,* ed. W. W. Hartup, vol. 2 (1972), 202–224. Washington, D.C.: National Association for the Education of Young Children. Reprinted with permission.

child-rearing practices of their parents could be contrasted. The findings of that study (Baumrind, 1967) can be summarized as follows:

1. Parents of the children who were the most self-reliant, self-controlled, explorative, and content were themselves controlling and demanding; but they were also warm, rational, and receptive to the child's communication. This unique combination of high control and positive encouragement of the child's autonomous and independent strivings can be called *authoritative* parental behavior.

2. Parents of children who, relative to the others, were discontent, withdrawn, and distrustful, were themselves detached and controlling, and somewhat less warm than other parents. These may be called *authoritarian* parents.

3. Parents of the least self-reliant, explorative, and self-controlled children were themselves noncontrolling, nondemanding, and relatively warm. These can be called *permissive* parents.

A second study, of an additional 95 nursery school children and their parents, also supported the position that "authoritative control can achieve responsible conformity with group standards without loss of individual autonomy or self-assertiveness" (Baumrind, 1966, p. 905). In a third investigation (Baumrind, 1971), patterns of parental authority were defined so that they would differ from each other as did the authoritarian, authoritative, and permissive combinations which emerged from the first study.

PATTERNS OF PARENTAL AUTHORITY

Each of these three authority patterns is described in detail below, followed by the subpatterns that have emerged empirically from the most recent study. The capitalized items refer to specific clusters obtained in the analysis of the parent behavior ratings.

The *authoritarian* parent[1] attempts:

to shape, control and evaluate the behavior and attitudes of the child in accordance with a set standard of conduct, usually an absolute standard, theologically motivated and formulated by a higher authority. She values obedience as a virtue and favors punitive, forceful measures to curb self-will at points where the child's actions or beliefs conflict with what she thinks is right conduct. She believes in inculcating such instrumental values as respect for authority, respect for work, and respect for the preservation of order and traditional structure. She does not encourage verbal give and take, believing that the child should accept her word for what is right (Baumrind, 1968, p. 261).

Two subpatterns in our newest study correspond to this description; they differ only in the

[1]In order to avoid confusion, when I speak of the parent I will use the pronoun "she," and when I speak of the child, I will use the pronoun "he," although, unless otherwise specified, the statement applies to both sexes equally.

degree of acceptance shown the child. One subpattern identifies families who were Authoritarian but Not Rejecting. They were high in Firm Enforcement, low in Encourages Independence and Individuality, low in Passive-Acceptance, and low in Promotes Nonconformity. The second subpattern contained families who met all the criteria for the first subpattern except that they scored high on the cluster called Rejecting.

The *authoritative* parent, by contrast with the above, attempts:

to direct the child's activities but in a rational, issue-oriented manner. She encourages verbal give and take, and shares with the child the reasoning behind her policy. She values both expressive and instrumental attributes, both autonomous self-will and disciplined conformity. Therefore, she exerts firm control at points of parent-child divergence, but does not hem the child in with restrictions. She recognizes her own special rights as an adult, but also the child's individual interests and special ways. The authoritative parent affirms the child's present qualities, but also sets standards for future conduct. She uses reason as well as power to achieve her objectives. She does not base her decisions on group consensus or the individual child's desires; but also, does not regard herself as infallible, or divinely inspired (Baumrind, 1968, p. 261).

Two subpatterns corresponded to this description, differing only in the parents' attitudes towards normative values. One subpattern contained families who were Authoritative and Conforming. Like the Authoritarian parents described above, these parents had high scores in Passive-Acceptance. However, they also had high scores in Encourages Independence and Individuality. The second subpattern contained parents who met the criteria for the first subpattern, but who also scored high in Promotes Nonconformity.

The *permissive* parent attempts:

to behave in a nonpunitive, acceptant and affirmative manner towards the child's impulses, desires, and actions. She consults with him about policy decisions and gives explanations for family rules. She makes few demands for household responsibility and orderly behavior. She presents herself to the child as a resource for him to use as he wishes, not as an active agent responsible for shaping or altering his ongoing or future behavior. She allows the child to regulate his own activities as much as possible, avoids the exercise of control, and does not encourage him to obey externally-defined standards. She attempts to use reason but not overt power to accomplish her ends (Baumrind, 1968, p. 256).

We were able to locate three subpatterns reflecting different facets of this prototypic permissiveness. One subpattern, called Nonconforming, typified families who were nonconforming but who were not extremely lax in discipline and who did demand high performance in some areas. The second subpattern, called Permissive, contained families who were characterized by lax discipline and few demands, but who did not stress nonconformity. The third subpattern contained families who were both nonconforming and lax in their discipline and demands; hence, they are referred to as Permissive-Nonconforming.

INSTRUMENTAL COMPETENCE

Instrumental Competence refers to behavior which is socially responsible and independent. Behavior which is friendly rather than hostile to peers, cooperative rather than resistive with adults, achievement rather than nonachievement-oriented, dominant rather than submissive, and purposive rather than aimless, is here defined as instrumentally competent. Middle-class parents clearly value instrumentally competent behavior. When such parents were asked to rank those attributes that they valued and devalued in children, the most valued ones were assertiveness, friendliness, independence, and obedience, and those least valued were aggression, avoidance, and dependency (Emmerich & Smoller, 1964). Note that the positively valued attributes promote successful achievement in United States society and, in fact, probably have survival value for the individual in any subculture or society.

There are people who feel that, even in the United States, those qualities which define instrumental competence are losing their survival value

in favor of qualities which may be called *Expressive Competence*. The author does not agree. Proponents of competence defined in terms of expressive, rather than instrumental, attributes, value feelings more than reason, good thoughts more than effective actions, "being" more than "doing" or "becoming," spontaneity more than planfulness, and relating intimately to others more than working effectively with others. At present, however, there is no evidence that emphasis on expressive competence, at the expense of instrumental competence, fits people to function effectively over the long run as members of any community. This is not to say that expressive competence is not essential for effective functioning in work as well as in love, and for both men and women. Man, like other animals, experiences and gains valid information about reality by means of both noncognitive and cognitive processes. Affectivity deepens man's knowledge of his environment; tenderness and receptivity enhance the character and effectiveness of any human being. But instrumental competence is and will continue to be an essential component of self-esteem and self-fulfillment.

One subdimension of instrumental competence, here designated *Responsible vs. Irresponsible*, pertains to the following three facets of behavior, each of which is related to the others:

(a) *Achievement-oriented vs. Nonachievement-oriented.* This attribute refers to the willingness to persevere when frustration is encountered, to set one's own goals high, and to meet the demands of others in a cognitive situation as opposed to withdrawal when faced with frustration and unwillingess to comply with the teaching or testing instructions of an examiner or teacher. Among older children, achievement-orientation becomes subject to autogenic motivation and is more closely related to measures of independence than to measures of social responsibility. But in the young child, measures of cognitive motivation are highly correlated with willingness to cooperate with adults, especially for boys. Thus, in my study, resistiveness towards adults was highly negatively correlated with achievement-oriented behavior for boys, but not for girls. Other investigators (Crandall, Orleans, Preston & Rabson, 1958; Haggard, 1969) have also found that compliance with adult values and demands characterizes young children who display high achievement efforts.

(b) *Friendly vs. Hostile Behavior Towards Peers.* This refers to nurturant, kind, altruistic behavior displayed toward agemates as opposed to bullying, insulting, selfish behavior.

(c) *Cooperative vs. Resistive Behavior Towards Adults.* This refers to trustworthy, responsible, facilitative behavior as opposed to devious, impetuous, obstructive actions.

A second dimension of child social behavior can be designated *Independent vs. Suggestible.* It pertains to the following three related facets of behavior:

(a) *Domineering vs. Tractable Behavior.* This attribute consists of bold, aggressive, demanding behavior as opposed to timid, nonintrusive, undemanding behavior.

(b) *Dominant vs. Submissive Behavior.* This category refers to individual initiative and leadership in contrast to suggestible, following behavior.

(c) *Purposive vs. Aimless Behavior.* This refers to confident, charismatic, self-propelled activity vs. disoriented, normative, goalless behavior.

The present review is limited to a discussion of instrumental competence and associated antecedent parental practices and is most applicable to the behavior of young children rather than adolescents.

. . . .

SOCIALIZATION PRACTICES RELATED TO RESPONSIBLE VS. IRRESPONSIBLE BEHAVIOR

The reader will recall that I have defined Responsible vs. Irresponsible Behavior in terms of Friendliness vs. Hostility Towards Peers, Cooperation vs. Resistance Towards Adults, and High vs. Low Achievement Orientation. Socialization seems to have a clearer impact upon the development of social responsibility in boys than in girls, probably because girls vary less in this particular attribute. In my own work, parents who were authoritative and relatively conforming, as compared with parents who were permissive or authoritarian, tended to have children who were more friendly, cooperative, and achievement-oriented. This was especially true for boys. Nonconformity in parents was not necessarily associated with resistant and hostile behavior in children. Neither did firm control and high maturity demands produce rebelliousness. In fact, it has generally been found that close supervision, high demands for obedience and personal neatness, and pressure upon the child to share in household responsibilities are associated with responsible behavior rather than with chronic rebelliousness. The condition most conducive to antisocial aggression, because it most effectively rewards such behavior, is probably one in which the parent is punitive and arbitrary in his demands, but inconsistent in responding to the child's disobedience.

Findings from several studies suggest that parental demands provoke rebelliousness only when the parent both restricts autonomy of action and does not use rational methods of control. For example, Pikas (1961), in a survey of 656 Swedish adolescents, showed that differences in the child's acceptance of parental authority depended upon the reason for the parental directive. Authority based on rational concern for the child's welfare was accepted well by the child, but arbitrary, domineering, or exploitative authority was rejected. Pikas' results are supported by Middleton and Snell (1963) who found that discipline regarded by the child as either very strict or very permissive was associated with rebellion against the parents' political views. Finally, Elder (1963), working with adolescents' reports concerning their parents, found that conformity to parental rules typified subjects who saw their parents as having ultimate control (but who gave the child leeway in making decisions) and who also provided explanations for rules.

Several generalizations and hypotheses can be drawn from this literature and from the results of my own work concerning the relations of specific parental practices to the development of social responsibility in young children. The following list is based on the assumption that it is more meaningful to talk about the effects of *patterns* of parental authority than to talk about the effects of single parental variables.

1. *The modeling of socially responsible behavior facilitates the development of social responsibility in young children, and more so if the model is seen by the child as having control over desired resources and as being concerned with the child's welfare.*

The adult who subordinates his impulses enough to conform with social regulations and is himself charitable and generous will have his example followed by the child. The adult who is self-indulgent and lacking in charity will have his example followed even if he should preach generous, cooperative behavior. Studies by Mischel and Liebert (1966) and by Rosenhan, Frederick and Burrowes (1968) suggest that models who behave self-indulgently produce similar behavior in children and these effects are even more extensive than direct reward for self-indulgent behavior. Further, when the adult preaches what he does not practice, the child is more likely to do what the adult practices. This is true even when the model preaches unfriendly or uncooperative behavior but behaves toward the child in an opposite manner. To the extent that the model for socially responsible behavior is perceived as having high social status (Bandura, Ross & Ross, 1963), the model will be most effective in inducing responsible behavior.

In our studies, both authoritative and authori-

tarian parents demanded socially responsible behavior and also differentially rewarded it. As compared to authoritative parents, however, authoritarian parents permitted their own needs to take precedence over those of the child, became inaccessible when displeased, assumed a stance of personal infallibility, and in other ways showed themselves often to be more concerned with their own ideas than with the child's welfare. Thus, they did not exemplify prosocial behavior, although they did preach it. Authoritative parents, on the other hand, both preached and practiced prosocial behavior and their children were significantly more responsible than the children of authoritarian parents. In this regard, it is interesting that nonconforming parents who were highly individualistic and professed anticonforming ideas had children who were more socially responsible than otherwise. The boys were achievement-oriented and the girls were notably cooperative. These parents were themselves rather pacific, gentle people who were highly responsive to the child's needs even at the cost of their own; thus, they modeled but did not preach prosocial behavior.

2. *Firm enforcement policies, in which desired behavior is positively reinforced and deviant behavior is negatively reinforced, facilitate the development of socially responsible behavior, provided that the parent desires that the child behave in a responsible manner.*

The use of reinforcement techniques serves to establish the potency of the reinforcing agent and, in the mind of the young child, to legitimate his authority. The use of negative sanctions can be a clear statement to the child that rules are there to be followed and that to disobey is to break a known rule. Among other things, punishment provides the child with information. As Spence (1966) found, nonreaction by adults is sometimes interpreted by children as signifying a correct response. Siegel and Kohn (1959) found that nonreaction by an adult when the child was behaving aggressively resulted in an increased incidence of such acts. By virtue of his or her role as an authority, the sheer presence of parents when the child misbehaves cannot help but affect the future occurrence of such behavior. Disapproval should reduce such actions, while approval or nonreaction to such behavior should increase them.

In our studies, permissive parents avoided the use of negative sanctions, did not demand mannerly behavior or reward self-help, did not enforce their directives by exerting force or influence, avoided confrontation when the child disobeyed, and did not choose or did not know how to use reinforcement techniques. Their sons, by comparison with the sons of authoritative parents, were clearly lacking in prosocial and achievement-oriented behavior.

3. *Nonrejecting parents are more potent models and reinforcing agents than rejecting parents; thus, nonrejection should be associated with socially responsible behavior in children provided that the parents value and reinforce such behavior.*

It should be noted that this hypothesis refers to nonrejecting parents and is not stated in terms of passive-acceptance. Thus, it is expected that nonrejecting parental behavior, but not unconditionally acceptant behavior, is associated with socially responsible behavior in children. As Bronfenbrenner pointed out about adolescents, "It is the presence of rejection rather than the lack of a high degree of warmth which is inimical to the development of responsibility in both sexes" (1961, p. 254). As already indicated, in our study authoritarian parents were more rejecting and punitive, and less devoted to the child's welfare than were authoritative parents; their sons were also less socially responsible.

4. *Parents who are fair, and who use reason to legitimate their directives, are more potent models and reinforcing agents than parents who do not encourage independence or verbal exchange.*

Let us consider the interacting effects of punishment and the use of reasoning on the behavior of children. From research it appears that an accompanying verbal rationale nullifies the special effectiveness of immediate punishment, and also of relatively intense punishment (Parke, 1969). Thus, by symbolically reinstating the deviant act, explaining the reason for punishment, and telling the child exactly what he should do, the parent obviates the need for intense or instantaneous punishment. Immediate, intense punishment may have undesirable side effects, in that the child is conditioned through fear to avoid deviant behavior, and is not helped to control himself consciously and willfully. Also, instantaneous, intense punishment produces high anxiety which may interfere with performance, and in addition may increase the likelihood that the child will avoid the noxious agent. This reduces that agent's future effectiveness as a model or reinforcing agent. Finally, achieving behavioral conformity by conditioning fails to provide the child with information about cause and effect relations which he can then transfer to similar situations. This is not to say that use of reasoning alone, without negative sanctions, is as effective as the use of both. Negative sanctions give operational meaning to the consequences signified by reasons and to rules themselves.

Authoritarian parents, as compared to authoritative parents, are relatively unsuccessful in producing socially responsible behavior. According to this hypothesis, the reason is that authoritarian parents fail to encourage verbal exchange and infrequently accompany punishment with reasons rather than that they use negative sanctions and are firm disciplinarians.

SOCIALIZATION PRACTICES RELATED TO INDEPENDENT VS. SUGGESTIBLE BEHAVIOR

The reader will recall that Independent vs. Suggestible Behavior was defined with reference to: (a) Domineering vs. Tractable Behavior, (b) Dominance vs. Submission, (c) Purposive vs. Aimless Activity, and (d) Independence vs. Suggestibility. Parent behavior seems to have a clearer effect upon the development of independence in girls than in boys, probably because preschool boys vary less in independence.

In my own work, independence in girls was clearly associated with authoritative upbringing (whether conforming or nonconforming). For boys, nonconforming parent behavior and, to a lesser extent, authoritative upbringing were associated with independence. By independence we do not mean anticonformity. "Pure anticonformity, like pure conformity, is pure dependence behavior" (Willis, 1968, p. 263). Anticonforming behavior, like negativistic behavior, consists of doing anything but what is prescribed by social norms. Independence is the ability to disregard known standards of conduct or normative expectations in making decisions. Nonconformity in parents may not be associated in my study with independence in girls (although it was in boys) because females are especially susceptible to normative expectations. One can hypothesize that girls must be trained to act independently of these expectations, rather than to conform or to anticonform to them.

It was once assumed that firm control and high maturity demands lead to passivity and dependence in young children. The preponderance of evidence contradicts this. Rather, it would appear that many children react to parental power by resisting, rather than by being cowed. The same parent variables which increase the probability that the child will use the parent as a model should increase the likelihood that firm control will result in assertive behavior. For example, the controlling parent who is warm, understanding, and supportive of autonomy should generate less passivity (as well as less rebelliousness) than the controlling parent who is cold and restrictive. This should be the case because of the kinds of behavior reinforced, the traits modeled, and the relative effectiveness of the parent as a model.

Several generalizations and hypotheses can be offered concerning the relations between parental practices and the development of independence in young children:

1. *Early environmental stimulation facilitates the development of independence in young children.*

It took the knowledge gained from compensatory programs for culturally disadvantaged children to counteract the erroneous counsel from some experts to avoid too much cognitive stimulation of the young child. Those Head Start programs which succeed best (Hunt, 1968) are those characterized by stress on the development of cognitive skills, linguistic ability, motivational concern for achievement, and rudimentary numerical skills. There is reason to believe that middle-class children also profit from such early stimulation and enrichment of the environment. Fowler (1962) pointed out, even prior to the development of compensatory programs, that concern about the dangers of premature cognitive training and an overemphasis on personality development had delayed inordinately the recognition that the ability to talk, read, and compute increase the child's self-respect and independent functioning.

Avoidance of anxiety and self-assertion are reciprocally inhibiting responses to threat or frustration. Girls, in particular, are shielded from stress and overstimulation, which probably serves to increase preferences for avoidant rather than offensive responses to aggression or threat. By exposing a child to stress or to physical, social, and intellectual demands, he or she becomes more resistant to stress and learns that offensive reactions to aggression and frustration are frequently rewarding. In our studies, as the hypothesis would predict, parents who provided the most enriched environment, namely the nonconforming and the authoritative parents, had the most dominant and purposive children. These parents, by comparison with the others studied, set high standards of excellence, invoked cognitive insight, provided an intellectually stimulating atmosphere, were themselves rated as being differentiated and individualistic, and made high educational demands upon the child.

2. *Parental passive-acceptance and overprotection inhibits the development of independence.*

Passive-acceptant and overprotective parents shield children from stress and, for the reasons discussed above, inhibit the development of assertiveness and frustration tolerance. Also, parental anxiety about stress to which the child is exposed may serve to increase the child's anxiety. Further, willingness to rescue the child offers him an easy alternative to self-mastery. Demanding and nonprotective parents, by contrast, permit the child to extricate himself from stressful situations and place a high value on tolerance of frustration and courage.

According to many investigators (e.g., McClelland, Atkinson, Clark & Lowell, 1953), healthy infants are by inclination explorative, curious, and stress-seeking. Infantile feelings of pleasure, originally experienced after mild changes in sensory stimulation, become associated with these early efforts at independent mastery. The child anticipates pleasure upon achieving a higher level of skill, and the pleasure derived from successfully performing a somewhat risky task encourages him to seek out such tasks.

Rosen and D'Andrade (1959) found that high achievement motivation, a motivation akin to stress-seeking, was facilitated both by high maternal warmth when the child pleased the parent and high maternal hostility and rejection when the child was displeasing. Hoffman et al. (1960) found that mothers of achieving boys were more coercive than those who performed poorly, and it has also been found (Crandall, Dewey, Katkovsky & Preston, 1964) that mothers of achieving girls were relatively nonnurturant. Kagan and Moss (1962) reported that achieving adult women had mothers who in early childhood were unaffectionate, "pushy," and not protective. Also, Baumrind and Black (1967) found paternal punitiveness to be associated positively with independence in girls. Finally, in a recent study (Baumrind, 1971), there were indications for girls that parental non-

acceptance was positively related to independence. That is, the most independent girls had parents who were either not passive-acceptant or were rejecting.

Authoritarian control and permissive noncontrol both may shield the child from the opportunity to engage in vigorous interaction with people. Demands which cannot be met, refusals to help, and unrealistically high standards may curb commerce with the environment. Placing few demands on the child, suppression of conflict, and low standards may understimulate him. In either case, he fails to achieve the knowledge and experience required to desensitize him to the anxiety associated with nonconformity.

3. *Self-assertiveness and self-confidence in the parent, expressed by an individual style and by the moderate use of power-oriented techniques of discipline, will be associated with independence in the young child.*

The self-assertive, self-confident parent provides a model of similar behavior for the child. Also, the parent who uses power-oriented rather than love-oriented techniques of discipline achieves compliance through means other than guilt. Power-oriented techniques can achieve behavioral conformity without premature internalization by the child of parental standards. It may be that the child is, in fact, more free to formulate his own standards of conduct if techniques of discipline are used which stimulate resistiveness or anger rather than fear or guilt. The use of techniques which do not stimulate conformity through guilt may be especially important for girls. The belief in one's own power and the assumption of responsibility for one's own intellectual successes and failures are important predictors of independent effort and intellectual achievement (Crandall, Katkovsky & Crandall, 1965). This sense of self-responsibility in children seems to be associated with power-oriented techniques of discipline and with critical attitudes on the part of the adult towards the child, provided that the parent is also concerned with developing the child's autonomy and encourages independent and individual behavior.

In my study, both the authoritative and the nonconforming parents were self-confident, clear as well as flexible in their child-rearing attitudes, and willing to express angry feelings openly. Together with relatively firm enforcement and nonrejection, these indices signified patterns of parental authority in which guilt-producing techniques of discipline were avoided. The sons of nonconforming parents and the daughters of authoritative parents were both extremely independent.

4. *Firm control can be associated with independence in the child, provided that the control is not restrictive of the child's opportunities to experiment and to make decisions within the limits defined.*

There is no logical reason why parents' enforcing directives and demands cannot be accompanied by regard for the child's opinions, willingness to gratify his wishes, and instruction in the effective use of power. A policy of firm enforcement may be used as a means by which the child can achieve a high level of instrumental competence and eventual independence. The controlling, demanding parent can train the child to tolerate increasingly intense and prolonged frustration; to broaden his base of adult support to include neighbors, teachers, and others; to assess critically his own successes and failures and to take responsibility for both; to develop standards of moral conduct; and to relinquish the special privileges of childhood in return for the rights of adolescence.

It is important to distinguish between the effects on the child of restrictive control and of firm control. *Restrictive control* refers to the use of extensive proscriptions and prescriptions, covering many areas of the child's life; they limit his autonomy to try out his skills in these areas. By *firm control* is meant firm enforcement of rules,

effective resistance against the child's demands, and guidance of the child by regime and intervention. Firm control does not imply large numbers of rules or intrusive direction of the child's activities.

Becker (1964) has summarized the effects on child behavior of restrictiveness vs. permissiveness and warmth vs. hostility. He reported that warm-*restrictive* parents tended to have passive, well-socialized children. This author (Baumrind, 1967) found, however, that warm-*controlling* (by contrast with warm-*restrictive*) parents were not paired with passive children, but rather with responsible, assertive, self-reliant children. Parents of these children enforced directives and resisted the child's demands, but were not restrictive. Early control, unlike restrictiveness, apparently does not lead to "fearful, dependent and submissive behaviors, a dulling of intellectual striving, and inhibited hostility," as Becker indicated was true of restrictive parents (1964, p. 197).

5. *Substantial reliance upon reinforcement techniques to obtain behavioral conformity, unaccompanied by use of reason, should lead to dependent behavior.*

To the extent that the parent uses verbal cues judiciously, she increases the child's ability to discriminate, differentiate, and generalize. According to Luria (1960) and Vygotsky (1962), the child's ability to "order" his own behavior is based upon verbal instruction from the adult which, when heeded and obeyed, permits eventual *cognitive* control by the child of his own behavior. Thus, when the adult legitimizes power, labels actions clearly as praiseworthy, explains rules and encourages vigorous verbal give and take, obedience is not likely to be achieved at the cost of passive dependence. Otherwise, it may well be.

It is self-defeating to attempt to shape, by extrinsic reinforcement, behavior which by its nature is autogenic. As already mentioned, the healthy infant is explorative and curious, and seems to enjoy mild stress. Although independent mastery can be accelerated if the parent broadens the child's experiences and makes certain reasonable demands upon him, the parent must take care not to substitute extrinsic reward and social approval for the intrinsic pleasure associated with mastery of the environment. Perhaps the unwillingness of the authoritative parents in my study to rely solely upon reinforcement techniques contributed substantially to the relatively purposive, dominant behavior shown by their children, especially by their daughters.

6. *Parental values which stress individuality, self-expression, initiative, divergent thinking, and aggressiveness will facilitate the development of independence in the child, provided that these qualities in the parent are not accompanied by lax and inconsistent discipline and unwillingness to make demands upon the child.*

It is important that adults use their power in a functional rather than an interpersonal context. The emphasis should be on the task to be done and the rule to be followed rather than upon the special status of the powerful adult. By focusing upon the task to be accomplished, the adult's actions can serve as an example for the child rather than as a suppressor of his independence. Firm discipline for both boys and girls must be in the service of training for achievement and independence, if such discipline is not to facilitate the development of an overconforming, passive life style.

In our study, independence was clearly a function of nonconforming but nonindulgent parental attitudes and behaviors, for boys. For girls, however, nonconforming parental patterns were associated with independence only when the parents were also authoritative. The parents in these groups tended to encourage their children to ask for, even to demand, what they desired. They themselves acquiesced in the face of such demands provided that the demands were not at variance with parental policy. Thus, the children

of these parents were positively reinforced for autonomous self-expression. In contrast to these results, the authoritarian parents did not value willfulness in the child, and the permissive parents were clearly ambivalent about rewarding such behavior. Further, the permissive parents did not differentiate between mature or praiseworthy demands by the child and regressive or deviant demands. These permissive parents instead would accede to the child's demands until patience was exhausted; punishment, sometimes very harsh, would then ensue.

CONCLUSIONS

Girls in Western society are in many ways systematically socialized for instrumental incompetence. The affiliative and cooperative orientation of girls increases their receptivity to the influence of socializing agents. This influence, in turn, is often used by socializing agents to inculcate passivity, dependence, conformity, and sociability in young females at the expense of independent pursuit of success and scholarship. In my studies, parents designated as authoritative had the most achievement-oriented and independent daughters. However, permissive parents whose control was lax, who did not inhibit tomboy behavior, and who did not seek to produce sex-role conformity in girls had daughters who were nearly as achievement-oriented and independent.

The following adult practices and attitudes seem to facilitate the development of socially responsible and independent behavior in both boys and girls:

1. Modeling by the adult of behavior which is both socially responsible and self-assertive, especially if the adult is seen as powerful by the child and as eager to use the material and interpersonal resources over which he has control on the child's behalf.

2. Firm enforcement policies in which the adult makes effective use of reinforcement principles in order to reward socially responsible

behavior and to punish deviant behavior, but in which demands are accompanied by explanations, and sanctions are accompanied by reasons consistent with a set of principles followed in practice as well as preached by the parent.

3. Nonrejecting but not overprotective or passive-acceptant parental attitudes in which the parent's interest in the child is abiding and, in the preschool years, intense; and where approval is conditional upon the child's behavior.

4. High demands for achievement and for conformity with parental policy, accompanied by receptivity to the child's rational demands and willingness to offer the child wide latitude for independent judgment.

5. Providing the child with a complex and stimulating environment offering challenge and excitement as well as security and rest, where divergent as well as convergent thinking is encouraged.

These practices and attitudes do not reflect a happy compromise between authoritarian and permissive practices. Rather, they reflect a synthesis and balancing of strongly opposing forces of tradition and innovation, divergence and convergence, accommodation and assimilation, cooperation and autonomous expression, tolerance and principled intractability.

References

Aberle, D. F. & Naegele, K. D. Middle-class fathers' occupational role and attitudes toward children. *Am. J. Orthopsychiat.*, 1952, 22, 366–378.

Bandura, A., Ross, D. & Ross, S. A. A comparative test of the status envy, social power, and the secondary-reinforcement theories of identificatory learning. *J. abnorm. soc. Psychol.*, 1963, 67, 527–534.

Barry, H., Bacon, M. K. & Child, I. L. A cross-cultural survey of some sex differences in socialization. *J. abnorm. soc. Psychol.*, 1957, 55, 327–332.

Baumrind, D. Effects of authoritative parental control on child behavior. *Child Develpm.*, 1966, 37, 887–907.

———. Child care practices anteceding three patterns of preschool behavior. *Genet. Psychol. Monogr.*, 1967, 75, 43–88.

———. Authoritarian vs. authoritative parental control. *Adolescence*, 1968, 3, 255–272.

———. Current patterns of parental authority. *Develpm. Psychol. Monogr.*, 1971, 4(1), 1–102.

———. From each woman in accord with her ability. *School Rev.*, Feb. 1972, in press. (a)

———. An exploratory study of socialization effects on black children: Some black-white comparisons. *Child Develpm.*, 1972, in press. (b)

Baumrind, D. & Black, A. E. Socialization practices associated with dimensions of competence in preschool boys and girls. *Child Develpm.*, 1967, 38, 291–327.

Becker, W. C. Consequences of different kinds of parental discipline. In M. L. Hoffman & L. W. Hoffman (Eds.), *Review of Child Developmental Research*, Vol. 1. New York: Russell Sage Foundations 1964. Pp. 169–208.

Bronfenbrenner, U. Some familial antecedents of responsibility and leadership in adolescents. In L. Petrullo & B. M. Bass (Eds.), *Leadership and Interpersonal Behavior*. New York: Holt, Rinehart & Winston, 1961. Pp. 239–271.

Brown, D. Sex role development in a changing culture. *Psychol. Bull.*, 1958, 55; 232–242.

Crandall, V., Dewey, R., Katkovsky, W. & Preston, A. Parents' attitudes and behaviors and grade school children's academic achievements. *J. genet. Psychol.*, 1964, 104, 53–66.

Crandall, V., Katkovsky, W. & Crandall, V. J. Children's beliefs in their own control of reinforcements in intellectual-academic achievement situations. *Child Develpm.*, 1965, 36, 91–109.

Crandall, V., Orleans, S., Preston, A. & Rabson, A. The development of social compliance in young children. *Child Develpm.*, 1958, 29, 429–443.

Dinitz, S., Dynes, R. R. & Clarke, A. C. Preference for male or female children: Traditional or affectional. *Marriage & Family Living*, 1954, 16, 128–130.

Eiduson, B. T. *Scientists, Their Psychological World*. New York: Basic Books, 1962.

Elder, G. H. Parental power legitimation and its effect on the adolescent, *Sociometry*, 1963, 26, 50–65.

Emmerich, W. & Smoller, F. The role patterning of parental norms. *Sociometry*, 1964, 27, 382–390.

Fowler, W. Cognitive learning in infancy and early childhood. *Psychol. Bull.*, 1962, 59, 116–152.

Haggard, E. A. Socialization, personality, and academic achievement in gifted children. In B. C. Rosen, H. J. Crockett & C. Z. Nunn (Eds.), *Achieve-*

ment in American society. Cambridge, Mass.: Schenkman Publishing, 1969. Pp. 85–94.

Heilbrun, A. B. Sex differences in identification learning. J. genet. Psychol., 1965, 106, 185–193.

Hoffman, L., Rosen, S. & Lippitt, R. Parental coerciveness, child autonomy, and child's role at school. Sociometry, 1960, 23, 15–22.

Horner, M. S. Sex differences in achievement motivation and performance in competitive situations. Unpubl. doctoral dissertation, Univ. of Michigan, 1968.

Hunt, J. McV. Toward the prevention of incompetence. In J. W. Carter, Jr. (Ed.), Research Contributions from Psychology to Community Mental Health. New York: Behavioral Publications, 1968.

Kagan, J. & Moss, H. A. Birth to Maturity: A Study in Psychological Development. New York: John Wiley, 1962.

Keniston, E. & Keniston, K. An American anachronism: the image of women and work. Am. Scholar, 1964, 33, 355–375.

Luria, A. R. Experimental analysis of the development of voluntary action in children. In The Central Nervous System and Behavior. Bethesda, Md.: U.S. Dept. of Health, Education, & Welfare, National Institutes of Health, 1960. Pp. 529–535.

Maccoby, E. E. (Ed.), The Development of Sex Differences. Stanford, Calif.: Stanford Univ. Press, 1966.

McClelland, D., Atkinson, J., Clark, R. & Lowell, E. The Achievement Motive. New York: Appleton-Century-Crofts, 1953.

McKee, J. P. & Sherriffs, A. C. The differential evaluation of males and females. J. Pers., 1957, 25, 356–371.

Middleton, R. & Snell, P. Political expression of adolescent rebellion. Am. J. Sociol., 1963, 68, 527–535.

Mischel, W. & Liebert, R. M. Effects of discrepancies between observed and imposed reward criteria on their acquisition and transmission. J. pers. soc. Psychol., 1966, 3, 45–53.

Parke, R. D. Some effects of punishment on children's behavior. Young Children, 1969, 24, 225–240.

Pikas, A. Children's attitudes toward rational versus inhibiting parental authority. J. abnorm. soc. Psychol., 1961, 62, 315–321.

Roe, A. The Making of a Scientist. New York: Dodd, Mead, 1952.

Rosen, B. C. & D'Andrade, R. The psychological origins of achievement motivation. Sociometry, 1959, 22, 185–218.

Rosenhan, D. L., Frederick, F. & Burrowes, A. Preaching and practicing: Effects of channel discrepancy on norm internalization. Child Develpm., 1968, 39, 291–302.

Rossi, A. Women in science: why so few? In B. C. Rosen, H. J. Crockett, & C. Z. Nunn (Eds.), Achievement in American Society. Cambridge, Mass.: Schenkman Publishing, 1969. Pp. 470–486.

Siegel, A. E. & Kohn, L. G. Permissiveness, permission, and aggression: The effects of adult presence or absence on aggression in children's play. Child Develpm., 1959, 36, 131–141.

Spence, J. T. Verbal-discrimination performance as a function of instruction and verbal reinforcement combination in normal and retarded children. Child Develpm., 1966, 37, 269–281.

Terman, L. M. & Oden, H. H. The Gifted Child Grows Up. Stanford, Calif.: Stanford Univ. Press, 1947.

Vygotsky, L. S. Thought and Language. Cambridge, Mass.: M.I.T. Press, 1962.

Walberg, H. J. Physics, femininity, and creativity. Develpm. Psychol., 1969, 1, 47–54.

Willis, R. H. Conformity, independence, and anticonformity. In L. S. Wrightsman, Jr. (Ed.). Contemporary Issues in Social Psychology. Belmont, Calif.: Brooks/Cole Publishing, 1968. Pp. 258–272.

FAMILIAL VARIABLES

A WARM

B POWER   SEX TYPING

C AGGRESSION   IMITATION

PARENT-CHILD
SIMILARITY

REVIEW OF CAROLE DRENNAN

#23

The Effects of Familial Variables on Sex Typing, on Parent-Child Similarity, and on Imitation in Children

E. Mavis Hetherington

Sex typing is a process by which children acquire the values, motives, and behaviors appropriate to either males or females in their culture. Frequently it is considered to be one facet of the more general process of identification, whereby the child, through imitation or introjection, develops traits and standards similar to those of his parents. Since sex-typed behaviors appear early and since the child's initial social encounters are with the parents, identification theorists assume that the role of the parents is particularly relevant in the development of sex typing. Various theories of identification emphasize different aspects of the child's relationship with the parents in accounting for sex typing.

PARENTAL CHARACTERISTICS AND SEX TYPING

The three parental variables which most frequently have been thought to affect identification are warmth, aggression, and power. Learning theorists usually interpret identification as a process based on the child's desire to reproduce the behavior of an affectionate, rewarding parent. This is sometimes referred to as anaclitic identification. In contrast, traditional psychoanalytic theory has stressed defensive identification or identification with the aggressor, a process involving the acquisition of the behaviors of a punitive or aggressive model and based upon anticipated punishment and threat. A third theory (Parsons, 1955) emphasizes the importance of total parental power in the development of identifica-

NOTE: The research for this study was supported by the Research Committee of the Graduate School, University of Wisconsin, with funds provided by the Wisconsin Alumni Research Foundation.

SOURCE: Reprinted, in abridged form, from *Minnesota Symposia on Child Psychology,* Volume I, pp. 82–107, edited by J. P. Hill. University of Minnesota Press, Minneapolis © 1967 University of Minnesota. Reprinted by permission of the author and the publisher.

tion. According to Parsons, the child identifies with the parent because he has the power to dispense both rewards and punishments.

There is considerable evidence that warmth in the parent of the same sex does facilitate identification and appropriate sex typing (Payne & Mussen, 1956; Mussen & Distler, 1959, 1960; Mussen & Rutherford, 1963; P. S. Sears, 1953; Helper, 1955). In contrast, the evidence for identification with a powerful or an aggressive parent is scanty. Two studies (Mussen & Distler, 1959, 1960) show that total parental power, as measured by a composite score of the father's nurturance and punitiveness of the child, increases masculinity in boys; however, a similar study (Mussen & Rutherford, 1963) indicates that maternal nurturance, but not punitiveness, facilitates femininity in girls. Most of the support offered for defensive identification comes from clinical case studies, anecdotal evidence (Freud, 1937), or naturalistic observations such as the studies made in German concentration camps (Bettelheim, 1943).

Other parental characteristics and behaviors also may influence sex typing in children. If, as Kohlberg (1965) suggests, the formation of a concept of masculinity-femininity is basic in sex typing, parental behaviors and traits that clarify the discrimination between sex-appropriate behaviors should foster sex typing in both boys and girls. Thus masculinity of the father, femininity of the mother, and clarity of definitions of sex roles in the home should facilitate sex typing. On the basis of reinforcement theory, it also is predicted that if the parents approve of each other as models for the appropriately sexed children and encourage identification with the parent of like sex, stronger sex typing should ensue.

Differential Patterns of Identification for Male and Female Children

White (1960) has suggested that striving for competence is a basic developmental process. The child gains a sense of competence, with a consequent reduction in feelings of helplessness and anxiety, if he acquires a feeling of mastery over the environment and over sources of love and affection. Kagan (1958) states that it is the child's desire to command these goals which motivates him to identify with his parent. If mastery over the environment were the most salient motive for a child's identification, it might be expected that he would identify with the parent who controls resources he desires and who determines the dispensation of rewards and punishments in the family. If, on the other hand, the child's identification were more involved with the control of love and affection, parental warmth should be the most influential variable in the identification process, and parental power of secondary importance. The distinction between expressive and instrumental sex-role behavior is relevant here (Parsons, 1955; Johnson, 1963). The male role in our culture is basically an instrumental one in which the male is oriented toward controlling the environment and is encouraged not to permit affective responses toward or from others to deter him from this goal. The ability to cope with and manipulate others in a competitive society, the ability to deal independently and even aggressively with problems is considered appropriate masculine behavior. In contrast, the female role is a more expressive one, emphasizing sensitivity to the feelings and needs of others. Female competence is encouraged in the form of awareness of and responsiveness to the affect and attitudes of others. Thus, although both boys and girls seek the security of an increasing sense of control and competence, boys learn to respond relatively more to parental dominance and power, and girls to the affective behaviors of parents.

The role of power or dominance in the parent of the same sex should be particularly salient in the identification of boys for two reasons. First, both male and female children form an early anaclitic bond with the mother. As the boy becomes older and interaction with his father increases, paternal dominance will facilitate the boy's shift from the mother to the father as a model. If the father is perceived as a powerful figure, the combination of the boy's striving for mastery and competence and of the social sanctions reinforcing him for being masculine will lead him to identify with the father. If the mother is dominant, the boy will tend to sustain his original identification with her, in spite of the extrafamilial social pressures for masculine behavior.

The second reason that paternal dominance should be particularly important for boys is that the controlling of resources and of decision-making is regarded as a more characteristically masculine than feminine behavior. Thus, the dominant father offers his son a more appropriate model than the non-dominant father. Sons of dominant fathers should therefore manifest appropriate sex-typed behavior earlier and should be more similar to the father in both sex-typed and non-sex-typed traits than are sons of dominant mothers.

In contrast, girls need only to sustain and intensify their original anaclitic bond with the mother. They require no special impetus to facilitate a shift in models for identification. However, it has been proposed that an additional important factor in the development of femininity in girls is the internalizing of a reciprocal role relationship with the father. The girl learns to be feminine by interacting with a warm, masculine father. Several recent works have, indeed, suggested that the father may be particularly salient in the sex typing of girls as well as boys (Johnson, 1963; Mussen & Distler, 1959; Mussen & Rutherford, 1963; Sears et al., 1965).

Extrafamilial influences may also affect the development of sex typing in boys and girls differentially. Since family orientation and dependency are characteristic of girls (Kagan, 1964) and since the feminine role is less clearly culturally defined than the masculine role (McKee & Sherriffs, 1957), both sex-typed and non-sex-typed traits of girls should be more directly related to parental behaviors than those of boys. On the other hand, boys are encouraged to be independent and to be oriented toward issues and values external to the family; as a consequence they will be more strongly influenced by extrafamilial social sanctions defining appropriate sex role behavior. Since the masculine role is more clearly defined, boys should receive both greater and more consistent encouragement and pressures by peers and adults outside the family to develop appropriate sex-typed behaviors than do girls. It also is predicted that because of the greater prestige and privileges of males in our culture, girls will be slower and less consistent than boys in developing appropriate sex role preferences (Brown, 1956, 1958).

RELATIONS AMONG SEX TYPING, PARENT-CHILD SIMILARITY, AND IMITATION

Some of the characteristics children acquire in identifying with parents will be sex typed—that is, they will be more typical of males or of females in our culture. Other characteristics will not be sex typed—they will be equally appropriate to both males and females. The acquisition of sex-typed traits should be related not only to parental behavior but also to cultural expectations and pressures to conform, and to the value placed upon a given sex role within society. In contrast, parent-child similarity in non-sex-typed traits should be more consistently and directly related to family structure and parental behavior, since fewer extrafamilial sanctions will be brought to bear upon them.

As the child grows older, he increasingly meets members of society other than his immediate family. Consequently, in young children, identification of both sex-typed and non-sex-typed traits should be closely related to child-rearing practices and the imitative models provided by the parents. However, in older children, sex role preferences should be increasingly influenced by social norms. This may attenuate the relation between sex typing and parental behaviors.

Certain parental traits and child-rearing practices may be related directly to sex typing but related only tangentially to parent-child similarity on non-sex-typed traits. In addition to those previously cited parental characteristics and behaviors that facilitate learning of the sex role, some less obvious relations have been found. For example, the dimension of permissiveness-restrictiveness in child rearing has been shown to be fairly consistently related to behaviors that might be considered sex typed. Permissiveness tends to be related to the masculine characteristics of activity, aggression, assertiveness, achievement, and independence (Baldwin, 1949; Meyers, 1944; Sears, 1961; Watson, 1957). Restrictiveness leads to the feminine characteristics of submissiveness, dependency, compliance, politeness, conformity, and minimal aggression (Levy, 1943; Watson, 1957; Sears, 1961; Meyers, 1944). Thus it is expected that permissiveness in rearing boys and restrictiveness in rearing girls will lead to appropriate sex typing, but not necessarily influence parent-child similarity in non-sex-typed traits. Some support for this hypothesis is found in Sears et al. (1965).

Bandura (1962) has suggested that identification and imitation are synonymous since both encompass the tendency for a person to match the behavior, attitudes, or emotional reactions exhibited by models. If this assumption is valid, and if sex typing and parent-child similarity in non-sex-typed traits are a result of identification, children's performance on experimental tasks involving imitation of the parents, measures of sex role typing, and parent-child-similarity measures should be positively correlated with one another. Parental characteristics assumed to influence identification should be relevant to performance of these tasks. There should be a stronger relation between parental imitation and parent-child similarity in non-sex-typed traits than between either of these two variables and sex typing, since sex typing is also strongly influenced by cultural expectations.

. . . .

The Relation of Parental Characteristics and Child-Rearing Practices to Sex Typing, Parent-Child Similarity, and Imitation

This study was intended to investigate the effects of a [broad] range of parental characteristics and practices on the child's identification. . . . Most of the parental variables selected as having possible relevance to identification were discussed in the introduction above.

·SUBJECTS Subjects were 50 boys and 54 girls, ranging in age from three years and four months to six years and two months, and their parents.

·PARENTAL PROCEDURES Parent procedures were administered in two sessions in the home. In the first session parents took the SFIT [Structured Family Interaction Test developed by Farina, 1960] and an inventory consisting of some buffer items and the dominance and femininity scales from the California Personality Inventory. In the second session parents were interviewed separately about child-rearing practices and parent-child relations.

The measures obtained from the SFIT included . . . [a] dominance index ranging from 1 (dominant mother) to 5 (dominant father), a measure of severity of discipline, and ratings of permissiveness-restrictiveness and warmth-hostility. Measures of total severity of discipline for mother alone, for father alone, and for joint solution of the problem were obtained. A scale developed by Jackson was used as the basis of the yielding measure in the dominance index and also as the measure of severity of discipline. It consists of a series of seventeen types of discipline ordered by a group of clinical psychologists from 1 for least severe practices to 17 for most severe. Yielding was defined in terms of the number of scale points yielded by a parent in the shift from his or her initial position in the individual session to the final solution agreed upon in the joint session. Severity measures were based on the total scale ratings for all situations for each parent in the individual sessions and for the joint session.

Two judges rated the mothers and fathers on seven-point scales for permissiveness-restrictiveness and warmth-hostility. The first-named characteristic in each pair was rated 1. The inter-judge reliabilities for permissiveness-restrictiveness were .82 for mothers and .79 for fathers, and for warmth-hostility were .85 for mothers and .84 for fathers.

The CPI measure of dominance was used to assess general social dominance in contrast to the measure of dominance in child rearing obtained on the SFIT. The measures of parental femininity were used to assess the masculinity or femininity of interests of the parental models.

The interviews with parents were designed to elicit information about parent-child relationships and child-rearing practices. Although the interviews were composed to permit evaluation of a wide range of child-rearing variables, ratings were made only for eighteen variables which were assumed to be related to the child measures on the basis of theory and past research. Two judges rated all variables on seven-point scales. The mean inter-judge reliability was .78, with a range from .48 to .91. In interpreting the results of the ratings it should be noted that the first named characteristic is rated 1 and the last 7. Thus for a variable such as psychological versus physical punishment, a rating of 1 would be extreme use of psychological punishment, a rating of 7 would be extreme use of physical punishment. For the permissiveness variables a rating of 1 is extreme permissiveness, a rating of 7 extreme restrictiveness, paralleling the ratings on the structured family interaction tests. For the punishment variables 1 indicates low punishment, 7 high punishment.

·CHILD MEASURES Four procedures were used to assess diverse aspects of the child's behavior that were thought to be related to identification. Three of them were the previously described measures

—the It Test [a projective test of sex-role preference (See Brown, 1956)], the parent-child similarity measure on non-sex-typed adjectives, and imitation of parents on an aesthetic preference test.

In addition to the It Test, a second measure assumed to be related to sex typing was used, the Play Test. The Play Test is an instrument measuring the percentage of time in a twenty-minute period that a child plays with appropriate sex-typed toys in a room containing five standardized masculine and five feminine toys. The test was originally standardized on 20 girls and 20 boys ranging in age from three through six. The children individually entered a playroom containing twenty-four toys and were instructed to play freely with the toys for twenty minutes. Toys were classified as masculine if significantly more boys than girls played with them and if the mean playing time was greater for boys than girls; the reverse was true for feminine toys. In selecting the final ten toys, the amount of playing time by the appropriate sex was matched for each of five pairs of toys. The test was readministered to a group of 10 boys and 10 girls, and the amount of playing time with the appropriate sex-typed toys differed significantly for the two groups.

·RESULTS Table 1 presents the intercorrelations of the parental variables and the child variables for girls, and Table 2 for boys. All significance levels reported are based on two-tailed tests. At first the reader may be dazzled by the array of insignificant correlations; however, upon closer inspection, most of the significant findings occur where relations would be expected, and many of the insignificant ones occur where no relations were predicted. It should be noted that although the correlation between the It Test and the Play Test is significant for girls ($r = -.40$, $p < .01$) and the pattern of relations between the two sex-typing measures is similar, there are many more significant findings with the It Test. In interpreting the correlations involving sex typing, it must be remembered that a low score on the It Test indi-

Table 1. Correlations between parental behavior and girls' sex role behavior (N = 53)

PARENT MEASURES	IT TEST	PLAY TEST	SIMILARITY[a] TO		IMITATION[b] OF	
			MOTHER	FATHER	MOTHER	FATHER
SFIT						
Dominance	.060	.103	−.065	.520[d]	−.384[d]	.514[d]
Severity of discipline						
Mother	.098	−.165	.104	−.094	.261	.061
Father	.185	−.145	.072	.044	−.122	−.190
Together	.176	−.132	.129	−.081	.147	−.115
Permissiveness-restrictiveness						
Mother	−.147	.204	−.167	−.173	−.147	.077
Father	−.197	−.014	.064	.088	.268[c]	.090
Warmth-hostility						
Mother	.499[d]	−.038	−.156	.104	−.666[d]	.052
Father	.463[d]	−.147	−.191	−.122	−.230	−.338[c]
CPI						
Dominance						
Mother	.125	.301[c]	−.084	.019	.200	−.100
Father	.202	−.121	−.229	.157	−.048	.321[c]
Femininity						
Mother	−.085	.198	−.002	−.126	.114	−.138
Father	.378	−.111	−.059	−.017	−.139	.097
INTERVIEW MEASURES						
Permissiveness for sexual curiosity						
Mother	−.324[c]	−.046	.294[c]	−.024	.191	−.029
Father	−.243	.075	.053	−.047	−.076	−.081
Permissiveness for aggression against parents						
Mother	−.359[d]	−.058	.258	−.053	.316[c]	.030
Father	−.280[c]	.040	.198	.010	−.230	.112
Permissiveness for aggression against peers						
Mother	−.296[c]	.089	.326[c]	.012	.281[c]	−.056
Father	−.184	.173	.130	−.126	−.046	.111
Permissiveness for aggression in home						
Mother	−.164	−.219	.113	−.184	.088	.139
Father	−.292[c]	.216	.143	−.158	.150	−.128
Punishment for sexual curiosity						
Mother	−.309[c]	−.059	.205	.043	.086	−.046
Father	−.380[d]	.167	−.007	−.024	−.016	−.048
Punishment for aggression against parents						
Mother	−.354[c]	−.088	.156	.038	.246	−.012
Father	−.406[d]	.268	−.024	−.054	−.112	.062

Table 1. (Continued)

PARENT MEASURES	IT TEST	PLAY TEST	SIMILARITY[a] TO		IMITATION[b] OF	
			MOTHER	FATHER	MOTHER	FATHER
Punishment for aggression against peers						
Mother	−.280[c]	−.012	.231	.073	.154	−.101
Father	−.208	.094	−.019	−.116	−.081	−.130
Psychological vs. physical punishment						
Mother	.219	−.386[d]	.042	.129	−.066	−.280
Father	.242	−.316[c]	−.190	.304[c]	.008	.112
Warmth-hostility						
Mother	.375[d]	−.068	−.228	.147	−.460[d]	−.115
Father	.303[c]	−.115	−.313[c]	.099	−.106	−.360[d]
Permissiveness-control						
Mother	−.415[d]	−.036	.234	.133	.172	−.044
Father	−.394[d]	.177	.107	−.104	−.059	−.060
Amount of caretaking						
Mother	.002	.054	−.069	−.043	.004	−.084
Father	.039	−.086	−.091	.152	−.025	.115
Attitude toward spouse						
Mother	−.066	−.234	−.033	.053	−.009	.044
Father	.452[d]	−.583[d]	−.085	.138	−.064	.007
Attitude toward opposite sex						
Mother	−.099	.184	−.013	−.109	−.018	−.227
Father	.338[c]	−.246	−.075	−.027	−.118	.046
Dominance in child rearing						
Mother	.105	−.086	−.088	.432[d]	−.416[d]	.350[d]
Father	−.018	−.057	.097	.246	−.358[d]	.378[d]
Dominance in marriage						
Mother	−.170	.317[c]	−.199	−.326[c]	.177	−.222
Father	−.331[c]	.491[d]	.074	−.164	.146	.070
Reinforcement for sex-appropriate behavior						
Mother	−.171	.075	−.078	.155	.024	−.008
Father	−.371[d]	.399[d]	.056	.015	−.190	.039
Clarity of sex roles						
Mother	.321[c]	−.144	−.040	−.188	.067	−.115
Father	−.079	−.040	−.061	.149	.376[d]	.109
Acceptance of feminine role						
Mother	.128	.006	.013	.021	−.013	.055

[a]Similarity scores are based on the number of identical ratings on a checklist of adjectives given by friends of parents and teachers of the children.
[b]Imitation scores are based on the number of similar responses made by parent and child in an aesthetic preference test where parental choices are observed by the child before he makes his own choices.
[c]$p < .05$, when $r = .268$
[d]$p < .01$, when $r = .348$

Table 2. Correlations between parental behavior and boys' sex role behavior (N = 49)

PARENT MEASURES	IT TEST	PLAY TEST	SIMILARITY[a] TO		IMITATION[b] OF	
			MOTHER	FATHER	MOTHER	FATHER
SFIT						
Dominance	.439[d]	.156	−.369[d]	.528[d]	−.228	.431[d]
Severity of discipline						
Mother	.208	.154	.062	.066	.034	−.036
Father	.012	.131	−.147	.157	.052	.275[c]
Together	.171	.113	.021	.240	.068	.265
Permissiveness-restrictiveness						
Mother	.059	−.016	.023	−.132	.066	−.019
Father	−.064	−.046	.196	−.116	.181	−.224
Warmth-hostility						
Mother	−.034	.114	.157	−.012	−.263	−.177
Father	.204	.237	.114	−.182	.104	−.286[c]
CPI						
Dominance						
Mother	−.006	−.086	−.120	.032	−.016	.111
Father	.272	.003	−.044	.334[c]	−.177	.080
Femininity						
Mother	−.179	−.085	.042	−.165	−.048	.136
Father	−.287[c]	−.178	.192	−.154	.003	−.287[c]
INTERVIEW MEASURES						
Permissiveness for sexual curiosity						
Mother	−.078	−.163	−.121	−.001	.035	.096
Father	−.169	−.075	−.041	.009	−.132	.052
Permissiveness for aggression against parents						
Mother	−.150	−.115	−.090	−.176	−.145	.164
Father	−.142	−.179	−.048	.132	−.070	.209
Permissiveness for aggression against peers						
Mother	−.061	−.023	−.051	−.048	−.136	.170
Father	−.090	−.102	−.231	.142	−.275	.189
Permissiveness for aggression in home						
Mother	−.073	−.016	.057	−.251	−.017	−.069
Father	−.108	−.022	−.110	.159	−.290[c]	.240
Punishment for sexual curiosity						
Mother	.014	−.049	−.062	−.149	.004	.089
Father	−.099	−.200	−.121	.163	−.150	.202
Punishment for aggression against parents						
Mother	−.047	−.142	.004	−.188	.084	.009
Father	−.156	−.223	−.233	.063	−.241	.177

Table 2. (Continued)

PARENT MEASURES	IT TEST	PLAY TEST	SIMILARITY[a] TO		IMITATION[b] OF	
			MOTHER	FATHER	MOTHER	FATHER
Punishment for aggression against peers						
Mother	−.153	.053	−.033	−.178	.046	−.050
Father	.056	−.177	−.126	.020	−.297[d]	−.053
Psychological vs. physical punishment						
Mother	.118	−.055	−.188	−.086	.111	−.084
Father	−.065	−.186	−.178	−.033	.107	.142
Warmth-hostility						
Mother	.330[c]	.150	.113	−.109	−.046	−.156
Father	−.082	−.023	−.073	−.073	.145	−.257
Permissiveness-control						
Mother	−.120	−.070	−.116	−.237	−.143	.013
Father	−.169	−.108	−.096	.136	−.254	.173
Amount of caretaking						
Mother	.114	−.274	−.018	−.008	.063	−.115
Father	.276	.129	.205	−.001	.194	−.019
Attitude toward spouse						
Mother	−.265	.001	.117	.044	.176	.076
Father	.051	.099	.052	.050	−.073	.025
Attitude toward opposite sex						
Mother	−.109	−.148	.122	−.108	.276	−.006
Father	−.199	−.216	−.012	−.200	.076	−.173
Dominance in child rearing						
Mother	.310[c]	.190	−.360[c]	.330[c]	−.155	.080
Father	.083	.328[c]	−.241	.211	−.202	−.022
Dominance in marriage						
Mother	.279[c]	.214	−.137	.050	.187	−.139
Father	.209	.108	−.147	.089	.234	−.152
Reinforcement for sex-appropriate behavior						
Mother	.172	.162	.214	.185	.162	.135
Father	−.005	−.276[c]	.075	−.051	.204	−.168
Clarity of sex roles						
Mother	.230	.127	.144	.186	.048	−.143
Father	−.032	−.234	.056	.111	.148	−.015
Acceptance of feminine role						
Mother	−.189	−.058	−.038	−.210	−.276	.147

[a]Similarly scores based on the number of identical ratings on a checklist of adjectives given by friends of parents and teachers of the children.
[b]Imitation scores based on the number of similar responses made by parent and child in an aesthetic preference test where parental choices are observed by the child before he makes his own choices.
[c]$p < .05$, when $r = .279$
[d]$p < .01$, when $r = .361$.

cates femininity and a high score masculinity for both boys and girls. In contrast, a high score on the Play Test means appropriate sex-typed behavior for children of both sexes.

Some support is found for the hypothesis that femininity in girls is facilitated by warmth in the parents and by restrictiveness and punishment for sexual curiosity and aggressive behavior. The relation between restrictiveness in the interview measures and femininity is consistent with the findings of Sears, Rau, and Alpert (1965). Overt sexual and aggressive behaviors are inappropriate for girls; their inhibition should lead to more acceptable sex typing in girls. Physical punishment leads to less feminine behavior in girls as measured by the Play Test. It might be argued that parents who physically punish are aggressive and thus inappropriate models for female children.

The behavior and characteristics of the father appear to be particularly important for sex typing in girls. The father who is masculine and is dominant in his marriage has a feminine daughter. If he enjoys women and has a positive attitude toward them, particularly his wife, and if he reinforces his daughter for feminine behavior, we do indeed find greater femininity developing in the daughter. These findings offer some evidence for a reciprocal role theory of the development of sex typing in girls. The young girl learns to be feminine by interacting with a warm, masculine father who encourages and enjoys her femininity.

It is surprising to note that the mother's femininity and her reinforcement of the daughter's feminine behaviors are not related to the girl's sex typing. This is in agreement with Mussen and Rutherford's study (1963). Apparently the mother's warmth and disciplinary practices are determinants of the daughter's femininity, but the appropriate sexual characteristics and reinforcements of the mother are not.

Relative parental dominance over the child, as measured by the SFIT scale or by interview ratings of dominance in child rearing, does not influence sex typing in girls. However, maternal dominance is disruptive to sex typing in boys. It is striking that there are few significant relations between the parental variables and sex typing in boys. Only the parental dominance measures predict appropriate sex typing, and even these are not consistent for maternal and paternal interview measures. There is some indication that maternal hostility increases masculinity in boys. This relation is found only between the maternal interview measure and the It Test. The lack of relation between child-rearing variables and sex typing suggests that sex typing in boys is influenced more by factors outside the home than is sex typing in girls. The clear cultural definition, high value, and privileges of the masculine role in our society may be more influential in sex role typing in boys than is the family. Since girls are encouraged to be family oriented and boys to be independent, intrafamilial influences may be more salient for sex typing in girls and extrafamilial influences for boys.

If, as Bandura (1962) proposes, identification can be reduced to imitation, similar patterns of relations between child-rearing variables and imitation or parent-child similarity would be expected. In the imitation task, girls imitate the dominant parent, whether it is the mother or the father. In contrast, paternal dominance facilitates cross-sexed identification but does not interfere with same-sexed identification in girls. Father-daughter similarity is increased by father dominance; mother-daughter similarity is not affected by parental dominance.

Girls imitate parents who are warm, but warmth and parent-daughter similarity are not related. The data also suggest that in some areas maternal restrictiveness may lead to both imitation of the mother and mother-daughter similarity in girls. Paternal dominance, warmth, and masculinity all facilitate the boy's imitation of the father. In contrast, boys' similarity to parents' non-sex-typed traits is facilitated by parental dominance but not by warmth. There are few other relations between the parent variables and imitation or parent-child similarity for boys.

DISCUSSION AND SUMMARY

[This study indicates] that the rate, patterns, and salient variables in identification for boys and girls vary greatly. Although girls are slower in acquiring appropriate sex role preferences, once sex typing occurs there is a greater relation for girls than for boys between variables assumed to be related to identification. This suggests that the process of identification is a more integrated one in female than in male children. Sex typing in boys is not related to parental imitation or parent-child similarity in non-sex-typed traits at any age.

It is suggested that the relation between parental variables and the variables assumed to be measures of identification, and among the identification variables themselves, might be expected to be less strong for boys than for girls. This is based on the premise that boys are encouraged to be oriented more toward independence from the family and toward extrafamilial influences and values, whereas girls are encouraged to sustain their early orientation toward the family. Since there is greater clarity in the cultural definition of the masculine role, greater social pressures external to the family will be exerted upon boys to behave in an appropriately sex-typed manner. Thus the relation among identification variables will be affected by both familial and extrafamilial influences for boys, but mainly by familial influences for girls. The findings do seem to support this position.

Femininity in girls is related to many parental and child-rearing variables including warmth, restrictiveness, psychological forms of discipline, paternal masculinity, paternal dominance in the marriage, approval of the mother and of the feminine role, and reinforcement of feminine behaviors. In contrast, sex typing in boys seems to be influenced only by paternal dominance and masculinity and maternal hostility. These may facilitate the shift from the original anaclitic identification with the mother to an appropriately sex-typed identification with the father. It could be speculated that maternal hostility leads the boy to reject the mother as a model and forces him to accept the father as a model, or that a hostile mother may be manifesting behaviors more appropriately masculine than feminine.

The many relations between paternal characteristics and sex typing in girls suggests that one process in becoming feminine is that of learning how to interact and play the feminine role with a warm, approving, masculine father. It seems that for both boys and girls a favorable relation with the father is important in sex typing. This supports the reciprocal role theory of identification of Parsons (1955) and Johnson (1963).

Although dominance and warmth are important in the identification of both boys and girls, dominance appears to be relatively more important for boys and warmth for girls. Maternal dominance appears to be extremely disruptive to sex typing, father-child similarity, and father-son imitation in boys, although it enhances mother-son similarity and mother-son imitation. Parental dominance has no effect on sex typing in girls, although it facilitates parent-child similarity and imitation of the dominant parent. Parental warmth is an important factor in the imitation of the parents by both boys and girls, and in sex role typing in girls. In fact, both maternal and paternal warmth increases femininity in girls. Warmth appears to have no effect on parent-child similarity in non-sex-typed traits. The results of these investigations . . . suggest that paternal dominance for boys and maternal warmth for girls are critical in effective identification. Furthermore, because of the male's instrumental role and the female's emotional expressive role in our culture, males learn to value and become oriented toward dominance and mastery and females toward effective cues in the process of identification.

An open question is whether this differential responsiveness to warmth and dominance for girls and boys precedes or is a result of identification. It may be that from an early age girls are reinforced for emotional sensitivity and boys for assertiveness and mastery of the environment, and consequently become responsive to these characteristics in others. On the other hand, as is suggested by Kohlberg (1965), cognitive self-categorization as boy or girl may result in positively valuing objects and acts consistent with this sexual identity. Thus it is possible that sex role typing precedes greater responsiveness to warmth or dominance. The most appropriate approach to investigating this problem would be a developmental study of boys and girls which would evaluate relative responsiveness to warmth and power, and the relation of these variables to cognitive and behavioral measures of sex typing at various ages. Since sex-typed behaviors occur early, it would seem imperative to include young children, even infants, in such a study.

These studies appear to yield evidence in partial support of the three main theories of identification—identification based on power, positive reinforcement and warmth, and aggression. However, the results suggest that the effects of warmth and power are less restricted than those of aggression. The specific circumstances and situational variables such as home atmosphere, family structures, and child-rearing practices under which parental warmth, aggression, or dominance becomes particularly influential in the process of identification warrant further investigation. This might be done through further studies of the parent-child interactions and behavioral measures of identification, or through experimental analogues of these situations in the laboratory. . . .

References

Baldwin, A. L. The effect of home environment on nursery school behavior. *Child Development*, 1949, 20, 49–61.

Bandura, A. Social learning through imitation, in M. R. Jones, ed., *Nebraska symposium on motivation*, pp. 211–269. Lincoln: University of Nebraska Press, 1962.

——— & Aletha Huston. Identification as a process of incidental learning. *Journal of Abnormal and Social Psychology*, 1961, 63, 311–318.

Bandura, A., Dorothea Ross, & Sheila Ross. A comparative test of the status envy, social power and secondary reinforcement theories of identificatory learning. *Journal of Abnormal and Social Psychology*, 1963, 67, 527–534.

Bettelheim, B. Individual and mass behavior in extreme situations. *Journal of Abnormal and Social Psychology*, 1943, 38, 417–452.

Brown, D. G. Sex role preference in young children. *Psychological Monographs*, 1956, 70, No. 14 (Whole No. 421).

———. Sex role development in a changing culture. *Psychological Bulletin*, 1958, 55, 232–242.

Farina, A. Patterns of role dominance and conflict in parents of schizophrenic patients. *Journal of Abnormal and Social Psychology*, 1960, 61, 31–38.

Freud, Anna. *The ego and the mechanisms of defense.* London: Hogarth, 1937.

Helper, M. M. Learning theory and the self concept. *Journal of Abnormal Social Psychology*, 1955, 51, 184–194.

Hetherington, E. Mavis. Developmental study of the effects of sex of the dominant parent on sex role preference, identification and imitation in children. *Journal of Personality and Social Psychology*, 1965, 2, 188–194.

Jackson, P. W. Verbal solutions to parent-child problems and reports of experience with punishment. Unpublished Ph.D. thesis, Columbia University, 1955.

Johnson, Miriam. Sex role learning in the nuclear family. *Child Development*, 1963, 34, 319–333.

Kagan, J. The concept of identification. *Psychological Review*, 1958, 65, 296–305.

———. Acquisition and significance of sex typing, in M. L. Hoffman & Lois W. Hoffman, eds., *Review of child development research*, pp. 137–167. New York: Russell Sage, 1964.

——— & W. Phillips. Measurement of identification: a methodological note. *Journal of Abnormal and Social Psychology*, 1964, 69, 442–445.

Kohlberg, L. A cognitive developmental analysis of children's sex-role concepts and attitudes, in Eleanor E. Maccoby, ed., *The development of sex differences*, pp. 82–173. Stanford: Stanford University Press, 1966.

Levy, D. M. *Maternal overprotection*. New York: Columbia University Press, 1943.

McDavid, J. W. Imitative behavior in preschool children. *Psychological Monographs*, 1959, 73, No. 16 (Whole No. 486).

McKee, J. P., & A. C. Sherriffs. The differential evaluation of males and females. *Journal of Personality*, 1957, 25, 356–371.

Meyers, C. E. The effect of conflicting authority on the child. *University of Iowa Studies in Child Welfare*, 1944, 20, No. 409, 31–98.

Mischel, W., & Joan Grusec. Determinants of the rehearsal and transmission of neutral and aversive behaviors. *Journal of Personality and Social Psychology*, 1963, 3, 197–205.

Mussen, P., & L. Distler. Masculinity, identification and father-son relationships. *Journal of Abnormal and Social Psychology*, 1959, 59, 350–356.

———. Child rearing antecedents of masculine identification in kindergarten boys. *Child Development*, 1960, 31, 89–100.

Mussen, P., & A. Parker. Mother nurturance and girls' incidental imitative learning. *Journal of Personality and Social Psychology*, 1965, 2, 94–96.

Mussen, P., & E. Rutherford. Parent-child relations and parental personality in relation to young children's sex-role preferences. *Child Development*, 1963, 34, 489–607.

Parsons, T. Family structure and the socialization of the child, in T. Parsons and R. F. Bales, eds., *Family, socialization and interaction process*, pp. 35–131. Glencoe, Ill.: Free Press, 1955.

Payne, D. E., & P. H. Mussen. Parent child relations and father identification among adolescent boys. *Journal of Abnormal and Social Psychology*, 1956, 52, 358–362.

Sarnoff, I. Identification with the aggressor: some personality correlates of anti-Semitism among Jews. *Journal of Personality*, 1951, 20, 199–218.

Sears, Pauline S. Child-rearing factors related to playing of sex-typed roles. *American Psychologist*, 1953, 8, 431. (Abstract)

Sears, R. R. The relation of early socialization experiences to aggression in middle childhood. *Journal of Abnormal and Social Psychology*, 1961, 63, 466–492.

———, Lucy Rau, & R. Alpert. *Identification and child rearing*. Stanford, Calif.: Stanford University Press, 1965.

Watson, G. Some personality differences in children related to strict or permissive parental discipline. *Journal of Psychology*, 1957, 44, 227–249.

White, R. Competence and the psychosexual stages of development, in M. R. Jones, ed., *Nebraska symposium on motivation*, pp. 97–141. Lincoln: University of Nebraska Press, 1960.

24

Vicarious Extinction of
Avoidance Behavior

Albert Bandura

Joan E. Grusec

Frances L. Menlove

Recent investigations have shown that behavioral inhibitions (Bandura, 1965a; Bandura, Ross & Ross, 1963; Walters & Parke, 1964) and conditioned emotional responses (Bandura & Rosenthal, 1966; Berger, 1962) can be acquired by observers as a function of witnessing aversive stimuli administered to performing subjects. The present experiment was primarily designed to determine whether preexisting avoidance behavior can similarly be extinguished on a vicarious basis. The latter phenomenon requires exposing observers to modeled stimulus events in which a performing subject repeatedly exhibits approach responses toward the feared object without incurring any aversive consequences.

Some suggestive evidence that avoidance responses can be extinguished vicariously is furnished by Masserman (1943) and Jones (1924) in exploratory studies of the relative efficacy of various psychotherapeutic procedures. Masserman produced strong feeding inhibitions in cats, following which the inhibited animals observed a cage mate, that had never been negatively conditioned, exhibit prompt approach and feeding responses. The observing subjects initially cowered at the presentation of the conditioned stimulus, but with continued exposure to their fearless companion they advanced, at first hesitantly and then more boldly, to the goal box and consumed the food. Some of the animals, however, showed

NOTE: This research was supported by Public Health Research Grant M-5162 from the National Institute of Mental Health. The authors are indebted to Janet Brewer, Edith Dowley, Doris Grant, and Mary Lewis for their generous assistance in various phases of this research.

SOURCE: From *Journal of Personality and Social Psychology*, vol. 5, no. 1 (1967), 16—23. Copyright © 1967 by the American Psychological Association. Reprinted by permission.

little reduction in avoidance behavior despite prolonged food deprivation and numerous modeling trials. Moreover, avoidance responses reappeared in a few of the animals after the normal cat was removed, suggesting that in the latter cases the modeling stimuli served merely as temporary external inhibitors of avoidance responses. Jones (1924) similarly obtained variable results in extinguishing children's phobic responses by having them observe their peers behave in a nonanxious manner in the presence of the avoided objects.

If a person is to be influenced by modeling stimuli and the accompanying consequences, then the necessary observing responses must be elicited and maintained. In the foregoing case studies, the models responded to the most feared stimulus situation at the outset, a modeling procedure that is likely to generate high levels of emotional arousal in observers. Under these conditions any avoidance responses designed to reduce vicariously instigated aversive stimulation, such as subjects withdrawing or looking away, would impede vicarious extinction. Therefore, the manner in which modeling stimuli are presented may be an important determinant of the course of vicarious extinction.

Results from psychotherapeutic studies (Bandura[1]) and experiments with infrahuman subjects (Kimble & Kendall, 1953) reveal that avoidance responses can be rapidly extinguished if subjects are exposed to a graduated series of aversive stimuli that progressively approximate the original intensity of the conditioned fear stimulus. For the above reasons it would seem advisable to conduct vicarious extinction by exposing observers to a graduated sequence of modeling activities beginning with presentations that can be easily tolerated; as observers' emotional reactions to displays of attenuated approach responses are extinguished, the fear-provoking properties of the modeled displays might be gradually increased,

concluding with interactions capable of arousing relatively strong emotional responses.

If emotion-eliciting stimuli occur in association with positively reinforcing events, the former cues are likely to lose their conditioned aversive properties more rapidly (Farber, 1948) than through mere repeated nonreinforced presentation. It might therefore be supposed that vicarious extinction would likewise be hastened and more adequately controlled by presenting the modeling stimuli within a favorable context designed to evoke simultaneously competing positive responses.

The principles discussed above were applied in the present experiment, which explored the vicarious extinction of children's fearful and avoidant responses toward dogs. One group of children participated in a series of modeling sessions in which they observed a fearless peer model exhibit progressively longer, closer, and more active interactions with a dog. For these subjects, the modeled approach behavior was presented within a highly positive context. A second group of children was presented the same modeling stimuli, but in a neutral context.

Exposure to the behavior of the model contains two important stimulus events, that is, the occurrence of approach responses without any adverse consequences to the performer and repeated observation of the feared animal. Therefore, in order to control for the effects of exposure to the dog per se, children assigned to a third group observed the dog in the positive context but with the model absent. A fourth group of children participated in the positive activities, but they were never exposed to either the dog or the model.

In order to assess both the generality and the stability of vicarious extinction effects, the children were readministered tests for avoidance behavior toward different dogs following completion of the treatment series, and approximately 1 month later. It was predicted that children who had observed the peer model interact nonanxi-

[1]A. Bandura, "Principles of Behavioral Modification," unpublished manuscript, Stanford University, 1966.

ously with the dog would display significantly less avoidance behavior than subjects who had no exposure to the modeling stimuli. The largest decrements were expected to occur among children in the modeling-positive context condition. It was also expected that repeated behavioral assessments and the general disinhibitory effects of participation in a series of highly positive activities might in themselves produce some decrease in avoidance behavior.

METHOD

Subjects

The subjects were 24 boys and 24 girls selected from three nursery schools. The children ranged in age from 3 to 5 years.

Pretreatment Assessment of Avoidance Behavior

As a preliminary step in the selection procedure, parents were asked to rate the magnitude of their children's fearful and avoidant behavior toward dogs. Children who received high fear ratings were administered a standardized performance test on the basis of which the final selection was made.

The strength of avoidance responses was measured by means of a graded sequence of 14 performance tasks in which the children were required to engage in increasingly intimate interactions with a dog. A female experimenter brought the children individually to the test room, which contained a brown cocker spaniel confined in a modified playpen. In the initial tasks the children were asked, in the following order, to walk up to the playpen and look down at the dog, to touch her fur, and to pet her. Following the assessment of avoidance responses to the dog in the protective enclosure, the children were instructed to open a hinged door on the side of the playpen, to walk the dog on a leash to a throw rug, to remove the leash, and to turn the dog over and scratch her stomach. Although a number of the subjects were unable to perform all of the latter tasks, they were nevertheless administered the remaining test items to avoid any assumption of a perfectly ordered scale for all cases. In subsequent items the children were asked to remain alone in the room with the animal and to feed her dog biscuits. The final and most difficult set of tasks required the children to climb into the playpen with the dog, to pet her, to scratch her stomach, and

to remain alone in the room with the dog under the exceedingly confining and fear-provoking conditions.

The strength of the children's avoidant tendencies was reflected not only in the items completed, but also in the degree of vacillation, reluctance, and fearfulness that preceded and accompanied each approach response. Consequently, children were credited 2 points if they executed a given task either spontaneously or willingly, and 1 point when they carried out the task minimally after considerable hesitancy and reluctance. Thus, for example, children who promptly stroked the dog's fur repeatedly when requested to do so received 2 points, whereas subjects who held back but then touched the dog's fur briefly obtained 1 point. In the item requiring the children to remain alone in the room with the dog, they received 2 points if they approached the animal and played with her, and 1 point if they were willing to remain in the room but avoided any contact with the dog. Similarly, in the feeding situation children were credited 2 points if they fed the dog by hand, but a single point if they tossed the biscuits on the floor and thereby avoided close contact with the animal. The maximum approach score that a subject could attain was 28 points.

On the basis of the pretreatment assessment, the children in each nursery school were grouped into three levels of avoidance behavior, with the corresponding scores ranging from 0 to 7, 8 to 17, and 18 to 20 points. There were approximately the same number of children, equally divided between boys and girls, at each of the three avoidance levels. The subjects from each of these groups were then assigned randomly to one of four conditions.

Treatment Conditions

Children who participated in the *modeling-positive context* condition observed a fearless peer model display approach responses toward a cocker spaniel within the context of a highly enjoyable party atmosphere.

There were eight 10-minute treatment sessions conducted on 4 consecutive days. Each session, which was attended by a group of four children, commenced with a jovial party. The children were furnished brightly colored hats, cookie treats, and given small prizes. In addition, the experimenter read stories, blew large plastic balloons for the children to play with, and engaged in other party activities designed to produce strong positive affective responses.

After the party was well under way, a second experimenter entered the room carrying the dog, followed by a 4-year-old male model who was unknown to most of the children. The dog was placed in a playpen located across the room from a large table at which the children were seated. The model, who had been chosen because of his complete lack of fear of dogs, then performed prearranged sequences of interactions with the dog for approximately 3 minutes during each session. One boy served as the model for children drawn from two of the nursery schools, and a second boy functioned in the same role at the third school.

The fear-provoking properties of the modeled displays were gradually increased from session to session by varying simultaneously the physical restraints on the dog, the directness and intimacy of the modeled approach responses, and the duration of interaction between the model and his canine companion. Initially, the experimenter carried the dog into the room and confined her to the playpen, and the model's behavior was limited to friendly verbal responses ("Hi, Chloe") and occasional petting. During the following three sessions the dog remained confined to the playpen, but the model exhibited progressively longer and more active interactions in the form of petting the dog with his hands and feet, and feeding her wieners and milk from a baby bottle. Beginning with the fifth session, the dog was walked into the room on a leash, and the modeled tasks were mainly performed outside the playpen. For example, in addition to repeating the feeding routines, the model walked the dog around the room, petted her, and scratched her stomach while the leash was removed. In the last two sessions the model climbed into the playpen with the dog where he petted her, hugged her, and fed her wieners and milk from the baby bottle.

It would have been of interest to compare the relative efficacy of the graduated modeling technique with bold displays of approach behavior from the outset. However, pretest findings showed that when modeled displays are too fear provoking, children actively avoid looking at the performances and are reluctant to participate in subsequent sessions. The latter approach would therefore require additional procedures designed to maintain strong attending behavior to highly aversive modeling stimuli.

Children assigned to the *modeling-neutral context* condition observed the same sequence of approach responses performed by the same peer model except that the parties were omitted. In each of the eight sessions the subjects were merely seated at the table and observed the modeled performances.

In order to control for the influence of repeated exposure to the positive atmosphere and to the dog per se, children in the *exposure-positive context* group attended the series of parties in the presence of the dog with the model absent. As in the two modeling conditions, the dog was introduced into the room in the same manner for the identical length of time; similarly, the dog was confined in the playpen during the first four sessions and placed on a leash outside the enclosure in the remaining sessions.

Children in the *positive-context* group participated in the parties, but they were never exposed to either the dog or the model. The main purpose of this condition was to determine whether the mere presence of a dog had an adverse or a beneficial effect on the children. Like the third condition, it also provided a control for the possible therapeutic effects of positive experiences and increased familiarity with amiable experimenters, which may be particularly influential in reducing inhibitions in very young children. In addition, repeated behavioral assessments in which subjects perform a graded series of approach responses toward a feared object without any aversive consequences would be expected to produce some direct extinction of avoidance behavior. The inclusion of the latter two control groups thus makes it possible to evaluate the changes effected by exposure to modeling stimuli over and above those resulting from general disinhibition, direct extinction, and repeated observation of the feared object.

Posttreatment Assessment of Avoidance Behavior

On the day following completion of the treatment series, the children were administered the performance test consisting of the graded sequence of interaction tasks with the dog. In order to determine the generality of vicarious extinction effects, half the children in each of the four groups were tested initially with the experimental animal and then with an unfamiliar dog; the remaining were presented with the two dogs in the reverse order.[2] The testing sessions were separated by an interval of $1\frac{1}{2}$ hours so as to minimize any transfer of emotional reactions generated by one animal to the other.

The unfamiliar animal was a white mongrel, predominantly terrier, and of approximately the same size and activity level as the cocker spaniel. Two groups of 15 children, drawn from the same nursery-school population, were tested with either the mongrel or the spaniel in order to determine the aversiveness of the two animals. The mean approach scores with the spaniel ($M = 16.47$) and the mongrel ($M = 15.80$) were virtually identical ($t = .21$).

[2]The authors are especially indebted to Chloe and Jenny for their invaluable and steadfast assistance with a task that, at times, must have been most perplexing to them.

Follow-Up Assessment

A follow-up evaluation was conducted approximately 1 month after the posttreatment assessment in order to determine the stability of modeling-induced changes in approach behavior. The children's responses were tested with the same performance tasks toward both animals, presented in the identical order.

After the experiment was completed, the children were told that, while most dogs are friendly, before petting an unfamiliar dog they should ask the owner. This precautionary instruction was designed to reduce indiscriminate approach behavior by children who were in the modeling conditions toward strange dogs which they would undoubtedly encounter.

Measurement Procedure

The same female experimenter administered the pretreatment, posttreatment, and follow-up behavioral tests. To prevent any possible bias, the experimenter was given minimal information about the details of the study and had no knowledge of the conditions to which the children were assigned. The treatment and assessment procedures were further separated by the use of different rooms for each activity.

In order to provide an estimate of interscorer reliability, the performances of 25% of the children, randomly selected from pretreatment, posttreatment, and follow-up phases of the experiment, were scored simultaneously but independently by another rater who observed the test sessions through a one-way mirror from an adjoining observation room. The two raters were in perfect agreement on 97% of the specific approach responses that were scored.

A dog's activity level may partly determine the degree of fear and avoidance exhibited by the children; conversely, timorous or unrestrained approach responses might differentially affect the animals' reactivity. Therefore, during the administration of each test item, the animals' behavior was rated as either passive, moderately active, or vigorous. The raters were in perfect agreement in categorizing the dogs' activity levels on 81% of the performance tests.

Changes in children's approach-response scores across the different phases of the experiment, and the number of subjects in each treatment condition who were able to carry out the terminal performance task, served as the dependent measures.

RESULTS

The percentages of test items in which the animals behaved in a passive, moderately active, or vigorous manner were 55, 43, and 2, respectively, for the model-positive context groups; 53, 44, and 2 for children in the model-neutral context condition; 52, 45, and 3 for the exposure-positive context group; and 57, 41, and 2 for the positive-context subjects. Thus, the test animals did not differ in their behavior during the administration of performance tasks to children in the various treatment conditions.

Approach Responses

Table 1 presents the mean increases in approach behavior achieved by children in each of the treatment conditions in different phases of the experiment with each of the test animals.

The children's approach responses toward the two dogs did not differ either in the posttreatment assessment ($t = 1.35$) or in the follow-up phase ($t = .91$) of the study. Nor were there any signifi-

Table 1. Mean increases in approach responses as a function of treatment conditions, assessment phases, and test animals

PHASES	TREATMENT CONDITIONS			
	MODELING— POSITIVE CONTEXT	MODELING— NEUTRAL CONTEXT	EXPOSURE— POSITIVE CONTEXT	POSITIVE CONTEXT
Posttreatment				
Spaniel	10.83	9.83	2.67	6.08
Mongrel	5.83	10.25	3.17	4.17
Follow-up				
Spaniel	10.83	9.33	4.67	5.83
Mongrel	12.59	9.67	4.75	6.67
Combined data	10.02	9.77	3.81	5.69

cant effects ($t = 1.68$) due to the order in which the test animals were presented following completion of the treatment series. A t-test analysis also disclosed no significant change ($t = 1.50$) in mean approach scores between measurements conducted in the posttreatment and the follow-up phases of the experiment. Moreover, analysis of variance of the posttreatment scores revealed no significant Treatment × Dogs ($F = 2.15$) or Treatment × Order ($F = .30$) interaction effects. The data were therefore combined across phases and test animals in evaluating the major hypotheses.

An analysis of covariance, in which adjustments were made for differences in initial level of avoidance, was computed for mean approach responses performed by children in the various groups. The results reveal that the treatment conditions had a highly significant effect on the children's behavior ($F = 5.09$, $p < .01$). Tests of the differences between the various pairs of treatments indicate that subjects in the modeling-positive context condition displayed significantly more approach behavior than subjects in either the exposure ($F = 9.32$, $p < .01$) or the positive-context ($F = 8.96$, $p < .01$) groups. Similarly, children who had observed the model within the neutral setting exceeded both the exposure ($F = 6.57$, $p < .05$) and positive-context groups ($F = 4.91$, $p < .05$) in approach behavior. However, the data yielded no significant differences between either the two modeling conditions ($F = .04$) or the two control groups ($F = .76$).

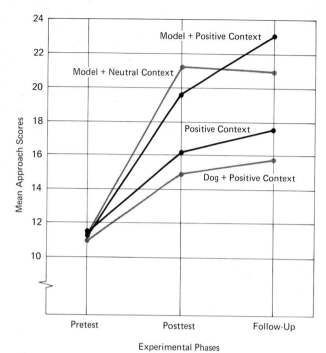

Figure 1 Mean approach scores achieved by children in each of the treatment conditions on the three different periods of assessment.

performance within the neutral setting ($t = 5.80$, $p < .001$). Although the positive-context group showed an increment in approach behavior ($t = 5.78$, $p < .001$), children who were merely exposed to the dog in the positive context achieved a small, but nonsignificant ($t = 1.98$), reduction in avoidance responses.

Within-Group Analysis of Approach Responses

The approach scores obtained by the different groups of children in preexperimental and subsequent tests are summarized graphically in Figure 1. Within-group analyses of changes between initial performance and mean level of approach behavior following treatment disclose significant increases in approach behavior for children in the modeling-positive context group ($t = 7.71$, $p < .001$) and for those who observed the modeling

Terminal Performances

Another measure of the efficacy of modeling procedures is provided by comparisons of the number of children in each condition who performed the terminal approach behavior at least once during the posttreatment assessment. Since the frequencies within the two modeling conditions did not differ, and the two control groups were essentially the same, the data for each of the two sets of subgroups were combined. The findings show that 67% of the children in the modeling treatment were able to remain alone in the room confined with the dog in the playpen, whereas the corresponding figure for the control subjects is 33%. The value χ^2 value for these data is 4.08, which is significant beyond the .025 level.

Within the control groups, the terminal performances were attained primarily by subjects who initially showed the weakest level of avoidance behavior. The differences between the two groups are, therefore, even more pronounced if the analysis is conducted on the subjects whose pretreatment performances reflected extreme or moderately high levels of avoidance behavior. Of the most avoidant subjects in each of the two pooled groups, 55% of the children in the modeling conditions were able to perform the terminal approach behavior following the experimental sessions, while only 13% of the control subjects successfully completed the final task. The one-tailed probability for the obtained $\chi^2 = 4.74$ is silghtly below the .01 level of significance.

The relative superiority of the modeling groups is also evident in the follow-up phase of the experiment. Based on the stringent criterion in which the most fearful task is successfully performed with *both* animals, a significantly larger number of children in the modeling conditions (42%) than in the control groups (12%) exhibited generalized extinction ($X^2 = 4.22$, $p < .025$). Moreover, not a single control subject from the two highest levels of avoidance behavior was able to remain alone in the room confined in the playpen with each of the dogs, whereas 33% of the most avoidant children in the modeling conditions successfully passed both terminal approach tasks ($\chi^2 = 4.02$, $p < .025$).

DISCUSSION

The findings of the present experiment provide considerable evidence that avoidance responses can be successfully extinguished on a vicarious basis. This is shown in the fact that children who experienced a gradual exposure to progressively more fearful modeled responses displayed extensive and stable reduction in avoidance behavior. Moreover, most of these subjects were able to engage in extremely intimate and potentially fearful interactions with test animals following the treatment series. The considerable degree of generalization of extinction effects obtained to the unfamiliar dog is most likely due to similar stimulus properties of the test animals. Under conditions where observers' avoidance responses are extinguished to a single animal, one would expect a progressive decrement in approach behavior toward animals of increasing size and fearfulness.

The prediction that vicarious extinction would be augmented by presenting the modeling stimuli within a highly positive context was not confirmed, although subjects in the latter condition differed more significantly from the controls than children who observed approach behavior under neutral conditions. It is entirely possible that a different temporal ordering of emotion-provoking modeling stimuli and events designed to induce anxiety-inhibiting responses would facilitate the vicarious extinction process. On the basis of evidence from conditioning studies (Melvin & Brown, 1964) the optimal treatment procedure might require repeated observational trials, in each of which aversive modeling stimuli are immediately followed by positively reinforcing experiences for the observers. These temporal prerequisites depend upon the abrupt presentation and termination of the two sets of stimulus events that cannot be readily achieved with live demonstrations. It would be possible, however, to study the effects of systematic variations in the temporal spacing of critical variables if modeling stimuli were presented pictorially. Apart from issues of economy and control, if pictoral stimulus material proved equally as efficacious as live modeling, then skillfully designed therapeutic films could be developed and employed in preventive programs for eliminating common fears and anxieties before they become well established and widely generalized.

Although children in both the exposure and

the positive-context groups showed some increment in approach behavior, only the changes in the latter group were of statistically significant magnitude. Apparently the mere presence of a dog had some mild negative consequences that counteracted the facilitative effects resulting from highly rewarding interactions with amiable experimenters, increased familiarity with the person conducting the numerous tests of avoidance behavior, and any inevitable direct extinction produced by the repeated performance of some approach responses toward the test animals without any adverse consequences. As might be expected, the general disinhibitory effects arising from these multiple sources incurred only in the early phase of the experiment, and no significant increases in approach behavior appeared between the post-treatment and follow-up assessments.

The data obtained in this experiment demonstrate that the fearless behavior of a model can substantially reduce avoidance responses in observers, but the findings do not establish the nature of the mechanism by which vicarious extinction occurs. There are several possible explanations of vicariously produced effects (Bandura, 1965b; Kanfer, 1965). One interpretation is in terms of the informative value of modeling stimuli. That is, the repeated evocation of approach responses without any adverse consequences to another person undoubtedly conveys information to the observer about the probable outcomes of close interactions with dogs. In the present study, however, an attempt was made to minimize the contribution of purely cognitive factors by informing children in all groups beforehand that the test animals were harmless.

The nonoccurrence of anticipated aversive consequences to a model accompanied by positive affective reactions on his part can also extinguish in observers previously established emotional responses that are vicariously aroused by the modeled displays (Bandura & Rosenthal, 1966). It is therefore possible that reduction in avoidance behavior is partly mediated by the elimination of conditioned emotionality.

Further research is needed to separate the relative contribution of cognitive, emotional, and other factors governing vicarious processes. It would also be of interest to study the effects upon vicarious extinction exercised by such variables as number of modeling trials, distribution of extinction sessions, mode of model presentation, and variations in the characteristics of the models and the feared stimuli. For example, with extensive sampling in the modeled displays of both girls and boys exhibiting approach responses to dogs ranging from diminutive breeds to larger specimens, it may be possible to achieve widely generalized extinction effects. Once approach behaviors have been restored through modeling, their maintenance and further generalization can be effectively controlled by response-contingent reinforcement administered directly to the subject. The combined use of modeling and reinforcement procedures may thus serve as a highly efficacious mode of therapy for eliminating severe behavioral inhibitions.

References

Bandura, A. Influence of models' reinforcement contingencies on the acquisition of imitative responses. *Journal of Personality and Social Psychology*, 1965, 1, 589–595. (a)

Bandura, A. Vicarious processes: A case of no-trial learning. In L. Berkowitz (Ed.), *Advances in Experimental Social Psychology*. Vol. 2, New York: Academic Press, 1965. Pp. 1–55. (b)

Bandura, A., & Rosenthal, T. L. Vicarious classical conditioning as a function of arousal level. *Journal of Personality and Social Psychology*, 1966, 3, 54–62.

Bandura, A., Ross, D., & Ross, S. A. Vicarious reinforcement and imitative learning. *Journal of Abnormal and Social Psychology*, 1963, 67, 601–607.

Berger, S. M. Conditioning through vicarious instigation. *Psychological Review*, 1962, 69, 450–466.

Farber, I. E. Response fixation under anxiety and nonanxiety conditions. *Journal of Experimental Psychology*, 1948, 38, 111–131.

Jones, M. C. The elimination of children's fears. *Journal of Experimental Psychology*, 1924, 7, 383–390.

Kanter, F. H. Vicarious human reinforcement: A glimpse into the black box. In L. Krasner & L. P.

Ullmann (Eds.), *Research in behavior modification.* New York: Holt, Rinehart and Winston, 1965. Pp. 244–267.

Kimble, G. A., & Kendall, J. W., Jr. A comparison of two methods of producing experimental extinction. *Journal of Experimental Psychology,* 1953, *45,* 87–90.

Masserman, J. H. *Behavior and neurosis.* Chicago: University of Chicago Press, 1943.

Melvin, K. B., & Brown, J. S. Neutralization of an aversive light stimulus as a function of number of paired presentations with food. *Journal of Comparative and Physiological Psychology,* 1964, *58,* 350–353.

Walters, R. H., & Parke, R. D. Influence of response consequences to a social model on resistance to deviation. *Journal of Experimental Child Psychology,* 1964, *1,* 269–280.

Part II

Contemporary Issues

Chapter 10

How to Teach Children

The kinds of teachers a child has and the instructional methods they use, as well as the child's own background, personality, and current life situation, play a part in determining whether the child's school experience will be personally rewarding and academically profitable or an exercise in frustration and discouragement. In general, children are happier and make better progress academically if their teachers are warm, flexible, competent, self-confident, and authoritative but not authoritarian, encouraging both responsibility **and** individual expression of ideas and feelings. Conversely, they do least well under teachers who are rigidly authoritarian, dogmatic, hostile, unresponsive to student needs, indecisive and uncertain, poorly trained, narcissistic, or preoccupied with their own anxieties and personal problems.

Unfortunately, teachers of socioeconomically disadvantaged students, compared with teachers of middle-class children, are more likely to display rigid attitudes toward child control and to be negative and dominating; they are less likely to encourage give-and-take relationships. To make matters worse, these teachers may further reinforce negative "teaching" behaviors used by a child's parents.

In the first of the readings in this chapter, N. D. Feshbach reports on studies of the "teaching" styles of 4-year-olds and their mothers. She demonstrates that the use of reinforcements in teaching situations are more characteristic of lower-class than of middle-class mothers and children (who, in the studies, instructed 3-year-olds on a task). Furthermore, among middle-class mothers, those whose children are problem readers tend to use negative reinforcements more often and to be more controlling and directive in instructing both their own and other children.

Among the most frequent complaints about many middle-class schools in this country is that they are engaged, in Charles Silberman's words, in "education for docility"[1] rather than the encouragement of curiosity, creativity, and individual initiative and responsibility. In an attempt to remedy this situation a number of schools, in both the United States and England, have attempted to develop curricula and instructional techniques that emphasize **individual** development.

(2) In the second selection in this chapter, C. Murrow and L. Murrow, two young American teachers, describe their impressions of some of the English "junior schools" that they recently spent a year studying. They quote Charity James, an English educator: "These are schools where it is not for the child to find out what the teacher wants and give it to him, but for the teacher to observe what the child is becoming and help him to find out what he needs."[2] Unlike some of the so-called free schools currently in vogue in some parts of the United States, classes in these junior schools, and the "infant schools" that precede them, remain "well structured—in their own ways—with the teacher making a number of conscious decisions about who should do what and when it should be done."[3] While this system obviously makes greater demands on the resourcefulness of teachers, the pupils' enthusiasm, personal development, and academic progress make the effort well worthwhile.

The relevance of the child's school experience and his readiness to profit from it will depend, not only on the nature of the experience itself, but on the child's background, motivations, prior skills, and personality. Many socioeconomically disadvantaged children enter school with motivations and skills far different from those demanded by traditional curricula, developed for the most part for middle-class children. In addition, many of the schools they enter are poorly staffed and physically inadequate. Consequently, children all too frequently become frustrated, lose self-esteem, and fail to make satisfactory aca-

1. C. E. Silberman, **Crisis in the Classroom: The Remaking of American Education** (New York: Random House, 1970), p. 113.
2. C. James, **Young Lives at Stake** (London: Collins, 1968), p. 19.
3. C. Murrow & L. Murrow, **Children Come First** (New York: McGraw-Hill, 1971), p. 277.

demic progress. They become educated, in Silberman's words, not for social mobility and success, but for "inequality."

(3)   The failure of too many of our schools to meet the special needs of economically disadvantaged, particularly minority-group students, and the formidable difficulties in the way of attempting to do so are illustrated in the sensitive essay by R. Coles that concludes this chapter.

Fortunately, some schools with economically disadvantaged minority-group children do succeed. The John H. Finley elementary school in Harlem, for example, has a student body that is predominantly black and Puerto Rican. The students entering this school score below the national median in reading readiness, but by the end of the second grade more than three-fourths of them score above the national median.

How are such results achieved? Silberman specifies several factors that appear to play a major role: (1) The atmosphere is warmer, and the environment both freer and more supportive, than in most schools. (2) Disruptive behavior is handled more gently and positively. (3) There is a conviction that the children can learn, and the principal and teachers hold themselves accountable if their students fail. (4) Innovative, imaginative, pupil-centered approaches to the development of reading and other skills are used flexibly. (5) Strong efforts are made to involve parents in their children's education. (6) Every opportunity is taken advantage of to enhance the child's self-esteem and pride in his cultural identity.[4]

4. Silberman, ibid., pp. 99–111.

Cross-Cultural Studies of Teaching Styles in Four-Year-Olds and Their Mothers

#25

Norma D. Feshbach

The series of investigations presented in this paper stem from a clinical and research interest in the relationship between parental socialization practices and the child's functioning in school, and the processes by which the school functions as a socializing agent. A related interest is the role of individual differences in the use of and response to variation in types of reinforcement. The common core of this interest pattern is the

NOTE: The early studies reported in this paper were supported by Contract 4-6-061646-1909 from the Office of Education, HEW, to the Research and Development Center, School of Education, University of California, Los Angeles, and the cross cultural research and the studies with parents of slow and problem readers was facilitated by UCLA faculty grants. I would like to thank Seymour Feshbach, Anne Singer, and Robert Singer for their critical and helpful reading of the manuscript.

SOURCE: From *Minnesota Symposia on Child Psychology*, vol. 7, edited by Anne D. Pick. University of Minnesota Press, Minneapolis. © 1973, University of Minnesota.

interaction between the socialization practices of the home and of the school, with the child being the active mediator between the two. Individual differences in response dispositions among children, resulting from differences in early socialization experiences, are presumed to interact with variations in teachers' programs and instructional styles. The studies described here represent efforts to delineate dimensions of parent, student, and teacher behaviors relevant to this interactional model and to specify relationships among these behaviors. These relationships are examined in the context of social class and ethnic differences within our own culture and in two other national settings.

But first, it may be helpful to explicate several theoretical assumptions and methodological strategies guiding our approach to this research problem. The most important initial decision was the choice of the response dimension—reinforcement style. Parents and children influence each other in many ways, children vary in a large number of personality traits, and teacher behaviors vary on many dimensions. The use of positive and negative reinforcement was seen as a response dimension that could be applied meaningfully to parent, teacher, and child behavior and that also would have explanatory value. A number of considerations went into the choice of this dimension. First, reinforcement is central in the learning process, having both motivational and informational functions. Second, there is much clinical and experimental evidence suggesting that the effects of positive reinforcement upon learning and performance are qualitatively and quantitatively different from the effects of negative reinforcement. These studies range from experimental analyses of achievement motivation (Weiner, 1972) to investigations of schizophrenics' avoidance responses to signs of maternal censure (Rodnick & Garmezy, 1957). The child who is motivated by negative reinforcement runs on a different course than the child who is motivated by positive reinforcement.

A third consideration in selecting the response dimension is the pervasiveness of reinforcement in social interaction. Teachers provide rewards and punishments, praise, and criticism in diverse academic contexts. Similarly, parents use rewards and punishments in a variety of social contexts; when they are training independence, when they are disciplining aggression, and when they are teaching a child how to button his clothes. Parental socialization practices and teacher instructional styles share important functions. The process of education and the process of socialization have some common characteristics and, at times, the processes are indistinguishable. Although society ostensibly assigns the teacher specific responsibility for the cognitive domain, and the parent specific responsibility for the social and affective domain, there is obviously considerable overlap in function. Teachers are concerned with the development of social skills, with the strength-

ening of behavioral controls, and with the acquisition of moral values. Parents shape their child's language performance and, directly or indirectly, teach their child to make appropriate discriminations and causal inferences. Many parents spend hours reading to their children and directly instructing them in matters clearly cognitive. This commonality between education and socialization makes the teacher a parent and the parent a teacher.

The fact that teachers and parents share functions is not meant to imply that the parent is a teacher in the narrow sense of providing instruction in academic skills pertinent to school achievement, although there are a number of current formulations of "parent as teacher" in this specific sense (e.g., Gordon, 1970; Schaefer, 1971). However, from a broader perspective, one can view almost all of socialization as education. Parents are teaching their child when they provide guidance, when they train for self-reliance and aggression control, when they instruct the child in proper handling of fork and spoon—no less than when they teach the child to count, to solve a simple puzzle, or to discriminate among the letters of the alphabet. In the context of this research program, all of these behaviors are seen as being able to be taught through the application of positive or negative reinforcements. The type of reinforcement employed by the parent is assumed to reflect a personality disposition or response style which characterizes many different teaching interactions. The validity of this assumption is, of course, an empirical question.

In addition to reinforcement style, social class and ethnicity were assessed in most of the studies to be reported. Social class was of interest because of its association with both cognitive performance and socialization practices as documented in the extensive literature relating economic level and academic functioning (Deutsch, Katz, & Jensen, 1968; Jensen, 1969) and in the substantial literature reporting differences in behavior patterns and socialization practices in parents of different social classes (Becker, 1964; Bronfenbrenner, 1958; Kohn, 1963; Miller & Swanson, 1960; Sears, Maccoby, & Levin, 1957).

However, a considerable theoretical gap exists between the socialization practices used by parents of different social classes and the cognitive performance of children from these social groups. Loosely defined constructs such as "cultural deprivation" which have been used to fill the gap have proved to have limited utility and are even considered by some investigators to be more misleading than helpful (e.g., Baratz & Baratz, 1970; Cole & Bruner, 1972). In my judgment, studies such as those stimulated by Bernstein (1961), in which an attempt is made to link directly specific patterns of parental behavior to the child's level and type of cognitive skill, are necessary for the identification of critical intervening processes.

Bernstein's work (1961), which emphasized the importance of maternal speech as a reflection of social context shaping the child's cognitive development, provided an impetus to the investigation of mechanisms mediating the effects of social class upon the child's cognitive performance. Bernstein identified two modes of linguistic style, the elaborate formal code found to be more characteristic of the middle-class parent, and the restricted code (manifested in a rigid and limited grammatical usage) found to be more typical of the lower-class parent. Bernstein's formulations regarding the relation between language modes and the social class structure in England have been supported empirically in American families by the research of Hess and Shipman (1965, 1967) and of Bee et al. (1969). More recently, however, linguists have challenged the cognitive implications of the two modes of linguistic style by questioning whether the two linguistic modes actually differ in communicative value. In addition, observed variations in linguistic behavior of black children, as a function of the social context in which their speech is assessed, raise a further question as to the generality of these linguistic modes (Labov, 1970).

Nevertheless, the research stimulated by Bern-

stein has made an important contribution by specifying processes by which social class membership can influence cognitive functioning. The importance of linguistic styles as mediators can be assessed by additional research. The same can be said of the behavioral parameter of reinforcement style which has been the object of my own research. However, I shall try to demonstrate that the concept of reinforcement style has generality across cultures and is a useful link between cognitive performance and social class or ethnic group.

IMITATION AND TEACHERS' REINFORCEMENT STYLES

The initial investigations of reinforcement styles in our laboratory entailed the experimental manipulation of positive and negative reinforcement and the assessment of the effects of this variable upon various indices of learning. The concern in these early studies was with the effects of differences in teacher's reinforcement style and in children's socioethnic background upon the imitative behavior of elementary school age children.

The paradigm used in these studies (Feshbach, 1967a&b; Portuges & Feshbach, 1972) was children's observation of teachers who used different modes of reinforcement and who manifested distinctive mannerisms incidental to the lesson presentation. The children's subsequent display of these incidental mannerisms was the measure of imitation. The teacher models were presented in two four-minute films. One film featured a positive reinforcing teacher, and the second showed a negative reinforcing teacher, each giving a geography lesson on Africa. After the child observed the two experimental films, counterbalanced for order of presentation, he or she was then required to teach a lesson like that observed in the films. In each of two experiments in which this procedure was used, a control group, consisting of children who were not shown the film but required to perform the same teaching task, was included to provide a base line for assessing degree of imitation. In the first study, the participants were nine-to ten-year-old boys with learning problems; in the second study, the subjects were a more representative group of both boys and girls. In each study, there was a middle-class sample which was predominantly white and a less economically advantaged sample which was predominantly black.

The results of the two studies were highly consistent. There was practically no imitation of the negative reinforcing teacher but considerable imitation of the positive reinforcing teacher. However, only the middle-class children imitated the positive teacher more than they imitated the negative teacher; the lower-class children showed little imitation of either teacher. The issues of ethnic differences in children's imitation is intriguing (Feshbach & Feshbach, 1972) but peripheral to the principal focus of the present paper. Of greater relevance here is the finding that the teachers' reinforcement style exerted a strong influence on one index of learning.

The fact that we found little or no observational learning of a negative reinforcing teacher could have important educational implications. A number of reports of teacher attitudes and behaviors in ghetto schools suggest that the learning environment in these schools is permeated with negative reinforcement (e.g., Kozol, 1965). Frequent resort to negative reinforcement by teachers and administrators may exaggerate existing avoidance patterns in the children, patterns which are incompatible with the assimilation of academic content and desired behavioral norms. There is evidence that children from economically disadvantaged backgrounds, before school attendance, have already been exposed to a negative reinforcing environment conducive to the development of avoidance behaviors. Reports from a number of studies of child-rearing practices have indicated that working-class parents tend to make greater use of physical punishment and related negative reinforcement than do middle-class parents (Becker, 1964; Bronfenbrenner, 1958). It seemed also possible, if these negative reinforcing behaviors are as pervasive as is indicated,

that through modeling and imitation, these negative behaviors might even extend to transactions among the children themselves.

REINFORCEMENT STYLES IN FOUR-YEAR-OLDS

Our next step, then, was to investigate patterns of reinforcement used by lower- and middle-class children in interaction situations involving cognitive learning concomitants (Feshbach & Devor, 1969). For these studies we required an age group sufficiently young that evidence of social class variations in behavior could not be attributed to school influences. Furthermore, the earlier the age at which social class and ethnic differences in reinforcement styles could be established, the greater could be the confidence in this variable as a contributor to cognitive differences between children of different social classes. Thus, there were methodological and theoretical constraints limiting the choice of the age of the sample. The children had to be at a level of social maturity and linguistic competence sufficiently advanced to permit the expression and assessment of positive and negative reinforcement. In addition, since imitation was a possible mechanism for the acquisition of reinforcement styles, the age level had to be one at which modeling effects had been demonstrated. For these various reasons, we decided to study four-year-old children to see if they demonstrated differences in patterns of reinforcements as a function of socioeconomic background.

In order to observe the children's reinforcement behavior, each four-year-old was asked to teach a three-year-old a simple puzzle. Previously, the experimenter demonstrated the puzzle to the four-year-old. During this familiarization period, the four-year-old teacher-child was given three trials in which to assemble the puzzle. During the first trial, the child was given active verbal assistance by the experimenter. During the second trial, the experimenter made one positive verbal remark, "that's very good," and one critical remark, "that's not right," about the child's performance. At the beginning of the third trial, the child completed the puzzle while the experimenter left to get the three-year-old pupil.

After being introduced to the younger child, the four-year-old was given the following instructions. "Now it's your turn to be the teacher. You're going to teach Andy how to do this puzzle. What does teach mean? It means to help. You may help Andy by using words but not your hands. Now you may begin by telling Andy how to do the puzzle."

The four-year-olds had no difficulty in understanding the teaching task they were being asked to perform, and most of them entered into the teaching role with great seriousness of purpose. Like their parents and their teachers, they wanted their three-year-old pupils to learn. One could see in these four-year-old teachers reactions of frustration, pleasure, disappointment, and excitement as their pupils shifted back and forth from persistent errors to flashes of insight.

The children's active engagement in the teaching task resulted in a range of verbal reinforcement behaviors which were recorded verbatim and which could readily be scored as positive or negative. Positive and negative reinforcing statements were defined in terms of their encouraging and discouraging connotations, rather than in the more formal, restricted sense of increasing or decreasing a specific response. The positive category included statements of praise, encouragement, and affirmation; the negative category included criticism, negations, and derogatory comments. Typical examples of positive comments were: "See, she can put it together." "That's better." "Yeah, like that. He did it." Frequent negative comments were: "Wrong way." "Not that way." "No, don't bang it." "You stupid." To determine the reliability of this dichotomous classification, eighty randomly selected statements were scored by two independent raters. There was only one instance in which the raters disagreed. The total number of positive and total number of negative statements were determined for each child and constituted the basic dependent measure. In addition, the performance of the three-year-olds was assessed in most of the studies by the number of errors made and time taken to complete the puzzle.

The four-year-olds in our first study were 50 boys and 52 girls, approximately equally distributed by ethnicity and social class. There were four combinations of race and social class: middle-class and lower-class whites and middle-class and lower-class blacks. The middle-class groups attended private nursery schools, lived in neighborhoods identified as middle to upper-middle class, and their fathers' occupations were professional and managerial. The lower-class children were enrolled in children's centers, lived primarily in neighborhoods identified as disadvantaged, and their parents were engaged in unskilled or semiskilled occupations.

In all instances, the ethnicity and social class of the three-year-old pupil was the same as that of the four-year-old teacher. In this first study, the sexes of the two children were varied so that within each grouping, half the pupils were of the same sex and half were of the opposite sex as their four-year-old teachers. However, the variation in sex of pupils did not affect the outcome and consequently will not be elaborated in the presentation of the results.

The mean frequencies of positive reinforcements used by each group were as follows: middle-class white children, 2.3; middle-class black children, .2; lower-class white children, .8; and lower-class black children, .7. Middle-class white children used a significantly greater number of positive reinforcements than did any of the other three groups. In contrast, the middle-class black children used significantly fewer positive reinforcements than either of the two lower-class groups. The overall pattern of social class and race differences was reflected by both sexes, and the strikingly greater use of positive reinforcement by the middle-class white boys and girls was consistent with expectation. The results for the middle-class blacks are an interesting deviation from the hypothesized relationship between social class and use of positive reinforcement.

The mean frequencies of negative reinforcement used by each group were as follows: middle-class whites, 1.6; middle-class blacks, 1.3; lower-class whites, 1.7; and lower-class blacks, 2.1. None of the group differences were statistically significant. However, if the two ethnic groups are combined and the children are categorized by those who did and did not use negative reinforcement, an interesting social class difference emerges. Of the 49 middle-class four-year-old teachers, 21 in comparison with only 10 of the 46 lower-class teachers did not use any negative reinforcement. Another way of viewing the data is to examine the relative frequency with which positive and negative reinforcement is used by each group. Here we find the greatest difference to be between middle-class whites and lower-class blacks. The middle-class white sample was the only group to use more positive than negative reinforcements when instructing the three-year-olds, whereas the lower-class black children displayed the largest preponderance of negative over positive reinforcements.

It is reasonable to ask whether these differences in the children's teaching behaviors could be attributed to differences in pupil performance. An analysis of the mean errors and of mean times to solution failed to reveal any significant performance differences among the groups. In addition, neither pupil performance measure was significantly correlated with either the number of positive or the number of negative reinforcements administered by the teacher-child.

The possible role of linguistic factors in the pattern of results is also of interest. Here, too, the performance of the various groups was comparable. There were no significant differences among the four-year-old groups in number of words used to make a positive or a negative reinforcing statement or in the grammatical complexity of the statements that were made. A possible explanation of the findings in terms of greater verbal facility on the part of the middle-class white child is rendered particularly unlikely by the fact that the mean number of words (3.5) used to make a negative comment was greater than the mean number of words (2.3) used to make a positive reinforcing statement.

The results of this first study of children's teaching styles suggested that as early as age four, children display different reinforcement patterns as a function of their socioethnic background. The findings were generally consistent with the assumption that the styles of reinforcement used by these four-year-olds are modeled after the socialization practices which they experience at home. The results also support the selection of reinforcement style as a fruitful dimension of individual difference which relates variations of socialization practices in the home and in the school with variations in cognitive performance. There have been studies of social class differences in learning in which the differential responsiveness of lower- and of middle-class children to various types of positive reinforcement and to praise and reproof has been emphasized (Kennedy & Willicut, 1964; Stevenson, 1967). The differences found here in reinforcement styles in four-year-old children suggested that a fuller understanding of social class and ethnic differences in learning required an assessment of the typical reinforcement contingencies present in the child's home and peer environments.

REINFORCEMENT STYLES IN FOUR-YEAR-OLDS AND THEIR MOTHERS

We next turned to an examination of social class and ethnic differences in parental reinforcement styles, specifically, in the type of reinforcement used by mothers in instructing their own four-year-old children (Feshbach, 1972). In addition, we wanted to replicate the results of the first experiment so that we might relate type of maternal reinforcement with the type used by the child. The second study included 109 four-year-olds and their mothers. An equal number of three-year-olds served as pupils.

The subjects were again divided into four groups, based on social class and ethnicity: middle-class white, lower-class white, middle-class black, and lower-class black. The mothers and children were drawn from eleven parent educational preschool centers distributed throughout Los Angeles. These are preschools run by the city which are attended one day a week by the child and his mother. The middle-class sample in this second study was less privileged and the lower-class sample less disadvantaged than their counterparts in the first study.

For the initial instructional sequence, we followed the same procedure as before, the four-year-olds' being asked to teach a puzzle to three-year-olds. A second instructional sequence occurred about an hour after the first. During this second session each mother was asked to teach her own four-year-old a similar but more complex puzzle than the puzzle used for the three-year-olds. The same measures used to analyze the child-child interactions were used to analyze the mother-child interactions. The reliability of the categorization of reinforcements was again very high, there being only one disagreement for sixty randomly selected statements.

The mean frequency of positive reinforcements used by each of the four-year-old groups while teaching the three-year-olds was as follows: middle-class white children, 2.4; middle-class black children, .08; lower-class white children, 1.9; and lower-class black children, .08. The pattern of these data, except for the relatively high number of positive reinforcements employed by lower-class whites, is similar to the pattern observed in the earlier study (Feshbach & Devor, 1969). Both middle- and lower-class white four-year-olds used a significantly greater number of positive reinforcements than did either middle- or lower-class black children.

There is less consistency between the results of the first and second study in the use of negative reinforcements than in the use of positive reinforcements by the four-year-old children. The mean frequencies of negative reinforcements for the four groups were as follows: middle-class white children, 2.3; middle-class black children,

.4; lower-class white children, 2.6; lower-class black children, 1.6. Although in the first study there were no significant differences in the frequency of negative reinforcements, the white children in the second study used significantly more negative reinforcements as well as positive reinforcements. However, the patterns of reinforcement—that is, the relative frequency of positive as compared with negative reinforcement—is similar in the results of both studies. The preponderance of negative over positive reinforcement was greatest for the lower-class black children and was least for the middle-class whites.

Some insight into the functional significance of the greater use of positive and negative reinforcements by the white four-year-olds is provided by an appraisal of the performance of the three-year-old pupils. Differences between middle- and lower-class white and black three-year-olds, both in time taken to complete the puzzle and in number of errors made, were small and statistically insignificant. However, pupil performance was not unimportant. For both the middle-class and lower-class white samples identical correlations of +.71 were obtained between the four-year-old teacher-child's negative reinforcement score and the number of errors made by his pupil. The corresponding correlations for the black samples were zero.

The mean frequencies of mothers' use of positive reinforcements in teaching the four-year-olds were as follows: middle-class white mothers, 6.5; middle-class black mothers, 4.7; lower-class white mothers, 4.7; lower-class black mothers, 4.8. The mean frequencies of mothers' use of negative reinforcements were: middle-class white mothers, 1.4; middle-class black mothers, 2.0; lower-class white mothers, 2.2; and lower-class black mothers, 5.4. Although middle-class white mothers tended to make greater use of positive reinforcements than did the other groups of mothers, none of the mean differences is significant. However, large and significant social class and ethnic differences are found in the frequency of mothers' use of negative reinforcement. Lower-class mothers use significantly more negative reinforcement than do middle-class mothers, and black mothers use significantly more negative reinforcements than do white mothers. The ethnic differences appear to be due largely to the high frequency with which lower-class black mothers use negative reinforcements in comparison with the other groups.

In contrast to the performance of the three-year-olds, ethnicity was a factor in the performance of four-year-olds. Middle- and lower-class black four-year-olds took significantly longer to complete the puzzle and made significantly more errors than did the white four-year-old groups. The mean error and time scores for lower- and middle-class groups within each ethnic category were quite similar. The frequency of the mothers' use of negative and also of positive reinforcement were significantly correlated with their children's time and error scores. Consequently, the ethnic differences found in the maternal use of negative reinforcement could be a function of the child's performance rather than a reflection of a stable maternal reinforcement style. However, an explanation of reinforcement styles in terms of the child's performance still would not account for the difference between lower- and middle-class black mothers in their use of negative reinforcement.

To summarize, the patterns of reinforcement used by four-year-old children and by their mothers vary as a function of ethnicity and, to a lesser extent, as a function of social class. In general, middle-class white children and their mothers used relatively more positive than negative reinforcement, lower-class black children and their mothers used more negative than positive reinforcement, with the other two groups falling between these two extremes.

The patterns of reinforcement used by children and by their mothers in each social class and ethnic group is but one index of degree of similarity. A more precise measure is provided by the correlations between mother's and child's use of positive and of negative reinforcement. For the total sample only, there is a small, although statistically reliable, correlation (+.22) between the child's and the mother's use of positive reinforcement. There is a correlation of similar magnitude between the child's use of negative reinforcement and the mother's use of positive reinforcement. However, neither correlation is readily interpretable since correlations for the total sample are influenced by social class and by ethnic differences in reinforcement frequencies. The meaningful mother-child correlations are those within each social class and ethnic group. These correlations are all small and statistically insignificant except for the correlation of +.65 ($p < .01$) between mother's and child's use of negative reinforcement in the middle-class white sample.

The findings concerning mothers' and children's reinforcement style suggest that the learning environment of the lower-class black child is more stressful than the environment of his white advantaged counterpart. On the basis of the mother-child interaction data, we can infer that the lower-class black child receives more negative reinforcements from his mother than do other children; and on the basis of the child-child interaction data, we can infer that the same child receives fewer positive reinforcements from his peers than does the middle-class white child.

By the age of four, the economically and socially disadvantaged child has already internalized aspects of this learning environment into his own behavioral repertoire. This child's mother is part of the environment but she is no less affected by it. Both have to cope in an environment replete with "no," "not that," "wrong," "can't you do anything right," and "what's the matter with you." It is reasonable to hypothesize that exposure to a primarily negative reinforcing environment can be disruptive of learning and can depress cognitive performance. Yet, a tenable alternative hypothesis is that these reinforcement styles merely reflect language dialect. They make it possible to distinguish between cultural groups, but may not contribute toward an explanation of group differences in cognitive skills and performance. Our understanding of the role of reinforcement style in cognitive development would be enhanced if reinforcement styles were shown to be more directly related to cognitive performance or if the relationship were evaluated in the context of other cultures. Clearly, reinforcement style is only one of many behavioral dimensions of socialization which would allow social class and ethnic differences to exert an influence on cognitive functioning and achievement. However, if the concept of reinforcement style is to have power, then there should be differences in patterns of reinforcement in other social groups who differ in cognitive achievements. Thus, our next study was carried out in Israel where one can find ethnic and economic divisions within the society associated with differences in children's academic levels.

ISRAELI REINFORCEMENT STYLES

The social division that exists in Israel between Israelis of Western origin and Israelis of Middle Eastern origin is somewhat comparable to socioethnic divisions in our own society. Middle Eastern Jews, whose dominant culture has been Arabic, are economically and socially disadvantaged in comparison with Israelis of Western origin. The former have less access to the resources of the society, are less well represented in positions of status and power, have lower mean incomes, more rarely attend institutions of higher learning, and, most germane to the hypothesis under investigation, perform more poorly on various measures of academic achievement (Smilansky & Yam, 1969). The discrepancy in academic achievement between Jews of Eastern and of Western origins has been of great concern to the Israeli educators and governmental authorities. The special educational programs that have been implemented for disadvantaged Israeli children and their families (Lombard, 1971; Smilan-

sky, 1968) have objectives and goals similar to compensatory and other intervention programs for disadvantaged groups in the United States.

Given these two economically and educationally disparate Israeli ethnic groups, there was an intriguing possibility that the reinforcement styles of four-year-olds and their mothers in the two groups would also be disparate. Consequently, it was decided to replicate in Israel the study of reinforcement styles that we had carried out with American four-year-olds and their mothers (Feshbach, 1973a).

The procedures developed for the American samples were followed as closely as possible in Israel. The principal difference was that it took longer to collect the data in Israel. The complexity of collecting parental data is compounded in another culture. Also, although Israel generally supports educational research, the government exercises thorough administrative control over experimentation in the schools. We began the study after receiving local approval but subsequently had to halt the procedures while awaiting separate administrative clearance for each of the facilities from which we drew our sample. About the time the final administrative clearance was obtained, the stopwatch broke; the decision then had to be made to complete the sample while administrative approval was in effect rather than to risk waiting for the stopwatch to be repaired or for a new one to be shipped from the United States. Hence, performance measures were not recorded for the children. So much for cross-cultural research on a shoestring.

Our final Israeli sample included 60 four-year-olds, their mothers, and an equal number of three-year-olds. The children were selected from eight preschools in Jerusalem and its environs. The sample was equally divided by sex and social class, the latter being determined by father's occupation. The lower-class children were predominantly from Yemenite and related ethnic backgrounds, whereas the middle-class sample were largely of Western origin. Again, two teaching interaction situations were used: in the first, a four-year-old taught a three-year-old of the same sex and social class; in the second instructional sequence, a mother taught her own four-year-old.

The mean frequencies of positive reinforcements used by the Israeli middle-class four-year-olds was 1.8 and that for the lower-class four-year-olds was .6. The mean frequencies of negative reinforcements for the middle-class children was 1.2, and the mean for the lower-class group was 1.0. The difference between the two groups in their use of positive reinforcement was highly significant; the middle-class Israeli child displayed about three times the frequency of positive reinforcements displayed by the lower-class child. On the other hand, the Israeli children made little use of negative reinforcement; the difference between the middle- and lower-class children was slight and insignificant. The differences between the two Israeli four-year-old groups are quite similar to the differences found between middle-class white and lower-class black American children in the first study of reinforcement styles (Fleshbach & Devor, 1969).

The Israeli middle-class mothers displayed a significantly greater frequency (mean = 6.7) of positive reinforcement than Israeli lower-class mothers (mean = 4.3) when instructing their four-year-olds. This finding is of special interest since the differences in maternal use of reinforcement among the various American socioethnic groups occurred primarily with negative rather than positive reinforcement. When the frequencies of negative reinforcement are compared, the results correspond in part to the American results. Israeli middle- and lower-class mothers use comparable amounts of negative reinforcement when instructing their four-year-old daughters (means = 3.5, 3.0, respectively), but they behave differently toward their four-year-old sons. Lower-class Israeli mothers used about twice as much negative reinforcement (mean = 4.6) as did the middle-class Israeli mothers (mean = 2.2) when teaching

their sons. We cannot ascertain whether this difference is related to sex differences in performance since, unfortunately, performance measures are not available for the Israeli sample. However, in view of the absence of prior sex differences on these tasks, sex differences in the performance of the Israeli four-year-olds seem unlikely.

In terms of the observed patterns of reinforcements, the environment of the Israeli lower-class child resembles that of the American lower-class black child, and the Israeli middle-class child and the American middle-class white child appear to share common experiences. Israeli lower-class children received fewer positive reinforcements from their peers, fewer positive reinforcements from their mothers, and, if they are male, more negative reinforcements from their mothers as compared with the middle-class Israeli children. The differences in reinforcement style between lower- and middle-class Israeli mothers and between lower- and middle-class Israeli children provide additional support for the hypothesis that reinforcement styles may be an important behavioral dimension linking socioethnic differences in socialization practices with socioethnic differences in cognitive performance.

Correlations were also obtained between the frequency of the mother's and of the child's use of positive and negative reinforcement in the two Israeli groups. Again, most of the correlations were small and statistically insignificant except for that found for Israeli middle-class mothers' and their four-year-olds' use of negative reinforcement (r = + .39; p < .05). In view of the restricted range of negative reinforcements used by the Israeli children, this finding was unexpected, although consistent with the similar relationship found for the American middle-class white children and mothers.

ENGLISH TEACHING STYLES

England was selected as a third culture in which to study socioeconomic group differences in reinforcement styles. I selected England partly because I was already involved in a study of English preschool education (Feshbach, Goodlad, & Lombard, 1973). In addition to having ready access to English nursery schools, I, like others, had been impressed by the striking difference in linguistic style between English middle- and working-class children, differences which had been extensively analyzed and documented by Bernstein (1961, 1962). Bernstein had proposed that social class differences in language exposure and usage are an important, if not the most important, determinant of social class differences in English children's cognitive performance and achievement. The question could be asked whether social class differences in reinforcement style could also be mediating the differential response of English middle- and lower-class children to the academic tasks they were required to master. And so the same procedures used in the United States and in Israel to assess reinforcement styles in four-year- olds and their mothers were also applied to an English sample (Feshbach, 1973b).

The English sample comprised 50 middle- and working-class mothers and their four-year-old children and 50 three-year-old pupils. The children were drawn from seven preschools in the greater London area; five were private nursery schools attended primarily by middle-class youngsters, and two were State-supported preschools attended primarily by working-class children. Father's occupation in conjunction with residential area were used as criteria for assigning a child to the middle-class or working-class group. Practically all of the English middle- and working-class samples were white and were native to England. Thus, in contrast to the Israeli sample, there were no ethnic differences between the English middle- and working-class groups; the distinctions were economic and social. Before considering the results, it should be noted that, in contrast to the American and Israeli children, a number of children in both of the English sam-

ples, apparently anxious about being left with the experimenter, had difficulty conforming to the experimental instructions.

The mean frequencies of positive reinforcement used by the children were 1.8 for the middle-class group and .7 for the lower-class group. The mean frequencies of negative reinforcement were 2.4 for the middle-class group and 2.5 for the lower-class group. The middle-class four-year-olds again used significantly more positive reinforcements than did the lower-class group. The means for the middle- and working-class English children for frequency of negative reinforcement were almost identical. Thus, the social class differences in reinforcement patterns observed in English four-year-olds are comparable to the socioethnic differences in children's reinforcement styles found in the Israeli and American samples.

The results for maternal use of reinforcements differ in several interesting respects from those obtained for the American and Israeli mothers, but the overall implications of the data are similar for all the groups. The middle-class English mothers teaching their sons made significantly greater use of positive reinforcement (mean = 6.1) than did the working-class English mothers teaching their sons (mean = 2.7). There was no difference in the frequency of use of positive reinforcement by the two groups of English mothers teaching their daughters (mean = 3.2 for both groups). It appears that middle-class English mothers shower their sons with positive reinforcement even though their sons perform no better than their daughters. In contrast to the findings for the Israeli and American mothers, there was no difference in the frequency with which the middle- and lower-class English mothers used negative reinforcement (means = 1.5, 2.0, respectively).

The performance times of the English children were longer than those obtained by the American children. This difference occurred for the entire three-year-old pupil sample and also for the middle-class four-year-olds. Since number of negative reinforcements is related to puzzle completion time, the greater time taken by these English children undoubtedly had some effect on the negative reinforcement scores. Perhaps for this reason the correlation between mother's and child's use of negative reinforcement, significant for both the middle-class Israeli and American white samples, was not significant for the English sample. In addition, none of the other correlations between mother's and child's reinforcement style were significant in the English sample.

CROSS-CULTURAL COMPARISONS

In describing reinforcement styles of four-year-olds and their mothers in the United States, Israel, and England, the focus has been on the similarity between cultures of socioethnic differences within each culture. The question of cultural differences in reinforcement styles has not been addressed. This approach was taken for primarily methodological reasons. We have much more confidence in the within-culture comparisons than in the between-culture comparisons. Within each culture, the same experimenters carried out the procedure with all socioethnic groups of mothers and children. However, different experimenters were used in different cultures. Although every effort was made to ensure that the same standardized procedures were followed in each cultural setting, experimenter effects may be included in the results. The degree of support provided by the central educational authority within each culture is another factor that varied between cultures and which could affect the degree of cooperation afforded by the mothers and children in the preschools.

The point is that caution must be exercised in drawing inferences from direct cross-cultural comparisons. In Table 1 the data are summarized for frequency of positive and of negative reinforcements by American, Israeli, and English four-year-olds when teaching their three-year-old pupils.

The number of positive reinforcements used by middle-class white American, Israeli, and English children are quite similar. The means for use of positive reinforcement for the lower-class children are also similar with the exception of the elevated score found for lower-class white children in the second American study. The most deviant children are the American middle-class black children, who consistently display less positive reinforcing behavior than do children in any of the other middle-class groups.

The frequencies of negative reinforcements reflect surprisingly little variation among cultures in the extent to which four-year-olds use negative

Table 1. Mean frequencies of reinforcement administered by American, Israeli, and English four-year-old teachers

CULTURE	MIDDLE-CLASS WHITE	MIDDLE-CLASS BLACK	LOWER-CLASS WHITE	LOWER-CLASS BLACK
POSITIVE REINFORCEMENT				
American (Study 1)	2.3	.2	.8	.7
American (Study 2)	2.4	.08	1.9	.08
Israeli	1.8		.6	
English	1.8		.7	
NEGATIVE REINFORCEMENT				
American (Study 1)	1.6	1.3	1.7	2.1
American (Study 2)	2.3	.4	2.6	1.6
Israeli	1.2		1.0	
English	2.4		2.5	

Table 2. Mean frequencies of reinforcements administered by American, Israeli, and English Mothers

CULTURE	MIDDLE-CLASS WHITE	MIDDLE-CLASS BLACK	LOWER-CLASS WHITE	LOWER-CLASS BLACK
POSITIVE REINFORCEMENT				
American	6.4	4.6	4.7	4.7
Israeli	6.7		4.3	
English	4.4		3.0	
NEGATIVE REINFORCEMENT				
American	1.4	1.8	2.2	5.4
Israeli	2.9		3.8	
English	1.5		2.0	

reinforcements in this teaching interaction situation. On the whole, the reinforcement styles characterizing the children within a socioethnic group are similar from culture to culture.

In Table 2 the results are summarized for the reinforcement styles of the mothers teaching their four-year-old children. The differences between cultures in mothers' use of positive reinforcement are relatively small. Although both samples of English mothers appear more conservative in their use of positive reinforcers, there is considerable variability within the English sample and the differences between cultures are not significant. When the mean frequencies of negative reinforcement are compared, one sees that the relative differences among groups are much larger than the relative differences among groups in the use of positive reinforcement. The American lower-class black mothers used much more negative reinforcement than did any other cultural subgroup. The scores of the Israeli mothers, both lower class and middle class, are also high relative to the English and American white subgroups. The possible contribution of differences in the children's performance to these cultural differences in maternal reinforcement frequency cannot be assessed inasmuch as performance measures were not obtained for the Israeli children.

It will be recalled that English three-year-olds took more time to complete the puzzle than any of the American three-year-olds. The English four-year-olds also took more time than American white four-year-olds. The data from this study do not help explain this difference. However, the finding is consistent with other observations made in connection with my study on early schooling in England. The philosophy and programs of English preschools were less oriented toward early cognitive stimulation and training than is the case for either the United States or Israel. The English curricula and materials reflected this orientation. Consequently, the English children's poorer performance on the puzzles could be due to a relative lack of familiarity and experience with this type of task.

Despite the longer times taken to complete the task by both middle- and lower-class English children, social class differences in types of reinforcement are still obtained for the English sample. Middle-class English four-year-olds and their mothers use more positive reinforcements than do lower-class English four-year-olds and their mothers. The finding for the mothers appears to differ from that obtained for the other cultures where the observed social class difference was in the frequency of negative reinforcement. However, the reinforcement pattern—that is, the relative use of positive and negative reinforcement—is similar.

In order to demonstrate the similarity in reinforcement pattern more directly, the proportion of positive reinforcements in relation to the total number of reinforcements was determined for each subject. This statistic consisted of the number of positive reinforcements divided by the number of positive plus negative reinforcements. In addition to providing a direct index of reinforcement pattern, the proportional analysis also controls for differences in absolute number of reinforcements.

A 3 × 2, culture by social class, analysis of variance was carried out for the entire sample of mothers and a comparable analysis was made for the four-year-old teacher-children. For each analysis, a significant main effect was obtained for social class, the middle-class samples displaying consistently higher proportions of positive reinforcement than the lower-class samples. Analyses of the mother data reflected significant social class differences for each of three countries. For the four-year-olds, the difference was significant for the Israeli and English teacher-children. When a further analysis for the American sample was carried out, a significant difference in the relative use of positive reinforcement was obtained between middle-class white children and lower-class black children.

In summary, the most consistent and least ambiguous aspect of the cross-cultural data are the socioethnic differences found in children's and mother's reinforcement styles within each culture. Middle-class children and middle-class mothers use more positive reinforcements than do lower-class children and their mothers, regardless of whether the culture is American, English, or Israeli. The socioeconomic differences that we have found in reinforcement styles are consistent with the socioethnic differences that have been observed in academic achievement. It seems reasonable then, to conclude that reinforcement style may be one factor—not the only factor or the most significant factor, but an important factor—mediating socioethnic differences in cognitive performance and academic achievement.

Reinforcement styles employed by parents and by children can be viewed as reflectors of more pervasive features of middle- and lower-class environments. The lower-class family, by reason of its impoverished economic status, is subject to more privation, frustration, illness, and in general, to more stressful events than is the middle-class family. The lower-class parent, who is trying to maintain at least a marginal level of social and economic adjustment, is confronted with more daily pressures and demands (including more pregnancies and children) than is the middle-class parent. Under these circumstances, we might expect the lower-class parent to be less tolerant and more critical of their child's errors and other deviant behaviors. It is difficult for a parent to be patient and encouraging when the family lives in crowded quarters and is beset with many, often conflicting demands. In brief, the economic circumstances under which lower- and middle-class families live render it likely that the lower-class family will make greater use of negative reinforcement than the middle-class family.

I am proposing that frequent resort to negative reinforcement by parents is a reflection of impatience, environmental pressure, and frustrations. These are conditions which are hardly conducive to the learning process. Rather, they are likely to discourage exploratory activities in the child and foster avoidance behaviors incompatible with effective learning.

Perhaps the most unfortunate consequence of these socialization experiences is the internalization by the child of these very response modes, which we have suggested interfere with effective learning. By age four, the genetics of poverty has already taken place, the process of identification and modeling being its DNA. The child is now prepared to duplicate the patterns of reinforcement of the parent in transactions with peers today and perhaps with his or her own offspring tomorrow.

I wish to re-emphasize that negative reinforcement and the environmental presses with which it is associated are seen as only one of a number of factors contributing to socioethnic group differences in cognitive performance. Also, I do not maintain that economic poverty inevitably leads to parental impatience, punishment, criticism, and other avoidance-producing behaviors detrimental to the child's cognitive development. These potential psychological effects of poverty may be mitigated or overridden by other factors operative in the family and in the culture. However, all other things being equal, one can expect a higher frequency of negative reinforcement and cognitive deficits among poor families than among middle-class families. Poverty, then, fosters psychological dispositions which place the poor child at an even further disadvantage in a society in which most avenues of economic reward have academic and related cognitive competencies as entrance requirements.

MATERNAL REINFORCEMENT STYLES AND LEARNING PROBLEMS

Although the major focus of this paper has been on cross-cultural similarities in patterns of reinforcements used by different socioethnic groups, the theoretical implications of positive and negative reinforcement usage are by no means restricted to cognitive differences between poor and more advantaged children. Differences in environmental stresses produced by variations in socioeconomic levels constitute but one possible source of differences in patterns of reinforcements employed by mothers and by their children. Differences in school economic resources, class size, school problems, and so forth should also contribute to differences in the patterns of reinforcements employed by teachers. Other possible antecedents of reinforcement style are variations in personality, in situational stresses, and in cultural mores. Whatever the source of reinforcement style, we should expect variations in reinforcement patterns to be associated with variations in cognitive performance. Thus, there

should be a relationship between reinforcement styles and cognitive competencies within a particular socioethnic group.

In the final study to be reviewed here the relationship between one facet of a child's cognitive competence, level of success in learning to read, and various maternal behaviors including reinforcement styles is investigated. In the previous studies, the principal independent variable had been socioeconomic and ethnic differences; the independent variable in the present study was the reading competence of the child. Successful and problem readers were drawn from equally comfortable middle-class, advantaged family backgrounds.

In a recent study undertaken in our laboratory (Bercovici & Feshbach, 1973), mothers of successful readers and of problem readers were observed while instructing children in several cognitive tasks. A reliable behavioral scoring scheme was developed which permitted the assessment of such maternal behaviors as controlling and directive statements, autonomy fostering statements, manual guidance, and verbal and nonverbal organization of task materials, in addition to the frequency of positive and negative reinforcing behaviors. An added methodological feature of this study was the broadening of the sample of children taught by individual mothers. Besides instructing their own child on two cognitive tasks, each mother also individually instructed two other children—one a problem reader, and the other a successful reader, on these same two tasks. This additional variation enables us to assess whether a particular maternal reinforcement pattern was specific to the mother's own child or reflected a more general mode of interaction with children. By having the mother teach both problem and successful readers, further information was obtained about the relevance of the child's performance to the mother's behavior. Finally, we used the opportunity provided by this project to investigate child-rearing attitudes and values that might relate to maternal reinforcement behavior and to children's reading competencies (Feshbach & Bercovici, in preparation). For this purpose the Child Rearing Practices Report measure, developed by Jean Block (1969), was completed by the participating mothers.

The total sample consisted of 40 first-grade children and their mothers, and 80 additional first-graders. Half the mothers had children categorized as problem readers, and the other half, successful readers. The designation of reading competence was made on the basis of both test data and teacher evaluation.[1] The successful and problem readers were matched for sex and IQ, and all children were of at least average intelligence with no manifest neurological impairment. Three-fourths of the sample in each group were male, and the total sample was drawn from schools in predominantly middle-class areas.

First, each mother was asked to instruct her own child on a task which required the matching of 12 simple line-drawn faces. Then the mother was asked to show her child how to fit pegs of different lengths into holes of different depths so that all the pegs would be level across the top. In the second experimental situation the mother taught the same two tasks to another child whose reading level was comparable with that of her own child. In the third experimental situation the mother instructed a third child, whose reading level was divergent from that of her own child. During the instruction of her own and the two other children a minute-by-minute time sampling of the mother's behavior was made by two observers. Finally, the mother was administered the Block Child Rearing Scale.

There were no significant differences among the groups of children—problem readers or successful readers, instructed by their own or an-

other mother—in task completion time. The only significant effect was the greater amount of time required to complete the more difficult second task as compared with the first task.

There were only slight, nonsignificant differences between the mothers of problem readers and the mothers of successful readers in the mean frequencies of positive reinforcement. A very different picture emerged when the mean frequencies of negative reinforcing behaviors were examined for tasks 1 and 2 combined (see the tabulation below). There were highly reliable and consistent differences between mothers of the problem readers and mothers of the successful readers. Mothers of the problem readers used much more negative reinforcement than did the mothers of the successful readers, both when instructing their own children and when instructing other children. The difference between amount of negative reinforcement used by the two sets of mothers occurred for both tasks, but it was greater for the second, more difficult task than it was for the first task.

These data support the suggested theoretical relationship between children's cognitive performance and the reinforcement style employed by their parents. The socioethnic differences obtained for the American, Israeli, and English samples demonstrated systematic differences in reinforcement styles between middle- and lower-socioethnic groups. There remains, however, a gap between these cross-cultural findings and the proposition that the social class differences in reinforcement styles are functionally related to social class differences in cognitive performance. The data of this last study, demonstrating greater

[1]The author wishes to thank Seymour Feshbach, Howard Adelman, and Will Fuller of the UCLA Early Prediction and Prevention of Reading Disability Project who made available data on children's IQ, tests of reading ability, and teachers' evaluation of class performance and competence.

	MOTHER OF PROBLEM READER	MOTHER OF SUCESSFUL READER
Own child	1.7	.8
Other problem reader	1.0	.4
Other successful reader	.5	.3
Mean	1.1	.4

use of negative reinforcement by mothers of problem readers as compared with mothers of successful readers, help fill this gap. The correlation between mother's behavior and children's reading competence is, of course, subject to alternative interpretations. However, it does provide a link in the chain of relationships that we believe exist between social class and socialization practices, as reflected in reinforcement styles, and between reinforcement styles and cognitive performance.

The detailed analyses made of the mother's instructional behaviors provide further insight into the behavior patterns denoted by a particular reinforcement style. For example, there was a greater frequency of controlling and directive statements made by the mothers of problem readers than by mothers of successful readers. The mothers of the problem readers were also much more likely to intervene verbally or manually when the child made an error or encountered some difficulty. Children taught by mothers of problem readers would sometimes complain about their instructor's intrusiveness and ask that they be allowed to solve the task themselves. The intrusiveness or impatience of these mothers was reflected particularly in the data for manual guidance. Manual guidance was scored whenever the mother manipulated the task materials after the child began the task or whenever she guided the child's hand. The difference was large between the frequency of manual guidance by the mothers of problem readers and by the mothers of successful readers. The mothers of problem readers had great difficulty in permitting the child to proceed at his or her own pace. In summary, mothers of problem readers used more negative reinforcement, were more directive and intrusive, and appeared to be less patient than mothers of successful readers when instructing their own and other children.

A thesis of this paper is that the behavior patterns observed are not idiosyncratic to the teaching of cognitive tasks but are characteristic of the mother-child interaction in many child-training situations. Thus, it is suggested that teaching styles displayed by mothers in these experimental situations constitute a dimension of socialization which has relevance for other child-rearing situations. To investigate reinforcement styles in these varied socialization situations, it would have been desirable to employ a methodology, comparable to that used in all of our studies, which allows for the direct observation of parental behaviors. We might have observed parents instructing their children on tasks ranging from eating routines to coping with frustration and conformity to adult controls. Our resources did not permit such an undertaking, and since our interest at this point was exploratory, we used instead a structured variation of an interview procedure, the Block Q sort measure. The mothers sorted 91 child-rearing items into seven piles ranging from least characteristic of their behavior to most characteristic.

Of the 91 items in the Q sort, 16 were considered applicable to the negative and positive reinforcement style dimension. The responses to these items were combined such that a higher score was indicative of more negative reinforcing attitudes and behaviors. Examples of items selected for inclusion in this reinforcement dimension are "I believe physical punishment to be the best way of disciplining," "I believe in praising the child when he is good and think it gets better results than punishing him when he is bad," and "I make sure my child knows that I appreciate what he tries or accomplishes."

The variance in response to the individual items was small, which probably reflected the influence of social desirability norms and the homogeneity of the parent population. Nevertheless, this response dimension did discriminate between the two groups of mothers; the mean score obtained by the mothers of problem readers was significantly higher than the mean score obtained by mothers of successful readers. Although the inventory difference was not large and certainly was much less dramatic than the behavioral differences manifested in the experimental tasks, the data support the proposition that the behaviors displayed by mothers in the teaching situations are indicative of more generalized reinforcement styles. The mothers of problem readers made greater use of negative reinforcement in the teaching situation and they also revealed more general punitive attitudes on the Q sort than did the mothers of successful readers.

SOME IMPLICATIONS

These findings, in conjunction with the cross-cultural data, increase our confidence in the utility of the construct of reinforcement style as a dimension of socialization with developmental implications for the cognitive growth of the child. One of the advantages of this construct is that as a structure or style variable, it cuts across many content areas. It can be applied with equal relevance to the interaction between parent and child, between teacher and child, and between child and peer. It provides a framework for the analysis of the developmental consequences of some of the behavioral practices of the socializing agencies of family, school, and peer culture. Finally, it suggests another promising approach to early intervention efforts designed to eliminate social class and ethnic differences in cognitive competency. It suggests that the way in which a child is taught may often be at least as important as what the child is taught.

Many current intervention efforts have moved in the direction of parent-training programs as a way of implementing cognitive and other developmental objectives (e.g., Gordon, 1969, 1970; Gray & Klaus, 1970; Karnes, 1970; Schaefer, 1969). Partly on the basis of the theoretical rationale for early intervention (Bloom, 1964; Hunt, 1961) and partly as a reaction to discouraging Head Start results (Westinghouse Learning Corporation, 1969) a number of these programs are attempting to reach the child under two. In general, the focus of the parent education programs has been primarily cognitive. Parents are trained and encouraged to instruct their young children before the child begins formal schooling, with cognitively related materials that are provided them. Occasionally, some emphasis is also placed on parental attitudes (Gordon, 1970).

We can expect that the development and implementation of parent-training programs will continue to expand and will constitute a major mode of early intervention for the very young child. However, these programs may prove to be ineffective if, in instructing the child, the parent teachers are impatient, intrusive, and use a high degree of negative reinforcement. These factors may be especially important when one considers that the target population of these programs are children in the first two years of life.

Before a new Jensen report (1969) or a new Westinghouse report (1969) or a new Hernstein report (1971) appears on the lack of success of these future infant/parent intervention programs, a re-examination of the critical dimensions of the curricula employed in these projects is in order. The thesis of this report suggests that modes of instruction as well as the content of instruction require attention and analysis and, further, that parental influences on the cognitive development of the child are not limited to cognitive training situations but encompass the full spectrum of parent-child interactions. The child's schooling may begin with day care, preschool, or kindergarten, but the child's education begins in the family. And the studies that have been reviewed suggest that the patterns of reinforcement and related modes of socialization used by the family are an integral part of this educational process.

References

Baratz, S., & Baratz, J. Early childhood intervention: The social science base of institutional racism. *Harvard Educational Review,* 1970, 40, 29–50.

Becker, W. C. Consequences of different kinds of parental discipline. In M. L. Hoffman & L. W. Hoffman (Eds.), *Review of child development research.* New York: Russell Sage, 1964, Pp. 169–208.

Bee, H. L., Egeren, L. F., Streisaguth, A. P., Nyman, B. A., & Leckie, M. S. Social class differences in maternal teaching strategies and speech patterns. *Developmental Psychology,* 1969, 1, 726–734.

Bercovici, A., & Feshbach, N. D. Teaching styles of mothers of successful and problem readers. Paper presented at the meeting of the American Educational Research Association, New Orleans, February 1973.

Bernstein, B. Social class and linguistic development: A theory of social learning. In A. H. Halsey, J. Floud, & C. A. Anderson (Eds.), *Education, economy, and society.* New York: Free Press, 1961.

————. Social class, linguistic codes, and grammatical elements. *Language and Speech,* 1962, 5, 221–240.

Block, J. Q-sort: *Child rearing attitudes.* MS., University of California, Berkeley, Department of Psychology, 1969.

Bloom, B. S. *Stability and change in human characteristics.* New York: Wiley, 1964.

Bronfenbrenner, U. Socialization and social class through time and space. In E. E. Maccoby, T. M. Newcomb, & E. L. Hartley (Eds.), *Readings in social psychology* (3rd ed.) New York: Holt, 1958.

Cole, M., & Bruner, J. S. Preliminaries to a theory of cultural differences. In I. J. Gordon (Ed.), *Early childhood education: The seventy-first yearbook of the National Society for the Study of Education.* Chicago: National Society for the Study of Education, University of Chicago Press, 1972.

Deutsch, M., Katz, I., & Jensen, A. *Social class, race, and psychological development.* New York: Holt, 1968.

Feshbach, N. D. The effects of teachers' reinforcement style upon children's imitation and preferences. *Proceedings of the 75th Annual Convention of the American Psychological Association,* 1967, 2, 281–282. (a)

————. Variations in teachers' reinforcement styles and imitative behavior of children differing in personality characteristics and social background. University of California, Los Angeles, Center for the Study of Evaluation, Technical Report No. 2, 1967. (b)

————. Teaching styles in four year olds and their mothers. Paper presented at the Meeting of the Western Psychological Research Association, Los Angeles, 1970. Reprinted in J. F. Rosenblith & W. Allinsmith (Ed.), *The causes of behavior: Readings in child development and educational psychology* (3rd ed.) New York: Allyn & Bacon, 1972.

————. Teaching styles of Israeli four-year-olds and their mothers: A cross-cultural comparison. Paper presented at the meeting of the American Educational Research Association, New Orleans, February 1973. (a)

————. A comparative study of teaching styles in American, Israeli, and English four-year-olds and their mothers. In preparation. (b)

———— & Bercovici, A. Maternal Reinforcement Behavior and First Grade Children's Reading Competence. In preparation.

Feshbach, N. D., & Devor, G. Teaching styles in four year olds. *Child Development,* 1969, 40, 183–190.

Feshbach, N. D., & Feshbach, S. Imitation of teacher preferences in a field setting. *Developmental Psychology,* 1972, 7, 84.

Feshbach, N. D., Goodlad, J., & Lombard, A. *Early schooling in England and Israel.* New York: McGraw-Hill, 1973.

Gordon, I. J. Early child stimulation through parent education. Final Report, Children's Bureau, Social and Rehabiltation Service, HEW, Grant No. PHS-R-306. June 30, 1969.

————. *Parent participation in compensatory education.* Urbana: University of Illinois Press, 1970.

Gray, S., & Klaus, R. *Early training project: The seventh year report.* John F. Kennedy Center for Research on Education and Human Development, George Peabody College for Teachers, Nashville, 1970.

Hernstein, R. J. I.Q. *Atlantic Monthly,* 1971, 228, 43–64.

Hess, R. D., & Shipman, V. C. Early experience and the socialization of cognitive modes in children. *Child Development,* 1965, 34, 869–886.

————. Cognitive elements in maternal behavior. In J. P. Hill (Ed.), *Minnesota symposia on child psychology.* Vol. 1. Minneapolis: University of Minnesota Press, 1967. Pp. 57–81.

Hunt, J. McV. *Intelligence and experience.* New York: Ronald Press, 1961.

Jensen, A. How much can we boost IQ and scholastic achievement? *Harvard Educational Review,* 1969, 39, 1–123.

Karnes, M., Reska, J., Hodgins, A., & Badger, E. Educational intervention at home by mothers of disadvantaged infants. *Child Development,* 1970, 41, 925–935.

Kennedy, W. A., & Willicut, W. C. Praise and blame in incentive. *Psychological Bulletin,* 1964, 62, 323–332.

Kohl, H. *36 Children.* New York: New American Library, 1967.

Kohn, M. L. Social class and parent-child relationship: An interpretation. *American Journal of Sociology,* 1963, 68, 471–480.

Kozol, J. *Death at an early age.* New York: Houghton, 1965.

Labov, W. The logical non-standard English. In F. Williams (Ed.), *Language and Poverty.* Chicago: Markham Press, 1970, Pp. 153–189.

Lombard, A. D. Home instruction program for pre-school children (Hippy). Interim Report 1969–1970. Center for Research in Education of the Disadvantaged, Hebrew University of Jerusalem, Israel, March 1971.

Miller, D. R., & Swanson, J. E. *Inner conflict and defense,* New York: Holt, 1960.

Portuges, S. H., & Feshbach, N. D. The influence of sex and socio-ethnic factors upon imitation of teachers by elementary school children. *Child Development,* 1972, 43, 981–989.

Rodnick, E. H., & Garmezy, N. An experimental approach to the study of motivation in schizophrenia. In M. R. Jones (Ed.), *Nebraska symposium on motivation.* Lincoln: University of Nebraska Press, 1957. Pp. 109–184.

Schaefer, E. S. Development of hierarchical, configurational models for parent behavior, and child behavior. In J. P. Hill (Ed.), *Minnesota symposia on child psychology.* Vol. 5. Minneapolis: University of Minnesota Press, 1971. Pp. 130–161.

———. Home tutoring program. *Children,* 1969, 16, 59–61.

Sears, R. R., Maccoby, E. E., & Levin, H. *Patterns of child rearing.* Evanston, Ill.: Row, 1957.

Smilansky, S. The effect of certain learning conditions on the progress of disadvantaged children of kindergarten age. *Journal of School Psychology,* 1968, 4, 68–81.

——— & Yam, Y. The relationship between family size, ethnic origin, father's education, and student's achievement. (Hebrew T. Megamot.) *Behavioral Sciences Quarterly,* 1969, 16, 248–273.

Stevenson, H. W. Developmental psychology. In P. R. Farnsworth, O. McNemar, & Q. McNemar (Eds.), *Annual review of psychology.* Palo Alto, Calif.: Annual Reviews, 1967. Pp. 87–128.

Weiner, B. Attribution theory, achievement motivation, and the educational process. *Review of Educational Research,* 1972, 42, 203–215.

Westinghouse Learning Corporation, Ohio University. The impact of Head Start: An evaluation of the effects of Head Start on children's cognitive and affective development, June 1969.

#26 *Days with Juniors*

Casey Murrow

Liza Murrow

In a few junior schools the switch to a more child-centered setting has stimulated a change in attitudes toward learning. Rather than attempting to impose the same set of facts and amount of knowledge on each child, teachers are concerned that their pupils develop new ways of thinking. They seek to extend the powers of observation and inquiry which the children bring with them from infant school. Charity James, a respected English educator, says of good primary schools: "These are schools where it is not for the child to find out what the teacher wants and give it to him, but for the teacher to observe what the child is becoming and help him to find out what he needs."[1]

SOURCE: From *Children Come First* by Casey & Liza Murrow. Used with permission of McGraw-Hill Book Company.

[1]C. James, *Young Lives at Stake* (London: Collins, 1968), p. 19.

Junior schools which think creatively about their students provide both a challenging and rigorous setting. Pupils undertake a great deal of hard work and attain a startling degree of excellence. The pride of accomplishment that these children show in their finished work is a joy to see, and it is important to note that this is usually work they have initiated and brought to fruition themselves, with the aid of their teacher.

We visited a large classroom in a junior school which illustrated the variety of work that can take place in one room. Six children grouped at a long table were making their conceptions of American Indian ritual masks out of paper, bits of cloth, and flexible reeds. The idea for the masks came from discussions and reading on Indians. Members of the class planned to use them in a dance later that week. The careful work of the maskmakers did not disturb a group gathered with a teacher at a round table. They had been reading some poetry written by members of the class and were talking about ideas for new poems.

Around the corner in this large room, other children were studying a collection of bones. A number of different animal skeletons had arrived on loan from the museum service. Some children were making accurate drawings of them, while others searched through reference books to identify the skeletons. ("Look, John, it's a mole, that's what it is!")

Still others handled the skeletons, running their fingers across a delicate structure or looking at it from many angles. Two girls wrote about the sheep's skull that lay on the table in front of them. All these children were talking, discussing, and thinking out loud about bones, animals, shapes. A typical reaction: "OOh, that's ugly. Think of a rabbit looking so ugly underneath!"

A boy at work near a window was building a scale model of a suspension bridge. He worked with papier-mâché, wood, wire, and other materials. This delicate task required a good deal of mathematics and a lot of reading. Open before him was an encyclopedia and a text on bridges. Why had he started this lengthy job? "I saw the new bridge over the Severn River and I wanted to make a model of it."

The sight of the bridge, on a weekend drive, initiated the thinking that resulted in a complex project. This ten-year-old's teacher had urged him to go deeper and deeper into the subject and to make as accurate a model as he could. The teacher told us he would not consider diverting the boy from the work. Making the model of the bridge had posed challenging mathematical problems, and the boy had thrown himself into some difficult reading and was culling from it the information that was applicable to the design. This was not the mindless copying of paragraphs for a report, which we see so often with children of this age.

This remarkable variety of work took place at once in a large classroom. For most of the time, there were thirty-seven children in the room with one teacher. Scenes of this nature are common in those few junior schools where the work is rooted in human needs and interests. Someone coming into these classrooms for a few moments might be alarmed that some children talked in a group in a corner, that others were painting and said they had been painting all morning, and that one child reported he had not done any math since two days before. Yet the children pursue and achieve excellence in many areas.

These junior schools have not organized their working days in any standard fashion. There are great differences, both from class to class and within the same room on different days. On any one day, children may come into a class and set to work on a task begun the day before while others will consult their teacher about work to be done or a new idea. A third group of children may like to begin their day by dealing with the chores of the classroom, cleaning the animal cages, and getting out special equipment. Tomorrow the membership of each group will probably be substantially different.

No class could ever work in this informal way and be successful if the teacher had to indicate the direction each child's work was to take every day. The teacher must respect the children's ideas and allow them to act upon them. This, in turn, permits the teacher to give his time where it is most needed, to children with immediate problems. Some children may finish a sequence of work and ask for advice on their next project. Others may have come to school depressed and in need of help. Family difficulties, an argument with a friend—anything may come into the open between child and teacher and lead to a discussion.

A whole class of thirty to forty children seldom does a specific thing at a set time in a school run this way. It is not unusual, however, for a teacher to bring the group together in order to discuss new materials, suggest new ways to approach a particular problem, or talk about the work that some children have completed. As was the case with the boy who built the model of the Severn Bridge, a teacher may allow a child to work for an extended period on one project, often skipping regular tasks, such as math, and sometimes ignoring meetings with the rest of the class. The good teacher seldom tries to lure a child back to any mainstream of work in the classroom, but attempts instead to extend and vary the child's interest within a range of subjects. The group that made the Indian masks, for example, went on to a further understanding of dance, ritual, and some of the history of American Indian tribes. They read extensively, wrote about aspects of what they had learned, and then combined it all in dance and drama using the masks, their own creations.

Because children in a few good junior schools often work from week to week, rather than day to day, it is nearly impossible to describe the typical day for a child of this age. Instead, the following examples illustrate the work undertaken by groups of children in one class over the course of three of four weeks.

These children were all younger juniors (eight- and nine-year-olds). At the beginning of the spring term, their teacher set up a display of yellow and gold items in a corner of the classroom. At the center of the display was a large bolt of cloth, which the teacher had tie dyed a startling bronze color. The material dominated one large corner of the room and seemed to magnify the sunlight that streamed in through the window. The dying created enormous white swirls in different parts of the cloth. On one of the first days of the term, the teacher talked with the children about the colors in the exhibit and how the gold was repeated in the shocks of wheat, photographs, and other yellow objects clustered near the cloth. Many children said that the display reminded them of sunlight and that the swirls in the material were like the sun.

Others concentrated on the gold color. They were reminded of Greek myths, and they heard the story of the Golden Fleece, Medusa, and Icarus, whose flight took him too close to the sun.

After further discussions, the class wrote a joint, impressionistic piece which included many of their thoughts on the display:

yellow is a light a burning sun
shining on the corn
it is a leaf in autumn, golden
on the ground
A heap of yellow fruit,
lemons, bananas, melons,
yellow is bees collecting pollen and
making honey.
yellow is a leaping tiger
a fish of brass.
it is a flaming fire or a cornish
ice cream on a hot day.
Yellow is a sandstorm
or shy daffodils a stabbing beak
a singing bird.
The colour of deep summer.

Following this effort, a number of children went on to write their own stories or poems.

Two girls in the class had different ideas about the display. They had immediately noticed that the circles in the cloth on the wall were like enormous eyes, and they asked the teacher if they might try to make some out of blue dye. With the teacher's help, they tie dyed two blue and white "eyes" on a piece of cloth, cut them out in the proper shape, mounted them, and framed them with paper lashes. The eyes, when mounted on the wall, were about two feet across and a foot high. Their dark "pupils" were piercing and seemed capable of sight.

The girls began to think about sight itself, and asked their teacher where they might find some real eyes to examine. They obtained a few frogs' eyes, which they dissected, drew, and wrote about:

The frog's eyes bulge out of his
head. He has no eyelashes.
Round his eye where the pupil is
he has a ring of gold. On a
human eye it is called an iris.
The rest of the eye is black.

It is joined to the head with a
strip of skin that reaches from the
head to the hind legs.

Their next interest was the human eye, which they read about, drew, and studied for some time. This project, beginning with the tie dying and ending with the human eye, absorbed them for three or four weeks. At the same time, they carried on with more conventional work in mathematics and reading.

Meanwhile, other members of the class branched off into different topics, all stimulated by the original discussion about sunlight and the stories of Jason, Icarus, and Medusa. A group interested in the monsters described in the myths began to talk about snakes, and their teacher brought a live one to school. This led to drawings of snakeskin, research on reptiles, and further work with frogs, toads, and newts. Some children built a vivarium to house the pet grass snake.

The tale of Icarus and his sad flight excited two other groups of children. Some were interested in the flight itself, wanting to know if Icarus really did fly and what allows birds and planes to leave the earth. They constructed models of a hot-air balloon and an airship, both involving mathematics and scale drawings.

A second group of boys was concerned about the ending of the myth, when Icarus flies too close to the sun, causing the wax on his wings to melt. They began to discuss the sun and its proximity to earth. The head teacher, hearing of this interest, brought in a book about the sun and encouraged some of the children to begin a study of the solar system.

They started with a flat diagram of the planets. After long hours of mathematical figuring, they worked out a chart that showed the planets' sizes to scale. They also did some reading and wrote a brief description of each planet. The teacher then urged them to try bigger, three-dimensional figures to show relative distances as well as accurate size. This they did, using papier-mâché to make the models. They read further about the planets so that they could paint their models accurately. They then hung them from the ceiling on fishing line, using a distance scale of one centimeter to one million miles. Their classroom was just long enough to accommodate this distance, from the flat paper sunburst they had made on the wall to the tiny, three-dimensional Pluto hanging at the other end of the room. When we saw the planets on display, hanging at the proper distances, the boys had yet another project in mind: they planned to work out a distance scale of ten thousand miles to the inch—which would take them beyond the school playground to the outskirts of town. The teacher hoped this would help them imagine the enormous distances in the solar system.

In all of these projects—the study of eyes, flight, and the exploration of the solar system—the teacher was directly involved. While he did not force these children to undertake their projects, he encouraged them to continue, throwing in new ideas when interest in one aspect failed. He was there to help one group with some very difficult math and to show the girls how to dissect the eye. He had sparked these interests with his original display and worked with the class as a whole before allowing them to take off on their own. As with so many junior projects in good schools, the children worked in a variety of ways —some preferred to work alone, others with a partner, while the boys studying the solar system formed a larger group.

At one point, the teacher consolidated many different activities by bringing the group together for a brief period. The children sat around the room facing the tie-dyed eyes. The teacher played a record of a piece of music called "The Planets" and asked the children to look into the eyes as they listened to it. At the end of the record, the pupils wrote about the feelings evoked by the experience. One child's impression was as follows:

> The blue eyes stare at me. They never
> look away. They make me scared.

The pupils look like blazing
fires.
They burn into me.
The eyelashes seem to pull me towards
them, like a powerful magnet
I try to run
The eyes are too strong for me
I can hardly take a step
I saw a pit.
Two more eyes were coming
out of the pit.
I fell to my knees and
crawled to a pond.
There was an old bucket there
I got some water in it and
threw water at one of the eyes
The eyes disappeared.
I threw water at the other
eyes. They disappeared
all their power had gone.
Then I ran home.

Aspects of these projects gave the child the sort of experience that Charity James feels is so greatly needed throughout the school years:

How much more profitable productive and critical thinking would be if it were demanded by the nature of the child's engagement, that is if the need for rigour arose from the creative purpose rather than the apparently arbitrary decision of the teacher; if the answer to the question, "Why are you doing that?" were not, "Because I was told to," or "Because we always do," but "Because I need to," whether the need is to test a hypothesis, to make one's dancing more skillful and expressive, or to get a pot ready for firing.[2]

Although James directs her comments toward secondary school, primary education must foster this kind of thinking as early as possible. For the child to be in a position to reply "Because I need to," his own needs must be the cornerstone of his entire school experience.

Most junior schools in England have not yet carried their children to this level of thinking. A few, however, have reached it by building on the successes of the infant schools. In many other areas, teachers would like to approach the chil-

dren this way, but are not sure how to go about it.

It does not appear that we are close to this kind of work in the overall curriculum of American elementary schools. In isolated instances, "Because I need to" might be heard. It is a reply that could accompany some work based upon an Elementary Science Study unit, for example, but there is seldom a carryover from work in one subject or project to include the child's work in other areas of the curriculum.[3] The work we describe throughout the rest of this chapter illustrates how a small number of schools have attempted to deal with the junior child's complete experience in learning.

EXPLORING THE SENSES

Sense experience . . . provides the raw material for reflection. . . . This work demands a rather special viewing of the classroom environment. We seek to entice, to fascinate, to encourage children to look into the heart of things. We want them to listen more carefully, look more closely and touch more sensitively.[4]

In the best English schools, junior children engage in a variety of activities that are sensory in nature. The descriptions that follow represent a few of the many ways that children and their teachers grow in their perceptions of themselves and each other as they explore the world around them.

We witnessed one aspect of sensory experience in an Oxfordshire school where different shapes, textures, and designs evoked varying responses in the children. An exhibit of metals was on display in a junior classroom. About fifteen children were eagerly handling and examining the items, each child absorbed by different aspects of the material. There were jugs, pitchers, plates of pewter, and iron implements for cook-

[2]C. James, Ibid., p. 107.

[3]Elementary Science Study (E.S.S.) was founded in 1959 and is now part of the Educational Development Center, Newton, Massachusetts.
[4]L. G. Marsh, *Alongside the Child in the Primary School* (London: A. & C. Black, 1970), p. 82.

ing, farming, and hand crafting. Objects of tin, brass, and copper stood on the display table. Some were complete items, others fragments that might or might not be identifiable.

The children who held the samples rubbed them, studied them, and talked about them with a neighbor. Some children were making careful, detailed drawings of the pieces they liked, using pencil first for accuracy. Others were more concerned with mathematical aspects of the display and spent time weighing and measuring particular pieces. A small group was clustered around the teacher, deep in a discussion about the strengths of different metals.

One child wrote about the texture, color, and size of a lovely brass pitcher. He used paper and pencil with the specific aim of recording the acute observations he had made. He hoped to describe the pitcher so that a person who had not seen it would gain an accurate image of it by reading about it. A girl by the window was concerned with the more emotive qualities of a twisted and pitted piece of iron which looked, she said, "like the arm of a monster."

The display of metals had been in the classroom for only a few days, and many children were just beginning to explore the materials. In the best junior classes, a child often involves his whole self in the work at hand. Much of his personality and feelings are revealed to the teacher as he creates a pottery bowl, makes a pattern of potato printings on a curtain, or writes about the piece of iron in his hand. The interaction of the teacher with the child is vital.

It is the teacher who makes an initial selection of materials, which either intrigue or bore the children. It is the interest of the teacher in the materials and in what the child is doing that encourages work of outstanding quality. The teacher's recognition of the needs of a particular child allow him to help the pupil toward a manner of working that is totally involving.

A friend teaching in Leicestershire described to us the dramatic change that took place in a boy who brought his rock collection, made outside school, into the classroom. While he had once been reticent and withdrawn from activities, this act of bringing an essential part of himself into the school transformed his relationships with the children. They were intensely interested in his collection and his knowledge. His teacher gained a new basis for working with him.

Many teachers can remember children bringing something of great importance into the classroom, but how many can say they seized upon this event to draw a part of the child's outside life into school? It is one of the accomplishments of some English schoolteachers that they often manage to do this. Both the philosophy behind their teaching and the freedom of the school day encourages them to draw upon the special interersts of one or more of the children.

Sometimes, the skills of the teacher will mesh with the interests of a group of children to provide a tremendously exciting working situation within a classroom. We witnessed such an event in a small village school where a new teacher had just arrived, bringing with her an enthusiasm for weaving and for unusual art effects. Her excitement caught the imagination of the children—a group of juniors who already had experience in the use of natural materials in art. Their common interests led to a number of different projects.

The class had previously studied some of the farm animals in the region with the head teacher. As part of their study of sheep, they collected samples of wool from barbed-wire fences and hedges, with little follow-up in the classroom. Now, with their new teacher, they planned to gather more wool and then to card, spin, and weave it, using dyes at different times to achieve particular effects. Although the teachers in the school could have dealt with weaving as simply one activity in a crafts period, they saw that their own interests and the interests of the children permitted a broader approach.

The children were engaged in all the mechanical and physical acts needed to transform the raw wool into finished fabric, and also asked questions about its history. Why were there certain towns with areas called wool markets in them, even though no one sold wool there now? The children came to these issues through their own natural curiosity and the sensory experiences of actually handling and working with the wool. Other children were more taken with the equipment involved in weaving than with the wool itself. Three boys gathered around the loom to talk and grew interested in its workings. Their teacher noticed them and brought over a pamphlet on building looms. For nearly an hour, they were engrossed in the book and the loom in front of them.

The teachers in this school made no special demands on the class as a whole. Most of the children worked very hard on weaving or subjects related to it. Some chose to use other materials, not connected to wool or weaving. Despite the skill of the new teacher in weaving and the interest of the head teacher who worked with her, neither would have chosen to coerce a child who was diligently engaged in something else to join the rest of the group.

We saw a different approach to the same subject at an Oxfordshire school. A group of children had decided to assemble some extensive displays about wool and what could be done with it. This exhibit formed as large a project as working with the wool itself. The children passed through many stages in dealing with the wool. They collected it from hedgerows, then washed it, carded it, and used two distinct methods to spin it. They experimented with a number of exciting dye techniques. A group collected natural materials (beets, elderberry, onionskin) and made dyes from them. At the end of the process, the wool was never quite the color the children had expected, leading them to investigate the chemical source of color in the materials they had used.

The finished display included wall posters that explained the qualities of certain colors and the natural method of obtaining them. Hanks of dyed wool hung near the posters to illustrate the points. Two girls sat on a low bench, below the posters, weaving a necktie from wool that they had prepared from its beginnings on the fences in the neighborhood. They were interested in the aesthetic qualities of the colors they were using, the feel of the material as it progressed from wool to cloth, and the patterns made as they passed shuttle back and forth.

As one might expect, a number of children in this class were involved in completely different activities. Four or five children, seated around a table, were drawing some pussy willows the teacher had brought in that morning. Now and then, a finger passed over the soft buds as a child studied their form carefully. On the walls of the classroom, in addition to the wool display, were recently completed examples of multicolored tie dying. Substantial painting took place at different times in this room and very graphic writing accompanied and complemented all the work.

Perhaps the most important features of sensory experiences such as these is the way they can develop unity in learning. The child learns to use his hands, his ears, his eyes, and his mind with equal proficiency. Unfortunately, only the best teacher is able to ensure that every child will have the chance to explore all the available areas of sensory experience. Yet it is remarkable how many teachers have encouraged their children to look at objects with great care and record what they see with imagination and skill, whether in writing, movement, or drawing.

The children have also begun to listen more carefully—although this is an area where many teachers could make further efforts. Music is sorely neglected in many schools, especially at the junior level. While a number of infant schools arouse children's interest in music with simple instruments, such as those designed by the musician Carl Orff, teachers in the junior schools are often unable to help the children to a more advanced level. The exceptions are local authorities, such as the West Riding of Yorkshire, which provide the schools with peripatetic teachers of music. These men and women are helping to fill the gap, but they need more assistance from the schools themselves.

We saw one instance where a teacher had coordinated music with other activities. His pupils made their own instruments, composed simple tunes, and filled their room with the sounds of recorders, xylophones, and other percussive instruments. In another small village school, every child from the age of five to eleven was able to play some instrument. This type of experience will gain in frequency only as hesitant teachers attend workshops and find that they can explore music without expertise.

The education of teachers has been essential to the development of more varied experiences for children. The best example is in the art that many children produce as juniors. The children are able to fire a pot or make an interesting collage only because their teacher has learned to appreciate art and has himself gained the ability to produce something worthwhile with his hands.

Art and the work it stimulates are very impressive in some junior schools. An observer expects to see intricate art work in infant classrooms. Many countries, the United States included, accept and encourage artistic expression in young children. We expect to see children painting in the first two or three grades of school and would be surprised to find a teacher who forbade it. But often, as American children reach the higher elementary grades, the amount of art work declines, sometimes to nil. This was once true in many English schools, and still is in some areas. But today, many teachers in England believe that art can form an integral part of the whole primary experience.

A good junior school teacher regards art as a means to enhance the work of the children in many fields. Such a teacher will try to lead the children into many varieties of art work. In the best schools, where a few teachers are proficient in one area or another, the children have access to many different media. Pottery, silk screening, prints made from wood or linocuts—all are a part of life in many exciting classrooms. The children will be encouraged to draw and sketch in detail as well as to paint large, expansive pictures. In some areas, handwriting is itself an art form. A child may make a book that involves many different methods of work. He will compose his own poems or stories, copying them neatly onto clean sheets of paper in his best handwriting. He will illustrate his work and then go on to make a cover for the book from material he has printed and dyed, or perhaps from a wood block he has perfected over the last few weeks.

The sensory experiences of working with art thus relate to more conventional school work. In one school, a class spent a few days talking about the Middle Ages. A group of ten- and eleven-year-olds became intrigued with illuminated writing practiced in the monasteries. Although they were unable to get to a museum where examples might be on display, they found some photographs in a number of books and began their own experiments. They revised and copied a report on some of the houses in their town. The margins and the first letter or word of each paragraph were enlarged and illuminated. A school report became a work of art. With the encouragement of their teacher, this group of children had explored an important part of the Middle Ages and had gone beyond mere historical curiosity to test out this art form with their own work.

The children whose work we discuss here have looked "into the heart of things," as Leonard Marsh suggests that they must. The work that we describe formed an important portion of these children's school experience. Each child reacted to these different activities in his own way. The sensory experiences they engaged in appeared to provide, from all we have been able to learn, valuable raw material for reflection which enhanced much of the rest of their efforts in school.

EXCELLENCE IN THE CURRICULUM

Teachers in English junior schools are faced with a difficult job. They are concerned with the excellence of both the specific pieces of work the children undertake and the caliber of their learning and development at the time they leave the school at the age of eleven. These teachers do not look upon their classroom methods as ends in themselves. They are valid only if the work is clearly beneficial to the children. Many teachers feel that an essential part of the learning process is the ability to communicate effectively with others. Some try to guide much of the work in the classroom toward this end. They argue that if a child has written poetry or practiced a piece of music, he can gain a great deal from the appreciation or criticism of his friends. For this reason, discussion takes place all the time in many classrooms. The child who looks over his friend's shoulder to comment on the accuracy of a drawing is helping the artist while increasing his own sense of how the work of another child differs from his own. Teachers often lead discussions that show the children, indirectly, the value of positive criticism as opposed to silly comments. The atmosphere or cooperation in a good classroom is of particular importance to this sort of talk.

Another very important way of sharing work is through displays of the finished product. Whether the walls are hung with paintings, poems, block prints, silk screening, poetry, descriptions of experiences, or complex geometric designs, the displays share a common characteristic in many of the best schools: they are of exceptional quality and reflect the degree of excellence achieved by the child on a certain piece of work. This does not mean that the same standard applies to all the children. The teacher must take differing abilities into account. If he is sensitive, he is careful to see that everyone is represented often in the changing exhibits. In some schools, children mount and prepare these displays themselves. In too many others, the teacher still does the finishing work, detracting from the child's overall feeling of accomplishment and pride.

The achievement of excellence is individual, and the best junior-school teachers emphasize their belief that there is no set standard which applies to every child. The teacher will, however, demand that the child do his best and that his work show a reasonable amount of improvement during the year. The idea that the children can improve upon and refine their own work is a valuable thought for them to grasp at this age. We had an opportunity to see children gain this sort of understanding in a school where a class had heard about the Norman invasion of England and where one group of children decided to pursue the topic further.

These children were interested in the way the Normans had become a part of the island and combined their way of life with that of the English. They began to do some reading, but soon tired of the books available. It was dry reading, which answered only a few of their questions. They sought a more direct way to approach the subject.

These nine-year-olds, working independently from the rest of their class, decided to build a model of a Norman village of the type that might have existed in their area. They collected the materials themselves. They received advice from teachers who knew something of model building. The job took a number of weeks, but when it was done they had completed a strikingly accurate, three-dimensional cardboard, wood, and styrofoam model of the main street of such a town. The details of each house were made to scale, involving extensive mathematics. The research had taken them far beyond the histories they had first read. The building and painting of the model required great manual dexterity. The team devoted far more care and time to this than they would have to any one painting or bit of wood-work that they might otherwise have worked on during those days. The model itself was of high quality and expressed, better than a teacher's grade ever could, the amount of care, involvement, and hard work that had gone into its construction. The excellence of this particular project, however, was not limited to the model making.

The children had also been drawn toward some writing. What they wrote was not a common report assigned by their teacher, but a series of papers on topics that had come to mind as a result of their work. Some sketched the history of Norman towns with facts gleaned from reading. Other children put themselves in the midst of their model, writing stories of themselves in their village. The children first did their writing without too much concern for grammar and spelling, but with a desire to get their ideas on paper. Once this was done, they showed their work to the teacher, who helped them with the technical side of the writing.

Aside from the generally high quality of this writing, it was impressive to see that the children using books for research had not copied material directly from the books, a problem that is common in more formal primary-school classrooms in England and the United States. Apparently, the experience of building the model and talking about their work had given them the confidence to be critical of what they read and the desire to put on paper exactly what they felt to be true, even when they were in disagreement with a book. They had broken through the barrier that so many children face of believing that what is in print cannot be contradicted and therefore might just as well be copied.

In outstanding junior schools, words that once helped to divide the curriculum (reading, spelling, history, geography, science) are losing their usefulness. Neither the boy who built the model of the Severn Bridge nor his teacher thought of his work as being divided into crafts, reading, mathe-matics, engineering, and geography—though he made use of each of these fields in completing his work. He was prepared to study any discipline that would help him to complete the bridge as he envisioned it. Yet, despite examples such as this, parts of the curriculum in many schools remain compartmentalized.

All teachers are concerned with the competence of their children in reading and mathematics. Historically, these two subjects have been taught independently, and in the bulk of English schools, math is still a separate subject. Reading, on the other hand, is only a distinct subject when it involves remedial work. A common approach to reading in quite a few junior schools is to integrate it as much as possible with other work. Reading is a pleasurable activity when the content is attractive to the child.

In the West Riding of Yorkshire, we talked to a ten-year-old girl who had become intrigued by the fact that some objects floated on water while others sank. She had noticed that of two, apparently similar, large crayons, one sank to the bottom of a tub of water while the other floated. Her teacher urged her to read two short science books about water, the density of objects, and the problems of getting a heavy object to float by designing it to do so. With the help of her teacher and a dictionary, she read the books carefully, improving her reading skills and vocabulary in the process. Fortunately, the school provided her with the proper books and with the facilities to experiment with flotation as she read.

She found a large plastic basin, filled it with water, and collected a number of different materials and objects to test, keeping notes as she did so. Her work, carried out in the classroom while other work was going on, caused no disturbance to the rest of the class. It did, however, draw some of her friends over to her corner to observe her work for a few minutes and get a glimpse of a problem they perhaps had not thought about before. Her work in one aspect of physics led her to pursue reading not as an end in itself, but for the explicit purpose of studying a subject that was important to her.

In other cases, where teachers strive to make reading a pleasurable activity, the school library plays an important role, as does the collection of reading books in each classroom. Head teachers of junior schools often devote substantial amounts of their budget to buying books, and although there are never enough, most schools have on hand a reasonable selection on varied subjects, aimed at different levels of reading competence. In a school run on informal lines, children can seek out books at many times during the day. They can visit the library if the school has one or ask in another class for a book they need. Collections of books are in greater demand and more extensively used in this setting than they can ever be in schools where going to the library is restricted to certain times or, worse, to a specific day of the week. This sort of arrangement is most unfortunate and can still be found in England as in America. It is unheard of in a junior school run along informal lines.

In junior schools, just as in some infant schools, many teachers try to provide a reading corner, where children can go to read in comfort and quiet. On occasion, we have seen children spend a whole day in a reading corner, enjoying an entire book with only an occasional interruption. These children are never exposed to readers or any reading text whatsoever. (Most of them would be as astounded to know that sometimes whole classes of children are forced to read the same story at the same time in a reading lesson.)

This practice also allows for far greater variety in books. The head teacher can afford to buy a few copies of many different books, rather than one or two full sets of readers for an entire class. The children are exposed to all sorts of fiction, poetry, reference books, and other literature in this way.

Junior schools face a major problem with their youngest children, who may have come from the infant school while in the midst of gaining confidence in their reading. The best solution, in the long run, may be to raise the age of leaving the infant school and to develop more effective means of communication between the infant and junior levels. At present, teachers are trying everything from formal reading programs—attempting to boost the child up—to informal approaches that give the child time to adjust to his new school. In the latter method, teachers recognize that a stimulating environment within the school is as important to the child's progress as additional help in areas where he is still weak.

We saw an example of this patience on the part of teachers in a school where many of the youngest children did some of their work in conjunction with the older nine-, ten-, and eleven-year-olds. There was initial concern, in the fall, that the youngest were not reading and writing enough and that they spent too much of their time working with the older children, observing superior writing and reading abilities without producing much on their own. Rather than assign these children to one type of reading or writing class, the decision was made to let them work as they were, with a great deal of support from their teachers. After two months of reticence on the part of the youngest junior group, many of them began to record their experiences spontaneously. They became involved in projects of deep importance to them, which led them to read on different subjects and induced them to write their feelings and impressions.

This approach reflects the careful thought being applied to the teaching of reading in many junior schools. It demonstrates the ability of the teachers to view learning as an experience that does not constantly include drill in such skills as reading and writing. The children's opportunity to observe and share in some of the work of their older classmates without being forced into any extended reading and writing of their own allowed them a period of growth without pressure and produced exciting results in the long run. When the children had branched out on projects that excited them, the teachers could help them with any specific reading problems that came up, in the context of other interests. They could thus approach their difficulties in a far less threatening way.

The kind of thinking applied to reading by some junior school teachers is sometimes extended to the teaching of mathematics, but less often. Just as in the United States, teachers are wary of modern mathematics and often unsure as to how it can best be taught. In the junior schools, it is the one subject that is almost invariably given a particular slot in each day's schedule, whereas other areas of the curriculum are dealt with more flexibly. We have spoken to mathematicians in colleges of education who contend that such scheduling is necessary. They argue that many teachers, because of their own backgrounds, remain most insecure with modern math. If they do not put it into the timetable, there is the danger it will be neglected for areas they find more enjoyable. In addition, some teachers feel—perhaps with justification—that many mathematical concepts can be learned only in isolation from other subjects.

In a substantial number of cases, junior-school teachers have treated modern math as a series of gimmicks to be larded on top of the traditional "basics." Some math books for children, designed to offer a very different approach, have been converted to texts and workbooks with which some children have to struggle just as they would with more traditional exercise books. This fate has befallen the very competent series of books *Let's Explore Mathematics,* by Leonard G. Marsh, which have become tattered exercise books in many schools rather than the innovative aids their author intended.[5] However, the picture of math teaching in junior schools is not completely bleak.

In many ways, the infant schools lead the junior schools in terms of work in mathematics.

[5]L. G. Marsh, *Let's Explore Mathematics* (London: A. & C. Black, 1964).

Many of the fine accomplishments in this area for juniors are derived from experiences the children have had in infant school. Children at the infant level learn the use of natural objects in some aspects of math. They also learn pictorial representation and some aspects of simple graphs. The junior schools are trying to build upon this knowledge, but it has taken them some time to develop the necessary materials.

Many teachers who experiment with modern math, and go beyond the workbook, use the Nuffield Mathematics Project as the basis of their work. Nuffield math leaves a great deal to the discretion of the teacher, who must make the decisions about the kind of work that specific children need. The series, which now consists of twelve published pamphlets, is neither a syllabus nor a text for children. It proposes a way of looking at mathematics that teachers must try to understand before they can use it with children. It is a tribute to the Nuffield Project that so many junior teachers are examining its work and trying to use it.

A few junior schools engage in math that is innovative and derived from children's interests. Outdoor Math, as it is known to some American teachers, has a strong foothold in many junior schools. Children deal with large-scale and difficult measuring and mapping with interest and competence. For example, the work that goes into accurately establishing the area of an irregularly shaped field can be both detailed and complex. Ten- and eleven-year-olds sometimes work toward an understanding of algebra, largely through the complexities of graphing. Despite the difficulties for some teachers (who may have had no exposure to these new concepts of math, even in college), it is safe to say that a few are beginning to consider the potentials of exciting mathematical thinking. Many of the more inventive materials may help an unsure teacher to realize that mathematics can be enjoyable and challenging.

It must be emphasized that the work of high quality described throughout this chapter is produced without the competition of grades or the pressure of homework. Junior schools which work informally believe that neither grades nor homework is necessary. The talks the teacher has with the child about his work, the sight of a favorite story or drawing on the wall, are in themselves far more satisfying to the child than an imposed grade could ever be. These are things he cares about deeply, and the teacher recognizes his concern. Who can judge that Susan's poem is worth B-plus while John's story of foxes, not his best work, merits only a C-minus? If John is not doing as well as he might, his teacher will certainly talk to him about it—and probably find that the cause goes deeper than laziness or lack of interest.

One thing common to good junior classes is the freshness with which the children start the day. Work that is not completed on one occasion is begun the following day with interest. One reason for this is that school work stops when the school day ends. Many junior schools have no regular homework. When a particular topic is exciting to a child, he may take home a relevant book to read. Poems and stories are often written at home, not because one is due the next day, but simply because the writer wanted to write and knew the work would receive attention and interest in school.

Many teachers find this hard to believe. Surely only the "best" children would take the time to write a poem at home unless they were asked to. But much of what we have seen—in good English schools—indicates that things do not work out this way. Writing and other projects are done for the child's pleasure and that of his peers, as well as for his teacher. Many children come to school with unsolicited work of all sorts and it does not necessarily go straight to the teacher. We have seen short stories handed around among friends in a classroom long before the teacher knows they have been written.

It is true that some children will never produce certain kinds of work without being required to do so. This is something the good teacher can deal with best in school. He can urge them to do their writing, or reading, or math, and keep a close watch on their work. In his mind, it would be a major error to pressure them to write something after school under the guise of homework. There is so much of life for a child of primary age to explore after school hours that many teachers in England have no desire to ask the child to sit at a desk at home.

The paramount focus on getting into secondary school is fading steadily in districts that have abolished the eleven-plus exam. There is growing confidence in the integral worth of junior schools themselves. Teachers want children to enjoy life now. Many head teachers and others deeply involved in the schools feel that a child who is happy in school is better prepared and equipped to deal with the future.

A good junior school gives its children confidence to cope with a wealth of different situations. The students will be accustomed to variety, to making choices and decisions. Many will have substantial self-assurance, and they will know some areas of study that interest them. They will hope and expect that the work they encounter in secondary school will relate to their own lives and concerns. Only if they are very lucky will this last wish be fulfilled.

Like It Is
in the Alley

Robert Coles

In the alley it's mostly dark, even if the sun is
out. But if you look around, you can find things. I
know how to get into every building, except that
it's like night once you're inside them, because
they don't have lights. So, I stay here. You're better
off. It's no good on the street. You can get hurt all
the time, one way or the other. And in buildings,
like I told you, it's bad in them, too. But here it's
o.k. You can find your own corner, and if someone
tries to move in you fight him off. We meet here
all the time, and figure out what we'll do next. It
might be a game, or over for some pool, or a coke
or something. You need to have a place to start out
from, and that's like it is in the alley; you can always know your buddy will be there, provided it's
the right time. So you go there, and you're on your
way, man.

SOURCE: Reprinted by permission of *Daedalus,* Journal of
the American Academy of Arts and Sciences, Boston,
Mass. "Conscience of the City," vol. 97 (Fall 1968), 1315–
1330.

Like all children of nine, Peter is always on
his way—to a person, a place, a "thing" he wants
to do. *"There's this here thing we thought we'd
try tomorrow,"* he'll say; and eventually I'll find
out that he means there's to be a race. He and his
friends will compete with another gang to see
who can wash a car faster and better. The cars
belong to four youths who make their money
taking bets, and selling liquor that I don't believe
was ever purchased, and pushing a few of those
pills that *"go classy with beer."* I am not completely sure, but I think they also have something
to do with other drugs; and again, I can't quite
be sure what their connection is with a "residence" I've seen not too far from the alley Peter
describes so possessively. The women come and
go—from that residence and along the street
Peter's alley leaves.

Peter lives in the heart of what we in contemporary America have chosen (ironically, so far as history goes) to call an "urban ghetto." The area was a slum before it became a ghetto, and there still are some very poor white people on its edges and increasing numbers of Puerto Ricans in several of its blocks. Peter was not born in the ghetto, nor was his family told to go there. They are Americans and have been here *"since way back before anyone can remember."* That is the way Peter's mother talks about Alabama, about the length of time she and her ancestors have lived there. She and Peter's father came north *"for freedom."* They did not seek out a ghetto, an old quarter of Boston where they were expected to live and where they would be confined, yet at least some of the time solidly at rest, with kin, and reasonably safe.

No, they sought freedom. Americans, they moved on when the going got *"real bad,"* and Americans, they expected something better someplace, some other place. They left Alabama on impulse. They found Peter's alley by accident. And they do not fear pogroms. They are Americans, and in Peter's words: *"There's likely to be another riot here soon. That's what I heard today. You hear it a lot, but one day you know it'll happen."*

Peter's mother fears riots too—among other things. The Jews of Eastern Europe huddled together in their ghettos, afraid of the barbarians, afraid of the *Goyim,* but always sure of one thing, their God-given destiny. Peter's mother has no such faith. She believes that *"something will work out one of these days."* She believes that *"you have to keep on going, and things can get better, but don't ask me how."* She believes that *"God wants us to have a bad spell here, and so maybe it'll get better the next time—you know in Heaven, and I hope that's where we'll be going."* Peter's mother, in other words, is a pragmatist, an optimist, and a Christian. Above all she is American:

Yes, I hear them talk about Africa, but it don't mean anything to us. All I know is Alabama and now it's in Massachusetts that we are. It was a long trip coming up here, and sometimes I wish we were back there, and sometimes I'd just as soon be here, for all that's no good about it. But I'm not going to take any more trips, no sir. And like Peter said, this is the only country we've got. If you come from a country, you come from it, and we're from it, I'd say, and there isn't much we can do but try to live as best we can. I mean, live here.

What is "life" like for her over there, where she lives, in the neighborhood she refers to as "here"? A question like that cannot be answered by the likes of me, and even her answer provides only the beginning of a reply:

Well, we does o.k., I guess. Peter here, he has it better than I did, or his daddy. I can say that. I tell myself that a lot. He can turn on the faucet over there, and a lot of the time, he just gets the water, right away. And when I tell him what it was like for us, to go fetch that water—we'd walk three miles, yes sir, and we'd be lucky it wasn't ten— well, Peter, it doesn't register on him. He thinks I'm trying to fool him, and the more serious I get the more he laughs, so I've stopped.

Of course it's not all so good, I have to admit. We're still where we were, so far as knowing where your next meal is coming from. When I go to bed at night I tell myself I've done good, to stay alive and keep the kids alive, and if they'll just wake up in the morning, and me too, well then, we can worry about that, all the rest, come tomorrow. So there you go. We do our best, and that's all you can do.

She may sound fatalistic, but she appears to be a nervous, hardworking, even hard-driven woman—thin, short, constantly on the move. I may not know what she "really" thinks and believes, because like the rest of us she has her contradictions and her mixed feelings. I think it is fair to say that there are some things that she can't say to me—or to herself. She is a Negro, and I am white. She is poor, and I am fairly well off. She is very near to illiterate, and I put in a lot of time worrying about how to say things.

But she and I are both human beings, and we both have trouble—to use that word—"communicating," not only with each other, but with ourselves. Sometimes she doesn't tell me something she really wants me to know. She has forgotten, pure and simple. More is on her mind than information I might want. And sometimes I forget too:

> Remember you asked the other day about Peter, if he was ever real sick. And I told you he was a weak child, and I feared for his life, and I've lost five children, three that was born and two that wasn't. Well, I forgot to tell you that he got real sick up here, just after we came. He was three, and I didn't know what to do. You see, I didn't have my mother to help out. She always knew what to do. She could hold a child and get him to stop crying, no matter how sick he was, and no matter how much he wanted food, and we didn't have it. But she was gone—and that's when we left to come up here, and I never would have left her, not for anything in the world. But suddenly she took a seizure of something and went in a half hour, I'd say. And Peter, he was so hot and sick, I thought he had the same thing his grandmother did and he was going to die. I thought maybe she's calling him. She always liked Peter. She helped him be born, she and my cousin, they did.

Actually, Peter's mother remembers quite a lot of things. She remembers the "old days" back South, sometimes with a shudder, but sometimes with the same nostalgia that the region is famous for generating in its white exiles. She also notices a lot of things. She notices, and from time to time will remark upon, the various changes in her life. She has moved from the country to the city. Her father was a sharecropper and her son wants to be a pilot (sometimes), a policeman (sometimes), a racing-car driver (sometimes), and a baseball player (most of the time). Her husband is not alive. He died one year after they came to Boston. He woke up vomiting in the middle of the night—vomiting blood. He bled and vomited and vomited and then he died. The doctor does not have to press very hard for "the facts." What-

ever is known gets spoken vividly and (still) emotionally:

> I didn't know what to do. I was beside myself. I prayed and I prayed, and in between I held his head and wiped his forehead. It was the middle of the night. I woke up my oldest girl and told her to go knocking on the doors. But no one would answer. They must have been scared, or have suspected something bad. I thought if only he'd be able to last into the morning, then we could get some help. I was caught between things. I couldn't leave him to go get a policeman. And my girl, she was afraid to go out. And besides, there was no one outside, and I thought we'd just stay at his side, and somehow he'd be o.k., because he was a strong man, you know. His muscles, they were big all his life. Even with the blood coming up, he looked too big and strong to die, I thought. But I knew he was sick. He was real bad sick. There wasn't anything else, no sir, to do. We didn't have no phone and even if there was a car, I never could have used it. Nor my daughter. And then he took a big breath and that was his last one.

When I first met Peter and his mother, I wanted to know how they lived, what they did with their time, what they liked to do or disliked doing, what they believed. In the back of my mind were large subjects like "the connection between a person's moods and the environment in which he lives." Once I was told I was studying "the psychology of the ghetto," and another time the subject of "urban poverty and mental health." It is hoped that at some point large issues like those submit themselves to lives; and when that is done, when particular but not unrepresentative or unusual human beings are called in witness, their concrete medical history becomes extremely revealing. I cannot think of a better way to begin knowing what life is like for Peter and his mother than to hear the following and hear it again and think about its implications:

> No sir, Peter has never been to a doctor, not unless you count the one at school, and she's a nurse I believe. He was his sickest back home before we came here, and you know there was no

doctor for us in the country. In Alabama you have to pay a white doctor first, before he'll go near you. And we don't have but a few colored ones. (I've never seen a one.) There was this woman we'd go to, and she had gotten some nursing education in Mobile. (No, I don't know if she was a nurse or not, or a helper to the nurses, maybe.) Well, she would come to help us. With the convulsions, she'd show you how to hold the child, and make sure he doesn't hurt himself. They can bite their tongues real, real bad.

Here, I don't know what to do. There's the city hospital, but it's no good for us. I went there with my husband, no sooner than a month or so after we came up here. We waited and waited, and finally the day was almost over. We left the kids with a neighbor, and we barely knew her. I said it would take the morning, but I never thought we'd get home near suppertime. And they wanted us to come back and come back, because it was something they couldn't do all at once—though for most of the time we just sat there and did nothing. And my husband, he said his stomach was the worse for going there, and he'd take care of himself from now on, rather than go there.

Maybe they could have saved him. But they're far away, and I didn't have money to get a cab, even if there was one around here, and I thought to myself it'll make him worse, to take him there.

My kids, they get sick. The welfare worker, she sends a nurse here, and she tells me we should be on vitamins and the kids need all kinds of check-ups. Once she took my daughter and told her she had to have her teeth looked at, and the same with Peter. So, I went with my daughter, and they didn't see me that day, but said they could in a couple of weeks. And I had to pay the woman next door to mind the little ones, and there was the carfare, and we sat and sat, like before. So, I figured, it would take more than we've got to see that dentist. And when the nurse told us we'd have to come back a few times—that's how many, a few—I thought that no one ever looked at my teeth, and they're not good, I'll admit, but you can't have everything, that's what I say, and that's what my kids have to know, I guess.

What *does* she have? And what belongs to Peter? For one thing, there is the apartment, three rooms for six people, a mother and five children. Peter is a middle child with two older girls on one side and a younger sister and still younger brother on the other side. The smallest child was born in Boston:

> It's the only time I ever spent time in a hospital. He's the only one to be born there. My neighbor got the police. I was in the hall, crying I guess. We almost didn't make it. They told me I had bad blood pressure, and I should have been on pills, and I should come back, but I didn't. It was the worst time I've ever had, because I was alone. My husband had to stay with the kids, and no one was there to visit me.

Peter sleeps with his brother in one bedroom. The three girls sleep in the living room, which is a bedroom. And, of course, there is a small kitchen. There is not very much furniture about. The kitchen has a table with four chairs, only two of which are sturdy. The girls sleep in one big bed. Peter shares his bed with his brother. The mother sleeps on a couch. There is one more chair and a table in the living room. Jesus looks down from the living room wall, and an undertaker's calendar hangs on the kitchen wall. The apartment has no books, no records. There is a television set in the living room, and I have never seen it off.

Peter in many respects is his father's successor. His mother talks things over with him. She even defers to him at times. She will say something; he will disagree; she will nod and let him have the last word. He knows the city. She still feels a stranger to the city. *"If you want to know about anything around here, just ask Peter,"* she once said to me. That was three years ago, when Peter was six. Peter continues to do very poorly at school, but I find him a very good teacher. He notices a lot, makes a lot of sense when he talks, and has a shrewd eye for the ironic detail. He is very intelligent, for all the trouble he gives his teachers. He recently summed up a lot of American history for me: *"I wasn't made for that school, and that school wasn't made for me."* It is an old school, filled with memories. The name of the school evokes Boston's Puritan past. Pictures and statues adorn the corridors—reminders of the soldiers and statesmen and writers who made New England so influential in the nineteenth century. And naturally one finds slogans on the walls, about freedom and democracy and the rights of the people. Peter can be surly and cynical when he points all that out to the visitor. If he is asked what kind of school he would *like,* he laughs incredulously.

> Are you kidding? No school would be my first choice. They should leave us alone, and let us help out at home, and maybe let some of our own people teach us. The other day the teacher admitted she was no good. She said maybe a Negro should come in and give us the discipline, because she was scared. She said all she wanted from us was that we keep quiet and stop wearing her nerves down, and she'd be grateful, because she would retire soon. She said we were becoming too much for her, and she didn't understand why. But when one kid wanted to say something, tell her why, she told us to keep still, and write something. You know what? She whipped out a book and told us to copy a whole page from it, so we'd learn it. A stupid waste of time. I didn't even try; and she didn't care. She just wanted an excuse not to talk with us. They're all alike.

Actually, they're all *not* alike, and Peter knows it. He has met up with two fine teachers, and in mellow moments he can say so:

> They're trying hard, but me and my friends, I don't think we're cut out for school. To tell the truth, that's what I think. My mother says we should try, anyway, but it doesn't seem to help, trying. The teacher can't understand a lot of us, but he does all these new things, and you can see he's excited. Some kids are really with him, and I am too. But I can't take all his stuff very serious. He's a nice man, and he says he wants to come and visit every one of our homes; but my mother says no, she wouldn't know what to do with him, when he came here. We'll just stand and have nothing to talk about. So she said to tell him not to come; and I don't think he will, anyway. I think he's getting to know.

What is that teacher getting to know? What *is* there to know about Peter and all the others like

him in our American cities? Of course Peter and his friends who play in the alley need better schools, schools they can feel to be theirs, and better teachers, like the ones they *have* in fact met on occasion. But I do not feel that a reasonably good teacher in the finest school building in America would reach and affect Peter in quite the way, I suppose, people like me would expect and desire. At nine Peter is both young and quite old. At nine he is much wiser about many things than my sons will be at nine, and maybe nineteen. Peter has in fact taught me a lot about his neighborhood, about life on the streets, about survival:

> I get up when I get up, no special time. My mother has Alabama in her. She gets up with the sun, and she wants to go to bed when it gets dark. I try to tell her that up here things just get started in the night. But she gets mad. She wakes me up. If it weren't for her shaking me, I might sleep until noon. Sometimes we have a good breakfast, when the check comes. Later on, though, *before* it comes it might just be some coffee and a slice of bread. She worries about food. She says we should eat what she gives us, but sometimes I'd rather go hungry. I was sick a long time ago, my stomach or something—maybe like my father, she says. So I don't like all the potatoes she pushes on us and cereal, all the time cereal. We're supposed to be lucky, because we get some food every day. Down South they can't be sure. That's what she says, and I guess she's right.
>
> Then I go to school. I eat what I can, and leave. I have two changes of clothes, one for everyday and one for Sunday. I wait on my friend Billy, and we're off by 8:15. He's from around here, and he's a year older. He knows everything. He can tell you if a woman is high on some stuff, or if she's been drinking, or she's off her mind about something. He knows. His brother has a convertible, a Buick. He pays off the police, but Billy won't say no more than that.
>
> In school we waste time until it's over. I do what I have to. I don't like the place. I feel like falling off all day, just putting my head down and saying good-bye to everyone until three. We're out then, and we sure wake up. I don't have to stop home first, not now. I go with Billy. We'll be in the alley, or we'll go to see them play pool. Then you know when it's time to go home. You hear some-

one say six o'clock, and you go in. I eat and I watch television. It must be around ten or eleven I'm in bed.

Peter sees rats all the time. He has been bitten by them. He has a big stick by his bed to use against them. They also claim the alley, even in the daytime. They are not large enough to be compared with cats, as some observers have insisted; they are simply large, confident, well-fed unafraid rats. The garbage is theirs; the land is theirs; the tenement is theirs; human flesh is theirs. When I first started visiting Peter's family, I wondered why they didn't do something to rid themselves of those rats, and the cockroaches, and the mosquitoes, and the flies, and the maggots, and the ants, and especially the garbage in the alley which attracts so much of all that "lower life." Eventually I began to see some of the reasons why. A large apartment building with many families has exactly two barrels in its basement. The halls of the building go unlighted. Many windows have no screens, and some windows are broken and boarded up. The stairs are dangerous; some of them have missing timber. (*"We just jump over them,"* says Peter cheerfully.) And the landowner is no one in particular. Rent is collected by an agent, in the name of a "realty trust." Somewhere in City Hall there is a bureaucrat who unquestionably might be persuaded to prod someone in the "trust"; and one day I went with three of the tenants, including Peter's mother, to try that "approach." We waited and waited at City Hall. (I drove us there, clear across town, naturally.) Finally we met up with a man, a not very encouraging or inspiring or generous or friendly man. He told us we would have to try yet another department and swear out a complaint; and that the "case" would have to be "studied," and that we would then be "notified of a decision." We went to the department down the hall, and waited some more, another hour and ten minutes. By then it was three o'clock, and the mothers wanted to go home. They weren't thinking of rats anymore, or poorly heated apartments,

or garbage that had nowhere to go and often went uncollected for two weeks, not one. They were thinking of their children, who would be home from school and, in the case of two women, their husbands who would also soon be home. *"Maybe we should come back some other day,"* Peter's mother said. I noted she didn't say *tomorrow,* and I realized that I had read someplace that people like her aren't precisely "future-minded."

Actually, both Peter and his mother have a very clear idea of what is ahead. For the mother it is *"more of the same."* One evening she was tired but unusually talkative, perhaps because a daughter of hers was sick:

I'm glad to be speaking about all these things tonight. My little girl has a bad fever. I've been trying to cool her off all day. Maybe if there was a place near here, that we could go to, maybe I would have gone. But like it is, I have to do the best I can and pray she'll be o.k.

I asked whether she thought her children would find things different, and that's when she said it would be *"more of the same"* for them. Then she added a long afterthought:

Maybe it'll be a little better for them. A mother has to have hope for her children, I guess. But I'm not too sure, I'll admit. Up here you know there's a lot more jobs around than in Alabama. We don't get them, but you know they're someplace near, and they tell you that if you go train for them, then you'll be eligible. So maybe Peter might someday have some real good steady work, and that would be something, yes sir it would. I keep telling him he should pay more attention to school, and put more of himself into the lessons they give there. But he says no, it's no good; it's a waste of time; they don't care what happens there, only if the kids don't keep quiet and mind themselves. Well, Peter has got to learn to mind himself, and not be fresh. He speaks back to me, these days. There'll be a time he won't even speak to me at all, I suppose. I used to blame it all on the city up here, city living. Back home we were always together, and there wasn't no place you could go, unless to Birmingham, and you couldn't do much for yourself there, we all knew. Of course, my momma, she knew how to make us behave. But I was thinking the other night, it wasn't so good back there either. Colored people, they'd beat on one another, and we had lot of people that liquor was eating away at them; they'd use wine by the gallon. All they'd do was work on the land, and then there'd be the next day—until they'd one evening go to sleep and never wake up. And we'd get the Bossman and he'd see to it they got buried.

Up here I think it's better, but don't ask me to tell you why. There's the welfare, that's for sure. And we get our water and if there isn't good heat, at least there's some. Yes, it's cold up here, but we had cold down there, too, only then we didn't have any heat, and we'd just die, some of us would, every winter with one of those freezing spells.

And I do believe things are changing. On the television they talk to you, the colored man and all the others who aren't doing so good. My boy Peter, he says they're puting you on. That's all he sees, people "putting on" other people. But I think they all mean it, the white people. I never see them, except on television, when they say the white man wants good for the colored people, I think Peter could go and do better for himself later on, when he gets older, except for the fact that he just doesn't *believe*. He don't believe what they say, the teacher, or the man who says it's getting better for us—on television. I guess it's my fault. I never taught my children, any of them, to believe that kind of thing; because I never thought we'd ever have it any different, not in this life. So maybe I've failed Peter. I told him the other day, he should work hard, because of all the "opportunity" they say is coming for us, and he said I was talking good, but where was my proof. So I went next door with him, to my neighbor's, and we asked her husband, and you know he sided with Peter. He said they were taking in a few here and a few there, and putting them in the front windows of all the big companies, but that all you have to do is look around at our block and you'd see all the young men, and they just haven't got a thing to do. Nothing.

Her son also looks to the future. Sometimes he talks—in his own words—"big." He'll one day be a bombardier or *"something like that."* At other times he is less sure of things:

I don't know what I'll be. Maybe nothing. I see the men sitting around, hiding from the welfare lady. They fool her. Maybe I'll fool her, too. I don't know what you can do. The teacher the other day

said that if just one of us turned out o.k. she'd congratulate herself and call herself lucky.

A while back a riot excited Peter and his mother, excited them and frightened them. The spectacle of the police being fought, of white-owned property being assaulted, stirred the boy a great deal: *"I figured the whole world might get changed around. I figured people would treat us better from now on. Only I don't think they will."* As for his mother, she was less hopeful, but even more apocalyptic: *"I told Peter we were going to pay for this good. I told him they wouldn't let us get away with it, not later on."* And in the midst of the trouble she was frightened as she had never before been:

I saw them running around on the streets, the men and women, and they were talking about burning things down, and how there'd be nothing left when they got through. I sat there with my children and I thought we might die the way things are going, die right here. I didn't know what to do: if I should leave, in case they burn down the building, or if I should stay, so that the police don't arrest us, or we get mixed up with the crowd of people. I've never seen so many people, going in so many different directions. They were running and shouting and they didn't know what to do. They were so excited. My neighbor, she said they'd burn us all up, and then the white man would have himself one less of a headache. The colored man is a worse enemy to himself than the white. I mean, it's hard to know which is the worst.

I find it as hard as she does to sort things out. When I think of her and the mothers like her I have worked with for years, when I think of Peter and his friends, I find myself caught between the contradictory observations I have made. Peter already seems a grim and unhappy child. He trusts no one white, not his white teacher, not the white policeman he sees, not the white welfare worker, not the white storekeeper, and not, I might add, me. There we are, the five of us from the 180,000,000 Americans who surround him and of course 20,000,000 others. Yet, Peter doesn't really trust his friends and neighbors, either. At nine he has learned to be careful, wary, guarded, doubtful, and calculating. His teacher may not know it, but Peter is a good sociologist, and a good political scientist, a good student of urban affairs. With devastating accuracy he can reveal how much of the "score" he knows; yes, and how fearful and sad and angry he is:

> This here city isn't for us. It's for the people downtown. We're here because, like my mother said, we had to come. If they could lock us up or sweep us away, they would. That's why I figure the only way you can stay ahead is get some kind of deal for yourself. If I had a choice I'd live someplace else, but I don't know where. It would be a place where they treated you right, and they didn't think you were some nuisance. But the only thing you can do is be careful of yourself; if not, you'll get killed somehow, like it happened to my father.

His father died prematurely, and most probably, unnecessarily. Among the poor of our cities the grim medical statistics we all know about become terrible daily experiences. Among the black and white families I work with—in nearby but separate slums—disease and the pain that goes with it are taken for granted. When my children complain of an earache or demonstrate a skin rash I rush them to the doctor. When I have a headache, I take an aspirin; and if the headache is persistent, I can always get a medical check-up. Not so with Peter's mother and Peter; they have learned to live with sores and infections and poorly mended fractures and bad teeth and eyes that need but don't have the help of glasses. Yes, they can go to a city hospital and get free care; but again and again they don't. They come to the city without any previous experience as patients. They have never had the money to purchase a doctor's time. They have never had free medical care available. (I am speaking now of Appalachian whites as well as southern blacks.) It may comfort me to know that every American city provides some free medical services for its "indigent," but Peter's mother and thousands like her have quite a different view of things:

> I said to you the other time, I've tried there. It's like at City Hall, you walk and wait and they pushes you and shove you and call your name, only to tell you to wait some more, and if you tell them you can't stay there all day, they'll say "lady go home, then." You get sick just trying to get there. You have to give your children over to people or take them all with you; and the carfare is expensive. Why if we had a doctor around here, I could almost pay him with the carfare it takes to get there and back all of us. And you know, they keep on having you come back and back, and they don't know what each other says. Each time they starts from scratch.

It so happens that recently I took Peter to a children's hospital and arranged for a series of evaluations which led to the following: a pair of glasses; a prolonged bout of dental work; antibiotic treatment for skin lesions; a thorough cardiac work-up, with the subsequent diagnosis of rheumatic heart disease; a conference between Peter's mother and a nutritionist, because the boy has been on a high-starch, low-protein, and low-vitamin diet all his life. He suffers from one attack of sinus trouble after another, from a succession of sore throats and earaches, from cold upon cold, even in the summer. A running nose is unsurprising to him—and so is chest pain and shortness of breath, due to a heart ailment, we now know.

At the same time Peter is tough. I have to emphasize again *how* tough and, yes, how "politic, cautious and meticulous," not in Prufrock's way, but in another way and for other reasons. Peter has learned to be wary as well as angry; tentative as well as extravagant; at times controlled and only under certain circumstances defiant:

> Most of the time, I think you have to watch your step. That's what I think. That's the difference between up here and down in the South. That's what my mother says, and she's right. I don't remember it down there, but I know she must be right. Here, you measure the next guy first and then make your move when you think it's a good time to.

He was talking about *"how you get along"* when you leave school and go *"mix with the guys"* and start *"getting your deal."* He was telling me what an outrageous and unsafe world he has inherited and how very carefully he has made his appraisal of the future. Were I afflicted with some of his physical complaints, I would be fretful, annoyed, petulant, angry—and moved to do something, see someone, get a remedy, a pill, a promise of help. He has made his "adjustment" to the body's pain, and he has also learned to contend with the alley and the neighborhood and us, the world beyond: *"The cops come by here all the time. They drive up and down the street. They want to make sure everything is o.k. to look at. They don't bother you, so long as you don't get in their way."*

So, it is live and let live—except that families like Peter's have a tough time living, and of late have been troubling those cops, among others. Our cities have become not only battlegrounds, but places where all sorts of American problems and historical ironics have converged. Ailing, poorly fed, and proud Appalachian families have reluctantly left the hollows of eastern Kentucky and West Virginia for Chicago and Dayton and Cincinnati and Cleveland and Detroit, and even, I have found, Boston. They stick close together in all-white neighborhoods—or enclaves or sections or slums or ghettos or whatever. They wish to go home but can't, unless they are willing to be idle and hungry all the time. They confuse social workers and public officials of all kinds because they both want and reject the city. Black families also have sought out cities and learned to feel frightened and disappointed.

I am a physician, and over the past ten years I have been asking myself how people like Peter and his mother survive in mind and body and spirit. And I have wanted to know what a twentieth-century American city "means" to them or "does" to them. People cannot be handed questionnaires and asked to answer such questions. They cannot be "interviewed" a few times and told to come across with a statement, a reply. But inside Peter and his brother and his sisters and his mother, and inside a number of Appala-

chian mothers and fathers and children I know, are feelings and thoughts and ideas—which, in my experience, come out casually or suddenly, by accident almost. After a year or two of talking, after experiences such as I have briefly described in a city hall, in a children's hospital, a lifetime of pent-up tensions and observation comes to blunt expression:

> Down in Alabama we had to be careful about ourselves with the white man, but we had plenty of things we could do by ourselves. There was our side of town, and you could walk and run all over, and we had a garden you know. Up here they have you in a cage. There's no place to go, and all I do is stay in the building all day long and the night, too. I don't use my legs no more, hardly at all. I never see those trees, and my oldest girl, she misses planting time. It was bad down there. We had to leave. But it's no good here, too, I'll tell you. Once I woke up and I thought all the buildings on the block were falling down on me. And I was trying to climb out, but I couldn't. And then the next thing I knew, we were all back South, and I was standing near some sunflowers—you know, the tall ones that can shade you if you sit down.
>
> No, I don't dream much. I fall into a heavy sleep as soon as I touch the bed. The next thing I know I'm stirring myself to start in all over in the morning. It used to be the sun would wake me up, but now it's up in my head. I guess. I know I've got to get the house going and off to school.

Her wistful, conscientious, law-abiding, devoutly Christian spirit hasn't completely escaped the notice of Peter, for all his hardheaded, cynical protestations:

> If I had a chance, I'd like to get enough money to bring us all back to Alabama for a visit. Then I could prove it that it may be good down there, a little bit, even if it's no good, either. Like she says, we had to get out of there or we'd be dead by now. I hear say we all may get killed soon; it's so bad here; but I think we did right to get up here, and if we make them listen to us, the white man, maybe he will.

To which Peter's mother adds:

> We've carried a lot of trouble in us, from way back in the beginning. I have these pains, and so

does everyone around here. But you can't just die until you're ready to. And I do believe something is happening. I do believe I see that.

To which Peter adds:

Maybe it won't be that we'll win, but if we get killed, everyone will hear about it. Like the minister said, before we used to die real quiet, and no one stopped to pay notice.

Two years before Peter spoke those words he drew a picture for me, one of many he has done. When he was younger, and when I didn't know him so well as I think I do now, it was easier for us to have something tangible to do and then talk about. I used to visit the alley with him, as I still do, and one day I asked him to draw the alley. That was a good idea, he thought. (Not all of my suggestions were, however.) He started in, then stopped, and finally worked rather longer and harder than usual at the job. I busied myself with my own sketches, which from the start he insisted I do. Suddenly from across the table I heard him say he was through. Ordinarily he would slowly turn the drawing around for me to see; and I would get up and walk over to his side of the table, to see even better. But he didn't move his paper, and I didn't move myself, I saw what he had drawn, and he saw me looking. I was surprised and a bit stunned and more than a bit upset, and surely he saw my face and heard my utter silence. Often I would break the awkward moments when neither of us seemed to have anything to say, but this time it was his turn to do so: *"You know what it is?"* He knew that I liked us to talk about our work. I said no, I didn't—though in fact the vivid power of his black crayon had come right across to me. *"It's that hole we dug in the alley. I made it bigger here. If you fall into it, you can't get out. You die."*

He had drawn circles within circles, all of them black, and then a center, also black. He had imposed an X on the center. Nearby, strewn across the circles, were fragments of the human body—two faces, an arm, five legs. And after I had taken the scene in, I could only think to myself that I had been shown *"like it is in the alley"* —by an intelligent boy who knew what he saw around him, could give it expression, and, I am convinced, would respond to a different city, a city that is alive and breathing, one that is not for many of its citizens a virtual morgue.

Chapter 11

Helping Disadvantaged Children

Socioeconomically disadvantaged children, including significant numbers of ethnic or racial minorities, typically obtain lower scores on IQ tests and perform more poorly in school than their more advantaged peers. Furthermore, their academic difficulties usually increase over the years and they are far more likely to drop out of school at an early age. Poorly prepared to cope with the world of work, many of them obtain only marginal types of jobs or are unemployed. Thus the cycle of poverty and, frequently, of ethnic or racial discrimination is likely to repeat itself in still another generation.

In an attempt to break this cycle, a number of programs of "compensatory education," such as Head Start, were begun on a broad scale in the 1960s. Taken together, the results of these programs, while still not entirely clear, do not appear to be very encouraging. Some children did not seem to profit from these preschool programs, which were generally of rather brief duration. Other children, while doing well upon entrance into regular school, subsequently dropped back to substandard levels of performance. Why?

In the view of Arthur Jensen, an educational psychologist at the University of California, socioeconomic and racial differences in IQ and academic performance are due primarily to genetic influences. Therefore, the chances of boosting IQ or scholastic achievement significantly through cultural enrichment programs or compensatory education are limited.

However, J. McV. Hunt argues in the first paper in this chapter that Jensen's conclusions are open to considerable question. Hunt presents an alternative hypothesis that may help to account for the lower performance of many disadvantaged children: "Given the necessary relationship between the physical structure of the nervous system and the behavior of the system (as in IQ), we must provide rich post-natal experience in order to develop the inherent structures" (p. 332). He offers analogies from animal research which suggest that the physical development of the brain is directly influenced by its information-processing activities, and he notes that these activities are particularly effective in neonatal organisms.

It well may be that the reason many efforts at compensatory education have failed to produce more encouraging results is that they were not intensive enough, relevant enough, begun early enough, or continued long enough to overcome the effects of countervailing influences (e.g., lack of early stimulation). This possibility has recently received rather dramatic support in a still unpublished, continuing study by Rick Heber and his colleagues in the Milwaukee Project at the University of Wisconsin.[1] The aim of the study is to see whether intellectual deficiency can be prevented by introducing an array of positive experiences in the early life of disadvantaged children, displacing those that appear to be negative or adverse. Subjects are disadvantaged black ghetto children, all of whose mothers had IQs of less than 75. Experimental subjects began receiving an intensive daily program of mental stimulation shortly after birth (about 3 months), which included individually supervised experiences, provided by specially trained workers, in language development, psychomotor skills, social interaction, and cultural enrichment. Programs to aid mothers in child care, homemaking, and vocational training were also instituted. A matched control group of children did not receive this training but was periodically tested, as the experimental group was, on a variety of measures of learning and performance, including language development and motor skills.

The results to date have been singularly impressive. At last report, the oldest children in the experimental group were over 5. They had rapidly built their vocabularies between 12 and 25 months of age; the control children were producing very little vocabulary (some were not speaking at all) at age 28 months. And by 32 months of age, while most control-

1. R. Heber, H. Garber, S. Herrington & C. Hoffman, **Rehabilitation of families at risk for mental retardation.** Progress Report, Rehabilitation Research and Training Center in Mental Retardation, University of Wisconsin, Madison, December 1972.

group children were still saying unconnected words, those in the experimental group were expressing themselves in complete sentences. On virtually every measure (e.g., matching and sorting, comprehension, motor skills, and IQ), the children in the experimental group have consistently outstripped controls and have generally surpassed the norms established for their age group. Despite the fact that their mothers all scored in the retarded range in intelligence, the average IQ of these children at 66 months was about 125 ("superior"), as contrasted with about 95 for control children.

In commenting on these results, Heber is both modest and cautious and admits that some of the results may be attributable, at least in part, to the children's becoming "test-wise." Furthermore, future performance as the children grow older remains to be determined. Nevertheless, it is difficult to conceive of the children in the experimental group falling back to the level of their peers in the control group.

(2) The second article in this chapter also tends to support the hypothesis that early stimulation can be effective, although the amount and persistence of the effect is a function of the intensity and duration of the stimulation. S. W. Gray and R. A. Klaus describe the results of an intervention program involving 10-week "summer school" experiences (over 2–3 summers) for disadvantaged black preschoolers, combined with weekly home visits when the summer school was not in session. The home visits aimed at helping the mothers provide continuing cognitive stimulation to their children. Children who had participated in the program performed significantly better than control subjects in measures of school achievement and intelligence in grade 1, but this superiority gradually declined in the following three grades. However, eight children who had transferred to a superior integrated school continued to make approximately "normal" progress in measures of school achievement. The authors conclude:

> The most effective intervention programs for preschool children that could possibly be conceived cannot be considered a form of inoculation whereby the child forever after is immune to the effects of a low-income home and of a school inappropriate to his needs. . . . Intervention programs, well conceived and executed, may be expected to make some relatively lasting changes. Such programs, however, cannot be expected to carry the whole burden of providing adequate schooling for children from deprived circumstances; they can provide only a basis for future progress in schools and homes that can build upon that early intervention" (p. 358).

#28 Has Compensatory Education Failed? Has It Been Attempted?

J. McV. Hunt

While Professor Hunt finds much of interest in parts of Jensen's article,[1] he objects strongly to some of its conclusions. Hunt fails to find satisfactory evidence that we may make the assertions about genetic differences determining the intelligence of Negroes and whites which Jensen has offered. He finds Jensen's claims about the high heritability of intelligence unsubstantiated; he finds Jensen's conclusion that observed group mean differences in IQ scores among Negro and white populations are genetically determined to be even less supportable. Hunt offers an alternative hypothesis: given the necessary relationship between the physical structure of the nervous system and the behavior of the system (as in IQ), we must

SOURCE: From *Harvard Educational Review*, vol. 39 (1969), 278–300. Copyright © 1969 by President and Fellows of Harvard College. Reprinted by permission.

[1]A. R. Jensen. How much can we boost IQ and scholastic achievement? *Harvard Educational Review*, 1969, 39, 1–123.

provide rich post-natal experience in order to develop the inherent structures. He offers analogies from animal research which suggest that the physical development of the brain is directly influenced by its information-processing activities—these activities are particularly effective in neo-natal organisms.

Jensen's paper is a critical effort to correct the currently wide-spread "belief in the almost indefinite plasticity of intellect." He asserts that "the ostrich-like denial of biological factors in individual differences, and the slighting of the role of genetics in the study of intelligence can only hinder investigation and understanding of the conditions, processes, and limits through which the social environment influences human behavior" (p. 29). He finds my term "fixed intelligence" to be rather misleading for two real and separate reasons: (1) the genetic basis of individual differences in intelligence and (2) the stability or the constancy of the IQ throughout the individual's life. A major share of his paper is devoted to explaining the heritability of traits and to the theoretical and empirical basis for the proposition that about 80% of the individual variance in intelligence (defined in terms of the IQ and/or Spearman's g) has a genetic basis. This, at least by implication, explains why compensatory education "apparently has failed" (p. 2). He examines class differences and race differences in these same terms. But there is more to his paper. In the end, he offers, from the results of his own investigations, a basis for some hope through education if educational practice is modified.

Honest criticism is useful, both in science and in the process of social change which the behavioral, biological, and social sciences have now begun to influence. It is always useful unless it serves to hamper freedom of and support for investigation and for the development of appropriate technologies for coping with social problems. On the whole, Jensen's criticism comes in a constructive spirit. Moreover, it is informative. I am glad for the invitation to respond to his paper, for it has motivated more careful reading and consideration than I might otherwise have given it. In responding, I would like to synopsize his argument and respond point by point, but in the pages allowed me, I must respond selectively.

It is worth noting that Professor Jensen's argument is highly sophisticated in terms of both psychometrics and population genetics. His explanations in these domains are as briefly clear and as uncluttered with unnecessary jargon as any I have seen. He defines intelligence operationally in terms of what the IQ tests measure, of what accounts for the co-variation among test scores (Spearman's g), and of the relations of these measures to scholastic ability (whence the tests come originally in the work of Binet and Simon), to occupational status, and to job success. What the IQ measures and what Spearman's g represents psychologically, he writes, "is prob-

ably best thought of as a capacity for abstract reasoning and problem-solving ability" (p. 19), and is also epitomized in cross-modality transfer. He recognizes clearly that intelligence is a phenotype, not a genotype:

> . . . the IQ is not constant, but, like all other developmental characteristics, is quite variable early in life and becomes increasingly stable throughout childhood. By age 4 or 5, the IQ correlates about .70 with IQ at age 17, which means that approximately half [r^2] of the variance in adult intelligence can be predicted as early as age 4 or 5. (p. 18)

He does not note here that this increasing stability is based on a part-whole relationship wherein the IQs of successive ages constitute increasing proportions of IQ of the criterion age. He asks the traditional geneticists' question of how much variation (*i.e.*, individual difference) in measures of the intelligence phenotype of our population can be accounted for in terms of variation in genetic factors. He then presents the evidence for heritability (H) approximating .80 in European and North American Caucasian populations. Jensen explicitly accepts that the value of H holds only for the population sampled, and that under changed conditions the value of H could be expected to change.

Despite this psychometric and genetic sophistication in Professor Jensen's discourse, I find little evidence of an inclination to broaden the nomological net to include evidence from social psychology, from the physiological effects of early experience in animals, and from history to help interpret the psychometric and genetic findings. I find wanting an appreciation of how what Sumner (1906) called the "folkways" and Sherif (1936) has called the "social norms" can operate to produce radically different ecological niches for developing infants and children of differing social classes and races. I find wanting also an appreciation of individual lives as dynamic processes in which the preprogrammed information in the genetic code gets cumulatively modified in both rate and direction by successive adaptations to the circumstances of the ecological niche. Thus, Professor Jensen's argument sums up to a sophisticated justification of what I have termed, and perhaps unfortunately, "fixed intelligence" and "predetermined development" (Hunt, 1961). Except for the educational significance he finds in the results of his own investigations, his argument allows only a eugenic approach to the problems of incompetence and poverty. With the exception of this loophole it is a counsel of despair, for our increasingly technological society cannot afford a century or two of selective breeding.

POINTS OF AGREEMENT

Even though my own theoretical predilections (or prejudices, perhaps) differ sharply from those of Professor Jensen, I have found many points in his paper with which I agree heartily. We agree, albeit for different reasons, that the concept of the "average child" is highly unfortunate in education. I find myself delighted with his thumbnail sketch of the central features of that traditional educational practice which has consequently evolved in Europe and America. It is the best I have ever seen. Unlike Jensen, however, I do not find imagining radically different forms so difficult even though I recognize that changing our educational folkways will be exceedingly difficult.

I agree that there is abundant evidence of genetic influences on behavior and that one can increase or decrease by selective breeding the measures of any phenotypic trait which has been investigated, but I believe from evidence omitted in Jensen's discourse that what Dobzhansky has termed the "range of reaction" (Sinott, Dunn, & Dobzhansky, 1958, p. 22ff) is probably greater for intelligence than it is for many other characteristics which depend less on what I suspect are cumulative effects of successive adaptations.

I agree that it is essentially meaningless to speak of "culture free" and of "culture fair" tests, and yet I also agree that Cattell (1963) has made, on the basis of differences within the intercorrelations, "a conceptually valid distinction between two aspects of intelligence, *fluid* and *crystallized*" (p. 13).

I agree with Jensen that the technological advances in our culture make it highly important to raise the intelligence, the educational attainments, and/or the general competence of those people who now comprise the bottom quarter of our population in measures of this cluster of characteristics. I agree that the national welfare policies we established in the 1930s have probably operated in disgenic fashion, and that it is highly important to establish welfare policies which will encourage initiative and probably, in consequence, help foster positive genotypic selection.

I could not agree more completely than I do with Professor Jensen's statement that:

> The variables of social class, race, and national origin are correlated so imperfectly with any of the valid criteria on which [social] decisions [with respect to individuals] should depend, or, for that matter, with any behavioral characteristic, that these background factors are irrelevant as a basis for dealing with individuals—as students, as employees, as neighbors. (p. 78)

Finally, for me the most interesting portion of Professor Jensen's paper is to be found in the results of his own investigations. The absence of class differences in what he calls "associative" learning, despite substantial differences in "cognitive" learning, is exceedingly interesting. Although I may well give a quite different interpretation of the basis for these findings than does Professor Jensen, I agree equally strongly with the educational implication he draws from his findings. *One does not provide equality of educational opportunity by submitting all children to the lock-step and by providing them with a single way in which to develop their genotype potential.* Variation in genotypes combines with variation in early experience to call for an increased individualization of education. (Jensen's discussion is on pp. 6–8, 111–117.)

POINTS OF DISAGREEMENT

Although I have found many points in Jensen's paper with which I can heartily agree, I have also found others with which I can just as heartily disagree. These are, first, several matters concerned with the measurement, the distribution, the development, and the nature of intelligence; second, the nature of his emphasis on biological versus psychological and social factors in behavioral development and the implications he draws for the relatively fixed nature of the existing norms for "intelligence." Third is Jensen's implicitly limited view of the learning process, coupled with his apparent lack of appreciation of the cumulative and dynamic implications of existing evidence of plasticity in the rate of behavioral development. Fourth are the implications which he draws for class and race differences from the measures of heritability of the IQ in European and American Caucasians. Finally, comes a disagreement about the wisdom of his opening sentence that "compensatory education has been tried and it apparently has failed" in the light of his avowed predilection for keeping all hypotheses open to investigation (and hopefully to technological development) as well as debate.

MATTERS CONCERNED WITH INTELLIGENCE

First, I find definitions of intelligence in terms of existing psychometric operations highly unsatisfying. Even though it was J. P. Guilford who introduced me to psychology and attracted me to the field largely with his discourse on aptitude testing and its implications for vocational guidance, I must confess that I have long distrusted the statistical operations of correlational analysis and averaging once they leave me without at least an intuitive connection with behavioral and biological observables. Thus, when Jensen remarks that Spearman's g-factor has "stood like a rock of Gibraltar," I find it hard to take seriously his avowance that "we should not reify g as an entity, of course, since it is only a hypothetical construct intended to explain covariation among

tests" (p. 9). The g-factor explains on the average some 50% of the total variation in individual differences. Jensen notes further that "as the tests change, the nature of g will also change, and a test which is loaded, say, .50 on g when factor analyzed among one set of tests may have a loading of .2% or .8%, or some other value, when factor analyzed among other sets of tests" (p. 11). Apparently g is the most malleable and ameoboid rock extant. Jensen, however, makes a partial escape from his self-made operational cul-de-sac by arguing that intelligence is but one component of ability and competence. Thus, his own investigative finding that children of lower-class background can manage "associative" learning as well as children of middle-class background provides him with a ray of educational hope.

Professor Jensen devotes a substantial portion of his paper to an explication of the existing distribution of IQs in the population. He makes much of the basic normality of the distribution and the deviations from normality for pathological retardates and the "bulge" between 70 and 90 which he attributes to "the combined effects of severe environmental disadvantages and of emotional disturbances that depress test scores" (p. 27). Professor Jensen acknowledges that the traditional procedures provided by Binet and Simon for determining the mental age of any test-item forces the scores to assume a normal distribution, and he honestly admits that "the argument about the distribution of intelligence thus appears to be circular" (p. 21). He then argues that the only way out is to look for evidence that intelligence scales behave like an "interval scale." He finds the most compelling evidence from studies of the inheritance of intelligence. Am I emitting a mere flippancy if I respond that apparently, for Jensen, going twice around the circular argument removes its circularity? Actually, I find no serious fault with this discussion of the existing distribution of IQs in the population until Jensen begins to draw from it the implication that this existing distribution is fixed in human nature for all time, or until selective breeding alters it. My reasons for finding fault with this implication are derived from enlarging the nomological net to include evidence from outside the domains of psychometrics and population genetics as applied to intelligence, and I hope my argument will gradually become both clear and forceful.

On the matter of the stability of the IQ, Professor Jensen disavows any claim for constancy. On the other hand, he appears to view intellectual development as a matter of static, largely predetermined, growth. Thus he takes the findings of Bloom (1964) and emphasizes that half of the variance in the IQ at age seventeen can be predicted from IQs at ages of four and five years. If one considers the development of intelligence to be in substantial degree a function of the cumulative effects of informational and intentional interaction with physical and social circumstances, and if one takes into account the fact that the longitudinal predictive value of the IQ involves part-whole relationships, the emphasis can readily be reversed. Thus, just as embryologists have said that half of the epigenetic changes in a human life occur between conception and the end of the embryonic phase after only two months of gestation, it is more than a mere analogy to say that half of the epigenetic changes in mental development have typically taken place by about age four. This latter position puts the emphasis on the importance of early experience (including the intrauterine and nutritional) as both Bloom and I have been wont to do.

Perhaps I am wrong in inferring that Professor Jensen at least implicitly conceives a sharp distinction between tests of intelligence and tests of educational achievement, for he emphasizes that the former has substantially a higher heritability (80%) than the latter (approximately 60%). Because the main thrust of his paper is to emphasize the high heritability of intelligence, one can understand his omission of the papers by both Ferguson (1954, 1956, 1959) on the relation of learning to human ability and Humphreys (1962a, 1962b)[2] on the point that tests of intelligence and tests of academic achievement differ only in degree, in the sense that the former assess the results of incidental learning typically distant in time from that of the testing while the latter assess the results of learning in specific educational situations near in time to the testing. When one combines the evidence and arguments from these papers with a conception of intelligence as a cumulative, dynamic product of the ongoing informational and intentional interaction of infants and young children with their physical and social circumstances, one must call into question the notion of intellectual development as essentially a static function of growth, largely predetermined in rate.

THE DUALISM OF BIOLOGICAL VERSUS PSYCHOLOGICAL (AND SOCIAL) FACTORS

Professor Jensen quotes with high approval a paragraph by Edward Zigler to the effect that:

> Not only do I insist that we take the biological integrity of the organism seriously, but it is also my considered opinion that our nation has more to fear from unbridled environmentalists than from those who point to such integrity as one factor in the determination of development. . . . It is the environmentalists who have placed on the defensive any thinker who, perhaps impressed by the revolution in biological thought stemming from discoveries involving DNA-RNA phenomena, has had the temerity to suggest that certain behaviors may be in part the product of read-out mechanisms residing within the programmed organism (p. 29).

[2]Professor Hunt calls attention to research that was omitted in the pre-publication draft on which this discussion is based. The Humphreys data is included in the printed version of Jensen's article as a note on page 58. The reader's attention is directed to the opposite interpretations each author draws from the research. In effect, Hunt argues that the correlation of IQ and academic achievement indicates that IQ is dynamic and cumulative; Jensen holds to his conception of IQ as largely predetermined, and suspects that he has overestimated the malleability of academic achievement.

I believe that I have regularly taken "the biological integrity of the organism" seriously. Taking seriously the biological integrity of the organism is the major reason for my repeated concern with what I call "the problem of the match" between what has been built into the organism—through the program of maturation and through previous informational interaction with circumstances—and how newly encountered circumstances affect his motivation and continuing development (see Hunt, 1961, pp. 268–288; 1965; 1966, 118–132). Also motivated by serious concern for the biological integrity of the organism is an extended effort to develop sequential scales of psychological development (Uzgiris & Hunt, 1969) and to look toward what one might term a "natural curriculum" for the fostering of early psychological development. In addition to these remarks, which may be regarded as defensive, it may be worth noting that the RNA (ribonucleic acid) phenomena are chiefly products of an organism's adaptation to circumstances.

Throughout his paper, and especially when he comes to the section on "how the environment works," the thrust of Professor Jensen's argument is to place psychological factors (and the social subset of these factors) in a kind of dualistic opposition to biological factors. Having implicitly constructed the dualism, he proceeds to denigrate the importance of the psychological set relative to the importance of biological set.

First, let me dispose of the dualism. Ample evidence has now accumulated to show that the consequences of informational interaction with circumstances, through the ears and the eyes (and especially the latter for the evidence extant), is quite as biological in nature as the effects of nutrition or of genetic constitution. Interaction through the eyes, especially early in life, has genuine neuroanatomical and neurochemical consequences.

Much of this evidence has its conceptual origin in the theorizing of Donald Hebb (1949). It was Hebb's hypothesis that the development of form-vision derives from sensory (S-S) integration that prompted Riesen and his colleagues to rear chimpanzees in the dark in order to determine the effect of light stimulation on the function and structure of the visual system. As is now widely known, a period of 16 or 18 months in total darkness produced drastic effects. On the functional side, there were a number of defects which proved essentially irreversible in those chimpanzees submitted to total darkness for 16 months or longer (see Riesen, 1958). On the side of anatomical structure, a defect was manifest during life as a pallor of the optic disc (Riesen, 1958). When these animals were sacrificed after some six years in full daylight, a histological examination brought out clear evidence of defects in the ganglion-cell layer of the retinae and in the optic nerve. These anatomical consequences within the visual system had themselves been irreversible (Chow, Riesen, & Newell, 1957). The histological examination also got evidence of a paucity of Mueller fibers within the retinal ganglia, and it should be noted that Mueller fibers are glia (Rasch, Swift, Riesen, & Chow, 1961).

Another line of investigation has stemmed from Hydén's (1961) biochemical hypothesis that memory and learning involve the metabolism of ribonucleic acid (RNA) in an interaction between neural and glial cells of the retina and brain. Hydén's hypothesis prompted Brattgård (1952) to rear rabbits in the dark. Histochemical analysis of the retinae of these dark-reared rabbits revealed a deficiency in RNA production of their retinal ganglion cells as compared with their light-reared litter-mates. Since then histological and histochemical effects of dark-rearing have been found not only in chimpanzees (Chow, et al., 1957) and rabbits, but also in kittens (Weiskrantz, 1958) and in rats (Liberman, 1962).

I have often expressed the wish that someone would extend this line of investigation centrally in the visual system to the lateral geniculate body of the thalamus and to the striate area of the occipital lobe. After regaling Robert Reichler of the National Institute of Mental Health with this evidence just outlined, I expressed again this wish to see an extension to the lateral geniculate body and to the striate area of the occipital lobe. Dr. Reichler responded excitedly that this had been done. In late October, he had attended an NIMH-supported conference on dyslexia where Dr. F. Valverde of Cajal's Institute in Madrid had presented a paper authored with Ruiz-Marcos which indeed reported such investigations with highly interesting findings. I am indebted to Dr. Reichler for letting me see a copy of the conference draft of the paper by Valverde and Ruiz-Marcos.

As yet I have had no opportunity to examine the evidence in detail, but their paper reviews an investigation by Wiesel and Hubel (1963), in which were described clearly evident defects in the cell areas of the lateral geniculate bodies on the thalami of kittens corresponding to the single eye deprived of vision for three months. Their paper also reviews evidence from investigations by Gyllesten (1959), by Coleman and Riesen (1968), by Ruiz-Marcos and Valverde (1968), by Valverde (1967, 1968), and by Valverde and Esteban (1968). All these investigations have shown clearly the effects of being reared in the dark, sometimes for only a very few days, on the fine structure of the striate area of the occipital lobe which is the center for visual reception. These effects show in the dendritic fields, and they show especially as a diminution in the number of spines on the dendrites of the large pyramidal cells in the striate area of the visual cortex (Valverde, 1967, 1968). Through electron-microscopy it was determined that the number of spines on these dendrites, in intervals at given distances from the wall of the cell body, is ordinarily very highly correlated with mouse age, but when mice are reared for various periods in the dark, this correlation is markedly diminished (Ruiz-Marcos & Valverde, 1968), and the diminution is especially marked for the days immediately after the eyes open. Clearly the psychological factor of dark-rearing produces neuroanatomical and neuro-

chemical effects not only in the eye but in the thalamus and in the visual area of the cortex. Thus, this psychological factor of visual function appears to be quite as biological in its consequences as are the consequences of nutrition and genotype.

Dark-rearing produces just the kind of anatomical effects one might envisage from Hebb's (1949) concepts of "cell assemblies" and "phase sequences." I see no reason to think that such processes should be less likely in human beings than in rodents. It takes little imagination, moreover, to extrapolate from these findings. I suspect that sensorimotor functioning, especially during the earliest phases of behavioral development in the first and second years, influences the development of such things as the spines on dendrites throughout the brain. The success of Hydén and Egyhazi (1962) in identifying with remarkable specificity the locus of the neuroanatomical and neurochemical effects of rats learning to climb a guy-rope suggests that each coordination, between vision-and-hand motion or between eye-function and ear-function, has its own neuro-electrical-chemical-anatomical equipment. I suspect that when such equipment has emerged as the consequence of a given bit of functional accommodation or learning, it can readily be employed in other functioning and thereby become the basis for the transfer of training. Moreover, as equipment has been developed in many domains, it can in all likelihood become one of the bases for the positive intercorrelation among tested abilities which Spearman called g.

In his section on "how the environment works" Professor Jensen contends that "below a certain threshold of environmental adequacy, deprivation can have a markedly depressing effect upon intelligence. But above this threshold, environmental variations cause relatively small differences in intelligence." He contends further: "The fact that the vast majority of the populations sampled in studies of the heritability of intelligence are above this threshold level of environmental adequacy accounts for the high values of the heritability estimates and the relatively small proportion of IQ variance attributable to environmental influences" (p. 60). The evidence of increase in the development of brain structures following enrichments of early experience is hardly consonant with this position. Altman and Das (1964), for instance, have reported a higher rate of multiplication of glial cells in the cerebral cortices of rats reared in "enriched environments" and in rats reared in the "impoverished environments" of laboratory cages. In another extended program of such investigation which has been underway for more than a decade at the University of California, Bennett, Diamond, Krech, and Rosenzweig (1964) and Krech, Rosenzweig, and Bennett (1966) have done a long series of studies which indicate that rats reared in relatively complex environments have shown cortical tissue greater in weight and thickness than that of litter-mates reared in the simpler environments of laboratory cages. Here "complexity" has been defined in terms of the variety of objects available for the rats to perceive and to manipulate and the variety of different kinds of space to be explored. These rats reared in complex environments have also shown histochemical effects in the form of higher total acetylcholinesterase activity of the cortex than the cage-reared rats. Associated with these neuroanatomical and neurochemical effects of the life history, moreover, is a higher level of maze-problem-solving ability in the rats reared under complex circumstances than in those reared in laboratory cages.

The definition "of a certain threshold of environmental adequacy" is unclear, but it can be said that cage-rearing is the standard ecological niche of laboratory rats and that it involves no serious absence of light and sound. Contrary to Jensen's position that it is only below "a certain threshold of environmental adequacy" that there can be a markedly depressing effect on intelligence, I am inclined to suspect that the basic central equipment for the inter-modal transfer which Jensen conceives to be a prime example of Spearman's g can be greatly modified by the informational interaction of the human infant and young child with his physical and social circumstances. I say that I suspect this is the state of affairs. This statement has not been proven, but the thrust of the existing evidence points strongly in the direction which I have indicated.

LEARNING AND THE CUMULATIVE IMPLICATION OF PLASTICITY IN EARLY DEVELOPMENT

The traditional view of heredity and environment held them to be essentially separate processes in development, and maturation was conceived to be the developmental representative of heredity, with learning the developmental representative of environment. We have just seen that the young organism's adaptations to the environment influence maturation, but we have not clarified the nature of learning.

Learning is typically conceived in terms of the ways it has been investigated in the laboratory. Investigations of learning still bear the marks of the pioneers: Ebbinghaus for rote learning, Bryan and Harter for skill learning, Pavlov for classical conditioning, and, for the fourth general category, C. Lloyd Morgan and E. L. Thorndike for trial-and-error with reinforcement, Clark L. Hull for instrumental learning motivated by drive and reinforced by drive-reduction, and B. F. Skinner for operant conditioning. If one examines the developmental observations of Piaget (1936, 1937), wherein accommodation and assimilation become the terms for learning, one finds several kinds of effects of encounters with circumstances which have failed to get investigated in psychological laboratories. If one examines the almost forgotten work on attention, the work of the ethologists, and the work of social psychologists on attitude change and communication, one finds other kinds of modification of function, and presumably of neuroanatomy and neurochemistry, through encounters with informational circumstances which do not get into the chapters on learning. I believe I have identified eight kinds of learning seldom studied for themselves which appear to be operative in psychological development (Hunt, 1966). The number is unimportant; the point is that Professor Jensen's distinction between associative learning and cognitive learning is but a conceptual drop in the bucket. His finding that the class-differences evident for cognitive learning are not evident for associative learning is exceedingly interesting, however.

What appears to be wrong with Professor Jensen's implicit conception of learning is that it consists only (or basically) of those minor changes of function which can be effected within short intervals of time in the laboratory. Thus, he speaks of learning ability as a kind of static trait which accounts for the number of trials required for the assimilation or mastery of relatively miniscule accommodations.

Except in the case where he calls for studies of the transfer of learning before age five to the cognitive functions after age six (in which I join him), I miss in his discourse any strong appreciation of what must be the cumulative dynamic effects of adaptations at one phase of development on the adaptations of later phases. Thus, he can write of the influence of the genotype "reading through the environmental overlay."

Although Professor Jensen acknowledges that such "extreme sensory and motor restrictions in environments such as those described by Skeels and Dye (1939) and Davis (1947), in which the subjects had little sensory stimulation of any kind and little contact with adults" (p. 60) resulted in large deficiencies in IQ, he tends to minimize their importance. He notes in favor of his view that the orphanage children of Skeels and Dye gained in IQ from an average of 64 at 19 months of age to 96 at age six as a result of being given "social stimulation and placement in good homes at between two and three years of age" (p. 60). He notes that when these children were followed up

as adults, they were found to be average citizens in their communities, and their own children had an average IQ of 105 and were doing satisfactorily in school. Similarly, Davis (1947) reported the more extreme case of Isabel, who had an IQ of 30 at age six, but who, when put into an intensive educational program at age six, developed a normal IQ by age eight. From these examples, he contends that even extreme environmental deprivation need not permanently result in below-average intelligence.

Professor Jensen neglects to report the results of the follow-up study of the adult status of the Skeels-Dye children left in the orphanage (Skeels, 1966). Those who were removed from the orphanage before they were 30 months old and placed on a women's ward at a state institution for the mentally retarded, and then later adopted, were all self-supporting and none became a ward of any institution. Their median educational attainment was 12th grade. Four had one or more years of college work, one received a bachelor's degree and went on to graduate school. On the other hand, of the 12 children who remained in the orphanage, one died in adolescence following continued residence in a state institution for the mentally retarded, and four remained on the wards of such institutions. With one exception, those employed were marginally employed, and only two had married. It is true that the effects of early experience can be reversed; the point to be made here, however, is that the longer any species of organism remains under any given kind of circumstances, the harder it is to change the direction of the effects of adaptation to those circumstances.

Even in infants reared in middle-class homes evidence exists of a remarkable degree of plasticity in early behavioral development. In my own laboratory, for instance, Greenberg, Uzgiris, and Hunt (1968) have shown that putting an attractive pattern over the cribs of such infants beginning when they are five weeks old, reduces the age at which the blink-response becomes regular for a target-drop of 11.5 inches from a mean of 10.4 weeks, in infants whose mothers agreed to put nothing over the cribs of their infants for 13 weeks, to a mean of 7 weeks. In the familiar terms of the IQ ratio this represents an increase of 48 points for the blink-response. The differences between the groups in mean age for drops of 7 inches and for drops of 3 inches becomes progressively less. Thus, the findings are quite consonant with those studies of the twenties and thirties which found the effects of practice on given skills to be evanescent. On the other hand, if one provides circumstances which permit the hastened looking schema, indicated by the blink-response, to be incorporated into a more complex sensorimotor organization, its early availability should be reflected in increased advancement. This is precisely the sort of thing one finds in the work of White and Held (1966). In their work, the capacity for visual accommodation permits looking to become incorporated into eye-hand coordination. In a normative study of successive forms of eye-hand coordination, top-level reaching failed to appear until the median age of the group was 145 days. The second enrichment program reduced the median age for top-level reaching from this 145 days to 87 days—an advance of 66 points in the familiar terms of the IQ ratio for this final level of eye-hand coordination. Hypothetically, at least, one should be able to extrapolate on this principle, but as yet experimental evidence is unavailable to confirm the hypothesis.

Cumulative and dynamic implications of this existing evidence of plasticity in the rate of behavioral development raises the question of what Dobzhansky has termed the "norm of reaction" (see Sinnott, Dunn, & Dobzhansky, 1958, p. 22ff) for the case of human intelligence. Although no one can now say how large the cumulative modifications in measurements of human intelligence might possibly be, Wayne Dennis (1966) has published a study which is highly relevant. The study examines the mean IQs from the Draw-a-Man Test for groups of typical children aged six and

seven years from some 50 cultures over the world. Florence Goodenough (1926) devised this test to be culture free. Its freedom from cultural influences was called into question, however, when typical Hopi Indian children of six and seven turned up with a mean of 124 on the test (Dennis, 1942). This mean of 124 equaled the mean IQ for samples of upper-middle-class suburban American children and for samples of children from Japanese fishing villages. The lower end of this distribution of mean IQs find nomadic Bedouin Arab children of Syria with a mean IQ of 52. Here, then, we find direct evidence of a norm of reaction of about 70 points in Draw-a-Man IQ. The most obvious correlate of this variation in mean IQ is amount of contact with the pictorial art. Among Moslem Arab children, whose religion prohibits representative art as graven images, the range in mean Draw-a-Man IQ is from 52 to 94, and the most obvious correlate of this norm of reaction is contact with groups of the Western culture. This is the most direct evidence concerning the norm of reaction for human intelligence of which I know. While the factor structure of the Draw-a-Man Test is probably considerably less complex than is that of either the Stanford-Binet or the Weschler Children's Scale, within our own culture Draw-a-Man scores correlate about as well with those from these other more complex scales as scores on them with each other.

In connection with this discussion of the norm of reaction, which Professor Jensen mentions but to which he gives little attention, it is interesting to note what he omits from a paragraph quoted from the geneticist, Dobzhansky (1968b, p. 554 quoted in Jensen, p. 30). The omitted portion reads:

Although the genetically-guaranteed educability of our species makes most individuals trainable for most occupations, it is highly probable that individuals have more genetic adaptability to some occupations than to others. Although almost everybody could become, if properly brought up and properly trained, a fairly competent farmer, or a craftsman of some sort, or a soldier, sailor, tradesman, teacher, or priest, certain ones would be more easily trainable to be soldiers and others to be teachers, for instance. It is even more probable that only a relatively few individuals would have the genetic wherewithal for certain highly specialized professions, such as musician, or singer, or poet, or high achievement in sports or wisdom or leadership.

Finally, I am among those few who are inclined to believe that mankind has not yet developed and deployed a form of early childhood education (from birth to age five) which permits him to achieve his full genotypic potential. Those studies which so sharply disconfirmed what R. B. Cattell (1937) once characterized as a "galloping plunge toward intellectual bankruptcy" (see Hunt, 1961, p. 337ff) can probably be repeated again after 20 to 25 years if our society supports the necessary research and development of educational technology to enable us to do early childhood education properly. In connection with this possibility of a general increase in intelligence, we should consider also what has happened to the stature of human beings. It appears to have increased by nearly a foot without benefit of selective breeding or natural selection. While visiting Festival Park in Jamestown, Virginia recently, we examined the reproductions of the ships which brought the settlers from England. They were astoundingly small. The guide reported that the average height of those immigrants was less than 5 feet, and that the still famous Captain John Smith was considered to be unusually tall at 5 feet 2 inches. The guide's "instruction book" puts the authority for these statements in the Sween Library at William and Mary. I have been unable to check the evidence, but scrutiny of the armor on display in various museums in England implies that the stature of the aristocrats who wore it must typically have been about the reported size of those immigrants to Jamestown. Also, the guide for the U.S. *Constitution* includes in his spiel the statement that the

headroom between decks needed to be no more than 5 feet and 6 inches. This increase in height can occur within a single generation. Among the families of German Russians whom I knew while growing up in Nebraska it was typical to find the average height of the children several inches above mid-parent height, and I can cite instances in which the increase was approximately a foot where all the children were sons. Inasmuch as Professor Jensen resorts repeatedly to the analogy between intelligence and stature, such evidence of an increase in the average height for human beings, the reasons for which are still a matter largely of conjecture, should have some force in increasing the credibility for the genetic potentiality for a general increase in intelligence.

IMPLICATIONS FROM EXISTING MEASURES OF HERITABILITY

Professor Jensen recognizes explicitly that measures of heritability may change as the nature of the population changes. Nevertheless, from these existing measures of heritability in European and American Caucasians, he draws implications for both class and race differences which, in view of the considerations already presented, I simply cannot accept at face value.

From the physiological evidence, from the fact that one can readily hasten the development of sensorimotor organizations in children of the middle class, and from the fact that technological advances have quite regularly increased the mean IQ of populations, I see no reason to believe that the current distribution of intelligence is fixed by the biological nature of man, despite the fact that heritability studies indicate that approximately 80% of the individual variance in the IQ can be attributed to variations in genotypes. Moreover, in view of the sharp contrast between the child-rearing practices of the middle class with those of the people of poverty, I see no reason to believe that the class differences now evident are inevitable. Finally, inasmuch as black people have had more than a century in slavery and then, since the war between the States, another century in both poverty and the bondage of "folkways," I see no reason to consider existing race differences as inevitable.

The contrast between the child-rearing of the middle class and that of the poor needs to be better understood. A study by Maxine Schoggen at the Demonstration and Research Center for Early Education at the George Peabody College for Teachers in Nashville is bringing out this contrast more forcefully than any other of which I know. The studies concern samples of eight families of professional status, eight of rural poverty, and eight of urban poverty. The families of rural poverty are white; those of urban poverty are black. In each family there is a 3-year-old who is the target-child. Observer-recorders become so well acquainted with these families that they become like furniture. They record for equal periods of time in functionally equivalent situations like meal time, bed time, and the time when the older children return from school. The observers record the instances of social interaction initiated by the older members of the family toward the target-child, and their reactions to the interaction initiated by the child. These are termed "environmental force units." From the evidence available, the older members of professional families initiated somewhat more than twice as many "environmental force units" per unit of time toward the 3-year-old in their family as did the older members in the families of either urban or rural poverty. I have asked Dr. Schoggen about how much difference there might be in the frequency of units in which the older members of the family would call upon a child to note the shape, the size, the color, or even the placement of objects and persons. She has indicated that this is quite common in professional families, but that it seldom occurs in the families of poverty except in connection with errands. Then the child usually gets castigated for his stupidity. On the verbal side, professional parents often call upon their three-year-olds to formulate such matters in language of their own, but families of either rural or urban poverty almost never do. One should recall in this connection that "warm democratic" rearing was associated with an average gain of 8 IQ points, over a three year period between the ages of approximately three or four to six or seven, in the study of Baldwin, Kalhorn, and Breese (1945), while the mean IQ dropped a point or two in the children of parents employing what these authors characterized as "passive-neglectful" and "actively-hostile" child-rearing (Baldwin, 1955, p. 523). This contrast between the rearing practices in families of professional status with those in families of either rural or urban poverty appears to be sharper than that between the families utilizing the various kinds of child-rearing identified by Baldwin, et al. Few if any of the studies of heritability have included the truly poor, so they have missed this portion of the variation in the circumstances of rearing.

At least a substantial portion of parents of poverty can be taught, however, to be effective teachers of their young when they are given models to imitate, when the actions of the models are explained, and when home visitors are provided to bring the new ways of child-rearng into the home (Gordon and associates, 1969; Karnes, 1969; Klaus & Gray, 1968; Miller, 1968). Moreover, when parents are involved in the education of their young children, they communicate newfound practices to their neighbors and the parents themselves take a new lease on life. In the Karnes project, the mothers agreed that if they were to give each child the attention needed, they dare not have a new baby each year, and so they all enrolled at the local Planned Parenthood Clinic. Miller (1968) reports that in the extension of the Early Training Project a majority of the mothers have upgraded their skills, and the families in the projects have formed clubs—one in which husbands and wives bowl regularly.

It will be no easy matter to spread this kind of training to all the families of poverty throughout this country, but a start has been made in the

Parent and Child Centers which the Office of Economic Opportunity has established on a pilot basis.

The enrolling in the Planned Parenthood clinic suggests that this kind of enterprise in early childhood education instigates help to prevent some of the disgenic processes with which Professor Jensen and I are both concerned.

I applaud Professor Jensen's proposal to develop a curriculum based upon his finding that children of lower-class background are equal in "associative" learning to children of middle-class background. In doing so, he may ultimately help to raise the general level of competence, and even the intelligence defined as Spearman's g, in the next generation of those who receive the benefit of his efforts to develop new educational technology. Moreover, since the effects of early experience can be reversed, at least in part, if and when Professor Jensen builds educationally upon the capacity of children from lower-class background for "associative" learning, he will probably increase measures of their g-factor gradually. His program will also probably increase measures of Cattell's "crystallized" intelligence in his pupils. To a lesser degree his program may also increase measures of their "fluid" intelligence. Moreover, Professor Jensen's program could well contribute to an increase in the intelligence of the next generation.

If one views societal evolution as a process, the mean of the IQ on the basis of existing standardizations and the existing measures of heritability can well be seen as the pre-measures to be compared with post-measures (based in the case of the IQ, of course, on today's standardizations) 10 or 20 years hence.

THE OPENING SENTENCE

At one point in his paper, Professor Jensen makes an ardent plea for keeping all hypotheses open for debate and investigation. With this plea, I heartily agree.

Unfortunately, since social change is a process,

one cannot settle the issue between my reading of the broad range of evidence and his reading of contemporary evidence from existing distributions of IQs and contemporary measures of heritability, until these changes in the ecological niche of infants and young children, to be accomplished by the research, the development, and the deployment of early childhood education, have been available for at least a decade or two. Saying outright that "compensatory education has been tried and it apparently has failed" is but a half-truth. Moreover, it is but a half-truth which can help to boost the forces of reaction which could halt support for research on how to foster psychological development, for the development of technology of early childhood education, and for the deployment of that technology across the USA. Insofar as it succeeds in boosting these forces of reaction, it will leave the issue open only for debate. Once the support for investigation, development, and deployment has been removed, the differences between our readings of the evidence will no longer be open for "investigation."

Perhaps I should explain why Professor Jensen's sentence is but a half-truth. In this sentence, "compensatory education" implies Head Start, for it is Head Start which has been tried—at least a little. Project Head Start did deploy a form of early childhood education for which many had hopes of compensatory effects. It was hoped that giving children of the poor a summer or two or a year of nursery school, beginning at age four, would overcome the handicaps of their earlier rearing. I hoped it would, but I feared from the beginning that such broad deployment of a technology untested for the purpose might lead to an "oversell" which, with failure of the hopes, would produce an "overkill" in which would be lost, for who knows how long, the opportunity to bring into the process of social change, in the form of early childhood education, the implications of the various lines of evidence indicating the importance of early experience for intellectual development. The 1967 report of the U.S. Commission of Civil Rights is correct in stating that Head Start has not appreciably raised the educational achievement of the children who participated. There is, however, a reason which absolves compensatory education as such.

Maria Montessori in Italy and Margaret Mc-Millan of England established nursery schools to aid the children of the poor. These were brought to America along with the intelligence tests and just as the emphasis on learning by doing was becoming established. Nursery schools did not survive in America as aids for children of the poor. Rather, they got adapted for the children of the well-to-do who could pay for them. Moreover, when the psychoanalytic movement coalesced with Froebel's kindergarten movement and with the Child Study movement of G. Stanley Hall, the goal became one of freeing young children, for at least part of each day, from their mothers' strict disciplinary controls. Free play became the mode. Since such nursery schools constituted the only early education model available when Project Head Start began, traditional nursery school practice was the kind of early education deployed for the most part.

But Head Start is not synonymous with compensatory education. Professor Jensen knows this for he reviews a number of the investigations of compensation in one of the later sections of his paper. Compensatory education has not failed. Investigations of compensatory education have now shown that traditional play school has little to offer the children of the poor, but programs which made an effort to inculcate cognitive skills, language skills, and number skills, whether they be taught directly or incorporated into games, show fair success. A substantial portion of this success endures. If the parents are drawn into the process, the little evidence available suggests that the effect on the children, and on the parents as well, increases in both degree and duration. All this in seven years sounds to me like substantial success. Yet, we still have a long way to go before we shall have learned what an appro-priate curriculum for infants from birth to five might be. Thus, Jensen's opening statement is a half-truth, and a dangerous half-truth, placed out of context for dramatic effect.

Insofar as the behavioral and educational sciences get involved in manning the tiller of social change, the practitioners of these sciences must learn to think in terms of processes and they must learn to think of political and social consequences of how and what they write and say. It does no good to plead for keeping all hypotheses open for debate and investigation if the form of the debate removes support for the relevant investigation and for the development and deployment required for a meaningful test of the hypotheses. I find it hard to forgive Professor Jensen for that half-truth placed out of context for dramatic effect at the beginning of his paper.

How much *can* we boost IQ and scholastic achievement by deliberately altering the ecological niche of infants and young children, from birth to age five, through early childhood education? Who knows? As I read the evidence, the odds are strong that we can boost both IQ and scholastic achievement substantially, but we cannot know how much for at least two decades. Moreover, we shall never find out if we destroy support for the investigation of how to foster early psychological development, for the development of educational technology, and for the deployment of that technology.

References

Altman, J. & Das, G. D. Autoradiographic examination of the effects of enriched environment on the rate of glial multiplication in the adult rat brain. *Nature, 1964; 204, 1161–1165.*

Baldwin, A. L. *Behavior and development in childhood.* New York: Dryden Press, 1955.

Baldwin, A. L., Kalhorn, J. & Breese, F. H. Patterns of parent behavior. *Psychological Monographs, 1945, 58, No. 3, 1–75.*

Bennett, E. L., Diamond, M. C., Krech, D., & Rosenzweig, M. R. Chemical and anatomical plasticity of the brain. *Science,* 146, No. 3644 (1964), 610–619.

Bereiter, C., & Engelmann, S. *Teaching disadvantaged children in the preschool.* New York: Prentice Hall, 1966.

Bloom, B. S. *Stability and change in human characteristics.* New York: John Wiley & Sons, Inc., 1964.

Brattgård, S. O. The importance of adequate stimulation for the chemical composition of retinal ganglion cells during early post-natal development. *Acta Radiological* (Stockholm), 1952, Supplement 96, 1–80.

Cattell, R. B. *The fight for our national intelligence.* London: King, 1937.

Cattell, R. B. Theory of fluid and crystallized intelligence: a critical experiment. *Journal of Education Psychology,* 1963, 54, 1–22.

Chow, K. L., Riesen, A. H., & Newell, F. W. Degeneration of retinal ganglion cells in infant chimpanzees reared in darkness. *Journal of Comparative Neurology,* 1957, 107, 27–42.

Coleman, P. D., & Riesen, A. H. Environmental effects on cortical dendritic fields. I. Rearing in the dark. *Journal of Anatomy* (London), 1968, 102, 363–374.

Davis, K. Final note on a case of extreme isolation. *American Journal of Sociology,* 1947, 57, 432–457.

Dennis, W. The performance of Hopi Indian children on the Goodenough Draw-a-Man Test. *Journal of Comparative Psychology,* 1942, 34, 341–348.

Dobzhansky, T. On genetics, sociology, and politics. *Perspectives in Biology and Medicine,* 1968, 11, 544–554.

Ferguson, G. A. Learning and human ability: A theoretical approach. *Factor analysis and related techniques in the study of learning.* Edited by P. H. DuBois, W. H. Manning, & C. J. Spies. A report of a conference held at Washington University in St. Louis, Missouri, February, 1959. Technical Report No. 7, Office of Naval Research Contract No. Nonr 816 (02).

Goodenough, F. L. *The measurement of intelligence by drawings.* Yonkers-on-Hudson, New York: World Book Co., 1926.

Gordon, I. J. (ed.) *Reaching the child through parent education: The Florida approach.* Gainesville: Institute for Development of Human Resources, College of Education, University of Florida, 1969.

Greenberg, D., Uzgiris, I., & Hunt, J. McV. Hastening the development of the blink-response with looking. *Journal of Genetic Psychology,* 1968, 113, 167–176.

Gyllensten, L. Postnatal development of the visual cortex in darkness (mice). *Acta Morphologica* (Neerlando-Scandinavica), 1959, 2, 331–345.

Hebb, D. O. *The organization of behavior.* New York: John Wiley & Sons, Inc., 1949.

Humphreys, L. G. The nature and organization of human abilities. *The 19th Yearbook of the National Council on Measurement in Education.* Edited by M. Katz. Ames, Iowa, 1962a.

Humphreys, L. G. The organization of human abilities. *American Psychologist,* 1962b, 17, 475–483.

Hunt, J. McV. *Intelligence and experience.* New York: Ronald Press, 1961.

Hunt, J. McV. Intrinsic motivation and its role in psychological development. *Nebraska Symposium on Motivation,* 13. Edited by D. Levine. Lincoln: University of Nebraska Press, 1965.

Hunt, J. McV. Toward a theory of guided learning in development. In *Giving emphasis to guided learning.* Edited by R. H. Ojemann & K. Pritchett. Cleveland, O.: Educational Research Council, 1966.

Hunt, J. McV. Poverty versus equality of opportunity. In *The challenge of incompetence and poverty.* Urbana: University of Illinois Press (in press).

Hydén, H. Biochemical aspects of brain activity. *Man and civilization: Control of the mind.* Edited by S. M. Farber & R. H. L. Wilson. New York: McGraw-Hill, 1961.

Hydén, H., & Egyhazi, E. Nuclear RNA changes of nerve cells during a learning experiment in rats. *Proceedings of the National Academy of Science,* 1962, 48, 1366–1373.

Karnes, M. B. *A new role for teachers: Involving the entire family in the education of preschool disadvantaged children.* Urbana: University of Illinois, College of Education, 1969.

Klaus, R. A., & Gray S. The early training project for disadvantaged children: A report after five years. *Monographs of the Society for Research in Child Development,* 1968, 33, No. 4.

Krech, D., Rosenzweig, M. R., & Bennett, E. L. Environmental impoverishment, social isolation, and changes in brain chemistry and anatomy. *Physiology and Behavior.* London: Pergamon Press, 1966.

Liberman, R. Retinal cholinesterase and glycolysis in rats raised in darkness. *Science,* 1962, 135, 372–373.

Miller, J. O. *Diffusion of intervention effects.* Urbana: ERIC Clearinghouse for Early Childhood Education, University of Illinois, 1968.

Rasch, E., Swift, H., Riesen, A. H., & Chow, K. L. Altered structure and compositon of retinal cells in dark-reared mammals. *Experimental Cellular Research,* 1961, 25, 348–363.

Riesen, A. H. Plasticity of behavior: Psychological aspects. In H. F. Harlow & C. N. Woolsey (Eds.), *Biological and biochemical bases of behavior.* Madison: University of Wisconsin Press, 1958, 425–450.

Ruiz-Marcos, A., & Valverde, F. Mathematical model

of the distribution of dendritic spines in the visual cortex of normal and dark-raised mice. *Journal of Comparative Neurology* (in press).

Sherif, M. *The psychology of social norms.* New York: Harper, 1936.

Sinnott, E. W., Dunn, L. C., & Dobzhansky, T. *Principles of genetics.* New York: McGraw-Hill, 1958.

Skeels, H. M. Adult status of children with contrasting early life experiences. *Monographs of the Society for Research in Child Development,* 1966, 31 (No. 3), 1–66.

Skeels, H. M., & Dye, H. B. A study of the effects of differential stimulation of mentally retarded children. *Proceedings of the American Association of Mental Deficiency,* 1939, 44, 114–136.

Sumner, W. G. *Folkways.* Boston: Ginn & Co., 1906 (1940).

Uzgiris, I. C., & Hunt, J. McV. *Toward ordinal scales of psychological development in infancy* (in press).

Valverde, F. Apical dendritic spines of the visual cortex and light deprivation in the mouse. *Experimental Brain Research,* 1967, 3, 337–352.

Valverde, F. Structural changes in the area striata of the mouse after enucleation. *Experimental Brain Research,* 1968, 5, 274–292.

Valverde, F., & Esteban, M. E. Peristriate cortex of mouse: Location and the effects of enucleation on the number of dendritic spines. *Brain Research,* 1968, 9, 145–148.

Weiskrantz, L. Sensory deprivation and the cat's optic nervous system. *Nature,* 1958, 181, 1047–1050.

White, B. L., & Held, R. Plasticity of sensorimotor development in the human infant. In J. F. Rosenblith & W. Allinsmith (Eds.), *The causes of behavior: Readings in child development and educational psychology* (2nd edition). Boston: Allyn & Bacon, 1966.

Wiesel, T. N., & Hubel, D. H. Effects of visual deprivation on morphology and physiology of cells in the cat's lateral geniculate body. *Journal of Neurophysiology,* 1963, 26, 978–993.

#29 The Early Training Project: A Seventh-Year Report

Rupert A. Klaus

Susan W. Gray

This is a report at the end of fourth grade of a pre-school intervention project for children from low-income homes. Its purpose was to investigate whether one could offset progressive retardation in elementary school. Special experiences provided for the 44 experimental children were based upon variables associated with attitudes and aptitudes conducive to school achievement. Intensive work was done for 3 summers; in the remaining months there were weekly home visits. Over the years the experimental children remained significantly superior to control children on intelligence tests. On measures of language and achievement, trends still remained, but differences were no longer significant by the end of fourth grade. There is a slight but parallel decline across groups. Evidence is presented on younger siblings.

NOTE: Major financial support for this study was received from the National Institute of Mental Health, under Mental Health Project grant 5-R11-MH-765. Additional support for research staff during the later phases of the study was made possible through grant HD-00973 from the National Institute of Child Health and Human Development, from the Office of Education, contract OEC 3-7-070706-3118, and grant 9174 from the Office of Economic Opportunity.

SOURCE: From *Child Development*, vol. 41 (1970), 909–924. Copyright © 1970 by the Society for Research in Child Development, Inc. Reprinted with permission.

The Early Training Project has been a field research study concerned with the development and testing over time of procedures for improving the educability of young children from low income homes. The rationale, the general design and methodology, and findings through the second year of schooling have been reported in some detail by Klaus and Gray (1968). A briefer report, up to school entrance, is given in Gray and Klaus (1965). The purpose of this report is to present the findings at the end of the fourth grade, 3 years after all experimental intervention had ceased.

The major concern of the Early Training Project was to study whether it was possible to offset the progressive retardation observed in the public school careers of children living in deprived circumstances. In addition, the writers undertook to study the spillover effect upon other children in the community and upon other family members.

The general research strategy was one of attempting to design a research "package" consisting of variables which—on the basis of research upon social class, cognitive development, and motivation—might be assumed to be relevant to the school retardation, which is observed in deprived groups which at the same time might be subject to the effects of manipulation. Because this was a problem with major social implications, we also tried to design a general treatment approach which would be feasible to repeat on a large scale in the event that the procedure proved successful.

Subjects were 88 children born in 1958. Sixty-one of these lived in a city of 25,000 in the upper South. The remaining 27, who served as a distal control group, resided in a similar city 65 miles away. The children were all Negro. When we initiated the study the schools of the city were still segregated; we chose to work with Negro children because in this particular setting we had reason to believe that our chances of success were greater with this group.

The children were selected on the basis of parent's occupation, education, income, and housing conditions. At the beginning of the study, incomes were considerably below the approximate $3,000 used as the poverty line for a family of four. Occupations were either unskilled or semi-skilled; the educational level was eighth grade or below; housing conditions were poor. The median number of children per family at the beginning of the study was five; in about one-third of the homes there was no father present.

From the 61 children in the first city three groups were constituted by random assignment. The first group (T1) attended, over a period of three summers, a 10-week preschool designed to offset the deficits usually observed in the performance of children from disadvantaged homes. In addition, this group had 3 years of weekly meetings with a specially trained home visitor during those months in which the preschool was not in session. The second group (T2) had a similar treatment, except that it began a year later; the children received two summers of the special preschool and 2 years of home visits. The third group (T3) became the local control group, which received all tests but no intervention treatment. The fourth group (T4), the distal control group, was added to the design because of the somewhat ghetto-type concentration of Negroes in the first city. The local and distal control groups also made possible the study of spillover effects upon children and parents living in proximity to the experimental children. The general layout of the experimental design is given in Table 1. By reading down the columns, one may see the particular treatment and testing sequence followed for each of the four groups. Periodic testing is continuing for the children through elementary school.

THE INTERVENTION PROGRAM

The overall rationale for the intervention program grew out of the literature on child-rearing patterns in different social classes, plus the writers' own observations in low-income homes. On the basis of this study, the intervention program for children was organized around two broad classes of variables: attitudes relating to achievement, and aptitudes relating to achievement. Under attitudes we were particularly interested in achievement motivation, especially as it concerns school-type activities, in persistence, in ability to delay gratification; generally interested in typical school materials, such as books, crayons, puzzles, and the like. We were also concerned with the parents' attitude toward achievement, particularly in their aspirations for their children, especially as they related to schooling.

In the broad class of aptitude variables relating to achievement, we were particularly inter-

Table 1. Layout of general research design

TREATMENT TIME	THREE SUMMER SCHOOLS (T1)	TWO SUMMER SCHOOLS (T2)	LOCAL CONTROLS (T3)	DISTAL CONTROLS (T4)
First winter (1961–1962)	Criterion development, curriculum planning, general tooling up			
First summer (1962)	Pretest, summer school, posttest	Pretest, posttest	Pretest, posttest	Pretest, posttest
Second winter (1962–1963)	Home visitor contacts	. . .	. . .	. . .
Second summer (1963)	Pretest, summer school, posttest	Pretest, summer school, posttest	Pretest, posttest	Pretest, posttest
Third winter (1963–1964)	Home visitor contacts	Home visitor contacts	. . .	. . .
Third summer (1964)	Pretest, summer school, posttest	Pretest, summer school, posttest	Pretest, posttest	Pretest, posttest
Fourth winter (1964–1965)	Home visitor contacts	Home visitor contacts	. . .	. . .
Fourth summer (1965)	Follow-up tests	Follow-up tests	Follow-up tests	Follow-up tests
Fifth summer (1966)	Follow-up tests	Follow-up tests	Follow-up tests	Follow-up tests
Seventh summer (1968)	Follow-up tests	Follow-up tests	Follow-up tests	Follow-up tests

ested in perceptual and cognitive development and in language. Children from low-income homes have been shown to have deficits in these areas, all of which appear closely related to school success in the primary grades.

In the summer months, for 10 weeks the children met in assembled groups. Each of the two experimental groups had a head teacher, who was an experienced Negro first-grade teacher. There were, in addition, three or four teaching assistants. These assistants were divided about equally as to race and sex.

The work with the parents in the project was carried on largely through a home-visitor program in which a specially trained preschool teacher made weekly visits to each mother and child. Both the home program and the school program are described in considerable detail in Gray, Klaus, Miller, and Forrester (1966) and in Klaus and Gray (1968).

Prior to and after summer session, children in all four groups were tested on several instru-

ments. From the first summer certain standardized tests of intelligence and language were used, along with a number of less formal instruments. At the end of first grade, achievement tests were added. This testing schedule is shown in Table 1. In general the .05 level of significance was used.

RESULTS

The detailed results of the testing program through May 1966, the end of the second grade for the children, are given in Klaus and Gray (1968). This paper gives the results as they relate to the spring and summer testings of 1968 with some additional information on performance of younger siblings. The same kinds of analyses were used for the 1968 data as were used in the earlier paper.

In 1968 the following tests were administered to all children still residing in middle Tennessee: the Stanford-Binet, the Peabody Picture Vocabulary Test, and the Metropolitan Achievement Test. The analyses here reported are based only upon those children available for testing with the exception of one child in the distal control group.

The Stanford-Binet scores are given in Table 2, and are portrayed graphically in Figure 1. A Lindquist (1953) Type 1 analysis of the results of 1962–1968, in terms of IQ, gave a significant F of 4.45 for the four groups, F of 16.81 for repeated measures, and F for interaction of groups over time of 3.51. All of these were significant at the .01 level or beyond. Next an analysis was made by the use of orthogonal comparisons. These are given in Table 3. Here it may be seen that the two experimental groups remained significantly superior to the two control groups. The comparison of the first and the second experimental groups for 1968 showed an F of less than 1.00.

The comparison of the two control groups, however, yielded an F that, although not conventionally significant, was still large enough (3.52 where $F_{.95} = 3.96$) to be suggestive of a sharper decline in the distal than in the local control group. As was true of earlier analyses, the larger part of the variance appeared to be carried by the second experimental group and the distal control group.

The scores across the 10 administrations of the Peabody Picture Vocabulary Test are given in Table 4 in MA and IQ form. A Lindquist (1953) Type 1 analysis of variance was performed for the MA scores. For groups F was 5.16, indicating a significant effect of the experimental treatment upon the children's performance. For repeated testings F was 376.73, an effect that would be

Table 2. Mean Stanford-Binet MA and IQ scores for the four treatment groups at each administration

DATE OF ADMINISTRATION	T1($N = 19$) MA (MO)	IQ	T2($N = 19$) MA (MO)	IQ	T3($N = 18$) MA (MO)	IQ	T4($N = 23$) MA (MO)	IQ
May 1962	40.7	87.6	43.8	92.5	40.3	85.4	40.3	86.7
August 1962	50.7	102.0	46.9	92.3	44.3	88.2	43.4	87.4
May 1963	55.6	96.4	56.0	94.8	53.2	89.6	50.4	86.7
August 1963	59.3	97.1	60.6	97.5	55.0	87.6	52.3	84.7
August 1964	68.0	95.8	71.6	96.6	62.3	82.9	59.4	80.2
August 1965	83.8	98.1	86.3	99.7	79.4	91.4	77.0	89.0
June 1966	88.7	91.2	93.4	96.0	86.8	87.9	82.9	84.6
July 1968	106.0	86.7	111.4	90.2	104.7	84.9	96.2	77.7

Table 3. Orthogonal comparisons of treatment-group sums for Stanford-Binet IQ scores for the eight administrations

DATE OF ADMINISTRATION	HYPOTHESIS: T1 = T2 + T3 + T4 F-RATIO	CONCLUSION	HYPOTHESIS: T2 = T3 + T4 F-RATIO	CONCLUSION	HYPOTHESIS: T3 = T4 F-RATIO	CONCLUSION
August 1962	12.67*	T1 > T2 + T3 + T4	1.44	T2 = T3 + T4	<1.00	T3 = T4
May 1963	2.91	T1 = T2 + T3 + T4	3.36	T2 = T3 + T4	<1.00	T3 = T4

DATE OF ADMINISTRATION	HYPOTHESIS: T1 + T2 = T3 + T4 F-RATIO	CONCLUSION	HYPOTHESIS: T1 = T2 F-RATIO	CONCLUSION	HYPOTHESIS: T3 = T4 F-RATIO	CONCLUSION
May 1962	2.07	T1 + T2 = T3 + T4	1.53	T1 = T2	<1.00	T3 = T4
August 1963	18.53*	T1 + T2 > T3 + T4	<1.00	T1 = T2	<1.00	T3 = T4
August 1964	29.94*	T1 + T2 > T3 + T4	<1.00	T1 = T2	<1.00	T3 = T4
August 1965	11.12*	T1 + T2 > T3 + T4	<1.00	T1 = T2	<1.00	T3 = T4
June 1966	5.99*	T1 + T2 > T3 + T4	1.18	T1 = T2	<1.00	T3 = T4
July 1968	7.50*	T1 + T2 > T3 + T4	<1.00	T1 = T2	3.53	T3 = T4

*$p < .05$; $F_{.95} = 3.97$.

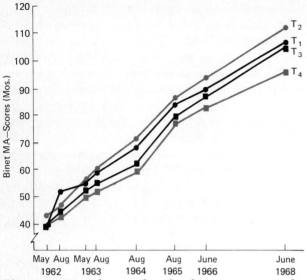

Figure 1 Mental ages for the four groups on the Stanford-Binet Test.

4, differences in mean scores were still apparent. Heterogeneity had increased over time, however, so that differences were no longer significant. In no analysis at any point of time was either experimental group significantly superior to the other. Nor did either control group show itself to be significantly superior to the other one.

The results for the Metropolitan Achievement Test are given in Table 5. A Lindquist (1953) Type 1 analysis was performed on each subtest, and orthogonal comparisons made. In the interest of brevity a table of orthogonal comparisons is not given. In 1965, at the end of the first grade, the experimental children were significantly superior on three of the four tests used at that time: word knowledge, word discrimination, and reading. For arithmetic computation score, F was less than 1.00. The local controls were also somewhat superior to the distal controls on these tests, an indication possibly of horizontal diffusion or, either in interaction or independently, a somewhat better instructional program. In 1966 five subtests were given. This time only two were significant, word knowledge and reading. On the other three tests, however, the F's ranged from 2.69 to 2.84, suggesting probabilities at about the .10 level. In neither year was T1 significantly superior to T2. The highest F was 1.16, where $F_{.95}$ is 3.97. In the comparisons of T3 and T4, T3 was

clearly expected when MA scores were used. These were selected in preference to IQ scores on this particular test since the IQ scores appear to lack discrimination at certain levels. The interaction between groups and time was nonsignificant. Orthogonals were next used. Here was found that T1 + T2 was significantly greater than T3 + T4 up until 1968, in which year differences were not significant. As may be seen from Table

Table 4. Mean PPVT mental age scores and IQ equivalents for the four treatment groups for the ten administrations

DATE OF ADMINISTRATION	TEST FORM	T1(N = 19) MA (MO)	IQ	T2(N = 19) MA (MO)	IQ	T3(N = 18) MA (MO)	IQ	T4(N = 23) MA (MO)	IQ
May 1962	A	30.0	69.5	30.6	70.1	29.4	66.4	32.2	74.0
August 1962	B	36.8	75.3	33.1	63.9	32.7	65.8	30.7	62.8
May 1963	A	44.8	79.0	40.7	69.6	39.1	69.3	39.5	69.8
August 1963	B	45.0	78.4	50.7	83.6	38.4	64.0	37.6	63.8
May 1964	B	55.6	81.2	60.1	85.5	45.8	65.4	48.7	70.9
August 1964	A	59.1	83.0	62.0	87.0	50.6	72.4	48.7	69.6
June 1965	B	74.2	89.0	76.2	90.3	67.6	83.0	67.3	84.0
August 1965	A	70.6	86.2	76.5	91.8	65.4	80.2	66.3	83.4
June 1966	A	78.1	86.7	81.9	89.3	75.4	83.9	71.2	80.7
July 1968	A	96.4	84.5	100.3	86.7	91.7	81.8	89.3	78.7

Table 5. Metropolitan achievement test grade equivalent mean scores for the various subtests for the three administrations

SUBTEST AND YEAR	T1	T2	T3	T4
Word knowledge:				
1965	1.69	1.73	1.79	1.37
1966	2.32	2.47	2.29	1.98
1968	3.58	3.90	3.54	3.27
Word discrimination:				
1965	1.68	1.81	1.82	1.37
1966	2.64	2.73	2.65	2.20
1968	3.73	3.95	3.76	3.47
Reading:				
1965	1.72	1.82	1.84	1.46
1966	2.52	2.75	2.56	2.11
1968	3.52	3.89	3.72	3.10
Arithmetic computation:				
1965	1.52	1.62	1.54	1.43
1966	2.41	2.55	2.49	2.05
1968	3.92	4.07	4.06	3.79
Spelling:				
1966	2.42	2.85	2.60	1.99
1968	4.26	4.69	4.24	3.67
Language:				
1968	3.52	4.00	3.63	3.17
Arithmetic problem solving and concepts:				
1968	3.31	3.54	3.75	3.26

superior to T4 on reading and arithmetic computation. On word knowledge, word discrimination, and spelling the F's ranged from 3.19 to 3.85, suggesting probabilities beyond the .10 level ($F_{.90}$ = 2.77). At the end of the fourth year no significant effects were found with the single exception of reading, on which T3 was superior to T4. There is some suggestion of residual effect since in six of the seven possible comparisons of experimentals and controls, the experimentals were superior. Also, on all seven possible comparisons the local control group was superior to the distal control group.

The Stanford-Binet was administered in all four groups to those younger siblings who were of testable age. This was first done in 1964 and again in 1966. Since the 1966 findings have not been previously reported, they are presented here in Table 6. In 1964, 57 children were tested. Fifty of these same children were tested again in 1966,

along with 43 additional siblings who were too young to test in 1964.

An analysis of covariance was performed on these scores, with the IQs at first testing of the target-age children used as the covariable. Also, where there were two young siblings in the same family, one was dropped, so that the analysis was based on 87 children. Separate analyses were also performed for the 1964 and the 1966 results of all children who were retested. In addition, an analysis was performed on the 1966 results for those children who were being tested for the first time.

On all younger siblings tested in 1966 F between groups was not significant at the .05 level (F = 3.97). It was significant beyond the .10 level, and therefore we made further analyses. Orthogonal comparisons were used, with the hypotheses shown in Table 7. This is the same general approach as used with the target children. All orthogonal comparisons showed significant differ-

Table 6. Initial Stanford-Binet scores of treatment group children and younger siblings in two testings

TESTING AND GROUPS	MEAN SCORES (FIRST TESTING, 1962) FOR TREATMENT GROUP CHILDREN WITH YOUNGER SIBLINGS			MEAN SCORES FOR YOUNGER SIBLINGS		
	N	CA	IQ	N	CA	IQ
1964 testing of younger siblings born in 1959 and 1960:						
T1	12	47	82	13	54	82
T2	16	46	89	21	53	83
T3	7	50	84	9	54	71
T4	12	48	88	14	62	74
1966 retesting of younger siblings initially tested in 1964:						
T1	12	47	82	13	78	85
T2	14	46	92	19	76	85
T3	5	46	82	7	76	78
T4	11	48	86	13	77	75
1966 testing of younger siblings born in 1961 and 1962:						
T1	10	44	87	11	58	84
T2	9	47	91	10	52	87
T3	7	48	83	9	56	76
T4	12	47	88	15	55	84
1966 testing of all younger siblings:						
T1	15	50	84	24	69	84
T2	17	46	91	29	68	86
T3	8	47	84	16	65	77
T4	15	47	86	28	63	80

ences for the testing of all younger siblings in 1966: the combined experimental group siblings were superior to the combined control group siblings; the T1 siblings were superior to the T2 siblings; and the T3 siblings were superior to the T4 siblings. When the children who were tested for the first time are separated out, it is clear, both in the 1966 and the 1964 data, that most of

Table 7. Orthogonal comparisons of Stanford-Binet scores of younger siblings

	HO:[a] T1 + T2 = T3 + T4		HO: T1 = T2		HO: T3 = T4	
	F-RATIO	CONCLUSION	F-RATIO	CONCLUSION	F-RATIO	CONCLUSION
All younger siblings 1966	3.48	T1 + T2 = T3 + T4	0.75	T1 = T2	0.00	T3 = T4
Younger siblings first tested in 1966	0.77	T1 + T2 = T3 + T4	0.04	T1 = T2	0.80	T3 = T4
Younger siblings re-tested in 1966:						
1964 results	8.13*	T1 + T2 > T3 + T4	0.74	T1 = T2	0.01	T3 = T4
1966 results	4.72*	T1 + T2 > T3 + T4	5.11*	T1 > T2	2.07	T3 = T4

[a]HO = hypothesis.
*$p < .05$; F .95 = 3.97.

the variance was being carried by younger siblings closer in age to the target-age children. There are some interesting implications of these general results on younger siblings which will be examined in more detail in the Discussion.

DISCUSSION

The results on the one test of intelligence which was used consistently, from the initiation of the program in 1962 until the testing at the end of the fourth grade in 1968, are very much in line with what might be expected. For this was an intervention program that used a broad-gauge approach and which was relatively successful in terms of improving the educability of young children from low-income homes. Intervention caused a rise in intelligence which was fairly sharp at first, then leveled off, and finally began to show decline once intervention ceased. The control groups on the other hand tended to show a slight but consistent decline with the single exception of a jump between entrance into public school and the end of first grade. Differences between experimentals and controls on Stanford-Binet IQ were still significant at the end of the third year after intervention ceased. All four groups have shown a decline in IQ after the first grade, but the decline, as shown in Figure 1, tended to be relatively parallel. Perhaps the remarkable thing is that with the relatively small amount of impact over time differences should still be significant. After all, the child experienced only five mornings of school a week for 10 weeks for two or three summers, plus weekly home visits during the other 9 months for 2 or 3 years. This suggests that the impact was not lost. It was not sufficient, however, to offset the massive effects of a low-income home in which the child had lived since birth onward.

The results on the PPVT showed a pattern that is not dissimilar. There was a rise during intervention, including the first grade, then a leveling off and a slight decline. Here, however, difference between groups, although consistent, was no longer significant.

The importance of the school situation for the maintenance or loss of a gain should be weighed. The children for the most part remained in schools in which the entire population was Negro. Eight of the local children at the end of first grade did enroll in schools that had previously been all white. Four more changed during the next 2 years. None of the distal children attended schools with white children. Since in this area, as in many places, race tends to be confounded with social class, the children in the study did not in general have the advantage of classmates with relatively high expectancies. There is some evidence that in both of the all-Negro schools the general teaching-learning situation, although fair, was less adequate than in the schools that have formerly been all white. This, plus the continuing effect of the home situation and the immediate community, took its toll. There are some data on achievement-test scores to be presented later which suggest the impact of the two all-Negro schools which most of the children attended.

On the one achievement battery administered from first to fourth grade, the Metropolitan Achievement Test (Table 5), significant differences did not appear in 1968 on any of the subtests with sole exception of the reading score, in which the local control group was superior to the distal control group. The experimentals had been superior to the controls on three tests in 1965 and on two tests in 1966. One might interpret this as showing that the intervention program did have measurable effects upon test performance at the end of first grade, but that by the end of fourth grade, the school program had failed to sustain at any substantial level the initial superiority. Although disappointing, this is perhaps not surprising in a test battery so dependent upon specific school instruction.

An interesting sidelight is thrown on this matter by looking at the performance on the Metropolitan Achievement Test of the eight children from the local school who enrolled in previously all-white schools at the end of first grade. An attempt was made, on the basis of first-grade achievement tests and home ratings of educational aspirations, to match these eight children with eight who remained in the Negro school. Admittedly, this is a chancy business, and one which should not be taken too seriously. Table 8 presents the gains in grade equivalents on the Metropolitan Achievement Tests from the end of first grade to the end of fourth grade. On the four subtests common to both grade levels, the picture is a clear one of more gain in the children who changed schools, varying from .8 to 1.4 years' greater gain. These data did not seem appropriate for subjection to statistical analysis. They do suggest, however, the fairly obvious: that performance on achievement tests is directly related to school experience. The children who changed schools have made approximately "normal" gain for their 3 years; the children who did not change have gained 2 years or less during the 3 years from first through fourth grade.

The results on the younger siblings are to the writers among the most interesting findings of the study. We have termed the process by which such results are achieved and the product of that process "vertical diffusion," to suggest that this is a spread of effect down the family from the mother and possibly the target-age child to a younger child. In this study the effects of the older sibling and the mother upon the younger child were confounded. Some research currently being carried on under the direction of one of the writers has made possible the separation of the influence of mother and older siblings. Results so far indicate that most of the effect is coming from the mother. It is plausible to assume that the role of the mother was the more influential since considerable effort was expended by the home visitor over a period of 3 years with the first experimental group and over 2 years with the second experimental group. The emphasis of the home intervention was on making the mother a more effective teacher, or more generally, an effective educational change agent for her target-age child. Also worthy of note is the finding that vertical diffusion appeared more clearly in the younger siblings born in 1959 and 1960, who were within 1–2½ years in age to the older siblings. The siblings born in 1961 and 1962, when pulled out for separate analysis, did not show an effect which approached statistical significance. Vertical diffusion also appeared more operative in the first than in the second experimental group. A plausible explanation is that intervention lasted a year longer with the first group and began a year earlier. There is also in the data some suggestion of a process we have examined in more detail elsewhere (Klaus & Gray 1968), one that may be termed horizontal diffusion, the spread of effect from one family to another. This we have in general analyzed by comparing the local and distal control groups. Here we find that the younger siblings in the local control group showed themselves to be superior to the distal control group.

To the extent that the findings on vertical diffusion have generality, they seem to point to the efficacy of a powerful process in the homes, presumably mediated by the parent, which may serve to improve the educability of young children. Before a second conclusion is reached by the reader, however, to the effect that "parent education" is the answer, we would like to point out that our procedure was clearly parent education with a difference. It was conducted in the homes; it was done by skilled preschool teachers with some experience in working in the homes; it was highly concrete and specific to a given mother's life situation; it was continuous over a long period of time. Indeed, parent education probably is the answer, but in low-income homes a very different kind of parent education from that usually provided may be needed.

Seven years after the Early Training Project began, in 1969, intervention programs for young children from low-income homes were nationwide. These programs differ tremendously in the length and timing of the intervention, in the objectives and consistency with which they are followed, in the degree of specificity of the pro-

Table 8. Mean gains on the MAT over a 3-year period for eight ETP children in integrated schools and matches in Negro schools

| | MEAN GAINS 1965–1968 | | | |
	WORD KNOWLEDGE	WORD DISCRIMINATION	READING	ARITHMETIC
ETP *Ss* integrated schools beginning Fall 1965	3.1	2.8	2.7	2.9
ETP *Ss* in Negro schools matched to the first group on Spring 1965 MAT and on verbal rating by home visitor	1.7	2.0	1.6	1.7
Difference	1.4	0.8	1.1	1.2

gram, and in the length and extent of follow-up study of the sample.

It is hardly surprising, with the wild heterogeneity of such programs, that nationwide assessment of programs, such as the Westinghouse Survey of Project Head Start (1969), would find relatively small evidence of positive effects upon the child's achievement and personal adequacy. Leaving aside all the problems of measuring personal adequacy and even achievement in young children, such lack of results is only to be expected in situations where the bad or inappropriate so cancels out the good that little positive effect can be found, especially if the evaluation is somewhat premature.

At this point in time it seems appropriate to look more closely at those programs which have clearly followed an adequate research design, specified and carefully monitored their treatments, and conducted adequate follow-up study of the sample. Such programs are relatively few in number, for their history is short.

In the Early Training Project we have been more fortunate than most. The study was initiated nearly 4 years before the tidal wave of interests in such early intervention that came about through such nationwide programs as Project Head Start and Titles I and III of the Elementary and Secondary Education Act. We have worked in a setting in which we have been free from administrative pressures either to

change our procedures or to make premature conclusions from our data. The two communities in which families live have had little outward mobility; even at the end of 7 years attrition is only a minor problem. For these reasons we believe the data collected over 7 years with our four groups of children do shed some light upon the problem of progressive retardation and the possibility that it can be offset.

Our answer as to whether such retardation can be offset is one of cautious optimism. The effects of our intervention program are clearly evidenced through the second year of public schooling, 1 year after intervention ceased. There is still an effect, most apparent in the Stanford-Binet, after 2 more years of nonintervention. Our data on horizontal and vertical diffusion, especially the latter, give us some hope that intervention programs can have a lasting effect that goes beyond the children that were the target of that intervention program.

Still, it is clear from our data, with a parallel decline across the four groups in the second through fourth grades, that an intervention program before school entrance, such as ours, cannot carry the entire burden of offsetting progressive retardation. By some standards the Early Training Project might be seen as one of relatively massive intervention. And yet a colleague of ours (Miller 1970) has estimated that in the years prior to school entrance the maximum amount of time that the children in the project could have spent with the Early Training Project staff was approximately 600 hours, less than 2 percent of their waking hours from birth to 6 years. Perhaps the remarkable thing is that the effect lasted as well and as long as it did. In a similar vein, we have estimated the amount of these contacts in the home as a maximum of 110 hours, or about 0.3 percent of the waking hours of the child from birth to 6 years. Surely it would be foolish not to realize that, without massive changes in the life situation of the child, home circumstances will continue to have their adverse effect upon the child's performance.

In 1968 we wrote:

> The most effective intervention programs for preschool children that could possibly be conceived cannot be considered a form of inoculation whereby the child forever after is immune to the effects of a low-income home and of a school inappropriate to his needs. Certainly, the evidence on human performance is overwhelming in indicating that such performance results from the continual interaction of the organism with its environment. Intervention programs, well conceived and executed, may be expected to make some relatively lasting changes. Such programs, however, cannot be expected to carry the whole burden of providing adequate schooling for children from deprived circumstances; they can provide only a basis for future progress in schools and homes that can build upon that early intervention.

References

Gray, S. W., & Klaus, R. A. An experimental preschool program for culturally deprived children. *Child Development,* 1965, 36, 887–898.

Gray, S. W.; Klaus, R. A.; Miller, J. O.; & Forrester, B. J. *Before first grade.* New York: Teachers College Press, Columbia University, 1966.

Klaus, R. A., & Gray, S. W. The early training project for disadvantaged children: a report after five years. *Monographs of the Society for Research in Child Development,* 1968, 33 (4, Serial No. 120).

Lindquist, E. F. *The design and analysis of experiments in psychology and education.* Boston: Houghton Mifflin, 1953.

Miller, J. O. Cultural deprivation and its modification; effects of intervention. In C. H. Haywood (Ed.), *Social-cultural aspects of mental retardation.* Boston: Appleton-Century-Croft, 1970.

Westinghouse Learning Corporation. *The impact of Head Start: an evaluation of the Head Start experience on children's cognitive and affective development.* Westinghouse Learning Corporation, Ohio University, 1969.

Chapter 12

Day-Care Centers

In response to public pressure, especially from working mothers, there has been an enormous increase in the number of day care facilities for young children, infants, and preschoolers in the United States. Advocates of more and better day care centers consider these institutions to be essentially capable of carrying out programs of "cognitive enrichment" for children from ghetto and poverty areas or at least "offsetting the developmental detriments" suffered by many children from low-income homes. In addition, proponents of day care claim that these centers may be helpful in improving the social and emotional adjustment of young children. In contrast, some authorities believe that day care centers may have deleterious effects on the child's subsequent development. They support their argument by citing studies that indicate that severe maternal deprivation and lack of strong mother-child attachments can adversely influence the child's later adjustment.

What, in fact, is known about the effects of day care programs? Unfortunately, definitive answers are not yet available because research on these important problems began only recently. But some doubts are being resolved. A recent study by R. B. Kearsley and his colleagues, described in the first article in this chapter, illustrates how these problems can be investigated systematically. The investigators focused their attention on separation protests (the onset and duration of distress manifested by an infant when his mother leaves him in an unfamiliar setting), presumably an index of mother-child attachment. The subjects were two groups of infants: One group spent 20–40 hours per week in a day care center during the first 20 months of their lives (beginning at $3\frac{1}{2}$ months of age); the other group of infants were exclusively home-reared. No group effects were discovered, indicating that "continuity of contact between the infant and his mother and the number of caretakers may not be major determinants of separation protest" (p. 363).

(2)   Further evidence supporting this conclusion is found in the second paper of this chapter. In it, B. M. Caldwell and her colleagues describe a day care program they have been conducting for infants and preschoolers for several years and report some preliminary findings on the outcomes. The broad aim of the program "was to create an environment which would foster optimal cognitive, social, and emotional development in young children from disadvantaged families" (p. 365). In an earlier published article, Caldwell and one of her colleagues reported that children attending this center increased between 10 and 14 IQ points during the first year in the program and 3 to 5 IQ points during the second. Although the children's scores dropped just prior to leaving the program, their performance level was still higher than that of a group of matched controls who had not attended the day care center.

Is there any evidence that early enrollment in the program resulted in emotional stress or maladjustment? Caldwell et al. report the results of a systematic test of the effects of attendance on strength of mother-child attachment. They found no differences in attachment patterns of infants enrolled in the day care center and the matched control children who were reared at home. There were significant associations, however, between strength of this attachment, amount of stimulation and support for development in the home, and developmental level achieved by the child.

Separation Protest in Day Care and Home Reared Infants

Richard B. Kearsley

Philip R. Zelazo

Jerome Kagan

Rebecca Hartmann

Separation sequences were observed at two-month intervals from age 3½ through 13½ months and at 20 months in 24 day care and 28 home-reared children. Day care infants spent 20 to 40 hours each week in a center where 35 children were cared for by 11 mature women. Day care and home-reared children showed similar patterns of protest over age, with sharp reductions in latency to cry at 9½ and 13½ months. The absence of a group effect implies that either separation protest is an ambiguous measure of attachment or that the frequency of maternal separation and the presence of multiple caretakers through the first 20 months of life failed to affect the mother-child attachment.

This study was supported by NIH grant HDO-4299; OCD grant OCD-CB-174; and the Spencer Foundation of Chicago. We thank L. M. Crary and the staff of the Tremont St. Infant Center.

SOURCE: From *Pediatrics* by permission of the authors and the American Academy of Pediatrics. In press.

SEPARATION PROTEST IN DAY CARE AND HOME-REARED INFANTS

The occurrence of distress in an infant when left alone by his mother in an unfamiliar setting has been used as an index of the quality or strength of the infant's emotional bond to his mother, a process that is usually called attachment (Ainsworth & Bell, 1970; Bowlby, 1969). Since the infant's bond to his primary caretaker is presumably established through dynamic interaction and the continuity of the caretaker's presence, some theorists regard repeated episodes of mother-infant separation as a major threat to the integrity of the infant's attachment to his mother and imply that such experiences should affect separation behavior (Blehar & Ainsworth, 1973; Heinecke & Westheimer, 1966). The present report is one of a series of studies whose aim is to examine the hypothesis that separation protest reflects the quality of the child's attachment. This paper summarizes data on the display of separation protest among day care and home-reared infants whose experiences differed markedly with respect to the frequency of maternal separation and the presence of multiple caretakers during the first 20 months of life. If such experiences affect the quality of maternal attachment, then these infants should, if separation protest indexes that bond, display different patterns of behavior to separation.

METHOD

Subjects

The subjects were 52 healthy infants, each of whom had a negative medical history and a normal pediatric examination at the time of entry into the study. One group ($N = 24$) was enrolled at $3\frac{1}{2}$ months of age in a day care center and continued in attendance for a minimum of four hours per day five days a week, while a second group ($N = 28$) was raised exclusively at home. Initial observations were obtained on most subjects at $3\frac{1}{2}$ months of age. No subject was older than $5\frac{1}{2}$ months when first tested. Observations were obtained for the entire sample through $13\frac{1}{2}$ months and for 11 day care and 13 home-reared infants at 20 months. The composition of the day care and home-reared groups was similar with respect to sex (12 males, 12 females in day care; 12 males, 16 females at home), ordinal position (either first- or second-born), and family background (predominantly working class). About half the children in each group were Caucasian and half were Chinese.

Rearing Conditions

Ninety-four percent of the children studied were from stable nuclear families who lived in urban south Boston, where the day care center was located. The center was an attractively furnished facility specifically designed to meet the needs of young children. The nursery was staffed by mature women from the community (all of whom were mothers) who had been given special training in child care that emphasized the importance of individualized social interaction. Upon enrollment each child was assigned to a specific caretaker, each of whom was primarily responsible for three infants. Between 13 and 15 months the child was transferred to the toddler section and assigned to another caretaker who was responsible for five children. The center was staffed to care for a maximum of 15 infants and 20 toddlers. While each child was assigned to a particular caretaker, his daily experience involved repeated and intimate contact with several other members of the nursery staff.

Procedure

Each of the day care and home-reared infants was observed through a one-way mirror during a two-minute period of isolated separation from the mother in a comfortably furnished unfamiliar room. The separation episode followed a battery of tests whose duration (one to three hours) varied as a function of the infant's age. The same room was used to make observations at two-month intervals from $3\frac{1}{2}$ to $13\frac{1}{2}$ months. A similarly equipped, equally unfamiliar room in a different building was used for the assessment at 20 months. Each separation episode conformed to the following protocol: When the child was content and playing on the floor with one of several toys the mother left her chair, attracted the child's attention, waved "bye-bye" and left the room, closing the door behind her. The onset and duration of overt distress by the infant (i.e., fretting or crying) were recorded and used as the measure of separation protest. The episode was terminated if intense crying persisted beyond 15 seconds.

RESULTS AND DISCUSSION

Figure 1 indicates that the average latency to the onset of the first instance of crying was similar for day care and home-reared infants. Analyses of variance for groups and sex with age as a repeated measure revealed that age was the only significant result ($F = 44.22$; 5/164; $p < .001$). Large decreases in latency to cry occurred from $7\frac{1}{2}$ to $9\frac{1}{2}$ months ($t = 4.62$, $p < .001$) and again from $11\frac{1}{2}$ to $13\frac{1}{2}$ months ($t = 5.39$, $p < .001$).

Figure 2 illustrates the percentage of infants in each group who displayed protest at any time during the separation episode. As with the latency measure the occurrence of protest following separation showed a similar pattern for the two groups, with marked increases in protest at $9\frac{1}{2}$ and $13\frac{1}{2}$ months.

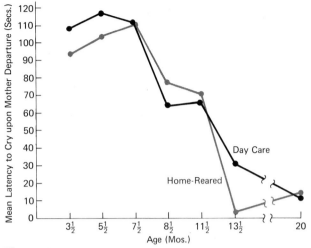

Figure 1

The fact that latency to and the occurrence of protest showed the same age function for day care and home-reared infants implies that the psychological processes which mediate separation distress may not be seriously affected by the number of caretakers an infant has or by repeated separations from his mother. This finding is consistent with the observations of Maccoby and Feldman (1972) that showed no difference in sepa-

ration protests between home-reared and kibbutz-reared children.

The dramatic increase in protest from $9\frac{1}{2}$ to 20 months has also been reported by other investigators who have found that crying to separation does not occur reliably until the last half of the first year (Schaffer & Emerson, 1964; Kotelchuck, 1973). These findings hold that the manifestation of such protest may be partially controlled by maturational factors that permit the infant to recognize but not resolve the discrepant nature of the separation event. As suggested by Kagan (1971) and Spelke, Zelazo, Kagan, and Kotelchuck (1973), the reliable occurrence of separation protest seems to parallel the appearance of a new cognitive competence that has been called *activation of hypothesis*. It may be that when the infant is faced with a discrepant situation during the latter part of the first year he not only detects and tries to assimilate it, but may also attempt to interpret it. If unable to generate an "explanation" —an attempt to understand the relation of the unfamiliar event to his knowledge—the infant becomes fearful and may cry.

The data of this study imply that the continuity of contact between the infant and his mother and the number of caretakers may not be major determinants of separation protest. However, since the mother's presence can prevent the occurrence of fear when her child is confronted with an unfamiliar situation, there is reason to believe that a special relationship does exist. We suggest that more sensitive measure of the quality of that relationship may be the caretaker's ability to placate the infant.

The results of this research do not deny the presence of an emotional bond between the primary caretaker or biological mother and the infant, but they do challenge the belief that protest to separation is an unambiguous index of that process. On the strength of these and other data (Spelke et al., 1973; Ainsworth & Bell, 1970), we suggest that separation protest no longer be used

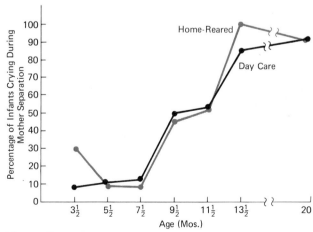

Figure 2

as an operational definition of maternal attachment.

References

Ainsworth, M. D. S., & Bell, S., Attachment, exploration, and separation: Illustrated by the behavior of one-year-olds in a strange situation. *Child Development,* 1970, 41, 49–67.

Blehar, M. P., & Ainsworth, M. D. S., Anxious attachment and defensive reactions associated with day care. Paper presented at the meeting of the Society for Research in Child Development, Philadelphia, March 1973.

Bowlby, J., *Attachment and Loss,* Vol. 1, New York: Basic Books, 1969.

Heinecke, C., & Westheimer, I., *Brief Separations,* New York: International University Press, 1966.

Kagan, J., *Change and Continuity in Infancy,* New York: Wiley, 1971.

Kotelchuck, M., The nature of a child's tie to his father. Paper presented at the meeting of the Society for Research in Child Development, Philadelphia, March 1973.

Maccoby, E. E., & Feldman, S. S., Mother-attachment and stranger-reactions in the third year of life. *Monographs of the Society for Research in Child Development,* 1972, 37 (Serial No. 146).

Schaffer, H. R., & Emerson, P. E., The development of social attachments in infancy. *Monographs of the Society for Research in Child Development,* 1964, 29 (Serial No. 94).

Spelke, E., Zelazo, P., Kagan, J., & Kotelchuck, M., Father interaction and separation protest. *Developmental Psychology,* 1973, 9, 83–90.

Infant Day Care
and Attachment

Bettye M. Caldwell

Charlene M. Wright

Alice S. Honig

Jordan Tannenbaum

A group of home-reared children and a group of children who had been enrolled in an infant day care center were examined at 30 months of age for differences in child-mother and mother-child attachment patterns. Essentially, no differences between the groups could be detected. However, an association was found between strength of attachment and developmental level of the child and between strength of attachment and amount of stimulation and support for development available in the home.

NOTE: *Presented at the 1969 meeting of the American Orthopsychiatric Association, New York, N.Y. This work was supported by Grant D-156 from the Children's Bureau, Social and Rehabilitation Services, Department of Health, Education, and Welfare.*

Day care for infants has had a slow crawl toward social respectability. Boosted on the one hand by zealots who see in it an antidote for many of today's social ills, it has been denounced on the other hand as destructive of a child's potential for normal social and emotional development. Such partisanship has made it somewhat difficult to operate innovative programs with sufficient objectivity to permit collection of the data needed to establish guidelines for current and future programs.

The authors and their colleagues have been engaged in operating a day care program for infants and preschoolers for four years. The broad aim of the program was to create an environment which would foster optimal cognitive, social, and emotional development in young children from disadvantaged families. As data from other studies suggested that by age 3 such children already showed cognitive deficits, the logic of the Syracuse program was to devise a delivery procedure which could get certain types of critical environmental experiences to the children prior to age 3 and thus hopefully circumvent the process of gradual decline. As there are few if any facilities through which large numbers of very young children in this society can be reached, it seemed necessary to devise a new kind of facility. The pressing clamor from working mothers for better child care facilities for their children presented the opportunity to set up a delivery process, and in 1964 the Children's Center, a day care center for infants and preschoolers, was established.

At that time the developers of the program (see Caldwell and Richmond[6]) were acutely aware that there might be certain inherent risks in group day care for infants. For one thing, little was known about the health consequences of bringing substantial numbers of infants into daily contact. For another, there was concern stemming from an awareness of the consistent findings that experiences which diluted the normal mother-infant relationship were likely to produce (be associated with) serious emotional, social, and cognitive impairment. When the plan to offer group day care for infants was announced, many persons expressed alarm that such an arrangement would surely produce deleterious social and emotional consequences, regardless of what benefits it might foster in the cognitive domain. Particularly it was feared that exposure of an infant to large numbers of adults might weaken his primary maternal attachment. If this were to happen, what price gains in any other area?

The quesiton of whether such dilution actually occurs as a consequence of infant day care cannot be answered overnight. It is much easier to report gains or losses in the cognitive area because they can be measured more precisely (though not necessarily more meaningfully) and because they might register at least temporary

effects more quickly. However, a certain passage of time is required before one can examine data for the relatively long-term effects upon the basic mother-child relationship of group day care for infants.

Informal checks have been made from the beginning, partly through the use of outside consultants who were experts in early development and objective and unbiased about possible effects of infant day care. Such impartial evaluations have on occasion identified areas of concern, yet offered reassurance that social and emotional development was not suffering. However, none of the outside consultants had the opportunity to observe the children interacting with their own mothers, seeing them instead with the day care staff. Accordingly, the Center staff members who were on duty at arrival and departure times were alerted to signs of healthy attachment. For example, resistance to separation upon being brought to the Center, calling for the mother during times of distress during the day, positive emotional responses shown upon sighting a returning parent, and scampering to gain proximity when the mother comes upon the scene have all been looked for and noted in the day care children. However, it still appeared necessary to conduct a formal evaluation to determine whether there were basic differences in the strength of attachment in a group of day care and a comparable group of home reared infants.

What Is Attachment?

Attachment is a term which is somewhat elusive of a conceptual definition and one about which there is not unanimity of opinion as to appropriate definition. Ainsworth[3] has attempted to distinguish among the terms *object relations*, *dependency*, and *attachment*. She suggests that attachment refers to an affectional tie to a specific person which may wax and wane as a function of the situation but which has an enduring quality which can survive even adverse socio-emotional circumstances. Attachment is characterized essentially by maintenance of proximity, by mutual pleasure in a relationship, and by reciprocal need gratification.

The importance of maternal attachment for healthy development has been perhaps more inferred than demonstrated. That is, some infants reared in circumstances which did not permit the formation of an exclusive child-mother attachment have developed deviant patterns of affective relationships with other people (see Goldfarb,[11] Provence and Lipton,[14] and summaries by Bowlby,[5] Yarrow,[17] and Ainsworth[1]). From such findings the inference has been drawn that the absence of a one-to-one relationship is the causative factor which explains the deviance. This inference has been challenged by Casler[9] and others, who proposed the alternative interpretation that the deficits shown in nonattached children are more the product of inadequate environmental stimulation than of maternal deprivation per se. The findings of Freud and Dann[10] that mother-separated children who have had prolonged contact with one another show intense peer attachment have been interpreted as indicating that reciprocal peer attachments can possibly substitute for maternal attachment. Also on the basis of his studies of nonhuman primates, Harlow[12] has suggested that peer attachments are actually more critical for subsequent species-normal social and sexual behavior than is maternal attachment. Mead,[13] referring to the need of children in today's world to be able to go many places wtihout fear and to interact with many people, questions the advocacy of a very close tie between mother and child, suggesting that perhaps wider experiences "in the arms of many individuals in different degrees of intimacy, if possible of different races," might represent the more adaptive experience for young children.

Empirical studies of attachment are scarce in the literature. Schaffer and Emerson[16] studied longitudinally 60 infants ranging in age from 21 to 78 weeks of age. They found indiscriminate attachment behavior during the second quarter and specific attachments during the third quarter of the first year of life. Mothers whose interaction with their children was more intense tended to have infants who were more intensely attached to them. Attachment was unrelated to whether the attachment object had had major responsibility for the child's physical care. Maternal availability to child did not differentiate significantly infants who formed exclusive attachments from those who attached to more than one object. Children who had extensive contacts with other people, independent of the nature of the mother-child relationship, tended to show broader attachment patterns than did children who had limited contacts with other people.

By far the greatest amount of empirical work on the topic of attachment has been carried out by Ainsworth[2,4] and her associates. In a group of 28 Uganda babies she categorized 15-month-old infants in terms of strength and security of attachment as: unattached, insecure-attached, and secure-attached. She then compared the infants in these groups on certain maternal variables. Warmth of the mother, care by people in addition to the mother, and use of scheduled versus demand feeding bore no relationship to strength of attachment. The only variables that showed a clear relationship were total amount of care given by the mother, mother's excellence as an informant, and positive attitudes toward breast feeding. Whether the mother had an ample milk supply was marginally related to attachment. In regard to the multiple caretaker variable, Ainsworth[2] concluded that "there is no evidence that care by several people necessarily interferes with the development of healthy attachment." In a sample of American babies and mothers studied throughout the first year of life, Ainsworth and Wittig[4] found that sensitivity of the mother in responding to the baby's signals and the amount and nature of the interaction between the mother and the infant were additional variables which bore a relationship to strength of attachment.

Attachment during the preschool years, at

which time the primary child-mother attachment should weaken somewhat and new attachments form, has been studied to only a very limited extent.

Objectives of This Study

The main question asked by the present study was: are there differences in child-mother attachment and mother-child attachment between a sample of home-reared children and a sample of children who have participated in a group day care program since infancy. Stated in the null version, the formal hypothesis would be that there are no differences between the groups. Additional questions addressed to the data related to whether there are associations between attachment and sex, race, and developmental level of child, and between attachment and stimulation and support available for development within the home.

METHOD

Subjects

Subjects for the study were 41 children who had been followed since early infancy in a longitudinal study relating infant and child development to the social and physical environment. Data for this study were collected as close to each child's 30-month birthday as possible. Twenty-three of the children had received their primary care from their mothers from birth until the time of data collection, except for brief periods during which the mother might have had temporary work or might have been out of the home because of illness. Eighteen of the children had been enrolled in the Children's Center from the time they were about a year old, with all but two of the children having been enrolled prior to 15 months of age. At the time data were collected for this study, the mean duration of day care attendance was 18.8 months, with a range of 5 to 24 months.

Demographic characteristics of the sample can be seen in Table 1. Most of the subjects were from lower-class families, with 25% being from one-parent families. As enrollment in the day care program was limited to children whose parents requested the service, certain desirable touches of methodological elegance—such as matching for sex and ethnicity—could not be achieved. The Home group contained a disproportion-

Table 1. Demographic characteristics of the sample

	HOME	DAY CARE	TOTAL
Sex			
Boys	14	4	18
Girls	9	14	23
Race			
White	19	9	28
Nonwhite	4	9	13
Parents in household			
1 parent	3	7	10
2 parents	20	11	31
No. of siblings			
None	6	6	12
One	11	6	17
Two	4	1	5
Three or more	2	5	7
Mother's education			
Some High School	9	12	21
High School Graduate	12	2	14
Some College	2	4	6
Father's education			
Some High School	10	7	17
High School Graduate	8	3	11
Some College	2	1	3
Not Applicable	3	7	10
Social class			
Lower Social Class	20	14	34
Middle Social Class	3	4	7
IQ (current mean)	107.2	108.8	
Stim score (current mean)	52.8	54.7	

ate number of males and Caucasian children.

On a gestalt of home characteristics the two groups were, at the time of the present analysis, quite comparable. This is perhaps best supported by current scores on the Inventory of Home Stimulation.[7] The Home sample had a mean of 52.8 and the Day Care sample a mean of 54.7 ($t = .98$, $p = NS$). However, Stimulation Inventory scores of 53.4 and 49.5 for the Home and Day Care samples when the study children were 12 months of age indicated a marginal difference ($t = 1.87$, $p = .10$) in favor of the Home sample at that time. The closer contact between the parents of the Day Care sample and staff of the project, plus continued exposure to the philosophy of the day care program, presumably (and hopefully) accounted for the higher Home Stimulation scores that were earned by the Day Care families at the current assessment. Objectively the Day Care group would be described as having been somewhat more "disadvantaged" in the customary connotation of that term at the time their children entered the day care program; clinically and subjectively, there was no doubt but that they were.

The Day Care Program

The generalizability of results from any scientific study is limited by the fidelity with which the sample represents the characteristics of the population from which it was drawn and by the replicability of the experimental procedures. At the outset it should be stated that the experimental procedure of the present study—the infant day care program—is not duplicated in every facility that advertises itself as a day care center. It is a very special day care center. A technical description of the program may be found in Caldwell and Richmond,[8] but at least a few descriptive sentences must be offered here.

The establishment of the Center effected a rather unique blend of social concern for the welfare of young children with the challenge of an intellectual idea—that disadvantaged children will benefit maximally if environmental supports are made available during the first three years of life. "Enrichment" in this carefully planned environment is not merely cognitive enrichment but is an atmosphere in which people and objects give proper levels and quantities of stimulation to young children in a context of emotional warmth, trust, and enjoyment. Teachers, research staff, and office personnel alike are selected partly on the basis of such personal characteristics as warmth and affection for children, empathy for (and often experience with) the problems of the poor, understanding of the complexities and difficulties of family life, and personal convictions about the importance of early experience. Visitors have repeatedly, over the years, commented on such things as the large number of rocking chairs (almost always containing an assortment of adults and children) in the Center, the fact that everybody seems to know everybody else's name, the apparent confidence in adults shown by the children, and the zest for their task displayed by all adults working in the program.

Vital statistics include an average daily attendance of 65 or 70 children ranging in age from 6 months to 5 years, with group assignment based roughly on developmental age. The largest group (the older children) contains 16 children, and the adult-child ratio is approximately one to four. The total group is racially balanced, but the goal of having approximately equal numbers of boys and girls is seldom achieved. Although some middle-class children are accepted into the program, preference for all openings is always given to socially and economically needy families.

The daily schedule is arranged to permit alternating cycles of action and rest, of adult-initiated and child-initiated activity, of group activities and pursuit of individualized interests, of playing for fun and working to learn. One cannot walk into a classroom without thinking, "This is a place where children will be happy." The authors are justified in offering this seemingly immodest and somewhat emotional description, as they are only peripherally involved in the daily programming and can take no credit for the creation of this special milieu for the children. It is hoped that the reader can forgive the immodesty, for knowledge about the program is essential to a correct interpretation of the material to follow.

Procedure

Primary data for the study were obtained from three sources: (1) an intensive, semistructured interview; (2) a home visit; and (3) developmental testing. All procedures were scheduled as close together in time as possible, with an interview and the developmental test usually administered on the same day. Also used in the data analysis was the developmental test administered to the subjects when they were one year of age.

·INTERVIEWS AND RATINGS Most of the assessment procedures employed in this project were designed to cover some specific and relatively circumscribed aspect of child and/or family functioning. The interview conducted for the present study was deliberately planned to achieve the opposite purpose—namely, to obtain a broad picture of the mother-child interaction and of child behavior in settings not ordinarily open to observation by the research staff. All interviews were conducted by a research-oriented social worker (CMW) in a room at the Children's Center comfortably furnished to encourage a relaxed atmosphere. The mothers were told simply, "We want to talk with you about your child's activities and about some of the things you and he (she) are doing now." The study child was present during the interview, and ratings were based on both maternal report and maternal and child behavior. The interview was observed through a one-way vision mirror by a second staff member, and immediately after the session the interviewer and the observer independently rated both mother and child.

Although the interview deliberately covered a broad array of topics, ratings made from the interviews mainly dealt with clusters of behavior representing attachment and achievement. For the present analysis only those concerned with attachment were used.

Each variable was defined as ranging along a 9-

point continuum, with all odd-numbered points described and behaviorally anchored in terms of either maternal or child behavior. The mothers were rated on all variables in terms of their behavior toward the study child, not toward other persons. For example, a mother might be very close to her husband but very distant and remote from the study child; only the latter behavior entered into the ratings used for this data analysis. Each child was rated on the attachment variables twice, once in terms of his relationship with his mother and once in terms of his behavior toward other people. These latter ratings were, of course, based entirely upon maternal report.

Both the interviewer and the observer rated the children and the mothers on these scales immediately following the interview and then, within a few hours, held a discussion and arrived at a rating consensus. Identical ratings were recorded on the final data sheet and were not discussed. Differences of one point were resolved in the direction of the more extreme rating (away from the midpoint of the scale), and differences of two points were reconciled by recording the intermediate rating. When the ratings differed by more than two points, the two raters reassessed the interview and defended their ratings until a consensus emerged. Although this form of rating obviates the need for conventional inter-rater reliability figures, a check was made on the extent of agreement between the raters. On four protocols across all scales the two raters agreed within two points on the material ratings on an average of 87% of the ratings (range 80% to 93%). On the child ratings the average agreement was 91% (range 83% to 96%).

It should be noted here that both the interviewer and the rater knew whether a particular mother-child dyad belonged in the Home or the Day Care sample. In a project like the present one, such knowledge will be unavoidable until a fiscal millenium is reached which permits the luxury of completely blind assessment by impartial assessors. However, the analytic strategy was not discussed with the interviewer until all the interviews had been completed and the ratings filed. She was not told at the outset that the interviews would be used for a comparison between the responses of the Home and Day Care samples. She knew only that the children's age (2½ years) had been designated as a major assessment point at the time the longitudinal study of the Home babies began. The interviewer's assignment was identical to that communicated to the mothers: to get a broad picture of the mother-child relationships and the development of the children, not to look for "strength of attachment." Furthermore, one of her major functions in the total project was to maintain rapport with the Home

families. Therefore, she was actually closer to and friendlier to the Home than to the Day Care mothers, and any bias might have been in their favor. Thus it is the honest conviction of the authors that as much objectivity was maintained as is possible under such circumstances.

·INVENTORY OF HOME STIMULATION This is an experimental procedure developed within the research program of which the present study is a component.[7] It represents an attempt to assess those qualities of the home environment impinging directly upon the young child which have the potential to inhibit or support development. The Inventory contains 72 binary items, about one-half of which depend entirely upon observation of home conditions for their score. It is scored on the basis of a home visit which usually lasts about two hours. Inter-observer reliability in terms of percent of agreement has been found to average around 95% for persons trained in the administration of the Inventory.

·DEVELOPMENTAL EXAMINATIONS The instrument used was the Stanford-Binet Intelligence Scale unless the child was somewhat slow and did not attain the basal age of two years. In such instances, and in all assessments of children younger than two, the Cattell Infant Intelligence Scale was used. Most of the examinations were given by the same person (ASH).

Operational Definition of Attachment

For this study attachment was defined operationally as involving the behavior characteristics sampled in the maternal interviews and rated on seven scales. The variables defined in terms of the behavior considered descriptive of the most intense manifestation for both mothers and children are as follows:

Affiliation. Mother: actively responsive to child; initiates nonroutine contacts; likes to be with child. Child: initiates contacts with mother with high frequency; protests being left alone; follows mother around; resists separation.

Nurturance. Mother: initiates support of child; tries to gratify needs; extremely helpful. Child: highly responsive to mother's activities; child's behavior reinforcement for mother's actions; is helpful.

Hostility. Mother: openly hostile; disapproves of much of child's behavior; imposes own schedule upon child; perceives child negatively. Child: expresses anger toward mother; demanding; negativistic, uncooperative; resists manipulation.

Permissiveness. Mother: lets child have own way much of time; invites manipulation and control by child. Child: extremely submissive to maternal control; yields to mother's wishes.

Dependency. Mother: hates to separate from child; extreme emotional involvement with this child to the exclusion of other persons; activities exclusively child-centered; enjoys company of child. Child: strong attachment to mother; is dependent upon mother; maintains proximity; resists separation when proximity is possible; likes to be with or near mother.

Happiness. Mother: expresses great happiness and pleasure in relation to child; child is the emotional high spot in mother's life. Child: extremely happy in interaction with mother; laughs, smiles, shows positive affect.

Emotionally. Mother: persistent extreme overt emotional expression displayed to child; frequently laughs or cries or becomes upset in interactive sessions. Child: persistent extreme overt emotional expression displayed to mother; interaction characterized by high affect rather than apathy and lack of involvement.

All scales except Hostility were expected to co-vary positively with attachment; low ratings on the Hostility scale were interpreted as indicative of strong attachment.

Data Analysis

For data analyses involving the behavior ratings, a distribution-free statistic was needed, and chi square and Fisher's exact test were used. When the developmental tests and the Inventory of Home Stimulation were examined internally, the *t* test for independent samples was used. For this type of study, it was felt that *t* Type II decision error (accepting the null hypothesis when it was actually false—i.e., inferring no difference when actually there were differences between the groups) carried greater interpretive risks. Therefore, it was decided to report and discuss p-values of .10.

RESULTS

Attachment and Early Child Care

·CHILD-MOTHER ATTACHMENT. The major hypothesis tested by the present study was that there would be no significant difference between child-mother attachment patterns shown by a sample of children who had been home-reared since birth and a sample who had been enrolled in a group day care program since roughly one year of age. The hypothesis was tested by dichotomizing the behavior ratings (above and below the median for the total sample of 41) and examining the obtained distributions for disproportionality related to membership in the Home or the Day Care samples by means of chi square. Results of this analysis are summarized in Table 2. From the first column it can be seen that there were no significant differences between the Home and Day Care samples on any of the ratings of the child's relationship with his mother. This failure to disconfirm the null hypothesis indicates that such group experience as that provided in our Center can occur without producing deviant child-mother relationship.

·CHILD-OTHER RELATIONSHIPS. In Column 2 of Table 2 are presented data on the way the children in the Home and Day Care samples relate to other people in their environment. These data were gathered and analyzed in order to determine whether children who see a larger number of people in an emotionally supportive context might not relate more positvely to other people. Schaffer and Emerson's[16] finding that infants who had more contact with persons other than the mother formed broader attachment patterns would lead to this prediction, as would Rheingold's[15] finding that infants in an experimentally mothered group

Table 2. Summary of chi square analyses of distribution of ratings (above and below median) for home and day care children*

	CHILD-MOTHER	CHILD-OTHER	MOTHER-CHILD
1. Affiliation	.24	.05	.00
2. Nurturance	.40	.20	.03
3. Hostility	.00	.96	.24
4. Permissiveness	.50	.17	5.49[b](H)
5. Dependency	1.45	3.39[a](DC)	.24
6. Happiness	1.04	.59	.96
7. Emotionality	.59	1.62	.09

[a]Significant at .10 level.
[b]Significant at .05 level.
*All chi squares have $df = 1$ and represent 4-cell tables enumerating numbers of persons in Home (H) and Day Care (DC) samples rated above or below the median of the total sample on the behavior ratings. Letters in parentheses (H, DC) after significant chi squares identify the group excessively represented in the above-median cell.

were more socially responsive than the controls to a neutral person in the environment as well as to the person who had supplied the extra mothering. In the present study there was only one scale on which a difference significant at the .10 level was found. This was on the Dependency scale, on which the Day Care children were found to have higher ratings than the Home children. As defined in the present scales, dependency connotes proximity-seeking more than help-seeking and perhaps indicates an enjoyment of interaction with others more than anything else. Although the difference is of marginal statistical significance, it offers some confirmation of previous findings relating to the breadth of interest in other people shown by children who have extensive nonfamily contacts.[1]

[1]In reacting to an earlier version of this paper, Dr. John Bowlby (personal communication) suggested that the slightly higher ratings of the day care children on the dependency scale in terms of their interactions with persons other than the mother might indicate that these children show an "overanxious" attachment. One manifestation of this would be apprehension about breaking contact with an adult and a tendency to maintain constant proximity with the adult at the expense of exploration. Experimental tests of this would have been desirable and will indeed be made in future studies.

MOTHER-CHILD ATTACHMENT. Of perhaps equal relevance to the child's attachment to the mother is the mother's attachment to the child. If early day care in any way diminishes the intensity of the emotion which the mother brings to the relationship with her baby, then this might also have negative consequences for the child no matter how normally the child's own attachment pattern might develop. The data in Column 3 of Table 2 indicate that this does not appear to be a valid threat. On six out of the seven ratings, there were no significant differences between the mothers of the Home and the Day Care samples. On the remaining scale, Permissiveness, the Day Care mothers were rated lower than were the Home mothers. Whether this reflects a general concern with achievement, "looking good" as a parent, or a basic personality characteristic of early Day Care mothers cannot be determined. It may reflect the fact that the Day Care mothers are more attuned to parent education literature and perceive permissiveness as being currently out of favor.

Sex and Race Differences

If the samples for the two groups had been more perfectly matched in terms of all possibly influential variables, the finding of only one significant difference as a function of group membership (Home or Day Care) could be interpreted more unequivocally. It will be recalled from Table 1 that girls were overrepresented in the Day Care sample and that Negroes were underrepresented in the Home group. Differences in either of these variables might conceivably mask differences related to early child care experience. As so many recent research studies have reported sex differences in behavioral characteristics measured during early childhood, an analysis by sex was considered especially relevant.

In order to determine whether there were differences in ratings as a function of sex or race, the same kind of analysis described above and summarized in Table 2 for infant care pattern was carried out for sex and then for race. In the child-mother and child-other ratings, there was only one significant disproportion. That was on the Nurturance scale in the child's relationships with his mother (see definition under Method). On this scale girls were found (chi square = 3.81, p = .10) to be more responsive and helpful to their mothers—a difference which certainly fits the cultural stereotype for sex-typed behavior. There were no significant differences as a function of sex in the child-other ratings or in the mother-child ratings.

On the racial variable there were no significant differences between the groups on the child-mother or child-other variables. On the mother-child attachment variables, however, there were three that attained significance: Affiliation (whites high: chi square = 3.35, p = .10), Permissiveness (whites high: chi square = 3.69, p = .10), and Emotionality (whites high: chi square = 10.81, p = .001). This appearance of a fairly consistent pattern on three out of the seven maternal attachment scales suggests that in this particular sample the Negro infants received slightly less intense affective responses from their mothers. These relationships also suggest that the earlier reported findings of relatively greater concern with control (low permissiveness) on the part of the Day Care mothers (see Table 2, Column 3) may be confounded by the fact that Negro infants are slightly overrepresented in the Day Care sample in relation to the Home sample.

In general these data strengthen the interpretation of no major differences in attachment patterns associated with Home or Day Care group membership. Unbalanced sex distribution made essentially no contribution, and racial differences in the mothers, if anything, should have increased the likelihood of significant differences as a function of group membership. Thus the unbalanced representation in the two infant care groups of sex and race cannot be cited as obscuring differences that might have existed as a function of child care group membership.

Developmental Level and Attachment

Although the major task of this project was to ascertain whether there were differences in attachment patterns of mothers and children as a function of child care history, the research program of which this project is but one part is concerned with broader aspects of child development. As stated previously, a major orientation of the program has been an attempt to develop a model of infant care that would support a child's development and provide certain critical experiences necessary to normalize development. It was conceivable that the child-mother and the mother-child attachment systems might in some way interact with the rate of development shown by the child.

Ratings on the attachment variables were examined for an association with child's developmental level at 30 months, with the results shown in Table 3. Only one of the maternal variables, Nurturance, achieved marginal significance, thus suggesting that in this sample child's developmental level bore little or no relation to strength of maternal attachment. In terms of child-mother attachment, however, there is a definite suggestion that the better developed infants tend to be more strongly attached to their mothers. This finding should be especially reassuring to those who are concerned that cognitive enrichment

Table 3. Summary of chi square analyses of attachment and child's developmental level

	CHILD-MOTHER	MOTHER-CHILD
Affiliation	.59	.00
Nurturance	3.69[a](HH)*	2.81[a](HH)
Hostility	3.69[a](HL)	.02
Permissiveness	1.77	.15
Dependency	1.77	1.95
Happiness	7.00[b](HH)	.12
Emotionality	.02	.33

[a]Significant at .10 level.
[b]Significant at .01 level.
*H (High) and L (Low) in parentheses indicate patterns of significant disproportionalities on the two variables.

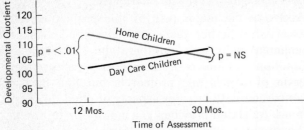

Figure 1 Time trends in developmental quotients for home and day care children at 12 and 30 months.

might be fostered at the expense of social and emotional development. These obtained associations suggest quite the contrary, namely, that rate of development and strength of attachment covary positively.

In view of the fact that cognitive enrichment was one of the goals of the research program, it appeared valid to examine the developmental quotients of the children in order to determine whether there were demonstrable differences between the Home and Day Care samples on this variable both in terms of current functioning and in terms of development prior to entering day care. The results of the analysis are shown in Figure 1. Data in Figure 1 show that the two groups were not comparable with respect to developmental level at 12 months of age (another situation that one must live with in research where random assignment of subjects is not possible). The difference between the DQ's obtained on the children at that time is significant at the .01 level of confidence. The Home children show the decline in DQ over time that has been consistently reported for disadvantaged children. The Day Care children, while not showing any astronomical rise in developmental level, have managed to avoid decline and have, in fact, shown a slight rise. The difference between the groups at 30 months is not statistically significant. This finding, coupled with the above results pointing to comparable attachment patterns in the two groups, demonstrates the feasibility of devising programs which circumvent developmental de-

cline without damaging the child's capacity to relate to his mother or her capacity to relate to him.

Home Characteristics and Attachment

The remaining assessment procedure used for this study was the Inventory of Home Stimulation. The score obtained by a given mother on this Inventory should provide some information about whether the verbal report and behavior which formed the basis for the attachment ratings were at all representative of child and maternal behavior. Accordingly, scores on the Inventory were dichotomized and related to dichotomized ratings on the attachment variables for the total sample of 41 children. Data from this analysis are presented in Table 4.

From Column 2 of Table 4 it is obvious that the mother-child ratings were rather consistently related to independent data about mother and child gathered during a visit to the home. On five of the seven attachment variables, high ratings on the interview data were associated with high scores on the Home Stimulation Inventory. Similarly, on two of the child-mother ratings, there was an association between amount of stimulation available in the home and the intensity of the child's attachment to his mother. These data give

Table 4. Summary of chi square analyses of home stimulation and attachment behavior (above and below median on STIM, above and below median on attachment scales)

	CHILD-MOTHER*	MOTHER-CHILD*
Affiliation	7.06[c]	3.38[a]
Nurturance	10.51[c]	5.11[b]
Hostility	1.71	.09
Permissiveness	.00	.85
Dependency	.00	7.06[c]
Happiness	.20	4.89[b]
Emotionality	1.95	6.93[c]

[a]Significant at .10 level.
[b]Significant at .05 level.
[c]Significant at .01 level.
*Significant disproportionalities were consistently of the High-High pattern.

support to the reliability of the behaviors sampled in the rating scales and also provide clues as to factors in the home situation which can be expected to correlate with strength of attachment.

Home Characteristics and Development

So far in this paper we have shown that child-mother and mother-child attachment were not adversely affected by the kind of early day care experience provided in this setting. We have further shown that attachment patterns are to some extent associated with developmental level of the child and are rather strongly associated with amount and quality of stimulation available to the child within the home. The data collected for this study also lent themselves to an examination of the relationship between home stimulation, pattern of early child care, and development. Results of this analysis are presented in Table 5. Here the association between child's developmental level (above or below a quotient of 100 at 30 months) and family score on the Home Stimulation Inventory (above or below the median) is examined separately for the Home sample, the Day Care sample, and the total group of children and families. The results of this analysis are again quite reassuring from the standpoint of the contribution that early day care can make to the total welfare of the developing child. In the Home sample, there is a statistically significant association (Fisher's exact test) between score on the Home Stimulation Inventory and developmental level—that is, children from homes low in stimulation tend to score below the median on the intelligence test. A similar association exists for the total sample. However, for the Day Care sample

the distribution of scores on the variables of home stimulation and developmental level is random. Thus it appears that infant day care intrudes into the relationship between home stimulation and developmental level; it can, in effect, offer at least some of the resources and some of the influences of a "second home." It is clearly not the absence of a home.

DISCUSSION AND CONCLUSIONS

At the time the project of which this study is a part was introduced to the scientific literature, the following statement of goals was made:

> This paper describes a recently initiated program which has as its aim the development of a day care program for children three years of age and under to foster their subsequent educability. In order to accomplish this aim, an attempt will be made to program an environment which will foster healthy social and emotional development as well as provide stimulation for cognitive growth during a developmental period that is critical for its priming. . . . The basic hypothesis to be tested is that an appropriate environment can be programmed which will offset any developmental detriment associated with maternal separation and possibly add a degree of environmental enrichment frequently not available in families of limited social, economic, and cultural resources.[6]

The data reported in this paper demonstrate that at least with respect to the social-emotional variables of child-mother and mother-child attachment, we can claim some success at this point. We *have* offered environmental enrichment, and we *have* shown that it is possible to do this without producing the classical picture of maternal deprivation. It is our hope that these

Table 5. Distribution of home stimulation scores and developmental quotients for home, day care, and total samples

	HOME		DAY CARE		TOTAL	
	HI STIM	LO STIM	HI STIM	LO STIM	HI STIM	LO STIM
Above 100	9	3	7	4	16	7
Below 100	3	8	4	3	7	11
	$p = .05$		*NS*		$p = .05$	

findings will offer encouragement and reassurance to all persons interested in obtaining for children the benefits of high quality infant day care but cautious about jumping into premature programming lest the welfare of the children be forgotten. We ourselves are reassured.

These findings do not guarantee that a socioemotional deficit would never be associated with infant day care. In the strict statistical sense, we can generalize only to samples participating in similar programs. As such programs are so scarce in America, the generalizability of the findings is sharply restricted. What they do show is that one *can* have infants in quality day care without having jeopardized the child's primary emotional attachment to his mother. In the present program, great pains were taken to avoid this jeopardy. For example, no infants were taken into the program prior to the age of six months, by which time rudimentary forms of attachment have developed. In point of fact, most children who enter the program during infancy do so around one year of age. Also the program is one which offers a generous adult-child ratio and which features in abundance the kinds of behavior shown to be associated with strength of attachment (intensity of response, sensitivity to child's needs, and general competence as adults).

Results of this study provide some extremely valuable information about the range of acceptable variability in patterns of social care for young infants which can be tolerated without damaging the developing children. The implicit equation of infant day care with institutionalization should be put to rest. Infant day care *may* be like institutionalization, but it does not have to be. Day care and institutional care have only one major feature in common: children in groups. Characteristics of institutional children that day care children do not share—prolonged family separation, a sameness of experience, absence of identity, isolation from the outside world, often *no* significant interpersonal relationship—undoubtedly far outweigh the one characteristic that the groups have in common.

The group with which we are working offers sufficient variation on both child and maternal dimensions to permit further investigations of factors influencing attachment and other important types of social and emotional development. For example, second in importance only to the development of child-mother and mother-child attachments is the development of peer attachments and other types of child-adult and adult-child attachments. One of the findings of the Schaffer and Emerson[16] study referred to earlier was that exclusivity of maternal care was not related to strength of child-mother attachment, but its opposite, wide child care experiences, bore a slight relationship to the tendency of the infant to develop broader attachment patterns. In this study our concern has been primarily with the influence of infant day care upon the basic child-mother attachment; only incidentally did we address ourselves to the influence of such an infant care experience upon attachment to others. We are currently designing new research strategies to determine whether infant day care tends to be associated with strong attachments to more than one person without weakening the basic child-mother attachment.

When we talk about "group care for infants," it is easy to sound as though we are proposing something radically deviant for the children. In the Western world of today with its tract houses, Dick and Jane and mother and dad readers, and our carefully nurtured concern for territoriality and for "mine" and "yours," it is easy to forget that until very recent times isolation of the nuclear family from relatives and friends was rare. Many children living and developing in a small amount of space was the rule, not the exception. Furthermore, the prevalence of extended family living arrangements made for interpersonal environmental settings not unlike that which exists in our infant day care setting: that is, a small group of infants cared for by several friendly and supportive adults but with never a question about who belongs to whom. Our teachers and nurses no more wish to usurp the maternal and paternal role than did relatives and friends who still help perform the child care functions in nonliterate societies and did so in our own country until some 60–70 years ago. We would like to claim that our program is truly innovative, but we must at least consider the possibility that it represents a return toward a pattern that is normal and adaptive for the species. At the same time, we fervently hope that it represents progression toward the goal of more complete utilization of society's resources to foster optimal development for its children.

References

1. Ainsworth, M. 1962. Reversible and irreversible effects of maternal deprivation on intellectual development. Child Welfare League of America: 42–62.
2. Ainsworth, M. 1967. Infancy in Uganda. Johns Hopkins Press, Baltimore.
3. Ainsworth, M. 1969. Object relations, dependency, and attachment: a theoretical review. Child Devel. 40:969–1026.
4. Ainsworth, M., and Wittig, B. 1968. Attachment and exploratory behavior of one-year-olds in a strange situation. *In* Determinants of Infant Behavior IV, B. M. Foss, ed. Methuen, London and John Wiley & Sons, New York.
5. Bowlby, J. 1952. Maternal Care and Mental Health. World Health Organization, Geneva, Switzerland.
6. Caldwell, B., and Richmond, J. 1964. Programmed day care for the very young child—a preliminary report. J. Mar. and Fam. 26:481–488.
7. Caldwell, B., Heider, J., and Kaplan, B. 1966. The Inventory of Home Stimulation. Paper presented at meeting of Amer. Psychol. Assn., Sept. 1966.
8. Caldwell, B., and Richmond, J. 1968. The Children's Center in Syracuse, New York. *In* Early Child Care: The New Perspectives, L. L. Dittmann, ed. Atherton Press, New York: 326–358.
9. Casler, L. 1961. Maternal deprivation: a critical review of the literature. Monographs of the Society for Research in Child Development, 26(2).
10. Freud, A. and Dann, S. 1951. An experiment in group upbringing. Psychoanal. Study of Child, 6:127–168.
11. Goldfarb, W. 1955. Emotional and intellectual consequences of psychologic deprivation in infancy: a revaluation. *In* Psychopathology of Childhood, P. H. Hoch and J. Zubin, eds. Grune and Stratton, New York: 105–119.
12. Harlow, H., and Harlow, M. 1966. Social deprivation in monkeys. *In* Human Development, M. L. Haimowitz and N. R. Haimowitz, eds. Thomas Crowell, New York: 230–235.
13. Mead, M. 1957. Changing patterns of parent-child relations in an urban culture. Int. J. Psychoanal. 38(6):1–10.
14. Provence, S., and Lipton, R. 1962. Infants in Institutions. International University Press, New York.
15. Rheingold, H. 1956. The modification of social responsiveness in institutional babies. Monograph of the Society for Research in Child Development 21(2).
16. Schaffer, H., and Emerson, P. 1964. The development of social attachments in infancy. Monograph of the Society for Research in Child Development, 29(3).
17. Yarrow, L. 1964. Separation from parents during early childhood. *In* Review of Child Development Research, Vol. I, M. L. Hoffman and L. W. Hoffman, eds. Russell Sage Foundation, New York: 89–130.

Chapter 13

Psychotherapy

Many preschool children manifest minor maladjustments, fears, anxieties, and behavior problems such as thumb-sucking, nail-biting, and temper tantrums. Fortunately, these are frequently transient, disappearing in time even without treatment. Furthermore, these maladaptive reactions may be considerably ameliorated—and desirable responses may be substituted and strengthened—by applying the basic principles of learning (rewarding desirable responses and failing to reward undesirable ones) in planned, systematic ways. This is the essence of "behavior therapy"; a parent or nursery school teacher may take the role of a behavior therapist.

(1) The first article in this chapter, by K. E. Allen, B. Hart, J. S. Buell, F. R. Harris, and M. M. Wolf, illustrates the effective use of the principles of behavior therapy by nursery school teachers who applied reinforcement principles consistently in guiding the behavior of a 4-year-old who showed persistent and marked isolate behavior. The positive social reinforcement used to modify her behavior, and to help her achieve and maintain more play relationships with peers, was **adult attention.** This is defined operationally as a teacher's going to the child, talking to her, smiling at her, touching, offering, and/or giving her assistance. Each teacher simply gave the child attention every time she interacted with one or more children (conversing, looking or smiling toward others, touching, helping, or working with others). The child's behavior changed radically as soon as this training was begun, and the changes were quite stable.

More serious, persistent maladjustments and behavioral symptoms may be manifesta-

tions of profound and complex emotional disturbances, often rooted in upset family relationships. Such symptoms and maladjustments are generally quite resistant to change.
Consequently, treatment is likely to require highly specialized techniques designed to help
the patient reveal and understand his deepest motives and conflicts. Then the psycho-
therapist can help him cope with his problems realistically and adjust more adequately
to the social world in which he lives.

There are numerous approaches to psychotherapy, many theories and many techniques. Well-trained psychotherapists, regardless of their theoretical orientation, attempt
to establish close relationships with their patients and provide an atmosphere of acceptance and security. In individual therapy the therapist works alone with the child
in a series of sessions, but he is also likely to confer with the child's parents, helping
them to facilitate the patient's acquisition of more adaptive behavior.

(2) In the second selection in this chapter, J. O. Palmer spells out some of the major
considerations involved in planning an individual psychotherapeutic program that fits
the needs of the child patient. The basic elements of therapy, elements that must be included in any effective therapeutic program, are briefly discussed, as are the difficulties
encountered in implementing plans for therapy.

Effects of Social Reinforcement on Isolate Behavior of a Nursery School Child

K. Eileen Allen

Betty Hart

Joan S. Buell

Florence R. Harris

Montrose M. Wolf

This report presents an application of reinforcement principles to guidance in a preschool. Teachers used systematic presentation of positive social reinforcement (adult attention) to help a child showing persistent and marked isolate behavior to achieve and maintain more play relationships with peers. Adult attention was defined as: a teacher's going to, talking to, smiling to, touching, offering and/or giving assistance to the child. Play relationships were defined as interactions between the subject and one or more children, such as conversing, looking or smiling toward each other, touching, helping, or working with each other on a project.

Reinforcement principles have been established in experiments with several subhuman species, and some applications have been made to human problems. Wolf, Risley, and Mees (7) and Ferster and DeMeyer (4) have applied them to the treatment of autism in children; Brady and Lind (3) to functional blindness; Ayllon and Michael (2) and Ayllon and Haughton (1) to psychotic behavior; Harris, Johnston, Kelley, and Wolf (5) to regressed motor behavior of a preschool child; and Hart, Allen, Buell, Harris, and Wolf (6) to operant crying. In each instance systematic improvement in behavior was achieved.

NOTE: Of inestimable value in planning and carrying out this study were the counsel and steady support of Sidney W. Bijou, Donald M. Baer, and Jay S. Birnbrauer. Refinement of observation techniques depended heavily on the collaboration of Robert G. Wahler, who is currently exploring and developing methods for recording behavior in the child clinical situation.

SOURCE: From *Child Development*, vol. 35, no. 2 (1964), 511–518. Copyright © 1964 by the Society for Research in Child Development, Inc. Reprinted with permission.

METHOD

Subject

Ann was 4.3 years old at the start of the study. She was enrolled at the Laboratory Preschool of the University of Washington in a group of eight boys and eight girls, homogeneous in terms of age (4 to 4.5 years), intelligence levels (higher than average), and family background (upper middle class).

During the first days of school, Ann interacted freely with adults but seldom initiated contact with children or responded to their attempts to play with her. She did not seem severely withdrawn or frightened; instead she revealed a varied repertory of unusually well-developed physical and mental skills that drew the interested attention of adults but failed to gain the companionship of chidren. Teachers gave warm recognition to her skilled climbing, jumping, and riding; her creative use of paints and clay; her original songs and rhythmic interpretations of musical selections; her collections of nature objects; her perceptive and mature verbalizations; and her willing and thorough help-with-cleanup behaviors.

With passing days she complained at length about minute or invisible bumps and abrasions. She often spoke in breathy tones at levels so low that it was difficult to understand what she said. Her innumerable, bulky collections of rocks or leaves seemed to serve as "conversation pieces" valued only so long as they drew adult comments. She spent increasing time simply standing and looking. Frequently she retired to a make-believe bed in a packing box in the play yard to "sleep" for several minutes. Mild, tic-like behaviors such as picking her lower lip, pulling a strand of hair, or fingering her cheek were apparent.

After six weeks of school, a period considered ample for adjustment to the nursery school situation, the teachers made a formal inventory of Ann's behaviors and appraised the time she spent with children, with adults, and by herself. The evaluation revealed that Ann's behavior consisted of isolating herself from children and indulging in many varied techniques for gaining and prolonging the attention of adults. Close scrutiny further revealed that most of the adult attention given to her was contingent upon behaviors incompatible with play behavior with peers.

A plan was instituted to give Ann maximum adult attention contingent on play with another child, and minimum attention upon isolate behavior or upon interactions with an adult when alone. Approximately the same total amount of adult attention was to be available to Ann each day provided she met the criteria for obtaining such behavior from the teachers.

Effort was made to hold all variables other than adult social reinforcement constant throughout the study: no changes were to be made in the regular nursery school program or in supervisional assignments of the three teachers. Teachers were to continue to be physically present, as usual. The only change instituted was in the conditions under which they were to give Ann attention, and this was governed by the schedule of reinforcement in effect at a given phase of the study.

Recording

In order to make assessments of changes in Ann's behavior, objective data were obtained each morning by two observers, the same throughout the study. Each observer worked half the morning. To ascertain rater reliability, they recorded jointly for two mornings. Their records showed 81 and 91 per cent agreement.

Proximity and interaction with adults and with children were recorded at 10-second intervals. A sample line from a data sheet is given in Figure 1. The sample shows 5 minutes of recorded behaviors. In the top row (a), the single strokes indicate four intervals of proximity to adults; the ×'s indicate seven intervals of interaction with adults. In the bottom row (c), single strokes indicate eight intervals of proximity to children; ×'s indicate seven intervals of interaction with children. Blank squares indicate intervals when Ann was neither in proximity to nor interacting with an adult (upper row) or a child (bottom row). A behavioral account might read as follows: Ann stood near a child when a teacher drew near (A). Ann talked to the child, and the teacher at once smiled at her and spoke to both children. Ann turned all her attention to the teacher, following her as she moved away. The teacher busied herself exclusivly with some other children, and Ann turned and walked to a gravel area where she started to gather pebbles alone. She moved near some children and a teacher (B), where she stayed for half a minute without interacting with them. Shortly after the teacher left the group, Ann moved away, continuing to gather pebbles by herself. A child approached her (C) and joined her in picking up pebbles. They smiled at each other. A teacher at once came and talked to both children. The teacher left after half a minute. Ann continued to play with the child for 20 seconds. After the child left, Ann continued picking up pebbles alone.

Behavior during a daily scheduled group activity which averaged about 15 minutes was excluded from the data. During this part of the nursery school pro-

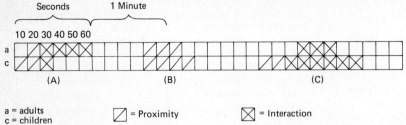

a = adults
c = children   ☐ = Proximity   ☒ = Interaction

Figure 1 A sample line from a data sheet which accommodated 12 such lines (1 hour of recording), spaced. Proximity was defined as physical closeness to adult or child (within 3 feet). Interaction was defined as conversing, smiling, or looking toward, touching, and/or helping an adult or a child. All interaction with adults was recorded in row a; interaction with children was recorded in row c. Notations were made every 10 seconds, by the observer, using a stop watch. Neither capital letters in parentheses nor time notations above the line appear on data sheets but merely facilitate explanations in the text.

gram the children were expected to sit in close proximity to each other and to the teacher.

Procedures

Before reinforcement procedures were initiated, an objective record was obtained of the actual amounts of time Ann was spending with children, adults, and alone.

After five days of baseline data had been secured, teachers were instructed to give attention to Ann whenever and only when she interacted with children. To begin with, any approximations to social interaction, such as standing near another child or playing beside another in the sandbox or at a table, were followed by teacher attention. As soon as Ann interacted with a child, an adult immediately gave her direct individual attention. A sample interaction was, "Ann, you are making dinner for the whole family." When she played alone, Ann was not given attention, and when she contacted an adult she was given minimum attention unless she was with another child.

It was immediately apparent that a direct approach to Ann tended to draw away from the play with children and into interaction with the adult. Original procedures were amended as follows: the teacher made comments and directed other attending behaviors to Ann, not individually, but as a participant in the ongoing group play; whenever possible, the adult approached the group prepared to give Ann an appropriate material or toy to add to the joint play project. A sample amended operation was, "You three girls have a cozy house! Here are some more cups, Ann, for your tea party." Whenever Ann began to leave the group, the teacher turned away from her and became occupied with some other child or with equipment. This procedure, which extended over six days, seemed to bring Ann into interaction with other children more frequently and for longer periods.

In order to substantiate whether the behavior changes effected by the above procedures had indeed been produced by the application of reinforcement principles, procedures were reversed for five days. Solitary pursuits and contacts made solely with an adult were once more made discriminative stimuli for adult attention. Ann was disregarded by adults whenever she interacted with children, and given only an unavoidable minimum of attention when she, in the company of another child, contacted them.

After this reversal, the previous contingencies were reinstated. For the next nine days teachers again gave (a) a maximum of attention for all play with children, (b) no attention when Ann was alone, and (c) a minimum of attention when she contacted adults, unless she was with a child. When she began spending longer periods in continuous interaction with children, adult reinforcement of interaction was gradually made more intermittent until she received adult attention in an amount normal for the group.

Following the last day of systematic reinforcement of interaction, the observers recorded Ann's behaviors on four days spaced at irregular intervals during the last months of school.

RESULTS

The data on interactions with adults and with children are shown in Figure 2. Since the total

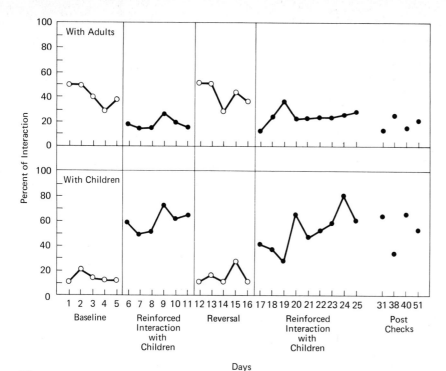

Days

Figure 2 Percentages of time spent in social interaction during approximately 2 hours of each morning session.

observation time each morning varied slightly (average of 114 minutes, with a range from 100 to 130 minutes), each dot on the graph represents a percentage of a morning Ann spent in interaction (a) with adults and (b) with children. Open dots represent periods in which baseline and reversal procedures were carried out. Closed dots represent periods in which interactions with children were reinforced by the teachers. The percentages of interactions on a given day sometimes total more than 100 per cent, since Ann often interacted with both an adult and a child in the same 10-second interval (see C, Figure 1).

As can be seen in Figure 2, the baseline data collected over five days showed that Ann was spending little more than 10 per cent of the time interacting with children and 40 per cent with adults. For at least half the time she was essentially solitary. Analysis of the data indicated that

her isolate behavior was being maintained and probably strengthened inadvertently by adult social reinforcement. Using traditional nursery school guidance techniques, the teachers responded warmly to Ann whenever she contacted them and remained in conversation with her for as long as she desired. When she stood about alone, they usually went to her and tried to get her into play with children. If they succeeded, they left shortly, to allow Ann to play freely with other children. All too frequently Ann was "out" again as soon as the teacher left, standing on the periphery, soliciting teacher attention, or playing alone.

On day 6, when Ann was first given teacher attention only when she was near children or interacting with them, an immediate change in her behavior took place. She spent almost 60 per cent of that morning first in approximations to interaction, and then in active play with children. Adult-child interaction, which was not followed by attention, dropped to less than 20 per cent. These levels of interactions varied little throughout the six-day period of continuous reinforcement of child-child interaction. Over the period, Ann spent increasing time in play with other children.

When procedures were reversed (12th day), Ann's previous patterns of behavior immediately reappeared. She spent the first few minutes after her arrival in close one-to-one interaction with a teacher, which was, of course, continuously reinforced. With this beginning, she spent the remainder of the morning much as she did during the baseline days. Over the five days of reversal she averaged less than 20 per cent of mornings in interaction with children and about 40 per cent in interaction with adults. She repeatedly ignored the contacts of other children and remained in some solitary activity where a teacher could attend to her. When she did enter play with children, she nearly always broke away after a few minutes to contact and remain with a teacher.

On the 17th day the final shift in contingencies was initiated and Ann was given adult attention only when she interacted with children. An immediate change in her behaviors again occurred. Less than 20 per cent of that morning was spent interacting with adults and 40 per cent interacting with children. Interaction with adults was for the most part adult-initiated, as when the teacher reinforced her play or gave routine instructions. Over the ensuing eight days of the study her interactions with adults stabilized at about 25 per cent of mornings; interactions with children rose to the previous level of about 60 per cent. During the last days of this reinforcement period, teachers gave increasingly intermittent (nonsystematic) attention for interaction with children. The schedule of nonreinforcement of adult contacts was similarly relaxed.

Six school days after the last day of reinforcement (25th day), the first post check of Ann's interactions with children and adults was made (Figure 2: 31st day, post checks). The data showed Ann to be spending more than 60 per cent of the morning in interaction with children, and only 12 per cent in interaction with adults. Further checks taken on the 13th, 15th, and 26th days subsequent to the last reinforcement day (25th day) indicated that Ann was maintaining an average interaction rate with other children of about 54 per cent per morning. Interaction with adults on these days averaged about 18 per cent per morning. On day 38, Ann's mother was present during school hours. Her presence seemed to influence Ann's behavior in the direction of less interaction with children, although the rate was higher than during either the baseline or the reversal periods.

DISCUSSION

Within the first half hour of the first morning of reinforcing interaction with children, Ann seemed to react to the contingencies for getting teacher attention. The immediate change may be attributed to the fact that she already had a repertory of skills readily adapted to play with peers. Similar studies in progress show that the development of adequate play behavior is not always so rapid as in Ann's case. Other children who tend to be off to themselves have taken several weeks to achieve similar levels of social play. During the six days of increasing interaction with children, other changes were noticed. Her speech rose in volume, tempo, and pitch, and complaints about abrasions and bumps dropped out entirely. She appeared to enjoy her play contacts, and the other children responded well to her.

When baseline procedures were again instituted, it immediately became apparent from the decrease in percentage that Ann's play with children was not yet so reinforcing as interaction with adults. Concurrently, her speech again became slow, drawling, and frequently almost inaudible. She again sought adult attention for various minor ills.

During the final period of reinforcing interaction with children, the inappropriate vocal and complaining behaviors quickly disappeared. At times Ann even took and held a strong, give-and-take role in play with five or six other children. Occasionally she defended herself vigorously. In general, her behavior indicated she had become a happy, confident member of the school group.

During the final period of the study teachers had further evidence of the care they must continue to exercise in judging how and under what circumstances to give adult social reinforcement to Ann: on the 19th day (see Figure 2) the children, with the help of a teacher, were making Easter baskets and dyeing eggs. Ann was in almost continuous proximity to both children and the teacher. But most of her interaction was with the adult, as can be seen from the sharp rise in child-adult interaction on this day. This tendency for Ann to gravitate readily to exclusive interaction with the reinforcing adult had been noted early in the study. Teachers had been trained to give attention and approval to Ann as a member of the group by commenting to the group on her contribution, offering some item which Ann could add to the group's play, or approving of the group activity as a unit. Such close pairing of adult reinforcement with children seemed effective in increasing the positive reinforcement values of Ann's peers.

Systematic application of reinforcement principles as a nursery school guidance technique seems to be an important advance toward more effective analysis and use of the existing knowledge about child behavior and development. Guidance measures such as "Encourage him to play with other children" are familiar to every parent and teacher. They imply that adults are to give attention to the child. Reinforcement principles offer a clear, objective guide for precisely discriminating occasions for giving and for withholding adult attention, a positive reinforcer for most young children. The only aspect of reinforcement principles that seems relatively new in nursery school guidance can be subsumed under the word *systematic*.

It seems noteworthy that this study was conducted by teachers in the course of their regular professional work with children. As they helped a child needing special guidance, they examined a guidance technique. Such a combination of the functions of research and service seems both practical and desirable.

References

1. Ayllon, T., & Haughton, E. Control of the behavior of schizophrenic patients by food. *J. exp. Anal. Behav.*, 1962, 5, 343–352.
2. Ayllon, T., & Michael, J. The psychiatric nurse as behavioral engineer. *J. exp. Anal. Behav.*, 1959, 2, 323–334.
3. Brady, J. P., & Lind, D. L. Experimental analysis of hysterical blindness. *Arch. gen. Psychiat.*, 1961, 4, 331–339.
4. Ferster, C. B., & DeMyer, M. K. The development of performance in autistic children in an automatically controlled environment. *J. chronic Dis.*, 1961, 13, 312–345.
5. Harris, F. R., Johnston, M. K., Kelley, C. S., & Wolf, M. M. Effects of positve social reinforcement on regressed crawling of a nursery school child. *J. Educ. Psychol.*, 1964, 55, 35–41.
6. Hart, B. M., Allen, K. E., Buell, J. S., Harris, F. R., & Wolf, M. M. Effects of social reinforcement on operant crying. *J. exp. Child Psychol.*, in press.
7. Wolf, M., Risley, T. R., & Mees, H. L. Application of operant conditioning procedures to the behavior problems of an autistic child. *Behav. Res. & Ther.*, in press.

#33 *Individualized Therapy—A Summary*

James O. Palmer

. . . Only occasionally do the child's needs correspond to the stated goals and criteria of any one therapeutic approach. There are often as many contraindications as indications. Rather than ask whether the child fits any particular therapeutic mold, it would seem much more reasonable to use the data from the assessment to design an individualized program to fit the needs of the child. An attempt will be made to outline the ways in which therapy might be so programmed to the child.

To design such individualized treatment requires a careful and thorough assessment and thoughtful planning. Individualized therapy does not consist merely of a random sampling of therapeutic techniques, nor is it simply an eclectic approach. The design should systematically take into account the following factors.

1. The needs and problems of the child.
2. The basic principles common to all forms of therapy.
3. The variations in techniques needed for the individual needs of the child.
4. The time sequence of the therapy.
5. The economic aspects of the therapy.
6. Some difficulties in implementing a plan for therapy.

1. . . . The overall need of every child is growth, that is, the development of a unique identity with an ego which is capable of independent need-gratification. The raison d'etre of any therapy is to promote such growth. Therapy, of

SOURCE: Reprinted, in abridged form, from *The Psychological Assessment of Children* by James O. Palmer (New York: Wiley, 1970), pp. 421–425. Copyright © 1970 by John Wiley & Sons, Inc. Reprinted by permission of John Wiley & Sons, Inc.

course, does not create the urge to grow; this drive is a central aspect of the biological and social nature of the child. Rather, therapy is aimed at eliminating the obstacles and limitations to the child's growth, and thus deals with those specific behavioral stresses and conflicts which impede the child's development.

If therapy is to be planned to meet these impediments, then the first step is a comprehensive assessment. The assessment should not be limited to the questions asked by the referrant, but should explore in depth all ramifications of the child's ego development, and should contain a list of the various problems, that is, the manifest disturbing behaviors. Next, it should specify the different ways in which development is being impeded, the stresses and conflicts which underlie the disturbances. There should follow some reasonable hypotheses about the possible interrelationships of these factors, the dynamics or interacting forces. To plan therapy, an assessment should uncover and delineate the leitmotiv of the child's development, the core patterns of events and conflicts. These dynamics should be stated in terms of the child's stage of development. In particular, the assessment should specify the degree and nature of the child's dependency on others, and the process of internalization. The kinds of therapy to be used depend in part on the stage of development of the child's experience balance. The assessment should also contain a summary estimate of the overall ego strength of the child, again in terms of development, for the kinds of therapy and their implementation depend on the ability of the child to absorb and use the treatment.

2. . . . There are certain aspects of psychotherapy which all forms have in common and which appear to be fundamental to behavioral change. The therapeutic "couch" need not be a Procrustean bed, but even though it comes in various shapes and sizes and designs, there are some basic elements. Any therapy must include to some degree and fashion, the following.

a. *A reflection or recognition of the child's affective states* or feelings. In behavior modification, which focuses on the environment, this recognition consists of the affective elements of the behavior of others in the environment and the affective responses of the child.

b. *The relationships between these affects and the environment.*

c. *The relationships between these affective states and the internal operations of the child.* In both client-centered therapy and behavior modification, this element of therapy is admittedly underestimated, since it is regarded as a constant.

d. *The relationship of these affective states to the motivations of the child* and of his parents and other authorities. All therapies are concerned with what the child is trying to do, learn, achieve, or obtain. His affective states reflect the frustration of these goals.

e. *The relationship between the child and the therapist.* In this relationship, the child both acts out the frustrations of his everyday life onto the therapist, and uses the therapist as a model.

f. *All therapists repeatedly reinforce* various aspects of the child's behaviors, in a working-through process, sometimes using simple operant rewards and punishments, sometimes using very complex verbal and behavioral situations.

g. Based chiefly on the therapeutic relationship, *all therapies use the therapeutic situation as a microcosm of everyday life.*

3. To design a therapeutic "couch" to fit the child, it is necessary to specify the variations needed in these basic dimensions of therapy. First, one needs to determine from the assessment which affective states need to be recognized and reflected. Which affective responses should be stressed? Which, possibly, ignored? Which are closest to the child's consciousness and are thus

most available for reflection? Which feelings does he hide at all costs? How much spontaneity and lability does he demonstrate? How much does he limit his affective awareness and expression? How sensitive is he? All these questions can and should be answered as best as possible if the reflection of affect is to be planned.

Second, the assessment should specify the relationships between these affects and observable environmental stresses. Are these affects a response to the environment, and to what degree? What stimuli set off these affective reactions? What stimuli inhibit them? Third, the assessment should specify the degree to which these affective responses reflect the internal state of the child. What memories, fantasies, impulses, and drives trigger off these feelings? Are these generalized affective states, or are they specific to certain external or internal stimuli? Assessment of these factors is basic to planning the degree to which the external and internal facts of behaviors are to be manipulated. Fourth, the therapist needs to be advised of the specific motivational patterns which drive the child to act and feel as he does. Where and why is the child frustrated in meeting his need-gratifications? How does he react to deprivation of needs? With knowledge of these motivational patterns, the therapist can make plans to help the child cope with his frustrations and to find effective means of gaining need-satisfactions. Usually the behaviors which require altering are these coping mechanisms. In other instances, the child may be very adept at coping, but needs to redirect his efforts.

The kinds of interactions that the therapist may initially expect from the child are those which the child currently conducts with other adults. These interactions appear during assessment, directly with the assessor and indirectly in the child's responses to various techniques, and parents may openly or inadvertently mention them. From assessment of these patterns, the therapist may be able to predict how the child

may react to him and his behavior. Finally, on the basis of the assessment, it is possible to plan out the kinds of reinforcements which may need to be used for the child under consideration. One may also estimate the frequency of these reinforcements and how they should be varied. With these variables in mind, the therapeutic situations or microcosms may be selected.

4. In all therapies, the timing and sequence of reinforcements are a major factor. Some learning has to be spaced; some consists of a rapid repetition of rewards and punishments. The question facing all therapists is: What is to be done first? Most often, therapy proceeds step by step from one element to the next, in the order listed above in paragraph 2: the therapist initially reflects the child's feelings, relating them to his environment and then to his own internal stresses. At the same time, the therapist begins to explore the child's motivations and their relationships to these affects. As these patterns of behavior are demonstrated in the therapy hour, the therapist uses his relationship with the child as a reinforcement. These and other reinforcements are repeated to obtain specific modifications of the child's behavior, externally and internally.

However, it is not possible to conduct all therapy in this exact order. Sometimes a program of operant conditioning has to be instituted before the child will respond to anything as, for example, in the case of so-called autistic children. With other children, for example, delinquent adolescents, a direct confrontation of motivations may be necessary, even before very much affect is dealt with. The planning of therapeutic strategy is made possible by the assessment of the child's modes of operation. If all of the child's functioning is overwhelmed by a habit, it may be necessary to begin with a program of behavior modification; thereafter, the feelings and motivations underlying the habit may be attacked. If the child has retreated to his daydream world, an exploration of that world may have to precede any alteration of his social environment, which then might be attacked through some form of group treatment. In other instances, it may be necessary to focus on the family and its interactions if that is where the child is operating, before turning to treatment of internal conflicts and affects.

5. The cost of the treatment in time and money also should be estimated. Unfortunately, there is no known basis for budgeting the cost of treatment. This important facet of treatment planning has yet to be studied. At best, one can make rough estimates of the number of sessions, the number of months over which these sessions will be spread, and the consequent cost in therapist's fees or salary. However, if the other aspects of treatment are systematically planned according to the assessment, and if these plans are effectively implemented, then it may be possible subsequently to determine the time and cost of various plans, much as the construction of buildings or highways are budgeted. The cost in terms of dropouts from treatment should decrease, and planned treatment should motivate more patients to remain. Conversely, the average length of treatment for those who do continue should also decrease. The number of wasted hours and misdirected efforts should be decreased by planning. The overall cost in terms of money spent on treatment may increase, but so should the number of successful outcomes.

6. *Difficulties and Objections.* If therapy is planned to meet the needs of the child, then there are no contraindications in the usual sense of the word. Each separate therapeutic endeavor is designed to be the indicated treatment of choice. However, this is not to deny that planning of therapy, in the present state of the scientific development, is often very difficult, if not nearly impossible. Admittedly, the above concepts of individually designed treatment are in many ways quite idealistic and only roughly outlined. Certainly, they are less specific than those proposed by advocates of other set plans, which do not take the variations of the individual into account. The only answer to this objection is that plans are necessary if treatment is not to be a hit-and-miss affair. Moreover, every expert in any kind of treatment does attempt to plan his therapy to fit the exigencies of the individual child. This proposal is intended to broaden such planning, so that by using the assessment, these individual variations may be made more definite and the opportunities for varying treatment may thus also be widened.

A second objection is that such individually designed treatment is, in effect, no treatment at all, but a potpourri of therapies. It does not seem to allow any one therapeutic technique to be completed. Admittedly, any plan must run its course to be effective. One might hesitate to cut a course of behavior modification short to begin a peer group or drop an individual psychoanalytic treatment in midstream to begin a conjoint family treatment. Any planned treatment has to allow for a completion of any component approach. However, these approaches may be considerably shortened by the very fact that more than one is being employed. Very often, any one approach is prolonged by the fact that there are other problems which cannot be easily handled by this single one. Moreover, it is often possible to conduct several therapeutic approaches at once— especially if a program is planned in advance. Reductio ad absurdum, a child might come daily for a therapeutic hour, but instead of receiving psychoanalytic treatment only, he might have such treatment only on Mondays; Tuesdays, he and his mother might be engaged in a behavior modification session; Wednesdays, he might meet in a peer group; Thursdays might be parents' day, for separate or joint sessions; and on Fridays, the whole family might gather for exploration of the family interactions. Unlikely as it is that any child should need such a mixture of treatments all at once, there is no reason that several approaches might not be used at once or in overlapping sequence. Moreover, through such a multiplex of treatment, the total time needed might well be reduced.

Although some therapists are skilled at several different approaches, it is rare that any one therapist can treat all the problems of a child. When a therapist is practicing by himself, he usually uses the methods which he knows best, hoping they will make sufficient changes in the child's behavior. If the child needs other forms of treatment, he may refer him elsewhere. Sometimes a child may be receiving a psychoanalytic treatment plus a conjoint family therapy from one therapist, but be attending some school or institute for learning difficulties where some form of operant conditioning is used. Unfortunately, in private practice, these forms of treatment are rarely coordinated. As a result, both in private practice and in public agencies there is an increasing trend toward the use of multiple therapies. Private practice is now being conducted by groups of several therapists of diverse training. The private school attempts to have several kinds of therapy available or the individual practitioner is associated with several colleagues or a private clinic. The implementation of a plan of therapy calls not only for a variety of therapists, but for a continuous administration of supervision and direction. Any such five-ring circus needs some kind of ringmaster. On the hospital ward, where such multiple treatment programs have long been used, the administrative director, usually a psychiatrist, is responsible for coordination of these treatment programs. However, the coordination of the treatment program for the individual child, within this milieu of treatments, is usually delegated to the individual therapist, the person who is working individually with the child. It is he who determines, in consultation with the staff, which treatments the child needs. Outpatient clinics seldom coordinate their treatment programs quite as closely, and more responsibility is placed on the individual therapist. Far too often, even in the best

of clinics, one therapist has only a slight idea of what is going on in other treatments of the child. Such miscellaneous uncoordinated treatment can be avoided if there is careful planning by the whole staff prior to instituting any therapy. The assessment should be available to the whole staff and be used by all in a coordinated plan.

Finally, it may be objected that no plan of treatment can possibly meet the many exigencies that arise. Even if one could detail all the current stresses and conflicts which the child is enduring, it can be predicted with a high level of certainty that other stresses will occur. For example, the therapist may leave the clinic; the groups will change in membership; the child may be expelled from school; one of his parents may leave the home; the child may fall ill or be injured. Often these emergencies call for a rapid change in plans. In many instances, such emergencies are visibly imminent and it may seem that no planning is possible. In fact, some families present one crisis after another for the therapist to solve, playing a long-range game of family uproar, which in effect prevents therapy from ever beginning. However, treatment needs to be planned if only to prevent the therapy from being overwhelmed by crises. In a carefully outlined plan of treatment, it is possible to include these events as natural experiences to be worked through in treatment. Such treatment plans have to be flexible enough to allow for emergencies. Moreover, when the treatment is interrupted or disrupted by a crisis, there is no reason that the child's situation should not be reassessed. . . . If a family operates by creating one crisis after another, this fact usually is revealed in the assessment and plans can be made for approaching this mode of operations.

These modes of treatment do not exhaust all the possibilities of changing children's behaviors. Often it is necessary to make changes in the child's environment as well as in his actions and attitudes. . . .

Chapter 14

Identity and Sex-Role Stereotypes

With the rise of the women's movement (itself a function of more general concerns with individual and group rights in society), there has been a renewed interest in research and theory in sex-role acquisition and sexual identity. As in the case of other socially volatile issues, discussions have sometimes generated more heat than light and there has been some blurring in terminology. Thus, for example, **sex identity** has at times been confused with **sex-role stereotyping,** although the meanings of these terms are distinct and have quite different implications for the individual's adjustment and the realization of his or her potential and capabilities. The two readings in this chapter do much to clarify the issues and point the way toward a perspective on traditionally sex-linked characteristics that can promote a fuller personal realization of individual potential, for both males and females, and a more harmonious and constructive society.

(1) In the first paper, J. M. Bardwick makes the important point that a secure sex identity does not mean the individual must exhibit or be restricted to exaggerated sex-stereotyped "masculine" or "feminine" characteristics. In some instances, male machismo or exaggerated female dependency and manipulation may be used as a defense against doubts about one's sex identity, that is, identification with one's biologically determined sex. The child or adult who fears or resents his gender, or has contempt for members of his own or the opposite sex, will obviously encounter significant problems since gender is a biological given that cannot be changed. ✳

On the other hand, being a male or female need not restrict the individual to play-

  ✳ 'Tain't necessarily so.

ing out stereotyped and limited sex roles (i.e., assertiveness, independence, task orientation, and an analytic orientation for males; nurturance, intuitiveness, sensitivity, and an interpersonal orientation for females). As Bardwick notes, "It seems . . . that men who are most confident in their masculinity are those who find it easiest to be nurturant; women who are most confident in their femininity need not limit their behaviors to stereotyped dependency and passivity" (p. 402).

Indeed as L. W. Hoffman suggests in the second article, both males and females —and society itself—may benefit from a better balance between traditional "masculine" and "feminine" characteristics within individuals of both sexes. Affiliative motives are personally desirable and socially needed in both males and females; however, excessive affiliative needs in girls, based on an insufficient sense of competence, may interfere with self-esteem, independence, and achievement of their potential. By the same token, while competence, independence, and a desire for mastery are useful characteristics in both sexes, premature pressures toward independence and a one-sided, single-minded preoccupation with achievement goals in boys may create neurotic difficulties, restrict flexibility, and limit one's ability to enjoy a richer, more varied life. "And from a social standpoint, a preoccupation with achievement goals can blot out consideration of the effect of one's work on the welfare of others and its meaning in the larger social scheme" (p. 416).

We would like to make an additional observation that seems indicated in view of the occasionally shrill dogmatisms encountered in discussions of this emotionally laden topic—dogmatisms that seem as confining as the rigid sex-stereotyping they were intended to replace: Some current efforts to insist that all women "act more like a man" (in Professor Higgins' words in **My Fair Lady**), or the reverse, seem equally inappropriate and limiting. The ultimate aim of socialization should be to permit each child or adolescent to develop his or her **unique** potential as a human being, consistent with the rights of others. As Anne Anastasi observed over 15 years ago, in a review of individual differences among both males and females, "the overlapping in all psychological characteristics is such that we need to consider men and women as individuals, rather than in terms of group stereotypes."[1]

1. Anastasi, A. **Differential Psychology.** New York: Macmillan, 1958, pp. 497–498.

The Ego and
Self-Esteem

Judith M. Bardwick

We have been discussing in a rather simplified way the personality qualities and ego skills of women as these characteristics derive from the models of identification. There has been an implicit assumption that femininity is a global or total characteristic, which is probably not true. The feminine woman has been described as passive, masochistic, nurturant, dependent, sensual, receptive, maternal, intuitive, emotional, labile, and empathic. But how generalized are these characteristics? Are feminine women high on all of these variables, in every situation? Or can a woman be "feminine" when she interacts with a man or her children and "nonfeminine" when she

works? As they grow up, do psychologically healthy girls evolve personality skills that are not in the feminine model? Does competitive success result in important subidentities within the image of the self that do not relate to the traditional female role-model? Do feminine women react in feminine ways in all roles, or do some situations bring out nonfeminine traits?

The self acts as a point of stability, a frame of reference, the main organizing principle available in dealings with the social and physical worlds. The self is an object to oneself as well as to others, and one conceives of oneself in the terms that have been learned in interaction with others. The self is a source of action, of motivation, of direction. How one perceives the value of the self determines the level of self-esteem, and the lower a person's self-esteem the greater the anxiety and the greater the response to pressures to assume a

SOURCE: From *Psychology of Women: A Study of Bio-Cultural Conflicts* by Judith M. Bardwick (New York: Harper & Row, 1971), pp. 154–166. Copyright © 1971 by Judith M. Bardwick. Reprinted by permission of Harper & Row, Publishers, Inc.

LABILE (LĀB'L) = LIABLE TO CHANGE

role. Boys may opt for more self-utilization, perceiving themselves as using skills or attributes that are encouraged by society. Because of role expectations, girls may not want to develop all their abilities (such as scholastic excellence). They may then perceive themselves as not using their potential skills or attributes, and as not approximating their ideal selves. It is not only that the culture values the achievements of the masculine world—a girl who has internalized these values will have an idealized self-concept partially dependent upon achievement-oriented skills. And wide divergence from one's ideal self-concept leads to low self-esteem. Girls who combine roles and who act on their various skills and attributes, and girls who are motivated only within the feminine model, are likely to have high feelings of self-esteem. Girls who defensively utilize only certain aspects of their potential but who are motivated to gratify the achievement aspects of themselves in addition to the feminine aspects are likely to have low feelings of self-esteem. A critical factor would seem to be the range of important motives a girl has developed, the diversity of her subidentities, and the extent to which she gratifies diverse aspects of her self-identity. *Role conflict, or the frustration of aspects of the self, does not exist unless diverse and conflicting motives have evolved.* Because role conflict is more likely to exist in women, in particular situations and in general women have lower self-esteem than men.

3   The basic sense of the self as a separate entity probably begins to develop around the age of 2, when a child begins referring to himself as "I." Because this concept develops when the child is very young, I suspect that feelings of aloneness, separation, and powerlessness are always part of the core self-concept—as well as feelings of object constancy (the permanence of the self), sex identity, trust, love, and acceptance. The core sense of self becomes fixed early in life; it is the residue of primary social learning and probably the more psychoanalytic mechanisms of identi-

fication. It includes the body image and the feelings of the body, sexual identification, basic techniques for enhancement of the self and defense of the self, and feelings of volition and responsibility. *It is the basic identity and it limits the subidentities that can be acquired later.* The core self is general; it crosses specific roles and subidentities, and it is not a verbal self so much as a psychological concept. This aspect of the self probably changes slowly with age, and because it is structured it results in a limitation upon the degrees of freedom for potential alternative behaviors. There is probably some kind of critical stage or time limit within which normal people develop this core concept or basic feeling of identity. The core sexual identification is the primary sexual identity but it will interact with a range of subidentities or roles. The social world one is in will define the opportunities or subidentities available, and these will change over the life cycle. In psychological theory, however, basic motivations evolve in childhood. If the basic core motivations have not evolved early, then motives to participate in different roles or subidentities later, when opportunities are available, will not evolve. For example, if the core self-concept is really completely traditionally feminine, there will be no motivation to participate in achievement roles nor will there be a perception of the opportunity.

4   Subidentities are also rather stable. They are acquired later than the core self, and they are acquired continuously within the roles that the person performs. The subidentity is the product of the basic expectations the society holds about each role, unique characteristics the person brings to the role, the experiences he has in the role, and his perceptions of himself in the role. This means that role behaviors will reflect a standard social personality (such as the mother role) and will also be idiosyncratic, reflecting the characteristics of the person who is acting within the role. While the social role is external to the individual, the subidentity is internal, part of the person's per-

ception of himself. The range of roles or subidentities is a function of both the sex and age of the individual. One can conceive of self-esteem as a function of how well one performs in each of the roles one participates in and the extent to which the range of roles and one's performance in them utilizes one's perceived capacity. For some women, the feeling that the traditional role does not permit them to use the range of their potential results in low feelings of self-esteem.

5   An independent sense of self develops later in women than in men. I think it possible that the core sense of self, the sense of female identity, develops relatively early. But the sense of self that evolves from role participations, from subidentities, develops later. Most of the critically important specifically feminine roles for women cannot be rehearsed—they must wait until the girl marries and has a child.

MOTIVES TO ACHIEVE AND TO AFFILIATE

6   Let us look at just two motives, the motive to achieve and the motive to affiliate. The achievement motive refers to the desire to do something, independent of others, according to some internal criteria of excellence. The affiliation motive refers to the need to acquire love and, perhaps, to give love. The role sources of self-esteem, which are critical in determining how one perceives and evaluates oneself, change for women over a period of time. Although there is a consistency in the personality and in the core roles, subidentities change and these changes are related to success in achieving or affiliating.

7   When children are very young their self-esteem is primarily related to their mastery of skills appropriate to their age, and the importance of their sex role is just beginning to become salient. Based upon a stable feeling that they are loved, I think their main preoccupations have to do with achievement. In prepuberty this is still true, but we begin to see girls anticipating adult sex roles by engaging in fantasies of dating, by discussing such matters as how many children

they want to have, and by real behaviors such as cooking or baby-sitting. These anticipations are still in terms of achievement if the girl feels basically loved by her family and liked by her friends. Although she is deeply motivated to continue receiving familial love, anxiety about love or affiliation will increase significantly when she turns for love to people outside of her family— especially when that love will be earned in competition with others and is not the result of simply being a member of a family.

8   For middle-class girls there is likely to be continued pressure for achievement, especially in academics (which has now become a part of the ideal self), and a new pressure for affiliation where affiliation is also seen as achievement and as an affirmation of the self. In adolescence the question of one's identity is a core anxiety and one's self-esteem is vulnerable. Because of parental, societal, and peer pressure, the girl will begin to perceive heterosexual affiliation as the dominant source of self-esteem as well as anxiety. For basic feelings of esteem she must be certain that she can achieve affiliatively, and this will become the more important motive. In addition, the nearness in time of being able to actually participate in the adult sex role will increase her motivation to secure the love of a man so that she can participate in the role.

9   In college, girls as well as boys seem preoccupied with questions about their identity, about their relations with others, their worth, their abilities, their goals, power, morality, and about the direction their life is taking. Boys are preoccupied with achievement, and affiliation is an important but secondary motive. For girls, adult sex-role identity depends upon their affiliative success; therefore, affiliative motives are dominant and achievement motives are important but secondary. Girls perceive heterosexual affiliation as the critical achievement for self-esteem.

10   In the early years of marriage women are not yet secure in the stability of the affiliative relationship and are motivated to succeed in the rela-

tionship because it is the major source of their esteem. They are vulnerable to the discord inevitable in any such important relationship, and they defer to the male in many ways in order not to jeopardize the marriage. They find fulfillment as well as frustration in their relationships with their husbands and children, and slowly they evolve a self-concept of being successful in the establishment of their most important affiliations.

After some years (some of the data suggest it may be as long as fifteen)—when women are secure in the nuclear family relationships and have feelings of self-esteem as females, when their husbands are secure in their achievements and affiliative relationships, when the children are in school—they will increasingly be motivated to achieve in the world of work. When a woman can take her family and the affiliative relationship for granted as a stable part of her life, as she did with her family in childhood, then she can extend herself in other directions, to assume new roles and new subidentities. If she has been feeling that her potential was not being realized in the traditional role, and therefore her self-esteem is low, participation in an occupation will seem to be the most relevant means to utilize her skills and attributes, to come closer to an ideal self which was formed in early childhood. I think that if a woman has a feminine and normal core identity, failure in the feminine roles will preclude feelings of self-esteem. Normally, women will not participate in roles which threaten their affiliative needs, because these needs are critical in their basic concept of themselves.

In early puberty the girl, like the boy, will see the parents as inhibitors and as representatives of childhood. She will devalue the parents and seek a more independent self through identification with persons outside the family. Because of guilt, anxiety, and long-term dependency relations her attempts at independence will not be as complete as the boy's. As she matures, she will transfer the dependent relation from her parents (especially her father) to her boyfriend, and then to her husband. Striving for some sense of independence, she will vacillate between independence and dependence. The greatest independent sense of self will be achieved when she has successfully realized her potential in the interdependent relationships of wife and mother.

Women continue to perceive the world in interpersonal terms and personalize the objective world in a way that men do not. Notwithstanding occupational achievements, they tend to esteem themselves only insofar as they are esteemed by those they love and respect. Unlike the man, who is considered successful when he has achieved within his occupation, the woman who achieves is generally not considered successful unless she also has a husband and children. Because of her needs and society's expectations, the woman who aims for career success assumes the responsibilities of two major roles. One wonders whether mores are changing. The college students I speak with at least voice a desire for a more equitable sharing of role responsibilities between the sexes. They view as offensive the image of the dependent woman whose self-esteem derives entirely from her familial commitment.

ROLE BEHAVIORS

It is probably clear by now that I believe the female's need to establish herself in a loving, intimate relationship, to love and be loved, is dominant. I also believe that the gratification of maternal needs are necessary for feelings of well-being. And I think that for most women in our society gratification of these needs, at home or at work (e.g., nursing, teaching), are dominant motives. I also think that for large groups of middle-class women, especially those who went to college or who learned that they are able to produce independently, gratification of the traditional needs is insufficient for a feeling of self-esteem. Their sense of identity is closely tied in with more traditional feminine needs, but the traditional feminine image—in which a sense of identity derives from an identification with a husband and from contributions to the welfare of a family—is inadequate.

15 Work is a situation to which many motives are brought and in which many gratifications are possible. So is maternity. The motives might be pregnancy, having someone to love who will love you and someone to nurture and protect, the generation of new life from the love relationship, and the certainty of successful femininity. Negative or aggressive motives are also brought to bear, and pregnancy and maternity can be a means of aggressing against the self, the husband, the parents, and the child. But no motives can prepare for the realities of housekeeping and child-rearing, the absorption of the husband in his roles, and the decreasing importance of the mother to her children as they grow and become more independent. If a woman's self-esteem then depends entirely upon a role whose functions diminish, or a role which almost anyone may be able to perform, a role where creativity, excitement, and pleasure are low compared with the total of routinized activity, she is going to be frustrated. On the other hand, few middle-class American women are willing to give up the pleasure and responsibility of being with their children in the early formative years and let someone else nurture them. In addition, the marital stresses of the early years and the crises of parenthood preclude taking for granted the stability of the new family.

16 In the reality of today, I think that the pattern of compromise in which the woman ... ... time, or works after children are in school, is both logical and least threatening. Or, to put it more positively, it is a more certain route to feelings of self-esteem and the utilization of one's potential–assuming that the woman does not need to be really preeminent in her career in order to feel fulfilled. The pattern of compromise means that the responsibilities of the traditional role are still most important and the commitment to work is secondary. For those very few women whose self-esteem derives predominantly from their independent achievements, the compromise pattern will be frustrating. For the majority of women whose primary commitment is to their feminine role, the compromise pattern will be satisfactory—especially if their work does not require personality qualities in strong opposition to characteristic feminine traits.

17 I am sometimes asked what is the effect upon the family when the wife returns to work. Good data on this topic are generally lacking. I think that the woman who is more secure in self-esteem does not need to demand reassurance from the family and make herself feel necessery by intruding into the lives of others. As a mother she is better able to let her children grow to independence and as a wife she is less psychologically demanding. The assignment of role behaviors alters somewhat from the clear traditional ones, but the assumption of most of the traditional roles still goes to the wife. Perhaps most difficult are the changes in subidentities as she goes from one role to another. Work creates new demands upon oneself, and the gratifications of work are proportionate to success and to the motives which led one to work in the first place.

18 If we go back to Douvan and Adelson's (1966) study of adolescents we read that the vocational plans and goals of girls were infused with the feminine needs of wanting to help others, to meet people, and to find some setting where they could meet husbands. In the same study, boys said that work achievement made them feel important, while girls listed acceptance, popularity, and praise.

19 Girls in college are also greatly concerned with feminine goals and with the realization that their identity will be closely tied to the man they marry. But they are concerned in addition with the conflict between their individual aspirations and the culture's definition of femininity. Middle-class college girls who are successful in school

think of themselves as students as well as members of a sex (Douvan and Gold, 1961). But the internalization of the culture's standards for femininity, the need to make identity certain, and the pressure from parents and peers serve to make affiliative needs critical for even the middle-class college girl.[1] For most women the need to gratify motives to achieve independently and occupationally can become important when affiliative gratification is certain and when feminine identity is achieved.

20   We might also mention here another idea which will be discussed in detail later. It is quite a different thing to develop self-esteem because of production in the competitive marketplace. As the self-esteem of most men is closely tied to their vocational achievements, so is the self-esteem of the working woman who is psychologically committed to achievement in her occupation. In work one is no longer applauded for who he is but for what he does. If a man fails in his achievement goals he fails publicly as well as in his private self-evaluation. Women who are motivated enough to enter the marketplace in spite of traditional role-demands and prejudiced expectations are putting themselves in a position where self-esteem may be lost instead of enhanced. It is probable that the motivation of these women to succeed is very high, especially because they have a lot to lose. This is psychologically quite different from the majority of the female working

20.1   [1]Two of the questions I recently asked female college students were "What would make you happiest?" and "What makes you sad or angry?" It rather surprised me that in this highly educated group of women all of the responses were interpersonal and never abstract. Things that would make them happy were to marry, to have children, to make someone happy, or to enable someone else to realize his potential. Anger and sadness were responses to rejection from other people, the death or illness of someone, or unfair treatment of someone. In a time when the university population was preoccupied with Vietnam, interracial conflict, personal freedoms, and the definition of citizen responsibility, not one of these more abstract causes was cited. It was also illuminating that not one girl in the university referred to her academic or professional role as a source of joy or sadness.

force who are content to take jobs with low ceilings of possible achievement, in which their responsibilities are clearly defined, and in which the tasks of the job are not very demanding.

21   It is common to see women, especially those who are college-educated, complaining when their children are young, looking forward to their return to the work force where they can "realize their potential." It is easy to talk but difficult to face potential failure and loss of self-esteem. As their children grow older and the possibility of entry into their profession becomes a reality, their interest declines. The logical and salient mechanisms for prohibiting entrance into the occupational world is a new "accidental" pregnancy. Once again, sometimes complaining loudly, they are forced by the new baby to remain within the easier confines of the house. In this case achievement aspirations are dulled by a fear of failure.

22   I should like to point out a derivative observation. Although I have posited a normal physiologically linked maternal motive, it should be obvious that maternity is an overdetermined behavior. That means that many different motives within the same person are gratified through maternity, and it also means that different people's motives to have a child may also be quite different. All of the important behaviors, such as academic achievement, vocational efforts, pregnancy and maternity, are similarly overdetermined. One cannot simply look at the behavior and assume the relevant motives that have been brought to bear . . . the importance of the reproductive functions in the self-identity of women will make this system a frequent site for the gratification of many motives and the expression of diverse anxieties.

23   Motherhood, for example, is an opportunity for women to act out all of the affects from sentimental, tender, and loving to authoritarian, punitive, and aggressive. Since gender identity is a core part of the self-image it is also true that a threat to one's self-esteem can be perceived as a

threat to one's masculinity or femininity. Adopting the behaviors of the sex-role *stereotype* allows one to ameliorate anxiety regarding femininity or masculinity.

24 Simplifying, we can say that there are basically four groups of adult women: women who are content within the traditional role; women who are wiling to enter the labor force at some time in their lives but who are not really committed to professional achievement and who perceive the job as an extension of their traditional role; a minority who, having achieved success within the traditional role, maintain a core commitment to achievement in a vocation; and women who are not motivated to achieve the traditional role responsibilities, who shy from marriage and children, and who work in order to achieve occupational status. All of the data lend support to the hypothesis that women in this culture are highly motivated to achieve an affiliative relationship although they may have "masculine" achievement strivings as well.

25 *In the reality of current socialization and expectations, I regard women who are not motivated to achieve the affiliative role with husband and children as not normal. The psychological needs that evolve from the body, the internalization of cultural expectation as part of the self-concept, and the pressure from parents and peers all converge to make marriage and children, love and nurturance, the most important of feminine psychological needs. When these needs are absent, denied, or defended against, my clinical observation is that there is evidence for pathological levels of anxiety, a distorted sex identity, and a neurotic solution.*

26 Nevertheless, we can currently see that the population explosion may well result in a change in values where parents are rewarded for producing only two children, or even none. Literature on the psychological and role effects of childlessness is extremely limited and we do not know what psychological or role changes are likely to occur because of this possible widespread change in values. Part of the question is to what extent are needs for nurturance, maternity, and paternity part of our mammalian heritage.

27 We started this chapter asking the question whether femininity is a global characteristic. Like many answers in psychology, the answer is yes and no. When we compare women with men, we could say that women are generally more nurturant, dependent, passive, receptive, maternal, intuitive, empathic, and labile, and that these characteristics become stronger as girls become women. But we could also say that these characteristics are seen mostly in interactive situations, in relationships with other people. It is likely that women are most "feminine" when they interact with their husbands, boyfriends, and children. It is also likely that women are not "feminine" when they are working. In other words, personality qualities of femininity will be present or absent partly depending upon the role, and partly depending upon individual personality traits. Most women I know are less feminine when they interact with other women than when they interact with men. Women often are verbally aggressive directly towards other women, obviously towards their children, and more or less subtly towards their husbands. And a woman can be nonfeminine in her feminine activities. For example, she can take pleasure in giving elaborate dinner parties while really competing for achievement within that role.

28 *Women are able to successfully compete in the masculine occupational world to the extent that they can bring "masculine" personality qualities to the role: objectivity and not subjectivity, assertion and not passivity, achievement motivation and not fears of success or commitment or ambition and drive. By temperament and socialization, relatively few women have these personality qualities. Success can be achieved by a greater number of women in less masculine occupations—those that professionalize interpersonal communication, subjectivity, empathy and nurturance—not simply because these are traditionally*

feminine fields but because the personality qualities women bring to these fields aid them in achieving.

③ EGO STYLES IN WOMEN

29 Women perceive the world differently from men; not only their skills but their interests and thought processes are in some ways different. Psychologically speaking, the easiest professions for women are those in which their interests, skills, and personality qualities are to their advantage, and this will minimize personality conflict within different roles. In terms of personality qualities, it is more difficult for most women to engage in vocations in which they need to be objective, aggressive, and independent. (These descriptions are, of course, simplistic. People are not simple and they develop personality qualities in diverse roles, and in different situations different aspects of the self will emerge.)

30 You may remember that in Chapter 6 we cited sex differences in infants and very young children. Let me briefly repeat them because they seem to be precursors of adult cognitive syles. Six-month-old girls have longer fixation times to visually presented stimuli, less motor activity, and larger magnitudes of cardiac deceleration—all correlates of a perceptual type that perceives similarities or relatedness. Girls show more attention to very complex stimuli, to social stimuli (faces), and to subtle differences in stimuli. These early differences between girls and boys seem to be constitutional; but whether or not they are genetic potentials, women develop attitudes based on perceptions that emphasize social cues, context, the subtle aspects of a situation, and the interpersonal expressions in the situation.

31 The way a person makes sense out of experience and develops his creative expression is called his "ego style." How ego style develops in adult women has been described in two papers by Gutmann (1965, 1968). "Various observers, whether psychologists, misanthropes, lovers or male chauvinists have noted a female tendency to leap to conclusions, to decide issues on emotional rather than rational grounds, and to disregard what men regard as the great necessities of existence" (1968).

32 Gutmann gave normal adult men and women the Thematic Apperception Test (TAT) in which the subject is asked to tell a story that describes the action in a picture.

32.1 I found that women were more erratic and personalizing in their handling of the TAT stimuli. Men tended to approach the cards as a task or as a puzzle, while women tended not to maintain such a rational perspective, such distance, and responded to the cards as if they actually were vivid, exciting or troubling events, rather than representations of such events. Women, for example, would be disturbed by situations which they first imparted to the cards and then experienced as an external reality. Thus, women would finish stories with, "I hope things turn out well for them," or "A boy like that should get what he deserves!" Women vented their immediate emotional reactions to the cards, "This one's horrible!" or, "He has a mean expression!"—and would then elaborate and justify their impulsive response to the subsequent story. Accordingly, by contrast to the male approach, the female approach tended to lack those qualities which are presumably the keystones of the secondary processes of the ego— delay, objectivity, and especially boundary. That is, for women, the boundary between the object and the emotion that pertained to that object, seemed more tenuous, or more permeable than was true of men. The world of women, as they mapped it on to the TAT, tended to be a metaphor, an extension of the affective reaction that it aroused in them. . . .

32.2 Most interesting was that women seemed to find this rather boundaryless mode congenial and perhaps even adaptive. Men who demonstrated an unboundaried approach to the TAT showed up as neurotic by other, independent measures. But women who featured the unboundaried TAT approach achieved higher scores on life satisfaction and morale than did their more contained and boundaried sisters. That is, the woman whose ego style resembled the normative male style was more apt than either the typical man or the typical woman to be anxious, depressed, neurotic. [1968]

33 Although men and women can and do agree on what is good and bad, possible and impossible, their experiences of self and other, space and

time, constancy and change may be very different. Men live in an impersonal world, women, in their domestic role, live in a very personal world. The female world is *autocentric,* which Gutmann defines as one where the individual has recurrent experiences of being the focus, the center, of communal events and ties. In the *allocentric* world of men, the individual has the feeling that the centers and sources of organization, social bonds, and initiatives are separate from him. In the perceptual world of women there is the feeling that she is a part of all that is worth being a part of, and the sense of self includes all of those others that persistently evoke action and affect from oneself. Whereas for men success depends upon the ability to perceive the world objectively, women can personalize the world, perceiving it without boundary.

34 The home environment of the American woman can also be described as autocentric. It is built upon the comparatively predictable and controllable events of the family, home, and neighborhood and reflects the wishes of the woman who is central to its running and the children who were once part of the mother.

34.1 In such a world porous ego boundaries might be a necessary precondition for contentment; and so-called strong ego boundaries could lead to alienation, a rupture of empathic bonds with one's children, and with the pleasant, self-confirming cycles of domestic life. [Gutmann, 1968]

34.2 This is not to say that women have no potential capacity for detached rationality nor men no potential for warm responsiveness; rather, women's affectional and response style is the one most relevant to the autocentric situation. Thus, the tendency of women, observed in their TAT responses, to override boundaries and to experience their own affective states in the world does not imply primitiveness, or regressive solutions to id problems. Rather, this tendency reflects a developed style, with its own sophistications, its own logic, its own version of creativity—a style that develops out of and is harmonious with its psychological ecology. [Gutmann, 1965]

35 We would only add that the origins for this ego style seem to lie not only in an adaptiveness

to the reality of the traditional female role but in an empathic, intuitive, person-oriented style of perception that had its origins in infantile styles of perceiving and in childhood reinforcements. It is not simply that women evaluate themselves in terms of others' appraisals—it is also that in a very real way their perceptual world is composed of their interactions with the subjective world of human relatedness. The subjective quality of feminine ego-functions is praised and valued in the warm mother-child and wife-husband relationships and in extensions of those relationships, such as nursing or voluntary activities in charities. But when this ego quality intrudes into the vocational sphere it is perceived negatively; in the more masculine world it is seen as dysfunctional (although, in fact, it may be functional). As the culture values vocational achievement and rewards ego styles more likely to result in that kind of success, the female may perceive her very personality qualities as second-rate.

36 The roles of men and women are traditionally different; the ego styles of men and women are also different. In their specific roles, some of the personality dispositions generally attributed to one sex or the other will make for greater success. Each sex has positive contributions to make to the welfare of both. But the pervasiveness of the masculine standards of excellence is so complete that we hardly notice its existence. McClelland (1965) has observed that women are perceived and defined as the opposite of men—and the adjectives describing men are all the positive ones. Both sexes describe men as "large," "strong," "hard," "heavy." The opposite adjectives, which characterize women, are "small," "weak," "soft," "light." The female image also includes the adjectives "dull," "peaceful," "relaxed," "cold," "rounded," "passive," and "slow." If male standards are esteemed, women seem inferior. The positive qualities and contributions which women make seem to be denied by men and women alike.

37 There is a school in psychology which feels that sex differences are attributable only to cul-

tural molding and that as culture changes what we perceive as the more basic differences between the sexes could be eliminated or even reversed. There is another school, or, if you like, a variant of the first, which feels that there is an incompatibility between a person's sense of identity as a human being and his sexual identity (Cohen, 1966). I suggest that the origin of the sex differences lies in cultural molding of a constitutional-physiological disposition, and that the overwhelmingly vast majority of cultures have defined the roles of the sexes in terms of the given disposition. It is not that genetics and the body automatically define the adult personality; on the other hand, cultures are not molding "tabula rasa" either. Men and women differ in abilities and traits, in motives, in interactions, in ego styles, and in the perception of what stimuli are relevant. But an insistence that the sexes are unable to effectively cross sex-lines in behaviors, that they are suited only for the traditional divisions of responsibility, seems wrong. It seems to me that men who are most confident in their masculinity are those who find it easiest to be nurturant; women who are most confident in their femininity need not limit their behaviors to stereotyped dependence and passivity. An exaggerated conformity to the stereotype of the sex roles in behaviors and personality traits is probably indicative of anxiety about one's core masculinity or femininity. The feminine core seems to me unchanged, although aspects may become emphasized, or specific behaviors may alter in different cultures and in different periods of history. In American society today women can work and participate in the masculine-occupational sphere without the connotation of protest against feminine functions or expressing a fear of those functions.

38   In our masculine-oriented culture a person is worth the market value of his skills and personality. One's esteem depends not on the human qualities which one possesses but on success in the competitive marketplace. Failure in this competition produces anxiety in the individual because it is one's worth as a person that is threatened. The striving for success is the striving for self-esteem. The individual with a stable self-concept and a high sense of self-esteem is better able to face the unknown, the changing demands of the market. The person whose sense of self is not stable nor well-defined, who has not achieved self-esteem, will fear the unknown as potentially dangerous to the self-concept he has, and he will cling to old patterns of dependence. In our culture we would expect much anxiety to occur in the striving for individual competitive success. This is an area of anxiety which women are able to avoid insofar as they do not put themselves into the marketplace competition, deriving their sense of self and their self-esteem from the traditional relationships. But like men, some American women perceive competitive achievement as a route to self-affirmation and self-realization, despite its being anxiety provoking.

References

Cohen, Mabel B. 1966. Personal identity and sexual identity. *Psychiatry* 29(19):1–14.

Douvan, Elizabeth, and J. Adelson 1966. *The adolescent experience.* Wiley, New York.

Douvan, Elizabeth, and M. Gold 1966. Model patterns in American adolescence. In Hoffman, M. L., and L. W. Hoffman (eds.), *Review of child development research,* vol. 2. Russell Sage Foundation, New York, pp. 469–528.

Gutmann, D. L. 1965. Women and the conception of ego strength. *Merrill-Palmer Quarterly* 11(3):229–240.

Gutmann, D. L. 1968. Female ego styles and generational conflict. Paper presented at the Midwestern Psychological Association, 3 May 1968, Chicago.

McClelland, D. C. 1965. Wanted: A new self-image for women. In Lifton, R. J. (ed.), *The Woman in America.* Houghton Mifflin, New York, pp. 173–192.

Silverman, J. Attentional Styles and the Study of Sex Differences, in Mostofsky, D. (ed), *Attention: Contemporary Studies and Analysis,* Appleton-Century-Croft, New York, in press.

Early Childhood Experiences and Women's Achievement Motives

Lois Wladis Hoffman

Research findings in child development are reviewed to shed light on female achievement motives. It is suggested that females have high needs for affiliation which influence their achievement motives and behavior, sometimes enhancing and sometimes blocking them. Since girls as compared to boys have less encouragement for independence, more parental protectiveness, less pressure for establishing an identity separate from the mother, and less mother-child conflict which highlights this separation, they engage in less independent exploration of their environments. As a result they develop neither adequate skills nor confidence but continue to be dependent upon others. Thus while boys learn effectance through mastery, the effectiveness of girls is contingent on eliciting the help of others. Affective relationships are paramount in females and much of their achievement behavior is motivated by a desire to please. If achievement threatens affiliation, performance may be sacrificed or anxiety may result.

The failure of women to fulfill their intellectual potential has been adequately documented. The explanations for this are so plentiful that one is almost tempted to ask why women achieve at all. Their social status is more contingent on whom they marry than what they achieve; their sense of femininity and others' perception of them as feminine is jeopardized by too much academic and professional success; their husband's masculinity, and hence their love relationship as well as their reciprocal sense of femininity, is threatened if they surpass him; discrimination against women in graduate school admittance and the professions puts a limit on what rewards their

SOURCE: From *Journal of Social Issues*, vol. 28 (1972), 129–155. Copyright © 1972 by the American Psychological Association. Reprinted by permission.

performance will receive; their roles as wives and mothers take time from their professional efforts and offer alternative sources of self-esteem. Perhaps most important, they have an alternative to professional success and can opt out when the going gets rough. A full scale achievement effort involves painful periods of effort and many a man would drop out if that alternative were as readily available as it is to women. (Indeed, the Vietnam war and the new distrust of the old goals have provided young men with just such an opportunity and many have grabbed it.) But women's underachievement must have roots deeper even than these, for the precursors of the underachieving woman can be seen in the female child.

Even at preschool age girls have different orientations toward intellectual tasks than do boys. Little girls want to please; they work for love and approval: if bright, they underestimate their competence. Little boys show more task involvement, more confidence, and are more likely to show IQ increments. Girls have more anxiety than boys and the anxiety they have is more dysfunctional to their performance. There are also differences in the specific skills of each sex: Males excel in spatial perceptions, arithmetical reasoning, general information, and show less set-dependency; girls excel in quick-perception of details, verbal fluency, rote memory, and clerical skills.

Boys and girls enter the world with different constitutional make-ups, and recent studies show that parents treat boys and girls differently even from birth. Social roles are first—and most impressively—communicated through parent-child relations and events in early childhood may have an impact that cannot later be duplicated in effectiveness.

As a result, interest in women's intellectual achievement has led a number of people to look to the child development data for insights. A few of the limitations of these data will be discussed first, for a number of extravagant generalizations are being drawn from them.

LIMITATIONS OF CHILD DEVELOPMENT DATA

Relativity

Child development data are often relative to a given group. Thus a statement about girls who are "high on aggression" usually means high relative to the other girls studied. If they are compared to boys who are "high on aggression" even in the same study, the actual aggressive behavior may be very different. Boys are considerably more aggressive than girls; a girl who is high on aggression may resemble a boy whose aggressive behavior is coded as average. She may also differ from the boys with respect to the form of aggression and the personality syndrome of which it is a part. It should not be surprising then to discover that the antecedent conditions of high aggression are different in boys and girls. They might very well be different even if the dependent variables were identical, but the fact is that they are not. We are comparing oranges with apples and discovering to our surprise that they grow on different trees.

This problem not only applies to the dependent variables, but also to the independent variables studied, usually parent behavior or the parent-child relationship. To use an actual finding, Kagan and Moss (1962) found that maternal protectiveness during the first three years was negatively related to adult achievement behavior for girls. This was not true for boys and in fact the relationship was positive although not statistically significant. This is an important finding to which we will return, but here it should be pointed out that we cannot tell from these correlations whether or not the actual maternal behavior is different for high achieving boys and girls. Girls are subject to more overprotection than boys and the same amount of protective behavior may be relatively low for a girl but average or high for a boy.

Baumrind (1970) has pointed out that obtaining data on the differential treatment (or behavior) of boys and girls is difficult because, even in behavioral observations, when the observer knows the sex of the child, "an automatic adjustment is made which tends to standardize judgments about the two sexes."

Generalizability

The problem of generalizing results obtained with one population to another occurs throughout the social sciences. It is particularly acute when the variables involve relative terms. "High parental coerciveness" in a middle class sample may not be considered high in a lower class sample. Furthermore, most empirical generalizations hold only within certain contexts. Variations in social class, parent education, rural-urban residence, family structure, and ethnicity—as well as changes over time—may make the generalizations inapplicable.

As an interesting case in point, it is impossible to generalize white sex differences to blacks for the patterns of sex differences are very different in the two groups. Studies of blacks will be important in interpreting the etiology of sex differences in intellectual performance for in many ways the black male resembles the white female. For both, school performance has been largely irrelevant to adult goals and there are interesting similarities in the patterns of achievement scores that may reflect this (Tulkin, 1968; Jensen, 1970). In a study of conformity and perceptual judgment by Iscoe, Williams, and Harvey (1964), black males and white females were more influenced by others than were black females and white males. Similarities between black males and white females argue against constitutional explanations, for these two groups share neither hormones nor race—but they do share environmental handicaps.

Maturation

Another difficulty in interpreting sex differences among children pertains to differences in the maturity of boys and girls. The newborn girl is one month to six weeks developmentally ahead of the boy. At school entrance she is about one year ahead, depending on the index of growth used. Growth does not proceed equally on all fronts and the intellectual growth rate is not related to the physical (Bayley, 1956). These different degrees of maturity complicate the comparison between the sexes.

Conceptualization

Ambiguous concepts are a problem in many fields. The so-called inconsistencies in the child development data often upon close examination turn out to be inconsistencies in the researcher's summaries and concluding statements rather than in the actual findings. If examined in terms of the operational definitions, contradictory studies sometimes turn out to be dealing with different phenomena that have been given the same label. Among the particularly troublesome concepts that are important in the sex-difference literature are identification and dependency (Bronfenbrenner, 1960; Maccoby & Masters, 1970).

FEMALE ACHIEVEMENT ORIENTATIONS

There are very few studies that have empirically connected socialization experiences to sex differences in achievement orientations. As a matter of fact, there are few studies of sex differences in child rearing practices in general, and existing data—most of which were originally collected for other purposes—are subject to the limitations mentioned above. Promising new approaches sensitive to identifying sex differences may be found in the studies of parent-child interaction with neonates (Moss, 1967; Moss & Robson, 1968; Moss, Robson, & Pedersen, 1969; Lewis, 1969; Goldberg & Lewis, 1969; Kagan, 1969; Kagan, Levine, & Fishman, 1967). These are mainly longitudinal studies which will make their most valuable contributions in the future, but some have already examined relationships between maternal behavior and cognitive orientations.

Probably the richest current area in the study of sex differences has to do with cognitive styles. Witkin, Dyk, Faterson, Goodenough, & Karp (1962) as well as other investigators have been interested in differences in perceptions of and approaches to problems. For example, some people are more affected by background stimuli than others. In a task in which the subject is asked to line up a rod until it is perpendicular, the fact that the frame around the rod is tilted will affect the judgment of some respondents more than others. Those most affected by the tilting frame are said to be field dependent. This body of research has revealed a number of personality traits that are associated with performance on the task, and a number of cognitive skills such as mathematical ability that seem to be closely tied to field independence. These personality traits describe differences between the sexes; the corresponding cognitive abilities similarly differentiate.

For example, Maccoby (1963, 1966)[1] has pointed out that girls are more conforming, suggestible, and dependent upon the opinions of others. These traits in turn have been related to field dependency, inability to break the set of a task, and IQ's that tend to decrease rather than increase over the years. She suggests that these same traits in females might also account for their superior performance on spelling and vocabulary tests, and their inferior performance on tests involving analytic thinking, spatial ability, and arithmetic reasoning. Additional discussion on this issue can be found in Kagan (1964), Sherman (1967), Silverman (1970), and Kagan and Kagan, 1970).

The actual linkage between these personality traits and the cognitive styles has not been established, nor has the etiology of sex differences in personality. Some of the infancy studies mentioned above are making inroads. Thus the finding that mothers spend more time in face-to-face verbalizations with infant girls (Kagan, 1969; Moss, 1967; Goldberg & Lewis, 1969) may be tied to the observation that female infants are more verbally responsive and to the later superiority of females in verbal ability. Verbal responsiveness may also result from the fact that girls' hearing is superior to that of boys (Garai & Scheinfeld, 1968). Also relevant is a study with 10-year-olds in which observations of mother-daughter interaction in task solving showed that girls good in math or spatial relations were left to solve tasks by themselves while the mothers of girls higher on verbal skills (the more typical female pattern) were more intrusive with help, suggestions, and criticism (Bing, 1963).

The present paper will focus on an area that is even less explored: the question of motivation for top intellectual performance. There are data that the very brightest women more often than comparable men stop short of operating at their top intellectual level. Terman and Oden (1947) have shown that gifted girls did not as adults fulfill their potential as often as gifted boys. Rossi (1965a, 1965b) has summarized data indicating that even those few women who do go into science and the professions rarely achieve eminence.[2]

These data reflect in part the factors mentioned earlier—alternative choices in life that have been available to women but not to men, barriers to career opportunities that exist because of women's family roles, and discrimination in the professions which limits the rewards obtainable. The concern here is not with these factors, however, but with a deeper, more psychologically-based motivation that occurs in women. The

---

[1]These reviews by Maccoby and reviews by Kagan (1964), Becker (1964), Glidewell, Kantor, Smith, and Stringer (1966), Oetzel (1966), Garai and Scheinfeld (1968), Silverman (1970), Kagan and Kogan (1970), and Bardwick (1971) will be referred to throughout the paper where a point is supported by several studies that are adequately reported in the review.

[2]Simon, Clark, and Galway (1970), on the other hand, have reported that the woman PhD who is employed full time publishes as much as her male colleagues.

most relevant data come from the work of Horner (1968, 1972) who has demonstrated with a projective story completion measure a "fear of success" among able college women. Furthermore, women who indicate fear of success show poorer performance in a competitive task than when the same task is performed alone. In interpreting her results, Horner suggests that this fear exists in women because their anticipation of success is accompanied by the anticipation of negative consequences in the form of social rejection or loss of femininity.

The idea that the affiliative motive can be dysfunctional to performance is supported by another of Horner's findings. Men who were motivated both to achieve and to affiliate showed a performance decrement when asked to compete with another man. Horner suggests this decrement may have resulted from a conflict of motives since "out-performing a competitor may be antagonistic to making him a friend."

AFFILIATIVE NEEDS AND ACHIEVEMENT

There is a great deal of evidence that females have greater affiliative needs than males (Oetzel, 1966; Walberg, 1969) and therefore the conflict between affiliation and achievement probably will occur more often for women. It seems that, apart from direct concerns with whether or not their behavior is sufficiently "feminine," academic and professional women frequently allow their concern with affective relationships to interfere with the full use of their cognitive capacities. In group discussion and in intellectual argument, women often seem to sacrifice brilliance for rapport.

However, while the findings of the Horner studies (1972) and our observations of professional women focus attention on the dysfunctions of affiliative motivations for performance, there are data indicating that the desire for love and approval can also have a positive effect. In fact, the Crandalls (V. J. Crandall, 1963; V. C. Crandall, 1964) as well as others (Garai & Scheinfeld, 1968) have suggested that achievement behavior in girls

is motivated not by mastery strivings as with boys, but by affiliative motives.

In two very different studies, nursery school and elementary school girls' achievement efforts were motivated by a desire for social approval to a greater extent than were boys'. In the nursery school study the attempt was also made to motivate the children by appeals to mastery strivings; this technique succeeded with boys but failed with girls (Lahtinen, 1964). In the study with elementary school children, achievement motives in boys were related positively to achievement test scores. Among the girls, affiliative motives, not achievement motives, were so related (Sears, 1962, 1963). Other studies with nursery school and elementary school children found affiliative behavior and achievement efforts positively related in girls, but boys showed no such relationship (Tyler, Rafferty, & Tyler, 1962; Crandall, Dewey, Katkovsky, & Preston, 1964). Similarly with adult women, the achievement arousal techniques that are effective with males have failed with females (Veroff, Wilcox, & Atkinson, 1953; Horner, 1968), but appeals to social acceptability have been successful (Field, 1951).

There are also several studies that indicate that throughout grade school boys are more motivated than girls to master challenging tasks when social approval is not involved. When given the opportunity to perform an easy or more difficult task, to work on a puzzle they had already solved or one they had failed, to pursue further or escape a difficult problem, boys are more likely to choose the more difficult and challenging, girls to choose the task that promises easy success or to leave the scene (Crandall & Rabson, 1960; Moriarty, 1961; McManis, 1965; Veroff, 1969).

From these studies it appears that female achievement behavior even at preschool or early grade school ages is motivated by a desire for love rather than mastery. When achievement goals conflict with affiliative goals, as was the case in Horner's projective responses and in the competitive situation in which her fear-of-success girls showed less competent performance, achievement behavior will be diminished and/or anxiety result. This does not mean that academic performance is lower for females in general since it is often compatible with affiliative motives. In elementary schools, excellence is rewarded with love and approval by parents, teachers, and peers. Even in the lower socioeconomic class, sociometric studies show that academic excellence in girls is rewarded with popularity (Glidewell et al., 1966; Pope, 1953). In college, however, and in professional pursuits, love is less frequently the reward for top performance. Driving a point home, winning an argument, beating others in competition, and attending to the task at hand without being side-tracked by concern with rapport require the subordination of affiliative needs.

In short, the qualities needed for sustained top performance—especially as an adult—are not typically part of a girl's makeup. She wants approval and so she performs well in school. She works for good grades. And indeed throughout grammar school, high school, and college, she obtains higher grades than boys (Oetzel, 1966; Garai & Scheinfeld, 1968). If overachievement is thought of as grades exceeding IQ's, then girls as a group are more overachieving than boys. But girls are less likely to become involved in their task; they are less motivated by strivings for mastery. In McClelland's sense of *achievement* (McClelland, Atkinson, Clark, & Lowell, 1953)—competition with a standard of excellence—they fall short.[3]

This affiliative need may be particularly germane to achievement patterns because it may be rooted in early experiences when the child is learning patterns of effectance. When little boys are expanding their mastery strivings, learning

[3]Women have obtained scores on McClelland's test of achievement motivation under neutral conditions that are as high or higher than those obtained by men under arousal conditions; however, researchers have questioned the validity of the measure for women (see McClelland et al., 1953; and Horner, 1968).

instrumental independence, developing skills in coping with their environment and confidence in this ability, little girls are learning that effectiveness—and even safety—lie in their affectional relationships. The idea expressed by Kagan (1964) that boys try to "figure the task" and girls try to "figure the teacher" seems rooted in early child-rearing practices and reinforced by later experiences.

STATEMENT OF THEORY

It is the thesis here that the female child is given inadequate parental encouragement in early independence strivings. Furthermore, the separation of the self from the mother is more delayed or incomplete for the girl because she is the same sex with the same sex role expectations, and because girls have fewer conflicts with their parents. As a result, she does not develop confidence in her ability to cope independently with the environment. She retains her infantile fears of abandonment; safety and effectiveness lie in her affective ties. These points will now be elaborated and supportive data brought in where available.

The Development of Independence, Competence, and Self-Confidence

All infants are dependent; as the child matures his independence strivings increase. Observers have often been impressed with what White (1960) calls the *effectance motive*—the child's need to have an effect upon his environment. Thus the child grasps and releases, reaches and pulls, and in the course of doing this he learns about his environment and his ability to manipulate it. He develops cognitive abilities, and he develops a sense of effectiveness—a sense of competence through increasingly successful interaction with his environment.

As the infant matures, the feats he undertakes get scarier. Increasingly they involve separating the self from the mother and leaving the security of that unity. Early independence explorations seem to take place most successfully with the parent present; the child moves toward independence so long as the "safety man" is in sight. As he gains confidence, the parent's presence becomes less and less necessary.

Very likely this period–somewhere between a year and three or four years of age—is critical in the development of independence and competence (Erikson, 1959; Veroff, 1969; White, 1960; Stendler, 1963). By critical, we mean a period when independence and competence orientations are more efficiently learned than at other times. There is a rapid building up of notions about the self and about the world.

Although theories differ as to the exact timing and differential importance of the events occurring in this period, all would probably agree on the minimal requirements for the development of independence and competence. Thus if the infant is deprived of affection, rejected, or prematurely pushed toward independence, he will not have a secure base from which to build true independence. The dependency that results from a short shrift in early affective ties is probably of a distinct kind (Stendler, 1963). We do not think it is more characteristic of girls, nor that it is sufficiently common to the nonpathogenic middle class family to be useful in understanding prevalent female achievement orientations.

Even with an adequate affective base, independent behavior does not happen automatically. It requires not only opportunities for independent behavior but also actual parental encouragement. Evidence for this can be found in Baumrind's research (Baumrind & Black, 1967; Baumrind, 1971) which indicates that competence comes not from permissiveness but from guidance and encouragement. The first steps a child takes are exciting but also frightening, and cues from the mother can greatly influence the subsequent behavior. The mother's delight is part of her independence training; her apprehension constitutes training in dependence.

Further, if the child's early independence be-

haviors are to be followed by more, these ventures must be reasonably in accord with his abilities. Repeated successes such as these will have the important effect of developing in the child a sense of competence. There may be a delicate timing mechanism—premature independence can backfire; but the parent who withholds independence opportunities too long and indeed does not encourage independent behavior will also fail to produce an independent child. (It is possible that the appropriate timing is different for boys than girls due to differences in abilities and maturation rates.)

The awareness that the mother is a separate person whose wishes are not the same as his serves to increase the child's striving for autonomy and independence. Both Erikson and White see the period between one and three as the battle for antonomy. At this age the child's motoric explorations often require parental interference. The span of consecutive action is such that interference can be frustrating for the child and completions gratifying. Toilet training usually occurs around this time. The child thus enters into conflict with his mother; out of this conflict, if it does not involve his humiliation and defeat, the child will emerge with "a lasting sense of autonomy and pride [Erikson, 1959]" and "a measure of confidence in his own strength [White, 1960]."

THE EMPIRICAL FINDINGS

Independence Training: Sex Differences
Early exploratory behaviors in which the child interacts effectively with his environment are seen here as crucial in building up a sense of competence. In this respect males have a number of advantages.

·INFANT STUDIES. Studies of neonates suggest a higher activity level on the part of the male, while females demonstrate greater tactile sensitivity and a lower pain threshold (Garai & Scheinfeld,

1968). From these predispositions alone we could expect more exploratory behavior on the part of male infants, but to compound the matter observations of mothers with neonates show that even controlling for the differences in activity levels, mothers handle and stimulate males more than females (Moss, 1967, undated). And a study by Rubenstein (1967) suggests that such maternal attentiveness facilitates exploratory behavior.

Kagan and Lewis and their associates have also reported differences in maternal behavior toward male and female infants (Kagan, Levine, & Fishman, 1967; Goldberg & Lewis, 1969). Whether the maternal behavior is primarily a response to infant predispositions or a cause of the differences is not definitely established, but there is some evidence that both influences occur. That maternal behavior is not entirely a response to the infant is indicated by relationships found between the mother's infant care and her orientations prior to the child's birth. For example, Moss (1967) reports that mothers were interviewed two years before they gave birth and rated on their attitudes toward babies. A positive attitude toward babies was found to relate significantly to the amount of responsiveness later shown to her 3-week-old infant. This same investigator also found mutual visual regard—one of the earliest forms of mother-infant communication—to be related to maternal attitudes expressed before the birth (Moss & Robson, 1968). On the other hand, that maternal behavior is not the sole determinant of the infant's behavior is indicated by the fact that the sex differences in tactile stimulation and pain thresholds mentioned above have been established for infants less than four days old and still in the hospital nursery (Garai & Scheinfeld, 1968; Silverman, 1970). An interaction hypothesis seems most tenable in the light of the present data.

One of Moss's mother-infant interaction findings is particularly pertinent to the theory presented in this paper (1967, undated). He reports data on the mother's responsiveness to the infant's cries and notes that this sequence—baby cries and mother responds with the needed care—is important in shaping the infant's response to the mother as a supplier of comfort. The more closely the mother's caretaking behavior is related to the infant's cries, the more effectively will the child "regard the mother as having reinforcing properties and respond to her accordingly [Moss, undated, p. 10]." The correlation obtained between maternal contact and infant irritability was statistically significant for females but not for males. The mothers did not attend to the female infants more than the male (less, in fact) but their attention was more closely linked to the infant's state of need as expressed by crying. This finding if borne out by further research could be very important for several reasons. First, it could signify the beginning of a pattern of interaction between mothers and daughters in which the daughters quickly learn that the mother is a source of comfort; and the mother's behavior is reinforced by the cessation of crying. The sheer presence of the mother would soon signal the satisfaction of the infant's needs. Second, there is agreement among most investigators that there are critical periods in infancy when learning takes place so efficiently that long range behaviors are effected by simple but pertinently timed events; this might be such a critical period. Third, even if this is not a critical period, the finding may reflect an orientation of mothers toward daughters that is often repeated beyond the infancy period.

In any case, one thing appears certain from this body of research on early mother-infant interaction: There are sex differences in both maternal and infant behavior during the first year of life. That sex role learning is begun so early should not be surprising. Sex is a primary status —the first one announced at birth. The mother is very much aware of it. Her early behaviors toward the infant are not deliberate efforts to teach the child his proper sex role, but she has internalized society's view and acts accordingly. She acts toward her son as though he were sturdy and active and she is more likely to show pleasure when his behavior fits this image. Her daughter is her doll—sweet and delicate and pink. The mother's behavior reflects this perception, and if the child exhibits behavior consistent with the female stereotype, such as dependency, she is not as likely to discourage it as she would with a son.

·INDEPENDENCE TRAINING IN CHILDHOOD. Moving from early infancy, we find studies that link independence training and the parent's achievement orientations to the child's competence (Baumrind & Black, 1967) and achievement orientations (Winterbottom, 1958; Rosen & D'Andrade, 1959), but few examining sex differences in the independence and achievement training children receive. It is our view that because of parental attitudes toward male and female children which reflect their culturally assigned roles, males receive more effective independence training and encouragement.

An adaptation of the Winterbottom measure for use with parents of younger children was developed by Torgoff (1958). Using this measure, Collard (1964) asked mothers of 4-year-olds to indicate the ages they thought parents should expect or permit certain child behaviors. For example, the parents were asked at what age they believed parents should: (a) begin to allow their child to use sharp scissors with *no* adult supervision, (b) begin to allow their child to play away from home for long periods of time during the day without first telling his parents where he will be. The answers to these questions yielded two measures—*independence granting* and *achievement induction*. Mothers of girls responded with later ages than mothers of boys. This difference was significant for the independence-granting items and it was particularly strong in the middle class. The achievement induction scores were not significantly different for the two sexes, but close inspection of the data revealed that, for the middle class, mothers of girls indicated an earlier age for only two of the 18 items making up the scale.

One of the two exceptions was "sharing toys" which may have more to do with inter-personal relationships than with achievement.

·PARENTAL ANXIETY AND PROTECTIVENESS. Still another difference in the independence training received by boys and girls may stem from parental ambivalence: Parents may show more unambivalent pleasure in sons' achievements than in daughters'. The young child's first motoric adventures can produce anxiety in the mother as well as the child, just as they produce pleasure for both. It seems likely that for the parent of a boy there is a particular pride in the achievement and less of a feeling of the child's fragility; as a result there is a clearer communication of pleasure in the achievement per se. A beaming mother when the child takes his first steps may have a very different effect than the mother who looks anxious while holding out loving arms. In the former case, the task itself becomes the source of pleasure (in reinforcement terms the reward is closer to the act). In the latter case, the mother is saying in effect, "You may break your neck en route, but I will give you love when you get here." The mother's indications of anxiety as the child moves toward independence make the child doubt his own competence, for mothers are still omniscient to the young child.

There is some indirect evidence for this view. Despite the greater maturity and sturdiness of the female infant (Garai & Scheinfeld, 1968), parents think of them as more fragile. Furthermore, behavioral observations of infants have shown that male infants are handled more vigorously (Moss, 1967). The setting of later ages for granting autonomy to girls, as indicated in the Collard (1964) study mentioned earlier, suggests that parents are more protective, if not more anxious, toward girls. For example, parents report allowing boys to cross busy streets by themselves earlier, though they are not motorically more advanced than girls and their greater motoric impulsivity would seem to make this more dangerous. And we do know that infants pick up the subtle attitudes of their caretakers. This was demonstrated in the well known study by Escalona (1945) in which the infant's preference for orange or tomato juice depended heavily on the preference of the nurse who regularly fed him. The infant had no way of knowing his nurse's preference except through sensing her attitude as she fed him.

Another kind of parent behavior that is detrimental to the development of independence might be called *over-help*. Mastery requires the ability to tolerate frustration. If the parent responds too quickly with aid, the child will not develop such tolerance. This shortcoming—the tendency to withdraw from a difficult task rather than to tackle the problem and tolerate the temporary frustration—seems to characterize females more than males. This has been demonstrated in the test situations mentioned earlier, and Crandall and Rabson (1960) have also found that, in free play, grade school girls are more likely than boys to withdraw from threatening situations and more frequently to seek help from adults and peers. The dysfunctions of this response for the development of skills and a sense of competence are clear. There are no data to indicate that over-help behavior is more characteristic of parents of girls, but such a difference seems likely in view of the greater emphasis placed on the independence training of boys.

Clearly more research is needed to identify differences in the independence and achievement training—and in any overprotection and over-help—that parents provide boys and girls. Even if the differences we have described are definitely established, it will still need to be shown that this pattern of parental protectiveness and insufficient independence training is a major contributor to an inadequate sense of personal competence in girls. It should be pointed out, however, that this inference is consistent with the findings that girls are more anxious than boys, more likely to underestimate their abilities, and more apt to lack confidence in their own judgment when it is contrary to that of others (Sarason, 1963; Sarason & Harmatz, 1965; Sears, 1964; Crandall, Katkovsky, & Preston, 1962; Hamm & Hoving, 1969). There is also evidence that the above pattern is reinforced by the later socialization experiences of girls. Several investigators report that while dependency in boys is discouraged by parents, teachers, peers, and the mass media, it is more acceptable in girls (Kagan & Moss, 1962; Kagan, 1964; Sears, Rau, & Alpert, 1965). Data from the Fels study (Kagan & Moss, 1962) are particularly interesting in this respect, reporting that childhood dependency predicted to adult dependency for females but not males, the converse being true for aggression. Their interpretation is that pressure is exerted on the child to inhibit behaviors that are not congruent with sex role standards (Kagan, 1964).

Establishing a Separate Self: Sex Differences

SAME SEX PARENT AS PRIMARY CARETAKER. Separation of the self is facilitated when the child is the opposite sex of the primary caretaker. Parsons (1949, 1965) and Lynn (1962, 1969), as well as others, have pointed out that both males and females form their first attachment to the mother. The girl's modeling of the mother and maintaining an identity with her is consistent with her own sex role, but the boy must be trained to identify with his father or to learn some abstract concept of the male role. As a result, the boy's separation from the mother is encouraged; it begins earlier and is more complete. The girl, on the other hand, is encouraged to maintain her identification with the mother; therefore she is not as likely to establish an early and independent sense of self. If the early experiences of coping with the environment independently are crucial in the development of competence and self-confidence, as suggested previously, the delayed and possibly incomplete emergence of the self should mitigate against this development.

There are no studies that directly test this

hypothesis. As indirect evidence, however, there are several studies showing that the more identified with her mother and the more feminine the girl is, the less likely she is to be a high achiever and to excel in mathematics, analytic skills, creativity, and game strategies. For example, Plank and Plank (1954) found that outstanding women mathematicians were more attached to and identified with their fathers than their mothers. Bieri (1960) found that females high on analytical ability also tended to identify with their fathers. Higher masculinity scores for girls are related positively to various achievement measures (Oetzel, 1961; Milton, 1957; Kagan & Kogan, 1970), as are specific masculine traits such as aggressiveness (Sutton-Smith, Crandall, & Roberts, 1964; Kagan & Moss, 1962). The relation between cross-sex identification and cognitive style for both boys and girls is discussed also by Maccoby (1966).

For several reasons the above studies provide only limited support for our view. First, there is some evidence, though less consistent, that "overly masculine" males, like "overly feminine" females, are lower on various achievement-related measures (Maccoby, 1966; Kagan & Kogan, 1970). Second, the definitions and measures of femininity may have a built-in anti-achievement bias. Third, the question of the mother's actual characteristics has been ignored; thus the significant factor may not be closeness to the mother and insufficient sense of self, as here proposed. The significant factor may be identifying with a mother who is herself passive and dependent. If the mother were a mathematician, would the daughter's close identification be dysfunctional to top achievement?

Clearly the available data are inadequate and further research is needed to assess the importance of having the same sex as the primary caretaker for personality and cognitive development.

·PARENT-CHILD CONFLICT. Establishing the self as separate from the mother is also easier for boys because they have more conflict with the mother than do girls. Studies of neonates suggest, as mentioned above, that males are more motorically active; this has also been observed with older children (Garai & Scheinfeld, 1968; Moss, 1967; Goldberg & Lewis, 1969). Furthermore, sex differences in aggressive behavior are solidly established (Oetzel, 1966; Kagan, 1964), and there is some evidence that this is constitutionally based (Bardwick, 1971). Because of these differences, the boy's behavior is more likely to bring him into conflict with parental authority. Boys are disciplined more often than girls, and this discipline is more likely to be of a power assertive kind (Becker, 1964; Sears, Maccoby, & Levin, 1957; Heinstein, 1965). These encounters facilitate a separation of the self from the parent. (While extremely severe discipline might have a very different effect, this is not common in the middle class.)

One implication of this is that girls need a little maternal rejection if they are to become independently competent and self-confident. And indeed a generalization that occurs in most recent reviews is that high achieving females had hostile mothers while high achieving males had warm ones (Bardwick, 1971; Garai & Scheinfeld, 1968; Maccoby, 1966; Silverman, 1970). This generalization is based primarily on the findings of the Fels longitudinal study (Kagan & Moss, 1962). In this study "maternal hostility" toward the child during his first three years was related positively to the adult achievement behavior of girls and negatively to the adult achievement behavior of boys. Maternal protection, on the other hand, as mentioned earlier, related negatively to girl's achievement and positively to boy's.

In discussions of these findings "maternal hostility" is often equated with rejection. There is reason to believe, however, that it may simply be the absence of "smother love." First, the sample of cooperating families in the Fels study is not likely to include extremely rejecting parents. These were primarily middle class parents who cooperated with a child development study for 25 years. They were enrolled in the study when the mother was pregnant, and over the years they tolerated frequent home visits, each lasting from 3 to 4 hours, as well as behavioral observations of their children in nursery school and camp. Second, we have already pointed out that what is "high hostility" toward girls, might not be so labeled if the same behavior were expressed toward boys. It is interesting to note in this connection that "high hostility" toward girls during these early years is related positively to "acceleration" (i.e., the tendency to push the child's cognitive and motoric development) and negatively to maternal protectiveness. Neither of these relationships is significant for the boys (Kagan & Moss, 1962, p. 207). Further, the mothers who were "hostile" to their daughters were better educated than the "nonhostile." In addition to being achievers, the daughters were "less likely to withdraw from stressful situations" as adults. The authors themselves suggest that the latter "may reflect the mother's early pressure for independence and autonomy [p. 213]."

Our interpretation of these findings then is that many girls experience too much maternal rapport and protection during their early years. Because of this they find themselves as adults unwilling (or unable) to face stress and with inadequate motivation for autonomous achievement. It is significant that the relationships described are strongest when the early years are compared to the adult behavior. Possibly the eagerness to please adults sometimes passes as achievement or maturity during the childhood years.

While excessive rapport between mother and son occurs, it is less common and usually of a different nature. The achievement of boys may be in greater danger from too much conflict with parents—there being little likelihood of too little.

The danger for girls of too much maternal nurturance has been pointed out by Bronfenbrenner (1961a, 1961b) and is consistent with data reported by Crandall, Dewey, Katkovsky, and Preston (1964). The finding that girls who are more impulsive than average have more analytic thinking styles while the reverse pattern holds for boys also fits this interpretation (Sigel, 1965; Kagan, Rosman, Day, Phillips, & Phillips, 1964). That is, impulsive girls may be brought into more conflict with their mothers, as in the typical pattern for boys. Maccoby (1966) has suggested that the actual relationship between impulsivity and analytic thinking is curvilinear: The extreme impulsivity that characterizes the very impulsive boys is dysfunctional, but the high impulsivity of the girls falls within the optimal range. In our view, the optimal range is enough to insure some conflict in the mother-child relationship but not so much as to interfere with the child's effective performance.

Inadequate Self-Confidence and Dependence on Others
Since the little girl has (a) less encouragement for independence, (b) more parental protectiveness, (c) less cognitive and social pressure for establishing an identity separate from the mother, and (d) less mother-child conflict which highlights this separation, she engages in less independent exploration of her environment. As a result she does not develop skills in coping with her environment nor confidence in her ability to do so. She continues to be dependent upon adults for solving her problems and because of this she needs her affective ties with adults. Her mother is not an unvarying supply of love but is sometimes angry, disapproving, or unavailable. If the child's own resources are insufficient, being on her own is frustrating and frightening. Fears of abandonment are very common in infants and young children even when the danger is remote. Involvement in mastery explorations and the increasing competence and confidence that results can help alleviate these fears, but for girls they may continue even into adulthood. The anticipation of being alone and unloved then may have a particularly desperate quality in women. The hypothesis we propose is that the all-pervasive

affiliative need in women results from this syndrome.

Thus boys learn effectance through mastery, but girls are effective through eliciting the help and protection of others. The situations that evoke anxiety in each sex should be different and their motives should be different.

The theoretical view presented in this paper is speculative but it appears to be consistent with the data. In the preceding sections we have reviewed the research on sex differences in early socialization experiences. The theory would also lead us to expect that owing to these differences females would show less self-confidence and more instrumental dependency than males.

The data on dependency are somewhat unclear largely because the concept has been defined differently in different studies. These findings have been summarized by Kagan (1964), Oetzel (1966), Garai and Scheinfeld, 1968), and the concept of dependency has been discussed by Maccoby and Masters (1970). The balance of the evidence is that females are more dependent, at least as we are using the concept here, and this difference appears early and continues into maturity. Goldberg and Lewis (1969) report sex differences in dependency among one-year-olds, but Crandall and his associates (Crandall, Preston, & Rabson, 1960; Crandall & Rabson, 1960) found such differences only among elementary school children and not among preschoolers. It should be noted, however, that even differences that do not show up until later can have their roots in early experiences. For example, independence training at a later age may require a sense of competence based on early successes if it is to be effective.

The findings on self-confidence show that girls, and particularly the bright ones, underestimate their own ability. When asked to anticipate their performance on new tasks or on repetition tasks, they give lower estimates than boys and lower estimates than their performance indicates Brandt, 1958; Sears, 1964; Crandall, Katkovsky, &

Preston, 1962; Crandall, 1968). The studies that show the girls' greater suggestibility and tendency to switch perceptual judgments when faced with discrepant opinions are also consistent with their having less self-confidence (Iscoe, Williams, & Harvey, 1963; Allen & Crutchfield, 1963; Nakamura, 1958; Hamm & Hoving, 1969; Stein & Smithells, 1969.[4] Boys set higher standards for themselves (Walter & Marzolf, 1951). As mentioned earlier, difficult tasks are seen as challenging to males, whereas females seek to avoid them (Veroff, 1969; Crandall & Rabson, 1960; Moriarty, 1961; McManis, 1965). Thus the research suggests that girls lack confidence in their own abilities and seek effectance through others (Crandall & Rabson, 1960). Affective relationships under these conditions would indeed be paramount.

The findings indicating that this is the case—that affective relationships are paramount in females—were summarized earlier in this paper. The data suggest that they have higher affiliative needs and that achievement behavior is motivated by a desire to please. If their achievement behavior comes into conflict with affiliation, achievement is likely to be sacrificed or anxiety may result.

IMPLICATIONS

If further research provides support for the present developmental speculations, many questions will still need answering before childrearing patterns used with girls can be totally condemned. Even from the standpoint of achievement behavior, I would caution that this paper has only dealt with the upper end of the achievement curve. Indices of female performance, like the female IQ scores, cluster closer to the mean and do not show the extremes in either direction that the male indices show. The same qualities that may

[4]Girls do not conform more to peer standards which conflict with adult norms (Douvan & Adelson, 1966), even though they conform more when group pressure is in opposition to their own perceptual judgments.

interfere with top performance at the highest achievement levels seem to have the effect of making the girls conscientious students in the lower grades. Is it possible for the educational system to use the positive motivations of girls to help them more fully develop their intellectual capacities rather than to train them in obedient learning? The educational system that rewards conformity and discourages divergent thinking might be examined for its role in the pattern we have described.

Although childrearing patterns that fail to produce a competent and self-confident child are obviously undesirable, it may be that boys are often prematurely pushed into independence. Because this paper has focused on achievement orientations, it may seem that I have set up the male pattern as ideal. This is not at all intended. The ability to suppress other aspects of the situation in striving for mastery is not necessarily a prerequisite for mental health or a healthy society. The more diffuse achievement needs of women may make for greater flexibility in responding to the various possibilities that life offers at different stages in the life cycle. A richer life may be available to women because they do not single-mindedly pursue academic or professional goals. And from a social standpoint, a preoccupation with achievement goals can blot out consideration of the effect of one's work on the welfare of others and its meaning in the larger social scheme.

A loss in intellectual excellence due to excessive affiliative needs, then, might seem a small price to pay if the alternative is a single-minded striving for mastery. But the present hypothesis suggests that women's affiliative needs are, at least in part, based on an insufficient sense of competence and as such they may have a compelling neurotic quality. While I have not made the very high achievement needs more characteristic of males the focus of this paper, they too may have an unhealthy base. By unraveling the childhood events that lead to these divergent orientations we may gain insights that will help both sexes develop their capacities for love and achievement.

References

Allen, V. L., & Crutchfield, R. S. Generalization of experimentally reinforced conformity. *Journal of Abnormal and Social Psychology.* 1963, 67, 326–333.

Bardwick, J. M. *The psychology of women: A study of biochemical conflict.* New York: Harper & Row, 1971.

Baumrind, D. Socialization and instrumental competence in young children. *Young Children,* 1970, December, 9–12.

Baumrind, D. Current patterns of parental authority. *Developmental Psychology Monograph,* 1971, 4 (1, Pt. 2).

Baumrind, D., & Black. A. E. Socialization practices associated with dimensions of competence in preschool boys and girls. *Child Development,* 1967, 38, 291–327.

Bayley, N. Growth curves of height and weight by age for boys and girls, scaled according to physical maturity. *Journal of Pediatrics,* 1956, 48, 187–194.

Bayley, N. Developmental problems of the mentally retarded child. In I. Phillips (Ed.), *Prevention and Treatment of mental retardation,* New York: Basic Books, 1966.

Becker, W. Consequences of different kinds of parental discipline. In M. L. Hoffman and L. W. Hoffman (Eds.), *Review of child development research.* Vol. 1. New York: Russell Sage, 1964.

Bieri, J. Parental identification, acceptance of authority and within-sex differences in cognitive behavior. *Journal of Abnormal and Social Psychology,* 1960, 60, 76–79.

Bing, E. Effect of childrearing practices on development of differential cognitive abilities. *Child Development,* 1963, 34, 631–648.

Brandt, R. M. The accuracy of self-estimate: A measure of self concept. *Genetic Psychology Monographs,* 1958, 58, 55–99.

Bronfenbrenner, U. Freudian theories of identification and their derivatives. *Child Development,* 1960, 31, 15–40.

Bronfenbrenner, U. Some familial antecedents of responsibility and leadership in adolescents. In L. Petrullo and B. M. Bass (Eds.), *Leadership and interpersonal behavior.* New York: Holt, Rinehart, & Winston, 1961. (a)

Bronfrenner, U. Toward a theoretical model for the analysis of parent-child relationships in a social context. In J. Glidewell (Ed.), *Parent attitudes and child behavior.* Springfield, Illinois: Thomas, 1961. (b)

Coleman, J. S. *The adolescent society.* Glencoe, Illinois: Free Press, 1961.

Collard, E. D. Achievement motive in the four-year-old child and its relationship to achievement expectancies of the mother. Unpublished doctoral dissertation, University of Michigan, 1964.

Crandall, V. C. Achievement behavior in young children. *Young Children,* 1964, 20, 77–90.

Crandall, V. C. Sex differences in expectancy of intellectual and academic reinforcement. In C. P. Smith (Ed.), *Achievement-related motives in children.* New York: Russell Sage, 1968.

Crandall, V. J. Achievement. In H. W. Stevenson (Ed.), *Child Psychology: The 62nd Yearbook of the National Society for the Study of Education.* Part I. Chicago: University of Chicago Press, 1963.

Crandall, V. J., Dewey, R., Katkovsky, W., & Preston, A. Parents' attitudes and behaviors and grade school children's academic achievements. *Journal of Genetic Psychology,* 1964, 104, 53–66.

Crandall, V. J., Katkovsky, W., & Preston, A. Motivational and ability determinants of young children's intellectual achievement behaviors. *Child Development,* 1962, 33, 643–661.

Crandall, V. J., Preston, A., & Rabson, A. Maternal reactions and the development of independence and achievement behavior in young children. *Child Development,* 1960, 31, 243–251.

Crandall, V. J., & Rabson, A. Children's repetition choices in an intellectual achievement situation following success and failure. *Journal of Genetic Psychology,* 1960, 97, 161–168.

Douvan, E. M., & Adelson, J. *The adolescent experience.* New York: Wiley, 1966.

Erikson, E. H. Identity and the life cycle. *Psychological Issues,* 1959, 1, 1–171.

Escalona, S. K. Feeding disturbances in very young children. *American Journal of Orthopsychiatry,* 1945, 15, 76–80.

Field, W. F. The effects of thematic apperception upon certain experimentally aroused needs. Unpublished doctoral dissertation, University of Maryland, 1951.

Garai, J. E., & Scheinfeld, A. Sex differences in mental and behavioral traits. *Genetic Psychology Monographs,* 1968, 77, 169–299.

Glidewell, J. C., Kantor, M. B., Smith, L. M., & Stringer, L. A., Socialization and social structure in the classroom. In L. W. Hoffman and M. L. Hoffman (Eds.), *Review of child development research.* Vol. 2. New York: Russell Sage, 1966.

Goldberg, S., & Lewis, M. Play behavior in the year old infant: Early sex differences. *Child Development,* 1969, 40, 21–31.

Hamm, N. K., & Hoving, K. L. Conformity of children in an ambiguous perceptual situation. *Child Development,* 1969, 40, 773–784.

Heinstein, M. *Child rearing in California.* Bureau of Maternal and Child Health, State of California, Department of Public Health, 1965.

Horner, M. S. Sex differences in achievement motivation and performance in competitive and non-competitive situations. Unpublished doctoral dissertation, University of Michigan, 1968.

Horner, M. S. Toward an understanding of achievement related conflicts in women. *Journal of Social Issues,* 1972, 28(2).

Iscoe, I., Williams, M., & Harvey, J. Modifications of children's judgments by a simulated group technique: A normative developmental study. *Child Development,* 1963, 34, 963–978.

Iscoe, I., Williams, M., & Harvey, J. Age, intelligence and sex as variables in the conformity behavior of Negro and White children. *Child Development,* 1964, 35, 451–460.

Jensen, A. R. The race × sex × ability interaction. Unpublished manuscript. University of California, Berkeley, 1970.

Kagan, J. Acquisition and significance of sex-typing and sex-role identity. In M. L. Hoffman and L. W. Hoffman (Eds.), *Review of child devlopment research.* Vol. 1, New York: Russell Sage, 1964.

Kagan, J. On the meaning of behavior: Illustrations from the infant. *Child Development,* 1969, 40, 1121–1134.

Kagan, J., & Kogan, N. Individuality and cognitive performance. In P. H. Mussen (Ed.), *Carmichael's manual of child psychology.* Vol. 1, New York: Wiley, 1970.

Kagan, J., Levine, J., & Fishman, C. Sex of child and social class as determinants of maternal behavior. Paper presented at the meeting of the Society for Research in Child Development, March 1967.

Kagan, J., & Moss, H. A. *Birth to maturity.* New York: Wiley, 1962.

Kagan, J., Rosman, B. L., Day, D., Phillips, A. J., & Phillips, W. Information processing in the child: Significance of analytic and reflective attitudes. *Psychological Monographs,* 1964, 78, 1.

Lahtinen, P. The effect of failure and rejection on dependency. Unpublished doctoral dissertation, University of Michigan, 1964.

Lewis, M. Infants' responses to facial stimuli during the first year of life. *Developmental Psychology,* 1969, 1, 75–86.

Lynn, D. B. Sex role and parental identification. *Child Development,* 1962, 33, 555–564.

Lynn, D. B. *Parental identification and sex role.* Berkeley: McCutchan, 1969.

Maccoby, E. E. Woman's intellect. In S. M. Farber and R. H. L. Wilson (Eds.), *The potential of woman.* New York. McGraw-Hill, 1963.

Maccoby, E. E. Sex differences in intellectual functioning. In E. E. Maccoby (Ed.), *The development of sex differences.* Stanford, California: Stanford University Press, 1966.

Maccoby, E. E., & Masters, J. C. Attachment and dependency. In P. H. Mussen (Ed.), *Carmichael's manual of child psychology.* Vol. 2, New York: Wiley, 1970.

McClelland, D. C., Atkinson, J. W., Clark, R. A., & Lowell, E. L. *The achievement motive.* New York: Appleton-Century-Crofts, 1953.

McManis, D. L. Pursuit-rotor performance of normal and retarded children in four verbal-incentive conditions. *Child Development,* 1965, 36, 667–683.

Milton, G. A. The effects of sex-role identification upon problem solving skill. *Journal of Abnormal and Social Psychology,* 1957, 55, 208–212.

Moriarty, A. Coping patterns of preschool children in response to intelligence test demands. *Genetic Psychology Monographs,* 1961, 64, 3–127.

Moss, H. A. Laboratory and field-studies of mother-infant interaction. Unpublished manuscript, NIMH, undated.

Moss, H. A. Sex, age, and state as determinants of mother-infant interaction. *Merrill-Palmer Quarterly,* 1967, 13, 19–36.

Moss, H. A., & Robson, K. S. Maternal influences in early social visual behavior. *Child Development,* 1968, 39, 401–408.

Moss, H. A., Robson, K. S., & Pedersen, F. Determinants of maternal stimulation of infants and consequences of treatment for later reactions to strangers. *Developmental Psychology,* 1969, 1, 239–247.

Nakamura, C. Y. Conformity and problem solving. *Journal of Abnormal and Social Psychology,* 1958, 56, 315–320.

Oetzel, R. M. The relationship between sex role acceptance and cognitive abilities. Unpublished masters thesis, Stanford University, 1961.

Oetzel, R. M. Annotated bibliography and classified summary of research in sex differences. In E. E. Maccoby (Ed.), *The development of sex differences.* Stanford, California: Stanford University Press, 1966.

Parsons, T. *Essays in sociological theory pure and applied.* Glencoe, Illinois: Free Press, 1949.

Parsons, T. Family structure and the socialization of the child. In T. Parsons and R. F. Bales (Eds.), *Family socialization and interaction process.* Glencoe, Illinois: Free Press, 1965.

Plank, E. H., & Plank, R. Emotional components in arithmetic learning as seen through autobiographies. In R. S. Eissler et al. (Eds.), *The psychoanalytic study of the child.* Vol. 9. New York: International Universities Press, 1954.

Pope, B. Socio-economic contrasts in children's peer culture prestige values. *Genetic Psychology Monographs,* 1953, 48, 157–220.

Rosen, B. C., & D'Andrade, R. The psychosocial origins of achievement motivations. *Sociometry,* 1959, 22, 185–218.

Rossi, A. S. Barriers to the career choice of engineering, medicine, or science among American women. In J. A. Mattfeld and G. G. Van Aken (Eds.), *Women and the scientific professions: Papers presented at the M.I.T. symposium on American Women in Science and Engineering, 1964.* Cambridge, Massachusetts: M.I.T. Press, 1965. (a).

Rossi, A. S. Women in science: Why so few? *Science,* 1965, 148, 1196–1202 (b)

Rubenstein, J. Maternal attentiveness and subsequent exploratory behavior in the infant. *Child Development,* 1967, 38, 1089–1100.

Sarason, I. G. Test anxiety and intellectual performance. *Journal of Abnormal and Social Psychology,* 1963, 66, 73–75.

Sarason, I. G., & Harmatz, M. G. Test anxiety and experimental conditions. *Journal of Personality and Social Psychology,* 1965, 1, 499–505.

Sears, P. S. Correlates of need achievement and need affiliation and classroom management, self concept, and creativity. Unpublished manuscript, Stanford University, 1962.

Sears, P. S. The effect of classroom conditions on the strength of achievement motive and work output of elementary school children. Final report, cooperative research project No. OE-873, U.S. Dept. of Health, Education, and Welfare, Office of Education, Washington, D.C., 1963.

Sears, P. S. Self-concept in the service of educational goals. *California Journal of Instructional Improvement,* 1964, 7, 3–17.

Sears, R. R., Maccoby, E. E., & Levin, H. *Patterns of child rearing.* Evanston, Illinois: Row, Peterson, 1957.

Sears, R. R., Rau, L., & Alpert, R. *Identification and child rearing.* Stanford: Stanford University Press, 1965.

Sherman, J. A. Problems of sex differences in space perception and aspects of intellectual functioning. *Psychological Review,* 1967, 74, 290–299.

Sigel, I. E. Rationale for separate analyses of male and female samples on cognitive tasks. *Psychological Record,* 1965, 15, 369–376.

Silverman, J. Attentional styles and the study of sex differences. In D. L. Mostofsky (Ed.), *Attention: Contemporary theory and analysis.* New York: Appleton-Century-Crofts, 1970.

Simon, R. J., Clark, S. M., & Galway, K. The woman Ph.D.: A recent profile. Paper prepared for a workshop of the New York Academy of Sciences, New York, February, 1970.

Stein, A. H., & Smithells, J. Age and sex differences in children's sex role standards about achievement. *Developmental Psychology,* 1969, 1, 252–259.

Stendler, C. B. Critical periods in socialization. In R. G. Kuhlen and G. G. Thompson (Eds.), *Psychological studies of human development.* New York: Appleton-Century-Crofts, 1963.

Sutton-Smith, B., Crandall, V. J., & Roberts, J. M. Achievement and strategic competence. Paper presented at the meeting of the Eastern Psychological Association, April 1964.

Terman, L. M., & Oden, M. H. *The gifted child grows up.* Stanford, California: Stanford University Press, 1947.

Torgoff, I. Parental developmental timetable. Paper presented at the meeting of the American Psychological Association, Washington, D.C., August 1958.

Tulkin, S. R. Race, class, family, and school achievement. *Journal of Personality and Social Psychology,* 1968, 9, 31–37.

Tyler, F. B., Rafferty, J. E., & Tyler, B. B. Relationships among motivations of parents and their children. *Journal of Genetic Psychology,* 1962, 101, 69–81.

Veroff, J. Social comparison and the development of achievement motivation. In C. P. Smith (Ed.), *Achievement-related matters in children.* New York: Russell Sage, 1969.

Veroff, J., Wilcox, S., & Atkinson, J. W. The achievement motive in high school and college age women. *Journal of Abnormal and Social Psychology,* 1953, 48, 108–119.

Walberg, H. J. Physics, femininity, and creativity. *Developmental Psychology,* 1969, 1, 47–54.

Walter, I. M., & Marzolf, S. S. The relation of sex, age, and school achievement to levels of aspiration. *Journal of Educational Psychology,* 1951, 42, 258–292.

White, R. W. Competence and the psychosexual stages of development. In M. Jones (Ed.), *Nebraska Symposium on Motivation.* Lincoln, Nebraska: University of Nebraska Press, 1960.

Winterbottom, M. R. The relation of need for achievement to learning experiences in independency and mastery. In J. W. Atkinson (Ed.), *Motives in fantasy, action, and society.* Princeton: Van Nostrand, 1958.

Witkin, H. A., Dyk, R. B., Faterson, H. F., Goodenough, D. R., & Karp, S. A. *Psychological differentiation.* New York: Wiley, 1962.

Chapter 15

Problems of Adolescence

The transition from childhood to adult status in our society is seldom simple. After years of dependency and limited responsibility within the family and of gradual and orderly physical growth and development, the adolescent is suddenly confronted with the necessity of adjusting to a variety of new demands—physiological, psychological, and social.

The onset of puberty brings a host of physiological changes, including increases in sex hormones and changes in body structure and function. These not only present special adjustment problems in themselves, but also challenge the individual's basic sense of self, or what Erik Erikson has called "ego identity." This sense of ego identity, in turn, requires a perception of the self as **separate** from others (despite similarities to them) and a feeling of wholeness, of self-consistency, not only in the sense of internal consistency at a particular moment but also over time. The adolescent (particularly the younger one) is faced with rapid increases in height, changing bodily dimensions, and the objective and subjective changes related to sexual maturation. Obviously, all of these developments disrupt the adolescent's ongoing feeling of self-consistency and he or she needs time to integrate them into a gradually emerging sense of a positive, self-confident ego identity.

At the same time that the adolescent is confronted with the uncertainties brought on by rapid physical and physiological changes and the flood of unfamiliar subjective feelings that accompany them, he is also faced with a whole set of societal demands from which he has heretofore been relatively protected. In the few short years between puberty and nominal adulthood, he is suddenly expected to prepare himself for a job; for changed political and social status as a citizen; for heterosexual relationships, including the possibility of marriage; for relatively complete separation from his parents and the setting up of an independent household; and for development of a system of values and a mature philosophy of life.

The task is not made easier by the fact that we are currently going through a period of rapid social change. Increasing urbanization and geographic mobility are altering the face of the nation and the nature of our social institutions. The result is an erosion in the stability and interdependence of communities, impaired communication between the family and other social and political institutions, increasing age-segregation throughout society, and a shrinking of the family unit from the extended family of an earlier day to the small and often socially isolated nuclear family. In addition, recent deep divisions and conflicts within society caused by war, socioeconomic and racial problems, and the growing destruction of the environment, combined with evidences of widespread corruption in government and business and among ordinary citizens, have led to a decline in adult authority in the eyes of many young people.

However, recent research indicates that despite these multiple stresses, a majority of young people make their way through the adolescent period, not without some problems, but without the high degree of emotional turmoil, violent mood swings, threatened loss of control, or serious acting-out behavior suggested by some clinical theorists. Significant numbers nevertheless do not, and they may become deeply alienated from society, emotionally disturbed, or delinquent.

In the first article in this chapter, T. J. Cottle discusses with sensitivity and understanding the mounting pressures on young people in a society divided in its allegiances and confused about its goals—a society seemingly filled with endless options, but one that often makes the problem of choosing a direction for one's life more difficult. As he observes, the failures of adult society to keep its house in order and the subsequent decline in adult authority have played a significant part in the increased incidence of adolescent alienation and emotional conflict. In his words, "the cat of the authority relationship is out of the bag."

But, as Cottle strongly emphasizes, the answer to this state of affairs is not a mea culpa and an abandonment of "the asymmetric structure of authority" on the part of parents and other adults responsible for young people. Still more important, the answer does not lie in an attempt to "tamper with the time of generations" through a regressive effort by parents and other adults to reembrace their own lost youth.

What is needed is not a renunciation of authority or generational separation, but a commitment to make adult authority responsible, particularly in child rearing. In D. Baumrind's terminology parents, teachers, and other caretakers need not—indeed should not—be authoritarian and inflexible, but they do need to be **authoritative,** unafraid to maintain their proper position in the life cycle and their own values, even at the risk of seeming "square or straight."[1] By doing so, with warmth and informed concern, they can strengthen rather than weaken the young person's efforts to find stability in an uncertain world.

Another manifestation of alienation in contemporary society, with both psychological and sociological roots, is the rising rate of juvenile delinquency. Delinquency is by no means a new problem, but there seems little doubt that it is an increasingly serious social concern in our ever more complex, fragmented society. And just as a **sense of identity** has its earliest roots in what Erikson calls the "basic trust" of infancy, so too does adolescent delinquency often find antecedents in the early years of childhood.

In the second paper of this chapter, J. J. Conger, W. C. Miller, and C. R. Walsmith show that the personality characteristics of future delinquents differ from those of nondelinquents even in the early school years and even after the possible effects of such factors as socioeconomic status, sex, intelligence, residence area, school background, and ethnic-group membership have been controlled through a matching technique. Perhaps most importantly, the authors demonstrate also that it may be relatively meaningless to speak of overall personality differences between delinquents and nondelinquents without first taking into account the social-class background and intelligence of the individual studied.

1. D. Baumrind, "Authoritarian vs. authoritative control," **Adolescence, Vol. 3** (1968), 255–272.

Of Youth and the Time of Generations

Thomas J. Cottle

Young people's involvement with adult authority—it's an old theme hammered to life almost daily in studies published on parents of adolescents, hippies, dropouts, druggies, militants, and the rest. Recently some writers "on youth" have openly chastised parents for failing to assume assertive roles with their children. Even some psychiatrists now argue for parental toughness, perhaps as a reaction to an oft-blamed emphasis on permissiveness.

Authority implies an inequality or what some prefer to call an asymmetry between the old and the young. There is no even exchange between generations, nor is there ever a possibility for it. Parents are by definition not peers, and their concern does not imply that they become colleagues.

SOURCE: From Thomas J. Cottle, *Time's Children: Impressions of Youth,* pp. 311–349. Copyright © 1967, 1969, 1970, 1971 by Thomas J. Cottle. Reprinted by permission of the author and Little, Brown and Company.

Yet the asymmetric structure of authority is not all bad, although parents and children are more than a bit ambivalent about it. Longing for the taste of adolescence, parents in many instances overstep the bounds that the asymmetry purports to guard. In some cases their intrusions are nothing short of disastrous. For some young people, a quiet inner strength vanishes when their parents trespass on the property of time and destroy the very same asymmetry that they themselves once wished to destroy.

The theme of authority is complicated, therefore, because young and old alike wish to tamper with the time of generations but realize the potentially devastating results of such an escapade. The asymmetry implies restraints on behavior, and the young, being today so profoundly aware of all the facts of life, recognize these restraints as well as anyone. Generally, the young seem more open than ever before, just as social reality seems more translucent. Perhaps there are fewer secrets today than yesterday, and perhaps too, our society honors revelation more than confident trust.

There is little doubt that young people extend, prolong, or simply react to their parents' demands, be they uttered or silently passed on. Erik Erikson, the American psychoanalyst, has said that one generation revives the repressions of the generation before it. But, equally important, adolescents have become brilliant readers of parental intentions, or adults generally—including parents, teachers, ministers, deans, and psychotherapists—have become predictable or transparent in their dealings with the young. High school students now portray the "shrink scene" with ease. They anticipate, with frightening accuracy, the words and moods of churlish school administrators. A fifteen-year-old Negro boy told me that he could not get help from his school guidance counselor: "I wouldn't say this to his face, but he doesn't like Negroes. He may not even know this, but we know it." I spoke to the counselor in question. The student had not only correctly interpreted the man's attitude—his impersonation of the man's behavior, right down to the speech pattern, was perfect.

All of this suggests that the cat of the authority relationship is out of the bag. The young understand and appreciate adult motivations, and, significantly, the sociological rationalizations for their actions in authority contexts. While they may protest against school principals and programs, they confess a sympathy for their elders' plight of being trapped in the policies of some greater bureaucratic establishment, "the system." They recognize a "sell-out" or "game player" a mile away, and a heady college freshman, if the matter concerns him at all, can differentiate between the authentic liberal and institutional brand from the last row of a lecture hall. Their language simplifications, such as "smarts,"

"head," "cool," "cop-out," are illustrations of an almost social-scientific terminology, which functions in reducing complex action patterns to succinct and manageable levels. Their language shows, moreover, the swiftness and clarity with which they can first interpret and then act upon personal and institutional demands. (Most students know that their parents' social class is still the best predictor of their own school success, and that the poor, and particularly the poor blacks, cannot hope to compete even with the omnipresent mediocrity found among the advantaged. Hence, their understanding of local school competition and mobility channels is profound, although frequently disillusioning and uninspiring.)

Perhaps the best illustration of language reflecting social sophistication and the apparent translucency of social reality is the expression "psyche out." A college junior assured me: "It's so easy to know what the teacher wants, or what he'll ask on a test. They never change. Give 'em what they want. You make them happy and you win." Even modest Phi Beta Kappa students claim they have "psyched out" their teachers and have emerged superior merely because they are better game players. The fact remains that to "psyche out" something is to stay one slender step ahead even of expectation. It is the ability to perceive the expression on the face of the future.

While it is hard for young people to be duped by authority figures, it is easy to be damaged by them, an act so often occurring when the superordinate—the elder, the parent, the teacher—wants to equalize what must remain as that asymmetric relationship. Again, asymmetry refers to relationships wherein the commodities exchanged are of unequal and, therefore, incomparable content, and the behavior of one person is not a call or demand for identical behavior in the other. In its most fundamental form, asymmetry describes relationships in which one of the members represents unquestioned authority in a particular context; hence, it refers to interactions engaging parents and children, teachers and students, and doctors and patients.

Several years ago, while leading a self-analytic group, I was invited to a party given by the members. As it was early in the group's history, it seemed reasonable that an informal evening together might loosen up and simplify all relationships. I was tempted to go, but a wiser man suggested that I not go. The asymmetry, he urged, ultimately must be preserved by the person holding authority. I may have lost something by declining, but I probably protected a valuable tension in the leader-member relationship. Moreover, the symbolic nature of the refusal reaffirmed the asymmetry, or inequality, which some of us working in groups feel is essential, and which members often confess, in their way, is preferred. The leader (or father) must in some sense forever remain the leader, and while this angers many, particularly those in groups, "humanness" is in no way automatically precluded by such a philosophy.

More recently, members of a self-analytic group observed their leader's participation in a political demonstration. At the following meeting they spoke of him with a newly discovered reverence. How good that he shares the same values; that he shows the courage to speak out against administrations. But they spoke, too, of a disgust for their mothers wearing mini-skirts and parents generally who act like kids. Anna, a mature young woman, told of a feeling of nausea that came over her when her roommate's mother reviewed the college courses she, the mother, was attending. Upon returning to her dormitory, Anna made a long-distance phone call home and luxuriated in the relief that her own mother still was pursuing mother-type activities: luncheons, museum visits, and food budgets.

The ambivalance is evident. Young people want to attack authority, and this is probably the way it must be. But in matters of human dealings, although not in issues of strict ideology, authority is not to "come down" to the child's level, as par-

ents once perceptively felt it necessary to kneel down, if only to attain a spatial equality of the generations. Authority is not to give in; it is to remain firm in its commitment to preserve the essential asymmetry and the indelible generational separation, even if this means being seen as a "square" or "straight arrow."

When a small child orders his parent out of his bedroom, he necessarily fears the enormity of the act. In a tearful rage, he can only pray that the parent will go no farther than the living room. Similarly, when members express the intense desire to kick out the leader of self-analytic groups (in symbolic re-enactment of the primal horde story perhaps), invariably they want to know would he really go and would he return.

There is, then, a primitive core, developing first in interactions with parents, that pleads for the overthrow of authority, yet simultaneously for the inability to do it by nature of the superordinate's strength in resisting. Parents simply cannot break down or retreat. They must prevail, and no one wants this more than the child. In terms of this infantile core that stays with us, parents are perfect, without problems, immortal. Relationships with them preclude both equality and peership. A college student said it this way: "No matter what I do in the face of authority, I end up a child. It happens even when I don't know the authority. Are we forever children to older persons?"

For children to out-achieve their parents, an event not uncommon among college students (let us not forget that women, too, are confronted with career aspirations and the ensuing competitions as much as men), means that they, the younger, must delicately initiate revisions in parental relationships so that the older generation will not interpret the younger's accomplishments as their own dismal and static ineptitude. What an incredible task it is for these young and talented students to return during Christmas and summer vacations to the rooms and persons of their childhood; to return where all of us know we cannot again return, then to battle the very essence of an unjust but immutable temporality.

Why is it that each of us believes in the development, even in the successes, of our surging expectations, but see only aging in our parents? Perhaps the eternal danger of the immediate future is that while it guarantees reports of our most present investments, it brings first our parents, then us, closer to some inexplicable end. But for the handful of "right nows," our youthful preoccupations make only our own movement in the life space visible. All the rest, parents and teachers included, remains unchanged, timeless: "It's like they've stood still. They bring me back to my childhood hang-ups. They know I've grown up; they know I'm at college, but they're used to me as I was when I was last there."

These last phenomena are so clearly not the sensations of regression. Although we all have fought back urges to feel once more, for even a bittersweet interval, the winds of childhood, returning must not be mistaken for regressing. On the contrary, returning is resuming. This is what is meant by bringing one back to childhood "hang-ups." It seems like regression, for only in our direct involvements does family time again move ahead. In our separation, that certain time stops, and the stillness augurs death. But the student returns and time jolts forward again, alive, just as the family itself becomes vitally alive, although now life becomes a bit more cumbersome.

The predicament confronting the child at these times is to help his parents resolve the problems that occur when the young out-achieve their elders. Variations in accomplishment must be reconciled in ways that legitimately reinforce parents' ultimate authority and special superiority. Regardless of their attainments, son and daughter want to remain in the child's role, at least in this one context. The parents know the child's task and, like the vaudeville joke, the child knows the parents know, and the parents know the child knows they know.

It is in interpersonal dilemmas and gestures of this sort, gestures made and carried out in such public yet at the same time secretive ways, that families reaffirm health. The gestures imply the mutual recognition and trust of which Professor Erikson has spoken so poetically and firmly. By these gestures the social and temporal gaps are preserved, sociologic and psychologic genes are somehow passed from one generation to the next and one is, in Erikson's words, able "to see one's own life in continuous perspective both in retrospect and in prospect" (*Young Man Luther*). The division, made first by time, permits the evolution of the adult and sanctifies the appropriateness and truth of the confirmation and the bar mitzvah. For sociological reasons, the gap between generations stays open. But it is all right because distance need not be construed as distrust, nor separateness as desertion.

For two years, I saw Kathy, who is now thirteen, in a hospital therapy setting. Her language and psychological test performance indicated a possible psychotic diagnosis. She had a recurring dream, one that intrigued us both, that she was in a forest being chased by a large bear. Up on its hind legs, it pursued and often caught her. The dream had become so terrifying that to prevent the bear from appearing, Kathy had resorted to magical powers symbolized in ritualized bedtime behavior. How terribly symbolic was this content: the personification of impulses at the same time sexual and aggressive. How literal was the content: her father, an alcoholic for all of Kathy's life, returning home at night, pitifully drunk, staggering toward her, his shirt off, the hair on his chest plain and exposed, his smell, his pants open; pleading for sex at a locked bedroom door, being rejected by his wife, until he promises to "grow up and behave like a man," masturbating as a little girl watches, bewildered and horrified.

Like Kathy, too many children have been freaked out by some form of family drama. Now, although nascent and unconscious, their strategy is to get out of their homes, out of their lives, and out of their minds. What a miracle it is that some stay, conjuring up reasons for the necessity of their remaining close. But the muffled aggression in their loyalty is unmistakable. The children and their parents are like the envied lovers in the old story who never stopped holding hands until just once, whereupon they beat each other to death. Holding on to a mother's skirt, after all, may be more than a wish to remain near and in touch. It may be playing the boxer who by staying in a clinch, prevents himself and his opponent from manning battle stations at arm's length.

When a thoughtless and angry Cambridge mayor's purge on young people led him to chastise hippies for having run away from home, I reacted by thinking on the contrary. The parents must have run away first, in some fashion, hence the children merely followed suit. Now, after examining life stories, I wonder whether, like the most domesticated of pets, "pre-hippies" ran because their parents rushed them and frightened them and got too close too soon. I wonder whether it was because they felt emotionally crowded by their parents that they "split." Still, even in unabandoned escape and angered protestation, children may be responding to or fulfilling some communicated need or directive. How curious is the thought, therefore, that protest and escape represent obeisance turned upside down.

It is equally curious that the familiar "need-to-escape-from-it-all" explanation of intoxication is used again when referring to serious drug-taking as a desire to repress. Mickey is a handsome, young high school dropout with an exceptional literary talent. When he was eleven, his parents fought so bitterly that he often found his mother lying in a pool of blood. Mickey would have to call for the ambulance and later on, after nursing his mother back to health, he would turn his attention to reuniting his parents.

During one cryptic account of a drug experience, he practically went into a swoon: "But when you come down, man, you come down hard, and that taking each moment one by one dissolves into that rotten other present, the one where you say, I gotta go back to my job. And you ask yourself, why do I do it, and you know, you gotta feel responsible. But It's OK because you think about the next high." I suggested to Mickey that coming down means having to think about tomorrow. "Wrong, man," he smiled for he had one on the shrink, "it's the past. It's on your back like you know what! . . . You say why did it have to happen to me?"

In speaking with Mickey and boys like him, one senses an ironical and twisted searching for insanity. Where the shocks of childhood were merely flirtations with craziness, by sixteen they have reappeared as an open willingness to consider "steady dating." At first only a couple of times a week; later on, every day and every night. The apparent psychotic quality or "way-outness" of the drugs is at once terrifying and exhilarating. The downs hurt but serve to affirm the lingering presence of sanity, or at least the ability to call upon it. If the user is sure it's still there, he goes back up on top again.

Not ironically, the very same strategy—"blowing the mind"—is used as a way of keeping out the mind-blowing experiences that might have urged persons toward this action in the first place. But just as drinking fails to induce forgetfulness, drugs seem to be failing many persons in their efforts to "repress" the past and keep it off their backs. If Timothy Leary is right, the next state will be electronic brain stimulation; hence, when pharmaceutical repression fails, attempts may be made at total memory ablation. At that time, a metaphysical present will evolve, free of any recollections and expectations, free of all regrets and despair.

Failing to understand so many of these complicated and gifted people, I often forget myself and remind them of their futures as parents. It is not that easy. For one thing, their very sense of future differs from mine. Moreover, the option to "start again" in marriage is highly problematic. Many fear they will repeat the desecrating scenes of their childhood: "I'll ruin my kid a helluva lot more than the drugs I take will"; "Are you kidding, man? Can you see me as a father? You gotta be nuts! And you a shrink!"; "A freak kid's gotta better chance than I did!"

If starting again were possible, most would probably opt for total recommencement. Knowing full well that their parents never wanted them in the first place, some almost cannot go back far enough to reach a time when their own histories might have started off on a good footing. No one admits it, however, for that would be to proclaim absolutely one's non-being. It would be to break the slim and delicate threads that now barely hold the generations pridefully together. Kathy told me that her mother was informed by doctors that she could have no more children after the birth of Kathy's nearest older sister. In fact, two more children were born. The mother admitted she had not wanted either one. Her "not wanting" became the daughter's description of herself as the "unexpected surprise." Kathy and I knew that she understood the conditions of her origin and the facts of her life. Indeed, I felt that her rather protracted inability to comprehend how children are born might have symbolized an even more profound reluctance and self-protection.

Regrettably, the concept of insanity pervades the worlds, however expansive, of many young people. What many want to know is utterly predictable: "Just tell me one thing, man; am I crazy? I mean, you know, am I crazy?" The word "crazy" is ubiquitous. It has lost its primeval jolt, but it holds on to an unmodifiable message. There is, however, plenty of insanity left over in television scripts and movies. Insanity is feared when witnessing the inexplicable behavior of those around us as they do nothing more than fight aggressively for social and private rights too long in coming. It is also feared when witnessing those well meaning men who seek to control those who protest. The young hear the President called mad and the war insane, and they puzzle over insanity's bewildering function in jury trials, and partly

because of this they seek it as a way of getting out of the draft.

In my day, not so long ago, a "joking" admonition for guaranteed military deferment was, when the army doctor examines you, kiss him. Now it's insanity. Naturally, the worry exists that they might carry forever the brand of insanity on their sleeves just about where the private stripe might have gone. To be crazy is to avoid military service. Like kissing the doc, it is the avoidance of maleness. An often cruel society rubs this in: A real man fights for his country. Ideologies and spirit react against this, but the doubt stays. American socialization patterns, normally instituting strict sex-role differentiations, take care of that. There will be a lingering doubt, although in much of their questioning and concern, perceptions and anguish, the young are supported. Many of the "knowing class," they come to learn, now prefer to think of "business as usual" as the real insanity course, and jail as an undesirable but honorable way out.

Earlier I spoke of a resistance to bearing children and the feeling that one cannot successfully assume responsibilities of parenthood. In some cases it seems as though the diffidence displayed in "going on" masks a wish to start anew. The present urge to keep the cycle from repeating and the intention to keep fresh life from beginning must be considered from the point of view of sexuality. Although the language remains unchanged, industries of "procuring" and "scoring" today refer to drugs. The prophylactic, its slick package dirtied by months in the seams of an old wallet, has been replaced by the nickel bag: "Always be prepared." A funny reversal regards sex-role functions in a new economic market, as girls now solicit funds to pay for their boyfriends' stuff. I was stopped by one of these girls in the street on a beautiful October day: "Excuse me, Sir," she began her proposal. "How about a quarter for a cup of God knows what?"

One cannot be certain of the sexual habits of the persons of whom I speak. Anyway, it's no one's business until they mention it. The subject, however, is close to the conversational surface. It is as intimate as it ever was, but beginning to be freed of its irrational ties to some mysterious and primordial secrecy. As with much of their behavior many of the young merely make overt what their elders do covertly. In so doing, they seem much more honest and far less foolish. However, the conspicuous consumption of other youngsters is little more than a mimicry of their parents.

Many young men on drugs confess their apprehensions about homosexuality. It is not simply that they fear their impulses; this seems more common among those actually engaged in heterosexual relationships. Instead, they tell of a lack of sexual impulses and a concern that perhaps drugs have destroyed the sex drive. Because of their sophistication, they comprehend the possibility that their activities generally could be interpreted as homosexual, but they manifest little panic about this. Some admit that they are able to "make it" with girls only when "high." They confess to fright, but it does not compare to the fear that they may be crazy.

This is the supreme danger, as it suggests again the complex reversal of not only competence in drug and sex work, but the associated interchange between the organs of sex and the "organ" of drugs, the mind. One almost wants to assert that a phallic phase of development has been temporarily supplanted or postponed by a "cephalic" phase. All life is fixated in the mind, and Leary spoke for the generation at least once when he advertised that each brain cell is capable of brilliant and repeating orgasms.

This then leaves one issue: "the freak-out," the ultimate reward—the ultimate punishment. It is total destruction, at once implosion and explosion. In their own words, it is brain damage and disintegration. It is, simultaneously, conception, pregnancy, childbirth, castration, and death. Some continue to believe that from the womb of the mind, a new child, a freak child is born.

By their own admission, the freak-out is also a premeditated cop-out. Like living with a woman unmarried, it is anticipated endingless and the preparation for a later recourse. Demanding no commitment, it is an out, permitting the luxury of retiring as undefeated champion. No one can find fault with the last-minute term paper writer or the hospital patient. Both have their excuses. Both wonder, presumably, about what their competence might be like void of recourse. Both wonder, too, about the lack of preparation for the equivocal future and the minimal confidence displayed in present endeavor.

Depicted in most of these notions is the mass communicative society in which we survive. The accomplishments by so many are so great, the knowledge and awareness so swift in arrival and so deep in meaning, that in a way we leave the young no excuse for failure other than severe illness and total collapse. Adlai Stevenson once confessed relief that career decisions were behind him. It's hard to be young today, he observed. So many good people are already so advanced in practically any area that one might choose for himself. Perhaps this is the reason why some drop out.

In sexual relations, the excuse that probably maintained the sanity of frightened generations of men no longer exists. Girls have "the pill," and aggressive action now swings both ways. Students offer apologies for not smoking pot and agonize over an inability to get excited, much less involved, in political enterprises. To be straight is to be square, and like it or not, the straight become defensive and tempted.

Our televised and instant-replay society also allows fewer secrets. We see the war; we see men murdered; and we become frustrated when we cannot discover the exact frame on which is recorded a President's death. Our newspapers pry and our movies reveal, and so too, apparently, do some parents. Where many children fantasize that the secrets they guard preserve some mysterious family integrity, others, in fact, are maintaining this integrity by biting a quivering lip in fear that exposure of their treasured secrets will cause their families to unravel. All the while, performance demands shriek for attention. One must compete and succeed often enough; make it on his own; and react to the war and the fact that he or a boyfriend will soon be drafted and, not so unlikely, killed! One must be good in school, good at home, good at sports, good at pot, and good in bed. Life becomes unmanageably meaningful. It is enough to make one (want to) go insane.

Most make it, however, even with the knowledge that their culture warns of belligerent Chinese, overkill, and an equivocal future. One cannot know when the next and final war will come, or when past experience with drugs will suddenly re-erupt in the form of a grotesque child or one's own psychotic demise. Unmistakably near, death becomes a real reality. Less fuzzy than ever before, its shape and sound hover about self-analytic groups, bull sessions, and coffee dates. Damn the future and the inevitable! It was better in the Thirties when gravelly throated heroes sang into megaphones. It was better, too, in the last century when men wore frock coats, beards, and long hair. It was better and easier because it was the past, and perception of the completed proves the validity of survival, if not achievement. At the very least, the past means having got this far. It also means the seat of much of the trouble.

Some young people reveal a peculiar attitude about the past. It is not merely a time that was, but the series of events that once were, yet somehow continue to remain as the present's lining. Neither recalled nor retrieved, the past has become the stuff of moment-to-moment encounter and the routine of day work. The past has not yet become past in the sense of being over, because its foundation, like a child's body, remains soft and unfinished. There are no completions, no triumphs, no guaranteed deferrals or subsistence.

No one as yet has studied the notes written by parents to their runaway children in New York's East Village or San Francisco's Haight-Ashbury district. These pitiful missives document so well the lack of generational space and the confession of failure in parenthood and adulthood. They could be the letters of children, who, wishing to come home, promise never again to misbehave. If they did not cause guilt or confusion in the recipients, hippies would have little need to prevent them from reaching the runaway child. (Those people whose self-appointed task is to maintain the separation and lack of communication between parent and child must fear the fruits of love's temptation, the very philosophy they profess. Moreover, they are reminiscent of professional mourners, who periodically remind the congregation or family of the recent loss by crying when others attain momentary composure.)

The "come back home; all is forgiven" notes stand as a testament to what must be seen by the young as a crumbling structure, or a tragic reversal of intentionality and interpersonal competence. They reflect adult pleas for help and forgiveness, and as such they represent a far worse social fact than hippie farm colonies or pot parties. The notes only document what the poets know so well: Of all rewards, youth is a supreme ideal. The old wish to be young, and the young are happy exactly where they are.

Few parents are able to accept the passing of adolescence, especially when their own children dramatize more vibrantly than ever the former gratifications and projected incompleteness of their own lives. It is inconceivable to think that young people have ever been simultaneously idolized and despised, worshiped and envied as they are presently. Without doubt, the problem of age-grading is now of paramount significance in the United States. It is *the* dimension: Good or bad, the old are preoccupied with the young, and the young are preoccupied with themselves.

When the activities of the young were secretive, adults were compelled to deal with their own imaginations. Now, when sexuality, in particular, screams at us from advertisements, fashions, television, movies, and magazines, it becomes increasingly difficult to decline youth's unintended invitation and accept the process and reality of aging. Adults must work hard to avoid the eternal seductions of the young, for these affairs simply do not work out. Time inevitably chaperones such liaisons, and the primordial strain that comes about through the separation of generations never will permit a successful consummation of these two hearts, the young and old.

The seduction does not stop with parents, however, for the succulence of youth is dreamed of each day by teachers, counselors, therapists, ministers, etc. A most dangerous tack for any of these persons is to be uncritically won over by youth's stated demands and ideologies or interpretations of them. An example of this point seems in order. We are emerging from an unfortunate era in which psychotherapy was viewed as either panacea or black magic. Psychotherapists finally have undertaken critical self-scrutinization, and for the most part, attacks on theory and procedure have resulted in clarifying statements for the practitioners. Still, there are some critics who expend a suspiciously great amount of energy communicating to youth the evils of psychotherapy and even more benign adult interventions. By acting this way, they signify their "stand with youth," a stand normally introduced by some phrase which seems an apologia, but which in truth is more a boastful pledge to be young like the young.

Frequently, these critics demonstrate a striking accuracy in their realignment of youth's goals, ambitions, and philosophies. Just as often, their arguments are indecorous and evil. Many young people, in fact, do find illness in themselves and do seek help. They despise the proverbial "shrink scene" and rightly so, but in their quest of a "hip shrink," they wish for a modification—or, better, modernization—of the psychotherapeutic relationship, but not its annihilation. They know it is no panacea, but in anticipation they feel it has worth and are willing to try. The best adults can do, therefore, is to experiment with the helping apparatus and not discourage the trying.

Those who aspire to speak for or understand youth must be aware of the seductive nature of their interests so that they will not reach the point where speaking for youth means no longer needing to listen to it. Genuine representation, after all, does not require reliving; it requires recalling.

One final point regards the heightened sophistication of the young, their eagerness to speak, their access to recesses of an experienced childhood, and their poignant observations of adulthood. While each generation can expect to live longer, much of society, as Erikson points out, demands that individuals be allotted less time for youth. Earnest young proto-professionals especially uphold this ethic. Scattered not so infrequently about, however, are those whose parents have denied them even this minuscule tenure. For most, the awareness is simply a function of a precocious curiosity and creative need to experience. For the ones knowingly in trouble, the most immediate and pressing action resembles an attempt to complete some poorly understood mission started long ago by someone else.

That time repeats itself is but a comforting saying. The concept of a family cycle, moreover, is misleading as it tends to slur over the individual cycles unwinding at various tempi within it. Individual cycles never repeat themselves, for in progressing or carrying on in any guise, healthy or sick, the young, as ingenious as they are, do little more than obey the wishes of others and the demands that time imposes. Typically, the directions given by those who were here before us are to wait patiently and not walk so fast.

Sociologists have written that a major function of social structures is to direct its members to appropriate goal states, means of attaining them, and attitudes that may be taken in evaluating goals and means. The desire to become a doctor or lawyer, indeed the need to achieve, does not come from out of the blue. These are learned. So too is the desire to rebel, have sex, take drugs, escape, and even "freak out." In their way, all of these actions are creative because they develop out of social forms of, as well as private needs for, expression. But they have not "sprung up"; like instincts, they have evolved.

For many today, the evolution is not satisfying, and the internal excursions and elaborations have become (and probably started out as), in David Riesman's terms, "other-directed" movements. Knowing exactly this, many young persons continue nonetheless, in their other-directed patterns, and thereby show themselves most willing to listen outward and upward. Considering much of our adult behavior, this fact is remarkable.

Recommended Additional Readings

Cottle, T. J. *Time's children: Impressions of youth.* Boston: Little, Brown, 1971.

Feuer, L. S. *The conflict of generations: The character and significance of student movements.* New York: Basic Books, 1969.

Lorenz, K. The enmity between generations and its probable ethological causes. *Psychoanalytic Review,* 1970, 57, 333–377.

Antecedents of Delinquency:
Personality, Social Class, and Intelligence

John Janeway Conger

Wilbur C. Miller

Charles R. Walsmith

A considerable number of studies have examined the relationship between delinquency and such variables as social class, intelligence, and residence area (2, 3, 5, 6, 9, 10, 11, 12, 13, 16). Many others, including such pioneering efforts as those of Healy and Bronner (8) and the Gluecks (6), have investigated the relationship of personality traits to delinquency within various populations (1, 7, 14, 15, 16).

It may well be, however, that the relationship of these variables to delinquency cannot properly be considered independently of their relation to one another. Thus, it is perfectly possible that personality characteristics which are related to delinquency in some intelligence and social-class subgroups may not be related in other subgroups. For example, traits which differentiate delinquents from nondelinquents in a high-IQ, socioeconomically favored subgroup may fail to be differentiating in a deprived subgroup of average intelligence.

If this is the case, it is not enough, in studying the relationship of antecedent personality characteristics to later delinquency, simply to control for the possible effects of other factors, such as socioeconomic status, residence area, intelligence, sex, educational background, and ethnic group membership. This is clearly a necessary step, and one which the more adequate studies in this field have attempted to take, but it is not a sufficient step.

NOTE: This study, and the more extended research project of which it is a part, was made possible by a grant (MH-03040) from the National Institute of Mental Health. We would like to express our indebtedness to the following colleagues and research assistants for their help in the conduct of this study: Joan Happel, Rosamond Putsch, Robert V. Rainey, Ann A. Shenefield, Joan Searles, and Donald Stilson.

SOURCE: By permission of the authors.

The study reported here in condensed form is a part of a larger, longitudinal study of personality, social class, and delinquency (4). The principle aims of the present study were to determine (1) whether personality traits manifested by boys in the period from kindergarten through the third grade are significantly related to future delinquency after the potential effects of other factors have been controlled through a matching technique, and (2) whether the nature, extent, and direction of such relationships may vary, depending on the intelligence and social class status of the child.

The population from which the subjects of this study were drawn comprised all males in the tenth grade of all high schools in a large Western city (N = 2,348). Subjects actually employed met several additional requirements, including presence in the school system of this city in the period from kindergarten through the third grade (K-3) and continued residence in this city, at least through age 18.

Teacher ratings of "personal-social behavior," made on a three-point scale twice yearly during the early school years, were available for use as antecedent variables, as were more informal, unstructured comments made by teachers about their pupils during the same period. The latter were subjected to a content analysis, from which the investigators derived a "Teacher Comment Check List," consisting of 97 discrete behavioral traits and environmental influences (e.g., "good attention, concentration," "distractable, poor attention, daydreams," "independent, self-sufficient," "resents and rejects authority," "parent interest and cooperation"), reflecting the principle kinds of statements which teachers tended to make spontaneously about their pupils at this age. Two trained judges, with experience both in psychology and in elementary education, then applied the check list independently to a sample of 100 sets of teacher comments. For purposes of the present study, a set comprised all of the comments made by teachers about a particular child

in the K-3 period. Only those check list items showing interjudge reliabilities of .65 and above at this age level were employed in the study.

Delinquency Criterion

All boys in the population who became delinquent prior to age 18 were subsequently identified. The criterion for delinquency employed in this study was formal acceptance of the case by the Juvenile Court. As we have noted elsewhere (4), and as Bandura and Walters (1) also note, delinquency as such is a sociolegal, rather than a psychological phenomenon. In fact, a primary purpose of this investigation was to determine what, if any, were the relationships of psychological variables to this sociolegal phenomenon. As a result, any operationally defined criterion of delinquency had to involve some degree of contact with law enforcement officials—either police or judicial.

Because of the organization of juvenile authorities in this particular city, we were faced with these alternatives: we could have defined as delinquent all youths who had any contact either with the court or juvenile bureau of the police department. This, however, would have meant including as "delinquents" a large number of boys who were involved in very trivial incidents, such as minor pranks, and who were talked to briefly, turned over to their parents or sent home, and never seen again. The local juvenile bureau of the police department has estimated that out of every five cases seen, only two are eventually considered serious enough, either because of the gravity of the offense or because of recidivism, to be turned over to the juvenile court.

In turn, of the youths carried on the records of the juvenile court, only about one in eight is brought to trial, convicted, and sentenced to an institution—either because of failure to respond to assistance by probation workers, or because of the gravity of the offense.

It was our belief that to have used the first of these possible criteria would have diluted the meaning of the term delinquency to the point of absurdity (e.g., calling a child delinquent because he was once involved in a minor bit of mischief which came to the attention of the police). On the other hand, we were convinced that it would be equally inappropriate to designate as delinquent only those youths whose offenses were extremely serious or chronic, and who proved completely refractory to help from juvenile workers. Not only would such a definition exclude many youths in considerable trouble with the law, but it

would also render subsequent comparisons between repeaters and nonrepeaters, or treatable and refractory cases, impossible.

It was our conclusion that selecting the middle ground, and defining delinquency as acceptance of the case by the juvenile court, had the greatest promise for this investigation, and was also in closest accord with common usage. The distribution of offenses and ages of offenses for males in our population are shown in Figure 1 and Table 1. As may be seen, the highest incidence of delin-

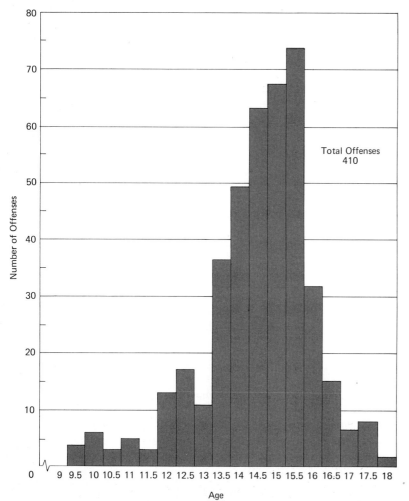

Figure 1 Distribution of number of offenses for 184 male delinquents, by age in half years, at time of offense.

Table 1. Distribution of 184 male delinquents by age in half-years at time of offense, and by type of offense

TYPE OF OFFENSE	AGE									
	9.5	10	10.5	11	11.5	12	12.5	13	13.5	14
Aggravated assault										2
Aggravated robbery										
Arson				1		1	1			
Assault and battery									1	3
Attempted car theft										
Burglary	1	2	1	2	1	3	3	5	7	4
Car prowl										
Car theft							1			2
Carrying concealed weapon										1
Cruelty to animals										
Curfew violation					1		1			1
Destroying city property										
Disturbances										
Escape from Juvenile Hall									1	
False fire alarm										
False registration										
Forgery										
Gangs										
Hit and run									1	1
Incorrigible	1	2	1	1		2	3	2	8	4
Indecent acts										1
Indecent language						1			1	1
Joyriding							1		1	1
Larceny	1			1	1	1	1	2	6	7
Loitering										
Malicious mischief	1					1	3	2	5	5
Receiving stolen goods						1	1			
Resisting arrest										
Runaway		1				1			2	2
Sex offenses						1			1	
Threats										1
Traffic violation										
Truancy		1					2		2	1
Vandalism						1				
Wearing women's clothing										
Witness to stabbing			1							
Total	4	6	3	5	3	13	17	11	36	49

quent offenses occurs at age 15.5, with a marked decline in number of offenses below age 14 and above age 16.

Selection of Study Samples

After identifying the delinquent males in our population for whom relatively complete records were available ($N = 271$), each was investigated individually to determine the following relevant characteristics: age, socioeconomic status (three levels: high, medium, low) residence area characteristics, IQ (seven levels: very superior, superior, bright normal, average, dull normal, borderline, mentally defective), school background (schools

Table 1. (Continued)

TYPE OF OFFENSE	AGE								TOTAL
	14.5	15	15.5	16	16.5	17	17.5	18	
Aggravated assault	1	1	5	1					10
Aggravated robbery	1	1	1						3
Arson									3
Assault and battery									4
Attempted car theft			2						2
Burglary	2	10	7	3	4		1		56
Car prowl	3	1							4
Car theft		5	5	6	1		1	1	22
Carrying concealed weapon	3	1							5
Cruelty to animals		1							15
Curfew violation	2	2	6				2		15
Destroying city property	1								1
Disturbances		1	3	1		1			6
Escape from Juvenile Hall			1						2
False fire alarm	1	1							2
False registration				1					1
Forgery					1	1			2
Gangs		1							1
Hit and run	2	2	1						7
Incorrigible	13	9	7	5	3	1	2		64
Indecent acts			1						2
Indecent language									3
Joyriding	17	18	12	5	3	1			71
Larceny	10	5	7	2	2	1			47
Loitering			2						2
Malicious mischief	3	3	5				1		29
Receiving stolen goods			1		1	1			5
Resisting arrest			1						1
Runaway	2	3	1	3					15
Sex offenses		1	2	3					8
Threats									1
Traffic violation		1	3						4
Truancy	1			1					8
Vandalism									1
Wearing women's clothing							1		1
Witness to stabbing									1
Total	62	67	73	31	15	6	8	1	N410

attended) and ethnic group membership. More detailed information regarding the techniques employed in determining such characteristics as socioeconomic status is available elsewhere (4).

Each delinquent was then matched *individually* with a nondelinquent on all the above variables. Because of the obvious impossibility of finding complete matches for all delinquents, this procedure reduced the number of potentially usable delinquents from 271 to 184.

Absence of teacher ratings or teacher comments on some of these boys during the K-3 period further reduced this number to 86. Thus, the final number of subjects employed in this study was 172, divided equally between delinquents and nondelinquents.

STUDY I: PERSONAL-SOCIAL BEHAVIOR OF FUTURE DELINQUENTS AND NONDELINQUENTS DURING THE EARLY SCHOOL YEARS

The first, and statistically much the simpler, of the two analyses presented in this paper involved a comparison of the personality characteristics of future delinquents and their nondelinquent matches in the period from kindergarten through the third grade. As noted above, two kinds of developmental personality measures were available in this period: teacher ratings of personal-social development and the Teacher Comment Check List. Each will be discussed in turn.

1. Ratings of Personal-Social Development

The behaviors rated here are listed in Table 2, and described in more detail elsewhere (4). Each

Table 2. Number of pairs in which both delinquent-nondelinquent pair members received ratings for each item of personal-social behavior at grade 3

TEACHER RATING	NUMBER OF DELINQUENT-NONDELINQUENT PAIRS
Physical skill	22
Creativeness	25
Clear thinking	20
Openmindedness	25
Leadership ability	50
Regard for persons	48
Sense of responsibility	52
Response to authority	49
Social acceptability	48
Work habits	49
Interests	15
Appreciations	4
Ideals (ambitions, wishes)	7
Physical health resources	12
Physical health problems	9
Home resources	5
Home problems	5
Overall	0

behavior was rated on a three-point scale: low (lower 25 percent), middle (middle 50 percent), and high (upper 25 percent). For purposes of statistical analysis, these ratings were given numerical values of 1, 2, and 3, respectively. Teachers were permitted to omit ratings where they did not feel that they had sufficient evidence to justify a judgment. While these same behaviors were rated at all elementary school grade levels, we selected the children's third grade ratings to represent the early school years. This was done for two reasons: (1) analyzing the ratings at all grade levels would have been prohibitive in terms of time and expense; (2) teachers apparently felt capable of rating more behaviors at this grade level than at earlier ones (though still less capable than at later grade levels). Thus, we had a greater total number of ratings with which to work at grade three.

It was our hypothesis, in view of the operational descriptions of these behaviors which were provided to teachers, that future nondelinquents would obtain higher scores on each of the traits rated. In testing this hypothesis we wanted to preserve the benefits of individual matching of delinquent and nondelinquent subjects and also to be able *later* to analyze for the effects, separately and in interaction, of social class-IQ subgroup membership. Consequently, for reasons to be described in more detail later in this paper, a 2 × 5 analysis of variance design for matched pairs (main effect for delinquency) was employed to test for the significance of delinquent-nondelinquent differences. For present purposes, and for the benefit of nonstatistically oriented readers, it is sufficient to note that this technique permitted us to test for the statistical significance of delinquent-nondelinquent differences on each personality measure.

Table 2 shows the number of times teachers rated *both* members of delinquent-nondelinquent pairs for each of the 18 traits rated at grade three. As may be seen, it appears that teachers felt little confidence at grade three in making ratings for

Table 3. Mean scores of male delinquents and nondelinquents on teacher ratings (Grade 3)

TEACHER RATING	DELINQUENT MEAN	NON-DELINQUENT MEAN	NUMBER OF MATCHED PAIRS	F-RATIO
Leadership	2.10	2.10	50	.00
Regard for persons	1.95	2.22	48	5.64[a]
Sense of responsibility	1.80	2.11	52	8.40[b]
Response to authority	2.10	2.28	49	2.48
Social acceptability	2.04	2.37	48	6.67[a]
Work habits	1.93	2.04	49	.62

[a]Significant at .05 level.
[b]Significant at .01 level.

most children on such variables as physical skill, creativeness, clear thinking, and open-mindedness (less than 30 pairs rated on each of these traits); and virtually no confidence in rating interest, appreciations, ideals, physical health resources, physical health problems, home resources, home problems, and overall adjustment (15 or fewer pairs rated).

On the other hand, they seemed to feel relatively confident (more than 45 pairs rated at this grade level) in rating: leadership ability, regard for persons, sense of responsibility, response to authority, social acceptability, and work habits. It is interesting to note that each of these six variables involves readily identifiable, relatively objective behaviors, common to the classroom situation; while many of the other variables involve behaviors or information not necessarily observable or known in the classroom, or they involve clinical inferences or unusually subtle judgments (e.g., "creativeness").

Nondelinquents scored higher than delinquents on 15 of the 18 traits, although, of course, in a fair number of instances the total number of ratings was too small to make statistical analysis possible. (Only on *interests, physical health resources,* and *physical health problems* did the delinquents obtain higher scores, and on none of these traits were more than 15 ratings made.)

However, as may be seen in Table 3, which presents means and significance levels for each rating involving over 45 pairs, of the six most commonly (and presumably most confidently) rated traits at the third grade level, three (*regard for persons, sense of responsibility,* and *social acceptability*) significantly differentiate nondelinquents from delinquents in the predicted direction at the .05[1] level or better, despite relatively small numbers. A fourth trait, *response to authority,* shows a possible trend toward significance (approaching the .10 level). Only two of the six variables, *work habits* and *leadership,* clearly fail to show any trend toward significance.[2]

2. Teacher Comment Check List

It may be recalled that only those items on the Teacher Comment Check List which had an interjudge reliability coefficient of .65 or higher at this age level were employed in the present

[1]A word of explanation for the nonstatistically oriented reader may be in order. A significance level of .025 simply means that there are only 25 chances in 1,000 that differences this large or larger would be obtained by chance alone. Similarly, a significance level of .01 indicated that there is only 1 chance in 100 that such results would occur by chance alone.

[2]*Statistical note:* These same data were also analyzed using a nonparametric sign test, based on the number of times the score of the nondelinquent member of a pair exceeded his match for each trait. Similar results were obtained, except that *response to authority,* discriminated in this latter analysis at the .05 level, rather than simply showing a possible trend. *Sense of responsibility* and *social acceptability* showed somewhat higher significance levels (.001 and .004, respectively) and *regard for persons* remained about the same (.035). *Work habits* and *leadership* continued to be nondiscriminating.

Table 4. Distribution of reliable teacher comment categories for matched pairs of male delinquents and nondelinquents, and D-score ratings for each category

TEACHER COMMENT CATEGORY	D-SCORE RATINGS	DELIN-QUENT ONLY	NON-DELIN-QUENT ONLY	BOTH	NEITHER	SIGNIFICANCE LEVEL (if p<.10)
1. Special ability or interest	−	7	15	5	59	.067
2. Below average ability	+	1	2[a]	0	83	
3. Slow learner	+	1	2	0	83	
4. Works up to capacity	−	2	4	0	80	
5. Underachieving	+	12	14	1	59	
6. Good reader	−	7	6[a]	3	70	
7. Poor reader	+	11	17[a]	9	49	
8. Good work habits	−	9	7[a]	1	69	
9. Careful worker	−	7	8	0	71	
10. Careless worker	+	6	4	3	73	
11. Good attention, concentration	−	6	8	0	72	
12. Distractible, poor attention, daydreams	+	21	9	4	52	.003
13. Shows effort to improve	−	16	23	11	36	
14. Lacks persistence, gives up easily	+	9	7	0	70	
15. Conscientious, dependable	−	9	11	2	64	
16. Cooperative	−	11	13	1	61	
17. Poor attitude toward school	+	2	2	1	81	
18. Good attendance	−	1	1	0	84	
19. Attendance problem	+	7	7	0	72	
20. Parent interest and cooperation	−	10	18	4	54	.093
21. Stable home	−	1	3	0	82	
22. Disturbed home environment	+	21	5	1	59	.002
23. Friendly, pleasant	−	11	26	6	43	.011
24. Considerate, fair to others	−	3	13	0	70	.011
25. Aggressive	+	10	4	1	71	.090
26. Resents and rejects authority	+	13	2	0	71	.004
27. Influenced by others	+	4	1	0	81	
28. Active group participation	−	6	13	3	64	.084
29. Well liked, accepted, gets along with peers	−	16	32	12	26	.027
30. Not well accepted, doesn't get along with peers	+	15	5	2	64	.021
31. Attention seeking	+	8	12[a]	0	66	
32. Well-behaved	−	2	4	0	80	
33. Unstable, insecure	+	12	7	2	65	
34. Nervous, restless	+	8	5	0	73	

Table 4. *(Continued)*

TEACHER COMMENT CATEGORY	D-SCORE RATINGS	DELIN-QUENT ONLY	NON-DELIN-QUENT ONLY	BOTH	NEITHER	SIGNIFICANCE LEVEL (if p<.10)
35. Mature (emotionally)	−	0	4	0	82	
36. Immature (emotionally)	+	6	17[a]	1	62	.017
37. Quiet, shy, tends to withdraw	−	12	11	2	61	
38. Physical defects	+	21	15	11	39	

[a]Not in predicted direction.

study. These are listed in Table 4, and are described in more detail elsewhere *(4)*.

The data emerging from the check list were analyzed in two ways. On the basis of a priori hypotheses about the relation to delinquency of specific personality traits, each trait was postulated as more likely to be associated with delinquency or more likely to be associated with non-delinquency. All instances of the former in a record were arbitrarily scored + 1, and all instances of the latter − 1. By summing all instances of the former and subtracting all instances of the latter, a hypothetical "D" (or delinquency) score was obtained for each subject. This procedure has, of course, both advantages and disadvantages. On the positive side, items occurring sufficiently infrequently that their individual validity cannot be assessed have an opportunity, if they are in fact valid, of contributing to the discriminating power of the overall D-score. On the other hand, even though the D-score itself proves capable of discriminating delinquents from nondelinquents, one cannot be sure just which rare items are making a valid (as opposed to a chance) contribution to this discrimination.

One can, however, test the individual significance of D-score items which occur frequently enough to make a statistical test of their discriminating power possible.

Table 4 shows the D-score rating (+1, or −1) for each of the reliable teacher comment categories, as well as the distribution of these categories for matched pairs of delinquents and non-

delinquents, for the period kindergarten through third grade. The D-scores for all subjects were obtained, means for delinquents and nondelinquents were computed, and the significance of the delinquent-nondelinquent difference was run.[3] A mean D-score of +.23 was found for delinquents and −1.23 for nondelinquents. The difference is clearly significant ($p < .001$).[4]

Among individual D-score items, 29 fell in the predicted direction, while eight fell in the opposite direction (Table 4). Of 26 cases where more than 15 ratings of delinquents and nondelinquents combined were made, *12 discriminated delinquents from nondelinquents at the .10 level or better, of which 8 were significant below the .05 level (sign test).*

SUMMARY OF FINDINGS

It appears that even at the third grade level future delinquents and nondelinquents as a group are viewed differently by their teachers. It should be stressed that we are speaking here only of differences above and beyond those which might be due to the effects of such variables as socioeconomic status, intelligence, and ethnic group membership, since the potential effects of these variables have already been controlled through matching. Had these not been controlled, even larger

[3]Based on the main effect for delinquency in an analysis of variance design for D-score.

[4]A nonparametric sign test, based on the number of instances in which delinquent pair members exceeded their nondelinquent matches, yielded similar results ($p = .003$).

differences would be anticipated, in view of the known relationship between these variables and both personality and delinquency, a relationship confirmed in this research *(4)*.

Nevertheless, even with such controls the differences are impressive, particularly at this early age—as evidenced, for example, by the fact that the overall D-score enables us to discriminate future delinquents and nondelinquents at the .001 level of significance.

In the period from kindergarten through third grade, future delinquent boys already appeared more poorly adapted than their classmates. They appeared to have less regard for the rights and feelings of their peers; less awareness of the need to accept responsibility for their obligations, both as individuals and as members of a group; and poorer attitudes toward authority, including the failure to understand the need for rules and regulations in any well-ordered social group, and to abide by them. They both resented and rejected authority in the school situation. Their overall social behavior was simply less acceptable; they had more difficulty in getting along with peers, both in individual 1-to-1 contacts and in group situations, and were less willing or able to treat others courteously and tactfully and less able to be fair in dealing with them. In return, they were less well liked and accepted by their peers.

In the academic situation itself, they were more easily distracted, daydreamed more, and, in general, had greater difficulty in maintaining attention and sticking to the task at hand until it was completed. They were less likely to display any special ability or interest.

Not surprisingly, these social and academic problems frequently appeared to reflect underlying emotional problems. In the opinion of teachers, as manifested by the ratings and teacher comments, future delinquents more often came from a disturbed home environment and were considered overly aggressive.

Future nondelinquents appeared in many ways as the other side of the coin. Socially, they were rated significantly more cooperative, dependable, friendly, pleasant, considerate, and fair. They were better liked by their peers and more accepted as members of the group.

In the school situation, they showed a considerably greater sense of individual and group responsibility, greater acceptance of constituted authority, and more acceptable social behavior generally.

Their parents appeared more often to show interest in the child's academic and social progress, and to cooperate more readily with school authorities. Emotionally, these boys appeared less aggressive.

STUDY II: SOCIOECONOMIC STATUS AND INTELLIGENCE

The question arising in our minds at this juncture was whether or not the general picture described above was equally applicable to all subgroups, or whether the picture might change as we proceeded from one social class-IQ subgroup to another. However, to approach this problem, it was necessary to subdivide our subjects, not only into the two matched groups of delinquents and nondelinquents employed in Study I, but also along the dimensions of socioeconomic status and intelligence.

For reasons which are elaborated elsewhere *(4)*, it appeared most appropriate, both for statistical reasons and because of the socioeconomic and IQ distributions of residents of this predominantly middle-class city, to employ two levels of socioeconomic status ("deprived" and "nondeprived"), and three levels of intelligence (below average, average [90–109 IQ], and above average). As may be seen in Figure 2, this yielded a $2 \times 2 \times 3$ design. The number of subjects falling into each of the cells of this design is shown in Table 5.

As statistically oriented readers are aware, the optimal method of analyzing a design of this sort involves a $2 \times 2 \times 3$ analysis of variance. Such

Table 5. Distribution of subjects according to socioeconomic levels, IQ, and delinquency status (K-3)

SOCIOECONOMIC LEVEL	DELINQUENTS			NONDELINQUENTS		
	BELOW AVERAGE IQ	AVERAGE IQ	ABOVE AVERAGE IQ	BELOW AVERAGE IQ	AVERAGE IQ	ABOVE AVERAGE IQ
Deprived	5	20	0	5	20	0
Nondeprived	13	33	15	13	33	15

an analysis would permit us simultaneously to determine not only if there are differences on a personality measure between delinquents and nondelinquents, between IQ categories, and between deprived and nondeprived subjects, but also whether there are *interaction effects* among two or more of these variables (i.e., in nonstatistical terms, and for present purposes, whether there are variations in the relationships of personality characteristics to delinquency as we proceed from one social class-IQ subgroup to another).

However, use of this one, maximally efficient method of analysis requires a basic minimum number of subjects in all cells of the design. Unfortunately, as Table 5 makes clear, this is not the case in our sample, since no subject fell in the above average IQ-deprived-delinquent cell. Apparently it is very unusual for a subject to be

delinquent, socioeconomically deprived, and still obtain an above average IQ score. (Examination of a *representative sample* of our entire population indicates that the combination of high IQ-deprived-nondelinquent is somewhat more common in the general population, but still relatively rare.)

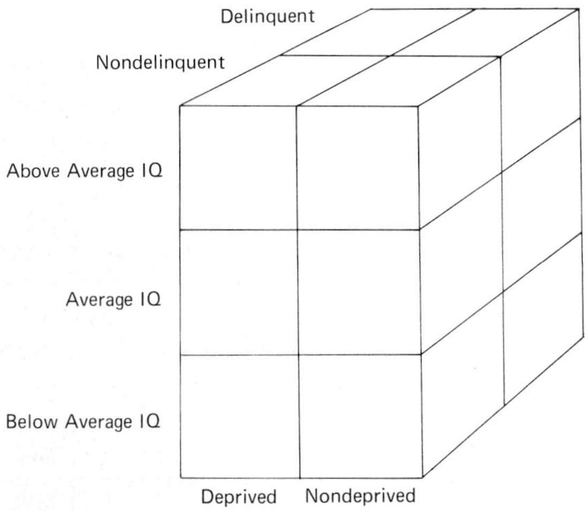

The absence of above average IQ-deprived cells forced us to modify our methods of analysis. This will become clear as we proceed. *The important fact for the reader (whether statistically oriented or not) to realize at this point is simply that the actual distribution of our subjects made it impossible to include an above average IQ-deprived subgroup in our comparisons of the personality characteristics of delinquents and nondelinquents.*

Teacher Comments and D-Score

Breaking down individual teacher comment check list items into social class-IQ subgroups was not feasible, because too few entries would have appeared in the various cells for any one trait to make statistical analysis meaningful. On the other hand, since a fairly large number of children (N-172) had D-scores, it was possible to analyze them further. Figure 3 shows the actual distribution of mean D-scores at this age level for future delinquents and nondelinquents in each of the social class-IQ subgroups, as well as in the group as a whole.

As may be seen, saying that delinquents have a mean D-score of +.23 while nondelinquents average −1.23 may be quite misleading when we come to a consideration of the various subgroups. Thus, for example, in the nondeprived-below

Figure 2 The basic 2 × 2 × 3 design.

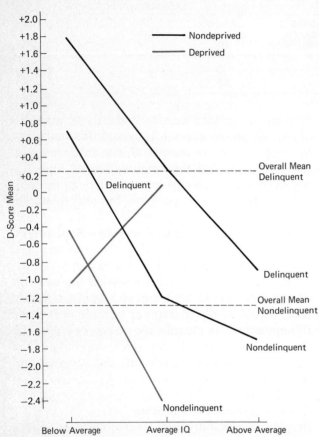

Figure 3 Distribution of mean D-scores for delinquents and matched nondelinquents by social class-IQ subgroup. N-172; K-3.

average IQ subgroup, nondelinquents are actually closer to the overall delinquent mean than to the nondelinquent. Conversely, delinquent youngsters in the nondeprived-above average and the deprived-below average IQ subgroups come much closer to the overall nondelinquent mean than to the delinquent. Such results appear to lend support to one of the basic tenets of this study, namely, that *personality factors may be differentially related to delinquency, depending on the social class and IQ status of the child.*

Analyses of Variance

Are the kinds of differences shown in Figure 3 meaningful, however, or do they simply reflect the effects of chance? In attempting to determine the statistical significance of the social class-IQ subgroup differences seen in Figure 3, it was not possible for reasons already stated, to use a straightforward 2 × 2 × 3 analysis of variance. Instead, we were forced to employ three partial analyses of variance in order to achieve as nearly as possible the same degree of information (see p. 443). These analyses will be described briefly in this section, although nonstatistically oriented readers may wish to proceed immediately to the next section, *Teacher Ratings.*

In the first place, a 2 × 5 analysis of variance was performed. This design involved two independent variables: (1) delinquency-nondelinquency and (2) five combinations of IQ level and socioeconomic status (e.g., "Deprived-below average IQ"). This analysis yielded significant differences between delinquents and nondelinquents as a group ($p < .001$, as previously noted) and between the various social class-IQ subgroups ($p < .001$). Interpreting these results in terms of Figure 3, it appears that an individual's D-score may be significantly elevated both by delinquency and by lower social class-IQ status, except in the case of deprived delinquents, where D-score actually decreases from average to below average IQ.

However, since this design confounds IQ and social class (each subgroup used in the preceding analysis involved a combination of the two), it did not permit an evaluation of the significance of each of these variables separately. In order to deal, at least partially, with this latter problem, two additional analyses of variance were performed. First, a 2 × 2 × 2 analysis of variance was carried out involving two levels of IQ (average, below average), two levels of socioeconomic status (deprived, nondeprived), and two levels of delinquency (delinquent, nondelinquent). This analysis yielded a significant overall difference between delinquents and nondelinquents ($p < .05$) and socioeconomic status ($p < .05$). In addition, there was some suggestion ($p < .20$) of an interaction effect between delinquency and intelligence, with the largest differences between delinquents and nondelinquents occurring in the average IQ range.

This type of analysis (unlike the 2 × 5 analysis) permitted us to consider the effects of intelligence and social class separately from one another at the average and below average IQ levels. However, it did not allow us to include above average IQ subjects. For this reason, one additional 2 × 3 analysis of variance was performed, involving only nondeprived subjects. This permitted us to include the above average IQ subjects and hence to cast additional light on the possible effects of IQ considered separately among nondeprived subjects. After the exclusion of deprived subjects, this analysis yielded a significant overall difference between delinquents and nondelinquents ($p < .025$), as in previous analyses. It also indicated that the D-score was strongly affected by intelligence ($p < .005$).

Teacher Ratings

It will be recalled that six items of personal-social behavior were noted fairly frequently by teachers at this age-grade level. These were: *work habits, social acceptability, response to authority, sense of responsibility, regard for persons, and leadership.* It has already been shown that three of these traits (*social acceptability, sense of responsibility,* and *regard for persons*) differentiated delinquents from nondelinquents at better than the .05 level.

There was no assurance, however, that each of these traits would discriminate in the same direction or to the same extent as we proceeded from one social class-IQ subgroup to another.

In fact, the findings from the D-score analysis suggested the likelihood that at least some of them would not. It appeared desirable, therefore,

to subject each of these traits to the same series of complementary analysis of variance designs that we had employed for D-scores, and this was done. Unfortunately, however, the results (or in some cases, the lack of results) at this age level have to be interpreted more cautiously, and also less fully for the following reason: The total number of pairs involved for each of these traits was consistently smaller than for D-score (ranging between 96 and 104, as contrasted with 172 for D-score). As it turned out, this had its greatest effect in the below average IQ-deprived subgroups, limiting the number of subjects to four in these analyses, as compared to ten in the D-score analysis. Other subgroups, while also reduced in number, still contained reasonable numbers of subjects.

At this age-grade level, therefore, the results of the D-score analysis appear deserving of greater confidence. Nevertheless, despite smaller numbers (both overall and particularly in the below average IQ-deprived subgroup), several traits still showed effects of variables other than delinquency status, and the statistically significant findings on these traits will be summarized briefly. Detailed results of the various analyses of variance supporting these statements are available elsewhere **(4)**.

Regard for Persons

Figure 4 shows the distribution of ratings for the five subgroups on this trait. As may be seen, as one progresses from below average to above average IQ among nondeprived subjects, favorableness of rating shows a (statistically significant) increase for both delinquents and nondelinquents, with the greatest increase occurring in the nondelinquent group. This has the effect of placing nondelinquents in the below average IQ subgroup closer to the actual delinquent mean, while placing above average IQ delinquents closer to the overall nondelinquent mean.

It may be observed that in the below average

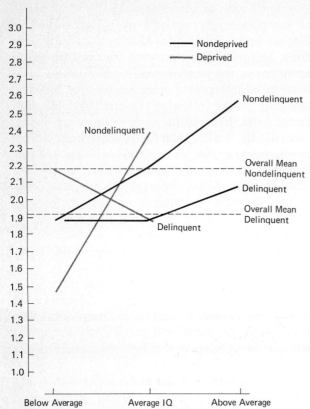

Figure 4 Distribution of mean teacher ratings of "regard for persons" for delinquents and matched nondelinquents by social class-IQ subgroup. N-96; K-3.

IQ-deprived subgroup, delinquents score more favorably than nondelinquents. This is interesting, since it corresponds to the findings for the D-score analysis and several other teacher ratings. However, in view of the small number of subjects in this subgroup, this observation must be viewed merely as suggestive; not surprisingly, it fails to find support in any of the analyses of variance.

Sense of Responsibility

Figure 5 shows the distribution of ratings on this trait. What appears to be reflected here, according

to the various analyses of variance, is a significant tendency for delinquents and nondelinquents (deprived and nondeprived) to show few differences at the below average IQ level, but marked differences at the average IQ level. Furthermore, among nondeprived subjects, there appears to be at least a tendency for favorableness of rating to increase with increases in IQ from below average to above average.

Again, as in the case of *regard for persons*, it would appear presumptuous to conclude that overall delinquent-nondelinquent differences on this trait are likely to be equally applicable to all

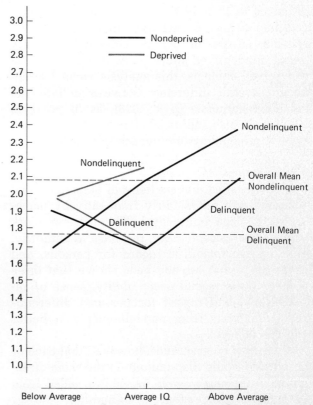

Figure 5 Distribution of mean teacher ratings of "social responsibility" for delinquents and matched nondelinquents by social class-IQ subgroup. N-104; K-3.

subgroups. For example, as may be seen, among nondeprived subjects, *delinquents* of above average IQ fell at the overall *nondelinquent* mean and *nondelinquents* of below average IQ actually fell below the overall *delinquent* mean. Furthermore, while fairly wide differences separating nondelinquents and delinquents occurred among all sub-groups at the average and above average IQ levels, at the below average IQ level there were either no differences or the direction of differences was actually reversed (though not significantly so).

Social Acceptability

Figure 6 shows the distribution of teacher ratings on this trait. In this case, it will be recalled from Study I that the significance level for overall delinquent-nondelinquent differences fell at the .025 level: As Figure 6 suggests, the failure to obtain a larger level of significance appears to have been due primarily to reversals in the direction of delinquent-nondelinquent differences among nondeprived subjects at the below average and above average IQ levels. This interpretation finds support in the various analyses of variance conducted for this trait.

Certainly, it would appear incautious, on the basis of these findings, to assume that overall delinquent and nondelinquent means for *social acceptability* could be applied to nondeprived subgroups of below average and above average intelligence, although they appear quite applicable to the other subgroups, both deprived and nondeprived.

Work Habits

The distribution of teacher ratings for this trait is shown in Figure 7. It will be recalled that this trait, unlike those discussed above, showed no significant overall mean difference between delinquents and nondelinquents. When one examines Figure 7, these results do not appear surprising. While in a number of subgroups fairly wide de-

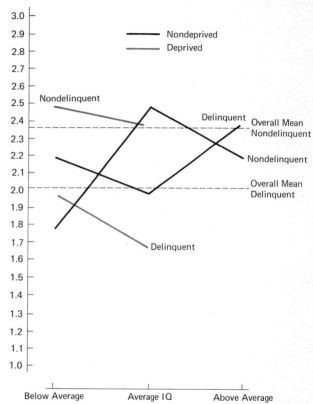

Figure 6 Distribution of mean teacher ratings of "social acceptability" for delinquents and matched nondelinquents by social class-IQ subgroup. N-96; K-3.

linquent-nondelinquent differences are seen (considerably wider than the *overall* mean difference), in the case of two of the three greatest differences, the delinquents scored more favorably.

These findings would appear to raise a warning of a different sort from those previously suggested. While the numbers of subjects involved in the subgroups showing reversals is quite small, making definitive statements suspect, it is at least possible (as a delinquency-intelligence *interaction effect* suggests) that the failure to obtain a significant overall delinquent-nondelinquent differ-

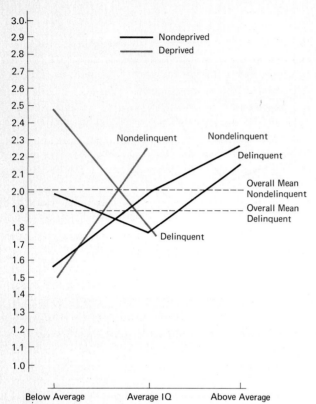

Figure 7 Distribution of mean teacher ratings of "work habits" for delinquents and matched nondelinquents by social class-IQ subgroup. N-98; K-3.

ence may have been due, not to the possibility that there were, in fact, no differences, but that the nature and distribution of these differences varied from one subgroup to another.

Obviously, this may be true of a number of personality characteristics. If so, investigations which confine themselves to studying only *overall* delinquent-nondelinquent differences (and this includes the great majority) may be ruling out as unrelated to delinquency, traits which, in some subgroups at least, and conceivably in all, actually may be strongly related to it.

The remaining two traits, *leadership* and *response to authority,* had originally shown no sig-

nificant overall mean differences between delinquents and nondelinquents, and also showed no other main or interaction effects in the various analyses of variance.

SUMMARY OF TEACHER RATINGS AND D-SCORE FINDINGS

Viewed together, the findings from the D-score analysis, supplemented by the more limited findings on individual teacher rating analyses, suggest that:

1. Personality trait ratings may be differentially related to delinquency, depending on socioeconomic status and IQ. As a result, *overall* means and mean differences between delinquents and nondelinquents may be quite misleading when applied to a particular social class-IQ subgroup. In many instances, delinquents in a particular subgroup scored closer to the overall nondelinquent mean than to the delinquent; conversely, in other subgroups nondelinquents scored closer to the overall delinquent mean than to the nondelinquent. This fact alone would appear to lend support to one of the basic hypotheses of this study; namely, that personality factors may be differentially related to delinquency, depending on the particular personality factor involved and on the social class and IQ status of the child.

2. On overall D-score, and on most individual traits, nondelinquents obtained more favorable mean ratings than delinquents in most subgroups. This would be expected, in view of the fact that significant overall differences between delinquents and nondelinquents (with nondelinquents scoring more favorably) were obtained for D-score, *social acceptability, sense of responsibility,* and *regard for persons.*

3. The largest mean differences between delinquents and nondelinquents occurred without exception among socioeconomically deprived children, either in the average IQ or below average IQ subgroups.

4. In some instances (e.g., *work habits*) where significant overall differences between delin-

quents and nondelinquents are *not* found, in this and other investigations, this may be due, at least partly, to variations in the direction of delinquent-nondelinquent differences from one social class-IQ subgroup to another.

5. In the case of boys of below average IQ, future delinquents *tended* to receive *more favorable* ratings than nondelinquents. This was especially likely to be true in the case of socioeconomically deprived subjects, although this observation must be viewed with considerable caution, due to the small number of subjects frequently present in the below average-IQ-deprived subgroups.

It would appear that in those instances where significant interaction effects between delinquency and intelligence were found on either the $2 \times 2 \times 2$ or 2×3 analyses of variance, absence of delinquent-nondelinquent differences, or reversals in the direction of these differences, among children of below average IQ were primarily responsible.

It should also be obvious that in *all* instances where delinquent subjects received the same or more favorable scores than nondelinquents, it would be a mistake to consider overall delinquent-nondelinquent differences as applicable to these subgroups, since the latter did not contribute to the size and significance of the overall difference, and in at least some cases (i.e., those where significant interaction effects were found) substantially reduced them.

6. There is some tendency among *nondeprived* subjects for favorableness of rating to increase with increases in IQ. This observation is supported by the fact that a highly significant main effect for intelligence was obtained on the 2×3 analysis of variance for D-score. Among individual teacher ratings on the 2×3 analysis, considerable variation was found, with significance levels for main effect for intelligence ranging from .05 to nonsignificance, with most traits showing a *trend* toward significance. No such tendency for favorableness of rating to increase

with intelligence could be observed among *deprived* subjects.

7. Except in the case of D-score, there is little *direct* relation between favorableness of teacher ratings and socioeconomic status, and even in the case of D-score, the expected direction of the difference is reversed, with deprived children scoring *more favorably* at both IQ levels, as the accompanying figures indicate. These statements are supported by the absence of a main effect for socioeconomic status in the $2 \times 2 \times 2$ analyses, except in the case of D-score where a significant effect was found.

This finding is of considerable general interest, in view of the contention of many sociologists and psychologists that teachers tend to rate lower-class children more unfavorably than middle-class children on personal-social traits in the school situation as a result of bias stemming from the average teacher's membership in middle-class culture. At least in this age-grade period, the most *favorable* teacher comments and ratings at the average IQ level characteristically were given to *deprived* nondelinquents.

It would appear that the apparent bias of teachers noted by some investigators may be due to a greater incidence of delinquent trends among socioeconomically deprived children. But where a deprived child, even though he may be identified with lower-class culture, appears capable of average intellectual performance and socially responsible future behavior, he tends to be rated, at least according to this investigation, as or more favorably than this middle-class peer.

SUMMARY

Even in the period from kindergarten through the third grade, future delinquents generally appeared more poorly adapted than nondelinquent peers of the same age, sex, IQ, socioeconomic status, residential background, and ethnic group membership, as measured by teacher ratings and a content analysis of informal teacher comments. As a group, they manifested less acceptable social behavior, more academic difficulty, and a greater incidence of emotional problems.

However, these general findings cannot be applied indiscriminately to all subgroups in the population. There were marked differences in the relationship of various personality traits to delinquency status from one social class-IQ subgroup to another. While in most subgroups nondelinquents received more favorable ratings from teachers on most traits, the size of delinquent-nondelinquent differences and the ranges in which these differences occurred varied considerably.

Furthermore, on some traits even the direction of delinquent-nondelinquent differences changed as one proceeded from one social class-IQ subgroup to another. Thus, on a majority of traits, future delinquents of below average IQ received more favorable teacher ratings than their nondelinquent peers. In short, ratings of personal-social behavior at this age were related, not only to future delinquency status, but also to socioeconomic status and intelligence, whether directly or through interaction with delinquency status.

References

1. Bandura, A., & Walters, R. H. *Adolescent aggression.* New York: Ronald, 1959.
2. Cloward, R. A., & Ohlin, L. *Delinquency and opportunity: a theory of delinquent groups.* Glencoe, Ill.: Free Press, 1960.
3. Conger, J. J., Miller, W. C., Gaskill, H. S., & Walsmith, C. R. *Progress report.* (Grant no. M–3040) National Institute of Mental Health, U.S.P.H.S., Washington, D. C., 1960.
4. Conger, J. J., & Miller, W. C., *Personality, social class, and delinquency.* New York: Wiley, 1966.
5. Glueck, S., & Glueck, E. T. *One thousand juvenile delinquents.* Cambridge: Harvard Univer. Press, 1934.
6. Glueck, S., & Glueck, E. T. *Unraveling juvenile delinquency.* New York: Commonwealth Fund, 1950.
7. Hathaway, S. R., and Monachesi, E. D. (Eds.) *Analyzing and predicting juvenile delinquency with the MMPI.* Minneapolis: Univer. Minnesota Press, 1953.
8. Healy, W., & Bronner, A. F. *New light on delinquency and its treatment.* New Haven: Yale Univer. Press, 1936.
9. Maccoby, Eleanor E., Johnson, J. P., & Church, R. M. Community integration and the social control of juvenile delinquency. *J. soc. Issues,* 1958, 14, 38–51.
10. Merrill, M. A. *Problems of child delinquency.* Boston: Houghton Mifflin, 1947.
11. Salisbury, H. E. *The shook-up generation.* New York: Harper (Crest Books), 1959.
12. Shaw, C. R. *Delinquency areas.* Chicago: Univer. Chicago Press, 1929.
13. Shaw, C. R., McKay, H. D., *et al. Juvenile delinquency and urban areas.* Chicago: Univer. Chicago Press, 1942.
14. Wattenberg, W. W. *The adolescent years.* New York: Harcourt Brace, 1955.
15. Werner, E. & Gallistel, E. Prediction of outstanding performances, delinquency, and emotional disturbance from childhood evaluations. *Child Developm.* 1961, 32, 255–260.
16. Wirt, R. D., & Briggs, P. F. Personality and environmental factors in the development of delinquency. *Psychol. Monogr.,* 1959, 73, No. 15, 1–47.

Chapter 16

Adolescent Sexuality

One of the more prominent aspects of the so-called youth culture of the 1960s, and apparently one of the more enduring, has been the development of a "new sexual morality." This new morality is based more on openness, honesty, and a greater concern for others in human relationships and less on conformity to institutionalized social norms. There has been a growing tendency among young people to view decisions about individual sexual values and behavior as more of a private and less of a public concern; they also tend to place a greater emphasis on individual self-discovery and self-expression in sex, as in other areas.

There is little doubt that the sexual attitudes and values of adolescents have been changing and are continuing to change, especially among middle- and upper-class youths. There is still considerable controversy, however, even among presumed experts, regarding the extent to which changing attitudes have been reflected in behavior.

In his article in this chapter, J. J. Conger reviews the relevant data (most of which are very recent) and concludes that while there was probably an initial lag, attitudinal changes are increasingly being reflected in the sexual behavior of contemporary adolescents. Furthermore, the **percentage increases** in premarital intercourse—in recent years from an initially lower baseline—have been greatest among middle- and upper-class young people, especially girls. He cautions, however, against unwarranted generalizations, pointing out that preoccupation with group trends can obscure the fact that there is still a wide, and probably growing, diversity of sexual attitudes and behavior in different sectors of the adolescent and youth population. Such factors as age, sex, socioeconomic and educational background, race, religion, and even geographical area are all strongly related to sexual attitudes, values, and behavior. For this reason, the results of any investigation dealing with adolescent sexuality will inevitably seem exaggerated to some young people and adults and minimized to others.

Conger concludes that the so-called sexual revolution appears likely to continue. While many of its results have been positive, there is still a danger that a significant number of adolescents may become involved in sexual relationships which they are too young, too poorly informed, or too vulnerable emotionally to be able to handle successfully.

A New Morality:
Sexual Attitudes and Behavior
of Contemporary Adolescents

John Janeway Conger

It has been apparent for some years now that the sexual attitudes and values of adolescents have been changing significantly, that a "new morality" has been developing in the United States and other Western countries (**3**, **16**, **20**). In comparison to their peers of earlier generations, today's adolescents place a greater emphasis on openness and honesty about sex (**4**, **16**, **29**). In a number of recent surveys (**8**, **9**, **10**, **33**, **34**), the majority (85% or more) of American adolescents expressed the view that young people need more and better sex education and that information about sex should be given in the schools—under most circumstances, in coeducational classes.

In one national survey of the confidential opinions of 1500 middle-class adolescent girls aged 13 to 19, 98 percent said they wanted sex

SOURCE: By permission of the author.

taught in school (**10**). When asked what was currently being taught and what *should* be taught, most girls responded that such topics as the anatomy and physiology of the female reproductive system and the menstrual cycle not only *should* be taught, but that they *were* being covered. Most girls also felt strongly that sex education classes should deal with such philosophical or scientific issues as premarital ethics, abortion, birth control and contraception, male and female sex drives, masturbation, homosexuality, loss of virginity, impotence and frigidity, fertility, and the nature of the orgasm. In *all* of these important areas, however, less than half of the sample reported having had school instruction.

In addition, there is a growing tendency among young people to view decisions about individual sexual behavior as more of a private and less of a public concern (**4**, **63**). In part, this appears to reflect a growing suspiciousness of or disenchantment with established social institutions and their proclaimed values, together with a shift among many young people in the direction of individual self-discovery and self-expression—of "doing one's thing." But it also reflects a greater emphasis on the importance of "meaningful," that is, genuine and sincere, interpersonal relationships in sex as in other areas.

In the view of a majority of contemporary adolescents, the acceptability of various forms and degrees of sexual behavior, including premarital intercourse, is highly dependent on the nature of the relationship between the individuals involved (16, 20, 26, 29). Eighty percent of adolescent boys and 72 percent of girls in this country agree with the statement, "It's all right for young people to have sex before getting married if they are in love with each other" (29). Seventy-five percent of all girls maintain that "I wouldn't want to have sex with a boy unless I loved him" (29). While only 47 percent of boys stated this stringent a requirement, 69 percent said, "I would not want to have sex with a girl unless I liked her as a person" (29). In contrast, most adolescents clearly oppose exploitation, pressure or force in sex, sex solely for the sake of physical enjoyment, and sex between people too young to understand what they are getting into (16, 20, 29). Nearly 75 percent of all adolescents concur that "when it comes to morality in sex, the important thing is the way people treat each other, not the things they do together" (29).

Despite a growing emphasis among adolescents on openness and honesty, there is little evidence of preoccupaion with sex, as many parents and other adults seem to think. Indeed, it may well be that the average adolescent of today is less preoccupied and concerned with sex than prior generations of young people, including his parents when they were the same age. Greater acceptance of sex as a natural part of life may well lead to less preoccupation than anxious concern in an atmosphere of secrecy and suppression. Most contemporary adolescents (87%) agree that "all in all, I think my head is pretty well together as far as sex is concerned" (29).

Furthermore, in ranking the relative importance of various goals, younger adolescent boys and girls (13–15) cited as most important: "Preparing myself to earn a good living when I get older," "Having fun," and "Getting along with my parents"; for younger girls, "Learning about myself" was also important. Older adolescents of both sexes (16–19) stressed "Learning about myself" as most important, followed by "Being independent so that I can make it on my own" and "Preparing myself to accomplish useful things." Among all age groups, "Having sex with a number of different boys (girls)" and "Making out" consistently ranked at or near the top among goals considered *least* important (29).

ARE CHANGING ATTITUDES REFLECTED IN BEHAVIOR?

Are the significant and apparently enduring changes in sexual attitudes and values among contemporary adolescents reflected in their behavior, and, if so, how? At least until very recently, a number of generally recognized authorities maintained that the overall behavior of today's adolescents and youth, though more open and in some respects probably freer, did not differ strikingly from that of their parents at the same age (20, 24, 28). Conversely, other observers have asserted that, although attitudinal changes may have been the more dramatic, there have also been marked changes in behavior (17, 20). What do the available data reveal? As will become evident, the answer appears to depend on *what* behaviors one is referring to, among *which* adolescents, and *how recently*.

Although current data are admittedly incomplete, the available information indicates that there has been relatively little if any change in the past few decades in the incidence of male masturbation (1, 21, 22, 27, 29); masturbation appears to have remained fairly stable over the years, with an estimated incidence of about 21 percent by age 12, 82 percent by age 15, and 92 percent by age 20 (**13, 27**). However, recent data (**9, 29**) indicates that there has been an increase in masturbation among girls at all age levels, with incidences of *at least* 36 percent by age 15 and 42 percent by age 19. In contrast, only about 17 percent of the mothers of today's adolescent girls had engaged in masturbation to orgasm by age 15, and by age 20, only about 30 percent (**12**).

One might be tempted to conclude that masturbation would occur most commonly among adolescents lacking other outlets. Interestingly, however, current masturbation experience among contemporary adolescents occurs about three times as frequently among those engaged in sexual intercourse or petting to orgasm as among the sexually inexperienced (**29**).

Petting does appear to have increased somewhat in the past few decades, and it tends to occur slightly earlier (**12, 13, 16, 20, 23, 24, 29**). The major changes, however, have probably been in the frequency of petting, degree of intimacy of techniques involved, the frequency with which petting leads to erotic arousal or orgasm, and, certainly, frankness about it (**2, 4, 16, 19, 28, 29**).

Premarital Intercourse

Currently, the greatest amount of public discussion (and parental and societal apprehension), as well as the most extensive data, deals with the incidence of sexual intercourse among contemporary youth. A favorite assertion among those who have claimed there have been few *recent* changes in adolescent sexual behavior is that, while there has indeed been a sexual revolution in this century, it took place, not among today's adolescents, but among their parents and grandparents. It does, in fact, appear that significant percentage increases in premarital intercourse occurred during this earlier period. For example, Kinsey's data indicate that only 2 percent of females born before 1900 had premarital intercourse prior to age 16, 8 percent prior to age 20, and only 14 percent prior to age 25 (**12**). In contrast, for the mothers of today's adolescents, the corresponding figures are 4 percent, 21 percent, and 37 percent, respectively (**12, 13**).

This, however, leaves unanswered the question of how the incidence of premarital intimacy among today's parents compares with that of their adolescent sons and daughters. Until very recently, relevant data for such a comparison were lacking, except in the case of college students. However, in a representative national study of adolescents aged 13 to 19, published in 1973, Robert Sorenson (**29**) found that 44 percent of boys and 30 percent of girls have had sexual intercourse prior to age 16. These figures increased to 72 percent of boys and 57 percent of girls by age 19. When compared with females of their mothers' generation in Kinsey's investigation (only 3% of whom had engaged in premarital intercourse by age 16 and less than 20% by age 19), this represents a very large increase, particularly at the younger age level. When compared with males of their fathers' generation (approximately 39% of whom had engaged in premarital intercourse by age 16 and 72% by age 19), contemporary adolescent boys as a whole show a much smaller change, mainly a tendency to have first intercourse at a slightly younger age. However, as will become apparent in the following section, these *overall* findings for boys obscure significant changes taking place among boys of higher socioeconomic and educational levels.

DIVERSITY OF SEXUAL ATTITUDES AND BEHAVIOR

Up to this point, our focus has been on *overall* trends in sexual attitudes and behavior among contemporary youth. Such group trends have meaning and usefulness in their own right, but they should not be allowed to distract our attention from an equally important phenomenon, namely, the diversity of sexual attitudes and behavior in different sectors of the adolescent and youth population. There is increasing evidence that this diversity is currently marked and probably growing (**5**, **16**, **20**, **29**). Such factors as age, sex, socioeconomic and educational level, race, religion, and even geographical area all appear to be related to sexual attitudes, values, and behavior. For this reason, the results of almost any survey dealing with adolescent sexuality will inevitably seem exaggerated to some young people and adults and minimized to others.

What do we know about some of these variations? As we have already noted, Sorenson's recent survey (**29**) shows that for the first time in such studies, a majority (52%) of American adolescents aged 13–19 reported having engaged in sexual intercourse. As significant as this evidence of a trend toward greater sexual freedom clearly is, it should not be allowed to obscure the complementary finding that a very substantial minority (48%) of adolescents had not as yet had such experience. Furthermore, neither of these broad groups was homogeneous. Thus, adolescents in the nonintercourse group ranged from those with virtually no sexual experience to those with a wide variety of experiences short of intercourse itself, including petting to orgasm.

Among the group with intercourse experience, two major subgroups emerge from the findings of this study: *serial monogamists* and *sexual adventurers*. The former "generally does not have intercourse with another during that relationship. We say 'serial' because one such relationship is often succeeded by another" (**29**, p. 121). The latter, on the other hand, "moves freely from one sex partner to the next and feels no obligation to be faithful to any sex partner" (**29**, p. 121). Among nonvirgins, serial monogamy was more frequent overall; it was also more frequent among girls, older adolescents, those from the northeast and west, and those from large metropolitan areas. The total number of partners was obviously far higher among sexual adventurers, although it is interesting to note that frequency of intercourse was higher among monogamists.

Not surprisingly, the two groups tended to vary significantly in attitudes, as well as in behavior. Most monogamists believe they love and are loved by their partners, believe in openness and honesty between partners, and deny that sex is the most important thing in a love relationship —although they also expressed greater satisfaction with their sex lives. At the same time their code stresses personal freedom and the absence of commitment to marriage, despite the fact that more than half believe they will or may marry their partner eventually. Sexual adventurers, in contrast, are primarily interested in variety of experience for its own sake, do not believe that love is a necessary part of sexual relationships, and feel no particular personal responsibility for their partners, although neither do they believe in hurting others. For many adventurers, sex itself is viewed as an avenue to communication; as one young adventurer stated, "Having sex together is a good way for two people to become acquainted."

As a group, monogamists tended to be more satisfied with themselves and life in general, to get along better with parents, and to be more conventional in social, political, and religious beliefs. Despite their greater emphasis on sex as a goal in itself, female adventurers report having orgasm during intercourse less frequently than monogamists.

In general, and contrary to recent popular impressions, both the attitudes and behavior of younger adolescents still appear more *conservative* than those of older adolescents (**4**, **6**, **8**, **10**, **29**). Younger adolescents may possibly, as some have speculated, end up less constrained by social mores than their older brothers and sisters. But the fact remains that for the great majority this is not presently the case.

Girls as a group are consistently more conservative than boys, both in attitudes and values and in behavior. In virtually all population subgroups, the incidence of all forms of intimate sexual behavior is less frequent among girls; girls are also more likely than boys to believe that partners in advanced forms of petting or intercourse should be in love, engaged, or married (**9**, **16**, **20**, **25**, **29**). Furthermore, girls are more likely than boys to be influenced by parental wishes and community social standards.

In Sorenson's study, 80 percent of the sexual adventurers were male; in contrast, 64 percent of serial monogamists were female. (The implication here is that a significant percentage of female monogamists were involved with males who were over 19, and hence not included in the study; the other possibility is that in some relationships the girl considered herself a monogamist, while the boy did not.) The greater emphasis among girls on love as a necessary component of sexual relationships is consistent with the stronger interpersonal orientation of girls generally. The extent to which a higher level of sexual activity among boys is a function of physiological differences, cultural influences, or (as seems most likely) both is still an unresolved question (**1**, **4**, **17**).

College youth emerge as consistently less conservative in their attitudes and values than noncollege peers of the same age. For example, in one study of American youth 17 and older (**35**), college youth were significantly less likely to express the view that premarital sexual relations "were not a moral issue." They were also more likely to believe that "sexual behavior should be bound by mutual feelings, not by formal ties," and they were more likely to express a desire for "more sexual freedom" than their noncollege peers.

Within the college population there appears to be considerable diversity in attitudes and values, both among geographical regions and types of schools attended—particularly in the case of girls. In general students from the east and west coasts emerge as less conservative than those from the Midwest (**16**, **20**, **25**). In a 1969 study more than two-thirds of midwestern students, but only about 40 percent of eastern students (both male and female), responded affirmatively to the question, "Do you feel that ideally it is still true that

a man and a girl who marry should have their first full sexual experience together?" Similarly, three-fourths of girls at midwstern schools, but less than a third of those at eastern schools, agreed that "coitus was reasonable 'only if married' for possible participants who would be in the 21- to 23-year-old age group" (**20**, p. 163). Students at permissive, liberally oriented colleges emerged as less conservative than those at more traditional colleges (**6**, **16**, **20**). Interestingly, the only apparent exception to the tendency for girls to have more conservative attitudes and values than boys occurs among students in some highly permissive, liberal colleges (**16**, **20**).

It is also among college youth that the greatest changes in sexual behavior have occurred since their parents' generation (**4**, **16**, **20**, **30**, **31**). This trend appears especially pronounced among some demographically distinguishable groups of female students. In the 1940s Kinsey and others (**12**, **13**, **23**) found that by the age of 21 the incidence of premarital experience among college-educated persons was 49 percent for males and 27 percent for females. In contrast several recent, broadly representative investigations of American college and university students of comparable ages, conducted between 1967 and 1971 (**9**, **16**, **20**, **30**, **31**), indicate a substantial upward shift, particularly among girls. Thus, for males, obtained incidence figures in these investigations ranged from a low of 58 percent to a high of 82 percent; comparable percentages for females ranged from a 43 percent to 56 percent. In both cases the highest percentages were obtained in the most recent samples (**9**, **30**, **31**, **36**).

Interestingly, whereas the percentage of male students engaging in premarital intercourse appeared to have reached a plateau (of about 80%) by 1970, among girls the incidence was apparently still increasing in 1971: Fifty-one percent of female students reported having had intercourse in 1970; 56 percent did so in 1971. Premarital relations are likely to be more frequent among those attending eastern colleges and universities than among those attending midwestern institutions (**20**) and among students attending private, "elite" colleges and universities.

Politically conservative youth are more conservative in sexual attitudes and values than "moderate reformers" and far more conservative than left-oriented "revolutionary" youth (**4, 9, 30, 31, 34**). Thus, among older adolescents *in general* (both college and noncollege), only 18 percent of conservative youth stated they would welcome more sexual freedom, as compared with 43 percent of moderate reformers and 80 percent of revolutionaries (**35**). Similarly, nearly two-thirds of conservative youth viewed premarital sexual relations as a moral issue, compared with one-third of moderate reformers and none of the revolutionaries!

Cultural differences are clearly reflected in the wide variations obtained between nations in various studies (**3, 11, 15, 16, 20**). Canada and the United States consistently rank lowest in incidence of premarital intercourse and England ranks highest, followed by the Scandinavian countries.

Even on the basis of the limited data discussed in this essay, it appears clear that adolescent attitudes and values regarding sex and sexual behavior itself are changing, although the extent of the changes varies widely from one segment of the youth population to another. Indeed, as in other areas of social concern, *the differences between some subgroups of youth appear wider than those between youth in general and adults in general*. There is a real and often ignored danger in generalizing too widely from specialized subgroups (e.g., a particular college campus or a particular urban high school) to youth in general. Furthermore, the greatest *relative* changes in both attitudes and behavior since their parents' generation have occurred among middle- and upper class adolescents, particularly girls. Not surprisingly it is among this socio-economically favored, and probably more socially conflicted, segment of the youth population that the "youth culture" of the 1960s took root and found its sustenance.

DISCUSSION

In brief, these findings, combined with general observation, do indicate an emerging new morality among contemporary adolescents. While this new morality has many positive aspects—a greater emphasis on openness and honesty, mutual respect and lack of dissembling or exploitation, and a more "natural" and better-informed approach to sex—it would be a mistake to conclude that the picture is wholly unclouded. Many experienced adolescents, particularly older adolescents, appear able to handle their sexual involvement and their relationships with themselves without undue stress. (Four out of five nonvirgins report getting "a lot of satisfaction" out of their sex lives; two-thirds of all nonvirgins and four out of five monogamists state that sex makes their lives more meaningful.) However, significant minorities report feelings of conflict and guilt, find themselves exploited or rejected, or discover belatedly that they have gotten in over their heads emotionally. Especially after the first experience of intercourse, girls are far more likely than boys to encounter negative feelings. While boys are most likely to report being excited, satisfied, and happy, girls most frequently report being afraid, guilty, worried, or embarrassed after their initial intercourse experience (**29**).

Obviously there are dangers, particularly for girls, with their generally stronger affiliative needs, in believing that sexual involvement is "okay as long as you're in love." Encouraged by such a philosophy among peers, a girl or boy may become more deeply involved emotionally than she or he can handle at a particular stage of maturity (**1, 4**). "An adolescent may also consciously think that his attitudes are more 'liberal' than they actually are, and involvement may lead to unanticipated feelings of guilt, anxiety or depression" (**18**, p. 643).

There also remain very practical problems, such as the possibility of pregnancy. Many girls today express the opinion that "now that science has given us the [birth control] pill, we no longer have to be frightened about pregnancy. We just have to decide what is right" (**4**, p. 254). Noble as this sentiment may be, the facts indicate that only a small percentage of unmarried girls having intercourse have used the contraceptive pill to prevent pregnancy (**7, 14, 29, 32**); a disturbingly high percentage—between 55 and 75 percent—used no contraceptive device whatever, at least in their first experience, and only a minority consistently use such a device thereafter (**14, 29, 36**). Even among monogomists, only two-thirds reported always using contraceptive devices. Furthermore, despite talk of the pill, less than a third of female nonvirgins have used this method.

Such lack of precaution against pregnancy results partly from ignorance or lack of availability of contraceptive devices. Far more often, however, it results from carelessness, impulsivenes of the moment, a magical conviction that pregnancy cannot really happen, a belief that the spontaneity of sex is impaired ("If the girl uses birth control pills or other forms of contraception, it makes it seem as if she were *planning* to have sex"), or a belief that the *other* partner has taken precautions. Furthermore, 40 percent of all nonvirgin girls in Sorenson's study agreed that "sometimes I don't really care whether or not I get pregnant." Rather astonishingly, he found that "10 percent of all American female adolescents and 23 percent of all nonvirgin girls report that they have been pregnant at least once" (**29**, p. 324).

It seems unlikely that the trend toward premarital intercourse as an accepted practice, and especially toward serial monogamy as the most frequent and the most socially approved pattern among sexually experienced adolescents, will be reversed. Of all residuals of the youth culture of the 1960s, greater sexual freedom and openness appear to be the more enduring. What one must hope is that adolescents entering sexual relationships can be helped to become mature enough, informed enough, responsible enough, sure enough of their own identities and value systems, and sensitive and concerned enough about the welfare of others so that the inevitable casualties in the "sexual revolution" can be reduced to a minimum. Sexuality as a vital part of human relationships should promote, rather than hinder, growth toward maturity and emotional fulfillment.

References

1. Bardwick, J. *Psychology of women: A study of bio-cultural conflicts.* Harper & Row, 1971.
2. Bell, R. R. Parent-child conflict in sexual values. *J. Soc. Issues*, 1966, 22, 34–44.
3. Christenson, H. T., & Carpenter, G. R. Value-behavior discrepancies regarding premarital coitus in three Western cultures. *Am. Sociol. Rev.*, 1962, 27, 66–74.
4. Conger, J. J. *Adolescence and youth: Psychological development in a changing world.* New York: Harper & Row, 1973.
5. Conger, J. J. A world they never knew: The family and social change. *Daedalus*, Fall 1971, 1105–1138.
6. Gallup poll, *Denver Post*, May 12, 1970.
7. Grinder, R. E., & Schmitt, S. S. Coeds and contraceptive information. *J. Marriage Fam.*, 1966, 28, 471–479.
8. Harris, L. Change, yes—upheaval, no. *Life*, January 8, 1971, 22–27.
9. Hunt, M. *Sexual behavior in the 1970s.* Chicago: Playboy Press, 1974.
10. Hunt, M. Special sex education survey. *Seventeen*, July 1970, 94 ff.
11. Karlsson, G. Karlsson, S., & Busch, K. Sexual habits and attitudes of Swedish folk high school students. Research Report No. 15. Uppsala, Sweden: Department of Sociology, Uppsala University, 1960.
12. Kinsey, A. C., Pomeroy, W. B., Martin, C. E., & Gebhard, P. H. *Sexual behavior in the human female.* Philadelphia: Saunders, 1953.
13. Kinsey, A. C., Pomeroy, W. B., & Martin, C. E. *Sexual behavior in the human male.* Philadelphia: Saunders, 1948.
14. Lake, A. Teenagers and sex: A student report. *Seventeen*, July 1967, 88.
15. Linner, B. *Sex and society in Sweden.* New York: Pantheon, 1967.
16. Luckey, E., & Nass, G. A comparison of sexual attitudes and behavior in an international sample. *J. Marriage Fam.*, 1969, 31, 364–379.

17. Money, J., & Ehrhardt, A. A. *Man and woman, boy and girl: The differentiation and dimorphism of gender identity from conception to maturity.* Baltimore: Johns Hopkins Press, 1972.

18. Mussen, P. H., Conger, J. J., & Kagan, J. *Child development and personality.* New York: Harper & Row, 1969 (3rd ed.).

19. Packard, V. . . . and the sexual behavior reported by 2100 young adults. In V. Packard, *The sexual wilderness: The contemporary upheaval in male-female relationships.* New York: Pocket Books, 1970, pp. 166–184.

20. Packard, V. *The sexual wilderness: The contemporary upheaval in male-female relationships.* New York: Pocket Books, 1970.

21. Pomeroy, W. B. *Boys and sex.* New York: Delacorte, 1969.

22. Pomeroy, W. B. *Girls and sex.* New York: Delacorte, 1969.

23. Reevy, W. R. Adolescent sexuality. In A. Ellis & A. Abarband (Eds.), *The encyclopedia of sexual behavior* (Vol. I). New York: Hawthorn, 1961, pp. 52–68.

24. Reiss, I. L. How and why America's sex standards are changing. In W. Simon and J. H. Gagnon (Eds.), *The sexual scene.* Chicago: Trans-action Books, 1970, pp. 43–57.

25. Reiss, I. L. The sexual renaissance in America. *J. Soc. Issues,* April 1966.

26. Reiss, I. L. The scaling of premarital sexual permissiveness. *J. Marriage Fam.,* 1964, 26, 188–199.

27. Simon, W., & Gagnon, J. H. Psychosexual development. In W. Simon & J. H. Gagnon (Eds.), *The sexual scene.* Chicago: Trans-action Books, 1970, pp. 23–41.

28. Simon, W., & Gagnon, J. H. (Eds.). *The sexual scene.* Chicago: Trans-action Books, 1970.

29. Sorenson, R. C. *Adolescent sexuality in contemporary America: Personal values and sexual behavior ages 13–19.* New York: World Publishing, 1973.

30. Student survey, 1971. *Playboy,* September 1971, 118 ff.

31. Student survey, *Playboy,* September 1970, 182 ff.

32. *The report of the Commission on Obscenity and Pornography.* New York: Bantam Books, 1970.

33. What people think of their high schools. *Life,* 1969, 66, 22–23.

34. Wilson, W. C. et al. *Technical report of the Commission on Obscenity and Pornography, Vol. VI: National survey.* Washington, D.C.: U.S. Government Printing Office, 1971.

35. Yankelovich, D. *Generations apart.* New York: CBS News, 1969.

36. Zelnik, M., & Kantner, J. E. Survey of female adolescent sexual behavior conducted for the Commission on Population, Washington, D.C., 1972.

Index of Names

Index of Subjects

75 76 77 9 8 7 6 5 4 3 2 1